Contemporary Mathematics

FOR BUSINESS AND CONSUMERS

6E

Contemporary Mathematics

FOR BUSINESS AND CONSUMERS

6E

Robert A. Brechner
Miami-Dade College

SOUTH-WESTERN
CENGAGE Learning

Australia • Brazil • Japan • Korea • Mexico • Singapore • Spain • United Kingdom • United States

SOUTH-WESTERN
CENGAGE Learning

**Contemporary Mathematics for
Business and Consumers, Sixth Edition**
Robert A. Brechner

Vice President of Editorial, Business: Jack W. Calhoun

Publisher: Joe Sabatino

Sr. Acquisitions Editor: Charles McCormick

Developmental Editor: Daniel Noguera

Editorial Assistant: Courtney Bavaro

Marketing Manager: Adam Marsh

Content Project Manager: Darrell E. Frye

Media Editor: Chris Valentine

Frontlist Buyer, Manufacturing: Miranda Klapper

Marketing Communications Manager: Libby Shipp

Production Service: Integra Software Services

Sr. Art Director: Stacy Jenkins Shirley

Internal and Cover Designer: Craig Ramsdell

Cover Image: ©iStock Photo

Rights Acquisitions Director: Audrey Pettengill

Rights Acquisitions Specialist: Deanna Ettinger

For product information and technology assistance, contact us at
Cengage Learning Customer & Sales Support, 1-800-354-9706

For permission to use material from this text or product, submit all requests online at **www.cengage.com/permissions**
Further permissions questions can be emailed to
permissionrequest@cengage.com

ExamView® is a registered trademark of eInstruction Corp. Windows is a registered trademark of the Microsoft Corporation used herein under license. Macintosh and Power Macintosh are registered trademarks of Apple Computer, Inc. used herein under license.
© 2008 Cengage Learning. All Rights Reserved.

Library of Congress Control Number: 2011920494

Student Edition package ISBN 13: 978-0-538-48125-0

Student Edition package ISBN 10: 0-538-48125-0

Student Edition book only ISBN 13: 978-0-538-48126-7

Student Edition book only ISBN 10: 0-538-48126-9

Brief Edition package ISBN 13: 978-1-111-52937-6

Brief Edition package ISBN 10: 1-111-52937-X

Brief Edition book only ISBN 13: 978-1-111-52936-9

Brief Edition book only ISBN 10: 1-111-52936-1

South-Western
5191 Natorp Boulevard
Mason, OH 45040
USA

Cengage Learning products are represented in Canada by Nelson Education, Ltd.

For your course and learning solutions, visit **www.cengage.com**

Purchase any of our products at your local college store or at our preferred online store **www.cengagebrain.com**

Printed in the United States of America
1 2 3 4 5 6 7 15 14 13 12 11

Dear Student:

Today's world of business revolves around numbers. From the profit margin of a corporation to the markup on a fast-food sandwich—using numbers is inescapable. The better you understand and feel comfortable working with numbers and basic math functions and principles, the better prepared you'll be to maximize your success in the business world.

That's why this book is in your hands. I created *Contemporary Mathematics for Business and Consumers* to give students like you a solid math foundation in an inviting, manageable way. Besides learning the principles, you'll also see why they are important to your success in other business courses and, ultimately, in your career. This is not a math book that uses a few business examples. It's a business book that uses math as a tool to further your journey to success.

As with any journey, there are ways to make the success—and a good grade—easier. Several important and valuable learning tools can make a tremendous difference for you.

The following pages illustrate the tools and resources available to help you understand the math principles—and to get the best grade possible—in the least amount of time. Math doesn't have to be intimidating no matter how long it's been since you studied it. With a little effort, you'll leave this course more confident in mathematics and much better equipped to succeed in your business career.

As part of my personal commitment to your success, I encourage you to contact me with questions or comments using my toll-free number 1-888-284-MATH or e-mailing me at bizmath@aol.com.

Warmest regards and best wishes,

Robert Brechner

Robert Brechner

Step into the Real Business World with the Strengths of *Contemporary Mathematics, 6e*

IN THE BUSINESS WORLD

New Federal Debit Card – In 2008, the U.S. Treasury introduced a debit card that people without traditional bank accounts can use to access federal benefits such as Social Security and disability payments.

Federal payments are credited to the cards each month, enabling users to make free withdrawals from in the government's Direct Expr network.

IN THE BUSINESS WORLD

Useful and interesting connections to the real business world. Many have useful information to help you manage your own personal finances.

LEARNING TIP

Frequently, the left side of an equation represents the "interaction" of the variables, and the right side shows the "result" of that interaction.

In this example, the left side is the interaction (in this case, addition) of the wax and wash sales. The right side is the result, or total.

$$\underset{X + X - 360}{\text{Interaction}} = \underset{920}{\text{Result}}$$

LEARNING TIPS

Helpful mathematical hints, shortcuts, and reminders to enhance your understanding of the chapter material.

FORMULA RECAP CHARTS

Lists of all-important formulas provide you with a quick reference for homework and test preparation.

DOLLARS AND SENSE

The Federal Deposit Insurance Corporation (FDIC) insures every depositor for at least $250,000 at each insured bank. People with more than $250,000 can split their cash among insured banks and remain fully protected. The FDIC insures more than 8,000 banks nationwide.

BUSINESS MATH TIMES

Appearing every three chapters beginning with Chapter 3, a page of current news items, cartoons, brain teasers, famous business and inspirational quotes, career information, and other interesting facts and figures related to business topics.

DOLLARS AND SENSE

The new "Dollars and Sense" feature stimulates your curiosity with current news items and statistics related to chapter topics. "Dollars and Sense" provides you with numerous personal finance and business money tips.

Additional Tools to Help You Succeed

ANSWERS TO ODD-NUMBERED EXERCISES

Answers to all of the odd-numbered Section Review Exercises and Assessment Test questions (except Business Decisions) allow you to easily check your progress on class assignments and homework.

TRY-IT EXERCISES with WORKED-OUT SOLUTIONS

provide you with immediate feedback as you evaluate your comprehension of each new topic.

TRY IT: EXERCISE SOLUTIONS F

	Numerical Form	Word Form
1a.	49,588	Forty-nine thousand, five hundred eighty-eight
1b.	804	Eight hundred four
1c.	1,928,837	One million, nine hundred twenty-eight thousand,
1d.	900,015	Nine hundred thousand, fifteen
1e.	6,847,365,911	Six billion, eight hundred forty-seven million, three
1f.	2,000,300,007	Two billion, three hundred thousand, seven

2a. 51,700   2b. 23,440   2c. 175,450,000   2d. 60,000

3a. 39,481   Verify
      5,594
   +11,029
     56,104

JUMPSTART

The all new "Jump Start" feature in each Section Review gives you the added advantage of seeing the worked-out solution to the first question of each new topic set. All Jump Start solutions are available on the website.

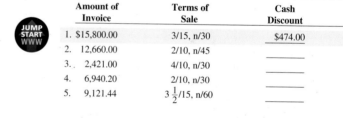

	Amount of Invoice	Terms of Sale	Cash Discount
1.	$15,800.00	3/15, n/30	$474.00
2.	12,660.00	2/10, n/45	
3.	2,421.00	4/10, n/30	
4.	6,940.20	2/10, n/30	
5.	9,121.44	$3\frac{1}{2}$/15, n/60	

For the following transactions, calculate the credit given for th ment and the net amount due on the invoice.

	Amount of Invoice	Terms of Sale	Partial Payment	Credit for Partial Payment
6.	$8,303.00	2/10, n/30	$2,500	$2,551.02
7.	1,344.60	3/10, n/45	460	
8.	5,998.20	4/15, n/60	3,200	
9.	7,232.08	$4\frac{1}{2}$/20, n/45	5,500	

EXCEL 1

25. Midtown Market received the following items at a discount of of canned peaches listing at $26.80 per case and 45 cases of ca $22.50 per case.

a. What is the total list price of this order?

b. What is the amount of the trade discount?

c. What is the net price of the order?

Shopper's Mart purchased the following items. Calculate the ex

EXCEL® EXERCISES

Each chapter includes 8–12 new Excel® exercises, with three levels of difficulty—beginner, intermediate, and advanced—that provide hands-on practice with realistic business calculations tailored to your developing skill levels. Student versions are available on the website.

DEDICATION

To my wife, Shari Joy.
You are my shining star
and constant inspiration.
I love you!

ABOUT THE AUTHORS

Robert Brechner

Robert Brechner is Professor Emeritus, School of Business, at Miami-Dade College, the largest multi-campus community college in the country. For the past 42 years, he has taught Business Math, Principles of Business, Marketing, Advertising, Public Relations, Management and Personal Finance. He has been Adjunct Professor at Florida Atlantic University, Boca Raton; International Fine Arts College, Miami; and Florida International University School of Journalism and Mass Communications.

Bob holds a Bachelor of Science degree in Industrial Management from the Georgia Institute of Technology in Atlanta, Georgia. He also has a Masters of Business Administration from Emory University in Atlanta. He has consulted widely with industrial companies and has published numerous books covering a variety of business topics.

Bob lives in Coconut Grove, Florida, with his wife, Shari Joy. His passions include travel, photography, sailing, tennis, and running. Bob encourages feedback and suggestions for future editions from those who use the text. Students as well as instructors can contact him toll-free at 1-888-284-MATH or e-mail him at bizmath@aol.com.

George Bergeman,
author of CengageNOW™ featuring MathCue.Business

The author of numerous software packages, George Bergeman has taught mathematics for more than 25 years. His teaching career began at a small college in West Africa as a Peace Corps volunteer and continued at Northern Virginia Community College, one of the largest multi-campus colleges in the country. Teaching awards include Faculty Member of the Year honors at his campus.

In an effort to enhance his instruction by incorporating computer support, George developed a small program for use in statistics classes. Students and instructors responded positively, and in 1985, an expanded version was published along with an accompanying workbook. Since then, George has developed a variety of software packages to accompany texts in statistics, calculus, developmental math, finite math, and—a special favorite—MathCue.Business for Robert Brechner's *Contemporary Mathematics for Business and Consumers*.

By drawing on his teaching experiences and contact with students and faculty, George has endeavored to develop software that provides targeted, effective, and easy-to-use support for instruction.

George lives with his wife, Clarissa, near Washington, D.C. They have one daughter, Jessy, who is currently in grad school in Colorado after previously working in San Francisco, Boston, and Brazil. In his free time, George enjoys accompanying his wife and their dog, Anny, to dog shows. Along those lines, and with Anny's help, George and his wife produced a dog-sport training video that has been distributed in the United States and in parts of Europe.

BRIEF CONTENTS

Contents

Chapter 6: Percents and Their Applications in Business 155

Chapter 7: Invoices, Trade Discounts, and Cash Discounts 191

Chapter 8: Markup and Markdown 232

Chapter 9: Payroll 265

Chapter 10: Simple Interest and Promissory Notes 307

Contemporary Mathematics

6E

istockphoto.com/SuperCreative

Whole Numbers

PERFORMANCE OBJECTIVES

Numbers are one of the primary tools used in business. The ability to read, comprehend, and manipulate numbers is an essential part of the everyday activity in today's complex business world. To be successful, business students should become competent and confident in dealing with numbers.

We will begin our study of business mathematics with whole numbers and their basic operations—addition, subtraction, multiplication, and division. The material in this chapter is based on the assumption that you have a basic working knowledge of these operations. Our goal is to review these fundamentals and build accuracy and speed. This arithmetic review will set the groundwork for our study of fractions, decimals, and percents. Most business math applications involve calculations using these components.

1-1 READING AND WRITING WHOLE NUMBERS IN NUMERICAL AND WORD FORM

decimal number system A system using the 10 Hindu-Arabic symbols 0 through 9. In this place-value system, the position of a digit to the left or right of the decimal point affects its value.

decimal point A dot written in a decimal number to indicate where the place values change from whole numbers to decimals.

whole numbers Any numbers 0 or greater that do not contain a decimal or fraction. Whole numbers are found to the left of the decimal point. Also known as an integer. For example, 6, 25, and 300 are whole numbers.

The number system most widely used in the world today is known as the Hindu-Arabic numeral system, or **decimal number system**. This system is far superior to any other for today's complex business calculations. It derives its name from the Latin words *decimus*, meaning 10th, and *decem*, meaning 10. The decimal system is based on 10s, with the starting point marked by a dot known as the **decimal point**. The decimal system uses the 10 familiar Hindu-Arabic symbols or digits:

$$0, 1, 2, 3, 4, 5, 6, 7, 8, 9$$

The major advantage of our decimal system over previous systems is that the position of a digit to the left or right of the decimal point affects its value. This enables us to write any number with only the 10 single-digit numbers, 0 through 9. For this reason, we have given names to the places or positions. In this chapter, we work with places to the left of the decimal point, **whole numbers**. The next two chapters are concerned with the places to the right of the decimal point, fractions and decimals.

When whole numbers are written, a decimal point is understood to be located on the right of the number. For example, the number **27** is actually

27.

The decimal point is not displayed until we write a decimal number or dollars and cents, such as 27.25 inches or $27.25.

Skills you acquire in this course will be applied frequently in your roles as a consumer and a businessperson.

Exhibit 1-1 illustrates the first 15 places, and five groups, of the decimal number system. Note that our system is made up of groups of three places, separated by commas, each with its own name. Whole numbers start at the understood decimal point and increase in value from right to left. Each group contains the same three places: ones, tens, and hundreds. Note that each place increases by a factor of "times 10." The group names are units, thousands, millions, billions, and trillions.

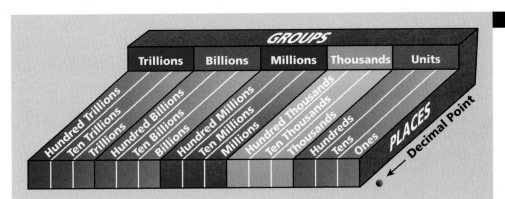

EXHIBIT 1-1

Whole Number Place Value Chart

STEPS FOR READING AND WRITING WHOLE NUMBERS

STEP 1. Beginning at the right side of the number, insert a comma every three digits to mark the groups.

STEP 2. Beginning from left to right, name the digits and the groups. The units group and groups that have all zeros are not named.

STEP 3. When writing whole numbers in word form, the numbers from 21 to 99 are hyphenated, except for the decades (e.g., thirty). For example, 83 would be written eighty-three.

Note: The word *and* should *not* be used in reading or writing whole numbers. It represents the decimal point and will be covered in Chapter 3.

LEARNINGTIP

Whole numbers with four digits may be written with or without a comma. For example, 3,400 or 3400 would be correct.

EXAMPLE1 READING AND WRITING WHOLE NUMBERS

Read and write the following whole numbers in numerical and word form.

a. 14296 b. 560
c. 2294857 d. 184910
e. 3004959001 f. 24000064

SOLUTIONSTRATEGY

Following the steps above, we insert the commas to mark the groups, then read and write the numbers from left to right.

INTHE BUSINESSWORLD

In text, large numbers, in the millions and greater, may be easier to read by writing the "zeros portion" in words. For example, 44,000,000,000,000 may be written as 44 trillion.

	Number	Numerical Form	Word Form
a.	14296	14,296	fourteen thousand, two hundred ninety-six
b.	560	560	five hundred sixty
c.	2294857	2,294,857	two million, two hundred ninety-four thousand, eight hundred fifty-seven
d.	184910	184,910	one hundred eighty-four thousand, nine hundred ten
e.	3004959001	3,004,959,001	three billion, four million, nine hundred fifty-nine thousand, one
f.	24000064	24,000,064	twenty-four million, sixty-four

TRYITEXERCISE1

Read and write the following whole numbers in numerical and word form.

a. 49588
b. 804
c. 1928837
d. 900015
e. 6847365911
f. 2000300007

CHECK YOUR ANSWERS WITH THE SOLUTIONS ON PAGE 24.

1-2 ROUNDING WHOLE NUMBERS TO A SPECIFIED PLACE VALUE

rounded numbers Numbers that are approximations or estimates of exact numbers. For example, 50 is the rounded number of the exact number 49.

In many business applications, an approximation of an exact number may be more desirable to use than the number itself. Approximations, or **rounded numbers**, are easier to refer to and remember. For example, if a grocery store carries 9,858 items on its shelves, you would probably say that it carries 10,000 items. If you drive 1,593 miles, you would say that the trip is 1,600 miles. Another rounding application in business involves money. If your company has profits of $1,302,201, you might refer to this exact amount by the rounded number $1,300,000. Money amounts are usually rounded to the nearest cent, although they could also be rounded to the nearest dollar.

estimate To calculate approximately the amount or value of something. The number 50 is an estimate of 49.

Rounded numbers are frequently used to **estimate** an answer to a problem before that problem is worked. Estimation approximates the exact answer. By knowing an estimate of an answer in advance, you will be able to catch many math errors. When using estimation to prework a problem, you can generally round off to the first digit, which is called **rounding all the way**.

rounding all the way A process of rounding numbers to the first digit. Used to prework a problem to an estimated answer. For example, 2,865 rounded all the way is 3,000.

Once you have rounded to the first digit, perform the indicated math procedure. This can often be done quickly and will give you a ballpark or general idea of the actual answer. In the example below, the estimated answer of 26,000 is a good indicator of the "reasonableness" of the actual answer.

	Estimated Solution	
Original Calculation	**(rounding all the way)**	**Actual Solution**
19,549	20,000	19,549
+ 6,489	+ 6,000	+ 6,489
	26,000	26,038

If, for example, you had mistakenly added for a total of 23,038 instead of 26,038, your estimate would have immediately indicated that something was wrong.

STEPS FOR ROUNDING WHOLE NUMBERS TO A SPECIFIED PLACE VALUE

STEP 1. Determine the place to which the number is to be rounded.

STEP 2a. If the digit to the right of the place being rounded is 5 or more, increase the digit in that place by 1.

STEP 2b. If the digit to the right of the place being rounded is 4 or less, do not change the digit in the place being rounded.

STEP 3. Change all digits to the right of the place being rounded to zeros.

EXAMPLE2 ROUNDING WHOLE NUMBERS

Round the following numbers to the indicated place.

a. 1,867 to tens
b. 760 to hundreds
c. 129,338 to thousands
d. 293,847 to hundred thousands
e. 97,078,838,576 to billions
f. 85,600,061 all the way

SOLUTIONSTRATEGY

Following the steps on page 4, locate the place to be rounded, use the digit to the right of that place to determine whether to round up or leave it as is, and change all digits to the right of the place being rounded to zeros.

		Place Indicated	Rounded Number
a.	1,867 to tens	1,867	1,870
b.	760 to hundreds	760	800
c.	129,338 to thousands	129,338	129,000
d.	293,847 to hundred thousands	293,847	300,000
e.	97,078,838,576 to billions	97,078,838,576	97,000,000,000
f.	85,600,061 all the way	85,600,061	90,000,000

TRYITEXERCISE2

Round the following numbers to the indicated place.

a. 51,667 to hundreds
b. 23,441 to tens
c. 175,445,980 to ten thousands
d. 59,561 all the way
e. 14,657,000,138 to billions
f. 8,009,070,436 to ten millions

CHECK YOUR ANSWERS WITH THE SOLUTIONS ON PAGE 24.

REVIEW EXERCISES   **SECTION I** **1**

Read and write the following whole numbers in numerical and word form.

Number	Numerical Form	Word Form
1. 22938	22,938	Twenty-two thousand, nine hundred thirty-eight
2. 1573	_____	_____
3. 184	_____	_____
4. 984773	_____	_____
5. 2433590	_____	_____
6. 49081472	_____	_____

Write the following whole numbers in numerical form.

7. One hundred eighty-three thousand, six hundred twenty-two   _____183,622_

8. Two million, forty-three thousand, twelve   _____

9. According to Globo's G1 website, it is estimated that the cost of the 2014 World Cup in Brazil will reach forty billion dollars. Write this number in numerical form.   _____

Match the following numbers in word form with the numbers in numerical form.

10. One hundred two thousand, four hundred seventy __b__   a. 12,743

11. One hundred twelve thousand, seven hundred forty-three _____   b. 102,470

12. Twelve thousand, seven hundred forty-three _____   c. 11,270

13. Eleven thousand, two hundred seventy _____   d. 112,743

14. According to NCR Corporation, retailers in America generate 228,700,000 pounds of paper receipts per year. Write this number in word form.

Round the following numbers to the indicated place.

15. 1,757 to tens   _____1,760_

16. 32,475 to thousands   _____

17. 235,376 to hundreds   _____

18. 559,443 to ten thousands   _____

19. 8,488,710 to millions   _____

20. 45,699 all the way   _____

21. 1,325,669,226 to hundred millions   _____

22. 23,755 all the way   _____

23. According to the American Wind Energy Association, Texas has the highest operating wind capacity, 8,797 megawatts. Iowa is second with 3,053 megawatts capacity.

    a. Write each of these numbers in word form.

    b. Round each of these numbers to the nearest hundred.

24. According to the *Financial Times*, in August 2009, outstanding consumer credit in the United States fell to $2,460,000,000,000— the seventh straight monthly decline. Most of the drop came as a result of consumers paying down revolving debt such as credit cards.

    a. Write this number in word form.

    b. Round this number to the nearest hundred billions.

BUSINESS DECISION: UP OR DOWN?

25. You are responsible for writing a monthly stockholders' report about your company. Your boss has given you the flexibility to round the numbers to tens, hundreds, thousands, and so on, or not at all, depending on which is most beneficial for the company's image. For each of the following monthly figures, make a rounding choice and explain your reasoning:

    a. 74,469—number of items manufactured   _____

    b. $244,833—your department's net sales for the month   _____

    c. 5,648—defective items manufactured   _____

    d. $649,341—total company profit   _____

    e. 149 new customers   _____

ADDITION AND SUBTRACTION OF WHOLE NUMBERS

SECTION II

1

Addition and subtraction are the most basic mathematical operations. They are used in almost all business calculations. In business, amounts of things or dollars are often combined or added to determine the total. Likewise, subtraction is frequently used to determine an amount of something after it has been reduced in quantity.

ADDING WHOLE NUMBERS AND VERIFYING YOUR ANSWERS

1-3

Addition is the mathematical process of computing sets of numbers to find their sum, or total. The numbers being added are known as **addends**, and the result or answer of the addition is known as the **sum**, **total**, or **amount**. The "+" symbol represents addition and is called the **plus sign**.

$$
\begin{array}{rl}
1,932 & \text{addend} \\
2,928 & \text{addend} \\
+\ 6,857 & \text{addend} \\
\hline
11,717 & \text{total}
\end{array}
$$

addition The mathematical process of computing sets of numbers to find their sum, or total.

addends Any of a set of numbers being added in an addition problem. For example, 4 and 1 are the addends of the addition problem 4 + 1 = 5.

sum, total, or amount The result or answer of an addition problem. The number 5 is the sum, or total, of 4 + 1 = 5.

plus sign The symbol "+" representing addition.

STEPS FOR ADDING WHOLE NUMBERS

STEP 1. Write the whole numbers in columns so that you line up the place values—units, tens, hundreds, thousands, and so on.

STEP 2. Add the digits in each column, starting on the right with the units column.

STEP 3. When the total in a column is greater than nine, write the units digit and carry the tens digit to the top of the next column to the left.

VERIFYING ADDITION

Generally, when adding the digits in each column, we add from top to bottom. An easy and commonly used method of verifying your addition is to add the numbers again, but this time from bottom to top. By adding the digits in the *reverse* order, you will check your answer without making the same error twice.

For illustrative purposes, addition verification will be rewritten in reverse. In actuality, you do not have to rewrite the numbers; just add them from bottom to top. As mentioned earlier, speed and accuracy will be achieved with practice.

LEARNINGTIP

Once you become proficient at verifying addition, you can speed up your addition by recognizing and combining two numbers that add up to 10, such as 1 + 9, 2 + 8, 6 + 4, and 5 + 5. After you have mastered combining two numbers, try combining three numbers that add up to 10, such as 3 + 3 + 4, 2 + 5 + 3, and 4 + 4 + 2.

Addition	Verification
8	6
3	3
+ 6	+ 8
17	17

A WORD ABOUT WORD PROBLEMS

In business math, calculations are only a part of the story! Business math, most importantly, requires the ability to (1) understand and analyze the facts of business situations, (2) determine what information is given and what is missing, (3) decide what strategy and procedure is required to solve for an answer, and (4) verify your answer. Business application word problems are an important part of each chapter's subject matter. As you progress through the course, your ability to analyze and solve these business situations will improve. Now start slowly and relax!

EXAMPLE3 ADDING WHOLE NUMBERS

Add the following sets of whole numbers. Verify your answers by adding in reverse.

a.   40,562   b. 2,293 + 121 + 7,706 + 20 + 57,293 + 4
     29,381
   + 60,095

c. Galaxy Industries, a furniture manufacturing company, has 229 employees in the design and cutting department, 439 employees in the assembly department, and 360 employees in the finishing department. There are 57 warehouse workers, 23 salespeople, 4 bookkeepers, 12 secretaries, and 5 executives. How many people work for this company?

SOLUTIONSTRATEGY

a.

    1 1 2
    40,562
    29,381
  + 60,095
   130,038 ◄

Verification:
    1 1 2
    60,095
    29,381
  + 40,562
   130,038 ─

Step 1. Write the numbers in columns so that the place values line up. In this example, they are already lined up.

Step 2. Add the digits in each column, starting with the units column.
- *Units column:* 2 + 1 + 5 = 8   Enter the 8 under the units column.
- *Tens column:* 6 + 8 + 9 = 23   Enter the 3 under the tens column and carry the 2 to the hundreds column.
- *Hundreds column:* 2 + 5 + 3 + 0 = 10   Enter the 0 under the hundreds column and carry the 1 to the thousands column.
- *Thousands column:* 1 + 0 + 9 + 0 = 10   Enter the 0 under the thousands column and carry the 1 to the ten thousands column.
- *Ten thousands column:* 1 + 4 + 2 + 6 = 13   Enter the 3 under the ten thousands column and the 1 under the hundred thousands column.

b.
Addition	Verification
11 21	11 21
2,293	4
121	57,293
7,706	20
20	7,706
57,293	121
+ 4	+ 2,293
67,437 ◄	67,437

c.
Addition	Verification
23	23
229	5
439	12
360	4
57	23
23	57
4	360
12	439
+ 5	+ 229
1,129 ◄	1,129

TRYITEXERCISE3

Add the following sets of whole numbers and verify your answers.

a. 39,481
    5,594
  + 11,029

b. 6,948 + 330 + 7,946 + 89 + 5,583,991 + 7 + 18,606

c. Anthony's Italian Restaurant served 183 meals on Monday, 228 meals on Tuesday, 281 meals on Wednesday, 545 meals on Thursday, and 438 meals on Friday. On the weekend, it served 1,157 meals. How many total meals were served that week?

CHECK YOUR ANSWERS WITH THE SOLUTIONS ON PAGE 24.

SUBTRACTING WHOLE NUMBERS AND VERIFYING YOUR ANSWERS

1-4

Subtraction is the mathematical computation of taking away, or deducting, an amount from a given number. Subtraction is the opposite of addition. The original or top number is the **minuend**; the amount we are subtracting from the original number is the **subtrahend**; and the answer is the **remainder**, or **difference**. The "−" symbol represents subtraction and is called the **minus sign**.

      2,495 minuend
  −   320 subtrahend
      2,175 difference

STEPS FOR SUBTRACTING WHOLE NUMBERS

STEP 1. Write the whole numbers in columns so that the place values line up.

STEP 2. Starting with the units column, subtract the digits.

STEP 3. When a column cannot be subtracted, you must "borrow" a digit from the column to the left of the one you are working in.

subtraction The mathematical process of taking away, or deducting, an amount from a given number.

minuend In subtraction, the original number. The amount from which another number, the subtrahend, is subtracted. For example, 5 is the minuend of the subtraction problem 5 − 1 = 4.

subtrahend The amount being taken or subtracted from the minuend. For example, 1 is the subtrahend of 5 − 1 = 4.

difference or remainder The number obtained when one number is subtracted from another. The answer or result of subtraction. For example, 4 is the difference or remainder of 5 − 1 = 4.

minus sign The symbol "−" representing subtraction.

VERIFYING SUBTRACTION

An easy and well-known method of verifying subtraction is to add the difference and the subtrahend. If you subtracted correctly, this total will equal the minuend.

Subtraction	Verification
200 minuend	150 difference
− 50 subtrahend	+ 50 subtrahend
150 difference	200 minuend

EXAMPLE4 SUBTRACTING WHOLE NUMBERS

Subtract the following whole numbers and verify your answers.

a. 4,968
  − 192

b. 189,440 − 1,347

c. On Monday morning, Appliance Depot had 165 microwave ovens in inventory. During the week, the store had a clearance sale and sold 71 of the ovens. How many ovens remain in stock for next week?

LEARNINGTIP ● SOLUTIONSTRATEGY

Because each place value increases by a factor of 10 as we move from right to left (units, tens, hundreds, etc.), when we borrow a digit, we are actually borrowing a 10.

a.
```
        8
    4,9̸68 ◄
  −   192
    4,776
```

Verification:
```
      1
    4,776
  +   192
    4,968 ─
```

Write the numbers in columns so that the place values are lined up. In this problem, they are already lined up.
Starting with the units column, subtract the digits.

Units column: 8 − 2 = 6. Enter the 6 under the units column.

Tens column: 6 − 9 can't be subtracted, so we must borrow a digit, 10, from the hundreds column of the minuend. This reduces the 9 to an 8 and gives us a 10 to add to the 6, making it 16.
Now we can subtract 9 from 16 to get 7. Enter the 7 under the tens column.

Hundreds column: 8 − 1 = 7. Enter the 7 under the hundreds column.

Thousands column: This column has no subtrahend, so just bring down the 4 from the minuend to the answer line.

b. **Subtraction**   **Verification**
```
      33                11
  189,4̸40 ◄         188,093
  −  1,347          +  1,347
   188,093            189,440
```

c. **Subtraction**   **Verification**
```
      0                 1
    1̸65 ◄             94
  −  71             +  71
     94               165
```

● TRYITEXERCISE4

Subtract the following whole numbers and verify your answers.

a.   98,117   b.   12,395 − 5,589
    −7,682

c. Joe Montgomery has $4,589 in his checking account. If he writes a check for $344, how much will be left in the account?

CHECK YOUR ANSWERS WITH THE SOLUTIONS ON PAGE 24.

SECTION II ①

REVIEW EXERCISES

Add the following numbers.

1.	2.	3.	4.	5.
45	548	339	2,359	733
27	229	1,236	8,511	401
+ 19	4,600	5,981	+ 14,006	1,808
91	+ 62,660	3,597		24,111
		+ 8,790		+ 10,595

6.   2,339 + 118 + 3,650 + 8,770 + 81 + 6 = _____

7.   12,554 + 22,606 + 11,460 + 20,005 + 4,303 = _____

Estimate the following by rounding each number all the way; then add to find the exact answer.

		Estimate	Rounded Estimate	Exact Answer
8.	288	300	6,800	6,694
	512	500		
	3,950	4,000		
	+ 1,944	+ 2,000		
	6,694	6,800		
9.	38,599		_____	_____
	3,116			
	+ 129			
10.	318,459		_____	_____
	+ 283,405			

11. City traffic engineers in Canmore are doing an intersection traffic survey. On Tuesday, a counter placed at the intersection of Armstrong Place and Three Sisters Blvd. registered the following counts: morning, 2,594; afternoon, 2,478; and evening, 1,863.
    a. Round each number to the nearest hundred and add to get an *estimate* of the traffic count for the day.

    b. What was the *exact* amount of traffic for the day?

12. While shopping, Tyler Hammond purchases items for $3, $24, $13, $2, and $175. How much did he spend?

13. The following chart shows the April, May, and June sales figures by service categories for Pandora's Beauty Salon. Total each row to get the category totals. Total each column to get the monthly totals. Calculate the grand total for the three-month period.

Pandora's Beauty Salon

Service Category	April	May	June	Category Totals
Cutting, Styling, Coloring	$13,515	$12,350	$14,920	_____
Manicure, Pedicure, Waxing	5,418	7,640	5,756	_____
Facials and Makeup	4,251	6,125	6,740	_____
Beauty Supplies	8,690	7,254	10,346	_____
Monthly Totals	_____	_____	_____	Grand Total

Service Sector
According to the *CIA World Factbook*, service sector businesses such as beauty salons and dry cleaners account for 79.6% of the U.S. economy's gross domestic product. Other sectors include industrial at 19.2% and agriculture at 1.2%. Service-providing industries are expected to account for approximately 15.7 million new wage and salary jobs over the 2006–2016 period.

14. At Cherry Valley Farms, a farmer plants 350 acres of soybeans, 288 acres of corn, 590 acres of wheat, and 43 acres of assorted vegetables. In addition, the farm has 9 acres for grazing and 4 acres for the barnyard and farmhouse. What is the total acreage of the farm?

15. Service Masters Carpet Cleaners pays its sales staff a salary of $575 per month, plus commissions. Last month Alex Acosta earned commissions of $129, $216, $126, $353, and $228. What was Alex's total income for the month?

Subtract the following numbers.

16.	17.	18.	19.	20.
354	5,596	95,490	339,002	2,000,077
− 48	− 967	− 73,500	− 60,911	− 87,801
306				

21. $185 minus $47   22. 67,800 − 9,835   23. $308 less $169

24. Subtract 264 from 1,893   25. Subtract 8,906,000 from 12,396,700

26. The beginning inventory of the Designer Shoe Salon for August was 850 pairs of shoes. On the 9th, it received a shipment from the factory of 297 pairs. On the 23rd, another shipment of 188 pairs arrived. When inventory was taken at the end of the month, there were 754 pairs left. How many pairs of shoes were sold that month?

27. An electrician, Sparky Wilson, starts the day with 650 feet of wire on his truck. In the morning, he cuts off pieces 26, 78, 45, and 89 feet long. During lunch, he goes to an electrical supply warehouse and buys another 250 feet of wire. In the afternoon, he uses lengths of 75, 89, and 120 feet. How many feet of wire are still on the truck at the end of the day?

DOLLARS AND SENSE

In 2009, the AARP launched www.lifetuner.org, a website of financial advice targeting those in their 20s and 30s. According to *USA Today*, the site contains tips from financial experts as well as calculators to help you budget and determine ways to reduce debt.

28. Use the U.S. Postal Service Mail Volume graph on the next page to answer the following questions.
    a. How many pieces were delivered in 2005 and 2006 combined?

b. How many fewer pieces were delivered in 2009 than in 2007?

c. Write the number of pieces of mail for 2008 in numerical form.

29. Eileen Townsend is planting her flower beds. She initially bought 72 bedding plants at Home Depot.

   a. If she plants 29 in the front bed, how many plants remain unplanted?

   b. Eileen's remaining flower beds have room for 65 bedding plants. How many more plants must she buy to fill up the flower beds?

   c. How many total plants did she buy?

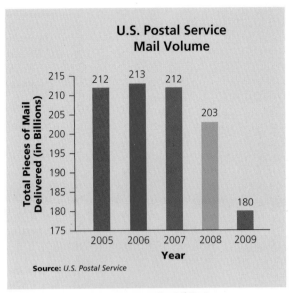

U.S. Postal Service Mail Volume

Source: *U.S. Postal Service*

Postal Facts

The **U.S. Postal Service** delivers billions of pieces of mail each year to more than 149 million residences, businesses, and Post Office Boxes in every state, city, town, and borough in America. In 2008, the USPS had over 656,000 career employees in 32,741 post offices, handling an average of 667 million pieces of mail each day.

The USPS has the largest civilian fleet of vehicles in the world, 221,000, driving over 1.2 billion miles each year and using 1.21 million gallons of fuel.

30. An Allied Vans Lines moving truck picks up loads of furniture weighing 5,500 pounds, 12,495 pounds, and 14,562 pounds. The truck weighs 11,480 pounds, and the driver weighs 188 pounds. If a bridge has a weight limit of 42,500 pounds, is the truck within the weight limit to cross the bridge?

BUSINESS DECISION: PERSONAL BALANCE SHEET

31. A personal *balance sheet* is the financial picture of how much "wealth" you have accumulated as of a certain date. It specifically lists your *assets* (i.e., what you own) and your *liabilities* (i.e., what you owe). Your current *net worth* is the difference between the assets and the liabilities.

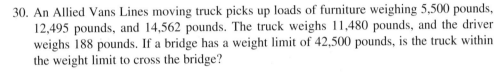

Net worth = Assets − Liabilities

Tom and Carol Jackson have asked for your help in preparing a personal balance sheet. They have listed the following assets and liabilities: current value of home, $144,000; audio/video equipment, $1,340; automobiles, $17,500; personal property, $4,350; computer, $3,700; mutual funds, $26,700; 401(k) retirement plan, $53,680; jewelry, $4,800; certificates of deposit, $19,300; stock investments, $24,280; furniture and other household goods, $8,600; balance on Wal-Mart and Sears charge accounts, $4,868; automobile loan balance, $8,840; home mortgage balance, $106,770; Visa and MasterCard balances, $4,211; savings account balance, $3,700; Carol's night school tuition loan balance, $2,750; checking account balance, $1,385; signature loan balance, $6,350.

Use the data provided and the personal balance sheet on page 14 to calculate the following for the Jacksons.

   a. Total assets

   b. Total liabilities

   c. Net worth

   d. Explain the importance of the personal balance sheet. How often should this information be updated?

"CAN YOU CALL BACK LATER? LORETTA'S GOING OVER THE BUDGET ... WAY, WAY OVER."

wmhoest@aol.com ©2003 WM. HOEST ENTERPRISES, INC. Distributed by King Features Syndicate.

PERSONAL BALANCE SHEET

ASSETS		LIABILITIES	
CURRENT ASSETS		**CURRENT LIABILITIES**	
Checking account	_____	Store charge accounts	_____
Savings account	_____	Credit card accounts	_____
Certificates of deposit	_____	Other current debt	_____
Other	_____	**Total Current Liabilities**	_____
Total Current Assets	_____	**LONG-TERM LIABILITIES**	
LONG-TERM ASSETS		Home mortgage	_____
Investments		Automobile loan	_____
Retirement plans	_____	Education loan	_____
Stocks	_____	Other loan	_____
Bonds	_____	Other loan	_____
Mutual funds	_____	**Total Long-Term Liabilities**	_____
Other	_____	**TOTAL LIABILITIES**	_____
Personal			
Home	_____		
Automobiles	_____		
Furniture	_____		
Personal property	_____		
Jewelry	_____	**NET WORTH**	
Other	_____	**Total Assets**	_____
Other	_____	**Total Liabilities**	_____
Total Long-Term Assets	_____		
TOTAL ASSETS	_____	**NET WORTH**	_____

Just as with corporate statements, **personal financial statements** are an important indicator of your financial position. The balance sheet, income statement, and cash flow statement are most commonly used. When compared over a period of time, they tell a story of where you have been and where you are going financially.

SECTION III — 1

MULTIPLICATION AND DIVISION OF WHOLE NUMBERS

Multiplication and division are the next two mathematical procedures used with whole numbers. Both are found in business as often as addition and subtraction. In reality, most business problems involve a combination of procedures. For example, invoices, which are a detailed list of goods and services sold by a company, require multiplication of items by the price per item and then addition to reach a total. From the total, discounts are frequently subtracted or transportation charges are added.

1-5 MULTIPLYING WHOLE NUMBERS AND VERIFYING YOUR ANSWERS

multiplication The combination of two numbers in which the number of times one is represented is determined by the value of the other.

multiplicand In multiplication, the number being multiplied. For example, 5 is the multiplicand of $5 \times 4 = 20$.

Multiplication of whole numbers is actually a shortcut method for addition. Let's see how this works. If a clothing store buys 12 pairs of jeans at $29 per pair, what is the total cost of the jeans? One way to solve this problem is to add $29 + $29 + . . . , 12 times. It's not hard to see how tedious this repeated addition becomes, especially with large numbers. By using multiplication, we get the answer in one step: $12 \times 29 = 348$.

Multiplication is the combination of two whole numbers in which the number of times one is represented is determined by the value of the other. These two whole numbers are known as factors. The number being multiplied is the **multiplicand**, and the number by which the multiplicand is multiplied is the **multiplier**. The answer to a multiplication problem is the **product**. Intermediate answers are called partial products.

$$
\begin{array}{r}
258 \\
\times \quad 43 \\
\hline
774 \\
10\ 32 \\
\hline
11{,}094
\end{array}
\quad
\begin{array}{l}
\text{multiplicand or factor} \\
\text{multiplier or factor} \\
\text{partial product 1} \\
\text{partial product 2} \\
\text{product}
\end{array}
$$

In mathematics, the **times sign**—represented by the symbols "$\times$" and "$\cdot$" and "( )"—is used to indicate multiplication. For example, 12 times 18 can be expressed as

$$12 \times 18 \qquad 12 \cdot 18 \qquad (12)(18) \qquad 12(18)$$

Note: The raised symbol $\cdot$ is *not* a decimal point.

multiplier The number by which the multiplicand is multiplied. For example, 4 is the multiplier of $5 \times 4 = 20$.

product The answer or result of multiplication. The number 20 is the product of $5 \times 4 = 20$.

times sign The symbol "$\times$" representing multiplication. Also represented by a raised dot "$\cdot$" or parentheses "( )".

STEPS FOR MULTIPLYING WHOLE NUMBERS

STEP 1. Write the factors in columns so that the place values line up.

STEP 2. Multiply each digit of the multiplier, starting with units, times the multiplicand. Each will yield a partial product whose units digit appears under the corresponding digit of the multiplier.

STEP 3. Add the digits in each column of the partial products, starting on the right with the units column.

MULTIPLICATION SHORTCUTS

The following shortcuts can be used to make multiplication easier and faster.

1. **When multiplying any number times 0,** the resulting product is *always* 0. For example,

$$573 \times 0 = 0 \qquad 0 \times 34 = 0 \qquad 1{,}254{,}779 \times 0 = 0$$

2. **When multiplying a number times 1, the product is that number itself.** For example,

$$1{,}844 \times 1 = 1{,}844 \qquad 500 \times 1 = 500 \qquad 1 \times 894 = 894$$

3. **When a number is multiplied by 10, 100, 1,000, 10,000, 100,000, and so on,** simply add the zeros of the multiplier to the end of that number. For example,

$$792 \times 100 = 792 + 00 = 79{,}200 \qquad 9{,}345 \times 1{,}000 = 9{,}345 + 000 = 9{,}345{,}000$$

4. **When the multiplier has a 0 in one or more of its middle digits,** there is no need to write a whole line of zeros as a partial product. Simply place a 0 in the next partial product row directly below the 0 in the multiplier and go on to the next digit in the multiplier. The next partial product will start on the same row one place to the left of the 0 and directly below its corresponding digit in the multiplier. For example, consider 554 times 103.

$$
\textit{Shortcut:}\quad
\begin{array}{r}
554 \\
\times\ 103 \\
\hline
1\ 662 \\
55\ 40 \\
\hline
57{,}062
\end{array}
\qquad\qquad
\textit{Long way:}\quad
\begin{array}{r}
554 \\
\times\ 103 \\
\hline
1\ 662 \\
0\ 00 \\
55\ 4 \\
\hline
57{,}062
\end{array}
$$

5. **When the multiplicand and/or the multiplier have zeros at the end,** multiply the two numbers without the zeros and add that number of zeros to the product. For example,

$$
130 \times 90 = \quad
\begin{array}{r}
13 \\
\times\ 9 \\
\hline
117 + 00 = 11{,}700
\end{array}
$$

$$
5{,}800 \times 3{,}400 = \quad
\begin{array}{r}
58 \\
\times\ 34 \\
\hline
232 \\
1\ 74 \\
\hline
1{,}972 + 0000 = 19{,}720{,}000
\end{array}
$$

VERIFYING MULTIPLICATION

To check your multiplication for accuracy, divide the product by the multiplier. If the multiplication was correct, this will yield the multiplicand. For example,

Multiplication	Verification	Multiplication	Verification
48		527	
× 7		× 18	
336	$336 ÷ 7 = 48$	4 216	
		5 27	
		9,486	$9,486 ÷ 18 = 527$

EXAMPLE5 MULTIPLYING WHOLE NUMBERS

Multiply the following numbers and verify your answers by division.

a. 2,293   b. 59,300   c. 436 × 2,027   d. 877 × 1   e. 6,922 × 0
    ×   45   ×   180

f. Maytag Industries has a new aluminum parts molding machine that produces 85 parts per minute. How many parts can this machine produce in an hour? If a company has 15 of these machines and they run for 8 hours per day, what is the total output of parts per day?

SOLUTIONSTRATEGY

a. 2,293   This is a standard multiplication problem with two partial products.
    ×   45   Always be sure to keep your columns lined up. The answer,
    11 465   103,185, can be verified by division: $103,185 ÷ 45 = 2,293$
    91 72
    103,185

b. 593   In this problem, we remove the three zeros, multiply,
    × 18   and then add back the zeros.
    4 744   Verification: $10,674 ÷ 18 = 593$
    5 93
    $10,674 + 000 = \underline{10,674,000}$

c. 2,027   This is another standard multiplication problem. Note
    × 436   that the larger number was made the multiplicand (top)
    12 162   and the smaller number became the multiplier. This
    60 81   makes the problem easier to work.
    810 8   Verification: $883,772 ÷ 436 = 2,027$
    883,772

d. $877 × 1 = \underline{877}$ Remember, any number multiplied by 1 is that number.

e. $6,922 × 0 = \underline{0}$ Remember, any number multiplied by 0 is 0.

f. 85 parts per minute × 60 minutes per hour = $\underline{5,100}$ parts per hour

5,100 parts per hour × 15 machines = 76,500 parts per hour, all machines

76,500 parts per hour × 8 hours per day = $\underline{612,000}$ parts per day, total output

TRYITEXERCISE5

Multiply the following numbers and verify your answers.

a. 8,203   b. 5,400   c. 3,370   d. 189 × 169
    × 508   × 250   × 4,002

e. Howard Martin, a plasterer, can finish 150 square feet of interior wall per hour. If he works 6 hours per day
    • How many square feet can he finish per day?
    • If a contractor hires four plasterers, how many feet can they finish in a 5-day week?

CHECK YOUR ANSWERS WITH THE SOLUTIONS ON PAGE 25.

DIVIDING WHOLE NUMBERS AND VERIFYING YOUR ANSWERS

1-6

Just as multiplication is a shortcut for repeated addition, division is a shortcut for repeated subtraction. Let's say while shopping you want to know how many $5 items you can purchase with $45. You could get the answer by finding out how many times 5 can be subtracted from 45. You would begin by subtracting 5 from 45 to get 40, then subtracting 5 from 40 to get 35, subtracting 5 from 35 to get 30, and so on, until you got to 0. Quite tedious, but it does give you the answer, 9. By using division, we simply ask how many $5 are contained in $45. By dividing 45 by 5, we get the answer in one step ($45 \div 5 = 9$). Because division is the opposite of multiplication, we can verify our answer by multiplying 5 times 9 to get 45.

Division of whole numbers is the process of determining how many times one number is contained within another number. The number being divided is called the **dividend**, the number doing the dividing is called the **divisor**, and the answer is known as the **quotient**. When the divisor has only one digit, as in 100 divided by 5, it is called short division. When the divisor has more than one digit, as in 100 divided by 10, it is known as long division.

The "$\div$" symbol represents division and is known as the **division sign**. For example, $12 \div 4$ is read "12 divided by 4." Another way to show division is

$$\frac{12}{4}$$

This is also read as "12 divided by 4." To actually solve the division, we use the sign $\overline{)}$. The problem is then written as $4\overline{)12}$. As in addition, subtraction, and multiplication, proper alignment of the digits is very important.

$$\frac{\text{Divided}}{\text{Divisor}} = \text{Quotient} \qquad \text{Divisor }\overline{)\text{Dividend}}^{\text{Quotient}}$$

When the divisor divides evenly into the dividend, it is known as even division. When the divisor does not divide evenly into the dividend, the answer then becomes a quotient plus a **remainder**. The remainder is the amount left over after the division is completed. This is known as uneven division. In this chapter, a remainder of 3, for example, will be expressed as R 3. In Chapter 2, remainders will be expressed as fractions, and in Chapter 3, remainders will be expressed as decimals.

division The mathematical process of determining how many times one number is contained within another number.

dividend In division, the quantity being divided. For example, 20 is the dividend of $20 \div 5 = 4$.

divisor The quantity by which another quantity, the dividend, is being divided. The number doing the dividing. For example, 5 is the divisor of $20 \div 5 = 4$.

quotient The answer or result of division. The number 4 is the quotient of $20 \div 5 = 4$.

division sign The symbol "$\div$" representing division.

remainder In uneven division, the amount left over after the division is completed. For example, 2 is the remainder of $22 \div 5 = 4$, R 2.

VERIFYING DIVISION

To verify even division, multiply the quotient by the divisor. If the problem was worked correctly, this will yield the dividend. To verify uneven division, multiply the quotient by the divisor and add the remainder to the product. If the problem was worked correctly, this will yield the dividend.

EVEN DIVISION ILLUSTRATED

$$\frac{850 \text{ (dividend)}}{25 \text{ (divisor)}} = 34 \text{ (quotient)}$$

$$\begin{array}{r} 34 \\ 25\overline{)850} \\ 75\downarrow \\ \hline 100 \\ 100 \\ \hline 0 \end{array}$$

Verification: $34 \times 25 = 850$

UNEVEN DIVISION ILLUSTRATED

$$\frac{850 \text{ (dividend)}}{20 \text{ (divisor)}} = 42 \text{ R } 10 \text{ (quotient)}$$

$$\begin{array}{r} 42 \text{ R } 10 \\ 20\overline{)850} \\ 80\downarrow \\ \hline 50 \\ 40 \\ \hline 10 \end{array}$$

Verification: $\begin{array}{r} 42 \times 20 = 840 \\ + 10 \\ \hline 850 \end{array}$

DIVISION SHORTCUT

When both the dividend and the divisor end in one or more zeros, you can remove an *equal* number of zeros from each and then divide. This gives the same answer with much less work. For example, 7,000 divided by 200 is the same as 70 divided by 2. *Note:* Although 7,000 has three zeros, you can't remove three zeros, because 200 has only two zeros.

$$\frac{70\cancel{00}}{2\cancel{00}} = 35 \qquad \frac{70}{2} = 35$$

 STEPS FOR DIVIDING WHOLE NUMBERS

STEP 1. Determine the first group of digits in the dividend that the divisor will divide into at least once. Divide and place the partial quotient over the last digit in that group.

STEP 2. Multiply the partial quotient by the divisor. Place it under the first group of digits and subtract.

STEP 3. From the dividend, bring down the next digit after the first group of digits.

STEP 4. Repeat Steps 1, 2, and 3 until all of the digits in the dividend have been brought down.

EXAMPLE 6 DIVIDING WHOLE NUMBERS

Divide the following numbers and verify your answers.

a. $210 \div 7$ b. $185 \div 9$ c. $\dfrac{1,508}{6}$ d. $\dfrac{14,000}{3,500}$

e. On an assembly line, a packing machine uses rolls of rope containing 650 feet. How many 8-foot pieces can be cut from each roll?

SOLUTION STRATEGY

a.
$$\begin{array}{r} 30 \\ 7\overline{)210} \\ 21\downarrow \\ \hline 00 \end{array}$$

This is an example of even division. Note that there is no remainder.

Verification: $30 \times 7 = 210$

b.
$$\begin{array}{r} 20\ R\ 5 \\ 9\overline{)185} \\ 18\downarrow \\ \hline 5 \end{array}$$

This example illustrates uneven division. Note that there is a remainder.

Verification:
$$\begin{array}{r} 20 \times 9 = 180 \\ +\ 5 \\ \hline 185 \end{array}$$

c.
$$\begin{array}{r} 251\ R\ 2 \\ 6\overline{)1508} \\ 12 \\ \hline 30 \\ 30\downarrow \\ \hline 08 \\ 6 \\ \hline 2 \end{array}$$

This is another example of uneven division. Be sure to keep the digits properly lined up.

Verification:
$$\begin{array}{r} 251 \times 6 = 1,506 \\ +\ \ 2 \\ \hline 1,508 \end{array}$$

d.
$$\begin{array}{r} 4 \\ 35\overline{)140} \\ 140 \\ \hline 0 \end{array}$$

In this example, we simplify the division by deleting two zeros from the dividend and the divisor.

Verification: $4 \times 35 = 140$

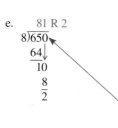

e.
$$
\begin{array}{r}
81\ R\ 2 \\
8\overline{)650} \\
64 \\
\hline
10 \\
8 \\
\hline
2
\end{array}
$$

In this word problem, we want to know how many 8-foot pieces of rope are contained in a 650-foot roll. The dividend is 650, and the divisor is 8. The quotient, 81 R 2, means that 81 whole pieces of rope can be cut from the roll with some left over, but not enough for another whole piece.

Verification: $81 \times 8 = 648$
$$
\begin{array}{r}
+\ 2 \\
\hline
650
\end{array}
$$

● TRYITEXERCISE6

Divide the following numbers and verify your answers.

a. $910 \div 35$
b. $1,503 \div 160$
c. $\dfrac{3,358}{196}$
d. $\dfrac{175,000}{12,000}$

e. Delta Industries has 39 production line workers, each making the same amount of money. If last week's total payroll amounted to $18,330, how much did each employee earn?

CHECK YOUR ANSWERS WITH THE SOLUTIONS ON PAGE 25.

REVIEW EXERCISES

SECTION III   **1**

Multiply the following numbers and verify your answers.

JUMP START WWW

1. 589	2. 1,292	3. 327	4. 76,000	5. 56,969
$\times\ 19$	$\times\ 158$	$\times\ 900$	$\times\ 45$	$\times\ 1,000$
11,191				

6. Multiply $4 by 501
7. 23×570
8. What is 475 times 12?

Estimate the following by rounding each number all the way; then multiply to get the exact answer.

JUMP START WWW

	Estimate	Rounded Estimate	Exact Answer
9. 202	200	100,000	98,980
$\times\ 490$	$\times\ 500$		
98,980	100,000		
10. 515		_____	_____
$\times\ 180$			
11. 17		_____	_____
$\times\ 11$			

12. Dazzling Designs made custom drapery for a client using 30 yards of material.
    a. At $5 per yard, what is the cost of the material?

    b. If the company received 4 more orders of the same size, how much material will be needed to fill the orders?

13. On April 29, 2010, a new U.S. Department of Transportation rule went into effect. It states that airlines must let passengers off domestic flights when they have waited three hours without taking off. Airlines that don't comply can be fined up to $27,500 per passenger.

    If a Premium Airlines 767 aircraft with 254 passengers on board was fined the maximum penalty for waiting four hours on the tarmac at JFK before takeoff last Tuesday, what was the amount of the fine?

14. There are 34 stairs from bottom to top in each of five stairways in the football bleachers at Waycross Stadium. If each track team member is to run four complete sets up and down each stairway, how many stairs will be covered in a workout?

15. To earn extra money while attending college, you work as a cashier in a restaurant.
    a. Find the total bill for the following food order: three sirloin steak dinners at $12 each; two baked chicken specials at $7 each; four steak burger platters at $5 each; two extra salads at $2 each; six drinks at $1 each; and tax of $7.

    b. How much change will you give back if the check is paid with a $100 bill?

16. Bob Powers, a consulting electrical engineer, is offered two different jobs. Abbott Industries has a project that pays $52 per hour and will take 35 hours to complete. Micro Systems has a project that pays $44 per hour and will take 45 hours to complete. Which offer has a greater gross income and by how much?

Divide the following numbers.

17. 4,500 ÷ 35   18. 74,770 ÷ 5,700   19. $\dfrac{60,000}{250}$ 20. $\dfrac{236,500,000}{4,300,000}$

```
        128 R 20
   35) 4500
        35
        ___
        100
         70
        ___
        300
        280
        ___
         20
```

Estimate the following by rounding each number to hundreds; then divide to get the exact answer.

	Estimate	Rounded Estimate	Exact Answer
21. 890 ÷ 295	$\dfrac{900}{300}$	3	3 R 5
22. 1,499 ÷ 580		_____	_____
23. 57,800 ÷ 102		_____	_____

24. Tip-Top Roofing has 50,640 square feet of roofing material on hand. If the average roof requires 8,440 square feet of material, how many roofs can be installed?

25. A calculator uses eight circuit boards, each containing 450 parts. A company has 421,215 parts in stock.

   a. How many calculators can it manufacture?

   b. How many parts will be left?

26. Eric Shotwell borrows $24,600 from the Mercantile Bank and Trust Co. The interest charge amounts to $8,664. What equal monthly payments must Eric make in order to pay back the loan, with interest, in 36 months?

27. A 16-person college basketball team is going to a tournament in Boston. As the team manager, you are trying to find the best price for hotel rooms. The Windsor Hotel is quoting a price of $108 for 2 people in a room and $10 for each extra person. The Royale Hotel is quoting a price of $94 for 2 people in a room and $15 for each extra person. If the maximum number of people allowed in a room is 4, which hotel would be more economical?

Hotel Choice Factors

Price 49.57%
Location 23.61%
Star Rating 16.52%
Amenities 10.30%

Hotels.com Survey
When selecting a hotel, what do you consider most important?

© hotels.com/PR Newswire Photo Service/NewsCom

28. You have just purchased a 65-acre ranch for a price of $780 per acre. In addition, the house was valued at $125,000 and the equipment amounted to $22,300.

   a. What was the total price of your purchase?

   b. Since the owner was anxious to sell, he offered to finance the ranch for you with a no-interest mortgage loan. What would your monthly payments be to pay off the loan in 10 years?

   c. Besides the mortgage payment, you are required to make monthly property tax and insurance payments. If property tax is $3,000 per year and insurance is $2,400 per year, how much would these items add to your monthly expenses for the ranch?

29. You are the IT manager for Liberty Industries. In 2002, you purchased 12 laptop computers and 15 desktop computers for your office staff. Using the graph Average PC Prices, answer the following:

   a. What was the total amount of the purchase for these computers in 2002?

   b. In 2009, you replaced all of the computers with new ones. What was the total amount of the purchase for these computers?

   c. In total, how much did you save in 2009 over 2002 because of falling computer prices?

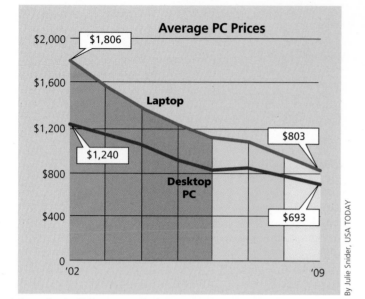

Average PC Prices

By Julie Snider, USA TODAY

According to Gartner research, the top five worldwide PC vendors by market share are Hewlett-Packard – 19.9%, Acer – 15.4%, Dell Inc. – 12.8%, Lenovo – 8.5%, and Toshiba – 5.0%.

BUSINESS DECISION: ESTIMATING A TILE JOB

30. You are the owner of Decorama Flooring. Todd and Claudia have asked you to give them an estimate for tiling four rooms of their house. The living room is 15 feet × 23 feet, the dining room is 12 feet × 18 feet, the kitchen is 9 feet × 11 feet, and the study is 10 feet × 12 feet.
   a. How many square feet of tile are required for each room? (Multiply the length by the width.)

   b. What is the total number of square feet to be tiled?

   c. If the tile for the kitchen and study costs $4 per square foot and the tile for the living and dining rooms costs $3 per square foot, what is the total cost of the tile?

   d. If your company charges $2 per square foot for installation, what is the total cost of the tile job?

   e. If Todd and Claudia have saved $4,500 for the tile job, by how much are they over or under the amount needed?

CHAPTER SUMMARY

Section I: The Decimal Number System: Whole Numbers

Topic	Important Concepts	Illustrative Examples
Reading and Writing Whole Numbers in Numerical and Word Form **Performance Objective 1-1, Page 2**	1. Insert the commas every three digits to mark the groups, beginning at the right side of the number. 2. From left to right, name the digits and the units group. The units group and groups that have all zeros are not named. 3. When writing whole numbers in word form, the numbers from 21 to 99 are hyphenated, expect for the decades (e.g., thirty). *Note:* The word *and* should not be used in reading or writing whole numbers.	Write each number in numerical and word form. The number 15538 takes on the numerical form 15,538 and is read, "fifteen thousand, five hundred thirty-eight." The number 22939643 takes on the numerical form 22,939,643 and is read, "twenty-two million, nine hundred thirty-nine thousand, six hundred forty-three." The number 1000022 takes on the numerical value 1,000,022 and is read, "one million, twenty-two."
Rounding Whole Numbers to a Specified Place Value **Performance Objective 1-2, Page 4**	1. Determine the place to which the number is to be rounded. 2a. If the digit to the right of the one being rounded is 5 or more, increase the digit in the place being rounded by 1. 2b. If the digit to the right of the one being rounded is 4 or less, do not change the digit in the place being rounded. 3. Change all digits to the right of the place being rounded to zeros.	Round as indicated. 1,449 to tens = 1,450 255 to hundreds = 300 345,391 to thousands = 345,000 68,658,200 to millions = 69,000,000 768,892 all the way = 800,000

Section II: Addition and Subtraction of Whole Numbers

Topic	Important Concepts	Illustrative Examples
Adding Whole Numbers and Verifying Your Answers **Performance Objective 1-3, Page 7**	1. Write the whole numbers in columns so that the place values line up. 2. Add the digits in each column, starting on the right with the units column. 3. When the total in a column is greater than 9, write the units digit and carry the tens digit to the top of the next column to the left. To verify addition, add the numbers in reverse, from bottom to top.	Add 2 11 1,931 addend 2,928 addend + 5,857 addend 10,716 sum ◄ Verification: 2 11 5,857 2,928 + 1,931 10,716
Subtracting Whole Numbers and Verifying Your Answers **Performance Objective 1-4, Page 9**	1. Write the whole numbers in columns so that the place values line up. 2. Starting with the units column, subtract the digits. 3. When a column cannot be subtracted, borrow a digit from the column to the left of the one you are working in. To verify subtraction, add the difference and the subtrahend; this should equal the minuend.	Subtract 34,557 minuend ◄ − 6,224 subtrahend 28,333 difference Verification: 28,333 + 6,224 34,557

Section III: Multiplication and Division of Whole Numbers

Topic	Important Concepts	Illustrative Examples
Multiplying Whole Numbers and Verifying Your Answers **Performance Objective 1-5, Page 14**	1. Write the multiplication factors in columns so that the place values are lined up. 2. Multiply each digit of the multiplier, starting with units, times the multiplicand. Each will yield a partial product whose units digit appears under the corresponding digit of the multiplier. 3. Add the digits in each column of the partial products, starting on the right, with the units column. To verify multiplication, divide the product by the multiplier. If the multiplication is correct, it should yield the multiplicand.	Multiply 258×43 $\quad 258$ multiplicand or factor $\times\ 43$ multiplier or factor $\quad 774$ partial product 1 $10\ 32\ \ $ partial product 2 $11,094$ product Verification: $$\dfrac{11,094}{43} = 258$$
Dividing Whole Numbers and Verifying Your Answers **Performance Objective 1-6, Page 17**	1. The number being divided is the dividend. The number by which we are dividing is the divisor. The answer is known as the quotient. $$\text{Divisor}\overline{)\,\text{Dividend}}^{\text{Quotient}}$$ 2. If the divisor does not divide evenly into the dividend, the quotient will have a remainder. To verify division, multiply the divisor by the quotient and add the remainder. If the division is correct, it will yield the dividend.	Divide six hundred fifty by twenty-seven. $$650 \div 27 = \dfrac{650}{27} = 27\overline{)650}^{\ 24\ R\ 2}$$ $\quad\quad\quad\quad\quad\quad\ \ \underline{54}$ $\quad\quad\quad\quad\quad\quad\ 110$ $\quad\quad\quad\quad\quad\quad\ \underline{108}$ $\quad\quad\quad\quad\quad\quad\quad\ 2$ Verification: $27 \times 24 = 648 + 2 = 650$

TRY IT: EXERCISE SOLUTIONS FOR CHAPTER 1

Numerical Form	**Word Form**
1a. 49,588	Forty-nine thousand, five hundred eighty-eight
1b. 804	Eight hundred four
1c. 1,928,837	One million, nine hundred twenty-eight thousand, eight hundred thirty-seven
1d. 900,015	Nine hundred thousand, fifteen
1e. 6,847,365,911	Six billion, eight hundred forty-seven million, three hundred sixty-five thousand, nine hundred eleven
1f. 2,000,300,007	Two billion, three hundred thousand, seven

2a. 51,700   **2b.** 23,440   **2c.** 175,450,000   **2d.** 60,000   **2e.** 15,000,000,000   **2f.** 8,010,000,000

3a.
```
  39,481     Verify:   11,029
   5,594                5,594
 +11,029              + 39,481
  56,104                56,104
```

3b.
```
   6,948     Verify:   18,606
     330                    7
   7,946              5,583,991
      89                   89
 5,583,991             7,946
       7                  330
 + 18,606             +  6,948
 5,617,917            5,617,917
```

3c.
```
     183     Verify:    1,157
     228                  438
     281                  545
     545                  281
     438                  228
 + 1,157               +  183
   2,832 Meals          2,832 Meals
```

4a.
```
  98,117     Verify:   90,435
 -  7,682             +  7,682
   90,435               98,117
```

4b.
```
  12,395     Verify:    6,806
 -  5,589             +  5,589
    6,806               12,395
```

4c.
```
  $4,589     Verify:   $4,245
 -    344             +    344
  $4,245 Left in account  $4,589
```

5a.
$$\begin{array}{r} 8{,}203 \\ \times\ 508 \\ \hline 65\ 624 \\ 4\ 101\ 50 \\ \hline 4{,}167{,}124 \end{array}$$

Verify:
$$\frac{4{,}167{,}124}{508} = 8{,}203$$

5b.
$$\begin{array}{r} 5{,}400 \\ \times\ 250 \\ \hline 270\ 000 \\ 1\ 080\ 00 \\ \hline 1{,}350{,}000 \end{array}$$

Verify:
$$\frac{1{,}350{,}000}{250} = 5{,}400$$

5c.
$$\begin{array}{r} 3{,}370 \\ \times\ 4{,}002 \\ \hline 6\ 740 \\ 13\ 480\ 00 \\ \hline 13{,}486{,}740 \end{array}$$

Verify:
$$\frac{13{,}486{,}740}{4{,}002} = 3{,}370$$

5d. 189×169
$$\begin{array}{r} 189 \\ \times\ 169 \\ \hline 1701 \\ 1134 \\ 189 \\ \hline 31{,}941 \end{array}$$

Verify:
$$\frac{31{,}941}{169} = 189$$

5e.
$$\begin{array}{r} 150 \\ \times\ 6 \\ \hline 900 \end{array} \text{ sq ft per day}$$

$$\begin{array}{r} 900 \\ \times\ 4 \\ \hline 3{,}600 \end{array} \text{ Plasterers} \quad \text{sq ft per day}$$

$$\begin{array}{r} 3{,}600 \\ \times\ 5 \\ \hline 18{,}000 \end{array} \text{ Days} \quad \text{sq ft in 5 days}$$

6a.
$$\begin{array}{r} 26 \\ 35\overline{)910} \\ 70 \\ \hline 210 \\ 210 \\ \hline 0 \end{array}$$

Verify:
$26 \times 35 = 910$

6b.
$$\begin{array}{r} 9\ \text{R}\ 63 \\ 160\overline{)1{,}503} \\ 1440 \\ \hline 63 \end{array}$$

Verify:
$$\begin{array}{r} 160 \times 9 = 1{,}440 \\ +\ \ 63 \\ \hline 1{,}503 \end{array}$$

6c.
$$\begin{array}{r} 17\ \text{R}\ 26 \\ 196\overline{)3{,}358} \\ 1\ 96 \\ \hline 1\ 398 \\ 1\ 372 \\ \hline 26 \end{array}$$

Verify:
$$\begin{array}{r} 196 \times 17 = \ 3{,}332 \\ +\ \ 26 \\ \hline 3{,}358 \end{array}$$

6d.
$$\begin{array}{r} 14\ \text{R}\ 7 \\ 12\overline{)175} \\ 12 \\ \hline 55 \\ 48 \\ \hline 7 \end{array}$$

Verify:
$$\begin{array}{r} 12 \times 14 = \ 168 \\ +\ \ 7 \\ \hline 175 \end{array}$$

6e. $\dfrac{18{,}330}{39} = \underline{\$470}$ Per employee

$$\begin{array}{r} 470 \\ 39\overline{)18{,}330} \\ 15\ 6 \\ \hline 2\ 73 \\ 2\ 73 \\ \hline 0 \end{array}$$

Verify: $39 \times 470 = 18{,}330$

CONCEPT REVIEW

1. The number system most widely used in the world today is known as the Hindu-Arabic numeral system, or _____ number system. (1-1)

2. Our number system utilizes the 10 Hindu-Arabic symbols _____ through _____ to write any number. (1-1)

3. The set of numbers 1, 2, 3, 4 . . . are known as _____ numbers. (1-1)

4. On the place-value chart, whole numbers appear to the _____ of the decimal point. (1-1)

5. A(n) _____ number is an approximation or estimate of an exact number. (1-2)

6. Rounding all the way is a process of rounding numbers to the _____ digit. (1-2)

7. In addition, the numbers being added are known as _____; the answer is known as the _____ . (1-3)

8. When performing addition, we write the addends in columns so that the place values are aligned _____ . (1-3)

9. The mathematical process of taking away, or deducting, an amount from a given number is known as _____ . (1-4)

10. In subtraction, when a column cannot be subtracted, we must _____ a digit from the column to the left. (1-4)

11. In multiplication, the product of any number and 0 is _____ . (1-5)

12. In multiplication, the product of any number and _____ is the number itself. (1-5)

13. The amount left over after division is completed is known as the _____ . (1-6)

14. Show four ways to express 15 divided by 5. (1-6)

CHAPTER 1

ASSESSMENT TEST

Read and write the following whole numbers in numerical and word form.

Number	Numerical Form	Word Form

1. 200049 _____ _____

2. 52308411 _____ _____

Write the following whole numbers in numerical form.

3. Three hundred sixteen thousand, two hundred twenty-nine

4. Four million, five hundred sixty thousand

Round the following numbers to the indicated place.

5. 18,334 to hundreds

6. 3,545,687 all the way

7. 256,733 to ten thousands

Perform the indicated operation for the following.

8.
$$\begin{array}{r} 1,860 \\ 429 \\ 133 \\ + 1,009 \\ \hline \end{array}$$

9.
$$\begin{array}{r} 927 \\ - 828 \\ \hline \end{array}$$

10.
$$\begin{array}{r} 207 \\ \times 106 \\ \hline \end{array}$$

11. $42\overline{)1876}$

12.
$$\begin{array}{r} 3,505 \\ \times 290 \\ \hline \end{array}$$

13.
$$\begin{array}{r} 6,800 \\ 919 \\ 201 \\ + 14,338 \\ \hline \end{array}$$

14. $150,000 \div 188$

15. $1,205 - 491$

16. The following chart shows the number of meals served at the Gourmet Diner last week. Use addition and subtraction to fill in the blank spaces. What is the week's grand total?

Gourmet Diner

	Monday	Tuesday	Wednesday	Thursday	Friday	Saturday	Total Units
Breakfast	82	___	68	57	72	92	427
Lunch	29	69	61	___	82	75	___
Dinner	96	103	71	108	112	159	___
Daily Totals	___	___	___	223	___	**Grand** ___ **Total** ___

17. You are the bookkeeper for the Gourmet Diner in Exercise 16. If breakfasts average $4 each, lunches average $7 each, and dinners average $13 each, calculate the total dollar sales for last week.

18. The stadium parking lot at Fairview College contained 5,949 cars last Saturday for the homecoming football game.
    a. If there are 3 entrances to the lot, what was the average number of cars that came through each entrance?

    b. If, on average, each car brought 4 people and 2,560 people walked to the stadium from the dormitories and fraternity houses, how many people attended the game?

19. Camp Minnewonka, a summer camp in the Rocky Mountains, has budgeted $85,500 for a new fleet of sailboats. The boat selected is a deluxe model costing $4,500.
    a. How many boats can be purchased by the camp?

    b. If, instead, a standard model was chosen costing $3,420, how many boats could be purchased?

20. According to *USA Today*, in 2009, Facebook dominated the world of snapshot sharing with an estimated 2 billion photographs uploaded per month. That averages to about 750 photographs per second!
    a. At that rate, how many photographs are uploaded per hour?

    b. Write the number of photographs per hour in word form.

facebook

Facebook helps you connect and share with the people in your life.

Facebook

Facebook is a social networking website with more than 350 million active users. Users can add friends, send them messages, and update their personal profiles to notify friends about themselves. Additionally, users can join networks organized by city, workplace, school, and region.

21. You are in charge of organizing the annual stockholders' meeting and luncheon for your company, Tundra Industries, Inc. The meal will cost $13 per person, entertainment will cost $2,100, facility rental is $880, invitations and annual report printing costs are $2,636, and other expenses come to $1,629. If 315 stockholders plan to attend:
    a. What is the total cost of the luncheon?

    b. What is the cost per stockholder?

22. According to the U.S. Department of Education, 1,508,000 students were home-schooled in 2007 compared with 850,000 students in 1999. How many more students were home-schooled in 2007 than 1999?

23. Katie Jergens had $868 in her checking account on April 1. During the month, she wrote checks for $15, $123, $88, $276, and $34. She also deposited $45, $190, and $436. What is the balance in her checking account at the end of April?

CHAPTER

1

24. A banana nut bread recipe calls for 5 cups of flour. If 4 cups of flour weigh a pound, how many recipes can be made from a 5-pound bag of flour?

25. Brian Hickman bought 2,000 shares of stock at $62 per share. Six months later he sold the 2,000 shares at $87 per share. If the total stockbroker's commission was $740, how much profit did he make on this transaction?

26. The Canmore Mining Company produces 40 tons of ore in an 8-hour shift. The mine operates continuously—3 shifts per day, 7 days per week. How many tons of ore can be extracted in 6 weeks?

27. Last week the *More Joy,* a commercial fishing boat in Alaska, brought in 360 pounds of salmon, 225 pounds of halibut, and 570 pounds of cod. At the dock, the catch was sold to Pacific Seafood Wholesalers. The salmon brought $3 per pound; the halibut, $4 per pound; and the cod, $5 per pound. If fuel and crew expenses amounted to $1,644, how much profit did Captain Bob make on this trip?

Photo by Robert Brechner

Alaskan Fishing Boats

According to the Alaska Department of Fish & Game, Alaska supports one of the most productive commercial fishing economies in the world, with over 9,600 licensed vessels as well as 20,500 licensed crewmembers. In 2008, the Alaskan fishing industry generated $76 million in taxes and license fees.

Alaskan fishermen typically receive well over $1 billion for their catch, while the value of Alaskan seafood sold at first wholesale easily tops $2 billion per year.

28. The Iberia Corporation purchased a new warehouse for $165,000. After a down payment of $45,600, the balance was paid in equal monthly payments, with no interest.
   a. If the loan was paid off in 2 years, how much were the monthly payments?

   b. If the loan was paid off in 5 years, how much *less* were the monthly payments?

29. A flatbed railroad car weighs 150 tons empty and 420 tons loaded with 18 equal-weight trailers. How many tons does each trailer weigh?

30. The Spring Creek Police Department has been asked to provide protection support for a visiting politician. If it has to provide 2 officers at the airport for motorcycle escort, 7 officers for intersection control along the planned route of travel, and 14 officers at the high school auditorium during the speech,
   a. How many officers are to be assigned to the protection detail?

b. If each officer is to be paid $75 extra for this duty, what is the total officer payroll for the protection detail?

31. The following ad for Tire King shows the original and sale prices of certain tires. If 2 tires of each size are to be bought, what will be the total amount saved by purchasing at the sale prices rather than at the original prices?

Tire Size	Original Price	Sale Price
14 in.	$36	$32
15 in.	$40	$34

32. John Rock has narrowed down his selection of a new cell phone to two models with similar features. Model 800 is plug-compatible with his existing car charger and remote earbud/ microphone and will cost $140. There is a $35 mail-in rebate for the Model 800. His other choice is the Model 300, which is not plug-compatible with his existing accessories. The price of the Model 300 is $89, and it has a $20 mail-in rebate. But if he buys the Model 300, he will also have to buy the car charger for $30 and an earbud/microphone for $23.

a. All considered, which model would be the least expensive choice? By how much?

b. For either cell phone choice, the monthly charge will be $34 per month with a $5 rebate if fewer than 250 minutes are used during the month. Government fees and taxes will be $9, the access fee is $7, and the Internet connection charge is $15. Based on last year's usage, John estimates that he will use fewer than 250 minutes in May, June, August, and October. If John's service starts on January 1, how much will he spend in the next year on cellular phone services?

BUSINESS DECISION: CIRQUE DU SOLEIL – ACROBATIC MAGIC

33. As a professional event planner, you have been hired to put together a family reunion at a local performance of Cirque du Soleil. There will be 25 adults, 30 children, and 15 senior citizens attending the reunion.

a. Assuming a ticket budget of $6,500, use the price schedule below to determine the *best* ticket level available for the reunion without going over the budget.

Ticket Prices

Ticket Level	Adult	Child	Senior
1 – Premium	$125	$88	$115
2 – Standard	$95	$66	$85
3 – Budget	$85	$59	$76

© ITAR-TASS Photo Agency/Alamy

Cirque du Soleil

Cirque du Soleil (French for "Circus of the Sun," in English pronounced Serk-doo-Solay), is a Canadian entertainment company, self-described as a "dramatic mix of circus arts and street entertainment." Starting with 20 street performers and 73 employees in 1984, Cirque du Soleil today employs more than 4,000 people from 40 different countries.

Since 1984, Cirque shows have visited more than 200 cities around the world. Nearly 200 million people have seen at least one Cirque du Soleil show. In 2009 alone, more than 15 million people attended one of the 20 touring shows. Estimated annual revenue exceeds $810 million.

b. In addition to the tickets, each person is expected to average $8 in food costs and $29 in bus transportation charges. Your service fee is $250. Calculate the total cost of the reunion.

COLLABORATIVE LEARNING ACTIVITY

Using Math in Business

As a team, discuss and list the ways that math is used in the following types of business. Report your findings to the class.

a. Supermarket

b. Car dealership

c. Beauty salon

d. Dog-walking service

e. Restaurant

f. Additional team choice _____

Image copyright erwinova 2010. Used under license from Shutterstock.com

Fractions

PERFORMANCE OBJECTIVES

SECTION I   ② UNDERSTANDING AND WORKING WITH FRACTIONS

fractions A mathematical way of expressing a part of a whole thing. For example, $\frac{1}{4}$ is a fraction expressing one part out of a total of four parts.

Fractions are a mathematical way of expressing a part of a whole thing. The word *fraction* comes from a Latin word meaning "break." Fractions result from breaking a unit into a number of equal parts. This concept is used quite commonly in business. We may look at sales for $\frac{1}{2}$ the year or reduce prices by $\frac{1}{4}$ for a sale. A new production machine in your company may be $1\frac{3}{4}$ times faster than the old one, or you might want to cut $5\frac{3}{4}$ yards of fabric from a roll of material.

Just like whole numbers, fractions can be added, subtracted, multiplied, divided, and even combined with whole numbers. This chapter introduces you to the various types of fractions and shows you how they are used in the business world.

2-1   DISTINGUISHING AMONG THE VARIOUS TYPES OF FRACTIONS

numerator The number on top of the division line of a fraction. It represents the dividend in the division. In the fraction $\frac{1}{4}$, 1 is the numerator.

denominator The number on the bottom of the division line of a fraction. It represents the divisor in the division. In the fraction $\frac{1}{4}$, 4 is the denominator.

division line The horizontal or slanted line separating the numerator from the denominator. The symbol representing "divided by" in a fraction. In the fraction $\frac{1}{4}$, the line between the 1 and the 4 is the division line.

Technically, fractions express the relationship between two numbers set up as division. The **numerator** is the number on the top of the fraction. It represents the dividend in the division. The **denominator** is the bottom number of the fraction. It represents the divisor. The numerator and the denominator are separated by a horizontal or slanted line, known as the **division line**. This line means "divided by." For example, the fraction 2/3 or $\frac{2}{3}$, read as "two-thirds," means 2 divided by 3, or 2 ÷ 3.

$$\frac{\text{Numerator}}{\text{Denominator}} \qquad \frac{2}{3}$$

Remember, fractions express parts of a whole unit. The unit may be dollars, feet, ounces, or anything else. The denominator describes how many total parts are in the unit. The numerator represents how many of the total parts we are describing or referring to. For example, an apple pie (the whole unit) is divided into eight slices (total equal parts, denominator). As a fraction, the whole pie would be represented as $\frac{8}{8}$. If five of the slices were eaten (parts referred to, numerator), what fraction represents the part that was eaten? The answer would be the fraction $\frac{5}{8}$, read "five-eighths." Because five slices were eaten out of a total of eight, three slices, or $\frac{3}{8}$, of the pie is left.

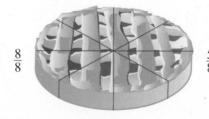 

$\frac{8}{8}$ $\frac{5}{8}$ $\frac{3}{8}$

common or **proper fractions** Fractions in which the numerator is less than the denominator. Represent less than a whole unit. The fraction $\frac{1}{4}$ is a common or proper fraction.

Fractions such as $\frac{3}{8}$ and $\frac{5}{8}$, in which the numerator is smaller than the denominator, represent less than a whole unit and are known as **common** or **proper fractions**. Some examples of proper fractions would be

$$\frac{3}{16} \text{ three-sixteenths} \qquad \frac{1}{4} \text{ one-fourth} \qquad \frac{9}{32} \text{ nine-thirty-seconds}$$

improper fraction A fraction in which the denominator is equal to or less than the numerator. Represents one whole unit or more. The fraction $\frac{4}{1}$ is an improper fraction.

When a fraction's denominator is equal to or less than the numerator, it represents one whole unit or more and is known as an **improper fraction**. Some examples of improper fractions are

$$\frac{9}{9} \text{ nine-ninths} \qquad \frac{15}{11} \text{ fifteen-elevenths} \qquad \frac{19}{7} \text{ nineteen-sevenths}$$

mixed number A number that combines a whole number with a proper fraction. The fraction $10\frac{1}{4}$ is a mixed number.

A number that combines a whole number with a proper fraction is known as a **mixed number**. Some examples of mixed numbers are

$$3\frac{1}{8} \text{ three and one-eighth} \qquad 7\frac{11}{16} \text{ seven and eleven-sixteenths}$$

$$46\frac{51}{60} \text{ forty-six and fifty-one-sixtieths}$$

EXAMPLE1 IDENTIFYING AND WRITING FRACTIONS

For each of the following, identify the type of fraction and write it in word form.

a. $\dfrac{45}{16}$ b. $14\dfrac{2}{5}$ c. $\dfrac{11}{12}$

SOLUTIONSTRATEGY

a. $\dfrac{45}{16}$ This is an <u>improper fraction</u> because the denominator, 16, is less than the numerator, 45. In word form, we say "<u>forty-five-sixteenths</u>." It could also be read as "45 divided by 16" or "45 over 16."

b. $14\dfrac{2}{5}$ This is a <u>mixed number</u> because it combines the whole number 14 with the fraction $\dfrac{2}{5}$. In word form, this is read "<u>fourteen and two-fifths</u>."

c. $\dfrac{11}{12}$ This is a <u>common or proper fraction</u> because the numerator, 11, is less than the denominator, 12. This fraction is read "<u>eleven-twelfths</u>." It could also be read "11 over 12" or "11 divided by 12."

TRYITEXERCISE1

For each of the following, identify the type of fraction and write it in word form.

a. $76\dfrac{3}{4}$ b. $\dfrac{3}{5}$ c. $\dfrac{18}{18}$ d. $\dfrac{33}{8}$

CHECK YOUR ANSWERS WITH THE SOLUTIONS ON PAGE 58.

LEARNINGTIP

A complex fraction is one in which the numerator, the denominator, or both are fractions.

Examples: $\dfrac{\frac{2}{3}}{6}$, $\dfrac{9}{\frac{3}{4}}$, $\dfrac{\frac{7}{8}}{\frac{1}{4}}$

Can you solve them?

(Answers: $\frac{1}{9}$, 12, $3\frac{1}{2}$)

CONVERTING IMPROPER FRACTIONS TO WHOLE OR MIXED NUMBERS

2-2

It often becomes necessary to change or convert an improper fraction to a whole or mixed number. For example, final answers cannot be left as improper fractions; they must be converted.

STEPS FOR CONVERTING IMPROPER FRACTIONS TO WHOLE OR MIXED NUMBERS

STEP 1. Divide the numerator of the improper fraction by the denominator.

STEP 2a. If there is no remainder, the improper fraction becomes a whole number.

STEP 2b. If there is a remainder, write the whole number and then write the fraction as

$$\text{Whole number } \dfrac{\text{Remainder}}{\text{Divisor}}$$

EXAMPLE2 CONVERTING FRACTIONS

Convert the following improper fractions to whole or mixed numbers.

a. $\dfrac{30}{5}$ b. $\dfrac{9}{2}$

SOLUTIONSTRATEGY

a. $\dfrac{30}{5} = \underline{6}$ When we divide the numerator, 30, by the denominator, 5, we get the whole number 6. There is no remainder.

b. $\frac{9}{2} = 2\overline{)9} = 4\frac{1}{2}$ This improper fraction divides 4 times with a remainder of 1; therefore, it will become a mixed number. In this case, the 4 is the whole number. The remainder, 1, becomes the numerator of the new fraction; the divisor, 2, becomes the denominator.

● TRYITEXERCISE2

Convert the following improper fractions to whole or mixed numbers.

a. $\frac{8}{3}$ b. $\frac{25}{4}$ c. $\frac{39}{3}$

CHECK YOUR ANSWERS WITH THE SOLUTIONS ON PAGE 58.

2-3 ## CONVERTING MIXED NUMBERS TO IMPROPER FRACTIONS

STEPS FOR CONVERTING A MIXED NUMBER TO AN IMPROPER FRACTION

STEP 1. Multiply the denominator by the whole number.

STEP 2. Add the numerator to the product from Step 1.

STEP 3. Place the total from Step 2 as the "new" numerator.

STEP 4. Place the original denominator as the "new" denominator.

● EXAMPLE3 CONVERTING FRACTIONS

Convert the following mixed numbers to improper fractions.

a. $5\frac{2}{3}$ b. $9\frac{5}{6}$

● SOLUTIONSTRATEGY

a. $5\frac{2}{3} = \frac{17}{3}$ In this example, we multiply the denominator, 3, by the whole number, 5, and add the numerator, 2, to get 17 ($3 \times 5 + 2 = 17$). We then place the 17 over the original denominator, 3.

b. $9\frac{5}{6} = \frac{59}{6}$ In this example, we multiply the denominator, 6, by the whole number, 9, and add the numerator, 5, to get 59 ($6 \times 9 + 5 = 59$). We then place the 59 over the original denominator, 6.

● TRYITEXERCISE3

Convert the following mixed numbers to improper fractions.

a. $2\frac{3}{4}$ b. $9\frac{1}{5}$ c. $22\frac{5}{8}$

CHECK YOUR ANSWERS WITH THE SOLUTIONS ON PAGE 58.

INTHE BUSINESSWORLD

Certain calculators have a fraction key, $a\frac{b}{c}$, that allows you to enter fractions. For example, $\frac{2}{3}$ would be entered as 2 $a\frac{b}{c}$ 3 and would appear as 2⌐3. The mixed fraction $25\frac{2}{3}$ would be entered as 25 $a\frac{b}{c}$ 2 $a\frac{b}{c}$ 3 and would appear as 25⌐2⌐3.

Fraction calculators express answers in fractional notation and are a handy tool for measuring materials without having to convert fractions to decimals. They are particularly useful in the construction, medical, and food industries.

REDUCING FRACTIONS TO LOWEST TERMS

2-4

Reducing a fraction means finding whole numbers, called common divisors or common factors, that divide evenly into both the numerator and denominator of the fraction. For example, the fraction $\frac{24}{48}$ can be reduced to $\frac{12}{24}$ by the common divisor 2. The new fraction, $\frac{12}{24}$, can be further reduced to $\frac{4}{8}$ by the common divisor 3 and to $\frac{1}{2}$ by the common divisor 4. When a fraction has been reduced to the point where there are no common divisors left, other than 1, it is said to be **reduced to lowest terms**.

The largest number that is a common divisor of a fraction is known as the **greatest common divisor**. It reduces the fraction to lowest terms in one step. In the example of $\frac{24}{48}$ above, we could have used 24, the greatest common divisor, to reduce the fraction to $\frac{1}{2}$.

reduced to lowest terms The process of having divided whole numbers, known as common divisors or common factors, into both the numerator and denominator of a fraction. Used for expressing fractions as final answers. For example, $\frac{5}{20}$ is reduced to $\frac{1}{4}$ by the common divisor 5.

greatest common divisor The largest number that is a common divisor of a fraction. Used to reduce a fraction to lowest terms in one step. For example, 5 is the greatest common divisor of $\frac{5}{20}$.

A. REDUCING FRACTIONS BY INSPECTION

Reducing fractions by inspection or observation is often a trial-and-error procedure. Sometimes a fraction's common divisors are obvious; other times they are more difficult to determine. The following rules of divisibility may be helpful:

RULES OF DIVISIBILITY

A Number Is Divisible by	Conditions
2	If the last digit is 0, 2, 4, 6, or 8.
3	If the sum of the digits is divisible by 3.
4	If the last two digits are divisible by 4.
5	If the last digit is 0 or 5.
6	If the number is divisible by 2 and 3 or if it is even and the sum of the digits is divisible by 3.
8	If the last three digits are divisible by 8.
9	If the sum of the digits is divisible by 9.
10	If the last digit is 0.

Construction workers must accurately measure and calculate various lengths of building materials by using fractions.

Image copyright Diego Cervo 2010. Used under license from Shutterstock.com

EXAMPLE4 REDUCING FRACTIONS TO LOWEST TERMS USING INSPECTION

Use observation and the rules of divisibility to reduce $\frac{48}{54}$ to lowest terms.

SOLUTIONSTRATEGY

$\frac{48}{54} = \frac{48 \div 2}{54 \div 2} = \frac{24}{27}$ Because the last digit of the numerator is 8 and the last digit of the denominator is 4, they are both divisible by 2.

$\frac{24}{27} = \frac{24 \div 3}{27 \div 3} = \frac{8}{9}$ Because the sum of the digits of the numerator, 2 + 4, and the denominator, 2 + 7, are both divisible by 3, the fraction is divisible by 3.

$\frac{48}{54} = \frac{8}{9}$ Because no numbers other than 1 divide evenly into the new fraction $\frac{8}{9}$, it is now reduced to lowest terms.

TRYITEXERCISE4

Reduce the following fractions to lowest terms.

a. $\frac{30}{55}$ b. $\frac{72}{148}$

CHECK YOUR ANSWERS WITH THE SOLUTIONS ON PAGE 58.

B. REDUCING FRACTIONS BY THE GREATEST COMMON DIVISOR METHOD

The best method for reducing a fraction to lowest terms is to divide the numerator and the denominator by the greatest common divisor because this accomplishes the task in one step. When the greatest common divisor is not obvious to you, use the following steps to determine it:

STEPS FOR DETERMINING THE GREATEST COMMON DIVISOR OF A FRACTION

STEP 1. Divide the numerator of the fraction into the denominator.

STEP 2. Examine the remainder.

- If it is 0, stop. The divisor is the greatest common divisor.
- If it is 1, stop. The fraction cannot be reduced and is therefore in lowest terms.
- If it is another number, divide the remainder into the divisor.

STEP 3. Repeat Step 2 as needed.

EXAMPLE5   REDUCING FRACTIONS TO LOWEST TERMS USING THE GREATEST COMMON DIVISOR METHOD

Reduce the fraction $\frac{63}{231}$ by finding the greatest common divisor.

SOLUTIONSTRATEGY

$$\begin{array}{r} 3 \\ 63\overline{)231} \\ 189 \\ \hline 42 \end{array}$$

Divide the numerator, 63, into the denominator, 231. This leaves a remainder of 42.

$$\begin{array}{r} 1 \\ 42\overline{)63} \\ 42 \\ \hline 21 \end{array}$$

Next, divide the remainder, 42, into the previous divisor, 63. This leaves a remainder of 21.

$$\begin{array}{r} 2 \\ 21\overline{)42} \\ 42 \\ \hline 0 \end{array}$$

Then divide the remainder, 21, into the previous divisor, 42. Because this leaves a remainder of 0, the last divisor, 21, is the greatest common divisor of the original fraction.

$$\frac{63 \div 21}{231 \div 21} = \frac{3}{11}$$

By dividing both the numerator and the denominator by the greatest common divisor, 21, we get the fraction, $\frac{3}{11}$, which is the original fraction reduced to lowest terms.

TRYITEXERCISE5

Reduce the following fractions to lowest terms.

a. $\frac{270}{810}$ b. $\frac{175}{232}$

CHECK YOUR ANSWERS WITH THE SOLUTIONS ON PAGE 58.

RAISING FRACTIONS TO HIGHER TERMS

Raising a fraction to higher terms is a procedure sometimes needed in addition and subtraction. It is the opposite of reducing fractions to lower terms. In reducing, we used common divisors; in raising fractions, we use common multiples. To **raise to higher terms**, simply multiply the numerator and denominator of a fraction by a **common multiple**.

For example, if we want to raise the numerator and denominator of the fraction $\frac{3}{4}$ by factors of 7, multiply the numerator and the denominator by 7. This procedure raises the fraction to $\frac{21}{28}$.

$$\frac{3 \times 7}{4 \times 7} = \frac{21}{28}$$

It is important to remember that the value of the fraction has not changed by raising it; we have simply divided the "whole" into more parts.

raise to higher terms The process of multiplying the numerator and denominator of a fraction by a common multiple. Sometimes needed in addition and subtraction of fractions. For example, $\frac{5}{20}$ is the fraction $\frac{1}{4}$ raised to higher terms, 20ths, by the common multiple 5.

common multiple Whole number used to raise a fraction to higher terms. The common multiple 5 raises the fraction $\frac{1}{4}$ to $\frac{5}{20}$.

STEPS FOR RAISING A FRACTION TO A NEW DENOMINATOR

STEP 1. Divide the original denominator into the new denominator. The resulting quotient is the common multiple that raises the fraction.

STEP 2. Multiply the numerator and the denominator of the original fraction by the common multiple.

EXAMPLE6 RAISING FRACTIONS TO HIGHER TERMS

Raise the following fractions to higher terms as indicated.

a. $\frac{2}{3}$ to fifteenths   b. $\frac{3}{5}$ to fortieths

SOLUTIONSTRATEGY

a. $\frac{2}{3} = \frac{?}{15}$ In this example, we are raising the fraction $\frac{2}{3}$ to the denominator 15.

$15 \div 3 = 5$ Divide the original denominator, 3, into 15. This yields the common multiple 5.

$\frac{2 \times 5}{3 \times 5} = \frac{10}{15}$ Now multiply both the numerator and denominator by the common multiple, 5.

b. $\frac{3}{5} = \frac{?}{40}$ Here the indicated denominator is 40.

$40 \div 5 = 8$ Dividing 5 into 40, we get the common multiple 8.

$\frac{3 \times 8}{5 \times 8} = \frac{24}{40}$ Now raise the fraction by multiplying the numerator, 3, and the denominator, 5, by 8.

LEARNINGTIP

Sometimes it is difficult to determine which of two fractions is the larger or smaller number. By converting them to **like fractions** (same denominator), the answer will become evident.

For example:

Which fraction is larger, $\frac{4}{5}$ or $\frac{5}{6}$?

$\frac{4}{5} = \frac{24}{30}$, whereas $\frac{5}{6} = \frac{25}{30}$

Therefore, $\frac{5}{6}$ is larger than $\frac{4}{5}$.

TRYITEXERCISE6

Raise the following fractions to higher terms as indicated.

a. $\frac{7}{8}$ to sixty-fourths   b. $\frac{3}{7}$ to thirty-fifths

CHECK YOUR ANSWERS WITH THE SOLUTIONS ON PAGE 59.

SECTION I **2** **REVIEW EXERCISES**

For each of the following, identify the type of fraction and write it in word form.

1. $23\frac{4}{5}$ 2. $\frac{12}{12}$ 3. $\frac{15}{9}$ 4. $\frac{7}{16}$ 5. $2\frac{1}{8}$

$\underline{\underline{\text{Mixed}}}$
Twenty-three
and four-fifths

Convert the following improper fractions to whole or mixed numbers.

6. $\frac{26}{8} = 3\frac{2}{8} = 3\frac{1}{4}$ 7. $\frac{20}{6}$ 8. $\frac{92}{16}$

9. $\frac{64}{15}$ 10. $\frac{88}{11}$ 11. $\frac{33}{31}$

Convert the following mixed numbers to improper fractions.

12. $6\frac{1}{2} = \frac{13}{2}$ 13. $11\frac{4}{5}$ 14. $25\frac{2}{3}$
$(6 \times 2 + 1 = 13)$

15. $18\frac{5}{8}$ 16. $1\frac{5}{9}$ 17. $250\frac{1}{4}$

Use inspection or the greatest common divisor to reduce the following fractions to lowest terms.

18. $\frac{21}{35}$ 19. $\frac{9}{12}$ 20. $\frac{18}{48}$ 21. $\frac{216}{920}$
$\frac{21 \div 7}{35 \div 7} = \frac{3}{5}$

22. $\frac{27}{36}$ 23. $\frac{14}{112}$ 24. $\frac{9}{42}$ 25. $\frac{95}{325}$

26. $\frac{8}{23}$ 27. $\frac{78}{96}$ 28. $\frac{30}{150}$ 29. $\frac{85}{306}$

Raise the following fractions to higher terms as indicated.

30. $\frac{2}{3}$ to twenty-sevenths   31. $\frac{3}{4}$ to forty-eighths   32. $\frac{7}{8}$ to eightieths

$\frac{2}{3} = \frac{18}{27}$ $\left(\begin{array}{l} 27 \div 3 = 9 \\ 9 \times 2 = 18 \end{array}\right)$

33. $\frac{11}{16}$ to sixty-fourths   34. $\frac{1}{5}$ to hundredths   35. $\frac{3}{7}$ to ninety-eighths

36. $\frac{3}{5} = \frac{}{25}$ 37. $\frac{5}{8} = \frac{}{64}$ 38. $\frac{5}{6} = \frac{}{360}$ 39. $\frac{9}{13} = \frac{}{182}$

"I'd like to meet you halfway, but I'm terrible with fractions."

40. What fraction represents the laptops in this group of computers?

41. What fraction represents the screwdrivers in this group of tools?

42. A wedding cake was cut into 40 slices. If 24 of the slices were eaten, what fraction represents the eaten portion of the cake? Reduce your answer to lowest terms.

43. Jasmine Marley's swimming pool holds 16,000 gallons of water, and her spa holds 2,000 gallons of water. Of all the water in the pool and spa,
    a. What fraction is the spa water?

    b. What fraction is the pool water?

44. You work in the tool department of a Home Depot store. Your manager asks you to set up a point-of-purchase display for a set of 10 wrenches that are on sale this week. He asks you to arrange them in order from smallest to largest on the display board. When you open the box, you find the following sizes in inches: $\frac{9}{32}, \frac{5}{8}, \frac{5}{16}, \frac{1}{2}, \frac{3}{16}, \frac{3}{4}, \frac{7}{8}, \frac{5}{32}, \frac{1}{4}, \frac{3}{8}$.

    a. Rearrange the wrenches by size from smallest to largest.

    b. Next your manager tells you that the sale will be "1/3 off" the regular price of $57 and has asked you to calculate the sale price to be printed on the sign.

    c. After the sale is over, your manager asks you for the sales figures on the wrench promotion. If 150 sets were sold that week, what amount of revenue will you report?

    d. If $6,000 in sales was expected, what reduced fraction represents the sales actually attained?

The Home Depot, with 2,242 stores, 322,000 employees and in 2009 sales of over $66.2 billion, is the world's largest home improvement chain.

Lowe's, the #2 home improvement chain, has more than 1,650 stores, with 228,000 employees. Sales in 2009 were $47.2 billion.

BUSINESS DECISION: EVALUATING THE QUESTION

45. You are on an academic committee appointed by the governor of your state to evaluate state employment math test questions. The following question has come to the attention of the committee:

> "Each of the four digits 2, 4, 6, and 9 is placed in one of the boxes to form a fraction. The numerator and the denominator are two-digit whole numbers. What is the smallest value of all the common fractions that can be formed? Express your answer as a reduced fraction."

Adapted from the NCTM Calendar, November 2004.

Some committee members contend that this is not a valid question. For the next committee meeting, solve the problem and explain the solution to prove (or disprove) the question's validity.

SECTION II 2 ADDITION AND SUBTRACTION OF FRACTIONS

Adding and subtracting fractions occurs frequently in business. Quite often we must combine or subtract quantities expressed as fractions. To add or subtract fractions, the denominators must be the same. If they are not, we must find a common multiple, or **common denominator**, of all the denominators in the problem. The most efficient common denominator to use is the least common denominator, or LCD. By using the LCD, you avoid raising fractions to terms higher than necessary.

common denominator A common multiple of all the denominators in an addition or subtraction of fractions problem. A common denominator of the fractions $\frac{1}{4} + \frac{3}{5}$ is 40.

2-6 DETERMINING THE LEAST COMMON DENOMINATOR (LCD) OF TWO OR MORE FRACTIONS

Determining the **least common denominator (LCD)** involves a series of divisions using prime numbers. A **prime number** is a whole number divisible only by itself and 1. Following are the prime numbers:

$$2, 3, 5, 7, 11, 13, 17, 19, 23, 29, 31, \text{ and so on}$$

least common denominator (LCD) The smallest and, therefore, most efficient common denominator in addition or subtraction of fractions. The least common denominator of the fractions $\frac{1}{4} + \frac{3}{5}$ is 20.

prime number A whole number divisible only by itself and 1. For example, 2, 3, 5, 7, and 11 are prime numbers.

STEPS FOR DETERMINING THE LEAST COMMON DENOMINATOR OF TWO OR MORE FRACTIONS

STEP 1. Write all the denominators in a row.

STEP 2. Find a prime number that divides evenly into any of the denominators. Write that prime number to the left of the row and divide. Place all quotients and undivided numbers in the next row down.

STEP 3. Repeat this process until the new row contains all ones.

STEP 4. Multiply all the prime numbers on the left to get the LCD of the fractions.

EXAMPLE 7 — DETERMINING THE LEAST COMMON DENOMINATOR (LCD)

Determine the least common denominator of the fractions $\frac{3}{4}$, $\frac{1}{5}$, $\frac{4}{9}$, and $\frac{5}{6}$.

SOLUTION STRATEGY

The following chart shows the solution. Note that the first row contains the original denominators. The first prime number, 2, divides evenly into the 4 and the 6. The quotients, 2 and 3, and the non-divisible numbers, 5 and 9, are brought down to the next row.

The same procedure is repeated with the prime numbers 2, 3, 3, and 5. When the bottom row becomes all ones, we multiply all the prime numbers to get the LCD, 180.

Prime Number	Denominators			
2	4	5	9	6
2	2	5	9	3
3	1	5	9	3
3	1	5	3	1
5	1	5	1	1
	1	1	1	1

$2 \times 2 \times 3 \times 3 \times 5 = \underline{180} = \text{LCD}$

TRY IT EXERCISE 7

Determine the least common denominator of the fractions $\frac{3}{8}$, $\frac{4}{5}$, $\frac{4}{15}$, and $\frac{11}{12}$.

CHECK YOUR ANSWER WITH THE SOLUTION ON PAGE 59.

CHECK YOUR ANSWER WITH THE SOLUTION ON PAGE 59.

LEARNING TIP

Answers to fraction problems should be reduced to lowest terms.

ADDING FRACTIONS AND MIXED NUMBERS

2-7

Now that you have learned to convert fractions to higher and lower terms and find least common denominators, you are ready to add and subtract fractions. We will learn to add and subtract fractions with the same denominator, fractions with different denominators, and mixed numbers.

ADDING FRACTIONS WITH THE SAME DENOMINATOR

Proper fractions that have the same denominator are known as **like fractions**.

like fractions Proper fractions that have the same denominator. For example, $\frac{1}{4}$ and $\frac{3}{4}$ are like fractions.

STEPS FOR ADDING LIKE FRACTIONS

STEP 1. Add all the numerators and place the total over the original denominator.

STEP 2. If the result is a proper fraction, reduce it to lowest terms.

STEP 3. If the result is an improper fraction, convert it to a whole or mixed number.

EXAMPLE 8 — ADDING LIKE FRACTIONS

Add $\frac{4}{15} + \frac{2}{15}$.

SOLUTION STRATEGY

$\frac{4}{15} + \frac{2}{15} = \frac{4+2}{15} = \frac{6}{15} = \frac{2}{5}$

Because these are like fractions, we simply add the numerators, $4 + 2$, and place the total, 6, over the original denominator, 15. This gives us the fraction $\frac{6}{15}$, which reduces by 3 to $\frac{2}{5}$.

TRYITEXERCISE8

Add and reduce to lowest terms.

$$\frac{3}{25} + \frac{9}{25} + \frac{8}{25}$$

CHECK YOUR ANSWER WITH THE SOLUTION ON PAGE 59.

ADDING FRACTIONS WITH DIFFERENT DENOMINATORS

unlike fractions Proper fractions that have different denominators. For example, $\frac{1}{4}$ and $\frac{1}{3}$ are unlike fractions.

Proper fractions that have different denominators are known as **unlike fractions**. Unlike fractions must be converted to like fractions before they can be added.

STEPS FOR ADDING UNLIKE FRACTIONS

STEP 1. Find the least common denominator of the unlike fractions.

STEP 2. Raise all fractions to the terms of the LCD, making them like fractions.

STEP 3. Follow the same procedure used for adding like fractions.

EXAMPLE9 ADDING UNLIKE FRACTIONS

Add $\frac{3}{8} + \frac{5}{7} + \frac{1}{2}$.

SOLUTIONSTRATEGY

Prime Number	Denominators		
2	8	7	2
2	4	7	1
2	2	7	1
7	1	7	1
	1	1	1

These are unlike fractions and must be converted to obtain the same denominator.

First, find the LCD, 56.

$$2 \times 2 \times 2 \times 7 = 56$$

$$\frac{3}{8} = \frac{21}{56}$$

$$\frac{5}{7} = \frac{40}{56}$$

Next, raise each fraction to fifty-sixths.

$$+ \frac{1}{2} = \frac{28}{56}$$

$$\frac{89}{56} = 1\frac{33}{56}$$

Then add the fractions and convert the answer, an improper fraction, to a mixed number.

TRYITEXERCISE9

Add and reduce to lowest terms.

$$\frac{1}{6} + \frac{3}{5} + \frac{2}{3}$$

CHECK YOUR ANSWER WITH THE SOLUTION ON PAGE 59.

DOLLARS AND SENSE

When buying gas, the price per gallon is frequently quoted as a fraction. The price of $285\frac{9}{10}$ is read as "two dollars, eighty-five and 9/10ths cents."

Photo by Robert Brechner

ADDING MIXED NUMBERS

STEPS FOR ADDING MIXED NUMBERS

STEP 1. Add the fractional parts. If the sum is an improper fraction, convert it to a mixed number.

STEP 2. Add the whole numbers.

STEP 3. Add the fraction from Step 1 to the whole number from Step 2.

STEP 4. Reduce the answer to lowest terms if necessary.

EXAMPLE10 ADDING MIXED NUMBERS

Add $15\frac{3}{4} + 18\frac{5}{8}$.

SOLUTIONSTRATEGY

$$15\frac{3}{4} = 15\frac{6}{8}$$
$$+\ 18\frac{5}{8} = 18\frac{5}{8}$$
$$\overline{\qquad\qquad 33\frac{11}{8} = 33 + 1\frac{3}{8} = \underline{\underline{34\frac{3}{8}}}}$$

First, add the fractional parts using 8 as the LCD. Because $\frac{11}{8}$ is an improper fraction, convert it to the mixed number $1\frac{3}{8}$.

Next, add the whole numbers: $15 + 18 = 33$. Then add the fraction and the whole number to get the answer, $34\frac{3}{8}$.

TRYITEXERCISE10

Add and reduce to lowest terms.

$$45\frac{1}{4} + 16\frac{5}{9} + \frac{1}{3}$$

CHECK YOUR ANSWER WITH THE SOLUTION ON PAGE 59.

SUBTRACTING FRACTIONS AND MIXED NUMBERS

2-8

In addition, we add the numerators of like fractions. In subtraction, we subtract the numerators of like fractions. If the fractions have different denominators, first raise the fractions to the terms of the least common denominator and then subtract.

STEPS FOR SUBTRACTING LIKE FRACTIONS

STEP 1. Subtract the numerators and place the difference over the original denominator.

STEP 2. Reduce the answer to lowest terms if necessary.

EXAMPLE 11 SUBTRACTING LIKE FRACTIONS

Subtract $\frac{9}{16} - \frac{5}{16}$.

SOLUTIONSTRATEGY

$$\frac{9}{16} - \frac{5}{16} = \frac{9-5}{16}$$

$$= \frac{4}{16} = \underline{\underline{\frac{1}{4}}}$$

In this example, the denominators are the same; so we simply subtract the numerators, $9 - 5$, and place the difference, 4, over the original denominator, 16. Then we reduce the fraction $\frac{4}{16}$ to lowest terms, $\frac{1}{4}$.

TRYITEXERCISE 11

Subtract $\frac{11}{25} - \frac{6}{25}$.

CHECK YOUR ANSWER WITH THE SOLUTION ON PAGE 59.

SUBTRACTING FRACTIONS WITH DIFFERENT DENOMINATORS

Unlike fractions must be converted to like fractions before they can be subtracted.

STEPS FOR SUBTRACTING UNLIKE FRACTIONS

STEP 1. Find the least common denominator.

STEP 2. Raise each fraction to the denominator of the LCD.

STEP 3. Follow the same procedure used to subtract like fractions.

EXAMPLE 12 SUBTRACTING UNLIKE FRACTIONS

Subtract $\frac{7}{9} - \frac{1}{2}$.

SOLUTIONSTRATEGY

$$\frac{7}{9} = \frac{14}{18}$$

In this example, we must first find the least common denominator. By inspection, we can see that the LCD is 18.

$$-\frac{1}{2} = \frac{9}{18}$$
$$\underline{\underline{\frac{5}{18}}}$$

Next, raise both fractions to eighteenths. Now subtract the numerators, $14 - 9$, and place the difference, 5, over the common denominator, 18. Because it cannot be reduced, $\frac{5}{18}$ is the final answer.

TRYITEXERCISE 12

Subtract $\frac{5}{12} - \frac{2}{9}$.

CHECK YOUR ANSWER WITH THE SOLUTION ON PAGE 59.

SUBTRACTING MIXED NUMBERS

STEPS FOR SUBTRACTING MIXED NUMBERS

STEP 1. If the fractions of the mixed numbers have the same denominator, subtract them and reduce to lowest terms.

STEP 2. If the fractions do not have the same denominator, raise them to the denominator of the LCD and subtract.

Note: When the numerator of the fraction in the minuend is less than the numerator of the fraction in the subtrahend, we must *borrow* one whole unit from the whole number of the minuend. This will be in the form of the LCD/LCD and is added to the fraction of the minuend.

STEP 3. Subtract the whole numbers.

STEP 4. Add the difference of the whole numbers and the difference of the fractions.

EXAMPLE 13 SUBTRACTING MIXED NUMBERS

Subtract.

a. $15\frac{2}{3} - 9\frac{1}{5}$ b. $7\frac{1}{8} - 2\frac{3}{4}$

SOLUTION STRATEGY

a. $15\frac{2}{3} = 15\frac{10}{15}$ In this example, raise the fractions to fifteenths; LCD = 5 × 3 = 15.

$-9\frac{1}{5} = -9\frac{3}{15}$ Then subtract the fractions to get $\frac{7}{15}$.

$\phantom{15-9\frac{1}{5}}6\frac{7}{15}$ Now subtract the whole numbers, 15 − 9, to get the whole number 6.

By combining the 6 and the $\frac{7}{15}$, we get the final answer $6\frac{7}{15}$.

b. $7\frac{1}{8} = 7\frac{1}{8} = 6\frac{1}{8} + \frac{8}{8} = 6\frac{9}{8}$ $6\frac{9}{8}$ In this example, after raising $\frac{3}{4}$ to $\frac{6}{8}$, we find that we cannot subtract $\frac{6}{8}$ from $\frac{1}{8}$. We must *borrow* one whole unit, $\frac{8}{8}$, from the whole number 7, making it a 6 (8 ÷ 8 = 1).

$-2\frac{3}{4} = -2\frac{6}{8} =$ $-2\frac{6}{8}$

$\phantom{-2\frac{3}{4} = -2\frac{6}{8} =}4\frac{3}{8}$

By adding $\frac{8}{8}$ to $\frac{1}{8}$, we get $\frac{9}{8}$.

Now we can subtract $\frac{9}{8} - \frac{6}{8}$ to get $\frac{3}{8}$.

We now subtract the whole numbers 6 − 2 = 4. By combining the whole number 4 and the fraction $\frac{3}{8}$, we get the final answer $4\frac{3}{8}$.

LEARNING TIP

Remember, when you borrow "one" in subtraction, you are borrowing a whole unit expressed in terms of the common denominator.

For example, $\frac{4}{4}, \frac{5}{5}, \frac{8}{8}, \frac{24}{24}$

Don't forget to add this to the existing fraction.

TRY IT EXERCISE 13

Subtract the following mixed numbers and reduce to lowest terms.

a. $6\frac{3}{4} - 4\frac{2}{3}$ b. $25\frac{2}{9} - 11\frac{5}{6}$

CHECK YOUR ANSWERS WITH THE SOLUTIONS ON PAGE 59.

SECTION II 2 — REVIEW EXERCISES

Find the least common denominator for the following groups of fractions.

1. $\frac{4}{5}, \frac{2}{3}, \frac{8}{15}$

$$\begin{array}{c|ccc} 3 & 5 & 3 & 15 \\ 5 & 5 & 1 & 5 \\ \hline & 1 & 1 & 1 \end{array}$$

$3 \times 5 = \underline{\underline{15}}$ LCD

2. $\frac{1}{3}, \frac{4}{9}, \frac{3}{4}$

3. $\frac{5}{6}, \frac{11}{12}, \frac{1}{4}, \frac{1}{2}$

4. $\frac{1}{6}, \frac{19}{24}, \frac{2}{3}, \frac{3}{5}$

5. $\frac{21}{25}, \frac{9}{60}, \frac{7}{20}, \frac{1}{3}$

6. $\frac{5}{12}, \frac{9}{14}, \frac{2}{3}, \frac{7}{10}$

Add the following fractions and reduce to lowest terms.

7. $\frac{5}{6} + \frac{1}{2}$

$$\begin{array}{r} \frac{5}{6} \\ + \frac{3}{6} \\ \hline \frac{8}{6} = 1\frac{2}{6} = 1\underline{\underline{\frac{1}{3}}} \end{array}$$

8. $\frac{2}{3} + \frac{3}{4}$

9. $\frac{5}{8} + \frac{13}{16}$

10. $\frac{9}{32} + \frac{29}{32}$

11. $\frac{1}{2} + \frac{4}{5} + \frac{7}{20}$

12. $\frac{3}{4} + \frac{7}{8} + \frac{5}{16}$

13. $\frac{11}{12} + \frac{3}{5} + \frac{19}{30}$

14. $5\frac{4}{7} + \frac{2}{3}$

15. $7\frac{1}{2} + 2\frac{7}{8} + 1\frac{1}{6}$

16. $13\frac{5}{9} + 45\frac{1}{3} + 9\frac{7}{27}$

17. Chet Murray ran $3\frac{1}{2}$ miles on Monday, $2\frac{4}{5}$ miles on Tuesday, and $4\frac{1}{8}$ miles on Wednesday. What was Chet's total mileage for the 3 days?

18. Crate and Barrel shipped three packages to New York weighing $45\frac{1}{5}$, $126\frac{3}{4}$, and $88\frac{3}{8}$ pounds. What was the total weight of the shipment?

19. At the Fresh Market, you buy $6\frac{3}{10}$ pounds of yams and $4\frac{1}{3}$ pounds of corn. What is the total weight of the purchase?

20. BrewMasters Coffee Co. purchased $12\frac{1}{2}$ tons of coffee beans in January, $15\frac{4}{5}$ tons in February, and $34\frac{7}{10}$ tons in March. What was the total weight of the purchases?

Subtract the following fractions and reduce to lowest terms.

21. $\frac{5}{6} - \frac{1}{6}$
$= \frac{4}{6} = \frac{2}{3}$

22. $\frac{4}{7} - \frac{1}{8}$

23. $\frac{2}{3} - \frac{1}{18}$

24. $\frac{3}{4} - \frac{9}{16}$

25. $12\frac{3}{5} - 4\frac{1}{3}$

26. $8\frac{1}{4} - 5\frac{2}{3}$

27. $28\frac{4}{9} - 1\frac{4}{5}$

28. $8\frac{11}{12} - 8\frac{3}{8}$

29. Casey McKee sold $18\frac{4}{5}$ of his $54\frac{2}{3}$ acres of land. How many acres does Casey have left?

30. A particular dress requires $3\frac{1}{4}$ yards of fabric for manufacturing. If the matching jacket requires $\frac{5}{6}$ yard less fabric, how much fabric is needed for both pieces?

31. Robert Burkart bought a frozen, factory-processed turkey that included the giblets and neck. The package weighed $22\frac{3}{4}$ pounds. Robert thawed the bird and then removed and weighed the giblets and neck, which totaled $1\frac{1}{8}$ pounds. The liquid that he drained from the package weighed $\frac{1}{2}$ pound. How much did the turkey weigh going into the oven?

Gobble, Gobble

According to www.eatturkey.com, turkey is one of the most popular protein foods in the United States, with annual sales of over $3.6 billion.

In 2009, consumption amounted to over 273 million turkeys, or 17.6 pounds per person. The top turkey processor in the United States was Butterball, LLC, with 1.45 million pounds. Other major U.S. processors include Jennie-O Turkey Store and Cargill Meat Solutions.

© Richard Levine/Alamy

32. Brady White weighed $196\frac{1}{2}$ pounds when he decided to join a gym to lose some weight. At the end of the first month, he weighed $191\frac{3}{8}$ pounds.

    a. How much did he lose that month?

    b. If his goal is $183\frac{3}{4}$ pounds, how much more does he have to lose?

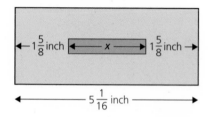

33. Hot Shot Industries manufactures metal heat shields for light fixture assemblies. What is the length, x, on the heat shield?

34. Tim Kenney, a painter, used $6\frac{4}{5}$ gallons of paint on the exterior of a house and $9\frac{3}{4}$ gallons on the interior.

    a. What is the total amount of paint used on the house?

    b. If an additional $8\frac{3}{5}$ gallons was used on the garage, what is the total amount of paint used on the house and garage?

    c. Rounding your answer from part b up to the next whole gallon, calculate the total cost of the paint if you paid $23 for each gallon.

BUSINESS DECISION: THE RED-EYE EXPRESS

35. You are an executive with the Varsity Corporation in Atlanta, Georgia. The company president was scheduled to make an important sales presentation tomorrow afternoon in Seattle, Washington, but has now asked you to take his place.

    The trip consists of a $2\frac{1}{2}$-hour flight from Atlanta to Dallas, a $1\frac{1}{4}$-hour layover in Dallas, and then a $3\frac{3}{4}$-hour flight to Portland. There is a $1\frac{1}{2}$-hour layover in Portland and then a $\frac{3}{4}$-hour flight to Seattle. Seattle is on Pacific Time, which is 3-hours earlier than Eastern Time in Atlanta.

    a. If you depart Atlanta tonight at 11:30 P.M. and all flights are on schedule, what time will you arrive in Seattle?

    b. If your return flight is scheduled to leave Seattle at 10:10 P.M. tomorrow night, with the same flight times and layovers in reverse, what time are you scheduled to arrive in Atlanta?

    c. If the leg from Dallas back to Atlanta is $\frac{2}{3}$ of an hour longer than scheduled due to headwinds, what time will you actually arrive?

World's Busiest Airports
As of July 28, 2009 (millions)

Rank	City (Airport)	Total Passengers
1.	Atlanta, GA (ATL)	90.03
2.	Chicago, IL (ORD)	69.35
3.	London, GB (LHR)	67.05
4.	Tokyo, JP (HND)	66.75
5.	Paris, FRA (CDG)	60.87
6.	Los Angeles, CA (LAX)	59.50
7.	Dallas/Fort Worth, TX (DFW)	57.09
8.	Beijing, CN (PEK)	55.93
9.	Frankfurt, DE (FRA)	53.47
10.	Denver, CO (DEN)	51.25

Source: www.airports.org, Airports Council International

MULTIPLICATION AND DIVISION OF FRACTIONS   SECTION III   **2**

In addition and subtraction, we were concerned with common denominators; however, in multiplication and division, common denominators are not required. This simplifies the process considerably.

MULTIPLYING FRACTIONS AND MIXED NUMBERS   **2-9**

STEPS FOR MULTIPLYING FRACTIONS

STEP 1. Multiply all the numerators to form the new numerator.

STEP 2. Multiply all the denominators to form the new denominator.

STEP 3. Reduce the answer to lowest terms if necessary.

A procedure known as **cancellation** can serve as a useful shortcut when multiplying fractions. Cancellation simplifies the numbers with which we are dealing and often leaves the answer in lowest terms.

cancellation When multiplying fractions, cancellation is the process of finding a common factor that divides evenly into at least one numerator and one denominator. The common factor 2 can be used to cancel

$$\frac{1}{\overset{4}{\underset{2}{4}}} \times \frac{\overset{3}{6}}{7} \text{ to } \frac{1}{2} \times \frac{3}{7}.$$

STEPS FOR APPLYING CANCELLATION

STEP 1. Find a common factor that divides evenly into at least one of the denominators and one of the numerators.

STEP 2. Divide that common factor into the denominator and numerator, thereby reducing it.

STEP 3. Repeat this process until there are no more common factors.

STEP 4. Multiply the fractions as before.

EXAMPLE14 MULTIPLYING FRACTONS

Multiply the following fractions.

a. $\dfrac{5}{7} \times \dfrac{3}{4}$ 　　　　b. $\dfrac{2}{3} \times \dfrac{7}{8}$

SOLUTIONSTRATEGY

a. 　　$\dfrac{5}{7} \times \dfrac{3}{4}$ 　　In this example, there are no common factors between the numerators and the denominators; therefore, we cannot use cancellation.

$\dfrac{5 \times 3}{7 \times 4} = \dfrac{15}{28}$ 　　Multiply the numerators, 5×3, to form the new numerator 15 and multiply the denominators, 7×4, to form the new denominator 28. This fraction does not reduce.

b. 　　$\dfrac{2}{3} \times \dfrac{7}{8}$ 　　In this example, the 2 in the numerator and the 8 in the denominator have the common factor of 2.

$\dfrac{\overset{1}{\cancel{2}}}{3} \times \dfrac{7}{\underset{4}{\cancel{8}}}$ 　　Dividing each by the common factor reduces the 2 to a 1 and the 8 to a 4.

$\dfrac{1 \times 7}{3 \times 4} = \dfrac{7}{12}$ 　　Now multiply the simplified numbers; 1×7 forms the numerator 7 and 3×4 forms the denominator 12. The resulting product is $\dfrac{7}{12}$.

TRYITEXERCISE14

Multiply and reduce to lowest terms.

$\dfrac{12}{21} \times \dfrac{7}{8}$

CHECK YOUR ANSWER WITH THE SOLUTION ON PAGE 59.

MULTIPLYING MIXED NUMBERS

STEPS FOR MULTIPLYING MIXED NUMBERS

STEP 1. Convert all mixed numbers to improper fractions.

Note: When multiplying fractions by whole numbers, change the whole numbers to fractions by placing them over 1.

STEP 2. Multiply as before, using cancellation wherever possible.

STEP 3. If the answer is an improper fraction, convert it to a whole or mixed number.

STEP 4. Reduce the answer to lowest terms if necessary.

EXAMPLE15 MULTIPLYING MIXED NUMBERS

Multiply.

a. $3\frac{3}{4} \times 5\frac{1}{2}$ b. $12\frac{5}{6} \times 4$

SOLUTIONSTRATEGY

a.

$3\frac{3}{4} \times 5\frac{1}{2}$

In this example, convert the mixed numbers to improper fractions; $3\frac{3}{4}$ becomes $\frac{15}{4}$, and $5\frac{1}{2}$ becomes $\frac{11}{2}$.

$\frac{15}{4} \times \frac{11}{2}$

$\frac{15 \times 11}{4 \times 2} = \frac{165}{8} = 20\frac{5}{8}$

After multiplying the numerators together and the denominators together, we get the improper fraction $\frac{165}{8}$, which converts to the mixed number $20\frac{5}{8}$.

b.

$12\frac{5}{6} \times 4$

This example demonstrates a mixed number multiplied by a whole number.

$\frac{77}{6} \times \frac{4}{1}$

The mixed number $12\frac{5}{6}$ converts to the improper fraction $\frac{77}{6}$. The whole number 4 expressed as a fraction becomes $\frac{4}{1}$.

$\frac{77}{\underset{3}{\cancel{6}}} \times \frac{\overset{2}{\cancel{4}}}{1}$

Before multiplying, cancel the 4 in the numerator and the 6 in the denominator by the common factor 2.

$\frac{77 \times 2}{3 \times 1} = \frac{154}{3} = 51\frac{1}{3}$

After multiplying, convert the improper fraction $\frac{154}{3}$ to the mixed number $51\frac{1}{3}$.

TRYITEXERCISE15

Multiply and reduce to lowest terms.

a. $8\frac{2}{5} \times 6\frac{1}{4}$ b. $45 \times \frac{4}{9} \times 2\frac{1}{4}$

CHECK YOUR ANSWERS WITH THE SOLUTIONS ON PAGE 59.

DIVIDING FRACTIONS AND MIXED NUMBERS

2-10

In division of fractions, it is important to identify which fraction is the dividend and which is the divisor. In whole numbers, we found that a problem such as $12 \div 5$ is read "12 divided by 5." Therefore, the 12 is the dividend and the 5 is the divisor. Fractions work in the same way. The number *after* the "÷" sign is the divisor. In the problem $\frac{3}{4} \div \frac{2}{3}$, for example, $\frac{3}{4}$ is the dividend and $\frac{2}{3}$ is the divisor.

$$\text{Dividend} \div \text{Divisor} = \frac{\text{Dividend}}{\text{Divisor}} = \text{Divisor}\,\overline{)\text{Dividend}}$$

Division of fractions requires that we **invert** the divisor. To invert means to turn upside down. By inverting a fraction, the numerator becomes the denominator and the denominator becomes the numerator. For example, the fraction $\frac{5}{12}$ becomes $\frac{12}{5}$ when inverted. These fractions are also known as **reciprocals**. Therefore, $\frac{5}{12}$ and $\frac{12}{5}$ are reciprocals of each other.

As in multiplication, division requires that mixed numbers be converted to improper fractions.

STEPS FOR DIVIDING FRACTIONS

STEP 1. Identify the fraction that is the divisor and invert.

STEP 2. Change the "divided by" sign, ÷, to a "multiplied by" sign, ×.

STEP 3. Multiply the fractions.

STEP 4. Reduce the answer to lowest terms if necessary.

LEARNINGTIP

The number *after* the "÷" sign is the divisor.
   This is the number that gets inverted when dividing.

invert To turn upside down. For example, $\frac{1}{4}$ inverted becomes $\frac{4}{1}$. In division of fractions, the divisor is inverted.

reciprocals Numbers whose product is 1. Inverted numbers are also known as reciprocals of each other. The fractions $\frac{1}{4}$ and $\frac{4}{1}$ are reciprocals because $\frac{1}{4} \times \frac{4}{1} = 1$.

EXAMPLE16 DIVIDING FRACTIONS

Divide the following fractions.

a. $\dfrac{4}{5} \div \dfrac{2}{3}$ b. $6\dfrac{3}{8} \div 2\dfrac{1}{2}$ c. $12\dfrac{1}{6} \div 3$

SOLUTIONSTRATEGY

a. $\dfrac{4}{5} \div \dfrac{2}{3} = \dfrac{4}{5} \times \dfrac{3}{2}$.

In this example, invert the divisor, $\dfrac{2}{3}$, to form its reciprocal, $\dfrac{3}{2}$, and change the sign from "÷" to "×."

$\dfrac{\overset{2}{\cancel{4}}}{5} \times \dfrac{3}{\underset{1}{\cancel{2}}} = \dfrac{6}{5} = 1\dfrac{1}{5}$

Now multiply in the usual manner. Note that the 4 in the numerator and the 2 in the denominator can be reduced by the common factor 2. The answer, $\dfrac{6}{5}$, is an improper fraction and must be converted to the mixed number $1\dfrac{1}{5}$.

b. $6\dfrac{3}{8} \div 2\dfrac{1}{2} = \dfrac{51}{8} \div \dfrac{5}{2}$

First, convert the mixed numbers to the improper fractions $\dfrac{51}{8}$ and $\dfrac{5}{2}$; then state them again as division.

$\dfrac{51}{8} \times \dfrac{2}{5}$

Next, invert the divisor, $\dfrac{5}{2}$, to its reciprocal, $\dfrac{2}{5}$, and change the sign from "÷" to "×."

$\dfrac{51}{\underset{4}{\cancel{8}}} \times \dfrac{\overset{1}{\cancel{2}}}{5} = \dfrac{51}{20} = 2\dfrac{11}{20}$

Now multiply in the usual way. Note that the 2 in the numerator and the 8 in the denominator can be reduced by the common factor 2. The answer, $\dfrac{51}{20}$, is an improper fraction and must be converted to the mixed number $2\dfrac{11}{20}$.

c. $12\dfrac{1}{6} \div 3 = \dfrac{73}{6} \div \dfrac{3}{1}$

In this example, we have a mixed number that must be converted to the improper fraction $\dfrac{73}{6}$ and the whole number 3, which converts to $\dfrac{3}{1}$.

$\dfrac{73}{6} \times \dfrac{1}{3}$

The fraction $\dfrac{3}{1}$ is the divisor and must be inverted to its reciprocal, $\dfrac{1}{3}$. The sign is changed from "÷" to "×."

$\dfrac{73}{6} \times \dfrac{1}{3} = \dfrac{73}{18} = 4\dfrac{1}{18}$

The answer is the improper fraction $\dfrac{73}{18}$, which converts to the mixed number $4\dfrac{1}{18}$.

TRYITEXERCISE16

Divide the following fractions and mixed numbers.

a. $\dfrac{14}{25} \div \dfrac{4}{5}$ b. $11\dfrac{3}{16} \div 8\dfrac{2}{3}$ c. $18 \div 5\dfrac{3}{5}$

CHECK YOUR ANSWERS WITH THE SOLUTIONS ON PAGE 59.

SECTION III   2   REVIEW EXERCISES

Multiply the following fractions and reduce to lowest terms. Use cancellation whenever possible.

JUMP START
WWW

1. $\dfrac{2}{3} \times \dfrac{4}{5} = \dfrac{8}{15}$ 2. $\dfrac{5}{6} \times \dfrac{1}{4}$ 3. $\dfrac{1}{2} \times \dfrac{4}{9}$ 4. $\dfrac{7}{8} \times \dfrac{1}{3} \times \dfrac{4}{7}$

5. $\dfrac{16}{19} \times \dfrac{5}{8}$ 6. $\dfrac{25}{51} \times \dfrac{2}{5}$ 7. $\dfrac{8}{11} \times \dfrac{33}{40} \times \dfrac{4}{1}$ 8. $\dfrac{2}{3} \times \dfrac{2}{3} \times \dfrac{6}{1}$

9. $8\dfrac{1}{5} \times 2\dfrac{2}{3}$ 10. $\dfrac{1}{2} \times \dfrac{2}{3} \times \dfrac{4}{5} \times \dfrac{3}{4} \times \dfrac{5}{1}$

11. $\dfrac{1}{5} \times \dfrac{1}{5} \times \dfrac{1}{5}$ EXCEL 1   12. $\dfrac{2}{3} \times 5\dfrac{4}{5} \times 9$

13. A recent market research survey showed that $\frac{3}{8}$ of the people interviewed preferred decaffeinated coffee over regular.

    a. What fraction of the people preferred regular coffee?

    b. If 4,400 people were interviewed, how many preferred regular coffee?

14. Wendy Wilson planned to bake a triple recipe of chocolate chip cookies for her office party. If the recipe calls for $1\frac{3}{4}$ cups of flour, how many cups will she need?

15. A driveway requires $9\frac{1}{2}$ truckloads of gravel. If the truck holds $4\frac{5}{8}$ cubic yards of gravel, how many total cubic yards of gravel are used for the driveway?

16. Melissa Silva borrowed $4,200 from the bank. If she has already repaid $\frac{3}{7}$ of the loan, what is the remaining balance owed to the bank?

17. Amy Richards' movie collection occupies $\frac{5}{8}$ of her computer's hard drive. Her photography takes up $\frac{1}{6}$ of the drive. The operating system, application software, and miscellaneous files take up another $\frac{1}{12}$ of the drive. If her hard drive's capacity is 120 gigabytes, how many gigabytes of free space remain on the hard drive?

18. Three partners share a business. Max owns $\frac{3}{8}$, Sherry owns $\frac{2}{5}$, and Duane owns the rest. If the profits this year are $150,000, how much does each partner receive?

Marketing Research
Market and survey researchers gather information about what people think. They help companies understand what types of products and services people want and at what price. By gathering statistical data on competitors and examining prices, sales, and methods of marketing and distribution, they advise companies on the most efficient ways of marketing their products.

According to the U.S. Bureau of Labor Statistics, overall employment of market and survey researchers is projected to grow 28 percent from 2008 to 2018. Median annual wages of market research analysts in May 2008 were $61,070.

Divide the following fractions and reduce to lowest terms.

19. $\frac{5}{6} \div \frac{3}{8}$

$$\frac{5}{\underset{3}{6}} \times \frac{\overset{4}{8}}{3} = \frac{20}{9} = 2\frac{2}{9}$$

20. $\frac{7}{10} \div \frac{1}{5}$

21. $\frac{2}{3} \div \frac{5}{8}$

22. $7 \div \frac{4}{5}$

23. $\frac{1}{3} \div \frac{5}{6}$

24. $\frac{9}{16} \div \frac{9}{16}$

25. $4\frac{4}{5} \div \frac{7}{8}$

26. $21\frac{1}{2} \div 5\frac{2}{3}$

27. $18 \div \frac{18}{19}$

28. $12 \div 1\frac{3}{5}$

29. $\frac{15}{60} \div \frac{7}{10}$

30. $1\frac{1}{5} \div 10$

31. Frontier Homes, Inc., a builder of custom homes, owns $126\frac{1}{2}$ acres of undeveloped land. If the property is divided into $2\frac{3}{4}$-acre pieces, how many homesites can be developed?

32. An automobile travels 365 miles on $16\frac{2}{3}$ gallons of gasoline.
    a. How many miles per gallon does the car get on the trip?

    b. How many gallons would be required for the car to travel 876 miles?

The U.S. Environmental Protection Agency (EPA) and U.S. Department of Energy (DOE) produce the *Fuel Economy Guide* to help car buyers choose the most fuel-efficient vehicle that meets their needs. The EPA compiles the fuel economy data, and the DOE publishes them in print and on the Web at www.fueleconomy.gov.

33. Pier 1 Imports purchased 600 straw baskets from a wholesaler.
    a. In the first week, $\frac{2}{5}$ of the baskets are sold. How many are sold?

    b. By the third week, only $\frac{3}{20}$ of the baskets remain. How many baskets are left?

34. At the Cattleman's Market, $3\frac{1}{2}$ pounds of hamburger are to be divided into 7 equal packages. How many pounds of meat will each package contain?

35. Super Value Hardware Supply buys nails in bulk from the manufacturer and packs them into $2\frac{4}{5}$-pound boxes. How many boxes can be filled from 518 pounds of nails?

36. The chef at the Sizzling Steakhouse has 140 pounds of sirloin steak on hand for Saturday night. If each portion is $10\frac{1}{2}$ ounces, how many sirloin steak dinners can be served? Round to the nearest whole dinner. (There are 16 ounces in a pound.)

37. Regal Reflective Signs makes speed limit signs for the state department of transportation. By law, these signs must be displayed every $\frac{5}{8}$ of a mile. How many signs will be required on a new highway that is $34\frac{3}{8}$ miles long?

38. Engineers at Triangle Electronics use special silver wire to manufacture fuzzy logic circuit boards. The wire comes in 840-foot rolls that cost $1,200 each. Each board requires $4\frac{1}{5}$ feet of wire.
    a. How many circuit boards can be made from each roll?

    b. What is the cost of wire per circuit board?

39. At Celtex Manufacturing, a chemical etching process reduces $2\frac{13}{16}$-inch copper plates by $\frac{35}{64}$ of an inch.

   a. What is the thickness of each copper plate after the etching process?

   b. How many etched copper plates can fit in a box 25 inches high?

BUSINESS DECISION: DINNER SPECIAL

40. You are the owner of The Gourmet Diner. On Wednesday nights, you offer a special of "Buy one dinner, get one free dinner—of equal or lesser value." Michael and Wayne come in for the special. Michael chooses chicken Parmesan for $15, and Wayne chooses a $10 barbecue-combo platter.

   a. Excluding tax and tip, how much should each pay for his proportional share of the check?

   b. If sales tax and tip amount to $\frac{1}{5}$ of the total of the two dinners, how much is that?

   c. If they decide to split the tax and tip in the same ratio as the dinners, how much more does each owe?

CHAPTER
2
CHAPTER SUMMARY

Section I: Understanding and Working with Fractions

Topic	Important Concepts	Illustrative Examples
Distinguishing among the Various Types of Fractions **Performance Objective 2-1, Page 32**	**Common or proper fraction:** A fraction representing less than a whole unit where the numerator is less than the denominator. **Improper fraction:** A fraction representing one whole unit or more where the denominator is equal to or less than the numerator. **Mixed number:** A number that combines a whole number with a proper fraction.	Proper fraction $\frac{4}{7}, \frac{2}{3}, \frac{93}{124}$ Improper fraction $\frac{5}{4}, \frac{7}{7}, \frac{88}{51}, \frac{796}{212}, \frac{1,200}{1,200}$ Mixed number $12\frac{2}{5}, 4\frac{5}{9}, 78\frac{52}{63}$
Converting Improper Fractions to Whole or Mixed Numbers **Performance Objective 2-2, Page 33**	**To convert improper fractions to whole or mixed numbers:** 1. Divide the numerator of the improper fraction by the denominator. 2a. If there is no remainder, the improper fraction becomes a whole number. 2b. If there is a remainder, write the whole number and then write the fraction as $\text{Whole Number } \frac{\text{Remainder}}{\text{Divisor}}$	Convert the following to whole or mixed numbers. a. $\frac{68}{4} = 17$ b. $\frac{127}{20} = 6\frac{7}{20}$
Converting Mixed Numbers to Improper Fractions **Performance Objective 2-3, Page 34**	**To covert mixed numbers to improper fractions:** 1. Multiply the denominator by the whole number. 2. Add the numerator to the product from Step 1. 3. Place the total from Step 2 as the "new" numerator. 4. Place the original denominator as the "new" denominator.	Convert $15\frac{3}{4}$ to an improper fraction. $15\frac{3}{4} = \frac{(15 \times 4) + 3}{4} = \frac{63}{4}$
Reducing Fractions to Lowest Terms by Inspection **Performance Objective 2-4a, Page 35**	**Reducing a fraction** means finding whole numbers, called common divisors or common factors, that divide evenly into both the numerator and denominator of the fraction. When a fraction has been reduced to the point where there are no common divisors left other than 1, it is said to be **reduced to lowest terms**.	Reduce $\frac{24}{120}$ to lowest terms by inspection. $\frac{24}{120} = \frac{24 \div 3}{120 \div 3} = \frac{8}{40}$ $\frac{8}{40} = \frac{8 \div 2}{40 \div 2} = \frac{4}{20}$ $\frac{4}{20} = \frac{4 \div 4}{20 \div 4} = \frac{1}{5}$
Finding the Greatest Common Divisor (Reducing Shortcut) **Performance Objective 2-4b, Page 36**	The largest number that is a common divisor of a fraction is known as the **greatest common divisor (GCD)**. It reduces the fraction to lowest terms in one step. **To find the GCD:** 1. Divide the numerator of the fraction into the denominator. 2. Examine the remainder. • If it is 0, stop. The divisor is the greatest common divisor. • If it is 1, stop. The fraction cannot be reduced and is therefore in lowest terms. • If it is another number, divide the remainder into the divisor. 3. Repeat Step 2 as needed.	What greatest common divisor will reduce the fraction $\frac{48}{72}$? $\begin{array}{r} 1 \\ 48\overline{)72} \\ 48 \\ \hline 24 \end{array} \quad \begin{array}{r} 2 \\ 24\overline{)48} \\ 48 \\ \hline 0 \end{array}$ The greatest common divisor is 24.
Raising Fractions to Higher Terms **Performance Objective 2-5, Page 37**	**To raise a fraction to a new denominator:** 1. Divide the original denominator into the new denominator. The resulting quotient is the common multiple that raises the fraction. 2. Multiply the numerator and the denominator of the original fraction by the common multiple.	Raise $\frac{5}{8}$ to forty-eighths. $\frac{5}{8} = \frac{?}{48}$ $48 \div 8 = 6$ $\frac{5 \times 6}{8 \times 6} = \frac{30}{48}$

Section II: Addition and Subtraction of Fractions

Topic	Important Concepts	Illustrative Examples
Understanding Prime Numbers Performance Objective 2-6, Page 40	A **prime number** is a whole number greater than 1 that is divisible only by 1 and itself. Prime numbers are used to find the least common denominator of two or more fractions.	Examples of prime numbers: 2, 3, 5, 7, 11, 13, 17, 19, 23, 29
Determining the Least Common Denominator (LCD) of Two or More Fractions Performance Objective 2-6, Page 40	1. Write all the denominators in a row. 2. Find a prime number that divides evenly into any of the denominators. Write that prime number to the left of the row and divide. Place all quotients and undivided numbers in the next row down. 3. Repeat this process until the new row contains all ones. 4. Multiply all the prime numbers on the left to get the LCD of the fractions.	Find the LCD of $\frac{2}{9}$, $\frac{5}{6}$, $\frac{1}{4}$, and $\frac{4}{5}$. **Prime Number Denominators** 3 9 6 4 5 2 3 2 4 5 2 3 1 2 5 3 3 1 1 5 5 1 1 1 5 1 1 1 1 $LCD = 3 \times 2 \times 2 \times 3 \times 5 = 180$
Adding Like Fractions Performance Objective 2-7, Page 41	1. Add all the numerators and place the total over the original denominator. 2. If the result is a proper fraction, reduce it to lowest terms. 3. If the result is an improper fraction, convert it to a whole or mixed number.	Add $\frac{8}{9}$, $\frac{4}{9}$, and $\frac{1}{9}$. $\frac{8+4+1}{9} = \frac{13}{9} = 1\frac{4}{9}$
Adding Unlike Fractions Performance Objective 2-7, Page 42	1. Find the least common denominator of the unlike fractions. 2. Raise each fraction to the terms of the LCD, thereby making them like fractions. 3. Add the like fractions.	Add $\frac{2}{3} + \frac{5}{7}$. $LCD = 3 \times 7 = 21$ $\frac{2 \times 7}{21} + \frac{5 \times 3}{21} = \frac{14 + 15}{21} = \frac{29}{21} = 1\frac{8}{21}$
Adding Mixed Numbers Performance Objective 2-7, Page 43	1. Add the fractional parts. If the sum is an improper fraction, convert it to a mixed number. 2. Add the whole numbers. 3. Add the fraction from Step 1 to the whole number from Step 2. 4. Reduce the answer to lowest terms if necessary.	Add $3\frac{3}{4} + 4\frac{1}{8}$. $\frac{3}{4} + \frac{1}{8} = \frac{(3 \times 2) + 1}{8} = \frac{7}{8}$ $3 + 4 = 7$ $7 + \frac{7}{8} = 7\frac{7}{8}$
Subtracting Like Fractions Performance Objective 2-8, Page 43	1. Subtract the numerators and place the difference over the original denominator. 2. Reduce the fraction to lowest terms if necessary.	Subtract $\frac{11}{12} - \frac{5}{12}$. $\frac{11-5}{12} = \frac{6}{12} = \frac{1}{2}$
Subtracting Unlike Fractions Performance Objective 2-8, Page 44	1. Find the least common denominator. 2. Raise each fraction to the denominator of the LCD. 3. Subtract the like fractions.	Subtract $\frac{7}{8} - \frac{2}{3}$. $LCD = 8 \times 3 = 24$ $\frac{21}{24} - \frac{16}{24} = \frac{5}{24}$
Subtracting Mixed Numbers Performance Objective 2-8, Page 45	1. If the fractions of the mixed numbers have the same denominator, subtract them and reduce to lowest terms. 2. If the fractions do not have the same denominator, raise them to the denominator of the LCD and subtract. 3. Subtract the whole numbers. 4. Add the difference of the whole numbers and the difference of the fractions.	Subtract $15\frac{5}{8} - 12\frac{1}{2}$. $15\frac{5}{8} = \quad 15\frac{5}{8}$ $-12\frac{1}{2} = -12\frac{4}{8}$ $\phantom{-12\frac{1}{2}} = \quad 3\frac{1}{8}$
Subtracting Mixed Numbers Using Borrowing Performance Objective 2-8, Page 45	When the numerator of the fraction in the minuend is less than the numerator of the fraction in the subtrahend, we must borrow one whole unit from the whole number of the minuend. This will be in the form of the LCD/LCD and is added to the fraction of the minuend. Then subtract as before.	Subtract $6\frac{1}{7} - 2\frac{5}{7}$. $6\frac{1}{7} = 5\frac{7}{7} + \frac{1}{7} = 5\frac{8}{7}$ $-2\frac{5}{7} = \phantom{5\frac{7}{7} + \frac{1}{7} = } -2\frac{5}{7}$ $\phantom{-2\frac{5}{7} = } = 3\frac{3}{7}$

Section III: Multiplication and Division of Fractions

Topic	Important Concepts	Illustrative Examples
Multiplying Fractions **Performance Objective 2-9, Page 49**	1. Multiply all the numerators to form the new numerator. 2. Multiply all the denominators to form the new denominator. 3. Reduce the answer to lowest terms if necessary.	Multiply $\frac{5}{8} \times \frac{2}{3}$. $\frac{5}{8} \times \frac{2}{3} = \frac{10}{24} = \frac{5}{12}$
Multiplying Fractions Using Cancellation **Performance Objective 2-9, Page 50**	Cancellation simplifies the numbers and leaves the answer in lowest terms. 1. Find a common factor that divides evenly into at least one of the denominators and one of the numerators. 2. Divide that common factor into the denominator and the numerator, thereby reducing it. 3. Repeat this process until there are no more common factors. 4. Multiply the fractions. The resulting product will be in lowest terms.	Use cancellation to solve the multiplication problem above. Cancellation Method: $\frac{5}{8} \times \frac{2}{3} = \frac{5}{\overset{4}{8}} \times \frac{\overset{1}{2}}{3} = \frac{5}{12}$
Multiplying Mixed Numbers **Performance Objective 2-9, Page 50**	1. Convert all mixed numbers to improper fractions. 2. Multiply using cancellation wherever possible. 3. If the answer is an improper fraction, convert it to a whole or mixed number. 4. Reduce the answer to lowest terms if necessary. *Note:* When multiplying fractions by whole numbers, change the whole numbers to fractions by placing them over 1.	Multiply $3\frac{1}{2} \times 2\frac{3}{8}$. $3\frac{1}{2} = \frac{7}{2}$ $2\frac{3}{8} = \frac{19}{8}$ $\frac{7}{2} \times \frac{19}{8} = \frac{133}{16} = 8\frac{5}{16}$
Dividing Fractions and Mixed Numbers **Performance Objective 2-10, Page 51**	Division of fractions requires that we invert the divisor, or turn it upside down. The inverted fraction is also known as a reciprocal. **Dividing fractions:** 1. Convert all mixed numbers to improper fractions. 2. Identify the fraction that is the divisor and invert it. 3. Change ÷ to ×. 4. Multiply the fractions. 5. Reduce the answer to lowest terms if necessary.	Divide $\frac{11}{12} \div \frac{2}{3}$. $\frac{11}{12}$ is the dividend. $\frac{2}{3}$ is the divisor. $\frac{11}{12} \div \frac{2}{3} = \frac{11}{12} \times \frac{3}{2}$ $\frac{11}{\underset{4}{12}} \times \frac{\overset{1}{3}}{2} = \frac{11}{8} = 1\frac{3}{8}$

TRY IT EXERCISE SOLUTIONS FOR CHAPTER 2

1a. Mixed fraction   Seventy-six and three-fourths   **1b.** Common or proper fraction   Three-fifths

1c. Improper fraction   Eighteen-eighteenths   **1d.** Improper fraction   Thirty-three-eighths

2a. $8 \div 3 = 2\frac{2}{3}$ **2b.** $25 \div 4 = 6\frac{1}{4}$ **2c.** $39 \div 3 = \underline{\underline{13}}$

3a. $\frac{11}{4} \longleftarrow$ **3b.** $\frac{46}{5} \longleftarrow$ **3c.** $\frac{181}{8} \longleftarrow$

$(2 \times 4 + 3 = 11)$ $(9 \times 5 + 1 = 46)$ $(22 \times 8 + 5 = 181)$

4a. $\frac{30 \div 5}{55 \div 5} = \frac{6}{\underline{\underline{11}}}$ **4b.** $\frac{72 \div 2}{148 \div 2} = \frac{36 \div 2}{74 \div 2} = \frac{18}{\underline{\underline{37}}}$ **5a.** $\frac{270 \div 270}{810 \div 270} = \frac{1}{\underline{\underline{3}}}$ **5b.** At lowest terms

$$\begin{array}{r} 3 \\ 270\overline{)810} \\ 810 \\ \hline 0 \end{array}$$

$$\begin{array}{r} 1 \\ 175\overline{)232} \\ 175 \\ \hline 57 \end{array}$$

$$\begin{array}{r} 3 \\ 57\overline{)175} \\ 171 \\ \hline 4 \end{array}$$

$$\begin{array}{r} 14 \\ 4\overline{)57} \\ 4 \\ \hline 17 \\ 16 \\ \hline 1 \end{array}$$

6a. $\dfrac{7 \times 8}{8 \times 8} = \dfrac{56}{64}$ (64 ÷ 8 = 8)   **6b.** $\dfrac{3 \times 5}{7 \times 5} = \dfrac{15}{35}$ (35 ÷ 7 = 5)

7.

2	8	5	15	12
2	4	5	15	6
2	2	5	15	3
3	1	5	15	3
5	1	5	5	1
	1	1	1	1

$2 \times 2 \times 2 \times 3 \times 5 = \underline{120 = \text{LCD}}$

8. $\dfrac{3}{25} + \dfrac{9}{25} + \dfrac{8}{25} = \dfrac{3+9+8}{25} = \dfrac{20}{25} = \underline{\underline{\dfrac{4}{5}}}$

9.
$$\dfrac{1}{6} = \dfrac{5}{30}$$
$$\dfrac{3}{5} = \dfrac{18}{30}$$
$$+\dfrac{2}{3} = +\dfrac{20}{30}$$
$$\dfrac{43}{30} = \underline{\underline{1\dfrac{13}{30}}}$$

10.
$$45\dfrac{1}{4} = 45\dfrac{9}{36}$$
$$16\dfrac{5}{9} = 16\dfrac{20}{36}$$
$$+\dfrac{1}{3} = +\dfrac{12}{36}$$
$$61\dfrac{41}{36} = 61 + 1\dfrac{5}{36} = \underline{\underline{62\dfrac{5}{36}}}$$

11.
$$\dfrac{11}{25}$$
$$-\dfrac{6}{25}$$
$$\dfrac{5}{25} = \underline{\underline{\dfrac{1}{5}}}$$

12.
$$\dfrac{5}{12} = \dfrac{15}{36}$$
$$-\dfrac{2}{9} = -\dfrac{8}{36}$$
$$\underline{\underline{\dfrac{7}{36}}}$$

13a.
$$6\dfrac{3}{4} = 6\dfrac{9}{12}$$
$$-4\dfrac{2}{3} = -4\dfrac{8}{12}$$
$$\underline{\underline{2\dfrac{1}{12}}}$$

13b.
$$25\dfrac{2}{9} = \quad 25\dfrac{4}{18} = 24\dfrac{18}{18} + \dfrac{4}{18} = 24\dfrac{22}{18}$$
$$-11\dfrac{5}{6} = -11\dfrac{15}{18} = \qquad\qquad -11\dfrac{15}{18}$$
$$\underline{\underline{13\dfrac{7}{18}}}$$

14. $\dfrac{\overset{1}{\underset{3}{\cancel{12}}}}{\underset{\underset{1}{3}}{\cancel{21}}} \times \dfrac{7}{\underset{2}{\cancel{8}}} = \underline{\underline{\dfrac{1}{2}}}$

15a. $8\dfrac{2}{5} \times 6\dfrac{1}{4} = \dfrac{\overset{21}{\cancel{42}}}{\underset{1}{\cancel{5}}} \times \dfrac{\overset{5}{\cancel{25}}}{\underset{2}{\cancel{4}}} = \dfrac{105}{2} = \underline{\underline{52\dfrac{1}{2}}}$

15b. $45 \times \dfrac{4}{9} \times 2\dfrac{1}{4} = \dfrac{45}{1} \times \dfrac{4}{\underset{1}{\cancel{9}}} \times \dfrac{\overset{1}{\cancel{9}}}{\underset{1}{\cancel{4}}} = \dfrac{45}{1} = \underline{\underline{45}}$

16a. $\dfrac{14}{25} \div \dfrac{4}{5} = \dfrac{14}{\underset{5}{\cancel{25}}} \times \dfrac{\overset{1}{\cancel{5}}}{\underset{2}{\cancel{4}}} = \underline{\underline{\dfrac{7}{10}}}$ **16b.** $11\dfrac{3}{16} \div 8\dfrac{2}{3} = \dfrac{179}{16} \div \dfrac{26}{3} = \dfrac{179}{16} \times \dfrac{3}{26} = \dfrac{537}{416} = \underline{\underline{1\dfrac{121}{416}}}$

16c. $18 \div 5\dfrac{3}{5} = \dfrac{18}{1} \div \dfrac{28}{5} = \dfrac{\overset{9}{\cancel{18}}}{1} \times \dfrac{5}{\underset{14}{\cancel{28}}} = \dfrac{45}{14} = \underline{\underline{3\dfrac{3}{14}}}$

CONCEPT REVIEW

1. In fractions, the number above the division line is the _____; the number below the division line is the _____. (2-1)

2. The numerator of a proper fraction is _____ than the denominator. (2-1)

3. To convert an improper fraction to a whole or mixed number, we _____ the numerator by the denominator. (2-2)

4. To convert a mixed number to an improper fraction, we begin by multiplying the denominator by the _____ number. (2-3)

5. A fraction can be reduced to lowest terms by inspection or by the greatest common _____ method. (2-4)

6. Common multiples are whole numbers used to raise fractions to _____ terms. (2-5)

7. In addition and subtraction of fractions, the most efficient common denominator is the _____ common denominator. It is abbreviated _____. (2-6)

8. A whole number divisible only by itself and 1 is a(n) _____ number. The first five of these numbers are _____, _____, _____, _____, and _____. (2-6)

9. Like fractions have the same _____. (2-7)

10. When adding unlike fractions, we begin by finding the _____ common denominator of those fractions. (2-7)

11. When subtracting like fractions, we subtract the numerators and place the difference over the original _____. (2-8)

12. When subtracting unlike fractions, we _____ each fraction to the denominator of the LCD. (2-8)

13. When multiplying fractions, cancellation is the shortcut process of finding common factors that _____ evenly into at least one of the numerators and one of the denominators. (2-9)

14. When dividing fractions, we _____ the fraction that is the divisor and then _____ the fractions. (2-10)

CHAPTER

2

ASSESSMENT TEST

Identify the type of fraction and write it in word form.

1. $\dfrac{18}{11}$ **2.** $4\dfrac{1}{6}$ **3.** $\dfrac{13}{16}$

Convert to whole or mixed numbers.

4. $\dfrac{57}{9}$ **5.** $\dfrac{125}{5}$

Convert to improper fractions.

6. $12\dfrac{3}{4}$ **7.** $9\dfrac{5}{9}$

Reduce to lowest terms.

8. $\dfrac{96}{108}$ **9.** $\dfrac{26}{65}$

Convert to higher terms as indicated.

10. $\dfrac{4}{5}$ to twenty-fifths   **11.** $\dfrac{3}{13} = \dfrac{}{78}$

Find the least common denominator for the following fractions.

12. $\dfrac{3}{4}, \dfrac{19}{20}, \dfrac{1}{6}, \dfrac{3}{5}, \dfrac{8}{15}$

Solve the following problems and reduce to lowest terms.

13. $\dfrac{3}{4} - \dfrac{1}{18}$ **14.** $\dfrac{2}{3} + \dfrac{1}{6} + \dfrac{11}{12}$ **15.** $\dfrac{2}{3} \div \dfrac{1}{8}$ **16.** $\dfrac{5}{6} \times \dfrac{1}{4}$

17. $\dfrac{2}{5} \times 5\dfrac{3}{8} \times 2$ **18.** $6\dfrac{5}{6} - \dfrac{17}{18}$ **19.** $4\dfrac{1}{2} + 5\dfrac{5}{6} + 3$

20. $25\dfrac{1}{2} \div 1\dfrac{2}{3}$

21. The Bean Counters, an accounting firm, has 161 employees. If $\frac{3}{7}$ of them are certified public accountants, how many CPAs are there?

22. Ventura Coal mined $6\frac{2}{3}$ tons on Monday, $7\frac{3}{4}$ tons on Tuesday, and $4\frac{1}{2}$ tons on Wednesday. If the goal is to mine 25 tons this week, how many more tons must be mined?

23. A blueprint of a house has a scale of 1 inch equals $4\frac{1}{2}$ feet. If the living room wall measures $5\frac{1}{4}$ inches on the drawing, what is the actual length of the wall?

24. If $\frac{3}{8}$ of a 60-pound bag of ready-mix concrete is Portland cement, how many pounds of other materials are in the bag?

25. The total length of an extension cord measures $18\frac{9}{16}$ inches. The plug end measures $2\frac{3}{4}$ inches, and the receptacle end measures $5\frac{3}{8}$ inches. What is the length of the wire portion of the extension cord?

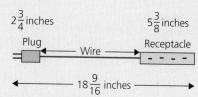

26. During a spring clearance sale, Sears advertises $\frac{1}{4}$ off the list price of Model II microwave ovens and an additional $\frac{1}{5}$ off the sale price for ovens that are scratched or dented.

a. If the list price of a Model II is $240, what is the sale price?

b. What is the price of a scratched one?

© B. O'Kane/Alamy

Sears Holdings Corporation, parent of **Kmart** and **Sears, Roebuck and Co.**, is the nation's fourth-largest broadline retailer with over 3,900 full-line and specialty retail stores in the United States and Canada. Sears is the leading home appliance retailer as well as a leader in tools, lawn and garden, home electronics, and automotive repair and maintenance.

As the nation's largest provider of home services, Sears makes more than 12 million service calls annually. Sales in 2009 were $44.0 billion.

27. You are a sales representative for Boater's Paradise. Last year you sold $490,000 in marine products.

a. If this year you expect to sell $\frac{1}{5}$ more, how much will your sales be?

b. If you are paid a commission of $\frac{1}{12}$ of sales, how much will you earn this year?

62

The National Association of Home Builders is a Washington, D.C.-based trade association representing more than 235,000 building industry members in more than 800 local associations. The NAHB represents the industry's interests and works with federal agencies when laws are made and policies are established.

Reflective of the housing downturn, according to the NAHB, 622,000 single-family homes were started in 2008, a 63.7% decrease from 2005. Multifamily homes fared better at 284,000, a 19.4% decrease from 2005.

28. A developer owns three lots measuring $1\frac{2}{3}$ acres each, four lots measuring $2\frac{1}{2}$ acres each, and one lot measuring $3\frac{3}{8}$ acres.

   a. What is the total acreage owned by the developer?

   b. If each acre is worth $10,000, what is the total value of the properties?

   c. If the company plans to build 8 homes per acre, how many homes will it build?

EXCEL 3

29. A house has 4,400 square feet. The bedrooms occupy $\frac{2}{5}$ of the space, the living and dining rooms occupy $\frac{1}{4}$ of the space, the garage represents $\frac{1}{10}$ of the space, and the balance is split evenly among three bathrooms and the kitchen.

   a. How many square feet are in each bath and the kitchen?

   b. If the owner wants to increase the size of the garage by $\frac{1}{8}$, how many total square feet will the new garage have?

Chefs and cooks measure, mix, and cook ingredients according to recipes, using a variety of pots, pans, cutlery, and other kitchen equipment.

A working knowledge of fractions is one of the job requirements for people employed in the culinary arts. Most foods and other recipe ingredients are measured and combined using fractions.

30. Among other ingredients, a recipe for linguini with red sauce calls for the following: 24 ounces linguini pasta, $6\frac{2}{5}$ tablespoons minced garlic, 5 cups fresh tomatoes, and 10 tablespoons Parmesan cheese. If the recipe serves eight people, recalculate the quantities to serve five people.

Pasta:

Garlic:

Tomatoes:

Cheese:

CHAPTER
2

31. You are an engineer with Ace Foundations, Inc. Your company has been hired to build a 165-foot foundation wall for the construction of a house. You have calculated that the drainage line around the wall will take 1 cubic yard of gravel for every 5 feet of wall.
   a. If a contractor's wheelbarrow has a $\frac{1}{3}$ cubic yard capacity, how many wheelbarrow loads of gravel will be needed?

   b. If your company typically builds this type of a wall at an average rate of $7\frac{1}{2}$ feet per hour, how many hours will it take to build the foundation wall?

   c. Each load of gravel costs $4. The wall materials cost $13 per foot, and labor costs $62 per hour. If $2,700 profit is to be added to the job, how much is the total charge to build the foundation wall?

BUSINESS DECISION: THE CUTTING EDGE

32. You have been given the job of cutting a supply of 2" × 4" pieces of lumber for a frame house. Each piece is to be $14\frac{1}{2}$ inches long. Each cut is $\frac{1}{8}$ inch wide. At Home Depot and Lowe's, the choices of stock length are 10 feet, 12 feet, and 14 feet. You have been asked to choose the length of stock that will have the least amount of waste after you cut as many pieces as you can from it. Which length of stock should you choose?

COLLABORATIVE LEARNING ACTIVITY

Knowing Fractions Is Half the Battle

As a team, investigate and share with the class how fractions are used in the following areas.
a. Cooking
b. Sports
c. Medicine or pharmacy
d. Architecture or building construction
e. Additional team choice _____
f. Additional team choice _____

CHAPTER 3

Andy Lyons/Getty Images

Decimals

PERFORMANCE OBJECTIVES

UNDERSTANDING DECIMAL NUMBERS

In Chapter 1, we learned that the position of the digits in our number system affects their value. In whole numbers, we dealt with the positions, or places, to the left of the decimal point. In decimal numbers, we deal with the places to the right of the decimal point. These places express values that are less than whole numbers.

As with fractions, decimals are a way of expressing *parts* of a whole thing. Decimals are used extensively in business applications. In this chapter, you learn to read, write, and work problems involving all types of decimal numbers.

READING AND WRITING DECIMAL NUMBERS IN NUMERICAL AND WORD FORM

3-1

By definition, **decimal numbers**, or **decimals**, are amounts less than whole, or less than one. They are preceded by a dot known as the **decimal point** and are written .31 or 0.31, for example. The zero is used to ensure that the decimal point is not missed. Often decimals are written in conjunction with whole numbers. These are known as **mixed decimals**. In mixed decimals, the decimal point separates the whole numbers from the decimal, such as 4.31.

The place value chart shown in Exhibit 3-1 expands the whole number chart from Chapter 1 to include the places representing decimals. In decimals, the value of each place starting at the decimal point and moving from left to right decreases by a factor of 10. The names of the places on the decimal side end in *ths*; they are tenths, hundredths, thousandths, ten-thousandths, hundred-thousandths, millionths, and so on.

To read or write decimal numbers in words, you must read or write the decimal part as if it were a whole number, then name the place value of the last digit on the right. For example, .0594 would be read as "five hundred ninety-four ten-thousandths."

In reading and writing mixed decimals, the decimal point should be read as "and." For example, 81.205 would be read as "eighty-one and two hundred five-thousandths." If the

decimal numbers, or decimals
Amounts less than whole, or less than one. For example, .44 is a decimal number.

decimal point A dot written in a decimal number to indicate where the place values change from whole numbers to decimal numbers.

mixed decimals Decimals written in conjunction with whole numbers. For example, 2.44 is a mixed decimal.

LEARNINGTIP

When reading numbers, remember that decimals start with the "tenths" place, whereas whole numbers start with the "ones" place.

Don't forget that the word *and* is used to represent the decimal point.

UPI Photo/Chad Cameron/Newscom

Margin of Victory
Decimals are used in all forms of racing to express the time differences among the competitors. The closest NASCAR finish to date occurred at the Darlington Raceway in 2003 when Ricky Craven finished ahead of Kurt Bush by a mere 0.002 of a second in the Carolina Dodge Dealers 400.

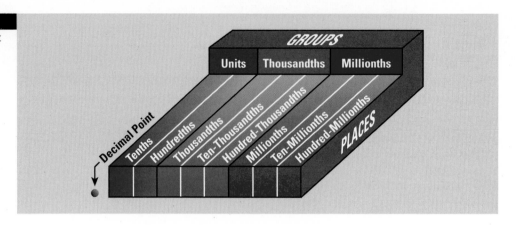

decimal has a fraction at the end, simply read them together using the place value of the last digit of the decimal. For example, $.12\frac{1}{2}$ would be read as "twelve and one-half hundredths."

When a dollar sign ($) precedes a number, the whole number value represents dollars and the decimal value represents cents. The decimal point is read as "and." For example, $146.79 would be read as "one hundred forty-six dollars and seventy-nine cents."

EXAMPLE 1 READING AND WRITING DECIMALS

Read and write the following numbers in word form.

a. .18   b. .0391   c. .00127   d. 34.892   e. 1,299.008   f. $.328\frac{2}{3}$

Read and write the following numbers in numerical form.

g. Three hundred seventy-two ten-thousandths
h. Sixteen thousand and forty-one hundredths
i. Twenty-five and sixty-three and one-half thousandths

SOLUTION STRATEGY

a. .18

Strategy: In this example, write the number eighteen. Because the last digit, 8, is in the hundredths place, the decimal would be written:

Eighteen hundredths

b. .0391

Strategy: Write the number three hundred ninety-one. The last digit, 1, is in the ten-thousandths place; therefore, the decimal would be written:

Three hundred ninety-one ten-thousandths

c. .00127

Strategy: Write the number one hundred twenty-seven. The last digit, 7, is in the hundred-thousandths place; therefore, the decimal would be written:

One hundred twenty-seven hundred-thousandths

d. 34.892

Strategy: This example is a mixed decimal. First, write the whole number: thirty-four. The decimal point is represented by the word *and.* Now write the decimal part as the number eight hundred ninety-two. The last digit, 2, is in the thousandths place; therefore, the mixed decimal is written:

Thirty-four and eight hundred ninety-two thousandths

e. 1,299.008

Strategy: This example is also a mixed decimal. Start by writing the whole number: one thousand, two hundred ninety-nine. Write *and* for the decimal point and write the number eight. Because the last digit, 8, is in the thousandths place, the mixed decimal is written:

One thousand, two hundred ninety-nine and eight thousandths

f. $.328\frac{2}{3}$

Strategy: This decimal has a fraction at the end. Start by writing the number three hundred twenty-eight. Write *and*; then write the fraction, two-thirds. Because the last digit of the decimal, 8, is in the thousandths place, it is written:

Three hundred twenty-eight and two-thirds thousandths

g. Three hundred seventy-two ten-thousandths

Strategy: Write three hundred seventy-two in numerical form. Place the last digit, 2, in the ten-thousandths place. Because ten thousand has four zeros, this is four places to the right of the decimal point. Note that we have to add a zero in the tenths place for the last digit, 2, to be in the ten-thousandths place.

.0372

h. Sixteen thousand and forty-one hundredths

Strategy: Write the whole number sixteen thousand. Place the decimal point for the word *and*. Write the number forty-one and place the last digit, 1, in the hundredths place. Note that hundred has two zeros; therefore, the hundredths place is two places to the right of the decimal point.

16,000.41

i. Twenty-five and sixty-three and one-half thousandths

Strategy: Write the whole number twenty-five. Place the decimal point for the word *and*. Write the number sixty-three and place the fraction one-half after it. Write the last digit, 3, in the thousandths place, three places to the right of the decimal point. Note that we have to add a zero in the tenths place for the last digit, 3, to be in the thousandths place.

$25.063\frac{1}{2}$

More IT Spending

Small and midsize businesses worldwide are expected to increase spending on information technology: (in billions)

$674.4

$487.4

'07   '13

Source: IDC SMB Research

In business, decimals are frequently used in writing large numbers.

TRYITEXERCISE1

Read and write the following numbers in word form.

a. .64   b. .492   c. .10019   d. 579.0004   e. 26.708   f. $.33\frac{1}{3}$

Write the following numbers in numerical form.

g. Twenty-one thousandths
h. Two hundred seventy-two and ninety-four hundred-thousandths
i. Eleven and three and one-quarter thousandths

CHECK YOUR ANSWERS WITH THE SOLUTIONS ON PAGE 84.

ROUNDING DECIMAL NUMBERS TO A SPECIFIED PLACE VALUE

3-2

Rounding decimals is important in business because numbers frequently contain more decimal places than necessary. For monetary amounts, we round to the nearest cent, or hundredth place. For other business applications, we usually do not go beyond thousandths as a final answer.

STEPS TO ROUND DECIMALS TO A SPECIFIED PLACE VALUE

STEP 1. Determine the place to which the decimal is to be rounded.

STEP 2a. If the digit to the right of the one being rounded is 5 or more, increase the digit in the place being rounded by 1.

STEP 2b. If the digit to the right of the one being rounded is 4 or less, do not change the digit in the place being rounded.

STEP 3. Delete all digits to the right of the digit being rounded.

EXAMPLE2 ROUNDING DECIMALS

Round the following numbers to the indicated place.

a. .0292 to hundredths
b. .33945 to thousandths
c. 36.798 to tenths
d. 177.0212782 to hundred-thousandths
e. $46.976 to cents
f. $66.622 to dollars

SOLUTIONSTRATEGY

Decimal Number	Indicated Place	Rounded Number
a. .0292	.0292	.03
b. .33945	.33945	.339
c. 36.798	36.798	36.8
d. 177.0212782	177.0212782	177.02128
e. $46.976	$46.976	$46.98
f. $66.622	$66.622	$67

TRYITEXERCISE2

Round the following numbers to the indicated place.

a. 5.78892 to thousandths
b. .004522 to ten-thousandths
c. $345.8791 to cents
d. 76.03324 to hundredths
e. $766.43 to dollars
f. 34,956.1229 to tenths

CHECK YOUR ANSWERS WITH THE SOLUTIONS ON PAGE 85.

SECTION I 3 REVIEW EXERCISES

Write the following numbers in word form.

1. .21

Twenty-one hundredths

2. 3.76
3. .092
4. 14.659
5. 98,045.045

6. .000033
7. .00938
8. $36.99\frac{2}{3}$
9. $.00057\frac{1}{2}$
10. $2,885.59

Write the following numbers in numerical form.

11. Eight tenths
   .8

12. Twenty-nine thousandths

13. Sixty-seven thousand, three hundred nine and four hundredths

14. Eleven hundred fifty-four dollars and thirty-four cents

15. On three consecutive laps at the Indianapolis Motor Speedway, a race car was timed at 41.507 seconds, 41.057 seconds, and 41.183 seconds. List these times in ascending order, from shortest to longest.

16. On an assembly line quality control test at Hi-Volt Electronics, silver wire measured 0.9 inches, 0.962 inches, 0.098 inches, and 0.9081 inches in diameter. List these measurements in descending order, from largest to smallest.

Super-Sized Speedway
The Indianapolis Motor Speedway, with a seating capacity of 250,000-plus and situated on more than 1,025 acres, is the largest race track in the country. According to *The Wall Street Journal*, the property could hold about 40 Yankee Stadiums or 12 Wimbledon tennis campuses or two Vatican Cities!

Round the following numbers to the indicated place.

17. .448557 to hundredths
    $0.448\underset{=}{5}57 = 0.45$

18. 123.0069 to thousandths

19. .9229388 to ten-thousandths

20. .0100393 to hundred-thousandths

21. $688.75 to dollars

22. $14.59582 to cents

23. 88.964 to tenths

24. 43.0056 to hundredths

25. 1.344 to hundredths

26. 45.80901 to a whole number

BUSINESS DECISION: TECH TALK

27. You are the assistant to the production manager for All American Industries. When you arrived at work, there was a message on your answering machine from an important client with a rush order. It stated the following:

    Hi! This is Lee Perry from Precision Fabricators. We need sixteen, three and three-quarter-inch widgets with a gap of fifty-seven thousandths; twenty, four and three-eighth-inch widgets with a gap of two hundred forty-nine ten-thousandths of an inch; and twenty-five widget connectors with clamps that adjust from one and twenty-three hundredths inches to five and three hundred seventy-six thousandths. Please bill and ship the order to the usual address. Thanks.

    a. Write this order in numerals for the production department to process.

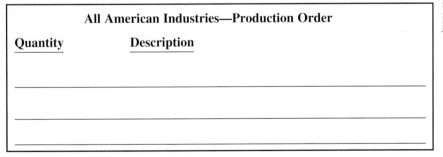

| | **All American Industries—Production Order** |
Quantity	**Description**

    b. If widgets cost $4.80 per inch regardless of gap size and connectors cost $17.95 each, calculate the total cost of the order.

A *micrometer* is a device used in science and engineering for precisely measuring minute distances or thicknesses.

A *micron* (also known as a *micrometer*) is a unit of length in the metric system equal to one-millionth of a meter. The diameter of a human hair measures 80–100 microns.

A *millimeter* (symbol mm) is a unit of length in the metric system equal to one-thousandth of a meter. One inch is equal to 25.4 mm.

A *centimeter* (symbol cm) is a unit of length in the metric system equal to one-hundredth of a meter. One inch is equal to 2.54 cm.

For complete coverage of business measurements and the metric system, see Chapter 22 on your text's website.

SECTION II **3** **DECIMAL NUMBERS AND THE FUNDAMENTAL PROCESSES**

In business, working with decimals is an everyday occurrence. As you will see, performing the fundamental processes of addition, subtraction, multiplication, and division on decimal numbers is very much like performing them on whole numbers. As before, the alignment of the numbers is very important. The difference is in the handling and placement of the decimal point.

3-3

ADDING AND SUBTRACTING DECIMALS

In adding and subtracting decimals, we follow the same procedure as we did with whole numbers. As before, be sure that you line up all the place values, including the decimal points.

STEPS **FOR ADDING AND SUBTRACTING DECIMALS**

STEP 1. Line up all the decimal points vertically.

STEP 2. (Optional) Add zeros to the right of the decimal numbers that do not have enough places.

STEP 3. Perform the addition or subtraction, working from right to left.

STEP 4. Place the decimal point in the answer in the same position (column) as in the problem.

EXAMPLE3 **ADDING AND SUBTRACTING DECIMALS**

a. Add 45.3922 + .0019 + 2.9 + 1,877.332   b. Add $37.89 + $2.76
c. Subtract 87.06 − 35.2   d. Subtract $67.54 from $5,400

SOLUTIONSTRATEGY

These examples are solved by lining up the decimal points, then performing the indicated operation as if they were whole numbers.

```
        45.3922
         .0019
a.       2.9000        b.  $37.89     c.    87.06      d.  $5,400.00
    + 1,877.3320           + 2.76         − 35.20          −  67.54
      1,925.6261           $40.65         51.86           $5,332.46
```

TRYITEXERCISE3

Perform the indicated operation.

a. 35.7008 + 311.2 + 84,557.54   b. $65.79 + $154.33
c. Subtract 57.009 from 186.7   d. $79.80 minus $34.61

CHECK YOUR ANSWERS WITH THE SOLUTIONS ON PAGE 85.

MULTIPLYING DECIMALS

3-4

Decimals are multiplied in the same way as whole numbers except we must now deal with placing the decimal point in the answer. The rule is that there must be as many decimal places in the product as there are total decimal places in the two factors, the multiplier and the multiplicand. This may require adding zeros to the product.

STEPS FOR MULTIPLYING DECIMALS

STEP 1. Multiply the numbers as if they were whole numbers. Disregard the decimal points.

STEP 2. Total the number of decimal places in the two factors, the multiplier and the multiplicand.

STEP 3. Insert the decimal point in the product, giving it the same number of decimal places as the total from Step 2.

STEP 4. If necessary, place zeros to the left of the product to provide the correct number of digits.

EXAMPLE4 MULTIPLYING DECIMALS

a. **Multiply 125.4 by 3.12.**

SOLUTIONSTRATEGY

```
    125.4   1 decimal place
  × 3.12    2 decimal places
   2 508
  12 54
 376 2
 391.248   3 decimal places
```

b. **Multiply .0004 by 6.3.**

SOLUTIONSTRATEGY

```
    6.3    1 decimal place
× .0004    4 decimal places
 .00252    5 decimal places
```

Here we had to add two zeros to the left of the product to make five decimal places.

Multiplication Shortcut

Whenever you are multiplying a decimal by a power of 10, such as 10, 100, 1,000, or 10,000, count the number of zeros in the multiplier and move the decimal point in the multiplicand the same number of places to the right. If necessary, add zeros to the product to provide the required places.

c. **Multiply 138.57 by 10, 100, 1,000, and 10,000.**

SOLUTIONSTRATEGY

$138.57 \times 10 = \underline{1,385.7}$	Decimal moved 1 place to the right
$138.57 \times 100 = \underline{13,857}$	Decimal moved 2 places to the right
$138.57 \times 1,000 = \underline{138,570}$	Decimal moved 3 places to the right—1 zero added
$138.57 \times 10,000 = \underline{1,385,700}$	Decimal moved 4 places to the right—2 zeros added

THE GOVERNMENT ANNOUNCED THAT TO REDUCE THE BUDGET DEFICIT, IT WILL MOVE THE DECIMAL TWO POINTS TO THE LEFT.

NEWS

SCHWADRON

TRYITEXERCISE4

Multiply the following numbers.

a. 876.66
    × .045

b. 4,955.8
    × 2.9

c. $65.79
    × 558

d. .00232 by 1,000

CHECK YOUR ANSWERS WITH THE SOLUTIONS ON PAGE 85.

3-5

DIVIDING DECIMALS

In division of decimals, be aware of the decimal points. The basic rule is that you cannot divide with a decimal in the divisor. If there is a decimal, you must convert it to a whole number before dividing.

STEPS FOR DIVIDING DECIMALS IF THE DIVISOR IS A WHOLE NUMBER

STEP 1. Place the decimal point in the quotient directly above the decimal point in the dividend.

STEP 2. Divide the numbers. Zeros may be added to the right of the dividend as needed.

LEARNINGTIP

When adding, subtracting, multiplying, or dividing decimals, numbers should not be rounded until the final answer—unless you are estimating.

If the situation involves money, final answers should be rounded to the nearest cent.

EXAMPLE5A DIVIDING DECIMALS

Divide: 8.50 ÷ 25.

SOLUTIONSTRATEGY

$$
\begin{array}{r}
.34 \\
8.50 \div 25 = 25\overline{)8.50} \\
\underline{7\ 5} \\
1\ 00 \\
\underline{1\ 00} \\
0
\end{array}
$$

In this example, the divisor, 25, is a whole number; so we place the decimal point in the quotient directly above the decimal point in the dividend and then divide. The answer is .34.

STEPS FOR DIVIDING DECIMALS IF THE DIVISOR IS A DECIMAL NUMBER

STEP 1. Move the decimal point in the divisor to the right until it becomes a whole number.

STEP 2. Move the decimal point in the dividend the same number of places as you moved it in the divisor. It may be necessary to add zeros to the right of the dividend if there are not enough places.

STEP 3. Place the decimal point in the quotient directly above the decimal point in the dividend.

STEP 4. Divide the numbers.

Note: All answers involving money should be rounded to the nearest cent. This means dividing until the quotient has a thousandths place and then rounding back to hundredths. For example, $45.671 = $45.67 and $102.879 = $102.88.

EXAMPLE5B DIVIDING DECIMALS

Divide: 358.75 ÷ 17.5.

SOLUTIONSTRATEGY

$358.75 \div 17.5 =$

$17.5 \overline{)358.75}$

$175 \overline{)3587.5}$

In this example, the divisor, 17.5, is a decimal with one place. To make it a whole number, move the decimal point one place to the right.

Then move the decimal point in the dividend one place to the right and place the decimal point in the quotient above the decimal point in the dividend.

$$\begin{array}{r} 20.5 \\ 175 \overline{)3587.5} \\ \underline{350} \\ 87\ 5 \\ \underline{87\ 5} \\ 0 \end{array}$$

Now divide the numbers. The answer is 20.5.

Division Shortcut

Whenever you divide a decimal by a power of 10, such as 10, 100, 1,000, or 10,000, count the number of zeros in the divisor and move the decimal point in the dividend the same number of places to the left. It may be necessary to add zeros to provide the required places.

EXAMPLE5C DIVIDING DECIMALS BY A POWER OF 10

Divide 43.78 by 10, 100, 1,000, and 10,000.

SOLUTIONSTRATEGY

$43.78 \div 10 = 4.378$ Decimal moved 1 place to the left

$43.78 \div 100 = .4378$ Decimal moved 2 places to the left

$43.78 \div 1,000 = .04378$ Decimal moved 3 places to the left—1 zero added

$43.78 \div 10,000 = .004378$ Decimal moved 4 places to the left—2 zeros added

TRYITEXERCISE5

Divide the following decimals.

a. $716.8 \div 16$ b. $21.336 \div .007$ c. $\$3,191.18 \div 42.1$ d. $2.03992 \div 1,000$

CHECK YOUR ANSWERS WITH THE SOLUTIONS ON PAGE 85.

REVIEW EXERCISES   SECTION II   3

Perform the indicated operation for the following.

1. $2.03 + 56.003$

$$\begin{array}{r} 2.030 \\ + 56.003 \\ \hline 58.033 \end{array}$$

2. $.006 + 12.33$

3. $24.66 + $19.72 + $.89

4. 54.669 + 121.3393 + 7.4

5. .000494 + 45.776 + 16.008 + 91

6. 495.09 − 51.05

7. 58.043 − 41.694

8. $70.55 − $12.79

9. $1.71 − $.84

10. 28.90922 − 16.41

11. Add seventy-five and twenty-six hundredths and forty-one and eighteen thousandths. Express your answer in numerical and word form.

12. Subtract fifteen and eighty-eight ten-thousandths from thirty-six. Express your answer in numerical and word form.

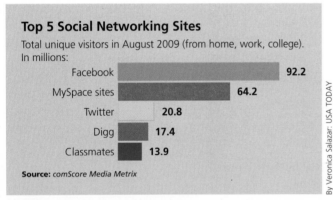

Top 5 Social Networking Sites

Total unique visitors in August 2009 (from home, work, college). In millions:

Facebook	92.2
MySpace sites	64.2
Twitter	20.8
Digg	17.4
Classmates	13.9

Source: *comScore Media Metrix*

By Veronica Salazar, USA TODAY

Facebook is a social networking website founded in 2004. It was originally designed for college students but is now open to anyone 13 years of age and older.

2009 Facebook Facts
- More than 300 million active users
- More than half of all users log in on any given day
- The average user had 130 friends on the site
- More than 8 billion minutes spent on Facebook each day, worldwide
- More than 45 million status updates each day
- More than 2 billion photos uploaded each month
- More than 14 million videos uploaded each month
- More than 65 million users access Facebook through their mobile devices

13. On a recent trip, Tony Segretto filled up his gas tank four times with the following quantities of gasoline: 23.4 gallons, 19.67 gallons, 21.008 gallons, and 16.404 gallons. How many gallons did Tony buy?

14. Use the chart "Top 5 Social Networking Sites" to calculate the total number of unique visitors in August 2009.

15. On the way home from work, Bill Kingman stopped at Chicken Delight to purchase dinner for the family. The chicken was $12.79. Drinks came to $4.84. Side dishes totaled $7.65, and desserts amounted to $4.97.

a. What was the total cost of the food?

b. If Bill had a coupon for "$2.50 off any purchase over $15," how much did he pay?

16. Last week Kate Burke ran a 5-kilometer race in 26.696 minutes. This week she ran a race in 24.003 minutes. What is the difference in Kate's times?

17. Jason Carlage needed a few groceries. At E-Z Shop Market, he bought a loaf of cinnamon raisin bread for $2.29, a quart of milk for $1.78, a bunch of bananas for $1.83, and a pound of butter for $2.96. How much change did he receive from a $20 bill?

18. Faith Sherlock received her monthly pension check of $1,348.26. From that amount, she transferred $180 to a savings account and paid the electricity bill for $156.33, the gas bill for $9.38, the water bill for $98.42, and the cable television bill for $48.54. How much remained of Faith's monthly pension?

19. Use the chart "The Pet Story" to answer the following questions.
   a. How many fewer birds are there than small animals? Express your answer in numerical form.

   b. How many more fish are there than cats and dogs combined? Express your answer in numerical form.

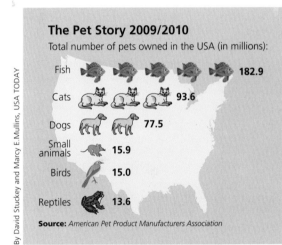

The Pet Story 2009/2010

Total number of pets owned in the USA (in millions):

Fish	182.9
Cats	93.6
Dogs	77.5
Small animals	15.9
Birds	15.0
Reptiles	13.6

Source: *American Pet Product Manufacturers Association*

By David Stuckey and Marcy E.Mullins, USA TODAY

According to the 2009/2010 National Pet Owners Survey, 62% of U.S. households owned a pet, which equates to 71.4 million homes. In 2009, $45.4 billion was spent on pets in the United States.

Multiply the following numbers.

20. $\begin{array}{r} 45.77 \\ \times\ 12 \\ \hline 549.24 \end{array}$ 21. $\begin{array}{r} 494.09 \\ \times\ .81 \\ \hline \end{array}$ 22. $\begin{array}{r} 2.311 \\ \times\ 3.2 \\ \hline \end{array}$ 23. $\begin{array}{r} 112.005 \\ \times\ 10,000 \\ \hline \end{array}$ 24. $\begin{array}{r} .00202 \\ \times\ 24 \\ \hline \end{array}$

25. 15.032×1.008 26. $45.0079 \times 1,000$ 27. $.3309 \times 100,000$

Divide the following numbers. Round to hundredths when necessary.

28. $24.6 \div 19$ 29. $.593 \div 8.6$ 30. $18.69 \div 1,000$ 31. $\$24.50 \div 9$
    $1.294 = \underline{\underline{1.29}}$

32. $72\overline{)266.4}$ 33. $23.18\overline{)139.08}$ 34. $.04\overline{)62.2}$ 35. $4.6\overline{)1000}$

36. Sam Estero received a $50 gift card to iTunes for his birthday. If he downloaded 12 songs at $0.99 per song, 5 songs at $1.29 per song, and 4 apps for his iPhone at $1.99 per app, how much credit remained on the gift card?

JUMP START WWW

JUMP START WWW

37. Ben Whitney bought a car at Auto Nation for $14,566.90. The sticker price was $17,047.88.
    a. How much did Ben save from the sticker price?

    b. The tax was $957.70, and the registration and license plate cost $65.40. What is the total cost of the car?

    c. If Ben makes a down payment of $4,550 and gets an interest-free car loan from the dealer, what will the equal monthly payments be for 48 months?

38. Jimmie Masters earns $4,825.50 per month as a manager at Berries Restaurant.
    a. How much does he earn in a year?

    b. If Jimmie gets a raise of $2,965 per year, what is his new annual and monthly salary?

39. In November 2009, *USA Today* reported that Ethiopian Airlines had confirmed a $3 billion order for 12 A350 aircrafts from Airbus.
    a. What was the average cost per plane?

    b. It was also reported that Airbus planned large wingtip devices on the A320 aircraft, reducing fuel burn by 3.5% and saving about $220,000 a year per plane. How much will this fuel savings per year amount to for a fleet of 12 of these aircraft?

Airbus is an aircraft manufacturing subsidiary of EADS, a European aerospace company. Based in Toulouse, France, and with significant activity across Europe, the company produces about half of the world's jet airliners.

In 2009, Airbus generated revenue of over 28.1 billion euros and employed around 57,000 people at 16 sites in four European Union countries: Germany, France, the United Kingdom, and Spain.

40. Last week you worked 18 hours and earned $256.50. What was your hourly rate?

41. Matt Menke purchased 153.6 square yards of carpeting on sale for $13.70 per yard.
    a. What was the cost of the carpet?

    b. Normally, this carpeting sells for $19.69 per yard. How much did Matt save by purchasing during the sale?

42. Edward Nolan has room for 26 bedding plants in his garden. He can get pansies for $1.89 each, marigolds for $1.29 each, and zinnias for $0.84 each. He plans to buy 10 of one type and 8 each of the other two types of plants.
    a. What is the minimum Edward will have to spend?

    b. What is the maximum Edward could spend?

43. Southern Telecom is offering a prepaid phone card that contains 200 minutes of time for 8 cents per minute. What is the cost of the card?

44. A developer, Fiesta Valley Homes, is building 13 townhouses at one time. Each roof measures 45.7 feet by 68.55 feet.

    a. What is the total square feet per roof? (Multiply length by width.)

    b. What is the total square feet of roof for the entire project?

    c. If the roofing company charges $4.15 per square foot, what is the total cost of the roofs?

45. Tim Meekma owns a PepsiCo vending truck that holds 360 quarts of soda. Last Saturday at a carnival, Tim sold out completely. He sells a 10-ounce Pepsi for $1.25. There are 16 ounces in a pint and 2 pints in a quart.

    a. How many drinks did he serve?

    b. How much revenue did he take in for the day?

    c. For the next carnival, Tim is considering switching to either a 12-ounce drink for $1.65 or a 16-ounce drink for $1.95. As his business adviser, what size do you recommend, assuming each would be a sellout?

© Richard Levine/Alamy

Cola Wars!
According to *Beverage Digest*, in 2008, Coca Cola had 42.7% and Pepsi had 30.8% of the $72.7 billion U.S. soft drink market.

BUSINESS DECISION: ADMINISTERING A GOVERNMENT PROGRAM

46. According to the Food and Nutrition Service of the U.S. Department of Agriculture, in 2008–2009, the National School Lunch Program served 31.2 million school lunches. Of these, 16.1 million students received free lunches, 3.2 million received lunches at a reduced price, and 11.9 million paid full price for their lunches.

    The federal government reimburses school districts $2.68 for each free lunch, $2.28 for each reduced-price lunch, and $0.25 for each paid lunch. In addition to cash reimbursements, schools are entitled to receive USDA foods called "entitlement" foods at a value of 19.50 cents for each lunch served.

    (*continued*)

The National School Lunch Program (NSLP) is a federally assisted meal program operating in public and nonprofit private schools and residential child care institutions. It provides nutritionally balanced, low-cost or free lunches to children each school day. The program was established under the National School Lunch Act and signed by President Harry Truman in 1946.

You are the administrator in charge of the school lunch program for your school district. Last month the schools in your district served 25,000 free lunches, 15,000 "reduced-price" lunches, and 50,000 regular priced lunches.

a. Calculate the amount of reimbursement you expect to receive from the NSLP for last month.

b. In addition to the lunch reimbursement, the NSLP program pays your district $.035 per one-half pint of milk served with each meal. If each student averaged 1 one-half pint of milk per meal, calculate the total amount of milk reimbursement you expect for last month.

c. **The Bottom Line**–What is the total amount of reimbursement your district will receive for last month?

d. **Red Tape** – The government paperwork you must submit requires that you report the average reimbursement per student for both lunch and milk combined last month. Calculate this amount.

SECTION III   3   CONVERSION OF DECIMALS TO FRACTIONS AND FRACTIONS TO DECIMALS

Changing a number from decimal form to its fractional equivalent or changing a number in fractional form to its decimal equivalent is common in the business world. For example, a builder or an architect may use fractions when dealing with the measurements of a project but convert to decimals when calculating the cost of materials.

3-6   CONVERTING DECIMALS TO FRACTIONS

Keep in mind that decimals are another way of writing fractions whose denominators are powers of 10 (10, 100, 1,000 . . .). When you are converting a mixed decimal, the whole number is added to the new fraction, resulting in a mixed fraction.

STEPS FOR CONVERTING DECIMALS TO THEIR FRACTIONAL EQUIVALENT

STEP 1. Write the numerator of the fraction as the decimal number, without the decimal point.

STEP 2. Write the denominator as 1 followed by as many zeros as there are decimal places in the original decimal number.

STEP 3. Reduce the fraction to lowest terms.

EXAMPLE6 CONVERTING DECIMALS TO FRACTIONS

Convert the following numbers to their reduced fractional equivalent.

a. .64　　　　　b. .125　　　　　c. .0457　　　　　d. 17.31

SOLUTIONSTRATEGY

a. $.64 = \frac{64}{100} = \frac{16}{25}$

In this example, 64 becomes the numerator. Because there are two decimal places, the denominator is 1 with two zeros. Then reduce the fraction.

b. $.125 = \frac{125}{1,000} = \frac{1}{8}$

Once again, the decimal becomes the numerator, 125. This decimal has three places; therefore, the denominator will be 1 followed by three zeros. The resulting fraction is then reduced to lowest terms.

c. $.0457 = \frac{457}{10,000}$

This fraction does not reduce.

d. $17.31 = 17 + \frac{31}{100} = 17\frac{31}{100}$

This mixed decimal results in a mixed fraction. It cannot be reduced.

TRYITEXERCISE6

Convert the following decimals to their fractional equivalent, reducing where possible.

a. .875　　　　　b. 23.076　　　　　c. .0004　　　　　d. 84.75

CHECK YOUR ANSWERS WITH THE SOLUTIONS ON PAGE 85.

LEARNINGTIP

When converting decimals to fractions, verbally say the decimal and then write down what you said as a fraction. For example:

- .85 would be verbally stated as "eighty-five hundredths" and written as $\frac{85}{100}$.

- .655 would be verbally stated as "six hundred fifty-five thousandths" and written as $\frac{655}{1,000}$.

CONVERTING FRACTIONS TO DECIMALS

3-7

In Chapter 2, we learned that fractions are actually a way of expressing division, with the line separating the numerator and the denominator representing "divided by."

$$\frac{\text{Numerator (dividend)}}{\text{Denominator (divisor)}} = \text{Denominator } \overline{)\text{Numerator}}$$

In business, decimal numbers are usually rounded to three places (thousandths) or less. When expressing money, round to the nearest hundredth, or cent.

STEPS FOR CONVERTING FRACTIONS TO DECIMALS

STEP 1. Divide the numerator by the denominator.
STEP 2. Add a decimal point and zeros, as necessary, to the numerator (dividend).

LEARNINGTIP

Try this for practice:
　　You are driving to a new restaurant in an unfamiliar area. A highway billboard directs you to make a right turn at an intersection $4\frac{3}{5}$ miles ahead. If your odometer reads 16,237.8, at what mileage should you make the turn?

Solution: $4\frac{3}{5} = 4.6$　$16,237.8 + 4.6 =$ 16,242.4 miles

EXAMPLE7 CONVERTING FRACTIONS TO DECIMALS

Convert the following fractions to their decimal equivalents, rounding to hundredths.

a. $\frac{3}{5}$　　　　　b. $\frac{1}{3}$　　　　　c. $\frac{23}{9}$　　　　　d. $15\frac{3}{8}$

SOLUTIONSTRATEGY

a. $\dfrac{3}{5} = 5\overline{)3.0}^{.6} = \underline{.6}$

In this example, the numerator, 3, becomes the dividend, with a decimal point and zero added. The denominator, 5, becomes the divisor.

b. $\dfrac{1}{3} = 3\overline{)1.0000}^{.3333} = \underline{.33}$

In this example, the division is uneven and goes on and on; so we round the quotient to hundredths.

c. $\dfrac{23}{9} = 9\overline{)23.00000}^{2.55555} = \underline{2.56}$

Improper fractions result in mixed decimals. Note that the quotient was rounded because of an endlessly repeating decimal.

d. $15\dfrac{3}{8} = 15 + 8\overline{)3.000}^{.375} = \underline{15.38}$

This example contains a whole number. Remember to add it to the resulting decimal.

TRYITEXERCISE7

Convert the following fractions to their decimal equivalents, rounding to hundredths where necessary.

a. $\dfrac{4}{5}$ b. $84\dfrac{2}{3}$ c. $\$6\dfrac{3}{4}$ d. $\dfrac{5}{2}$ e. $\dfrac{5}{8}$

CHECK YOUR ANSWERS WITH THE SOLUTIONS ON PAGE 85.

LEARNINGTIP

When fractions such as $\frac{2}{3}$ are converted to decimals, the result is a *repeating decimal*. These may be written as .666; for business applications, they may be rounded to tenths or hundredths.

Others include $\dfrac{1}{3}, \dfrac{1}{6}, \dfrac{5}{6}, \dfrac{1}{9}, \dfrac{4}{9}, \dfrac{23}{9}$.

SECTION III **3** REVIEW EXERCISES

Pizza, Pizza!
According to the NPD group, pizza sales from June 2008 to June 2009 were $36.6 billion, with 67,554 pizzerias in the United States. Pizzerias account for 11.7% of all restaurants.

Each man, woman, and child in America eats an average of 46 slices (23 pounds) of pizza per year. The equivalent of 100 acres of pizza is consumed daily, or about 350 slices per second.

Source: www.pmq.com, *Pizza Magazine*

Convert the following decimals to fractions and reduce to lowest terms.

1. .125
  $\dfrac{125}{1,000} = \dfrac{1}{8}$

2. 4.75

3. .008

4. 93.0625

5. 14.82

Convert the following fractions to decimals. Round the quotients to hundredths when necessary.

6. $\dfrac{9}{16}$
  $.5625 = \underline{.56}$

7. $5\dfrac{2}{3}$

8. $24\dfrac{1}{8}$

9. $\dfrac{55}{45}$

10. $\dfrac{3}{5}$

For the following numbers, perform the indicated operation.

11. $34.55 + 14.08 + 9\dfrac{4}{5}$

12. $565.809 - 224\dfrac{3}{4}$

13. $12\dfrac{1}{2} \div 2.5$

14. $\$35.88 \times 21\dfrac{1}{4}$

15. a. You are planning a party for your bowling league at Upper Crust Pizza. How many eight-slice pizzas must you order to feed 24 women who eat $2\dfrac{1}{8}$ slices each and 20 men who eat $3\dfrac{3}{4}$ slices each? Round to the nearest whole pizza.

    b. If each pizza costs $11.89, what is the total cost?

JUMP START WWW

16. Catalina Jewelers has 147 ounces of 14-carat gold in stock.
    a. How many custom necklaces can be manufactured if each requires $2\frac{3}{8}$ ounces of gold?

    b. If gold is currently selling for $1,050 per ounce, how much is the gold in each necklace worth?

17. a. What is the total cost of fuel for a 3,003 mile trip if your vehicle gets 15.4 miles per gallon and the average cost of gasoline is 2.50\frac{9}{10}$? Round to the nearest cent.

    b. While on the trip, you paid $368.50 for engine repairs and $37.80 for a new battery. In addition, tolls amounted to $45.75 and parking averaged $4.50 per day for nine days. What was the cost per mile for the trip? Round to the nearest tenth of a cent.

18. Ever Ready taxicabs charge $1.20 for the first $\frac{1}{4}$ of a mile and $0.35 for each additional $\frac{1}{4}$ of a mile. What is the cost of a trip from the airport to downtown, a distance of $8\frac{3}{4}$ miles?

19. You are the purchasing manager for Five Star Graphics, a company that uses specially treated photo paper. The yellow paper costs $.07$\frac{1}{5}$ per sheet, and the blue paper costs $.05$\frac{3}{8}$ per sheet. If you order 15,000 yellow sheets and 26,800 blue sheets, what is the total cost of the order?

20. You are the manager of Rally Rent-a-Car. A customer, Sandy Furrow, has asked you for an estimate of charges for a nine-day rental of an SUV. She expects to drive 670 miles. If Rally charges $53.50 per day plus $18\frac{1}{2}$ cents per mile for this category of vehicle, what would be the total rental charge for Sandy's trip?

BUSINESS DECISION: QUALIFYING FOR A MORTGAGE

21. You are a loan officer at the West Elm Savings and Loan. Mr. and Mrs. Brady are in your office to apply for a mortgage loan on a house they want to buy. The house has a market value of $180,000. Your bank requires $\frac{1}{5}$ of the market value as a down payment.
    a. What is the amount of the down payment?

    b. What is the amount of the mortgage for which the Bradys are applying?

(*continued*)

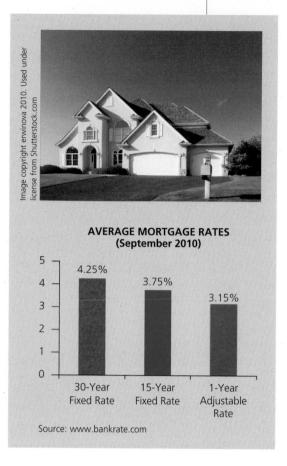

AVERAGE MORTGAGE RATES
(September 2010)

4.25% — 30-Year Fixed Rate
3.75% — 15-Year Fixed Rate
3.15% — 1-Year Adjustable Rate

Source: www.bankrate.com

c. The current annual interest rate for a 30-year mortgage is 5 percent. At that rate, the monthly payments for principal and interest on the loan will be $5.37 for every $1,000 financed. What is the amount of the principal and interest portion of the Bradys' monthly payment?

d. What is the total amount of interest that will be paid over the life of the loan?

e. Your bank also requires that the monthly mortgage payments include property tax and homeowners insurance payments. If the property tax is $1,710 per year and the property insurance is $1,458 per year, what is the total monthly payment for PITI (principal, interest, taxes, and insurance)?

f. To qualify for the loan, bank rules state that mortgage payments cannot exceed $\frac{1}{4}$ of the combined monthly income of the family. If the Bradys earn $3,750 per month, will they qualify for this loan?

g. What monthly income would be required to qualify for this size mortgage payment?

"As an alternative to the traditional 30-year mortgage, we also offer an interest-only mortgage, balloon mortgage, reverse mortgage, upside down mortgage, inside out mortgage, loop-de-loop mortgage, and the spinning double axel mortgage with a triple lutz."

CHAPTER SUMMARY

Section I: Understanding Decimal Numbers

Topic	Important Concepts	Illustrative Examples
Reading and Writing Decimal Numbers in Numerical and Word Form **Performance Objective 3-1, Page 65**	In decimals, the value of each place starting at the decimal point and moving from left to right decreases by a factor of 10. The names of the places end in *ths;* they are tenths, hundredths, thousandths, ten-thousandths, hundred-thousandths, millionths, and so on. 1. To write decimal numbers in words, write the decimal part as a whole number; then add the place value of the last digit on the right. 2. When writing mixed decimals, the decimal point should be read as "and." 3. If the decimal ends in a fraction, read them together using the place value of the last digit of the decimal. 4. When a dollar sign ($) precedes a number, the whole number value represents dollars, the decimal value represents cents, and the decimal point is read as "and."	*Decimal Numbers* .0691 is six hundred ninety-one ten-thousandths Twenty-one ten-thousandths is .0021 *Mixed Decimals* 51.305 is fifty-one and three hundred five thousandths Eighteen and thirty-six thousandths is 18.036 *Decimals with Fractions* .22$\frac{1}{2}$ is twenty-two and one-half hundredths Seventeen and one-half hundredths is .17$\frac{1}{2}$ *Dollars and Cents* $946.73 is nine hundred forty-six dollars and seventy-three cents Six dollars and twelve cents is $6.12
Rounding Decimal Numbers to a Specified Place Value **Performance Objective 3-2, Page 67**	1. Determine the place to which the decimal is to be rounded. 2a. If the digit to the right of the one being rounded is 5 or more, increase the digit in the place being rounded by 1. 2b. If the digit to the right of the one being rounded is 4 or less, do not change the digit in the place being rounded. 3. Delete all digits to the right of the one being rounded.	Round as indicated: .645 rounded to hundredths is .65 42.5596 rounded to tenths is 42.6 .00291 rounded to thousandths is .003 $75.888 rounded to cents is $75.89

Section II: Decimal Numbers and the Fundamental Processes

Topic	Important Concepts	Illustrative Examples
Adding and Subtracting Decimals **Performance Objective 3-3, Page 70**	1. Line up all the place values, including the decimal points. 2. The decimal point in the answer will appear in the same position (column) as in the problem. 3. You may add zeros to the right of the decimal numbers that do not have enough places.	Addition: $\begin{array}{r} 2,821.049 \\ 12.500 \\ +\ 143.008 \\ \hline 2,976.557 \end{array}$ Subtraction: $\begin{array}{r} 194.1207 \\ -\ 45.3400 \\ \hline 148.7807 \end{array}$
Multiplying Decimals **Performance Objective 3-4, Page 71**	1. Multiply the numbers as if they were whole numbers, disregarding the decimal points. 2. Total the number of decimal places in the multiplier and the multiplicand. 3. Insert the decimal point in the product, giving it the same number of decimal places as the total from Step 2. 4. If necessary, place zeros to the left of the product to provide the correct number of digits. *Note:* If the situation involves money, answers should be rounded to the nearest cent.	Multiply 224.5 by 4.53. $\begin{array}{r} 224.5 \\ \times\ 4.53 \\ \hline 6\ 735 \\ 112\ 25 \\ 898\ 0 \\ \hline 1,016.985 \end{array}$ 224.5 1 decimal place 4.53 2 decimal places 1,016.985 3 decimal places

Section II (continued)

Topic	Important Concepts	Illustrative Examples
Multiplication Shortcut: Powers of 10 **Performance Objective 3-4, Page 71**	When multiplying a decimal times a power of 10 (such as 10, 100, 1,000, or 10,000): 1. Count the number of zeros in the multiplier and move the decimal point in the multiplicand the same number of places to the right. 2. If necessary, add zeros to the product to provide the required places.	Multiply $.064 \times 10 = .64 $ 1 place $.064 \times 100 = 6.4 $ 2 places $.064 \times 1,000 = 64 $ 3 places $.064 \times 10,000 = 640 $ 4 places $.064 \times 100,000 = 6,400$ 5 places
Dividing Decimals **Performance Objective 3-5, Page 72**	*If the divisor is a whole number:* 1. Place the decimal point in the quotient directly above the decimal point in the dividend. 2. Divide the numbers. *If the divisor is a decimal number:* 1. Move the decimal point in the divisor to the right until it becomes a whole number. 2. Move the decimal point in the dividend the same number of places you moved it in the divisor. It may be necessary to add zeros to the right of the dividend if there are not enough places. 3. Place the decimal point in the quotient directly above the decimal point in the dividend. 4. Divide the numbers. *Note:* All answers involving money should be rounded to the nearest cent.	Divide: $9.5 \div 25$ $\begin{array}{r} .38 \\ 25\overline{)9.50} \\ 7\,5 \\ \hline 2\,00 \\ 2\,00 \\ \hline 0 \end{array}$ Divide: $14.3 \div 2.2$ $2.2\overline{)14.3}$ $\begin{array}{r} 6.5 \\ 22\overline{)143.0} \\ 132 \\ \hline 110 \\ 110 \\ \hline 0 \end{array}$
Division Shortcut: Powers of 10 **Performance Objective 3-5, Page 73**	When dividing a decimal by a power of 10 (such as 10, 100, 1,000, or 10,000): 1. Count the number of zeros in the divisor and move the decimal point in the dividend the same number of places to the left. 2. It may be necessary to add zeros to provide the required number of decimal places.	Divide $21.69 \div 10 = 2.169 $ 1 place $21.69 \div 100 = .2169 $ 2 places $21.69 \div 1,000 = .02169 $ 3 places $21.69 \div 10,000 = .002169$ 4 places

Section III: Conversion of Decimals to Fractions and Fractions to Decimals

Topic	Important Concepts	Illustrative Examples
Converting Decimals to Fractions **Performance Objective 3-6, Page 78**	1. Write the numerator of the fraction as the decimal number without the decimal point. 2. Write the denominator as "1" followed by as many zeros as there are decimal places in the original decimal number. 3. Reduce the fraction to lowest terms.	$.88 = \dfrac{88}{100} = \dfrac{22}{25}$ $5.57 = 5 + \dfrac{57}{100} = 5\dfrac{57}{100}$
Converting Fractions to Decimals **Performance Objective 3-7, Page 79**	1. Divide the numerator by the denominator. 2. Add a decimal point and zeros, as necessary, to the numerator.	$\dfrac{4}{5} = 5\overline{)4.0}^{\,.8}$ $\dfrac{22}{4} = 4\overline{)22.0}^{\,5.5}$

TRY IT: EXERCISE SOLUTIONS FOR CHAPTER 3

1a. Sixty-four hundredths

b. Four hundred ninety-two thousandths

c. Ten thousand nineteen hundred-thousandths

d. Five hundred seventy-nine and four ten-thousandths

e. Twenty-six and seven hundred eight thousandths

f. Thirty-three and one-third hundredths

g. .021

h. 272.00094

i. $11.003\frac{1}{4}$

2a. $5.78892 = 5.789$ **b.** $.004522 = .0045$ **c.** $\$345.8791 = \$345.88$

d. $76.03324 = 76.03$ **e.** $\$766.43 = \$766$ **f.** $34,956.1229 = 34,956.1$

3a.
$$
\begin{array}{r}
35.7008 \\
311.2000 \\
+\ 84,557.5400 \\
\hline
84,904.4408
\end{array}
$$

b.
$$
\begin{array}{r}
65.79 \\
+154.33 \\
\hline
\$220.12
\end{array}
$$

c.
$$
\begin{array}{r}
186.700 \\
-\ 57.009 \\
\hline
129.691
\end{array}
$$

d.
$$
\begin{array}{r}
79.80 \\
-\ 34.61 \\
\hline
\$45.19
\end{array}
$$

4a.
$$
\begin{array}{r}
876.66 \\
\times\ .045 \\
\hline
4\ 38330 \\
35\ 0664 \\
\hline
39.44970
\end{array}
$$

b.
$$
\begin{array}{r}
4,955.8 \\
\times\ 2.9 \\
\hline
4\ 460\ 22 \\
9\ 911\ 6 \\
\hline
14,371.82
\end{array}
$$

c.
$$
\begin{array}{r}
65.79 \\
\times\ 558 \\
\hline
526\ 32 \\
3\ 289\ 5 \\
32\ 895 \\
\hline
\$36,710.82
\end{array}
$$

d. $.00232 \times 1,000 = 2.32$

5a.
$$
\begin{array}{r}
44.8 \\
16\overline{)716.8} \\
64 \\
\hline
76 \\
64 \\
\hline
12\ 8 \\
12\ 8 \\
\hline
0
\end{array}
$$

b.
$$
\begin{array}{r}
3048 \\
7\overline{)21336} \\
21 \\
\hline
33 \\
28 \\
\hline
56 \\
56 \\
\hline
0
\end{array}
$$

c.
$$
\begin{array}{r}
75.8 = \$75.80 \\
421\overline{)31911.8} \\
2947 \\
\hline
2441 \\
2105 \\
\hline
336\ 8 \\
336\ 8 \\
\hline
0
\end{array}
$$

d. $2.03992 \div 1,000 = .00203992$

6a. $\dfrac{875}{1,000} = \dfrac{7}{8}$ **b.** $23\dfrac{76}{1,000} = 23\dfrac{19}{250}$ **c.** $\dfrac{4}{10,000} = \dfrac{1}{2,500}$ **d.** $84\dfrac{75}{100} = 84\dfrac{3}{4}$

7a. $\dfrac{4}{5} = .8$
$$
\begin{array}{r}
.8 \\
5\overline{)4.0} \\
4\ 0 \\
\hline
0
\end{array}
$$

b. $84\dfrac{2}{3} = 84.67$
$$
\begin{array}{r}
.666 \\
84 + 3\overline{)2.000} \\
1\ 8 \\
\hline
20 \\
18 \\
\hline
20 \\
18 \\
\hline
2
\end{array}
$$

c. $\$6\dfrac{3}{4} = \$6.75$
$$
\begin{array}{r}
.75 \\
6 + 4\overline{)3.00} \\
2\ 8 \\
\hline
20 \\
20 \\
\hline
0
\end{array}
$$

d. $\dfrac{5}{2} = 2.5$
$$
\begin{array}{r}
2.5 \\
2\overline{)5.0} \\
4 \\
\hline
1\ 0 \\
1\ 0 \\
\hline
0
\end{array}
$$

e. $\dfrac{5}{8} = .63$
$$
\begin{array}{r}
.625 \\
8\overline{)5.000} \\
4\ 8 \\
\hline
20 \\
16 \\
\hline
40 \\
40 \\
\hline
0
\end{array}
$$

CONCEPT REVIEW

1. As with fractions, _____ are a way of expressing parts of a whole thing. (3-1)

2. The _____ _____ separates the whole number part from the decimal part of a mixed decimal. It is read as the word _____. (3-1)

3. When rounding decimals, we delete all digits to the _____ of the digit being rounded. (3-2)

4. When rounding monetary amounts, we round to the nearest _____, or _____ place. (3-2)

5. When adding or subtracting decimals, we begin by lining up all the _____ _____ vertically. (3-3)

6. When adding or subtracting decimals, we work from _____ to _____. (3-3)

7. In the multiplication of decimals, the product has as many decimal places as the total number of decimal places in the two _____, the multiplier and the multiplicand. (3-4)

8. When multiplying a decimal by a power of 10, as a shortcut, move the decimal point to the right the same number of places as there are _____ in the power of 10. (3-4)

9. When dividing decimals, the basic rule is that you cannot divide with a decimal in the _____. (3-5)

10. When dividing a decimal by a power of 10, as a shortcut, move the decimal point in the dividend to the _____ the same number of places as there are zeros in the divisor. (3-5)

11. When converting a decimal to a fraction, we commonly _____ the fraction to lowest terms. (3-6)

12. To convert a fraction to a decimal, we divide the _____ by the _____. (3-7)

CHAPTER

3

ASSESSMENT TEST

Write the following numbers in word form.

1. .61   2. 34.581   3. $119.85   4. $.09\frac{3}{7}$ 5. .0495

Write the following numbers in numerical form.

6. Nine hundred sixty-seven ten-thousandths

7. Five and fourteen thousandths

8. Eight hundred forty-three and two tenths

9. Sixteen dollars and fifty-seven cents

Round the following numbers to the indicated place.

10. .44857 to hundredths   11. 995.06966 to thousandths

12. $127.94 to dollars   13. 4.6935 to tenths

Perform the indicated operation for the following.

14. 6.03 + 45.168   15. $1.58 + $15.63 + $19.81 + $.17

16. .0031 + 69.271 + 193.55 + 211   17. 23.0556 − 15.35

18. $95.67 − $2.84   19. .802 − .066

20. 14.74
    × 15

21.   .008
    × .024

22. .9912 × 100,000

23. .503 ÷ 1.2575   24. 79.3 ÷ 10,000   25. $150.48 ÷ 7.5

Convert the following decimals to fractions and reduce to lowest terms.

26. 12.035   27. .0441

EXCEL1

Convert the following fractions to decimals. Round the quotients to hundredths.

28. $\frac{8}{29}$

29. $3\frac{1}{9}$

30. $\frac{95}{42}$

31. Gary Scott can buy a box of 40 Blu-ray discs for $18.99 and a box of 40 jewel cases for $9.98. Alternatively, he can purchase two boxes of 20 Blu-ray discs already in jewel cases for $16.95 each. Which is the better buy, and by how much—the box of 40 Blu-ray discs and a box of 40 cases or the two boxes of 20 Blu-ray discs with jewel cases included?

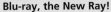

Blu-ray, the New Ray!
Blu-ray format offers more than five times the storage capacity of traditional DVDs and can hold up to 25GB on a single-layer disc and 50GB on a dual-layer disc. While optical disc technologies such as DVD rely on a red laser to read and write data, the new format uses a blue-violet laser instead, hence the name Blu-ray

Blu-ray discs software accounted for 3% of consumer disc spending in 2008. Blu-ray discs are projected to reach half of consumer disc spending by 2013.

32. Two Wheeler-Dealer Bike Shop has a 22-inch off-road racer on sale this month for $239.95. If the original price of the bike was $315.10, how much would a customer save by purchasing it on sale?

33. The chief financial officer of Allied Corporation is setting up two production work shift pay schedules. Swing shift workers are to receive $\frac{1}{12}$ more pay than day shift workers. If the day shift workers are to receive average pay of $18.36 per hour, what is the average pay for the swing shift workers?

34. A ream of paper contains 500 sheets and costs $7.50. What is the cost per sheet?

35. Liz Thorton has signed up for a one-semester class that meets twice a week. The semester is 16 weeks long. She knows that she will miss three classes during her vacation. She has a choice of buying a semester parking pass for $41.50, or she can pay $1.75 daily for parking. How much will Liz save if she buys the parking pass?

36. At Mager's Market, a 24-bottle case of spring water is on sale for $5.99. If the regular price for the case is $6.97,

   a. How much is saved if a customer buys the case at the sale price?

   b. What is the sale price per bottle? Round to the nearest cent.

   c. Which sales strategy earns more revenue for Mager's Market, selling 400 cases of water per week at the sale price or selling 300 cases per week at the regular price?

37. Maria Lopez shares an apartment with a friend. They divide all expenses evenly. Maria's monthly take-home pay is $2,792.15. The apartment expenses this month are $985.50 for rent, $192.00 for maintenance fees, $56.31 for electricity, and $28.11 for telephone. How much remains from Maria's check after she pays her share of the monthly rent and expenses?

CHAPTER

3

38. Ryan Miller wanted to make some money at a flea market. He purchased 55 small orchids from a nursery for a total of $233.75, three bags of potting soil for $2.75 each, and 55 ceramic pots at $4.60 each. After planting the orchids in the pots, Ryan sold each plant for $15.50 at the flea market.

    a. What was his total cost per potted plant?

    b. How much profit did Bill make on this venture?

39. A cargo ship, *The Caribbean Trader*, has a cargo area of 23,264 cubic feet.

    a. How many 145.4 cubic foot storage containers can the ship hold?

    b. The shipping cost per storage container is $959.64 for a trip from Miami to Nassau. What is the cost per cubic foot?

40. As the food manager for a local charity, you are planning a fund-raising pasta party. Spaghetti sells for $1.79 per 16-ounce box.

    a. If the average adult serving is $5\frac{3}{4}$ ounces and the average child eats $3\frac{1}{2}$ ounces, how many boxes will you have to purchase to serve 36 adults and 46 children?

    b. What is the total cost of the spaghetti?

Maersk Line is the core liner shipping activity of the A.P. Moller – Maersk Group and the leading container shipping company in the world. Maersk employs about 16,900 and has 7,600 seafarers. In 2009, revenue totaled $20.6 billion.

    The Maersk Line fleet comprises more than 500 vessels and a number of containers corresponding to more than 2 million TEU (twenty-foot equivalent unit – a container 20 feet long).

EXCEL 2

BUSINESS DECISION: THE INTERNATIONAL BUSINESS TRIP

41. U.S. dollars are legal currency only in the United States. International investment, travel, and trade require that dollars be exchanged for foreign currency. In today's global economy, a floating exchange rate system is used to value major currencies compared to each other. Because the values of these currencies vary continually, exchange rate tables are published daily by numerous business sources. The table below reflects the currency exchange rates on November 19, 2009.

Currency Exchange Rates – November 19, 2009

Country – Currency	Dollar	Euro	Pound	SFranc	Peso	Yen	CdnDlr
Canada – Canadian dollar	1.0625	1.5793	1.7663	1.0445	0.0814	0.0120	....
Japan – Yen	88.777	132.08	147.70	87.277	6.8018	....	83.537
Mexico – Peso	13.052	19.411	21.701	12.830	....	0.1470	12.280
Switzerland – Swiss Franc	1.0170	1.5132	1.6924	....	0.0779	0.0115	0.9580
Britain – Pound	0.6010	0.8941	....	0.5911	0.0461	0.0068	0.5659
Euro – Euro	0.6721	....	1.1187	0.6610	0.0515	0.0076	0.6334
U.S. – Dollar	....	1.4877	1.6639	0.9839	0.0767	0.0113	0.9420

For example, on that date, $100 U.S. dollars was worth 67.21 euros.

$$\$100 \times 0.6721 = 67.21 \text{ euros}$$

STEPS TO CONVERT BETWEEN FOREIGN CURRENCIES

STEP 1. Locate the *currency exchange rate* at the intersection of the column of the currency you are changing from (old currency) and the row of the currency you are changing to (new currency).

STEP 2. Multiply the number of units you are changing from (old currency) by the currency exchange rate.

New currency = Old currency × Currency exchange rate

DOLLARS AND SENSE

Up-to-the-minute currency exchange rates can be found at www.xe.com.

You are the sales manager of Republic Enterprises, Inc., a company that sells motor parts in many countries. For the next two weeks, you are going on a selling trip to Canada and the United Kingdom. Your airline fare and hotel bill will be charged on company credit cards. Your boss has allotted an additional $2,500 for out-of-pocket expenses during the trip.

a. A few days before your trip, you exchange the $2,500 U.S. dollars for British pounds to be used while you are in London. How many pounds will you have for the British portion of your trip? Round to the nearest pound.

b. When you finish your business in London, you have 800 pounds left. Your next stop is Toronto, Canada. How many Canadian dollars will those British pounds purchase? Round to the nearest Canadian dollar.

c. After completing your business in Canada, you have $375 Canadian dollars left. How many U.S. dollars will those Canadian dollars purchase? Round to the nearest U.S. dollar.

"KEEP GOING, LEROY. THE DOLLAR'S NOT THAT STRONG."

Lockhorns © 2001 WM Hoest Enterprises, inc.
King Features Syndicate

d. Before you left on the trip, you price-checked a particular camera at Best Buy for $358. You then used the Internet to find that the same camera model is available in London for 266 British pounds and in Toronto for $362 Canadian dollars. Where should you buy the camera to get the lowest price—at home or in one of the cities on the trip? Round each figure to the nearest U.S. dollar.

COLLABORATIVE LEARNING ACTIVITY

Sports Math

As a team, choose two sports.
a. Investigate how fractions and decimals are used in their record keeping and statistics.
b. Prepare a visual presentation of your findings to share with the class.

Business Math Times

TIPS FOR TAKING MATH TESTS

BEFORE THE TEST

- Know what material will be covered on the test and pace your study schedule accordingly.
- Get a good night's sleep. (Don't study all night.)
- Get up earlier than usual on test day to review your notes.
- Have a positive mental attitude about doing well on the test.
- Bring all necessary materials—calculator, pencils, erasers, paper, ruler, etc.

DURING THE TEST

- Listen to all verbal instructions. If you have a question or don't understand something, ask for clarification.
- If you feel nervous, close your eyes and take a few deep breaths.
- Read all written directions carefully.
- If there is an answer sheet, make sure you write your answers in the proper place.
- Budget your time. Spend the most time on those portions if the test that are worth the most points.
- Skip questions you don't know and come back to them. Place a check mark next to the questions you must return to.
- Be sure your answers are logical. On multiple-choice tests, eliminate the answers you know can't be right and work from there.
- If time permits, double-check your answers.

AFTER THE TEST

- If you did well, reward yourself.
- If you didn't do so well, reward yourself for a good effort and learn from your mistakes.

OVERCOMING ANXIETY IN BUSINESS MATH

Math! It makes throats lumpy, stomachs queasy, and palms sweaty. Each year in thousands of classrooms around the country, math causes anxiety in many students.

"I would like to be able to refer to this statistical graph, but I have math anxiety."

© Aaron Bacall, Reproduction rights obtainable from www.CartoonStock.com

What can you do? To begin, understand that math isn't just another course you have to take in school and then not deal with any more. On the contrary, math skills, particularly in business, are an integral part of what it takes to build a successful career.

Even as a consumer, today's complex marketplace requires math skills if you are to function in an informed and prudent manner. Make the commitment – Learn It Now!

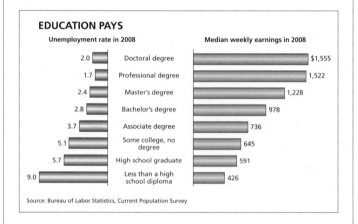

EDUCATION PAYS

Unemployment rate in 2008		Median weekly earnings in 2008
2.0	Doctoral degree	$1,555
1.7	Professional degree	1,522
2.4	Master's degree	1,228
2.8	Bachelor's degree	978
3.7	Associate degree	736
5.1	Some college, no degree	645
5.7	High school graduate	591
9.0	Less than a high school diploma	426

Source: Bureau of Labor Statistics, Current Population Survey

ISSUES & ACTIVITIES

1. Change as follows: Use the chart above to:
   a. Calculate the annual earnings for each education category.
   b. Calculate the annual difference in earnings between the categories: some college, associate degree, and bachelor's degree.
2. Locate the most recent edition of the *Current Population Survey* published by the Bureau of Labor Statistics. For the associate degree and bachelor's degree categories, calculate the difference in annual earnings found in the chart above and in the latest figures.
3. In teams, research the Internet to find current trends in "value of education" statistics. List your sources and visually report your findings to the class.

BRAINTEASER – "GET THE POINT"

What mathematical symbol can you place between the number 1 and the number 2 to yield a new number larger than 1 but less than 2?

See the end of Appendix A for the solution.

© Jim West/Alamy

Checking Accounts

PERFORMANCE OBJECTIVES

SECTION I: Understanding and Using Checking Accounts

4-1: Opening a checking account and understanding how the various forms are used (p. 92)

4-2: Writing checks in proper form (p. 95)

4-3: Endorsing checks by using blank, restrictive, and full endorsements (p. 96)

4-4: Preparing deposit slips in proper form (p. 98)

4-5: Using check stubs or checkbook registers to record account transactions (p. 99)

SECTION II: Bank Statement Reconciliation

4-6: Understanding the bank statement (p. 106)

4-7: Preparing a bank statement reconciliation (p. 108)

Checking accounts are among the most useful and common banking services available today. They provide a detailed record of monetary transactions and are used by most businesses and individuals to purchase goods and services and to pay bills. When a checking account is opened, banks often require an initial minimum deposit of $50 or $100. Certain types of accounts require a minimum *average monthly balance* in the account. If the balance falls below the minimum, the bank may charge a fee.

Checking account transactions are processed in our banking system using a combination of paper checks and electronic options such as automated teller machines (ATMs), debit cards, automatic bill paying, and electronic funds transfer (EFT). Online banking uses today's technology to give account holders the option of bypassing some of the time-consuming paper-based aspects of traditional banking. Exhibit 4-1, Preferred Banking Method – 2009, illustrates the results of an American Bankers Association survey showing that for the first time, when compared to any other method, more bank customers (25 percent) prefer to do their banking online.

Mobile banking (also known as M-Banking), the next-generation banking experience, is projected to increase rapidly over the next few years. *Mobile banking* is a term used for performing balance checks, account transactions, payments, etc., via a mobile device such as a mobile phone. According to *Bank Technology News*, 58% of the U.S. population, or 108 million adults, are expected to be mobile bankers by 2012.

According to Forrester.com, between 2009 and 2014, the total number of U.S. online banking households will increase from 54 million to 66 million.

stockphoto.com/YinYang

4-1   OPENING A CHECKING ACCOUNT AND UNDERSTANDING HOW THE VARIOUS FORMS ARE USED

deposits Funds added to a checking account.

depositor A person who deposits money in a checking account.

check, or **draft** A written order to a bank by a depositor to pay the amount specified on the check from funds on deposit in a checking account.

payee The person or business named on the check to receive the money.

payor The person or business issuing the check.

After you have chosen a bank, the account is usually opened by a new accounts officer or a clerk. After the initial paperwork has been completed, the customer places an amount of money in the account as an opening balance. Funds added to a checking account are known as **deposits**. The bank will then give the **depositor** a checkbook containing checks and deposit slips.

A **check**, or **draft**, is a negotiable instrument ordering the bank to pay money from the checking account to the name written on the check. The person or business named on the check to receive the money is known as the **payee**. The person or business issuing the check is known as the **payor**.

EXHIBIT 4-1
Preferred Banking Method – 2009

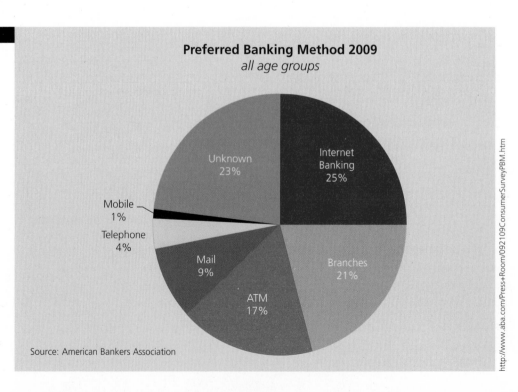

Preferred Banking Method 2009
all age groups

- Internet Banking 25%
- Branches 21%
- ATM 17%
- Mail 9%
- Telephone 4%
- Mobile 1%
- Unknown 23%

Source: American Bankers Association

http://www.aba.com/Press+Room/092109ConsumerSurveyPBM.htm

Checks are available in many sizes, colors, and designs; however, they all contain the same fundamental elements. Exhibit 4-2 shows a check with the major parts labeled. Look at the illustration carefully and familiarize yourself with the various parts of the check.

Deposit slips, or deposit tickets, are printed forms with the depositor's name, address, account number, and space for the details of the deposit. Deposit slips are used to record money, both cash and checks, being *added* to the checking account. They are presented to the bank teller along with the items to be deposited. When a deposit is completed, the depositor receives a copy of the deposit slip as a receipt, or proof of the transaction. The deposit should also be recorded by the depositor on the current check stub or in the check register. Exhibit 4-3 is an example of a deposit slip.

Either **check stubs** or a **check register** can be used to keep track of the checks written, the deposits added, and the current account balance. It is very important to keep these records accurate and up to date. This will prevent the embarrassing error of writing checks with insufficient funds in the account.

deposit slips Printed forms with the depositor's name, address, account number, and space for the details of the deposit. Used to record money, both cash and checks, being added to the checking account.

check stubs A bound part of the checkbook attached by perforation to checks. Used to keep track of the checks written, deposits, and current account balance of a checking account.

check register A separate booklet of blank forms used to keep track of all checking account activity. An alternative to the check stub.

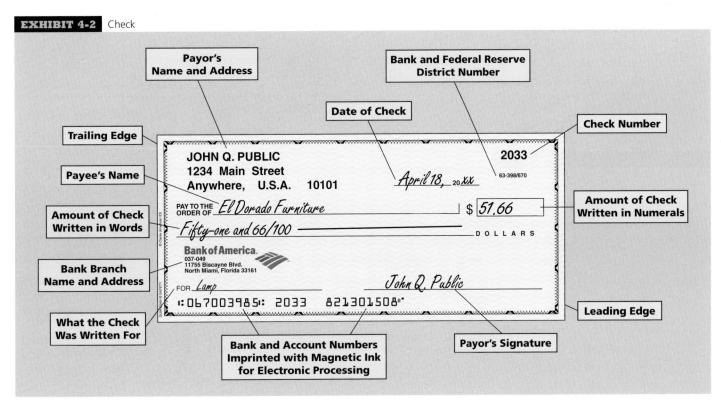

"Gentlemen, this bank's profits are about to go sky high! I've invented the *fee* fee!"

© Andy White Reproduction Rights obtainable from www.cartoonstock.com

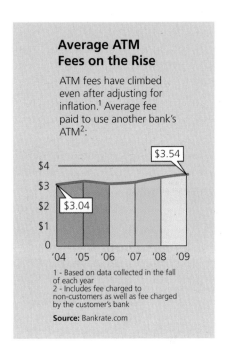

Average ATM Fees on the Rise

ATM fees have climbed even after adjusting for inflation.[1] Average fee paid to use another bank's ATM[2]:

1 - Based on data collected in the fall of each year
2 - Includes fee charged to non-customers as well as fee charged by the customer's bank

Source: Bankrate.com

EXHIBIT 4-2 Check

Payor's Name and Address

Bank and Federal Reserve District Number

Date of Check

Check Number

Trailing Edge

Payee's Name

Amount of Check Written in Words

Bank Branch Name and Address

What the Check Was Written For

Bank and Account Numbers Imprinted with Magnetic Ink for Electronic Processing

Payor's Signature

Amount of Check Written in Numerals

Leading Edge

JOHN Q. PUBLIC
1234 Main Street
Anywhere, U.S.A. 10101

2033

63-398/670

April 18, 20 *XX*

PAY TO THE ORDER OF *El Dorado Furniture* $ *51.66*

Fifty-one and 66/100 ————— D O L L A R S

Bank of America.
037-049
11755 Biscayne Blvd.
North Miami, Florida 33161

FOR *Lamp*   *John Q. Public*

⑈067003985⑈ 2033 821301508⑈

Check stubs, with checks attached by perforation, are usually a bound part of the checkbook. A sample check stub with a check is shown in Exhibit 4-4. Note that the check number is preprinted on both the check and the attached stub. Each stub is used to record the issuing of its corresponding check and any deposits made on that date.

Check registers are the alternative method for keeping track of checking account activity. They are a separate booklet of forms rather than stubs attached to each check. A sample check register is shown in Exhibit 4-5. Note that space is provided for all the pertinent information required to keep an accurate and up-to-date running balance of the account.

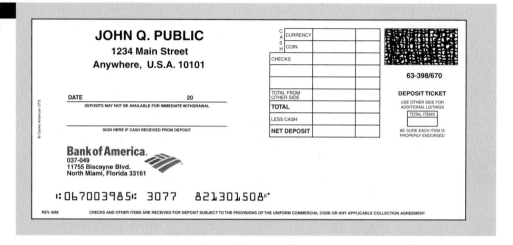

EXHIBIT 4-3

Deposit Slip

EXHIBIT 4-4 Check Stub with Check

EXHIBIT 4-5

Check Register

CHECK NUMBER	DATE	DESCRIPTION OF TRANSACTION	AMOUNT OF PAYMENT OR WITHDRAWAL (-)	✓	AMOUNT OF DEPOSIT OR INTEREST (+)	BALANCE FORWARD	
		To					
		For				Bal.	
		To					
		For				Bal.	
		To					
		For				Bal.	
		To					
		For				Bal.	
		To					
		For				Bal.	
		To					
		For				Bal.	

PLEASE BE SURE TO **DEDUCT** ANY BANK CHARGES THAT APPLY TO YOUR ACCOUNT.

WRITING CHECKS IN PROPER FORM

When a checking account is opened, you will choose the color and style of your checks. The bank will then order custom-printed checks with your name, address, and account number identifications. The bank will provide you with some blank checks and deposit slips to use until your printed ones arrive.

Checks should be typed or neatly written in ink. There are six parts to be filled in when writing a check.

STEPS FOR WRITING CHECKS IN PROPER FORM

STEP 1. Enter the *date* of the check in the space provided.

STEP 2. Enter the name of the person or business to whom the check is written, the payee, in the space labeled *pay to the order of*.

STEP 3. Enter the amount of the check in numerical form in the space with the dollar sign, $. The dollar amount should be written close to the $ so additional digits cannot be added. The cents may be written as xx/100 or .xx.

STEP 4. Enter the amount of the check, this time written in word form, on the next line down, labeled *dollars*. As before, the cents should be written as xx/100 or .xx. A horizontal line is then drawn to the end of the line.

STEP 5. The space labeled *for* is used to write the purpose of the check. Although this step is optional, it's a good idea to use this space so you will not forget why the check was written.

STEP 6. The space in the lower right-hand portion of the check is for the signature.

IN THE BUSINESS WORLD

When there is a discrepancy between the numerical and written word amount of a check, banks consider the *written word amount* as official.

EXAMPLE 1 WRITING A CHECK

Write a check for Walter Anderson to the Falcon Tire Center for a front-end alignment in the amount of $83.73 on June 7, 20xx.

SOLUTION STRATEGY

Here is the check for Walter Anderson written in proper form. Note that the amount, $83.73, is written $83 73/100 and the name is signed as it is printed on the check.

LEARNING TIP

Don't forget, when writing the amount of a check in word form, the word *and* represents the decimal point.

© 2010 Keith Brofsky/Jupiterimages Corporation

● TRYITEXERCISE1

1. Use the following blank to write a check for Natalie Eldridge to Whole Foods for a party platter in the amount of $41.88 on April 27.

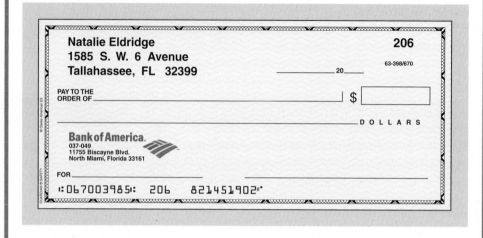

CHECK YOUR ANSWER WITH THE SOLUTION ON PAGE 116.

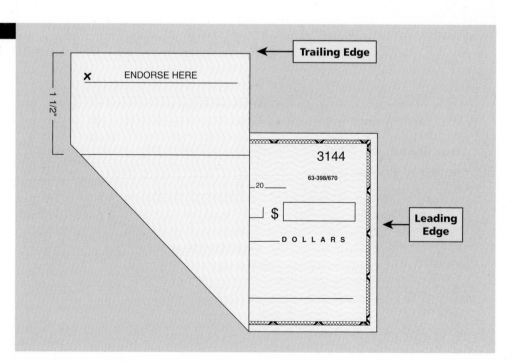

4-3

ENDORSING CHECKS BY USING BLANK, RESTRICTIVE, AND FULL ENDORSEMENTS

endorsement The signature and instructions on the back of a check instructing the bank on what to do with that check.

When you receive a check, you may cash it, deposit it in your account, or transfer it to another party. The **endorsement** on the back of the check instructs the bank on what to do. Federal regulations require that specific areas of the reverse side of checks be designated for the payee and bank endorsements. Your endorsement should be written within the $1\frac{1}{2}$-inch space at the trailing edge of the check, as shown in Exhibit 4-6. The space is usually labeled "ENDORSE HERE."

There are three types of endorsements with which you should become familiar: blank endorsements, restrictive endorsements, and full endorsements, which are shown in Exhibits 4-7, 4-8, and 4-9, respectively.

blank endorsement An endorsement used when the payee wants to cash a check.

A **blank endorsement** is used when you want to cash the check. You, as the payee, simply sign your name exactly as it appears on the front of the check and write your account number. Once you have endorsed a check in this manner, anyone who has possession of the check can cash it. For this reason, you should use blank endorsements cautiously.

EXHIBIT 4-6

Endorsement Space

In the Business World

New Federal Debit Card – In 2008, the U.S. Treasury introduced a debit card that people without traditional bank accounts can use to access federal benefits such as Social Security and disability payments.

Federal payments are credited to the cards each month, enabling users to make free withdrawals from ATMs in the government's Direct Express network.

EXHIBIT 4-7
Blank Endorsement

John Q. Public
82-1301-508

EXHIBIT 4-8
Restrictive Endorsement

for deposit only
John Q. Public
82-1301-508

EXHIBIT 4-9
Full Endorsement

pay to the order of
Cindy J. Citizen
John Q. Public
82-1301-508

A **restrictive endorsement** is used when you want to deposit the check in your account. In this case, you endorse the check "for deposit only," sign your name as it appears on the front, and write your account number.

A **full endorsement** is used when you want to transfer the check to another party. In this case, you endorse the check "pay to the order of," write the name of the person or business to whom the check is being transferred, sign your name, and write your account number.

restrictive endorsement An endorsement used when the payee wants to deposit a check in his or her account.

full endorsement An endorsement used when the payee wants to transfer a check to another party.

EXAMPLE2 ENDORSING A CHECK

You have just received a check. Your account number is #2922-22-33-4. Write the following endorsements and identify what type they are.

a. Allowing you to cash the check.
b. Allowing you to deposit the check in your checking account.
c. Allowing the check to be transferred to your partner Sam Johnson.

SOLUTIONSTRATEGY

a.
Blank Endorsement
Your Signature
2922-22-33-4

b.
Restrictive Endorsement
for deposit only
Your Signature
2922-22-33-4

c.
Full Endorsement
pay to the order of
Sam Johnson
Your Signature
2922-22-33-4

TRYITEXERCISE2

You have just received a check. Your account number is #696-339-1028. Write the following endorsements in the space provided and identify what type they are.

a. Allowing the check to be transferred to your friend Roz Reitman.
b. Allowing you to cash the check.
c. Allowing you to deposit the check in your checking account.

a. _____   b. _____   c. _____

CHECK YOUR ANSWERS WITH THE SOLUTIONS ON PAGE 117.

PREPARING DEPOSIT SLIPS IN PROPER FORM

4-4

Deposit slips are filled out and presented to the bank along with the funds being deposited. They are dated and list the currency, coins, individual checks, and total amount of the deposit. Note on the sample deposit slip, Exhibit 4-10, that John Q. Public took $100 in cash out of the deposit, which required him to sign the deposit slip.

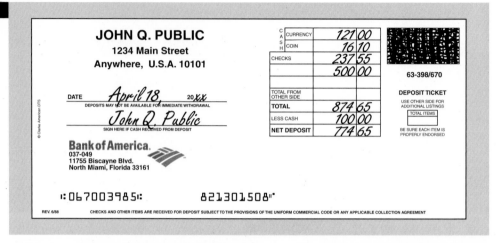

EXAMPLE 3 — PREPARING A DEPOSIT SLIP

Prepare a deposit slip for Jamie McCallon based on the following information.

a. Date: June 4, 20xx.
b. $127 in currency.
c. $3.47 in coins.
d. A check for $358.89 and a check for $121.68.

SOLUTION STRATEGY

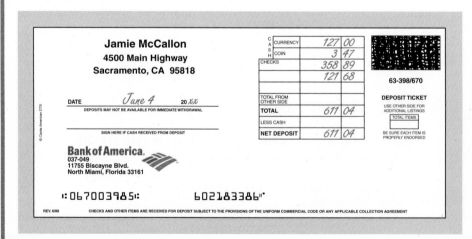

TRY IT EXERCISE 3

Fill out the deposit slip for Hi-Volt Electronics based on the following information.

a. Date: November 11, 20xx.
b. $3,549 in currency.
c. 67 quarters, 22 dimes, and 14 nickels.
d. A check for $411.92 and a check for $2,119.56.

HI-VOLT ELECTRONICS
12155 Miller Road
New Orleans, LA 70144

DATE _____ 20 _____
DEPOSITS MAY NOT BE AVAILABLE FOR IMMEDIATE WITHDRAWAL

SIGN HERE IF CASH RECEIVED FROM DEPOSIT

Bank of America.
037-049
11755 Biscayne Blvd.
North Miami, Florida 33161

⑆067003985⑆   536101902⑈

REV. 6/88   CHECKS AND OTHER ITEMS ARE RECEIVED FOR DEPOSIT SUBJECT TO THE PROVISIONS OF THE UNIFORM COMMERCIAL CODE OR ANY APPLICABLE COLLECTION AGREEMENT

C A S H	CURRENCY		
	COIN		
CHECKS			

63-398/670

TOTAL FROM OTHER SIDE
DEPOSIT TICKET
TOTAL
USE OTHER SIDE FOR ADDITIONAL LISTINGS
LESS CASH
TOTAL ITEMS
NET DEPOSIT
BE SURE EACH ITEM IS PROPERLY ENDORSED

CHECK YOUR ANSWER WITH THE SOLUTION ON PAGE 117.

USING CHECK STUBS OR CHECKBOOK REGISTERS TO RECORD ACCOUNT TRANSACTIONS

4-5

In Performance Objective 4-1, we learned that some people use check stubs to keep records and some use check registers. Exhibit 4-11 shows a check and its corresponding stub properly filled out. Note that the check number is printed on the stub. The stub is used to record the amount of the check, the date, the payee, and the purpose of the check. In addition, the stub also records the balance forwarded from the last stub, deposits made since the previous check, and the new balance of the account after the current check and any other charges are deducted.

Check registers record the same information as the stub but in a different format. Exhibit 4-12 shows a check register properly filled out. The starting balance is located in the upper right-hand corner. In keeping a check register, it is your option to write it single spaced or double spaced. Remember, in reality, you would use *either* the check stub or the checkbook register.

EXHIBIT 4-11 Check with Filled-Out Stub

IF TAX DEDUCTIBLE CHECK HERE ☐ $ _183.12_

3078

May 26 20 _XX_
TO _Walmart_
FOR _Stereo_

	DOLLARS	CENTS
BAL. FWD.	1,240	89
DEPOSIT	300	00
DEPOSIT		
TOTAL	1,540	89
THIS ITEM	183	12
SUB-TOTAL	1,357	77
OTHER DEDUCT. (IF ANY)		
BAL. FWD.	1,357	77

RICK UNGERMAN
299 Williams Road
Dallas, TX 75208

May 26 20 _XX_   63-398/670

PAY TO THE ORDER OF _Walmart_ $ _183.72_

One Hundred Eighty-Three and ¹²/100 ——————— D O L L A R S

Bank of America.
037-049
11755 Biscayne Blvd.
North Miami, Florida 33161

FOR _Stereo_   _Rick Ungerman_

⑆067003985⑆ 3078 53678792⑈

EXHIBIT 4-12
Filled-Out Check Register

CHECK NUMBER	DATE		DESCRIPTION OF TRANSACTION	AMOUNT OF PAYMENT OR WITHDRAWAL (–)		✓	AMOUNT OF DEPOSIT OR INTEREST (+)		BALANCE FORWARD	
			PLEASE BE SURE TO **DEDUCT** ANY BANK CHARGES THAT APPLY TO YOUR ACCOUNT.						560	00
450	1/6	To	MasterCard	34	60					
		For							Bal. 525	40
451	1/8	To	Allstate Insurance	166	25					
		For							Bal. 359	15
	1/12	To	Electronic Payroll Deposit				340	00		
		For							Bal. 699	15
452	1/13	To	CVS Pharmacy	15	50					
		For							Bal. 683	65
	1/15	To	Deposit				88	62		
		For							Bal. 772	27
	1/17	To	ATM–Withdrawal	100	00					
		For							Bal. 672	27
	1/21	To	Debit Card—AMC Theater	24	15					
		For							Bal. 648	12

IN THE BUSINESS WORLD

A new rule issued by the Federal Reserve prohibits banks from charging overdraft fees on ATM and debit card transactions unless customers "opt-in" to a protection program. If customers don't "opt in" to a protection program, any debit or ATM transactions that overdraw their accounts will be denied.

The rule responds to complaints that overdraft fees for debit cards and ATMs are unfair because many people assume they can't spend more than is in their account. Instead, many banks allow the transactions to go through and then charge overdraft fees of up to $35.

Source: *The Miami Herald*, "Customer consent will be a must for overdraft fees," by Christopher S. Rugaber, Nov. 13, 2009, page 3C.

EXAMPLE 4 — RECORDING ACCOUNT TRANSACTIONS

From the following information, complete the two check stubs and the check register in proper form.

a. Starting balance $1,454.21.
b. January 14, 20xx, check #056 in the amount of $69.97 issued to Paints & Pails Hardware for a ladder.
c. January 19, 20xx, deposit of $345.00.
d. February 1, 20xx, check #057 in the amount of $171.55 issued to Northern Power & Light for electricity bill.
e. February 1, 20xx, debit card purchase—groceries, $77.00.

SOLUTION STRATEGY

Below are the properly completed stubs and register. Note that the checks were subtracted from the balance and the deposits were added to the balance.

Profitable Penalties

Banks reap record revenue from overdraft fees for checking accounts, ATMs, and debit cards—far outstripping their fees from credit card penalties.
(fees in billions)

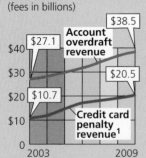

Account overdraft revenue: $27.1 (2003) → $38.5 (2009)
Credit card penalty revenue[1]: $10.7 (2003) → $20.5 (2009)

1- Includes late fees and over-limit fees
Sources: Moebs Services and R.K. Hammer Investment Bankers

Check Stub 056

IF TAX DEDUCTIBLE CHECK HERE ☐	$ 69.97
056	
Jan. 14 20xx	
TO Paints & Pails	
FOR ladder	

	DOLLARS	CENTS
BAL. FWD.	1,454	21
DEPOSIT		
DEPOSIT		
TOTAL	1,454	21
THIS ITEM	69	97
SUB-TOTAL	1,384	24
OTHER DEDUCT. (IF ANY)		
BAL. FWD.	1,384	24

Check Stub 057

IF TAX DEDUCTIBLE CHECK HERE ☐	$ 171.55
057	
Feb. 1 20xx	
TO Northern P & L	
FOR electricity bill	

	DOLLARS	CENTS
BAL. FWD.	1,384	24
DEPOSIT 1/19	345	00
DEPOSIT		
TOTAL	1,729	24
THIS ITEM	171	55
SUB-TOTAL	1,557	69
OTHER DEDUCT. (IF ANY)	77	00
BAL. FWD.	1,480	69

CHECK NUMBER	DATE		DESCRIPTION OF TRANSACTION	AMOUNT OF PAYMENT OR WITHDRAWAL (–)		✓	AMOUNT OF DEPOSIT OR INTEREST (+)		BALANCE FORWARD	
			PLEASE BE SURE TO **DEDUCT** ANY BANK CHARGES THAT APPLY TO YOUR ACCOUNT.						1,454	21
056	1/14	To	Paints & Pails Hardware	69	97					
		For							Bal. 1,384	24
	1/19	To	Deposit				345	00		
		For							Bal. 1,729	24
057	2/1	To	Northern Power & Light	171	55					
		For							Bal. 1,557	69
	2/1	To	Debit Card—Groceries, $77.	77	00					
		For							Bal. 1,480	69

TRYITEXERCISE4

From the following information, complete the two check stubs and the check register in proper form.

a. Starting balance $887.45.

b. March 12, 20xx, check #137 issued to Nathan & David Hair Stylists for a permanent and manicure in the amount of $55.75.

c. March 16, 20xx, deposits of $125.40 and $221.35.

d. March 19, 20xx, check #138 issued to Complete Auto Service for car repairs in the amount of $459.88.

e. March 20, 20xx, debit card purchase—post office, $53.00.

IF TAX DEDUCTIBLE CHECK HERE ☐	$ ____			IF TAX DEDUCTIBLE CHECK HERE ☐	$ ____	
137				**138**		
_____ 20 ____				_____ 20 ____		
TO _____				TO _____		
FOR _____				FOR _____		
BAL. FWD.	DOLLARS	CENTS		BAL. FWD.	DOLLARS	CENTS
DEPOSIT				DEPOSIT		
DEPOSIT				DEPOSIT		
TOTAL				TOTAL		
THIS ITEM				THIS ITEM		
SUB-TOTAL				SUB-TOTAL		
OTHER DEDUCT. (IF ANY)				OTHER DEDUCT. (IF ANY)		
BAL. FWD.				BAL. FWD.		

PLEASE BE SURE TO **DEDUCT** ANY BANK CHARGES THAT APPLY TO YOUR ACCOUNT.

CHECK NUMBER	DATE	DESCRIPTION OF TRANSACTION	AMOUNT OF PAYMENT OR WITHDRAWAL (−)	✔	AMOUNT OF DEPOSIT OR INTEREST (+)	BALANCE FORWARD	
		To					
		For				Bal.	
		To					
		For				Bal.	
		To					
		For				Bal.	
		To					
		For				Bal.	
		To					
		For				Bal.	
		To					
		For				Bal.	

CHECK YOUR ANSWER WITH THE SOLUTION ON PAGE 117.

SECTION I

4

REVIEW EXERCISES

You are the owner of the Busy Bee Launderette. Using the blanks provided, write out the following checks in proper form.

1. Check #2550, September 14, 20xx, in the amount of $345.54 to the Silky Soap Company for 300 gallons of liquid soap.

```
BUSY BEE LAUNDERETTE                                    2550
   214 Collings Blvd.
   Durham,  NC   27704        Sept. 14  20 xx      63-398/670

PAY TO THE
ORDER OF ___Silky Soap Company_____  $ | 345.54 |

Three Hundred Forty-Five and 54/100_____ D O L L A R S

Bank of America
037-049
11755 Biscayne Blvd.
North Miami, Florida 33161

FOR ___300 gals. Soap___        ___Your Signature___

⑆067003985⑆ 2550   821301508⑈
```

2. Check #2551, September 20, 20xx, in the amount of $68.95 to the Tidy Towel Service for six dozen wash rags.

```
BUSY BEE LAUNDERETTE                                    2551
   214 Collings Blvd.
   Durham,  NC   27704        _____ 20____       63-398/670

PAY TO THE
ORDER OF _____  $ |        |

_____ D O L L A R S

Bank of America
037-049
11755 Biscayne Blvd.
North Miami, Florida 33161

FOR _____        _____

⑆067003985⑆ 2551   821301508⑈
```

You have just received a check. Your account number is #099-506-8. Write the following endorsements in the space provided below and identify what type they are.

3. Allowing you to deposit the check in your account.

4. Allowing you to cash the check.

5. Allowing you to transfer the check to your friend David Sporn.

3. _____   4. _____   5. _____

6. Properly fill out the deposit slip for The Star Vista Corp. based on the following information:
   a. Date: July 9, 20xx.
   b. $1,680 in currency.
   c. $62.25 in coins.
   d. Checks in the amount of $2,455.94, $4,338.79, and $1,461.69.

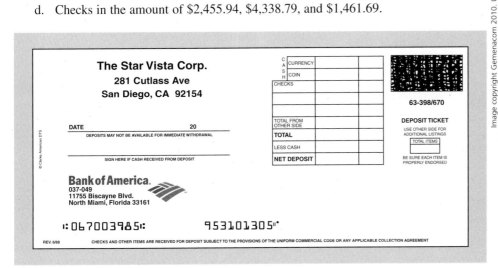

7. Properly fill out the deposit slip for Howard Lockwood, based on the following information:
   a. Date: December 18, 20xx.
   b. A check for $651.03.
   c. $150 cash withdrawal.

The deposit slip for Howard Lockwood

HOWARD LOCKWOOD
5700 S. W. 4th St.
Reno, NV 89501

DATE _____ 20 _____
DEPOSITS MAY NOT BE AVAILABLE FOR IMMEDIATE WITHDRAWAL

SIGN HERE IF CASH RECEIVED FROM DEPOSIT

Bank of America.
037-049
11755 Biscayne Blvd.
North Miami, Florida 33161

⑆067003985⑆   450912507⑈

REV. 6/88   CHECKS AND OTHER ITEMS ARE RECEIVED FOR DEPOSIT SUBJECT TO THE PROVISIONS OF THE UNIFORM COMMERCIAL CODE OR ANY APPLICABLE COLLECTION AGREEMENT

CASH CURRENCY / COIN / CHECKS
TOTAL FROM OTHER SIDE
TOTAL
LESS CASH
NET DEPOSIT

63-398/670

DEPOSIT TICKET
USE OTHER SIDE FOR ADDITIONAL LISTINGS
TOTAL ITEMS
BE SURE EACH ITEM IS PROPERLY ENDORSED

DOLLARS AND SENSE

Safe-deposit boxes are a type of safe usually located inside a bank vault or in the back of a bank or post office. These boxes are typically used to store things such as valuable gemstones, precious metals, currency, or important documents. In the typical arrangement, a renter pays the bank a fee for the use of the box, which can be opened only with the assigned key, the bank's key, the proper signature, or perhaps a code of some sort.

The contents of the safe-deposit boxes are not insured unless you cover them in your homeowner's or renter's insurance policy. According to the AARP, in 2009, there was close to $33 billion of property abandoned or otherwise unclaimed in safe-deposit boxes.

A "cyber backup" is a good way to protect your important documents. Banks and online vendors offer "virtual safe-deposit boxes," where digital copies of documents can be stored.

Source: *AARP The Magazine*, "Not-so-safe deposits," Nov./Dec. 2009, page 20.

8. From the following information, complete the three check stubs on page 104 in proper form.
   a. Starting balance $265.73.
   b. February 12, 20xx, check #439 in the amount of $175.05 to The Fidelity Bank for a car payment.
   c. February 15 deposit of $377.10.
   d. February 18 check #440 in the amount of $149.88 to Apex Fitness Equipment for a set of dumbbells.
   e. February 22 deposit of $570.00.
   f. February 27 check #441 in the amount of $23.40 to Royalty Cleaners for dry cleaning.
   g. March 3 debit card purchase—tires, $225.10.

IF TAX DEDUCTIBLE CHECK HERE ☐	$ _____
439	
_____ 20 _____	
TO _____	
FOR _____	

BAL. FWD.	DOLLARS	CENTS
DEPOSIT		
DEPOSIT		
TOTAL		
THIS ITEM		
SUB-TOTAL		
OTHER DEDUCT. (IF ANY)		
BAL. FWD.		

IF TAX DEDUCTIBLE CHECK HERE ☐	$ _____
440	
_____ 20 _____	
TO _____	
FOR _____	

BAL. FWD.	DOLLARS	CENTS
DEPOSIT		
DEPOSIT		
TOTAL		
THIS ITEM		
SUB-TOTAL		
OTHER DEDUCT. (IF ANY)		
BAL. FWD.		

IF TAX DEDUCTIBLE CHECK HERE ☐	$ _____
441	
_____ 20 _____	
TO _____	
FOR _____	

BAL. FWD.	DOLLARS	CENTS
DEPOSIT		
DEPOSIT		
TOTAL		
THIS ITEM		
SUB-TOTAL		
OTHER DEDUCT. (IF ANY)		
BAL. FWD.		

9. From the following information, complete the checkbook register:
    a. Starting balance $479.20.
    b. April 7, 20xx, deposit of $766.90.
    c. April 14, 20xx, debit card purchase in the amount of $45.65 to Mario's Market for groceries.
    d. April 16 ATM withdrawal, $125.00.
    e. April 17, check #1208 in the amount of $870.00 to Banyan Properties, Inc., for rent.
    f. April 21, 20xx, electronic payroll deposit of $1,350.00.
    g. April 27, check #1209 in the amount of $864.40 to Elegant Decor for a dining room set.

PLEASE BE SURE TO **DEDUCT** ANY BANK CHARGES THAT APPLY TO YOUR ACCOUNT.							
CHECK NUMBER	DATE	DESCRIPTION OF TRANSACTION	AMOUNT OF PAYMENT OR WITHDRAWAL (–)	✓	AMOUNT OF DEPOSIT OR INTEREST (+)	BALANCE FORWARD	
		To					
		For				Bal.	
		To					
		For				Bal.	
		To					
		For				Bal.	
		To					
		For				Bal.	
		To					
		For				Bal.	
		To					
		For				Bal.	

10. From the following information, complete the checkbook register on the next page through October 10.

Cheryl Roberts' account balance on September 26 was $1,196.19. On the first of October, she received $3,023.11 by electronic payroll deposit. Also on the first of October, she wrote check #1804 to pay her rent in the amount of $1,175.00. Cheryl used her debit card to make purchases on September 28 for $37.79, on October 2 for $311.86, and on October 3 for $164.26. On October 8, she paid her electricity bill, gas bill, and phone bill using her bank's online bill-paying service. Her electricity bill was $142.87. Gas was $18.46, and phone amounted to $38.52. On October 9, she deposited a rebate check for $50.

PLEASE BE SURE TO **DEDUCT** ANY BANK CHARGES THAT APPLY TO YOUR ACCOUNT.

CHECK NUMBER	DATE	DESCRIPTION OF TRANSACTION	AMOUNT OF PAYMENT OR WITHDRAWAL (–)	✔	AMOUNT OF DEPOSIT OR INTEREST (+)	BALANCE FORWARD	
		To					
		For				Bal.	
		To					
		For				Bal.	
		To					
		For				Bal.	
		To					
		For				Bal.	
		To					
		For				Bal.	
		To					
		For				Bal.	
		To					
		For				Bal.	
		To					
		For				Bal.	
		To					
		For				Bal.	
		To					
		For				Bal.	

BUSINESS DECISION: TELLER TRAINING

11. You are the training director for tellers at a large local bank. As part of a new training program that you are developing, you have decided to give teller trainees a "sample" deposit slip, check, and check register with common errors on them. The trainees must find and correct the errors. Your task is to create the three documents.

a. On a separate sheet of paper, list some "typical errors" that bank customers might make on a deposit slip, a check, and a check register.

b. Use the following blank deposit slip, check, and check register to create "filled-out" versions, each with one error you named for that document in part **a**. You make up all the details; names, dates, numbers, etc.

c. After completing part b, exchange documents with another student in the class and try to find and correct the errors. (If this is a homework assignment, bring a copy of each document you created to class for the exchange. If this is an in-class assignment, temporarily trade documents with the other student after completing part b.)

Bank Teller
According to the U.S. Department of Labor, bank tellers make up 28% of bank employees and conduct most of a bank's routine transactions.

In hiring tellers, banks seek people who enjoy public contact and have good numerical, clerical, and communication skills. Banks prefer applicants who have had courses in mathematics, accounting, bookkeeping, economics, and public speaking.

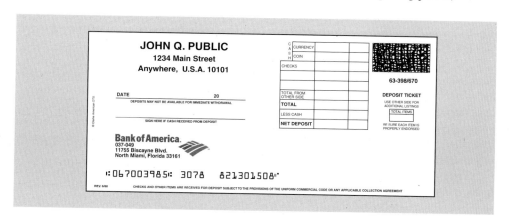

SECTION II 4 BANK STATEMENT RECONCILIATION

bank statement A monthly summary of the activities in a checking account, including debits, credits, and beginning and ending balance. Sent by the bank to the account holder.

Your monthly **bank statement** gives you a detailed review of the activity in your account for a specific period of time. It's your best opportunity to make sure your records match the bank's records. Be prepared to "match up" every activity (credits and debits) on the statement with your checkbook.

It is important that you review the bank statement in a timely fashion. If you find any discrepancies in ATM, debit card, or other electronic transactions, you must report them to the bank within 60 days of the date of the statement or the bank has no obligation to conduct an investigation. Another important reason to reconcile your checkbook with the statement is to look for debits you didn't make that might indicate that someone has access to your account.

4-6 UNDERSTANDING THE BANK STATEMENT

Bank statements vary widely in style from bank to bank; however, most contain essentially the same information. Exhibit 4-13 illustrates typical online and printed bank statements. Note that it shows the balance brought forward from the last statement, the deposits and credits that have been added to the account during the month, the checks and debits that have been subtracted from the account during the month, any service charges assessed to the account, and the current or ending balance.

credits Additions to a checking account, such as deposits and interest earned.

debits Subtractions from a checking account, such as service charges.

nonsufficient fund (NSF) fee A fee charged by the bank when a check is written without sufficient funds in the account to cover the amount of that check.

returned items checks Checks that you deposited but were returned to your bank unpaid because the person or business issuing the checks had insufficient funds to cover them.

Credits are additions to the account, such as interest earned, notes collected, and electronic funds transfers of direct deposit payroll checks. **Debits** are subtractions from the account, such as automatic teller machine (ATM) withdrawals, debit card transactions, monthly service charges, check printing charges, nonsufficient fund (NSF) fees, and returned items. A **nonsufficient fund (NSF) fee** is a fee charged by the bank when a check is written without sufficient funds in the account to cover the amount of that check. **Returned items** are checks from others that you deposited in your account but were returned to your bank unpaid because the person or business issuing the check had insufficient funds in its account to cover the check. Banks usually charge a returned item fee when this occurs.

EXHIBIT 4-13 Paper and Electronic Bank Statements

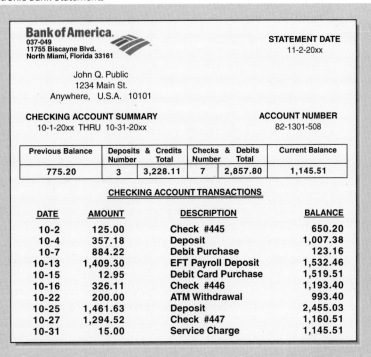

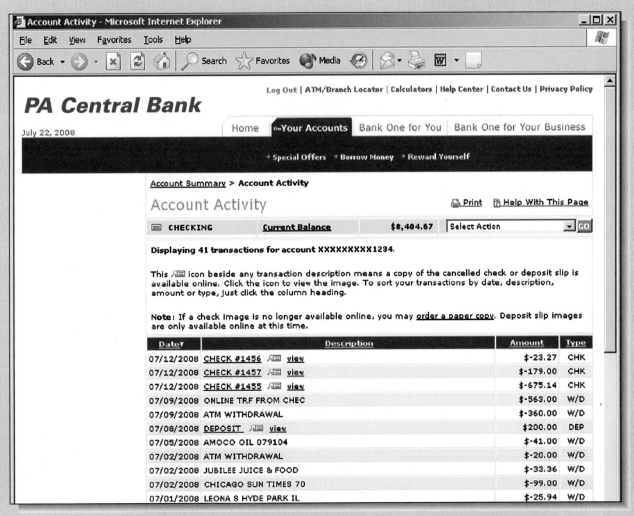

PREPARING A BANK STATEMENT RECONCILIATION

4-7

bank statement reconciliation The process of adjusting the bank and checkbook balances to reflect the actual current balance of the checking account.

outstanding checks Checks that have been written but have not yet reached the bank and therefore do not appear on the current bank statement.

deposits in transit Deposits made close to the statement date or by mail that do not clear in time to appear on the current bank statement.

adjusted checkbook balance The checkbook balance minus service charges and other debits plus interest earned and other credits.

adjusted bank balance The bank balance minus outstanding checks plus deposits in transit.

When the statement arrives from the bank each month, the depositor must compare the bank balance with the balance shown in the checkbook. Usually, the balances are not the same because during the month, some account activity has taken place without being recorded by the bank and other activities have occurred without being recorded in the checkbook. The process of adjusting the bank and checkbook balances to reflect the actual current balance is known as **bank statement reconciliation**. When we use the word *checkbook* in this chapter, we are actually referring to the records kept by the depositor on the check stubs or in the checkbook register.

Before a statement can be reconciled, you must identify and total all the checks that have been written but have not yet reached the bank. These are known as **outstanding checks**. Outstanding checks are found by comparing and checking off each check in the checkbook with those shown on the statement. Any checks not appearing on the statement are outstanding checks.

Sometimes deposits are made close to the statement date or by mail and do not clear the bank in time to appear on the current statement. These are known as **deposits in transit**. Just like outstanding checks, deposits in transit must be identified and totaled. Once again, this is done by comparing and checking off the checkbook records with the deposits shown on the bank statement.

A bank statement is reconciled when the **adjusted checkbook balance** is equal to the **adjusted bank balance**. Most bank statements have a form on the back to use in reconciling the account. Exhibit 4-14 is an example of such a form and is used in this chapter.

STEPS FOR PREPARING A BANK STATEMENT RECONCILIATION

STEP 1. Calculate the adjusted checkbook balance:
   a. Look over the bank statement and find any credits not recorded in the checkbook, such as interest earned or notes collected, and *add* them to the checkbook balance to get a subtotal.
   b. From the bank statement, locate any charges or debits such as service charges, NSF fees, or returned items that have not been recorded in the checkbook and *subtract* them from the subtotal from Step 1a.

STEP 2. Calculate the adjusted bank balance:
   a. Locate all of the deposits in transit and *add* them to the statement balance to get a subtotal.
   b. Locate and total all outstanding checks and *subtract* them from the subtotal from Step 2a.

STEP 3. Compare the adjusted balances:
   a. If they are equal, the statement has been reconciled.
   b. If they are not equal, an error exists that must be found and corrected. The error is either in the checkbook or on the bank statement.

EXHIBIT 4-14 Bank Statement Reconciliation Form

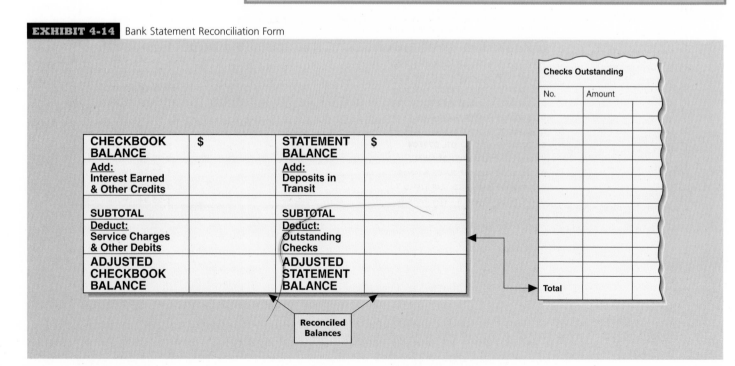

EXAMPLE5 RECONCILING A BANK STATEMENT

Prepare a bank reconciliation for Anita Gomberg from the bank statement and checkbook records below.

Grove Isle Bank

STATEMENT DATE
8-2-20xx

ANITA GOMBERG
8834 Kimberly Avenue
Surfside, FL 33154

CHECKING ACCOUNT SUMMARY
7-1-20xx THRU 7-31-20xx

ACCOUNT NUMBER
82-1301-508

Previous Balance	Deposits & Credits Number	Total	Checks & Debits Number	Total	Current Balance
1,233.40	3	2,445.80	7	2,158.92	1,520.28

CHECKING ACCOUNT TRANSACTIONS

DATE	AMOUNT	DESCRIPTION	BALANCE
7-3	450.30	Check #1209	783.10
7-6	500.00	Deposit	1,283.10
7-10	47.75	Check #1210	1,235.35
7-13	1,300.00	EFT Payroll Deposit	2,535.35
7-15	312.79	Check #1212	2,222.56
7-17	547.22	Check #1214	1,675.34
7-22	350.00	ATM Withdrawal	1,325.34
7-24	645.80	Deposit	1,971.14
7-28	430.86	Debit Card Purchase	1,540.28
7-30	20.00	Service Charge	1,520.28

PLEASE BE SURE TO **DEDUCT** ANY BANK CHARGES THAT APPLY TO YOUR ACCOUNT

CHECK NUMBER	DATE	DESCRIPTION OF TRANSACTION	AMOUNT OF PAYMENT OR WITHDRAWAL (−)	✓	AMOUNT OF DEPOSIT OR INTEREST (+)	BALANCE FORWARD
						1,233 40
1209	7/1	To Home Shopping Network	450 30			
		For			Bal.	783 10
	7/6	To Deposit			500 00	
		For			Bal.	1,283 10
1210	7/8	To Food Spot	47 75			
		For			Bal.	1,235 35
1211	7/10	To Delta Air Lines	342 10			
		For			Bal.	893 25
	7/13	To Payroll Deposit			1,300 00	
		For			Bal.	2,193 25
1212	7/13	To Hyatt Hotel	312 79			
		For			Bal.	1,880 46
1213	7/15	To Wall Street Journal	75 00			
		For			Bal.	1,805 46
1214	7/15	To Fashionista	547 22			
		For			Bal.	1,258 24
	7/21	To ATM Withdrawal	350 00			
		For			Bal.	908 24
	7/24	To Deposit			645 80	
		For			Bal.	1,554 04
	7/28	To J. Crew — Debit Card	430 86			
		For			Bal.	1,123 18
	7/31	To Deposit			550 00	
		For			Bal.	1,673 18

LEARNINGTIP

When a bank statement arrives, the balance on that statement will not agree with the checkbook balance until the account has been *reconciled*. Remember that *both* balances need to be adjusted.

To determine which balance, the checkbook or the bank, gets adjusted for various situations, ask "Who didn't know?" For example,

- The bank *"didn't know"* about outstanding checks and deposits in transit; therefore, these adjustments are made to the bank balance.
- The checkbook *"didn't know"* the amount of the service charges and other debits or credits. These adjustments are made to the checkbook.

SOLUTIONSTRATEGY

The properly completed reconciliation form is on page 110. Note that the adjusted checkbook balance equals the adjusted bank statement balance. The balances are now reconciled. After some practice, the format will become familiar to you and you should no longer need the form.

	Checks Outstanding	
No.	Amount	
1211	342	10
1213	75	00
Total	417	10

CHECKBOOK BALANCE	$ 1,673.18	STATEMENT BALANCE	$ 1,520.28
Add: Interest Earned & Other Credits		Add: Deposits in Transit	550.00
SUBTOTAL	1,673.18	SUBTOTAL	2,070.28
Deduct: Service Charges & Other Debits	20.00	Deduct: Outstanding Checks	417.10
ADJUSTED CHECKBOOK BALANCE	1,653.18	ADJUSTED STATEMENT BALANCE	1,653.18

Reconciled Balances

● TRYITEXERCISE5

Using the form provided, reconcile the following bank statement and checkbook records for Max Mangones.

North Star Bank

STATEMENT DATE
4-3-20xx

MAX MANGONES
4121 Pinetree Rd.
Bangor, Maine 04401

CHECKING ACCOUNT SUMMARY
3-1-20xx THRU 3-31-20xx

ACCOUNT NUMBER
097440

Previous Balance	Deposits & Credits		Checks & Debits		Current Balance
	Number	Total	Number	Total	
625.40	3	1,790.00	8	690.00	1,725.40

CHECKING ACCOUNT TRANSACTIONS

DATE	AMOUNT	DESCRIPTION	BALANCE
3-2	34.77	Debit Card Purchase	590.63
3-6	750.00	Payroll-EFT Deposit	1,340.63
3-10	247.05	Check #340	1,093.58
3-13	390.00	Deposit	1,483.58
3-15	66.30	Check #342	1,417.28
3-17	112.18	Check #343	1,305.10
3-22	150.00	ATM Withdrawal	1,155.10
3-24	650.00	Deposit	1,805.10
3-28	50.00	Check #345	1,755.10
3-30	17.70	Check printing charge	1,737.40
3-31	12.00	Service charge	1,725.40

PLEASE BE SURE TO **DEDUCT** ANY BANK CHARGES THAT APPLY TO YOUR ACCOUNT.

CHECK NUMBER	DATE	DESCRIPTION OF TRANSACTION	AMOUNT OF PAYMENT OR WITHDRAWAL (−)	✓	AMOUNT OF DEPOSIT OR INTEREST (+)		BALANCE FORWARD
							625 40
	3/2	To Naples Pet Shop — Debit Card	34 77				
		For				Bal.	590 63
	3/5	To Electronic Payroll Deposit			750 00		
		For				Bal.	1,340 63
339	3/5	To Alison Company	19 83				
		For				Bal.	1,320 80
340	3/9	To Tennis Warehouse	247 05				
		For				Bal.	1,073 75
	3/12	To Deposit			390 00		
		For				Bal.	1,463 75
341	3/12	To The Book Shelf	57 50				
		For				Bal.	1,406 25
342	3/13	To Walmart	66 30				
		For				Bal.	1,339 95
343	3/15	To Sports Authority	112 18				
		For				Bal.	1,227 77
	3/22	To ATM Withdrawal	150 00				
		For				Bal.	1,077 77
	3/24	To Deposit			650 00		
		For				Bal.	1,727 77
344	3/24	To Foot Locker	119 32				
		For				Bal.	1,608 45
345	3/28	To Cablevision, Inc.	50 00				
		For				Bal.	1,558 45
	3/30	To Deposit			240 23		
		For				Bal.	1,798 68

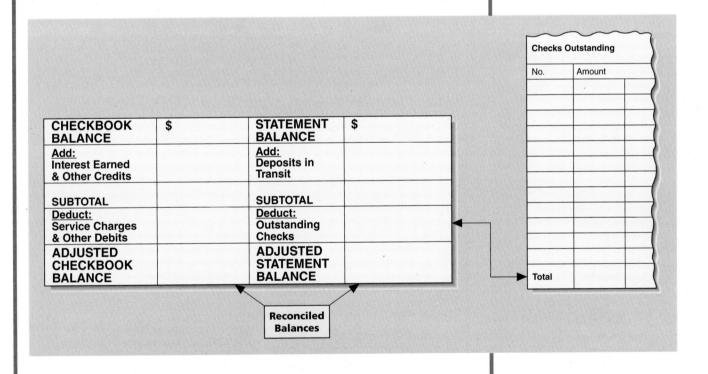

CHECKBOOK BALANCE	$	STATEMENT BALANCE	$
Add: Interest Earned & Other Credits		Add: Deposits in Transit	
SUBTOTAL		SUBTOTAL	
Deduct: Service Charges & Other Debits		Deduct: Outstanding Checks	
ADJUSTED CHECKBOOK BALANCE		ADJUSTED STATEMENT BALANCE	

Reconciled Balances

Checks Outstanding

No.	Amount	
Total		

CHECK YOUR ANSWERS WITH THE SOLUTIONS ON PAGE 118.

SECTION II **4** **REVIEW EXERCISES**

1. On April 3, Erin Gardner received her bank statement showing a balance of $2,087.93. Her checkbook showed a balance of $1,493.90. Outstanding checks were $224.15, $327.80, $88.10, $122.42, and $202.67. There was an $8.00 service charge, and the deposits in transit amounted to $813.11. There was an electronic payroll deposit of $450.00. Use the form below to reconcile Erin's account.

CHECKBOOK BALANCE	$	STATEMENT BALANCE	$		Checks Outstanding		
					No.	Amount	
Add: Interest Earned & Other Credits		Add: Deposits in Transit					
SUBTOTAL		SUBTOTAL					
Deduct: Service Charges & Other Debits		Deduct: Outstanding Checks					
ADJUSTED CHECKBOOK BALANCE		ADJUSTED STATEMENT BALANCE			Total		

Reconciled Balances

2. Bob Albrecht received his bank statement on July 5 showing a balance of $2,663.31. His checkbook had a balance of $1,931.83. The statement showed a service charge of $15.80 and an electronic payroll deposit of $200.00. The deposits in transit totaled $314.12, and the outstanding checks were for $182.00, $261.40, and $418.00. Use the form below to reconcile Bob's account.

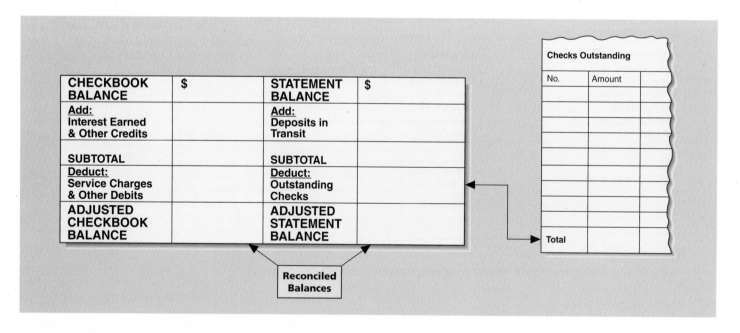

CHECKBOOK BALANCE	$	STATEMENT BALANCE	$		Checks Outstanding		
					No.	Amount	
Add: Interest Earned & Other Credits		Add: Deposits in Transit					
SUBTOTAL		SUBTOTAL					
Deduct: Service Charges & Other Debits		Deduct: Outstanding Checks					
ADJUSTED CHECKBOOK BALANCE		ADJUSTED STATEMENT BALANCE			Total		

Reconciled Balances

3. On December 2, John Leahy received his bank statement showing a balance of $358.97. His checkbook showed a balance of $479.39. There was a check printing charge of $13.95, and interest earned was $6.40. The outstanding checks were for $22.97, $80.36, $19.80, and $4.50. The deposits in transit totaled $240.50. Use the form below to reconcile John's account.

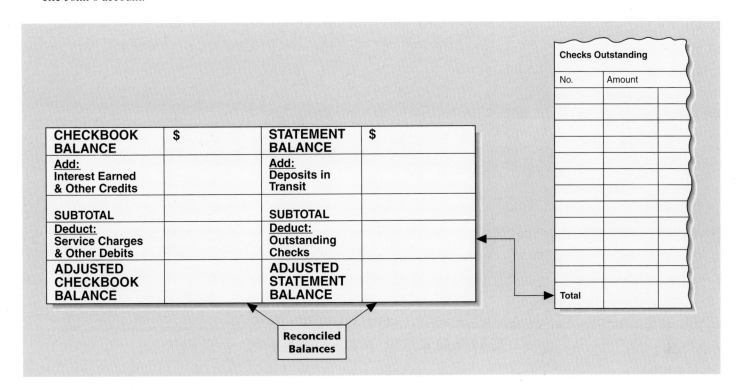

CHECKBOOK BALANCE	$	STATEMENT BALANCE	$
Add: Interest Earned & Other Credits		Add: Deposits in Transit	
SUBTOTAL		SUBTOTAL	
Deduct: Service Charges & Other Debits		Deduct: Outstanding Checks	
ADJUSTED CHECKBOOK BALANCE		ADJUSTED STATEMENT BALANCE	

Reconciled Balances

Checks Outstanding		
No.	Amount	
Total		

BUSINESS DECISION: CHOOSING A BANK

4. You are looking for a bank in which to open a checking account for your new part-time business. You estimate that in the first year, you will be writing 30 checks per month and will make three debit transactions per month. Your average daily balance is estimated to be $900 for the first six months and $2,400 for the next six months.

Use the following information to solve the problem.

Bank	Monthly Fees and Conditions
Intercontinental Bank	$15.00 with $1,000 min. daily balance -or- $25.00 under $1,000 min. daily balance
City National Bank	$4.50 plus $0.50 per check over 10 checks monthly $1.00 per debit transaction
Bank of America	$6 plus $0.25 per check $2.00 per debit transaction
First Union Bank	$9 plus $0.15 per check $1.50 per debit transaction

a. Calculate the cost of doing business with each bank for a year.

Intercontinental Bank:

City National Bank:

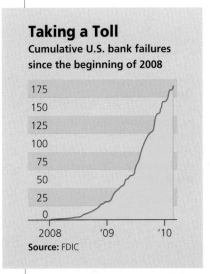

Taking a Toll
Cumulative U.S. bank failures since the beginning of 2008

Source: FDIC

Bank of America:

First Union Bank:

b. Which bank should you choose for your checking account?

CHAPTER

4

CHAPTER SUMMARY

Section I: Understanding and Using Checking Accounts

Topic	Important Concepts	Illustrative Examples
Checks **Performance Objectives 4-1 and 4-2, Pages 92–96**	Checks, or drafts, are negotiable instruments ordering the bank to pay money from the checking account to the name written on the check. The person or business named on the check to receive the money is known as the payee. The person or business issuing the check is known as the payor.	See Check with Parts Labeled, Exhibit 4-2, p. 93
Deposit Slips **Performance Objective 4-1, Pages 93** **Performance Objective 4-4, Page 98**	Deposit slips, or deposit tickets, are printed forms with the depositor's name, address, account number, and space for the details of the deposit. Deposit slips are used to record money, both cash and checks, being added to the checking account. They are presented to the bank teller along with the items to be deposited. When a deposit is completed, the depositor receives a copy of the deposit slip as a receipt, or proof of the transaction.	See Deposit Slip, Exhibit 4-3, p. 94 See Completed Deposit Slip, Exhibit 4-10, p. 98

Section I (continued)

Topic	Important Concepts	Illustrative Examples
Check Stubs **Performance Objective 4-1, Pages 93** **Performance Objective 4-5, Page 99**	Check stubs, with checks attached by perforation, are a bound part of the checkbook. The check number is preprinted on both the check and the attached stub. Each stub is used to record the issuing of its corresponding check and any deposits made on that date.	See Check Stub with Check, Exhibit 4-4, p. 94
Check Registers **Performance Objective 4-1, Pages 93** **Performance Objective 4-5, Page 99**	Check registers are the alternative method for keeping track of checking account activities. They are a separate booklet of forms rather than stubs attached to each check. Space is provided for all the pertinent information required to keep an accurate and up-to-date running balance of the account.	See Check Register, Exhibit 4-5, p. 94
Endorsements **Performance Objective 4-3, Page 96**	When you receive a check, you may cash it, deposit it in your account, or transfer it to another party. The endorsement on the back of the check tells the bank what to do. Your endorsement should be written within the $1\frac{1}{2}$-inch space at the trailing edge of the check.	See Endorsement Space, Exhibit 4-6, p. 96
Blank Endorsement **Performance Objective 4-3, Pages 96**	A blank endorsement is used when you want to cash the check. You, as the payee, simply sign your name exactly as it appears on the front of the check and write your account number. Once you have endorsed a check in this manner, anyone who has possession of the check can cash it.	See Blank Endorsement, Exhibit 4-7, p. 97 *John Q. Public* *82-1301-508*
Restrictive Endorsement **Performance Objective 4-3, Page 97**	A restrictive endorsement is used when you want to deposit the check in your account. In this case, you endorse the check "for deposit only," sign your name as it appears on the front, and write your account number.	See Restrictive Endorsement, Exhibit 4-8, p. 97 *for deposit only* *John Q. Public* *82-1301-508*
Full Endorsement **Performance Objective 4-3, Page 97**	A full endorsement is used when you want to transfer the check to another party. In this case, you endorse the check "pay to the order of," write the name of the person or business to whom the check is being transferred, and sign your name and account number.	See Full Endorsement, Exhibit 4-9, p. 97 *pay to the order of* *Cindy J. Citizen* *John Q. Public* *82-1301-508*

GO ONLINE FOR MORE ACTIVITIES • www.cengagebrain.com

Section II: Bank Statement Reconciliation

Topic	Important Concepts	Illustrative Examples
Bank Statements **Performance Objective 4-6, Pages 106**	Bank statements are a recap of the checking account activity for the month. They show the balance brought forward from the last statement, the deposits and credits that have been added to the account during the month, the checks and debits that have been subtracted from the account during the month, service charges assessed to the account, and the current or ending balance.	See Paper Bank Statement, Exhibit 4-13, p. 107 **Bank of America.** 037-049 11755 Biscayne Blvd. North Miami, Florida 33161 STATEMENT DATE 11-2-20xx John Q. Public 1234 Main St. Anywhere, U.S.A. 10101 CHECKING ACCOUNT SUMMARY ACCOUNT NUMBER 10-1-20xx THRU 10-31-20xx 82-1301-508 Previous Balance 775.20 · Deposits & Credits Number 3 Total 3,228.11 · Checks & Debits Number 7 Total 2,857.80 · Current Balance 1,145.51 CHECKING ACCOUNT TRANSACTIONS DATE · AMOUNT · DESCRIPTION · BALANCE 10-2 · 125.00 · Check #445 · 650.20 10-4 · 357.18 · Deposit · 1,007.38 10-7 · 884.22 · Debit Purchase · 123.16 10-13 · 1,409.30 · EFT Payroll Deposit · 1,532.46 10-15 · 12.95 · Debit Card Purchase · 1,519.51 10-16 · 326.11 · Check #446 · 1,193.40 10-22 · 200.00 · ATM Withdrawal · 993.40 10-25 · 1,461.63 · Deposit · 2,455.03 10-27 · 1,294.52 · Check #447 · 1,160.51 10-31 · 15.00 · Service Charge · 1,145.51
Bank Statement Reconciliation **Performance Objective 4-7, Page 108**	1. Calculate the adjusted checkbook balance: a. Locate any credits on the statement not recorded in the checkbook, such as interest earned or notes collected, and add them to the checkbook balance to get a subtotal. b. Subtract any debits or charges such as service charges, NSF fees, or returned items from the subtotal above. 2. Calculate the adjusted bank balance: a. Locate all the deposits in transit and add them to the bank statement balance to get a subtotal. b. Locate all outstanding checks and subtract them from the subtotal above. 3. Compare the adjusted balances: a. If they are equal, the statement has been reconciled. b. If they are *not* equal, an error exists that must be found and corrected. The error is either in the checkbook or on the bank statement.	See Bank Statement Reconciliation Form, Exhibit 4-14, p. 108

TRY IT: EXERCISE SOLUTIONS FOR CHAPTER 4

1.

Natalie Eldridge   206
1585 S. W. 6 Avenue
Tallahassee, FL 32399   *April 27* 20 *xx*   63-398/670

PAY TO THE ORDER OF ___ *Whole Foods* ___ $ *41.88*

Forty-one and 88/100 ___ DOLLARS

Bank of America.
037-049
11755 Biscayne Blvd.
North Miami, Florida 33161

FOR ___ *Party Platter* ___ *Natalie Eldridge*

⑉067003985⑉ 3077 821451902⑈

2. a.

Pay to the order of
Roz Reitman
Your Signature
696-339-1028

Full Endorsement

b.

Your Signature
696-339-1028

Blank Endorsement

c.

for deposit only
Your Signature
696-339-1028

Restrictive Endorsement

3.

HI-VOLT ELECTRONICS
12155 Miller Road
New Orleans, LA 70144

DATE *November 11* 20XX
DEPOSITS MAY NOT BE AVAILABLE FOR IMMEDIATE WITHDRAWAL

SIGN HERE IF CASH RECEIVED FROM DEPOSIT

Bank of America.
037-049
11755 Biscayne Blvd.
North Miami, Florida 33161

⑆067003985⑆   536101902⑈•

REV. 6/88   CHECKS AND OTHER ITEMS ARE RECEIVED FOR DEPOSIT SUBJECT TO THE PROVISIONS OF THE UNIFORM COMMERCIAL CODE OR ANY APPLICABLE COLLECTION AGREEMENT

CASH	CURRENCY	3,549	00
	COIN	19	65
CHECKS		411	92
		2,119	56
TOTAL FROM OTHER SIDE			
TOTAL		6,100	13
LESS CASH			
NET DEPOSIT		6,100	13

63-398/670

DEPOSIT TICKET
USE OTHER SIDE FOR
ADDITIONAL LISTINGS
TOTAL ITEMS
BE SURE EACH ITEM IS
PROPERLY ENDORSED

4.

IF TAX DEDUCTIBLE CHECK HERE ☐ $ *55.75*
137
March 12 20 XX
TO *Nathan & David*
FOR *perm & manicure*

	DOLLARS	CENTS
BAL. FWD.	887	45
DEPOSIT		
DEPOSIT		
TOTAL	887	45
THIS ITEM	55	75
SUB-TOTAL	831	70
OTHER DEDUCT. (IF ANY)		
BAL. FWD.	831	70

IF TAX DEDUCTIBLE CHECK HERE ☐ $ *459.88*
138
March 19 20 XX
TO *Complete Auto Service*
FOR *Car repairs*

	DOLLARS	CENTS
BAL. FWD.	831	70
DEPOSIT 3/16	125	40
DEPOSIT 3/16	221	35
TOTAL	1,178	45
THIS ITEM	459	88
SUB-TOTAL	718	57
OTHER DEDUCT. (IF ANY)	53	00
BAL. FWD.	665	57

PLEASE BE SURE TO **DEDUCT** ANY BANK CHARGES THAT APPLY TO YOUR ACCOUNT.

CHECK NUMBER	DATE	DESCRIPTION OF TRANSACTION	AMOUNT OF PAYMENT OR WITHDRAWAL (−)	✓	AMOUNT OF DEPOSIT OR INTEREST (+)	BALANCE FORWARD	
						887	45
137	3/12	To *Nathan & David Hair Stylists*	55	75				
		For				Bal. 831	70
	3/16	To *Deposit*			125	40		
		For				Bal. 957	10
	3/16	To *Deposit*			221	35		
		For				Bal. 1,178	45
138	3/19	To *Complete Auto Service*	459	88				
		For				Bal. 718	57
	3/20	To *Debit Card — Post Office*	53	00				
		For				Bal. 665	57

5.

CHECKBOOK BALANCE	$ 1,798.68	STATEMENT BALANCE	$ 1,725.40
Add: Interest Earned & Other Credits		Add: Deposits in Transit	240.23
SUBTOTAL	1,798.68	SUBTOTAL	1,965.63
Deduct: Service Charges & Other Debits	17.70 12.20	Deduct: Outstanding Checks	196.65
ADJUSTED CHECKBOOK BALANCE	1,768.98	ADJUSTED STATEMENT BALANCE	1,768.98

Reconciled Balances

Checks Outstanding

No.	Amount	
339	19	83
341	57	50
344	119	32
Total	196	65

CONCEPT REVIEW

1. A(n) _____ is a written order to a bank by a depositor to pay the amount specified from funds on deposit in a checking account. (4-1)

2. On a check, the _____ is the person or business issuing the check; the _____ is the person or business named on the check to receive the money. (4-1)

3. When a(n) _____ card is used, the amount of the transaction is deducted electronically from the checking account. (4-1)

4. Write the word form of $52.45 as it would appear on a check. (4-2)

5. The signature and instructions on the back of a check are known as the _____. (4-3)

6. There are three types of endorsements used on checks: the blank, the restrictive, and the _____ endorsement. (4-3)

7. The form used to record money being added to the checking account is a called a(n) _____. (4-4)

8. When cash is being withdrawn at the time of a deposit, a(n) _____ is required on the deposit slip. (4-4)

9. Attached by perforation to checks, check _____ are one method of tracking checking account activity. (4-5)

10. A check _____ is a separate booklet used to keep track of checking account activity. (4-5)

11. A bank _____ is a monthly summary of activities in a checking account. (4-6)

12. Additions to a checking account are called _____; subtractions from a checking account are called _____. (4-6)

13. A bank statement is reconciled when the adjusted checkbook balance _____ the adjusted bank balance. (4-7)

14. Checks that have not yet reached the bank are called _____ checks. Deposits that have not reached the bank are called deposits in _____. (4-7)

ASSESSMENT TEST

1. As the purchasing manager for Fuzzy Logic Industries, write a check dated April 29, 20xx, in the amount of $24,556.00, to Outback Electronics, Inc., for circuit boards.

FUZZY LOGIC INDUSTRIES   **206**
12221 Keystone Blvd
Greenville, SC 29610   _____ 20 _____   63-398/670

PAY TO THE
ORDER OF _____ $ _____

_____ D O L L A R S

Bank of America.
037-049
11755 Biscayne Blvd.
North Miami, Florida 33161

FOR _____   _____

⑈067003985⑈   206   731021807⑈

---

2. You have just received a check. Your account number is #9299-144-006. Write the following endorsements in the space provided below and identify what type they are.

   a. Allowing the check to be transferred to Expo, Inc.
   b. Allowing you to cash the check.
   c. Allowing you to deposit the check in your account.

   a. _____   b. _____   c. _____

"We're not a bank anymore.
Care for a latte?"

3. As cashier for Cellini's Pizza, it is your responsibility to make the daily deposits. Complete the deposit slip below based on the following information.

   a. Date: January 20, 20xx.
   b. Checks totaling $344.20.
   c. Currency of $547.00.
   d. Coins: 125 quarters, 67 dimes, 88 nickels, and 224 pennies.

CELLINI'S PIZZA
1470 Fleetwood St.
Madison, WI 53704

	CURRENCY		
C A S H	COIN		
CHECKS			

63-398/670

DEPOSIT TICKET
USE OTHER SIDE FOR
ADDITIONAL LISTINGS

DATE _____ 20 _____
DEPOSITS MAY NOT BE AVAILABLE FOR IMMEDIATE WITHDRAWAL

TOTAL FROM OTHER SIDE	
TOTAL	
LESS CASH	
NET DEPOSIT	

TOTAL ITEMS

_____
SIGN HERE IF CASH RECEIVED FROM DEPOSIT

BE SURE EACH ITEM IS
PROPERLY ENDORSED

Grove Isle Bank

⑈067003985⑈   730451408⑈

REV. 6/88   CHECKS AND OTHER ITEMS ARE RECEIVED FOR DEPOSIT SUBJECT TO THE PROVISIONS OF THE UNIFORM COMMERCIAL CODE OR ANY APPLICABLE COLLECTION AGREEMENT

CHAPTER 4

4. When Heather Gott went online to check her account balance in the morning, it was $823.71. During the day, she used her debit card for the following purchases: groceries—$48.38, flowers—$13.86, prescription refill—$28.00, and gasoline—$56.28. There was a $0.45 charge to use her debit card for the gas purchase. She also used her debit card to buy a roll of stamps for $44.00. In her mail was a birthday card with a $75 check from her uncle. Heather took the check to the bank and deposited it. What should she expect her account balance to be the following morning?

5. From the following information, complete the two check stubs and the check register below.

   a. Starting balance: $463.30.

   b. April 15, 20xx, check #450 issued to the Keystone Market for groceries in the amount of $67.78.

   c. April 17 debit card purchase of $250.

   d. April 19 deposit of $125.45.

   e. April 20 deposit of $320.00.

   f. April 27, check #451 in the amount of $123.10 to Ace Appliance, Inc., for refrigerator repair.

DOLLARS AND SENSE

Rewards Checking

Recently, a new type of checking account has been offered by banks and credit unions. These accounts, known as **rewards checking**, promise to pay high interest rates and are without any fees. Rewards checking accounts typically require that you use your debit card at least 10 times per month and that you give up paper bank statements in favor of online ones.

You can research various checking account offers at such sites as:
- www.bankrate.com
- www.bankdeals.com
- www.bankingmyway.com

Check stub 450

IF TAX DEDUCTIBLE CHECK HERE ☐	$ _____
450	
_____ 20 ____	
TO _____	
FOR _____	

	DOLLARS	CENTS
BAL. FWD.		
DEPOSIT		
DEPOSIT		
TOTAL		
THIS ITEM		
SUB-TOTAL		
OTHER DEDUCT. (IF ANY)		
BAL. FWD.		

Check stub 451

IF TAX DEDUCTIBLE CHECK HERE ☐	$ _____
451	
_____ 20 ____	
TO _____	
FOR _____	

	DOLLARS	CENTS
BAL. FWD.		
DEPOSIT		
DEPOSIT		
TOTAL		
THIS ITEM		
SUB-TOTAL		
OTHER DEDUCT. (IF ANY)		
BAL. FWD.		

PLEASE BE SURE TO **DEDUCT** ANY BANK CHARGES THAT APPLY TO YOUR ACCOUNT.

CHECK NUMBER	DATE	DESCRIPTION OF TRANSACTION	AMOUNT OF PAYMENT OR WITHDRAWAL (−)	✔	AMOUNT OF DEPOSIT OR INTEREST (+)	BALANCE FORWARD	
		To					
		For				Bal.	
		To					
		For				Bal.	
		To					
		For				Bal.	
		To					
		For				Bal.	
		To					
		For				Bal.	
		To					
		For				Bal.	

6. On October 1, Jessica Clay received her bank statement showing a balance of $374.52. Her checkbook records indicate a balance of $338.97. There was a service charge for the month of $4.40 on the statement. The outstanding checks were for $47.10, $110.15, $19.80, and $64.10. The deposits in transit totaled $125.50. There was a $75.70 debit for automatic payment of her telephone bill. Use the following form to reconcile Jessica's checking account.

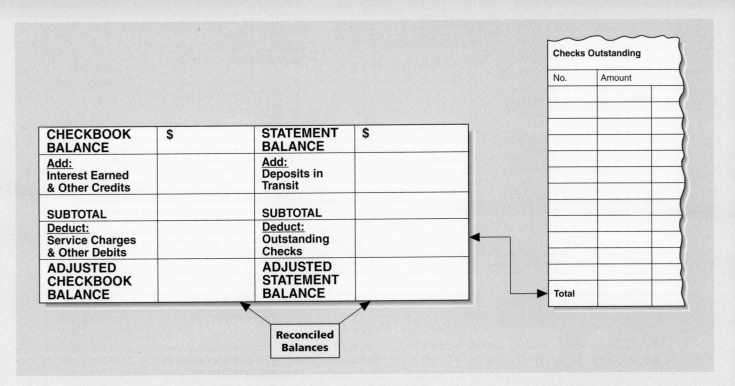

CHECKBOOK BALANCE	$	STATEMENT BALANCE	$
Add: Interest Earned & Other Credits		Add: Deposits in Transit	
SUBTOTAL		SUBTOTAL	
Deduct: Service Charges & Other Debits		Deduct: Outstanding Checks	
ADJUSTED CHECKBOOK BALANCE		ADJUSTED STATEMENT BALANCE	

Reconciled Balances

Checks Outstanding

No.	Amount	
Total		

7. Using the form on page 122, prepare a bank reconciliation for Kali Loi from the following checkbook records and bank statement.

PLEASE BE SURE TO **DEDUCT** ANY BANK CHARGES THAT APPLY TO YOUR ACCOUNT.

CHECK NUMBER	DATE	DESCRIPTION OF TRANSACTION	AMOUNT OF PAYMENT OR WITHDRAWAL (−)	✓	AMOUNT OF DEPOSIT OR INTEREST (+)	BALANCE FORWARD	
						879	36
801	10/1	To H & H Jewelers	236	77			
		For				Bal. 642	59
	10/6	To Deposit			450 75		
		For				Bal. 1,093	34
802	10/8	To L.L. Bean	47	20			
		For				Bal. 1,046	14
803	10/10	To Cashé	75	89			
		For				Bal. 970	25
	10/13	To Deposit			880 34		
		For				Bal. 1,850	59
804	10/13	To Four Seasons Hotel	109	00			
		For				Bal. 1,741	59
805	10/15	To American Express	507	82			
		For				Bal. 1,233	77
	10/20	To ATM Withdrawal	120	00			
		For				Bal. 1,113	77
	10/24	To Deposit			623 50		
		For				Bal. 1,737	27
	10/27	To Deposit			208 40		
		For				Bal. 1,945	67
	10/28	To Home Depot — Debit Card	48	25			
		For				Bal. 1,897	42

CHAPTER 4

Aloha Bank

Kali Loi
1127 Pineapple Place
Honolulu, HI 96825

STATEMENT DATE
11-2-20xx

CHECKING ACCOUNT SUMMARY
10-1-20xx THRU 10-31-20xx

ACCOUNT NUMBER
449-56-7792

Previous Balance	Deposits & Credits Number	Total	Checks & Debits Number	Total	Current Balance
879.36	3	1,954.59	7	1,347.83	1,486.12

CHECKING ACCOUNT TRANSACTIONS

DATE	AMOUNT	DESCRIPTION	BALANCE
10-3	236.77	Check #801	642.59
10-6	450.75	Deposit	1,093.34
10-10	324.70	Returned Item	768.64
10-13	880.34	EFT Payroll Deposit	1,648.98
10-15	75.89	Check #803	1,573.09
10-17	507.82	Check #805	1,065.27
10-22	120.00	ATM Withdrawal	945.27
10-24	623.50	Deposit	1,568.77
10-28	48.25	Debit Card Purchase	1,520.52
10-30	34.40	Check Printing Charge	1,486.12

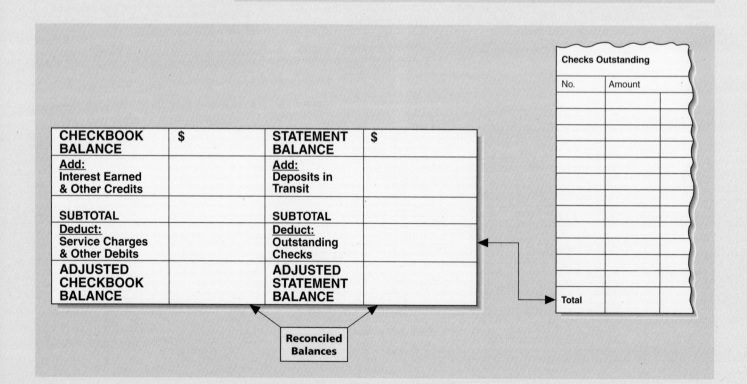

CHECKBOOK BALANCE	$	STATEMENT BALANCE	$
Add: Interest Earned & Other Credits		Add: Deposits in Transit	
SUBTOTAL		SUBTOTAL	
Deduct: Service Charges & Other Debits		Deduct: Outstanding Checks	
ADJUSTED CHECKBOOK BALANCE		ADJUSTED STATEMENT BALANCE	

Reconciled Balances

Checks Outstanding

No.	Amount	
Total		

BUSINESS DECISION: CHOOSING A BANK WITH INTEREST

8. Sometimes banks offer checking accounts that earn interest on the average daily balance of the account each month. This interest is calculated using a formula known as the simple interest formula. The formula is written as:

$$\text{Interest} = \text{Principal} \times \text{Rate} \times \text{Time} \qquad I = PRT$$

The formula states that the amount of **interest** earned on the account is equal to the **principal** (average daily balance) multiplied by the **rate** (interest rate per year—expressed as a decimal) multiplied by the **time** (expressed in years—use $\frac{1}{12}$ to represent one month of a year).

a. If you have not already done so, complete the Business Decision, Choosing a Bank on page 113.

b. Use the simple interest formula to calculate the amount of interest you would earn per month if the Intercontinental Bank was offering 2% (.02) interest per year on checking accounts. (Note that your average daily balance changes from $900 to $2,400 in the last six months of the year.)

c. How much interest would you earn per month at Bank of America if it were offering 1.5 percent (.015) interest per year on checking accounts? Round to the nearest cent when necessary.

d. Recalculate the cost of doing business with Intercontinental Bank and Bank of America for a year.

e. Based on this new information, which of the four banks should you choose for your checking account?

Largest U.S. Banks and Thirfts – by Assets

Bank (stock symbol)	Assets (billions)
Bank of America Corp. (BAC)	$2,344
JPMorgan Chase & Co. (JPM)	2,031
Citigroup, Inc. (C)	1,938
Wells Fargo & Co. (WFC)	1,226
HSBC North America (HBC)	334
U.S. Bancorp (USB)	283
PNC Financial Services (PNC)	260
Bank of New York Mellon Corp. (BK)	238
Capital One Financial Corp. (COF)	198
SunTrust Banks, Inc. (STI)	171

Source: http://finance.yahoo.com, 2nd Quarter, 2010

COLLABORATIVE LEARNING ACTIVITY

Choosing a Checking Account

Have each team member research a local bank, a credit union, or another financial institution offering checking accounts to find the types of checking accounts they have and other banking services they offer. As a team, look over the material and answer the following:

a. How do the accounts compare regarding monthly service charges, interest paid, account minimums, debit and ATM charges, and other rules and regulations?

b. Do the banks offer any incentives such as a no-fee Visa or MasterCard, bounce-proof checking, or a line of credit?

c. Based on your team's research, which bank would you recommend for each of the following:
   • College student. Why?
   • Small business. Why?
   • Family with three teenagers. Why?

d. Because many banks have failed in recent years, check your bank's health by looking up its "star rating" at www.bauerfinancial.com or www.bankrate.com. Also look over your bank's financial statements filed quarterly with the government at www.fdic.gov. What can you conclude from your findings?

Using Equations to Solve Business Problems

PERFORMANCE OBJECTIVES

SECTION I: Solving Basic Equations

SECTION II: Using Equations to Solve Business-Related Word Problems

SOLVING BASIC EQUATIONS

One of the primary objectives of business mathematics is to describe business situations and solve business problems. Many business problems requiring a mathematical solution have been converted to formulas. A **formula** is a mathematical statement describing a real-world situation in which letters represent number quantities. A typical example of a formula follows:

Business Situation:	Revenue less expenses is profit
Mathematical Formula:	Revenue − Expenses = Profit

or

$$R - E = P$$

By knowing the numerical value of any two of the three parts, we can use the formula to determine the unknown part. Formulas are a way of standardizing repetitive business situations. They are used in almost every aspect of business activity and are an essential tool for the businessperson. Later in the book, we see formulas applied to topics such as markup and markdown, percents, interest rates, financial ratios, inventory, and depreciation.

As valuable and widespread as formulas are, they cannot anticipate all business situations. Today businesspeople must have the ability to analyze the facts of a situation and devise custom-made formulas to solve business problems. These formulas are actually mathematical **equations**.

In this important chapter, you learn to write and solve equations. At first, some of the concepts may seem a bit strange. Equations use letters of the alphabet as well as numbers. Do not be intimidated! After some practice, you will be able to write and solve equations comfortably.

formula A mathematical statement describing a real-world situation in which letters represent number quantities. An example is the simple interest formula $I = PRT$, where *interest* equals *principal* times *rate* times *time*.

equations Mathematical statements expressing a relationship of equality; usually written as a series of symbols that are separated into left and right sides and joined by an equal sign. $X + 7 = 10$ is an equation.

UNDERSTANDING THE CONCEPT, TERMINOLOGY, AND RULES OF EQUATIONS

5-1

In English, we write by using words to form complete thoughts known as sentences. Equations convert written sentences describing business situations into mathematical sentences. When the statement contains an equal sign ($=$), it is an equation. If it does not contain an equal sign, it is simply an **expression**. Equations express business problems in their simplest form. There are no adjectives or words of embellishment, just the facts.

$$S + 12 \text{ is an } expression \qquad S + 12 = 20 \text{ is an } equation$$

An equation is a mathematical statement using numbers, letters, and symbols to express a relationship of equality. Equations have an expression on the left side and an expression on the right side connected by an equal sign.

Letters of the alphabet are used to represent unknown quantities in equations and are called **variables**. In the equation above, S is the variable, or the **unknown**. The 12 and the 20 are the **constants**, or **knowns**. Variables and constants are also known as the **terms** of the equation. The plus sign and the equal sign separate the terms and describe the relationship between them.

To **solve an equation** means to find the numerical value of the unknown. From our equation $S + 12 = 20$, what value of S would make the equation true? Is it 6? No, 6 plus 12 is 18, and 18 does not equal 20. Is it 10? No, 10 plus 12 is 22, and 22 does not equal 20. How about 8? Yes, 8 plus 12 does equal 20.

$$S + 12 = 20$$
$$8 + 12 = 20$$
$$20 = 20$$

expression A mathematical operation or a quantity stated in symbolic form, not containing an equal sign. $X + 7$ is an expression.

variables, or **unknowns** The parts of an equation that are not given. In equations, the unknowns, or variables, are represented by letters of the alphabet. In the equation $X + 7 = 10$, X is the unknown, or variable.

constants, or **knowns** The parts of an equation that are given. In equations, the knowns are constants (numbers), which are quantities having a fixed value. In the equation $X + 7 = 10$, 7 and 10 are the knowns, or constants.

terms The knowns (constants) and unknowns (variables) of an equation. In the equation $X + 7 = 10$, the terms are X, 7, and 10.

solve an equation To find the numerical value of the unknown in an equation.

solution, or root The numerical value of the unknown that makes the equation true. In the equation $X + 7 = 10$, for example, 3 is the solution because $3 + 7 = 10$.

By substituting 8 for the variable, S, we have found the value of the unknown that satisfies the equation and makes it true: 20 equals 20. The numerical value of the variable that makes the equation true (in this case, 8) is known as the **solution**, or **root**, of the equation.

5-2 SOLVING EQUATIONS FOR THE UNKNOWN AND PROVING THE SOLUTION

In solving equations, we use the same basic operations we used in arithmetic: addition, subtraction, multiplication, and division. The meanings of the signs $+$, $-$, $\times$, and $\div$ are still the same. Equations have a few new designations, however, that we must learn.

Multiplication of 5 times Y, for example, may be written as

$$5 \times Y$$
$$5 \cdot Y$$
$$5(Y)$$
$$5Y$$

Today managers must have the ability to analyze the facts of a business problem and devise custom-made formulas to solve them.

The number 5 in the term $5Y$ is known as the **coefficient** of the term. In cases in which there is no numerical coefficient written, such as W, the coefficient is understood to be a 1. Therefore,

$$1W = W.$$

Division in equations is indicated by the fraction bar, just as in Chapter 2. For example, the term 5 divided by Y would be written as

$$\frac{5}{Y}$$

It is important to remember that an equation is a statement of *equality*. The left side must always *equal* the right side. To solve equations, we must move or **transpose** all the unknowns to one side and all the knowns to the other side. It is customary for the unknowns to be on the left side and the knowns to be on the right side, such as $X = 7$.

Transposing involves the use of inverse, or opposite, operations. To transpose a term in an equation, (1) note the operation indicated and (2) apply the *opposite* operation to both sides of the equation as follows:

coefficient A number or quantity placed before another quantity, indicating multiplication. For example, 4 is the coefficient in the expression $4C$. This indicates 4 multiplied by C.

transpose To move a term from one side of an equation to the other. Whenever addition or subtraction is used for moving the term, a corresponding change of sign occurs.

Operation Indicated		Opposite Operation
Addition	$\longrightarrow$	Subtraction
Subtraction	$\longrightarrow$	Addition
Multiplication	$\longrightarrow$	Division
Division	$\longrightarrow$	Multiplication

STEPS FOR SOLVING EQUATIONS AND PROVING THE SOLUTION

STEP 1. Transpose all the *unknowns* to the left side of the equation and all the *knowns* to the right side of the equation by using the following "**order of operations**" for solving equations.

- *Parentheses,* if any, must be cleared before any other operations are performed. To clear parentheses, multiply the coefficient by each term inside the parentheses.

$$3(5C + 4) = 2 \qquad 3(5C) + 3(4) = 2 \qquad 15C + 12 = 2$$

- To solve equations with more than one operation:
  - First, perform the additions and subtractions.
  - Then perform the multiplications and divisions.

STEP 2. Prove the solution by substituting your answer for the letter or letters in the original equation. If the left and right sides are *equal*, the equation is true and your answer is correct.

Image copyright visi.stock 2010. Used under license from Shutterstock.com

EXAMPLE 1 SOLVING EQUATIONS

Solve the equation $X + 4 = 15$ and prove the solution.

SOLUTIONSTRATEGY

The equation $X + 4 = 15$ indicates addition ($+4$). To solve for X, apply the opposite operation, subtraction. Subtract 4 from each side.

$$
\begin{aligned}
X + 4 &= 15 \\
-\ 4\quad &-4 \\
\hline
X\quad\ &= 11
\end{aligned}
$$

$$X = 11$$

Proof: The solution can easily be proven by substituting our answer (11) for the letter or letters in the original equation. If the left and right sides are equal, the equation is true and the solution is correct.

$$
\begin{aligned}
X + 4 &= 15 \\
11 + 4 &= 15 \\
15 &= 15
\end{aligned}
$$

TRYITEXERCISE 1

Solve the following equations for the unknown and prove your solutions.

a. $W + 10 = 25$ b. $Q + 30 = 100$

CHECK YOUR ANSWERS WITH THE SOLUTIONS ON PAGE 148.

CHECK YOUR ANSWERS WITH THE SOLUTIONS ON PAGE 148.

LEARNINGTIP

Remember, an equation is a statement of "equality." The left side must always equal the right side. The word *equation*, in fact, is derived from the word *equal*.

INTHE BUSINESSWORLD

The equal sign, two parallel lines ($=$), was invented in the sixteenth century by Robert Recorde. He stated, "Nothing can be more equal than parallel lines!"

   Other related mathematical symbols are:

$\approx$ is approximately equal to
$\neq$ is not equal to
$\geq$ is greater than or equal to
$\leq$ is less than or equal to

EXAMPLE 2 SOLVING EQUATIONS

Solve the equation $H - 20 = 44$ and prove the solution.

SOLUTIONSTRATEGY

The equation $H - 20 = 44$ indicates subtraction (-20). To solve for H, apply the opposite operation, addition. Add 20 to each side of the equation.

$$
\begin{aligned}
H - 20 &= 44 \\
+\ 20\quad &+20 \\
\hline
H\quad\ &= 64
\end{aligned}
$$

$$H = 64$$

Proof: Substitute 64 for H.

$$
\begin{aligned}
H - 20 &= 44 \\
64 - 20 &= 44 \\
44 &= 44
\end{aligned}
$$

TRYITEXERCISE 2

Solve the following equations for the unknown and prove your solutions.

a. $A - 8 = 40$ b. $L - 3 = 7$

CHECK YOUR ANSWERS WITH THE SOLUTIONS ON PAGE 148.

CHECK YOUR ANSWERS WITH THE SOLUTIONS ON PAGE 148.

EXAMPLE 3 SOLVING EQUATIONS

Solve the equation $9T = 36$ and prove the solution.

SOLUTIONSTRATEGY

The equation $9T = 36$ indicates multiplication. $9T$ means 9 times T. To solve for T, apply the opposite operation. Divide both sides of the equation by 9.

$$9T = 36$$

$$\frac{9T}{9} = \frac{36}{9}$$

$$T = 4$$

Proof:

$$9T = 36$$

$$9(4) = 36$$

$$36 = 36$$

TRYITEXERCISE 3

Solve the following equations for the unknown and prove your solutions.

a. $15L = 75$ b. $16F = 80$

CHECK YOUR ANSWERS WITH THE SOLUTIONS ON PAGE 148.

EXAMPLE 4 SOLVING EQUATIONS

Solve the equation $\frac{M}{5} = 4$ and prove the solution.

SOLUTIONSTRATEGY

The equation $\frac{M}{5} = 4$ indicates division. To solve for M, do the opposite operation. Multiply both sides of the equation by 5.

$$(5)\frac{M}{5} = 4(5)$$

$$M = 20$$

Proof:

$$\frac{M}{5} = 4$$

$$\frac{20}{5} = 4$$

$$4 = 4$$

TRYITEXERCISE 4

Solve the following equations for the unknown and prove your solutions.

a. $\frac{Z}{8} = 2$ b. $\frac{C}{9} = 9$

CHECK YOUR ANSWERS WITH THE SOLUTIONS ON PAGE 148.

EXAMPLE5 SOLVING EQUATIONS CONTAINING MULTIPLE OPERATIONS

Solve the equation $7R - 5 = 51$ and prove the solution.

SOLUTIONSTRATEGY

The equation $7R - 5 = 51$ indicates subtraction and multiplication. Following the order of operations for solving equations, begin by adding 5 to each side of the equation.

$$\begin{array}{rcr} 7R - 5 = & & 51 \\ + 5 & & + 5 \\ \hline 7R \quad = & & 56 \end{array}$$

$$7R = 56$$

Next, divide both sides of the equation by 7.

$$\frac{7R}{7} = \frac{56}{7}$$

$$R = 8$$

Proof:

$$\begin{array}{rcl} 7R - 5 &=& 51 \\ 7(8) - 5 &=& 51 \\ 56 - 5 &=& 51 \\ 51 &=& 51 \end{array}$$

TRYITEXERCISE5

Solve the following equations for the unknown and prove the solutions.

a. $12N + 14 = 50$ b. $3W - 4 = 26$

CHECK YOUR ANSWERS WITH THE SOLUTIONS ON PAGE 148.

EXAMPLE6 SOLVING EQUATIONS CONTAINING MULTIPLE OPERATIONS

Solve the equation $\frac{X}{2} + 20 = 34$ and prove the solution.

SOLUTIONSTRATEGY

The equation $\frac{X}{2} + 20 = 34$ indicates addition and division. Following the order of operations for solving equations, begin by subtracting 20 from each side.

$$\begin{array}{rcr} \frac{X}{2} + 20 = & & 34 \\ - 20 & & - 20 \\ \hline \frac{X}{2} \quad = & & 14 \end{array}$$

$$\frac{X}{2} = 14$$

Next, multiply each side by 2.

$$(2)\frac{X}{2} = 14(2)$$

$$X = 28$$

Proof:

$$\frac{X}{2} + 20 = 34$$

$$\frac{28}{2} + 20 = 34$$

$$14 + 20 = 34$$

$$34 = 34$$

● **TRYITEXERCISE6**

Solve the following equations for the unknown and prove the solutions.

a. $\dfrac{F}{3} - 6 = 2$ b. $\dfrac{Z}{5} + 15 = 24$

CHECK YOUR ANSWERS WITH THE SOLUTIONS ON PAGE 148.

Parentheses

Sometimes parentheses are used in equations. They contain a number just outside the left-hand parentheses known as the coefficient and two or more terms inside the parentheses. An example is $5(3X + 6) = 20$.

Parentheses Rule

In solving equations, parentheses must be removed before any other operations are performed. To remove parentheses, multiply the coefficient by each term inside the parentheses.

  To apply this rule to the example above,

$$5(3X + 6) = 20$$

$$5(3X) + 5(6) = 20$$

$$15X + 30 = 20$$

● **EXAMPLE7** SOLVING EQUATIONS CONTAINING PARENTHESES

Solve the equation 8(2*K* − 4) = 48 and prove the solution.

● **SOLUTIONSTRATEGY**

Because this equation contains parentheses, we must begin there. Following the rule for removing parentheses, multiply the coefficient, 8, by each term inside the parentheses.

$$8(2K - 4) = 48$$

$$8(2K) - 8(4) = 48$$

$$16K - 32 = 48$$

Now solve the equation as before by isolating the unknown, K, on the left side of the equal sign. Remember, add and subtract first, then multiply and divide.

$$
\begin{array}{rcr}
16K - 32 = & & 48 \\
+\,32 & & +\,32 \\
\hline
16K \quad = & & 80
\end{array}
$$

$$16K = 80$$

$$\frac{\cancel{16}K}{\cancel{16}} = \frac{80}{16}$$

$$\underline{K = 5}$$

Proof:

$$8(2K - 4) = 48$$

$$8(2\{5\} - 4) = 48$$

$$8(10 - 4) = 48$$

$$8(6) = 48$$

$$\underline{48 = 48}$$

TRYITEXERCISE7

Solve the following equations for the unknown and prove the solutions.

a. $4(5G + 6) = 64$ b. $6(3H - 5) = 42$

CHECK YOUR ANSWERS WITH THE SOLUTIONS ON PAGE 149.

When equations contain unknowns that appear two or more times, they must be combined.

STEPS FOR COMBINING MULTIPLE UNKNOWNS

STEP 1. To combine unknowns, they must be on the same side of the equation. If they are not, move them all to the same side.

$$5X = 12 + 2X$$
$$5X - 2X = 12$$

STEP 2. Once the unknowns are on the same side of the equation, add or subtract their coefficients as indicated.

$$5X - 2X = 12$$
$$3X = 12$$

EXAMPLE8   SOLVING EQUATIONS CONTAINING MULTIPLE UNKNOWNS

Solve the equation $4C + 7 - C = 25 - 6C$ and prove the solution.

SOLUTIONSTRATEGY

To solve this equation, we begin by combining the two terms on the left side that contain C: $4C - C = 3C$. This leaves

$$3C + 7 = 25 - 6C$$

Next, move the $-6C$ to the left side by adding $+6C$ to both sides of the equation.

$$
\begin{array}{rcl}
3C + 7 & = & 25 - 6C \\
+6C & & +6C \\
\hline
9C + 7 & = & 25
\end{array}
$$

Now that all the terms containing the unknown, C, have been combined, we can solve the equation.

$$
\begin{array}{rcl}
9C + 7 & = & 25 \\
-7 & & -7 \\
\hline
9C & = & 18 \\
\dfrac{9C}{9} & = & \dfrac{18}{9} \\
C & = & 2
\end{array}
$$

Proof:

$$4C + 7 - C = 25 - 6C$$
$$4(2) + 7 - 2 = 25 - 6(2)$$
$$8 + 7 - 2 = 25 - 12$$
$$13 = 13$$

TRYITEXERCISE8

Solve the following equations for the unknown and prove the solutions.

a. $X + 3 = 18 - 4X$ b. $9S + 8 - S = 2(2S + 8)$

CHECK YOUR ANSWERS WITH THE SOLUTIONS ON PAGE 149.

5-3

WRITING EXPRESSIONS AND EQUATIONS FROM WRITTEN STATEMENTS

Expressions and equations are created from written statements by identifying the unknowns and the knowns and then determining the mathematical relationship between them. The variables are assigned letters of the alphabet. The letter X is commonly used to represent the unknown. The relationship between the knowns and the unknowns involves addition, subtraction, multiplication, or division or a combination of two or more of these.

STEPS FOR WRITING EXPRESSIONS AND EQUATIONS

STEP 1. Read the written statement carefully.

STEP 2. Using the following list, identify and underline the key words and phrases.

STEP 3. Convert the words to numbers and mathematical symbols.

Key Words and Phrases for Creating Equations

Equal Sign	Addition	Subtraction	Multiplication	Division	Parentheses
is	and	less	of	divide	times the quantity of
are	added to	less than	multiply	divided by	
was	totals	smaller than	times	divided into	
equals	the sum of	minus	product of	quotient of	
gives	plus	difference	multiplied by	ratio of	
giving	more than	decreased by	twice		
leaves	larger than	reduced by	double		
results in	increased by	take away	triple		
produces	greater than	loss of	at		
yields	exceeds	fewer than	@		

EXAMPLE 9 WRITING EXPRESSIONS

For the following statements, underline the key words and translate into *expressions*.

a. A number increased by 18   b. 19 times W

c. 12 less than S d. $\frac{2}{3}$ of Y

e. 9 more than 2 times R f. 4 times the quantity of X and 8

SOLUTIONSTRATEGY

Key Words	Expression
a. A number <u>increased by</u> 18	$N + 18$
b. 19 <u>times</u> W	$19W$
c. 12 <u>less than</u> S	$S - 12$
d. $\frac{2}{3}$ <u>of</u> Y	$\frac{2}{3}Y$
e. 9 <u>more than</u> 2 <u>times</u> R	$2R + 9$
f. 4 <u>times the quantity</u> of X <u>and</u> 8	$4(X + 8)$

TRYITEXERCISE9

For the following statements, underline the key words and translate into *expressions.*

a. The sum of twice E and 9

b. 6 times N divided by Z

c. 8 less than half of F

d. $45.75 more than the product of X and Y

e. The difference of Q and 44

f. R times A times B

CHECK YOUR ANSWERS WITH THE SOLUTIONS ON PAGE 149.

EXAMPLE10 WRITING EQUATIONS

For the following statements, underline the key words and translate into *equations.*

a. A number decreased by 14 is 23.

b. 8 less than $3D$ leaves 19.

c. A number totals 4 times the quantity of V and N.

d. The cost of X lb at $3 per lb is $12.

e. Cost is the product of price and quantity.

f. The sum of liabilities and capital is assets.

SOLUTIONSTRATEGY

Key Words	Equations
a. A number decreased by 14 is 23.	$X - 14 = 23$
b. 8 less than $3D$ leaves 19.	$3D - 8 = 19$
c. A number totals 4 times the quantity of V and N.	$X = 4(V + N)$
d. The cost of X lb at $3 per lb is $12.	$3X = 12$
e. Cost is the product of price and quantity.	$C = PQ$
f. The sum of liabilities and capital is assets.	$L + C = A$

TRYITEXERCISE10

For the following statements, underline the key words and translate into *equations.*

a. What number increased by 32 yields 125?

b. 21 less than twice C gives 9.

c. 5 more than 6 times a number plus 3 times that number is 25.

d. The cost of G gallons at $1.33 per gallon equals $34.40.

e. The area of a rectangle is the length times the width.

f. (Challenge) What number less 12 is the average of A, B, and C?

CHECK YOUR ANSWERS WITH THE SOLUTIONS ON PAGE 149.

REVIEW EXERCISES

SECTION I 5

Solve the following equations for the unknown and prove your solutions.

JUMP
START
WWW

1. $B + 11 = 24$

   $B = \underline{13}$

2. $C - 16 = 5$

3. $S + 35 = 125$

4. $M - 58 = 12$

5. $21K = 63$

6. $\dfrac{Z}{3} = 45$

7. $50Y = 375$ 8. $\dfrac{L}{5} = 8$ 9. $6G + 5 = 29$

10. $\dfrac{D}{3} - 5 = 15$ 11. $25A - 11 = 64$ 12. $\dfrac{R}{5} + 33 = 84$

13. $3(4X + 5) = 63$ 14. $C + 5 = 26 - 2C$ 15. $12(2D - 4) = 72$

16. $14V + 5 - 5V = 4(V + 5)$ 17. $Q + 20 = 3(9 - 2Q)$

For the following statements, underline the key words and translate into *expressions*.

18. 5 <u>times</u> G <u>divided by</u> R

$$\dfrac{5G}{R}$$

19. The sum of 5 times F and 33

20. 6 less than one-fourth of C

21. 550 more than the product of H and P

22. T times B times 9

23. The difference of $8Y$ and 128

24. 7 times the quantity of X and 7

25. 40 more than $\frac{3}{4}$ of B

For the following statements, underline the key words and translate into *equations*.

26. A number <u>increased by</u> 24 <u>is</u> 35.

$$X + 24 = 35$$

27. A number totals 5 times B and C.

28. 12 less than $4G$ leaves 33.

29. The cost of R at \$5.75 each is \$28.75.

30. Cost per person is the total cost divided by the number of persons.

31. 4 more than 5 times a number plus 2 times that number is that number increased by 40.

BUSINESS DECISION: GROUPING SYMBOLS

32. Grouping symbols are used to arrange numbers, variables, and operations. In this chapter, you learned to use the grouping symbols known as parentheses ( ). In addition to parentheses, other symbols used for grouping are brackets [ ] and braces { }. When solving equations with multiple grouping symbols, always start with the innermost symbols and work to the outside.

    In business, you may encounter situations that require you to set up equations with more than just parentheses. For practice, solve the following equation.

$$X = 6(2 + [3\{9 - 3\} + \{8 + 1\} - 4])$$

$x^2 + 2 = 6$

"If 'x' is unknown, why should I rock the boat?"

USING EQUATIONS TO SOLVE BUSINESS-RELATED WORD PROBLEMS

SECTION II **5**

In business, most of the math encountered is in the form of business-situation word problems. Variables such as profits, production units, inventory, employees, money, customers, and interest rates are constantly interacting mathematically. Your boss will not ask you simply to add, subtract, multiply, or divide, but will ask for information requiring you to perform these functions in a business context. Business students must be able to analyze a business situation requiring math, set up the situation in a mathematical expression or equation, and work it out to a correct solution.

LEARNINGTIP

This is the real "bottom line" of equations: the ability to analyze a business situation, convert it to an equation, and solve it. Proficiency will come with practice.

SETTING UP AND SOLVING BUSINESS-RELATED WORD PROBLEMS BY USING EQUATIONS

5-4

In Section I of this chapter, we learned to create and solve equations from written statements. Let's see how to apply these skills in business situations. You will learn a logical procedure for setting up and solving business-related word problems. Some problems have more than one way to arrive at an answer. The key, once again, is not to be intimidated. Learning to solve word problems requires practice, and the more you do it, the easier it will become and the more comfortable you will feel with it.

STEPS **FOR SETTING UP AND SOLVING WORD PROBLEMS**

STEP 1. Understand the situation. If the problem is written, read it carefully, perhaps a few times. If the problem is verbal, write down the facts of the situation.

STEP 2. Take inventory. Identify all the parts of the situation. These parts can be any variables, such as dollars, people, boxes, tons, trucks, anything! Separate them into knowns and unknowns.

STEP 3. Make a plan—create an equation. The object is to solve for the unknown. Ask yourself what math relationship exists between the knowns and the unknowns. Use the chart of key words and phrases on page 132 to help you write the equation.

STEP 4. Work out the plan—solve the equation. To solve an equation, you must move the unknowns to one side of the equal sign and the knowns to the other.

STEP 5. Check your solution. Does your answer make sense? Is it exactly correct? It is a good idea to estimate an approximate answer by using rounded numbers. This will let you know if your answer is in the correct range. If it is not, either the equation is set up incorrectly or the solution is wrong. If this occurs, you must go back and start again.

EXAMPLE11 SOLVING BUSINESS-RELATED EQUATIONS

On Tuesday, Double Bubble Car Wash took in $360 less in wash business than in wax business. If the total sales for the day were $920, what were the sales for each service?

SOLUTIONSTRATEGY

Reasoning: Wax sales <u>plus</u> wash sales <u>equal</u> the total sales, $920.

Let X = $ amount of wax sales

Let $X - 360$ = $ amount of wash sales

$$X + X - 360 = 920$$
$$\underline{ + 360 \quad + 360}$$
$$X + X = 1{,}280$$

LEARNING TIP

Frequently, the left side of an equation represents the "interaction" of the variables and the right side shows the "result" of that interaction.

In this example, the left side is the interaction (in this case, addition) of the wax and wash sales. The right side is the result, or total.

$$\frac{\text{Interaction}}{X + X - 360} = \frac{\text{Result}}{920}$$

$$2X = 1,280$$

$$\frac{\cancel{2}X}{\cancel{2}} = \frac{1,280}{2}$$

$$X = 640 \quad \underline{\text{Wax sales} = \$640}$$

$$X - 360 = 640 - 360 = 280 \quad \underline{\text{Wash sales} = \$280}$$

Proof:

$$X + X - 360 = 920$$

$$640 + 640 - 360 = 920$$

$$\underline{920 = 920}$$

● TRYITEXERCISE11

Don and Chuck are salespeople for Security One Alarms. Last week Don sold 12 fewer alarm systems than Chuck did. Together they sold 44. How many did each sell?

CHECK YOUR ANSWERS WITH THE SOLUTIONS ON PAGE 149.

● EXAMPLE12 SOLVING BUSINESS-RELATED EQUATIONS

Dynamic Industries, Inc., spends $\frac{1}{4}$ of total revenue on employee payroll expenses. If last week's payroll amounted to $5,000, what was the revenue for the week?

● SOLUTIONSTRATEGY

Reasoning: $\frac{1}{4}$ of revenue is the week's payroll, $5,000.

Let R = revenue for the week

$$\frac{1}{4}R = 5,000$$

$$(\cancel{4})\frac{1}{\cancel{4}}R = 5,000(4)$$

$$R = 20,000 \quad \underline{\text{Revenue for the week} = \$20,000}$$

Proof:

$$\frac{1}{4}R = 5,000$$

$$\frac{1}{4}(20,000) = 5,000$$

$$\underline{5,000 = 5,000}$$

● TRYITEXERCISE12

One-third of the checking accounts at the Community Bank earn interest. If 2,500 accounts are this type, how many total checking accounts does the bank have?

CHECK YOUR ANSWER WITH THE SOLUTION ON PAGE 149.

IN THE BUSINESS WORLD

According to the Math Worksheet Center, formulas are a part of our lives. Whether you drive a car and need to calculate the distance of travel or need to work out the volume in a milk container, you use algebraic formulas everyday without even realizing it.

Let's say, for example, that you have a total of $100 to spend on video games. When you go to the video store, you find that each game sells for $20. How many games can you buy? This scenario provides the equation $20X = 100$, where X is the number of games you can buy. Most people don't realize that this type of calculation is algebra; they just subconsciously do it!

● EXAMPLE13 SOLVING BUSINESS-RELATED EQUATIONS

United Dynamics, Inc., has 25 shareholders. If management decides to split the $80,000 net profit equally among the shareholders, how much will each receive?

SOLUTIONSTRATEGY

Reasoning: Profit per shareholder <u>is</u> the net profit, $80,000, <u>divided by</u> the number of shareholders.

Let P = Profit per shareholder

$$P = \frac{80,000}{25}$$

$$P = 3,200 \quad \underline{\text{Profit per shareholder} = \$3,200}$$

Proof:

$$P = \frac{80,000}{25}$$

$$3,200 = \frac{80,000}{25}$$

$$3,200 = 3,200$$

TRYITEXERCISE13

Century Manufacturing, Inc., fills an order for 58 cartons of merchandise weighing a total of 7,482 pounds. What is the weight per carton?

CHECK YOUR ANSWER WITH THE SOLUTION ON PAGE 150.

EXAMPLE14 SOLVING BUSINESS-RELATED EQUATIONS

A local Best Buy store sold 144 TVs last week. If five times as many LCD models sold as compared to plasma models, how many of each were sold?

SOLUTIONSTRATEGY

Reasoning: Plasma models <u>plus</u> LCD models <u>equals</u> total TVs sold, 144.

Let X = plasma models

Let $5X$ = LCD models

$$X + 5X = 144$$

$$6X = 144$$

$$\frac{\cancel{6}X}{\cancel{6}} = \frac{144}{6}$$

$$X = 24 \qquad \underline{\text{Plasma models sold} = 24}$$

$$5X = 5(24) = 120 \qquad \underline{\text{LCD models sold} = 120}$$

Proof:

$$X + 5X = 144$$

$$24 + 5(24) = 144$$

$$24 + 120 = 144$$

$$144 = 144$$

TRYITEXERCISE14

Dollar Discount Department Store sells three times as much in soft goods, such as clothing and linens, as it sells in hard goods, such as furniture and appliances. If total store sales on Saturday were $180,000, how much of each category was sold?

CHECK YOUR ANSWERS WITH THE SOLUTIONS ON PAGE 150.

© David Zanzinger/Alamy

Best Buy is the largest retailer of consumer electronics in the United States and Canada, with over 155,000 employees. The company operates more than 3,900 stores throughout North America, Europe, China, and now Mexico.

Best Buy stores sell a wide variety of electronic gadgets, movies, music, computers, and appliances. In addition to selling products, the stores offer installation and maintenance services, technical support, and subscriptions for cell phone and Internet services. Fiscal 2009 revenues were $45.02 billion, with net income of over $1 billion.

Source: www.bestbuy.com

Recycling Bins

Municipal solid waste (MSW)—more commonly known as garbage—consists of everyday items we throw away. According to the U.S. Environmental Protection Agency (EPA), in 2008, Americans generated about 250 million tons of trash and recycled and composted 83 million tons of this material. On average, we recycled and composted 1.5 pounds of our individual waste generation of 4.5 pounds per person per day.

Recycling and composting 83 million tons of MSW saved 1.3 quadrillion Btu of energy, the equivalent of more than 10.2 billion gallons of gasoline and reduced CO_2 emissions by 182 million metric tons, comparable to the annual emissions from more than 33 million passenger vehicles.

Source: www.epa.gov

EXAMPLE 15   SOLVING BUSINESS-RELATED EQUATIONS

Yesterday the Valley Vista recycling van picked up a total of 4,500 pounds of material. If newspaper weighed three times as much as aluminum cans and aluminum weighed twice as much as glass, what was the weight of each material?

SOLUTIONSTRATEGY

Reasoning: Glass <u>plus</u> aluminum <u>plus</u> newspaper <u>amounts to</u> the total material, 4,500 pounds.

Hint: Let the least (smallest) element equal X. That way the larger ones will be multiples of X. By doing this, you avoid having fractions in your equation.

$$\text{Let } X = \text{pounds of glass}$$
$$\text{Let } 2X = \text{pounds of aluminum}$$
$$\text{Let } 3(2X) = \text{pounds of newspaper}$$
$$X + 2X + 3(2X) = 4{,}500$$
$$X + 2X + 6X = 4{,}500$$
$$9X = 4{,}500$$
$$\frac{\cancel{9}X}{\cancel{9}} = \frac{4{,}500}{9}$$
$$X = 500$$
$$2X = 2(500) = 1{,}000$$
$$3(2X) = 3(1{,}000) = 3{,}000$$

Glass collected = 500 pounds
Aluminum collected = 1,000 pounds
Newspaper collected = 3,000 pounds

Proof:
$$X + 2X + 3(2X) = 4{,}500$$
$$500 + 2(500) + 3(2\{500\}) = 4{,}500$$
$$500 + 1{,}000 + 3{,}000 = 4{,}500$$
$$4{,}500 = 4{,}500$$

TRYITEXERCISE 15

Last week Comfy Cozy Furniture sold 520 items. It sold twice as many sofas as chairs and four times as many chairs as tables. How many were sold of each product?

CHECK YOUR ANSWERS WITH THE SOLUTIONS ON PAGE 150.

EXAMPLE 16   SOLVING BUSINESS-RELATED EQUATIONS

Chicken Delight sells whole chicken dinners for $12 and half chicken dinners for $8. Yesterday it sold a total of 400 dinners and took in $4,200. How many of each size dinner were sold? What were the dollar sales of each size dinner?

SOLUTIONSTRATEGY

Reasoning: The <u>sum of</u> the price <u>multiplied by</u> the quantity of each item <u>is</u> total sales, $4,200.

Hint: This type of problem requires that we multiply the price of each item by the quantity. We know that a total of 400 dinners were sold; therefore,

$$\text{Let } X = \text{quantity of whole chicken dinners}$$
$$\text{Let } 400 - X = \text{quantity of half chicken dinners}$$

Note: By letting X equal the quantity related to the more expensive item, we avoid dealing with negative numbers.

$$\text{Price times quantity of whole chicken dinners} = \$12X$$
$$\text{Price times quantity of half chicken dinners} = \$8(400 - X)$$

$$12X + 8(400 - X) = 4,200$$
$$12X + 3,200 - 8X = 4,200$$
$$4X + 3,200 = 4,200$$
$$\underline{- 3,200 \quad - 3,200}$$
$$4X = 1,000$$
$$\frac{\cancel{4}X}{\cancel{4}} = \frac{1,000}{4}$$

$$X = 250 \quad \underline{\text{Quantity of whole chicken dinners} = 250}$$
$$400 - X = 400 - 250 = 150 \quad \underline{\text{Quantity of half chicken dinners} = 150}$$

Proof:

$$12X + 8(400 - X) = 4,200$$
$$12(250) + 8(400 - 250) = 4,200$$
$$3,000 + 8(150) = 4,200$$
$$3,000 + 1,200 = 4,200$$
$$\underline{4,200 = 4,200}$$

Now that we have calculated the quantity sold of each size dinner, we can find the dollar sales.

Reasoning: Dollar sales <u>are</u> the price per dinner <u>multiplied by</u> the quantity sold.

Let S = dollar sales

Whole chicken dinners: $\quad S = \$12(250) = \underline{\$3,000 \text{ in sales}}$

Half chicken dinners: $\quad S = \$8(150) = \underline{\$1,200 \text{ in sales}}$

TRYITEXERCISE16

AutoZone sells a regular car battery for $70 and a heavy-duty model for $110. If it sold 40 batteries yesterday for a total of $3,400, how many of each type battery were sold? What were the dollar sales of each type?

CHECK YOUR ANSWERS WITH THE SOLUTIONS ON PAGE 150.

Eddie Seal/Bloomberg via Getty Images

As of August 2009, **AutoZone** operated 4,417 auto parts stores, including 188 in Mexico, with over 60,000 employees. Each store carries an extensive product line, including automotive parts, maintenance items, accessories, and non-automotive products.

In many of its domestic stores, AutoZone also has a commercial sales program that provides credit and delivery of parts and other products to repair garages, dealers, and service stations. Fiscal 2009 sales were over $6.8 billion with net income of over $657 million.

Source: www.autozone.com

UNDERSTANDING AND SOLVING RATIO AND PROPORTION PROBLEMS

5-5

Many business problems and situations are expressed as ratios. A **ratio** is a fraction that describes a comparison of two numbers or quantities. In business, numbers often take on much more meaning when compared with other numbers in the form of a ratio.

For example, a factory has an output of 40 units per hour. Is this good or bad? If we also know that the industry average is 20 units per hour, we can set up a ratio of our factory, 40, compared with the industry average, 20.

$$\frac{\text{Factory}}{\text{Industry}} = \frac{40}{20} = 40:20 \qquad \text{Expressed verbally, we say, "40 to 20."}$$

Because ratios are fractions, we can reduce our fraction and state that our factory output is 2 to 1 over the industry average. If the industry average changed to 40, the ratio would be $\frac{40}{40}$, or 1 to 1. Had the industry average been 80, the ratio would have been $\frac{40}{80}$, or 1 to 2.

Ratios can compare anything: money, weights, measures, output, or individuals. The units do not have to be the same. If we can buy 9 ounces of shampoo for $2, this is actually a ratio of ounces to dollars, or $9:2$.

A **proportion** is a statement showing that two ratios are equal. Proportions are equations, with *as* being the equal sign. For example, we could say, "9 is to 2 as 18 is to 4."

$$\frac{9}{2} = \frac{18}{4} \quad \text{or} \quad 9:2 = 18:4$$

ratio A fraction that describes a comparison of two numbers or quantities. For example, five cats for every three dogs would be a ratio of 5 to 3, written as 5:3.

proportion A mathematical statement showing that two ratios are equal. For example, 9 is to 3 as 3 is to 1, written as $9:3 = 3:1$.

This means that if we can buy 9 ounces for $2, we can buy 18 ounces for $4. Proportions with three knowns and one unknown become a very useful business tool. For example, if we can buy 9 ounces for $2, how many ounces can we buy for $7? This proportion, 9 is to 2 as X is to 7, would be written as

$$\frac{9 \text{ ounces}}{\$2} = \frac{X \text{ ounces}}{\$7} \quad \text{or} \quad 9:2 = X:7$$

STEPS FOR SOLVING PROPORTION PROBLEMS USING CROSS-MULTIPLICATION

STEP 1. Assign a letter to represent the unknown quantity.

STEP 2. Set up the proportion with one ratio (expressed as a fraction) on each side of the equal sign.

STEP 3. Multiply the numerator of the first ratio by the denominator of the second and place the product to the left of the equal sign.

STEP 4. Multiply the denominator of the first ratio by the numerator of the second and place the product to the right of the equal sign.

STEP 5. Solve for the unknown.

EXAMPLE 17 SOLVING PROPORTIONS

On a recent trip, a car used 16 gallons of gasoline to travel 350 miles. At that rate, how many gallons of gasoline would be required to complete a trip of 875 miles?

SOLUTIONSTRATEGY

This situation can be solved by setting up and solving a proportion. The proportion reads:

"16 gallons is to 350 miles as X gallons are to 875 miles"

$$\frac{16}{350} = \frac{X}{875}$$

Using cross-multiplication to solve the proportion,

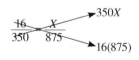

$$350X = 16(875)$$
$$350X = 14{,}000$$
$$X = \frac{14{,}000}{350}$$
$$\underline{X = 40 \text{ gallons}}$$

TRYITEXERCISE 17

If Steve earns $87.50 for 7 hours of work, how much can he expect to earn in a 35-hour week?

CHECK YOUR ANSWER WITH THE SOLUTION ON PAGE 150.

REVIEW EXERCISES

Set up and solve equations for the following business situations.

1. Kathy and Karen work in a boutique. During a sale, Kathy sold eight fewer dresses than Karen did. If together they sold 86 dresses, how many did each sell?

$$X + X - 8 = 86 \qquad \frac{2X}{2} = \frac{94}{2}$$

Karen $= X$ $2X - 8 = 86$

Kathy $= X - 8$ $\underline{+ 8 \quad +8}$ $X = \underline{\underline{47}}$ Karen's sales

          $2X \quad = 94$ $X - 8 = 47 - 8 = \underline{\underline{39}}$ Kathy's sales

2. One-fifth of the employees of Delta Industries, Inc., work in the Southeastern region. If the company employs 252 workers in that region, what is the total number of employees working for the company?

3. Walter's salary this year is $23,400. If this is $1,700 more than he made last year, what was his salary last year?

4. The Book Nook makes four times as much revenue on paperback books as on hardcover books. If last month's sales totaled $124,300, how much was sold of each type book?

5. BHphotovideo.com sells 16-gigabyte Apple iPod Nanos for $190 and 4-gigabyte iPod Shuffles for $80. Last week it sold three times as many Shuffles as Nanos. Combined sales totaled $3,440. How many Nanos and Shuffles did it sell?

6. You are moving to a new home and have rented a truck to assist you with the move. Trailside Truck Rentals charges $39.95 per day plus 68 cents per mile. You will need the truck for 3 days and will travel 460 miles. If you have budgeted $400 for the truck rental, will this amount be sufficient to cover the cost?

The Toy Industry

According to the Toy Industry Association, Inc., in 2008, total toy sales amounted to $21.6 billion. Video games added another $21.4 billion.

Toys"R"Us, Inc., employs nearly 70,000 associates and is the world's leading dedicated toy and baby products retailer. It currently sells merchandise in more than 1,550 stores, including 848 Toys"R"Us and Babies"R"Us stores in the United States and more than 700 international stores in 33 countries.

In August 2009, Toys"R"Us, Inc., acquired the KB Toys brand, which includes its URL, KBToys.com.

Source: www.toysrus.com

7. Kid's Kingdom, a retail toy chain, placed a seasonal order for stuffed animals from Stuffed Stuff, a distributor. Large animals cost $20, and small ones cost $14.

   a. If the total cost of the order was $7,320 for 450 pieces, how many of each size were ordered?

   b. What was the dollar amount of each size ordered?

8. PC Solutions sells regular keyboards for $84 and wireless keyboards for $105. Last week the store sold three times as many regular keyboards as wireless. If total keyboard sales were $4,998, how many of each type were sold?

9. An estate is to be distributed among a wife, three children, and two grandchildren. The children will each receive three times as much as each grandchild, and the wife will receive four times as much as each child. If the estate amounts to $115,000, how much will each person receive?

"THESE ARE THE HAPPIEST YEARS OF MY LIFE, EH?--YOU OBVIOUSLY HAVEN'T MET MY ALGEBRA TEACHER!"

10. E-Z Stop Fast Gas sold $10,957 worth of gasoline yesterday. Regular sold for $2.30 a gallon, and premium sold for $2.55 a gallon. If the station sold 420 more gallons of regular than of premium:

a. How many gallons of each type of gasoline were sold?

b. If the profit on regular gas is $0.18 per gallon and on premium is $0.20 per gallon, what was the station's total profit?

11. Yesterday Tween Teen Fashions had seven less than three-fourths of its sales transactions paid for by credit cards. If 209 transactions were charged, how many total transactions took place?

12. You are the administrator of an annual essay contest scholarship fund. This year a $48,000 college scholarship is being divided between the top two contestants so that the winner receives three times as much as the runner-up. How much will each contestant receive?

13. The Cookie Monster sells oatmeal cookies for $1.30 per pound and peanut butter cookies for $1.60 per pound.

a. If total cookie sales last week amounted to 530 pounds, valued at $755, how many pounds of each type of cookie were sold?

b. What dollar amount of each type was sold?

14. If a 48-piece set of stainless steel flatware costs $124.80 at Bed Bath & Beyond, what is the cost per piece?

15. The U.S. Congress has a total of 535 members. If the number of representatives is 65 less than five times the number of senators, how many senators and how many representatives are in Congress?

Bed Bath & Beyond Inc., together with its subsidiaries, operates a chain of retail stores. It sells a range of domestic merchandise (e.g., bed linens and related items, bath items, and kitchen textiles) and home furnishings, including kitchen and tabletop items, fine tabletop, basic housewares, and general home furnishings.

16. One-ninth of Polymer Plastics' sales are made in New England. If New England sales amount to $600,000, what are the total sales of the company?

As of February 27, 2010, the company operated 1,100 stores and had 41,000 full-time employees. Fiscal 2010 revenues were $7.82 billion with net income over $600 million.

Source: Yahoo Finance

17. You are the shipping manager for World Imports. Calculate the total cost to ship an order of glassware weighing 1,860 pounds if the breakdown is $0.04 per pound for packing, $0.02 per pound for insurance, $0.13 per pound for transportation, and $132.40 for the crate.

18. Scott Mason purchased a 4-unit apartment building as an investment before he retired. From the rent he collects each month, Scott pays out $600 for expenses. How much rent must he charge for each of the 4 apartments if he wants to make $500 profit each month? The amount of rent is the same for each of the apartments.

19. You are the facilities director of the Carnival Shopping Mall. You have been asked to rope off a rectangular section of the parking lot for a car show next weekend. The area to be roped off is 250 feet long by 300 feet wide. Rubber traffic cones are to be placed every 25 feet around the lot. How many cones are needed?

Use ratio and proportion to solve the following business situations.

20. If the interest on a $4,600 loan is $370, what would be the interest on a loan of $9,660?

21. At Fancy Fruit Distributors, Inc., the ratio of fruits to vegetables sold is 5 to 3. If 1,848 pounds of vegetables are sold, how many pounds of fruit are sold?

FedEx Office (formerly FedEx Kinko's and earlier simply Kinko's) is a chain of stores that provides a retail outlet for FedEx Express and FedEx Ground shipping as well as printing, copying, and binding services. Many stores also provide videoconferencing facilities.

The primary clientele consists of small business and home office clients. There are more than 2,000 centers in Asia, Australia, Europe, and North America. With over $2 billion in revenues and 20,000 employees, the company is the 7th largest printing company in North America. FedEx Office's primary competitors include The UPS Store, OfficeMax, Alpha Graphics, Staples, Sir Speedy, and VistaPrint.
Source: www.fedex.com

22. A local FedEx Office store has a press that can print 5,800 brochures per hour. How many can be printed during a $3\frac{1}{4}$-hour run?

23. A recipe for turkey stuffing calls for three eggs for every $12\frac{1}{2}$ ounces of corn bread. If a dinner party requires $87\frac{1}{2}$ ounces of corn bread for stuffing, how many eggs should be used?

24. An architect uses a scale of $\frac{3}{4}$ inch to represent 1 foot on a blueprint for a building. If the east wall of the building is 36 feet long, how long will the line be on the blueprint?

25. According to the *New York Daily News*, in December 2008, nearly 300,000 people had applied for the approximately 7,000 available jobs in President Barack Obama's new administration. At that rate, on average, how many people had applied for each job? Round to the nearest whole person.

26. If auto insurance costs $6.52 per $1,000 of coverage, what is the cost to insure a car valued at $17,500?

27. Blue Sky International Airport handles passenger to cargo traffic in a ratio of 8 to 5. If 45 cargo planes landed yesterday, how many passenger flights came in?

28. Eighty ounces of Lazy Lawn fertilizer covers 1,250 square feet of lawn.
   a. How many ounces would be required to cover a 4,000-square-foot lawn?

   b. If Lazy Lawn costs $1.19 for a 32-ounce bag, what is the total cost to fertilize the lawn?

29. You have just been hired as advertising manager of *The Daily Chronicle*, a not-very-successful newspaper. In the past, *The Chronicle* contained one-half advertising and one-half news stories. Current industry research indicates a newspaper must have three times as much advertising as news stories to make money. In addition, the advertising must be divided in the following ratio: 5 to 3 to 1, retail advertising to national advertising to classified advertising. *The Chronicle* is typically 48 pages in length.

   a. How many pages should be advertising, and how many should be news stories?

b. Based on the industry ratios, how should the pages be divided among the three types of advertising?

Photo by Robert Brechner

c. After you made the changes in the advertising distributions ratios, your newspaper began making a profit—for the first time in years. If last year's total advertising revenue was $810,000, how much was earned by each type of advertising?

Top 10 Weekday Newspapers by Circulation – 2009

1. *The Wall Street Journal*	2,024,269
2. *USA Today*	1,900,116
3. *The New York Times*	927,851
4. *Los Angeles Times*	657,467
5. *The Washington Post*	582,844
6. *New York Daily News*	544,167
7. *New York Post*	508,042
8. *Chicago Tribune*	465,892
9. *Houston Chronicle*	384,419
10. *The Philadelphia Enquirer*	361,480

Source: Audit Bureau of Circulations

d. When you accepted the job of advertising manager, in addition to your salary, you were promised a $\frac{1}{50}$ share of each year's revenue from retail and classified advertising and a $\frac{1}{75}$ share for national. What bonus will you receive for last year's sales?

BUSINESS DECISION: HELPING CAR MANUFACTURERS— SAVING THE PLANET!

30. According to *USA Today*, in April 2009, President Obama announced that the government was stepping up efforts to help U.S. car manufacturers by purchasing 17,600 new fuel-efficient vehicles for its fleet. The new fleet, which includes 2,500 hybrid sedans, will be paid for with $285 million from the economic stimulus package.

As an accountant in the White House Budget Office (WHBO), you have been asked to calculate the following:

a. If each hybrid vehicle will have an average cost of $24,000, what will be the average cost per non-hybrid vehicle? Round to the nearest whole dollar.

b. Further, the White House said that by replacing less efficient vehicles, the government will reduce gasoline consumption by 1.3 million gallons per year and prevent 26 million pounds of carbon dioxide from entering the atmosphere. On average, how many gallons of gasoline and how many pounds of carbon dioxide will be "saved" per year per vehicle? Round to the nearest whole gallon and whole pound.

CHAPTER

5

CHAPTER SUMMARY

Section I: Solving Basic Equations

Topic	Important Concepts	Illustrative Examples
Solving Equations for the Unknown and Proving the Solution **Performance Objective 5-2, Page 126**	To solve equations, we must move or transpose all the unknowns to one side and isolate all the knowns on the other side. It is customary for the unknowns to be on the left side and the knowns to be on the right side, such as $X = 33$. To solve for the unknown value, apply an inverse, or opposite, operation to both sides of the equation. **Operation—Opposite** Addition $\longrightarrow$ Subtraction Subtraction $\longrightarrow$ Addition Multiplication $\longrightarrow$ Division Division $\longrightarrow$ Multiplication	Solve the equation $R + 7 = 12$ The equation indicates addition; therefore, use the opposite operation: subtract 7 from both sides: $$\begin{aligned} R + 7 &= 12 \\ -7 &= -7 \\ \hline R &= 5 \end{aligned}$$ $\underline{R = 5}$ Solve the equation $W - 4 = 30$ The equation indicates subtraction; therefore, use the opposite operation: add 4 to both sides: $$\begin{aligned} W - 4 &= 30 \\ +4 &= +4 \\ \hline W &= 34 \end{aligned}$$ $\underline{W = 34}$ Solve the equation $3G = 18$ The equation indicates multiplication; therefore, use the opposite operation: divide both side by 3: $$\frac{3G}{3} = \frac{18}{3}$$ $\underline{G = 6}$ Solve the equation $\frac{T}{5} = 9$ The equation indicates division; therefore, use the opposite operation: multiply both sides by 5: $$(5)\frac{T}{5} = 9(5)$$ $\underline{T = 45}$
Solving Equations Containing Multiple Operations **Performance Objective 5-2, Page 129**	Order of Operations: To solve equations with more than one operation, transpose the terms by performing the *additions* and *subtractions* first, then the *multiplications* and *divisions*.	Solve the equation $5X - 4 = 51$ $$\begin{aligned} 5X - 4 &= 51 \\ +4 &= +4 \\ \hline 5X &= 55 \end{aligned}$$ $$\frac{5X}{5} = \frac{55}{5}$$ $\underline{X = 11}$
Solving Equations Containing Parentheses **Performance Objective 5-2, Page 130**	To remove parentheses, multiply the coefficient by each term inside the parentheses. Sign Rules: When like signs are multiplied, the result is positive. For example, $5(5) = 25$ and $-5(-5) = 25$. When unlike signs are multiplied, the result is negative. For example, $5(-5) = -25$.	Solve the equation $3(4S - 5) = 9$ To remove the parentheses, multiply the coefficient, 3, by both terms inside the parentheses: $$\begin{aligned} 3(4S - 5) &= 9 \\ 3(4S) - 3(5) &= 9 \\ 12S - 15 &= 9 \\ 12S &= 24 \end{aligned}$$ $\underline{S = 2}$
Solving Equations by Combining Multiple Unknowns **Performance Objective 5-2, Page 131**	To combine unknowns in an equation, add or subtract their coefficients and retain their common variable. For example, $6B + 4B = 10B$. If the unknowns are on opposite sides of the equal sign, first move them all to one side.	Solve the equation $3B + 5 - B = 7$ $$\begin{aligned} 3B + 5 - B &= 7 \\ 2B + 5 &= 7 \\ 2B &= 2 \end{aligned}$$ $\underline{B = 1}$
Writing Expressions and Equations from Written Statements **Performance Objective 5-3, Page 132**	Expressions and equations are created from written statements by identifying the unknowns and the knowns and determining the mathematical relationship between them. The variables are assigned letters of the alphabet. The relationship between the knowns and the unknowns involve addition, subtraction, multiplication, and division or a combination of two or more. Key words indicate what relationship exists between the terms (see list, page 132). If the written statement has a verb such as *is*, the statement is an equation.	A number <u>increased by</u> 44 $\qquad \underline{X + 44}$ 6 <u>more than</u> 3 <u>times</u> U $\qquad \underline{3U + 6}$ 3 <u>times</u> the <u>sum of</u> C and 9 $\qquad \underline{3(C + 9)}$ 7 <u>less than</u> 4 <u>times</u> M <u>leaves</u> 55. $\quad \underline{4M - 7 = 55}$ 2 <u>less than</u> 5 <u>times</u> a number <u>plus</u> 9 <u>times</u> that number <u>is</u> 88. $\underline{5X - 2 + 9X = 88}$

Section II: Using Equations to Solve Business-Related Word Problems

Topic	Important Concepts	Illustrative Examples
Solving Business-Related Equations **Performance Objective 5-4, Page 135**	Example 1: Mary and Beth sell furniture at Contempo Designs. Last week Mary sold eight fewer recliner chairs than Beth sold. Together they sold 30. How many chairs did each sell?	Solution: *Reasoning*: Beth's sales plus Mary's sales equal total sales, 30. Let X = Beth's sales Let $X - 8$ = Mary's sales $X + X - 8 = 30$ $\quad 2X - 8 = 30$ $\qquad 2X = 38$ $\qquad\quad X = 19$ Chairs—Beth's sales $\quad X - 8 = 11$ Chairs—Mary's sales
	Example 2: One-fourth of the employees at Atlas Distributors work in the accounting division. If there are 45 workers in this division, how many people work for Atlas?	Solution: *Reasoning*: $\frac{1}{4}$ of the total employees are in accounting, 45. Let X = total employees Let $\frac{1}{4}X$ = accounting employees $\quad \frac{1}{4}X = 45$ $(4)\,\frac{1}{4}X = 45(4)$ $\qquad X = 180$ Total employees
	Example 3: Frontier Industries, a small manufacturing company, made a profit of \$315,000 last year. If the nine investors decide to evenly split this profit, how much will each receive?	Solution: *Reasoning*: Each investor's share is the total profit divided by the number of investors. Let X = each investor's share $\quad X = \dfrac{315{,}000}{9}$ $\quad X = \$35{,}000$ Investor's share
	Example 4: The Pet Carnival sells four times as much in cat supplies as in fish supplies. If total sales last week were \$6,800, how much of each category was sold?	Solution: *Reasoning*: Fish supplies plus cat supplies equal total, \$6,800. Let X = fish supplies Let $4X$ = cat supplies $X + 4X = 6{,}800$ $\quad 5X = 6{,}800$ $\qquad X = \$1{,}360$ Fish supplies $\quad 4X = \$5{,}440$ Cat supplies
	Example 5: The Male Image, a clothing store, sells suits for \$275 and sport coats for \$180. Yesterday it made 20 sales, for a total of \$4,360. a. How many suits and how many sport coats were sold? b. What were the dollar sales of each?	Solution a: *Reasoning*: The sum of the price multiplied by the quantity of each item is the total sales, \$4,360. Let X = suit sales Let $20 - X$ = sport coat sales $\quad 275X + 180(20 - X) = 4{,}360$ $\quad 275X + 3{,}600 - 180X = 4{,}360$ $\qquad\quad 95X + 3{,}600 = 4{,}360$ $\qquad\qquad\qquad 95X = 760$ $X = 8$ Number of suits sold $20 - X = 12$ Sports coats sold Solution b: 8 suits $\times$ \$275 each = \$2,200 Suits sales 12 coats $\times$ \$180 each = \$2,160 Coats sales

Section II (continued)

Topic	Important Concepts	Illustrative Examples

Understanding and Solving Ratio and Proportion Problems
 	
Performance Objective 5-5, Page 139
	A ratio is a fraction that describes a comparison of two numbers or quantities.
	
	  A proportion is a statement showing that two ratios are equal. Proportions are equations with "as" being the equal sign and "is to" being the division bar.
	
	  Proportion problems are solved by cross-multiplication:
	1. Let X represent the unknown quantity.
	2. Set up the equation with one ratio on each side of the equal sign.
	3. Multiply the numerator of the first ratio by the denominator of the second and place the product to the left of the equal sign.
	4. Multiply the denominator of the first ratio by the numerator of the second and place the product to the right of the equal sign.
	5. Solve the equation for X.
		Example 1:
		12 is to 42 as 6 is to X
		$\dfrac{12}{42} = \dfrac{6}{X}$
		$12X = 42(6)$
		$12X = 252$
		$\underline{X = 21}$
		
		Example 2:
		If Larry works 6 hours for \$150, how much can he expect to earn in a 42-hour week?
		$\dfrac{6}{150} = \dfrac{42}{X}$
		$6X = 150(42)$
		$6X = 6,300$
		$\underline{X = \$1,050}$ Larry's salary for 42 hours of work

TRY IT: EXERCISE SOLUTIONS FOR CHAPTER 5

1a.
$$W + 10 = \ \ 25$$
$$\begin{aligned}W + 10 &= \ \ 25\\ -10 \ \ &\ -10\\ \hline W \ \ \ \ \ &= \ \ 15\end{aligned}$$
$$\underline{W = \ \ 15}$$

Proof:
$$W + 10 = 25$$
$$15 + 10 = 25$$
$$\underline{25 = 25}$$

1b.
$$Q + 30 = \ \ 100$$
$$\begin{aligned}Q + 30 &= \ \ 100\\ -30 \ \ &\ -30\\ \hline Q \ \ \ \ \ &= \ \ 70\end{aligned}$$
$$\underline{Q = \ \ 70}$$

Proof:
$$Q + 30 = 100$$
$$70 + 30 = 100$$
$$\underline{100 = 100}$$

2a.
$$A - 8 = \ \ 40$$
$$\begin{aligned}A - 8 &= \ \ 40\\ +8 \ \ &\ +8\\ \hline A \ \ \ \ \ &= \ \ 48\end{aligned}$$
$$\underline{A = \ \ 48}$$

Proof:
$$A - 8 = 40$$
$$48 - 8 = 40$$
$$\underline{40 = 40}$$

2b.
$$L - 3 = \ \ 7$$
$$\begin{aligned}L - 3 &= \ \ 7\\ +3 \ \ &\ +3\\ \hline L \ \ \ \ \ &= \ \ 10\end{aligned}$$
$$\underline{L = \ \ 10}$$

Proof:
$$L - 3 = 7$$
$$10 - 3 = 7$$
$$\underline{7 = 7}$$

3a.
$$15L = 75$$
$$\frac{\cancel{15}L}{\cancel{15}} = \frac{75}{15}$$
$$\underline{L = 5}$$

Proof:
$$15L = 75$$
$$15(5) = 75$$
$$\underline{75 = 75}$$

3b.
$$16F = 80$$
$$\frac{\cancel{16}F}{\cancel{16}} = \frac{80}{16}$$
$$\underline{F = 5}$$

Proof:
$$16F = 80$$
$$16(5) = 80$$
$$\underline{80 = 80}$$

4a.
$$\frac{Z}{8} = 2$$
$$(8)\frac{Z}{8} = 2(8)$$
$$\underline{Z = 16}$$

Proof:
$$\frac{Z}{8} = 2$$
$$\frac{16}{8} = 2$$
$$\underline{2 = 2}$$

4b.
$$\frac{C}{9} = 9$$
$$(9)\frac{C}{9} = 9(9)$$
$$\underline{C = 81}$$

Proof:
$$\frac{C}{9} = 9$$
$$\frac{81}{9} = 9$$
$$\underline{9 = 9}$$

5a.
$$12N + 14 = \ \ 50$$
$$\begin{aligned}12N + 14 &= \ \ 50\\ -14 \ \ &\ -14\\ \hline 12N \ \ \ \ &= \ \ 36\end{aligned}$$
$$\frac{\cancel{12}N}{\cancel{12}} = \frac{36}{12}$$
$$\underline{N = 3}$$

Proof:
$$12N + 14 = 50$$
$$12(3) + 14 = 50$$
$$36 + 14 = 50$$
$$\underline{50 = 50}$$

5b.
$$3W - 4 = \ \ 26$$
$$\begin{aligned}3W - 4 &= \ \ 26\\ +4 \ \ &\ +4\\ \hline 3W \ \ \ \ &= \ \ 30\end{aligned}$$
$$\frac{3W}{3} = \frac{30}{3}$$
$$\underline{W = 10}$$

Proof:
$$3W - 4 = 26$$
$$3(10) - 4 = 26$$
$$30 - 4 = 26$$
$$\underline{26 = 26}$$

6a.
$$\frac{F}{3} - 6 = \ \ 2$$
$$\begin{aligned}\frac{F}{3} - 6 &= \ \ 2\\ +6 \ \ &\ +6\\ \hline \frac{F}{3} \ \ \ &= \ \ 8\end{aligned}$$
$$(3)\frac{F}{3} = 8(3)$$
$$\underline{F = 24}$$

Proof:
$$\frac{F}{3} - 6 = 2$$
$$\frac{24}{3} - 6 = 2$$
$$8 - 6 = 2$$
$$\underline{2 = 2}$$

6b.
$$\frac{Z}{5} + 15 = \ \ 24$$
$$\begin{aligned}\frac{Z}{5} + 15 &= \ \ 24\\ -15 \ \ &\ -15\\ \hline \frac{Z}{5} \ \ \ &= \ \ 9\end{aligned}$$
$$(5)\frac{Z}{5} = 9(5)$$
$$\underline{Z = 45}$$

Proof:
$$\frac{Z}{5} + 15 = 24$$
$$\frac{45}{5} + 15 = 24$$
$$9 + 15 = 24$$
$$\underline{24 = 24}$$

7a.

$$4(5G + 6) = 64$$
$$20G + 24 = 64$$
$$20G + 24 = 64$$
$$\underline{\quad -24 \quad -24\quad}$$
$$20G \quad = 40$$
$$\frac{20G}{20} = \frac{40}{20}$$
$$\underline{G = 2}$$

Proof:

$$4(5G + 6) = 64$$
$$4(5\{2\} + 6) = 64$$
$$4(10 + 6) = 64$$
$$4(16) = 64$$
$$\underline{64 = 64}$$

7b.

$$6(3H - 5) = 42$$
$$18H - 30 = 42$$
$$18H - 30 = 42$$
$$\underline{\quad +30 \quad +30\quad}$$
$$18H \quad = 72$$
$$\frac{18H}{18} = \frac{72}{18}$$
$$\underline{H = 4}$$

Proof:

$$6(3H - 5) = 42$$
$$6(3\{4\} - 5) = 42$$
$$6(12 - 5) = 42$$
$$6(7) = 42$$
$$\underline{42 = 42}$$

8a.

$$X + 3 = 18 - 4X$$
$$X + 3 = 18 - 4X$$
$$\underline{+4X \qquad\quad + 4X}$$
$$5X + 3 = 18$$
$$5X + 3 = 18$$
$$\underline{\quad - 3 \quad -3\quad}$$
$$5X \quad = 15$$
$$\frac{5X}{5} = \frac{15}{5}$$
$$\underline{X = 3}$$

Proof:

$$X + 3 = 18 - 4X$$
$$3 + 3 = 18 - 4(3)$$
$$6 = 18 - 12$$
$$\underline{6 = 6}$$

8b.

$$9S + 8 - S = 2(2S + 8)$$
$$9S + 8 - S = 4S + 16$$
$$8S + 8 = 4S + 16$$
$$8S + 8 = 4S + 16$$
$$\underline{\quad - 4S \qquad\quad -4S\quad}$$
$$4S + 8 = \qquad + 16$$
$$4S + 8 = 16$$
$$\underline{\quad - 8 \quad -8\quad}$$
$$4S \quad = 8$$
$$\frac{4S}{4} = \frac{8}{4}$$
$$\underline{S = 2}$$

Proof:

$$9S + 8 - S = 2(2S + 8)$$
$$9(2) + 8 - 2 = 2(2\{2\} + 8)$$
$$18 + 8 - 2 = 2(4 + 8)$$
$$24 = 2(12)$$
$$\underline{24 = 24}$$

9a. The sum of twice E and 9

$$\underline{2E + 9}$$

9b. 6 times N divided by Z

$$\underline{\frac{6N}{Z}}$$

9c. 8 less than half of F

$$\underline{\frac{1}{2}F - 8}$$

9d. \$45.75 more than the product of X and Y

$$\underline{XY + \$45.75}$$

9e. The difference of Q and 44

$$\underline{Q - 44}$$

9f. R times A times B

$$\underline{RAB}$$

10a. What number increased by 32 yields 125?

$$\underline{X + 32 = 125}$$

10b. 21 less than twice C gives 9.

$$\underline{2C - 21 = 9}$$

10c. 5 more than 6 times a number plus 3 times that number is 25.

$$\underline{6X + 5 + 3X = 25}$$

10d. The cost of G gallons at \$1.33 per gallon equals \$34.40.

$$\underline{\$1.33G = \$34.40}$$

10e. The area of a rectangle is the length times the width.

$$\underline{A = LW}$$

10f. What number less 12 is the average of A, B, and C?

$$\underline{X - 12 = \frac{A + B + C}{3}}$$

11. *Reasoning:* Don's sales and Chuck's sales equal total sales, 44.
Let X = Chuck's sales
Let $X - 12$ = Don's sales

$$X + X - 12 = 44$$
$$2X - 12 = 44$$
$$2X = 56$$
$$\frac{2X}{2} = \frac{56}{2}$$
$$X = 28 \qquad \underline{\text{Chuck's sales} = 28 \text{ Alarm systems}}$$
$$X - 12 = 28 - 12 = 16 \qquad \underline{\text{Don's sales} = 16 \text{ Alarm systems}}$$

Proof:

$$X + X - 12 = 44$$
$$28 + 28 - 12 = 44$$
$$\underline{44 = 44}$$

12. *Reasoning:* $\frac{1}{3}$ of the total checking accounts are interest-earning, 2,500.
Let C = total checking accounts

$$\frac{1}{3}C = 2{,}500$$
$$(3)\frac{1}{3}C = 2{,}500(3)$$
$$C = 7{,}500$$
$$\underline{\text{Total checking accounts} = 7{,}500}$$

Proof:

$$\frac{1}{3}C = 2{,}500$$
$$\frac{1}{3}(7{,}500) = 2{,}500$$
$$\underline{2{,}500 = 2{,}500}$$

13. *Reasoning:* Weight per carton equals the total weight divided by the number of cartons.

Let W = weight per carton

$W = \dfrac{7{,}482}{58}$

$W = 129$

Proof:

$W = \dfrac{7{,}482}{58}$

$129 = \dfrac{7{,}482}{58}$

Weight per carton = 129 pounds

$129 = 129$

14. *Reasoning:* Soft goods plus hard goods equals total store sales, $180,000.

Let X = hard goods

Let $3X$ = soft goods

$X + 3X = \$180{,}000$

$4X = 180{,}000$

$\dfrac{4X}{4} = \dfrac{180{,}000}{4}$

$X = 45{,}000$ Hard goods = $45,000

$3X = 3(45{,}000) = 135{,}000$ Soft goods = $135,000

Proof: $X + 3X = 180{,}000$

$45{,}000 + 3(45{,}000) = 180{,}000$

$45{,}000 + 135{,}000 = 180{,}000$

$180{,}000 = 180{,}000$

15. *Reasoning:* Tables plus chairs plus sofas equals total items sold, 520.

Let X = tables

Let $4X$ = chairs

Let $2(4X)$ = sofas

$X + 4X + 2(4X) = 520$

$X + 4X + 8X = 520$

$13X = 520$

$\dfrac{13X}{13} = \dfrac{520}{13}$

$X = 40$

$4X = 4(40) = 160$

$2(4X) = 2(4\{40\}) = 2(160) = 320$

Tables sold = 40

Chairs sold = 160

Sofas sold = 320

Proof:

$X + 4X + 2(4X) = 520$

$40 + 4(40) + 2(4\{40\}) = 520$

$40 + 160 + 2(160) = 520$

$40 + 160 + 320 = 520$

$520 = 520$

16. *Reasoning:* The sum of the price of each item multiplied by the quantity of each item is the total sales, $3,400.

Remember: Let X equal the more expensive item, thereby avoiding negative numbers.

Let X = Quantity of heavy-duty batteries

Let $40 - X$ = Quantity of regular batteries

Price times quantity of heavy-duty batteries = $110X$

Price times quantity of regular batteries = $70(40 - X)$

$110X + 70(40 - X) = 3{,}400$

$110X + 2{,}800 - 70X = 3{,}400$

$40X + 2{,}800 = 3{,}400$

$40X = 600$

$\dfrac{40X}{40} = \dfrac{600}{40}$

$X = 15$

$40 - X = 40 - 15 = 25$

Proof:

$110X + 70(40 - X) = 3{,}400$

$110(15) + 70(40 - 15) = 3{,}400$

$1{,}650 + 70(25) = 3{,}400$

$1{,}650 + 1{,}750 = 3{,}400$

$3{,}400 = 3{,}400$

Quantity of heavy-duty batteries = 15

Quantity of regular batteries = 25

Now that we have calculated the quantity of each size battery, we can find the dollar sales.

Reasoning: Dollar sales are the price per battery multiplied by the quantity sold.

Let S = dollar sales

Heavy-duty battery: $S = \$110(15) = \$1{,}650$ in sales

Regular battery: $S = \$70(25) = \$1{,}750$ in sales

17. $\dfrac{87.50}{7} = \dfrac{X}{35}$

$7X = 87.50(35)$

$7X = 3{,}062.50$

$\dfrac{7X}{7} = \dfrac{3{,}062.50}{7}$

$X = 437.50$ Steve would earn $437.50 for 35 hours of work.

Proof: $\dfrac{87.50}{7} = \dfrac{X}{35}$

$\dfrac{87.50}{7} = \dfrac{437.50}{35}$

$12.50 = 12.50$

CONCEPT REVIEW

1. A(n) ＿＿ is a mathematical statement describing a real-world situation in which letters represent number quantities. (5-1)

2. A mathematical statement expressing a relationship of equality is known as a(n) ＿＿. (5-1)

3. The parts of an equation that are *given* are called the constants, or ＿＿. (5-1)

4. The variables, or unknowns, of an equation are represented by letters of the ＿＿. (5-1)

5. The numerical value of the unknown that makes an equation true is called the ＿＿, or ＿＿. (5-1)

6. A coefficient is a number or quantity placed before another quantity, indicating ＿＿. (5-2)

7. To transpose means to bring a term from one side of an equation to the other. When addition or subtraction is used for moving the term, a corresponding change of ＿＿ occurs. (5-2)

8. List the "order of operations" for solving equations. (5-2)

9. To prove the solution of an equation, we substitute the solution for the ＿＿ in the original equation. (5-2)

10. When writing an equation from a written statement, a verb such as *is* represents the ＿＿ ＿＿ in the equation. (5-3)

11. When writing an equation from a written statement, the word *difference* means ＿＿, while the word *of* means ＿＿. (5-3)

12. A comparison of two quantities by division is known as a(n) ＿＿. (5-5)

13. A mathematical statement showing that two ratios are equal is known as a(n) ＿＿. (5-5)

14. Proportions are solved using a process known as ＿＿ multiplication. (5-5)

CHAPTER

5

ASSESSMENT TEST

Solve the following equations for the unknown and prove your solutions.

1. $T + 45 = 110$

2. $G - 24 = 75$

3. $11K = 165$

4. $3(2C - 5) = 45$

5. $8X - 15 = 49$

6. $\dfrac{S}{7} = 12$

7. $B + 5 = 61 - 6B$

8. $\dfrac{N}{4} - 7 = 8$

9. $4(3X + 8) = 212$

For the following statements, underline the key words and translate into *expressions*.

10. 15 less than one-ninth of P

11. The ＿＿＿＿ of $4R$ and 108

12. 3 times the quantity of H less 233

13. 24 more than the product of Z and W

For the following statements, underline the key words and translate into *equations*.

14. A number decreased by 4 is 25.

15. A number totals 4 times C and L.

CHAPTER 5

16. The cost of Q at \$4.55 each is \$76.21.   **17.** 14 less than $3F$ leaves 38.

18. The sum of 2 more than 6 times a number and 7 times that number is that number decreased by 39.

Set up and solve equations for each of the following business situations.

19. At a recent boat show, Boater's Paradise sold five more boats than Pelican Marine sold. If together they sold 33 boats, how many were sold by each company?

20. At TelePower Plus, long-distance phone calls to China cost \$0.59 for the first minute and \$0.25 for each additional minute plus an additional roaming charge of \$2.50. If the total charge of a call to Beijing was \$11.84, how long did the call last?

21. Discount Electronics ordered three dozen cell phones from the manufacturer. If the total order amounted to \$1,980, what was the cost of each phone?

22. The Cupcake Café makes $4\frac{1}{2}$ times as much revenue on doughnuts as muffins. If total sales were \$44,000 for May, what dollar amount of each was sold?

23. A regular lightbulb uses 20 watts less than twice the power of an energy-saver lightbulb. If the regular bulb uses 170 watts, how much does the energy-saver bulb use?

24. Do It Best Hardware is offering a 140-piece mechanic's tool set plus a \$65 tool chest for \$226. What is the cost per tool?

25. En Vogue Menswear ordered short-sleeve shirts for \$23.00 each and long-sleeve shirts for \$28.50 each from Hugo Boss.

  a. If the total order amounted to \$9,862.50 for 375 shirts, how many of each were ordered?

  b. What was the dollar amount of each type of shirt ordered?

Photo by Robert Brechner

Do it Best Corp. engages in the wholesale distribution of hardware, lumber, builder supplies, and related products. The company is a member-owned cooperative and is guided by the members of the board of directors. This group is entirely composed of and elected by Do it Best Corp. stockholders—those hardware, lumber, and home center store owners who make up the 4,100 member-retailers in the United States and in 45 countries around the world. In 2009, member purchases were close to \$3 billion.

Sources: www.doitbestcorp.com and www.businessweek.com

26. Austin and Kaitlyn Kojan invested $195,000 in a business venture. If Kaitlyn invested $2\frac{1}{4}$ times as much as Austin invested, how much did each invest?

27. You are planning to advertise your boat for sale on the Internet. *The Boat Mart* charges $1.30 for a photo plus $0.12 per word. *Boat Bargains* charges $1.80 for a photo plus $0.10 per word. For what number of words will the charges be the same?

28. A Cold Stone Creamery ice cream shop sells sundaes for $3.60 and banana splits for $4.25. The shop sells four times as many sundaes as banana splits.

   a. If total sales amount to $3,730 last weekend, how many of each dish were sold?

   b. What were the dollar sales of each?

Use ratio and proportion to solve the following business situations.

29. At Performance Sporting Goods, the inventory ratio of equipment to clothing is 8 to 5. If the clothing inventory amounts to $65,000, what is the amount of the equipment inventory?

30. You are interested in purchasing a wide-screen television set at Target. On this type of TV, the ratio of the width of the screen to the height of the screen is 16 to 9. If a certain model you are considering has a screen width of 48 inches, what would be the height of this screen?

31. The directions on a bag of powdered driveway sealant call for the addition of 5 quarts of water for every 30 pounds of sealant. How much water should be added if only 20 pounds of sealant will be used?

Cold Stone Creamery, Inc., is a private company that manufactures ice cream, cakes, smoothies, and shakes. In 1988, Donald and Susan Sutherland opened the first Cold Stone Creamery in Tempe, Arizona. Today there are more than 1,400 stores, with operations in the United States, Puerto Rico, Guam, Japan, Korea, China, and Taiwan.

   As of May 2007, Cold Stone Creamery, Inc., was acquired by Kahala Corp., one of the fastest-growing franchising companies in North America. The initial fee for opening a Cold Stone franchise is $42,000, with a total investment between $294,250 and $438,850.

Sources: www.coldstonecreamery.com, www.businessweek.com, http://kahalacorp.com

32. Angela Hatcher is planting flower bulbs in her garden for this coming summer. She intends to plant 1 bulb for every 5 square inches of flower bed.

   a. How many flower bulbs will she need for an area measuring 230 square inches?

   b. If the price is $1.77 for every 2 bulbs, how much will she spend on the flower bulbs?

CHAPTER 5

33. The Pizza Palace makes 30 pizzas every 2 hours to accommodate the lunch crowd.

    a. If lunch lasts 3 hours, how many pizzas does Pizza Palace make?

    b. If each pizza can serve 4 people, how many people are served during the 3-hour lunch period?

BUSINESS DECISION: DETERMINING THE "BEST BUY"

34. One special type of ratio is known as a *rate*. A rate is a ratio that compares two quantities that have different units, such as miles per hour, calories per serving, pounds per square inch, and price per unit. In consumer economics, expressing prices as "price per unit" allows us to determine the "best buy" when comparing various shopping choices. All else being equal, the best buy is the choice with the *lowest* price per unit (unit price).

    Donna Kelsch is comparing dry cat food brands for her cats Nicki and Nasty. If Nicki and Nasty's favorite, Funny Fish, comes in the three sizes listed below, which size is the best buy? Hint: Determine the unit price for each size. Round to the nearest cent if necessary.

Size	Price	Unit Price
5 pounds	$12.25	
10 pounds	$21.90	
20 pounds	$38.50	

COLLABORATIVE LEARNING ACTIVITY

Using Formulas in Business

Have each member of the team speak with someone in one of the following professions to determine how the person uses standardized formulas in his or her business.

a. Store owner or manager

b. Real estate or insurance salesperson

c. Advertising or marketing manager

d. Production manager

e. Accountant

f. Banker

g. Stockbroker

h. Additional choice: _____

istockphoto.com/Alpamayo Software, Inc.

Percents and Their Applications in Business

PERFORMANCE OBJECTIVES

SECTION I: Understanding and Converting Percents

6-1: Converting percents to decimals and decimals to percents (p. 156)

6-2: Converting percents to fractions and fractions to percents (p. 158)

SECTION II: Using the Percentage Formula to Solve Business Problems

6-3: Solving for the portion (p. 162)

6-4: Solving for the rate (p. 164)

6-5: Solving for the base (p. 166)

SECTION III: Solving Other Business Problems Involving Percents

6-6: Determining rate of increase or decrease (p. 171)

6-7: Determining amounts in increase or decrease situations (p. 174)

6-8: Understanding and solving problems involving percentage points (p. 177)

SECTION I

6 UNDERSTANDING AND CONVERTING PERCENTS

Percents are commonly used in retailing to advertise discounts.

percent A way of representing the parts of a whole. Percent means "per hundred" or "parts per hundred."

percent sign The symbol, %, used to represent percents. For example, 1 percent would be written 1%.

It takes only a glance at the business section of a newspaper or an annual report of a company to see how extensively percents are applied in business. Percents are the primary way of measuring change among business variables. For example, a business might report "revenue is up 6% this year" or "expenses have been cut by 2.3% this month." Interest rates, commissions, and many taxes are expressed in percent form. You may have heard phrases like these: "Sunnyside Bank charged 12% on the loan," "A real estate broker made 5% commission on the sale of the property," or "The state charges a $6\frac{1}{2}$% sales tax." Even price changes are frequently advertised as percents, "Sears Dishwasher Sale—All Models, 25% off!"

To this point, we have learned that fractions and decimals are ways of representing parts of a whole. Percents are another way of expressing quantity with relation to a whole. **Percent** means "per hundred" or "parts per hundred" and is represented by the **percent sign, %.**

Percents are numbers equal to a fraction with a denominator of 100. Five percent, for example, means five parts out of 100 and may be written in the following ways:

$$5 \text{ percent} \qquad 5\% \qquad 5 \text{ hundredths} \qquad \frac{5}{100} \qquad .05$$

Before performing any mathematical calculations with percents, they must be converted to either decimals or fractions. Although this function is performed automatically by the percent key on a calculator, Section I of this chapter covers the procedures for making these conversions manually. Sections II and III introduce you to some important applications of percents in business.

6-1 CONVERTING PERCENTS TO DECIMALS AND DECIMALS TO PERCENTS

Because percents are numbers expressed as parts per 100, the percent sign, %, means multiplication by $\frac{1}{100}$. Therefore, 25% means

$$25\% = 25 \times \frac{1}{100} = \frac{25}{100} = .25$$

 STEPS FOR CONVERTING A PERCENT TO A DECIMAL

STEP 1. Remove the percent sign.

STEP 2. Divide by 100.

Note: If the percent is a fraction such as $\frac{3}{8}$% or a mixed number such as $4\frac{3}{4}$%, change the fraction to a decimal; then follow Steps 1 and 2 above.

$$\frac{3}{8}\% = .375\% = .00375 \qquad 4\frac{3}{4}\% = 4.75\% = .0475$$

Note: If the percent is a fraction such as $\frac{2}{3}$%, which converts to a repeating decimal, .66666, round the decimal to hundredths, .67; then follow Steps 1 and 2 above.

$$\frac{2}{3}\% = .67\% = .0067$$

LEARNINGTIP

To divide a number by 100, move the decimal point two places to the left. Add zeros as needed.

Remember, if there is no decimal point, it is understood to be to the right of the digit in the ones place. (24 = 24.)

EXAMPLE1 CONVERTING PERCENTS TO DECIMALS

Convert the following percents to decimals.

a. 44%   b. 233%   c. 56.4%   d. .68%   e. $18\frac{1}{4}$%   f. $\frac{1}{8}$%   g. $9\frac{1}{3}$%

SOLUTIONSTRATEGY

Remove the percent sign and move the decimal point two places to the left.

a. 44% = .44

b. 233% = 2.33

c. 56.4% = .564

d. .68% = .0068

e. $18\frac{1}{4}$% = 18.25% = .1825

f. $\frac{1}{8}$% = .125% = .00125

g. $9\frac{1}{3}$% = 9.33% = .0933

TRYITEXERCISE1

Convert the following percents to decimals.

a. 27%

b. 472%

c. 93.7%

d. .81%

e. $12\frac{3}{4}$%

f. $\frac{7}{8}$%

CHECK YOUR ANSWERS WITH THE SOLUTIONS ON PAGE 184.

STEPS FOR CONVERTING A DECIMAL OR WHOLE NUMBER TO A PERCENT

STEP 1. Multiply by 100.

STEP 2. Write a percent sign after the number.

STEP 3. If there are fractions involved, such as $\frac{3}{4}$, convert them to decimals first; then proceed with Steps 1 and 2 above.

$$\frac{3}{4} = .75 = 75\%$$

EXAMPLE2 CONVERTING DECIMALS TO PERCENTS

Convert the following decimals or whole numbers to percents.

a. .5

b. 3.7

c. .044

d. $.09\frac{3}{5}$

e. 7

f. $6\frac{1}{2}$

SOLUTIONSTRATEGY

Move the decimal point two places to the right and add a percent sign.

a. .5 = 50%

b. 3.7 = 370%

c. .044 = 4.4%

d. $.09\frac{3}{5}$ = .096 = 9.6%

e. 7 = 700%

f. $6\frac{1}{2}$ = 6.5 = 650%

TRYITEXERCISE2

Convert the following decimals or whole numbers to percents.

a. .8

b. 1.4

c. .0023

d. $.016\frac{2}{5}$

e. 19

f. $.57\frac{2}{3}$

CHECK YOUR ANSWERS WITH THE SOLUTIONS ON PAGE 184.

LEARNINGTIP

To multiply a number by 100, move the decimal point two places to the right. Add zeros as needed. As a "navigational aid" to the direction of the decimal point, consider the words *decimal* and *percent* as written alphabetically, with *decimal* preceding *percent*.

- When converting from decimal to percent, the decimal moves **right**

    decimal ⟶ percent

- When converting from percent to decimal, the decimal moves **left**

    decimal ⟵ percent

6-2

CONVERTING PERCENTS TO FRACTIONS AND FRACTIONS TO PERCENTS

DOLLARS AND SENSE

If you have not already done so and your instructor allows it, this would be a good time to purchase a business calculator. There are many choices available today in the $10 to $40 price range. Popular brands include Hewlett-Packard, Texas Instruments, Canon, Sharp, and Casio.

To help you choose a calculator, go to www.shopzilla.com and enter *business calculators* in the "I'm Shopping for" box.

STEPS FOR CONVERTING PERCENTS TO FRACTIONS

STEP 1. Remove the percent sign.

STEP 2. (*If the percent is a whole number*) Write a fraction with the percent as the numerator and 100 as the denominator. If that fraction is improper, change it to a mixed number. Reduce the fraction to lowest terms.

or

STEP 2. (*If the percent is a fraction*) Multiply the number by $\frac{1}{100}$ and reduce to lowest terms.

or

STEP 2. (*If the percent is a decimal*) Convert it to a fraction and multiply by $\frac{1}{100}$. Reduce to lowest terms.

EXAMPLE3 CONVERTING PERCENTS TO FRACTIONS

Convert the following percents to reduced fractions, mixed numbers, or whole numbers.

a. 3%   b. 57%   c. $2\frac{1}{2}\%$ d. 150%   e. 4.5%   f. 600%

SOLUTIONSTRATEGY

a. $3\% = \frac{3}{100}$

b. $57\% = \frac{57}{100}$

c. $2\frac{1}{2}\% = \frac{5}{2} \times \frac{1}{100} = \frac{5}{200} = \frac{1}{40}$

d. $150\% = \frac{150}{100} = 1\frac{50}{100} = 1\frac{1}{2}$

e. $4.5\% = 4\frac{1}{2}\% = \frac{9}{2} \times \frac{1}{100} = \frac{9}{200}$

f. $600\% = \frac{600}{100} = 6$

TRYITEXERCISE3

Convert the following percents to reduced fractions, mixed numbers, or whole numbers.

a. 9%   b. 23%   c. 75%   d. 225%   e. 8.7%   f. 1,000%

CHECK YOUR ANSWERS WITH THE SOLUTIONS ON PAGE 184.

STEPS FOR CONVERTING FRACTIONS TO PERCENTS

STEP 1. Change the fraction to a decimal by dividing the numerator by the denominator.

STEP 2. Multiply by 100. (Move the decimal point two places to the right. Add zeros as needed.)

STEP 3. Write a percent sign after the number.

EXAMPLE4 CONVERTING FRACTIONS TO PERCENTS

Convert the following fractions or mixed numbers to percents.

a. $\dfrac{1}{10}$ b. $\dfrac{69}{100}$ c. $\dfrac{15}{4}$ d. $4\dfrac{3}{8}$ e. $\dfrac{18}{25}$ f. $13\dfrac{1}{2}$

SOLUTIONSTRATEGY

Change the fractions to decimals by dividing the denominator into the numerator; then move the decimal point two places to the right and add a percent sign.

a. $\dfrac{1}{10} = .10 = \underline{10\%}$ b. $\dfrac{69}{100} = .69 = \underline{69\%}$ c. $\dfrac{15}{4} = 3\dfrac{3}{4} = 3.75 = \underline{375\%}$

d. $4\dfrac{3}{8} = 4.375 = \underline{437.5\%}$ e. $\dfrac{18}{25} = .72 = \underline{72\%}$ f. $13\dfrac{1}{2} = 13.5 = \underline{1350\%}$

TRYITEXERCISE4

Convert the following fractions or mixed numbers to percents.

a. $\dfrac{1}{5}$ b. $\dfrac{70}{200}$ c. $\dfrac{23}{5}$ d. $6\dfrac{9}{10}$ e. $\dfrac{45}{54}$ f. $140\dfrac{1}{8}$

CHECK YOUR ANSWERS WITH THE SOLUTIONS ON PAGES 184.

LEARNINGTIP

Use the % key on your calculator to save the step of multiplying by 100.

For example: $\dfrac{44}{50} = .88 = 88\%$.

Calculator sequence:

44 ÷ 50 % = 88

Note: Scientific and business calculators require pushing the = button after the % key; common arithmetic calculators do not.

REVIEW EXERCISES   SECTION I   6

Convert the following percents to decimals.

1. 28%   2. 76%   3. 13.4%   4. 121%   5. 42.68%
   .28

6. $6\dfrac{1}{2}\%$ 7. .02%   8. $\dfrac{3}{5}\%$ 9. $125\dfrac{1}{6}\%$ 10. 2,000%

Convert the following decimals or whole numbers to percents.

11. 3.5   12. .11   13. 46   14. $.34\dfrac{1}{2}$

    350%

15. .00935   16. $.9\dfrac{3}{4}$ 17. 164   18. .04

19. 5.33   20. $1.15\dfrac{5}{8}$

Convert the following percents to reduced fractions, mixed numbers, or whole numbers.

21. 5%   22. 75%   23. 89%   24. 230%

$\dfrac{5}{100} = \dfrac{1}{20}$

25. 38%   26. 37.5%   27. $62\frac{1}{2}$%

28. 450%   29. 125%   30. .8%

Convert the following fractions or mixed numbers to percents.

31. $\frac{3}{4}$ 32. $\frac{1}{8}$ 33. $\frac{12}{5}$ 34. $6\frac{3}{10}$

    .75 = <u>75%</u>

35. $\frac{125}{100}$ 36. $\frac{78}{24}$ 37. $\frac{3}{16}$ 38. $4\frac{1}{5}$

39. $\frac{35}{100}$ 40. $\frac{375}{1,000}$

What is your favorite cookie?

Chocolate chip 53%
Peanut butter 16%
19% Oatmeal
11% Sugar shortbread
5% Other

Source: Impulse Research for Downtown Cookie Co. survey of 1,033 adults

Anne R. Carey and Sam Ward, *USA Today*

Use the pie chart "What is Your Favorite Cookie?" to find the decimal and reduced fraction equivalent for Exercises 41–45.

	Type of Cookie	Decimal	Reduced Fraction
41.	Chocolate chip		
42.	Peanut butter		
43.	Oatmeal		
44.	Sugar/Shortbread		
45.	Other		

BUSINESS DECISION: ENHANCING THE PIE

Disney Dollars

46. You have been asked to make a presentation about The Walt Disney Company. In your research, you locate the accompanying pie chart, which shows Disney revenue by segment expressed in billions of dollars.

    To enhance your presentation, you have decided to convert the dollar amounts to percents and display both numbers.

a. What is the total revenue?

b. For each category, write a fraction with the revenue from that category as the numerator and the total revenue as the denominator.

Media Networks   Parks and Resorts

Consumer Products   Studio Entertainment

The Walt Disney Company Segment Revenue, 2009
($ billions)

Media Neworks ____ $16.9

Parks and Resorts ____ $10.7

$6.1

$2.4

Consumer Products ____

Studio Entertainment ____

© Disney Enterprises, Inc.

c. Convert each fraction from part b to a percent rounded to the nearest tenth of a percent. Enter your answers on the red lines in the chart.

| Media Networks | Parks and Resorts | Consumer Products | Studio Entertainment |

USING THE PERCENTAGE FORMULA TO SOLVE BUSINESS PROBLEMS

SECTION II

6

Now that we have learned to manipulate percents, let's look at some of their practical applications in business. Percent problems involve the use of equations known as the percentage formulas. These formulas have three variables: the **base**, the **portion**, and the **rate**. In business situations, two of the variables will be given and are the *knowns*; one of the variables will be the *unknown*.

Once the variables have been properly identified, the equations are simple to solve. The variables have the following characteristics, which should be used to help identify them:

BASE: The base is the number that represents 100%, or the *whole thing*. It is the starting point, the beginning, or total value of something. The base is often preceded by the word *of* in the written statement of the situation because it is multiplied by the rate.

PORTION: The portion is the number that represents a *part* of the base. The portion is always in the same terms as the base. For example, if the base is dollars, the portion is dollars; if the base is people, the portion is people; if the base is production units, the portion will be production units. The portion often has a "unique characteristic" that is being measured or compared with the base. For example, if the base is the total number of cars in a parking lot, the portion could be the part of the total cars that are convertibles (the unique characteristic).

RATE: The rate is easily identified. It is the number with the *percent sign* or the word *percent*. It defines what part the portion is of the base. If the rate is less than 100%, the portion is less than the base. If the rate is 100%, the portion is equal to the base. If the rate is more than 100%, the portion is greater than the base.

base The variable of the percentage formula that represents 100%, or the whole thing.

portion The variable of the percentage formula that represents a part of the base.

rate The variable of the percentage formula that defines how much or what part the portion is of the base. The rate is the number with the percent sign.

The following percentage formulas are used to solve percent problems:

| Portion = Rate × Base | $P = R \times B$ |

| Rate = $\dfrac{\text{Portion}}{\text{Base}}$ | $R = \dfrac{P}{B}$ |

| Base = $\dfrac{\text{Portion}}{\text{Rate}}$ | $B = \dfrac{P}{R}$ |

STEPS FOR SOLVING PERCENTAGE PROBLEMS

STEP 1. Identify the two knowns and the unknown.

STEP 2. Choose the formula that solves for that unknown.

STEP 3. Solve the equation by substituting the known values for the letters in the formula.

Hint: By remembering the one basic formula, $P = R \times B$, you can derive the other two by using your knowledge of solving equations from Chapter 5. Because multiplication is indicated, we isolate the unknown by performing the inverse, or opposite, operation, division.

LEARNINGTIP

Don't confuse the word *percentage* with the percent, or rate. The *percentage* means the portion, not the rate.

To solve for rate, R, divide both sides of the equation by B:

$$P = R \times B \longrightarrow \frac{P}{B} = \frac{R \times \cancel{B}}{\cancel{B}} \longrightarrow \frac{P}{B} = R$$

To solve for base, B, divide both sides of the equation by R:

$$P = R \times B \longrightarrow \frac{P}{R} = \frac{\cancel{R} \times B}{\cancel{R}} \longrightarrow \frac{P}{R} = B$$

Another method for remembering the percentage formulas is by using the Magic Triangle.

The Magic Triangle

The triangle is divided into three sections representing the portion, rate, and base. By circling or covering the letter in the triangle that corresponds to the *unknown* of the problem, the triangle will "magically" reveal the correct formula to use.

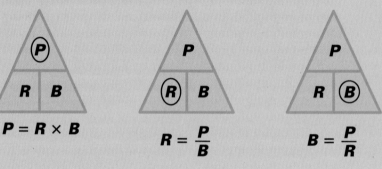

$$P = R \times B \qquad R = \frac{P}{B} \qquad B = \frac{P}{R}$$

6-3

SOLVING FOR THE PORTION

Remember, the portion is a part of the whole and will always be in the same terms as the base. It is found by multiplying the rate times the base: $P = R \times B$. The following examples will demonstrate solving for the portion.

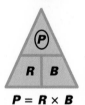

$$P = R \times B$$

EXAMPLE5 SOLVING FOR THE PORTION

What is the portion if the base is $400 and the rate is 12%?

SOLUTIONSTRATEGY

Substitute the knowns for the letters in the formula Portion = Rate × Base. In this problem, 12% is the rate and $400 is the base. Do not forget to convert the percent (rate) to a decimal by deleting the % sign and moving the decimal point two places to the left (12% = .12).

$$P = R \times B$$

$$P = 12\% \times 400 = .12 \times 400 = 48$$

$$\underline{\text{Portion} = \$48}$$

LEARNINGTIP

Shortcut
Remember to use the % key on your calculator.
12 % × 400 = 48

TRYITEXERCISE5

Solve the following for the portion.

What is the portion if the base is 980 and the rate is 55%?

CHECK YOUR ANSWER WITH THE SOLUTION ON PAGE 184.

EXAMPLE6 USING THE PERCENTAGE FORMULA

What number is 43.5% of 250?

SOLUTIONSTRATEGY

In this problem, the rate is easily identified as the term with the % sign. The base, or whole amount, is preceded by the word *of*. We use the formula Portion = Rate × Base, substituting the knowns for the letters that represent them.

$$P = R \times B$$

$$P = 43.5\% \times 250 = .435 \times 250 = 108.75$$

$$\underline{108.75}$$

TRYITEXERCISE6

Solve the following for the portion.

What number is 72% of 3,200?

CHECK YOUR ANSWER WITH THE SOLUTION ON PAGE 184.

EXAMPLE7 USING THE PERCENTAGE FORMULA

Republic Industries produced 6,000 stoves last week. If 2% of them were defective, how many defective stoves were produced?

SOLUTIONSTRATEGY

To solve this problem, we must first identify the variables. Because 2% has the percent sign, it is the rate. The terms are stoves; the total number of stoves (6,000) is the base. The unique characteristic of the portion, the unknown, is that they were defective.

$$P = R \times B$$

$$P = 2\% \times 6,000 = .02 \times 6,000 = 120$$

$$\underline{120} = \text{Number of defective stoves last week}$$

DOLLARS AND SENSE

Keeping it in Perspective!
In May 2009, President Obama ordered $100 million cut from his $3.5 trillion budget, representing a reduction of 0.0029 percent. If a family with an income of $100,000 cut a comparable amount from its budget, it would spend just $2.90 less over the course of a year!

Source: *The Week*

● TRYITEXERCISE7

Solve the following for the portion.

a. Premier Industries has 1,250 employees. 16% constitute the sales staff. How many employees are in sales?

b. Aventura Savings & Loan requires a 15% down payment on a mortgage loan. What is the down payment needed to finance a $148,500 home?

CHECK YOUR ANSWERS WITH THE SOLUTIONS ON PAGE 184.

6-4

$$R = \frac{P}{B}$$

SOLVING FOR THE RATE

The rate is the variable that describes what part of the base is represented by the portion. It is *always* the term with the percent sign. When solving for the rate, your answer will be a decimal. Be sure to convert the decimal to a percent by moving the decimal point two places to the right and adding a percent sign. We use the formula

$$\text{Rate} = \frac{\text{Portion}}{\text{Base}} \quad \text{or} \quad R = \frac{P}{B}$$

The following examples demonstrate solving for the rate.

LEARNINGTIP

Remember, the rate expresses "what part" the portion is of the base.
- When the rate is less than 100%, the portion is *less* than the base.
- When the rate is more than 100%, the portion is *more* than the base.
- When the rate is 100%, the portion *equals* the base.

● EXAMPLE8 SOLVING FOR THE RATE

What is the rate if the base is 160 and the portion is 40?

● SOLUTIONSTRATEGY

Substitute the knowns for the letters in the formula.

$$\text{Rate} = \frac{\text{Portion}}{\text{Base}}$$

$$R = \frac{P}{B}$$

$$R = \frac{40}{160} = .25 = 25\%$$

$$\underline{\text{Rate} = 25\%}$$

● TRYITEXERCISE8

Solve the following for the rate. Round to the nearest tenth when necessary.

What is the rate if the base is 21 and the portion is 9?

CHECK YOUR ANSWER WITH THE SOLUTION ON PAGE 184.

EXAMPLE9 USING THE PERCENTAGE FORMULA

What percent of 700 is 56?

SOLUTIONSTRATEGY

This problem asks what percent, indicating that the rate is the unknown. The 700 is preceded by the word *of* and is therefore the base. The 56 is part of the base and is therefore the portion. Once again we use the formula $R = P \div B$, substituting the knowns for the letters that represent them.

$$R = \frac{P}{B}$$

$$R = \frac{56}{700} = .08 = 8\%$$

$$\underline{\underline{8\%}}$$

TRYITEXERCISE9

Solve the following for the rate. Round to the nearest tenth when necessary.

67 is what percent of 142?

CHECK YOUR ANSWER WITH THE SOLUTION ON PAGE 184.

EXAMPLE10 USING THE PERCENTAGE FORMULA

Pet Supermarket placed an order for 560 fish tanks. If only 490 tanks were delivered, what percent of the order was received?

SOLUTIONSTRATEGY

The first step in solving this problem is to identify the variables. The statement asks "what percent"; therefore, the rate is the unknown. Because 560 is the total order, it is the base; 490 is a part of the total and is therefore the portion. Note that the base and the portion are in the same terms, fish tanks; the unique characteristic of the portion is that 490 tanks *were delivered*.

$$R = \frac{P}{B}$$

$$R = \frac{490}{560} = .875 = 87.5\%$$

$$\underline{87.5\% = \text{Percent of the order received}}$$

Note: Because 560 is the total order, it is the base and therefore represents 100% of the order. If 87.5% of the tanks were received, then 12.5% of the tanks were not received.

$$100\% - 87.5\% = \underline{12.5\% \text{ not received}}$$

TRYITEXERCISE10

Solve the following for the rate. Round to the nearest tenth when necessary.

a. A contract called for 18,000 square feet of tile to be installed in a shopping mall. In the first week, 5,400 feet of tile was completed.

What percent of the job has been completed?

What percent of the job remains?

b. During a recent sale, Sir John, a men's boutique, sold $5,518 in business suits. If total sales amounted to $8,900, what percent of the sales were suits?

CHECK YOUR ANSWERS WITH THE SOLUTIONS ON PAGE 184.

6-5

$$B = \frac{P}{R}$$

SOLVING FOR THE BASE

To solve business situations in which the whole or total amount is the unknown, we use the formula

$$\text{Base} = \frac{\text{Portion}}{\text{Rate}} \quad \text{or} \quad B = \frac{P}{R}$$

The following examples illustrate solving for the base.

LEARNINGTIP

Percentage problems can also be solved by using proportion. Set up the proportion

$$\frac{\text{Rate}}{100} = \frac{\text{Portion}}{\text{Base}}$$

and cross-multiply to solve for the unknown.

For example, at a Radio Shack store last week, 70 televisions were sold with built-in DVD players. If this represents 20% of all TVs sold, how many total TVs were sold?

$$\frac{20}{100} = \frac{70}{\text{base (total TVs)}}$$
$$20b = 100(70)$$
$$20b = 7,000$$
$$b = 350 \text{ Total TVs}$$

EXAMPLE11 SOLVING FOR THE BASE

What is the base if the rate is 21% and the portion is 58.8?

SOLUTIONSTRATEGY

In this basic problem, we simply substitute the known values for the letters in the formula. Remember, the rate must be converted from a percent to a decimal.

$$B = \frac{P}{R}$$
$$B = \frac{58.8}{21\%} = \frac{58.8}{.21} = 280$$
$$\underline{\text{Base} = 280}$$

TRYITEXERCISE11

Solve the following for the base. Round to hundredths or the nearest cent when necessary.

What is the base if the rate is 40% and the portion is 690?

CHECK YOUR ANSWER WITH THE SOLUTION ON PAGE 184.

EXAMPLE12 USING THE PERCENTAGE FORMULA

75 is 15% of what number?

SOLUTIONSTRATEGY

Remember, the base is usually identified as the value preceded by *of* in the statement. In this case, that value is the unknown. Because 15 has the percent sign, it is the rate, and 75 is the part of the whole, or the portion.

$$B = \frac{P}{R}$$

$$B = \frac{75}{15\%} = \frac{75}{.15} = 500$$

$$\underline{500}$$

TRYITEXERCISE12

Solve the following for the base. Round to hundredths or the nearest cent when necessary.

$550 is 88% of what amount?

CHECK YOUR ANSWER WITH THE SOLUTION ON PAGE 184.

EXAMPLE13 USING THE PERCENTAGE FORMULA

All Star Sporting Goods reports that 28% of total shoe sales are from Nike products. If last week's Nike sales were $15,400, what was the total amount of sales for the week?

SOLUTIONSTRATEGY

In this problem, the total amount of sales, the base, is unknown. Because 28% has the percent sign, it is the rate and $15,400 is the portion. Note again, the portion is in the same terms as the base, dollar sales; however, the unique characteristic is that the portion represents Nike sales.

$$B = \frac{P}{R}$$

$$B = \frac{15,400}{28\%} = \frac{15,400}{.28} = 55,000$$

$55,000 Total sales for the week

TRYITEXERCISE13

Solve the following for the base. Round to hundredths or the nearest cent when necessary.

a. In a machine shop, 35% of the motor repairs are for broken shafts. If 126 motors had broken shafts last month, how many total motors were repaired?
b. At Office Mart, 75% of the copy paper sold is letter size. If 3,420 reams of letter size were sold, how many total reams of copy paper were sold?

CHECK YOUR ANSWERS WITH THE SOLUTIONS ON PAGE 184.

REVIEW EXERCISES   SECTION II **6**

JUMP START www

Solve the following for the portion. Round to hundredths when necessary.

1. 15% of 380 is _____
    $P = R \times B = .15 \times 380 = \underline{57}$

2. 3.6% of 1,800 is _____

3. 200% of 45 is _____

4. $5\frac{1}{2}$% of $600 is _____

5. What is the portion if the base is 450 and the rate is 19%?

6. What is the portion if the base is 1,650 and the rate is 150%?

7. What number is 35.2% of 184?   **EXCEL 1**   8.   What number is .8% of 500?

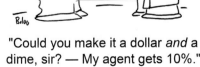

"Could you make it a dollar *and* a dime, sir? — My agent gets 10%."

9. What number is $15\frac{4}{5}\%$ of 360?   10. What number is 258% of 2,500?

Solve the following for the rate. Round to the nearest tenth of a percent when necessary.

11. 40 is _____ % of 125   12. _____ % of 50 is 23   13. 600 is _____ % of 240

$$R = \frac{P}{B} = \frac{40}{125} = .32 = \underline{\underline{32\%}}$$

14. What is the rate if the base is 288 and the portion is 50?

15. What is the rate if the portion is 21.6 and the base is 160?

16. What is the rate if the base is $3,450 and the portion is $290?

17. What percent of 77 is 23?   18. What percent of 1,600 is 1,900?

19. 68 is what percent of 262?   20. $7.80 is what percent of $58.60?

Solve the following for the base. Round to hundredths when necessary.

21. 69 is 15% of _____   22. 360 is 150% of _____   23. 6.45 is $18\frac{1}{2}\%$ of _____

$$B = \frac{P}{R} = \frac{69}{.15} = \underline{\underline{460}}$$

24. What is the base if the rate is 16.8% and the portion is 451?

25. What is the base if the portion is 10 and the rate is $2\frac{3}{4}\%$?

26. What is the base if the portion is $4,530 and the rate is 35%?

27. 60 is 15% of what number?   28. 160 is 130% of what number?

29. $46.50 is $86\frac{2}{3}\%$ of what number?   30. .55 is 21.4% of what number?

Solve the following word problems for the portion, rate, or base.

31. Alicia Kirk owns 37% of a travel agency.

   a. If the total worth of the business is $160,000, how much is Alicia's share?

   b. Last month Alicia's agency booked $14,500 in airline fares on Orbit Airline. If Orbit pays agencies a commission of 4.1%, how much commission should the agency receive?

32. What is the sales tax rate in a state where the tax on a purchase of $464 is $25.52?

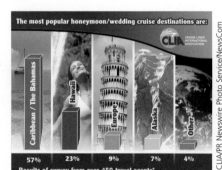

The most popular honeymoon/wedding cruise destinations are:

Caribbean / The Bahamas 57%   Hawaii 23%   Europe 9%   Alaska 7%   Other 4%

Results of survey from over 450 travel agents*   *Survey conducted January 2007

Travel Agent

According to the latest data from the U.S. Department of Labor, Bureau of Labor Statistics, travel agents held about 105,300 jobs in 2008 and are found in every part of the country. More than three out of five agents worked for travel agencies. Around 17% were self-employed.

Median annual earnings of travel agents were $30,570. The middle 50 percent earned between $23,940 and $38,390. The top 10% earned more than $47,860.

© CLIA/PR Newswire Photo Service/NewsCom

33. In August 2009, CNNMoney.com reported that for the first time in more than a decade, the size of the average newly built American house had shrunk to 2,065 square feet, or 93% of its original size. What was the original size before the decline? Round to the nearest square foot.

34. According to *The Miami Herald*, in January 2010, Barnes & Noble launched a textbook rental program for college students. The company said books would rent for 42.5% of their original price. If a chemistry textbook rents for $48, what was the original price of the text? Round to the nearest cent.

35. If Rob Winter, a real estate agent, earned $6\frac{1}{2}\%$ commission on the sale of property valued at $210,000, how much was Rob's commission?

36. As part of a report you are writing that compares living expenses in various cities, use the chart "Cities with the highest average monthly utility bills" to calculate the following:
    a. What percent is the Baltimore utility bill of the Las Vegas bill? Round to the nearest whole percent.

    b. What percent is the Orlando utility bill of the Dallas bill? Round to the nearest tenth of a percent.

Cities with the highest average monthly utility bills[1]

Baltimore	$390.44
Houston	$359.52
Dallas	$346.46
Orlando	$310.10
Las Vegas	$300.03

1 - Including home phone, television, high-speed Internet, electricity, and natural gas as of the third quarter.
Source: WhiteFence.com

37. Thirty percent of the inventory of a Nine West shoe store is high heels. If the store has 846 pairs of high heels in stock, how many total pairs of shoes are in the inventory?

38. Municipal Auto Sales advertised a down payment of $1,200 on a Mustang valued at $14,700. What is the percent of the down payment? Round to the nearest tenth of a percent.

39. According to *The Miami Herald* research, in 2009, for every dollar of tip left at South Florida restaurants, 74% went to the server, 5% went to the host, 6% went to the bartender, and 15% went to the busser. One night a large party spent $750 on dinner and left a 20% tip.
    a. How much tip was left?

    b. Use the research percents to distribute the tip between the server, the host, the bartender, and the busser.

40. A quality control process finds 17.2 defects for every 8,600 units of production. What percent of the production is defective?

41. The Parker Company employs 68 part-time workers. If this represents 4% of the total work force, how many individuals work for the company?

42. A medical insurance policy requires Ana to pay the first $100 of her hospital expense. The insurance company will then pay 80% of the remaining expense. Ana is expecting a short surgical stay in the hospital, for which she estimates the total bill to be about $4,500. How much will Ana's portion of the bill amount to?

43. A corporation earned \$457,800 last year. If its tax rate is $13\frac{3}{8}\%$, how much tax was paid?

44. In June, the New York Yankees won 15 games and lost 9. What percent of the games did they win? (*Hint:* Use total games played as the base.)

Use the pie chart "Century Mutual Fund – Investments" for Exercises 45–46.

45. What is the total amount invested in the Century Mutual Fund?

46. What percent does each investment category represent? Round your answers to the nearest tenth of a percent.

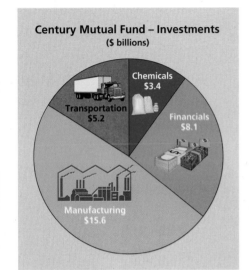

Century Mutual Fund – Investments
(\$ billions)

Chemicals
\$3.4

Transportation
\$5.2

Financials
\$8.1

Manufacturing
\$15.6

47. In 2009, Ford Motor Co. announced that it planned to sell a new police cruiser vehicle in the United States to replace its Crown Victoria "Police Interceptor." Ford sells about 45,000 police vehicles a year, or about 75% of all police vehicles sold in the United States. Based on this information, what is the total number of police vehicles sold in the United States each year?

48. Elwood Smith attends a college that charges \$1,400 tuition per semester for 12 credit hours of classes. If tuition is raised by 9% next year:
    a. How much more will he pay for two semesters of classes with the same course load?

    b. If Elwood works at a car wash earning \$8 per hour and pays 15% in taxes, how many extra hours must he work to make up for the tuition increase? Round to the nearest whole hour.

UpperCut Images/Getty Images

Nuptial Numbers
According to the Bridal Association of America, in 2009, there were over 2.3 million weddings in the United States, with a market value of over \$72 billion. The average cost of a wedding was almost \$31,000, with 169 guests. The average engagement time was 17 months.

In 1960, an American bride was typically 20 years old and a groom was 23. Today the average age of wedding couples is 26 for the bride and 28 for the groom. Approximately 75 percent of all wedding receptions take place at a hotel, country club, or catering facility.

BUSINESS DECISION: THE PARTY PLANNER

49. You are the catering manager for the Imperial Palace Hotel. Last Saturday your staff catered a wedding reception in the main ballroom, during which 152 chicken dinners, 133 steak dinners, and 95 fish dinners were served. All dinners are the same price. The hotel charges "per person" for catered events.
    a. What percent of the total meals served was each type of dinner?

    b. If \$13,300 was charged for all the meals, how much revenue did each type produce?

c. If a 20% price increase goes into effect next month, what will be the new price per meal?

d. When photographers, florists, DJs, bands, and other outside vendors are booked through your office for events at the hotel, a $5\frac{1}{2}$% "finder's fee" is charged. Last year $175,000 of such services were booked. How much did the hotel make on this service?

e. If your boss is expecting $11,000 in "finder's fee" revenue next year, what amount of these services must be booked?

SOLVING OTHER BUSINESS PROBLEMS INVOLVING PERCENTS

SECTION III **6**

In addition to the basic percentage formulas, percents are used in many other ways in business. Measuring increases and decreases, comparing results from one year with another, and reporting economic activity and trends are just a few of these applications.

The ability of managers to make correct decisions is fundamental to success in business. These decisions require accurate and up-to-date information. Measuring percent changes in business activity is an important source of this information. Percents often describe a situation in a more informative way than do the raw data alone.

For example, a company reports a profit of $50,000 for the year. Although the number $50,000 is correct, it does not give a perspective of whether that amount of profit is good or bad. A comparison to last year's figures using percents might reveal that profits are up 45% over last year or profits are down 66.8%. Significant news!

> **LEARNINGTIP**
>
> It is important to remember when solving percentage problems that involve "change" from an original number to a new number, the original number is always the *base* and represents 100%.

DETERMINING RATE OF INCREASE OR DECREASE

6-6

In calculating the rate of increase or decrease of something, we use the same percentage formula concepts as before. Rate of change means percent change; therefore, the *rate* is the unknown. Once again we use the formula $R = P \div B$. Rate of change situations contain an original amount of something, which either increases or decreases to a new amount.

In solving these problems, the original amount is always the base. The amount of change is the portion. The unknown, which describes the percent change between the two amounts, is the rate.

$$\text{Rate of change (Rate)} = \frac{\text{Amount of change (Portion)}}{\text{Original amount (Base)}}$$

STEPS FOR DETERMINING THE RATE OF INCREASE OR DECREASE

STEP 1. Identify the original and the new amounts and find the *difference* between them.

STEP 2. Using the rate formula $R = P \div B$, substitute the difference from Step 1 for the portion and the original amount for the base.

STEP 3. Solve the equation for R. Remember, your answer will be in decimal form, which must be converted to a percent.

Tropical Stom Force Wind Speed Probabilities
For the 120 hours (5 days) from 8am EDT Thu Aug 27 to 8am EDT Tue Sep 1

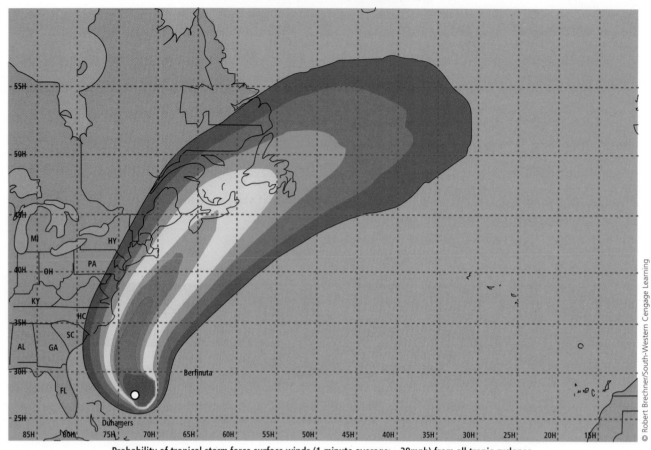

Probability of tropical storm force surface winds (1-minute average>=39mph) from all tropic cyclones
○ indicates TROPICAL STORM DANNY centter localion at 8AM EDT Thu Aug 27 2009 (Forecast/Advisory 05

| 5% | 10% | 20% | 30% | 40% | 50% | 60% | 70% | 80% | 90% | 100% |

Predicting the probability of an event occurring is often expressed as a percent. This graphic illustrates the probabilities of tropical storm force winds during Tropical Storm Danny in 2009.

EXAMPLE 14 FINDING THE RATE OF INCREASE

If a number increases from 60 to 75, what is the rate of increase?

SOLUTIONSTRATEGY

In this basic situation, a number changes from 60 to 75 and we are looking for the percent change; in this case, it is an increase. The original amount is 60; the new amount is 75.

The portion is the difference between the amounts, $75 - 60 = 15$, and the base is the original amount, 60. We now substitute these values into the formula.

$$R = \frac{P}{B} = \frac{15}{60} = .25 = 25\%$$

Rate of increase = 25%

TRYITEXERCISE 14

Solve the following problem for the rate of increase or decrease. Round to the nearest tenth of a percent when necessary.

If a number increases from 650 to 948, what is the rate of increase?

CHECK YOUR ANSWER WITH THE SOLUTION ON PAGE 184.

EXAMPLE15 FINDING THE RATE OF DECREASE

A number decreased from 120 to 80. What is the rate of decrease?

SOLUTIONSTRATEGY

This problem illustrates a number decreasing in value. The unknown is the rate of decrease. We identify the original amount as 120 and the new amount as 80.

The difference between them is the portion: $120 - 80 = 40$. The original amount, 120, is the base. Now apply the rate formula.

$$R = \frac{P}{B} = \frac{40}{120} = .333 = 33.3\%$$

Rate of decrease $= 33.3\%$

TRYITEXERCISE15

Solve the following problem for the rate of increase or decrease. Round to the nearest tenth of a percent when necessary.

If a number decreases from 21 to 15, what is the rate of decrease?

CHECK YOUR ANSWER WITH THE SOLUTION ON PAGE 184.

EXAMPLE16 FINDING THE RATE OF CHANGE

Last year Iberia Furniture had a work force of 360 employees. This year there are 504 employees. What is the rate of change in the number of employees?

SOLUTIONSTRATEGY

The key to solving this problem is to properly identify the variables. The problem asks "what is the rate"; therefore, the rate is the unknown. The original amount, 360 employees, is the base. The difference between the two amounts, $504 - 360 = 144$, is the portion. Now apply the rate formula.

$$R = \frac{P}{B} = \frac{144}{360} = .4 = 40\%$$

40% Increase in employees

TRYITEXERCISE16

Solve the following problem for the rate of increase or decrease. Round to the nearest tenth of a percent when necessary.

When Mike Veteramo was promoted from supervisor to manager, he received a salary increase from $450 to $540 per week. What was the percent change in his salary?

CHECK YOUR ANSWER WITH THE SOLUTION ON PAGE 184.

EXAMPLE 17 FINDING THE RATE OF CHANGE

Over-the-Top Roofing had revenue of $122,300 in May and $103,955 in June. What is the percent change in revenue from May to June?

SOLUTION STRATEGY

In this problem, the rate of change, the unknown, is a decrease. The original amount, $122,300, is the base. The difference between the two amounts, $122,300 − $103,955 = $18,345, is the portion. Now apply the rate formula.

$$R = \frac{P}{B} = \frac{18,345}{122,300} = .15 = 15\%$$

<u>15% Decrease in revenue</u>

TRY IT EXERCISE 17

Solve the following problem for the rate of increase or decrease. Round to the nearest tenth of a percent when necessary.

You are the production manager for the Berkshire Corporation. After starting a quality control program on the production line, the number of defects per day dropped from 60 to 12. Top management was very pleased with your results but wanted to know what percent decrease this change represented. Calculate the percent change in the number of defects per day.

CHECK YOUR ANSWER WITH THE SOLUTION ON PAGE 184.

6-7   DETERMINING AMOUNTS IN INCREASE OR DECREASE SITUATIONS

FINDING THE NEW AMOUNT AFTER A PERCENT CHANGE

Sometimes the original amount of something and the rate of change will be known and the new amount, after the change, will be the unknown. For example, if a store sold $5,000 in merchandise on Tuesday and 8% more on Wednesday, what are Wednesday's sales?

Keep in mind that the original amount, or beginning point, is always the base and represents 100%. Because the new amount is the total of the original amount, 100%, and the amount of increase, 8%, the rate of the new amount is 108% (100% + 8%). If the rate of change had been a decrease instead of an increase, the rate would have been 8% less than the base, or 92% (100% − 8%).

The unknown in this situation, the new amount, is the portion; therefore, we use the formula Portion = Rate × Base.

LEARNING TIP

Remember
- If the rate of change is an increase, *add* that rate to 100%.
- If the rate of change is a decrease, *subtract* that rate from 100%.

STEPS FOR DETERMINING THE NEW AMOUNT AFTER A PERCENT CHANGE

STEP 1. In the formula Portion = Rate × Base, substitute the original amount, or starting point, for the base.

STEP 2. If the rate of change is an increase, add that rate to 100% to get the rate.

or

STEP 2. If the rate of change is a decrease, subtract that rate from 100% to get the rate.

STEP 3. Solve the equation for the portion.

EXAMPLE18 FINDING THE NEW AMOUNT AFTER A PERCENT CHANGE

Affiliated Insurance estimated that the number of claims on homeowner's insurance would increase by 15% this year. If the company received 1,240 claims last year, how many can it expect this year?

SOLUTIONSTRATEGY

Last year's claims, the original amount, is the base. Because the rate of change is an increase, we find the rate by adding that change to 100% (100% + 15% = 115%). Now substitute these values in the portion formula.

$$P = R \times B$$

$$P = 115\% \times 1,240 = 1.15 \times 1,240 = 1,426$$

1,426 Homeowners' claims expected this year

TRYITEXERCISE18

Solve the following business situation for the new amount after a percent change.

Worldwide Imports had a computer with a 525 gigabyte hard drive. If it was replaced with a new model containing 60% more capacity, how many gigabytes would the new hard drive have?

CHECK YOUR ANSWER WITH THE SOLUTION ON PAGE 185.

EXAMPLE19 FINDING THE NEW AMOUNT AFTER A PERCENT CHANGE

Mel's Drive-in Restaurant sold 25% fewer milk shakes this week than last week. If the drive-in sold 380 shakes last week, how many did it sell this week?

SOLUTIONSTRATEGY

Because this situation represents a percent decrease, the rate is determined by subtracting the rate of decrease from 100% (100% − 25% = 75%). As usual, the base is the original amount.

$$P = R \times B$$

$$P = 75\% \times 380 = .75 \times 380 = 285$$

285 Milk shakes sold this week

TRYITEXERCISE19

Solve the following business situation for the new amount after a percent change.

Overland Express has delivery trucks that cover 20% fewer miles per week during the winter snow season. If the trucks average 650 miles per week during the summer, how many miles can be expected per week during the winter?

CHECK YOUR ANSWER WITH THE SOLUTION ON PAGE 185.

FINDING THE ORIGINAL AMOUNT BEFORE A PERCENT CHANGE

In another business situation involving percent change, the new amount is known and the original amount, the base, is unknown. For example, a car dealer sold 42 cars today. If this represents a 20% increase from yesterday, how many cars were sold yesterday? Solving for the original amount is a base problem; therefore, we use the formula

$$\text{Base} = \frac{\text{Portion}}{\text{Rate}}$$

STEPS **FOR DETERMINING THE ORIGINAL AMOUNT BEFORE A PERCENT CHANGE**

STEP 1. In the formula Base = Portion ÷ Rate, substitute the new amount for the portion.

STEP 2. If the rate of change is an increase, add that rate to 100% to get the rate.

or

STEP 2. If the rate of change is a decrease, subtract that rate from 100% to get the rate.

STEP 3. Solve the equation for the base.

© Christopher Griffin/Alamy

Costco Wholesale Corporation operates an international chain of membership warehouses, mainly under the "Costco Wholesale" name, that carry brand name merchandise at substantially lower prices than are typically found at conventional wholesale or retail sources.

As of March 2010, Costco had 567 warehouses. Membership included 56 million cardholders, 30.6 million households, and 5.7 million businesses. Costco employs 147,000 full- and part-time employees. Fiscal year 2009 revenue amounted to $71.4 billion.

Source: www.costco.com and annual report

EXAMPLE 20 FINDING THE ORIGINAL AMOUNT

At Costco, the price of a Sony HD camcorder dropped by 15% to $425. What was the original price?

SOLUTIONSTRATEGY

Because this situation represents a percent decrease, the rate is determined by subtracting the rate of decrease from 100%. 100% − 15% = 85%. The portion is the new amount, $425. The original price, the base, is the unknown. Using the formula for the base,

$$B = \frac{P}{R}$$

$$B = \frac{425}{85\%} = \frac{425}{.85} = 500$$

$\underline{\$500}$

TRYITEXERCISE 20

Solve the following business situation for the original amount before a percent change.

The water level in a large holding tank decreased to 12 feet. If it is down 40% from last week, what was last week's level?

CHECK YOUR ANSWER WITH THE SOLUTION ON PAGE 185.

EXAMPLE 21 FINDING THE ORIGINAL AMOUNT

Viking Technologies found that after an advertising campaign, business in April increased 12% over March. If April sales were $53,760, how much were the sales in March?

SOLUTIONSTRATEGY

April's sales, the new amount, is the portion. Because the rate of change is an increase, we find the rate by adding that change to 100%. 100% + 12% = 112%.

$$B = \frac{P}{R}$$

$$B = \frac{53,760}{112\%} = \frac{53,760}{1.12} = 48,000$$

$\underline{\$48,000}$

TRYITEXERCISE21

Solve the following business situation for the original amount before a percent change.

A John Deere harvester can cover 90 acres per day with a new direct-drive system. If this represents an increase of 20% over the conventional chain-drive system, how many acres per day were covered with the old chain-drive?

CHECK YOUR ANSWER WITH THE SOLUTION ON PAGE 185.

UNDERSTANDING AND SOLVING PROBLEMS INVOLVING PERCENTAGE POINTS

6-8

Percentage points are a way of expressing a change from an original amount to a new amount without using a percent sign. When percentage points are used, it is assumed that the original amount of percentage points is the base amount, or the whole to which the change is compared. For example, if a company's market share increased from 40 to 44 percent of a total market, this is expressed as an increase of 4 percentage points.

The actual percent change in business, however, is calculated by using the formula

percentage points A way of expressing a change from an original amount to a new amount without using a percent sign.

$$\text{Rate of change} = \frac{\text{Change in percentage points}}{\text{Original amount of percentage points}}$$

In this illustration, the change in percentage points is 4 and the original amount of percentage points is 40; therefore,

$$\text{Rate of change} = \frac{4}{40} = .10 = \underline{10\% \text{ increase in market share}}$$

LEARNINGTIP

Calculating percentage points is an application of the rate formula, Rate = Portion ÷ Base, with the change in percentage points as the *portion* and the original percentage points as the *base*.

EXAMPLE22 SOLVING A PERCENTAGE POINTS PROBLEM

When a competitor built a better mouse trap, a company's market share dropped from 55 to 44 percent of the total market, a drop of 11 percentage points. What percent decrease in market share did this represent?

SOLUTIONSTRATEGY

In this problem, the change in percentage points is 11 and the original market share is 55. Using the formula to find rate of change:

$$\text{Rate of change} = \frac{\text{Change in percentage points}}{\text{Original amount of percentage points}}$$

$$\text{Rate of change} = \frac{11}{55} = .2 = 20\%$$

$\underline{20\% \text{ Decrease in market share}}$

INTHE BUSINESSWORLD

According to a study by the Urban Institute, during the economic downturn in 2008 and 2009, each percentage point rise in the unemployment rate increased the number of Americans without health insurance by 1.1 million.

Source: *The Week, The New York Times*

TRYITEXERCISE22

Prior to an election, a political research firm announced that a candidate for mayor had gained 8 percentage points in the polls that month, from 20 to 28 percent of the total registered voters. What is the candidate's actual percent increase in voters?

CHECK YOUR ANSWER WITH THE SOLUTION ON PAGE 185.

SECTION III **6**   **REVIEW EXERCISES**

Solve the following increase or decrease problems for the unknown. Round decimals to hundredths and percents to the nearest tenth.

1. If a number increases from 320 to 440, what is the rate of increase?

   Portion = Increase = 440 − 320 = 120
   Base = Original number = 320 $R = \dfrac{P}{B} = \dfrac{120}{320} = .375 = \underline{\underline{37.5\%}}$

2. If a number decreases from 56 to 49, what is the rate of decrease?

3. What is the rate of change if the price of an item rises from \$123 to \$154?

4. What is the rate of change if the number of employees in a company decreases from 133 to 89?

5. 50 increased by 20% = _____   6. 750 increased by 60% = _____

   Rate = 100% + 20% = 120%
   Base = Original number = 50
   $P = R \times B = 1.2 \times 50 = \underline{\underline{60}}$

7. 25 decreased by 40% = _____   8. 3,400 decreased by 18.2% = _____

9. 2,500 increased by 300% = _____   10. \$46 decreased by $10\frac{1}{2}\%$ = _____

11. You are writing a report on the various specialty fields that medical school graduates are choosing. As part of your research, you have found the chart "Seniors in Family Medicine." Use the chart to calculate the percent decrease of seniors graduating from U.S. medical schools between 1997 and 2009 who chose residency spots in family medicine.

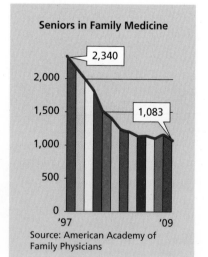

Seniors in Family Medicine

2,340

1,083

'97   '09

Source: American Academy of Family Physicians

12. Sunshine Honda sold 112 cars this month. If that is 40% greater than last month, how many cars were sold last month?

13. At a Sports King store, 850 tennis racquets were sold last season.

    a. If racquet sales are predicted to be 30% higher this season, how many racquets should be ordered from the distributor?

    b. If racquet sales break down into 40% metal alloy and 60% graphite, how many of each type should be ordered?

14. At a Safeway Supermarket, the price of yellow onions dropped from $0.59 per pound to $0.45 per pound.

    a. What is the percent decrease in the price of onions?

    b. Tomatoes are expected to undergo the same percent decrease in price. If they currently sell for $1.09 per pound, what will be the new price of tomatoes?

15. According to the American Association of Retired Persons, AARP, without healthcare reform, the number of people in the United States without healthcare insurance would have reached 61 million in 2020. This represents a 24.5% increase from 2010. How many people were uninsured in 2010? Round to the nearest million.

Top U.S. Supermarkets—2009 Revenue ($billions)

1. Walmart	**5. Safeway**
Bentonville, AR	Pleasanton, CA
$405 billion	$44.8 billion
Stores—2,601	Stores—1,743
2. Kroger	**6. Publix Super**
Cincinnati, OH	**Markets**
$77.2 billion	Lakeland, FL
Stores—2,477	$24.0 billion
	Stores—990
3. Costco	
Issaquah, WA	**7. Ahold USA**
$71.4 billion	Quincy, MA
Stores—567	$21.8 billion
	Stores—704
4. Supervalu	
Minneapolis, MN	
$45.0 billion	
Stores—2,491	

16. Housing prices in San Marino County have increased 37.5% over the price of houses five years ago.

    a. If $80,000 was the average price of a house five years ago, what is the average price of a house today?

Source: *Supermarket News*, company data

    b. Economists predict that next year housing prices will drop by 4%. Based on your answer from part **a**, what will the average price of a house be next year?

Photo by Robert Brechner

17. At Camper's Paradise, sales have increased 15%, 20%, and 10% over the past three years; that is, 15% three years ago, 20% two years ago, and 10% one year ago. If sales this year are $1,000,000, how much were sales three years ago? Round each year's sales to the nearest dollar.

18. According to the U.S. Census Bureau, in 1950, 39.3 million families had a child under 18 at home. By 2009, that number had decreased by 9.4 percent. How many families had a child under 18 at home in 2009? Round the number of millions to the nearest tenth.

19. After a vigorous promotion campaign, Crunchy Flakes Cereal increased its market share from 5.4% to 8.1%, a rise of 2.7 percentage points. What percent increase in sales does this represent?

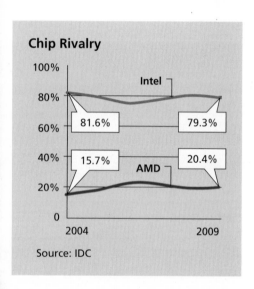

Chip Rivalry

Source: IDC

20. The chart "Chip Rivalry" illustrates the global market share of Intel and AMD processing chips shipped to PC makers. Use this chart to answer the following questions:

    a. From 2004 to 2009, Intel's market share dropped by 2.3 percentage points. What percent decrease in market share does this represent?

    b. From 2004 to 2009, AMD's market share increased by 4.7 percentage points. What percent increase in market share does this represent?

21. Economic reports indicate that during the recession of 2008–2010, unemployment in Ferndale Valley increased from 7.4% to 9.8%, an increase of 2.4 percentage points.

    a. What percent increase does this represent? Round to the nearest tenth of a percent.

    b. In 2011, the government's economic stimulus efforts provided infrastructure jobs, lowering unemployment in Ferndale Valley from 9.8% to 8.1%, a decrease of 1.7 percentage points. What percent decrease does this represent? Round to the nearest hundredth of a percent.

BUSINESS DECISION: CREATING AN ECONOMIC SNAPSHOT

22. You are the editor of your school newspaper. For the next edition, you are writing a story about inflation. You have located the following chart listing various consumer purchases and their costs in 2008 and 2009, as well as the percentage change. Unfortunately, portions of the chart are missing.

    Fill in the blank spaces to complete the chart for your story. Round percent answers to the nearest tenth of a percent. Round dollar amount answers to the nearest whole dollar.

	Consumer Purchase	2008	2009	Percent Change
	Single-Family Home Median resale price	$198,100	$172,700	_____
	Toyota Camry MSRP for the LE – manual transmission	$20,600	_____	+1.2%
	Unleaded Gasoline Average national price per gallon for all grades of unleaded – including taxes	$3.26	$2.40	_____
	Hospital Stay Average cost of one day in a semiprivate room (Cleveland)	_____	$6,838	+28.8%
	Pair of Jeans Gap's Easy Fit, stonewashed	$44.50	$54.50	_____
	Birth Average hospital cost for mother and child	_____	$10,121	+13.6%
	McDonald's Big Mac Average price at company-owned restaurants	$2.97	$3.20	_____
	A Year in College In-state including room and board and fees, Penn State undergraduate	$21,030	_____	+10.5%

Adapted from The *Wall Street Journal*, Jan. 4, 2010, page R4.

CHAPTER

CHAPTER FORMULAS

The Percentage Formula

$$\text{Portion} = \text{Rate} \times \text{Base}$$

$$\text{Rate} = \text{Portion} \div \text{Base}$$

$$\text{Base} = \text{Portion} \div \text{Rate}$$

Rate of Change

$$\text{Rate of change (Rate)} = \frac{\text{Amount of change (Portion)}}{\text{Original amount (Base)}}$$

Percentage Points

$$\text{Rate of change} = \frac{\text{Change in percentage points}}{\text{Original amount of percentage points}}$$

CHAPTER SUMMARY

Section I: Understanding and Converting Percents

Topic	Important Concepts	Illustrative Examples
Converting a Percent to a Decimal **Performance Objective 6-1, Page 156**	1. Remove the percent sign. 2. Move the decimal point two places to the left. *Note:* If the percent is a fraction such as $\frac{4}{5}\%$ or a mixed number such as $9\frac{1}{2}\%$, change the fraction part to a decimal; then follow Steps 1 and 2.	$28\% = .28$ $\qquad$ $\frac{4}{5}\% = .8\% = .008$ $159\% = 1.59$ $\qquad$ $9\frac{1}{2}\% = 9.5\% = .095$ $.37\% = .0037$
Converting a Decimal or Whole Number to a Percent **Performance Objective 6-1, Pages 157**	1. Move the decimal point two places to the right. 2. Write a percent sign after the number. *Note:* If there are fractions involved, convert them to decimals first; then proceed with Steps 1 and 2.	$.8 = 80\%$ $\qquad$ $3 = 300\%$ $2.9 = 290\%$ $\qquad$ $\frac{1}{2} = .5 = 50\%$ $.075 = 7.5\%$
Converting a Percent to a Fraction **Performance Objective 6-2, Page 158**	1. Remove the percent sign. 2. *(If the percent is a whole number)* Write a fraction with the percent as the numerator and 100 as the denominator. Reduce to lowest terms. or 2. *(If the percent is a fraction)* Multiply the number by $\frac{1}{100}$ and reduce to lowest terms. or 2. *(If the percent is a decimal)* Convert it to a fraction and multiply by $\frac{1}{100}$. Reduce to lowest terms.	$7\% = \frac{7}{100}$ $60\% = \frac{60}{100} = \frac{3}{5}$ $400\% = \frac{400}{100} = 4$ $2.1\% = 2\frac{1}{10}\% = \frac{21}{10} \times \frac{1}{100} = \frac{21}{1,000}$ $5\frac{3}{4}\% = \frac{23}{4} \times \frac{1}{100} = \frac{23}{400}$
Converting a Fraction or Mixed Number to a Percent **Performance Objective 6-2, Page 158**	1. Change the fraction to a decimal by dividing the numerator by the denominator. 2. Move the decimal point two places to the right. 3. Write a percent sign after the number.	$\frac{1}{8} = .125 = 12.5\%$ $\frac{16}{3} = 5.333 = 533.3\%$ $12\frac{3}{4} = 12.75 = 1,275\%$

Section II: Using the Percentage Formula to Solve Business Problems

Topic	Important Concepts	Illustrative Examples
Solving for the Portion Performance Objective 6-3, Page 162	The portion is the number that represents a part of the base. To solve for portion, use the formula $$\text{Portion} = \text{Rate} \times \text{Base}$$	15% of Kwik-Mix Concrete employees got raises this year. If 1,800 individuals work for the company, how many got raises? $$P = .15 \times 1{,}800 = 270$$ 270 employees got raises this year.
Solving for the Rate Performance Objective 6-4, Page 164	The rate is the variable that describes what part of the base is represented by the portion. It is always the term with the percent sign. To solve for rate, use the formula $$\text{Rate} = \frac{\text{Portion}}{\text{Base}}$$	28 out of 32 warehouses owned by Metro Distributors passed safety inspection. What percent of the warehouses passed? $$\text{Rate} = \frac{28}{32} = .875 = 87.5\%$$ 87.5% passed inspection.
Solving for the Base Performance Objective 6-5, Page 166	Base is the variable that represents 100%, the starting point, or the whole thing. To solve for base, use the formula $$\text{Base} = \frac{\text{Portion}}{\text{Rate}}$$	34.3% of Thrifty Tile's sales are from customers west of the Mississippi River. If those sales last year were $154,350, what are the company's total sales? $$\text{Base} = \frac{154{,}350}{.343} = \$450{,}000$$ Total sales = $450,000.

Section III: Solving Other Business Problems Involving Percents

Topic	Important Concepts	Illustrative Examples
Determining Rate of Increase or Decrease Performance Objective 6-6, Page 171	1. Identify the original and the new amounts and find the difference between them. 2. Using the rate formula $R = P \div B$, substitute the difference from Step 1 for the portion and the original amount for the base. 3. Solve the equation for R. $$\text{Rate of change } (R) = \frac{\text{Amount of change } (P)}{\text{Original amount } (B)}$$	A price rises from $45 to $71. What is the rate of increase? $$\text{Portion} = 71 - 45 = 26$$ $$\text{Rate} = \frac{P}{B} = \frac{26}{45} = .5778 = \underline{57.8\%}$$ What is the rate of decrease from 152 to 34? $$\text{Portion} = 152 - 34 = 118$$ $$\text{Rate} = \frac{P}{B} = \frac{118}{152} = .776 = \underline{77.6\%}$$
Determining New Amount after a Percent Change Performance Objective 6-7, Page 174	Solving for the new amount is a portion problem; therefore, we use the formula $$\text{Portion} = \text{Rate} \times \text{Base}$$ 1. Substitute the original amount for the base. 2. If the rate of change is an increase, add that rate to 100%. or 2. If the rate of change is a decrease, subtract that rate from 100%.	Prestige Plastics projects a 24% increase in sales for next year. If sales this year were $172,500, what sales can be expected next year? $$\text{Rate} = 100\% + 24\% = 124\%$$ $$P = R \times B = 1.24 \times 172{,}500$$ $$P = 213{,}900$$ Projected sales = $213,900
Determining Original Amount before a Percent Change Performance Objective 6-7, Page 176	Solving for the original amount is a base problem; therefore, we use the formula $$\text{Base} = \frac{\text{Portion}}{\text{Rate}}$$ 1. Substitute the new amount for the portion. 2. If the rate of change is an increase, add that rate to 100%. or 2. If the rate of change is a decrease, subtract that rate from 100%.	If a DVD was marked down by 30% to $16.80, what was the original price? $$\text{Portion} = 100\% - 30\% = 70\%$$ $$\text{Base} = \frac{P}{R} = \frac{16.80}{.7} = 24$$ Original price = $24

Section III (continued)

Topic	Important Concepts	Illustrative Examples
Solving Problems Involving Percentage Points **Performance Objective 6-8, Page 177**	Percentage points are a way of expressing a change from an original amount to a new amount without using the percent sign. When percentage points are used, it is assumed that the base amount, 100%, stays constant. The actual percent change in business, however, is calculated by using the formula $\text{Rate of change} = \dfrac{\text{Change in percentage points}}{\text{Original percentage points}}$	After an intensive advertising campaign, General Industries' market share increased from 21 to 27%, an increase of 6 percentage points. What percent increase in business does this represent? $\%\text{ change} = \dfrac{6}{21} = .2857 = 28.6\%$ $\%\text{ increase in business} = 28.6\%$

TRY IT: EXERCISE SOLUTIONS FOR CHAPTER 6

1a. $27\% = \underline{.27}$ **1b.** $472\% = \underline{4.72}$ **1c.** $93.7\% = \underline{.937}$ **1d.** $.81\% = \underline{.0081}$

1e. $12\frac{3}{4}\% = 12.75\% = \underline{.1275}$ **1f.** $\frac{7}{8}\% = .875\% = \underline{.00875}$ **2a.** $.8 = \underline{80\%}$ **2b.** $1.4 = \underline{140\%}$

2c. $.0023 = \underline{.23\%}$ **2d.** $.016\frac{2}{5} = .0164 = \underline{1.64\%}$ **2e.** $19 = \underline{1,900\%}$ **2f.** $.57\frac{2}{3} = .5767 = \underline{57.67\%}$

3a. $9\% = \underline{\frac{9}{100}}$ **3b.** $23\% = \underline{\frac{23}{100}}$ **3c.** $75\% = \frac{75}{100} = \underline{\frac{3}{4}}$ **3d.** $225\% = \frac{225}{100} = 2\frac{25}{100} = \underline{2\frac{1}{4}}$

3e. $8.7\% = 8\frac{7}{10}\% = \frac{87}{10} \times \frac{1}{100} = \underline{\frac{87}{1,000}}$ **3f.** $1,000\% = \frac{1,000}{100} = \underline{10}$ **4a.** $\frac{1}{5} = .2 = \underline{20\%}$

4b. $\frac{70}{200} = .35 = \underline{35\%}$ **4c.** $\frac{23}{5} = 4\frac{3}{5} = 4.6 = \underline{460\%}$ **4d.** $6\frac{9}{10} = 6.9 = \underline{690\%}$ **4e.** $\frac{45}{54} = .8333 = \underline{83.33\%}$

4f. $140\frac{1}{8} = 140.125 = \underline{14,012.5\%}$ **5.** $P = R \times B = .55 \times 980 = \underline{539}$ **6.** $P = R \times B = .72 \times 3,200 = \underline{2,304}$

7a. $P = R \times B = .16 \times 1,250 = \underline{200}$ Salespeople   **7b.** $P = R \times B = .15 \times 148,500 = \underline{\$22,275}$ Down payment

8. $R = \frac{P}{B} = \frac{9}{21} = .4285 = \underline{42.9\%}$ **9.** $R = \frac{P}{B} = \frac{67}{142} = .4718 = \underline{47.2\%}$ **10a.** $R = \frac{P}{B} = \frac{5,400}{18,000} = .3 = \underline{30\%}$ Completed

$100\% - 30\% = \underline{70\%}$ Remains

10b. $R = \frac{P}{B} = \frac{5,518}{8,900} = .62 = \underline{62\%}$ Suits   **11.** $B = \frac{P}{R} = \frac{690}{.4} = \underline{1,725}$ **12.** $B = \frac{P}{R} = \frac{550}{.88} = \underline{\$625}$

13a. $B = \frac{P}{R} = \frac{126}{.35} = \underline{360}$ Motors   **13b.** $B = \frac{P}{R} = \frac{3,420}{.75} = \underline{4,560}$ Reams of paper

14. Portion = Increase = 948 − 650 = 298   **15.** Portion = Decrease = 21 − 15 = 6

Base = Original number = 650   Base = Original number = 21

$R = \frac{P}{B} = \frac{298}{650} = .45846 = \underline{45.8\%}$ Increase $R = \frac{P}{B} = \frac{6}{21} = .2857 = \underline{28.6\%}$ Decrease

16. Portion = Increase = \$540 − \$450 = \$90   **17.** Portion = Decrease = 60 − 12 = 48

Base = Original number = \$450   Base = Original number = 60

$R = \frac{P}{B} = \frac{90}{450} = .2 = \underline{20\%}$ Increase $R = \frac{P}{B} = \frac{48}{60} = .8 = \underline{80\%}$ Decrease

18. Rate = 100% + 60% = 160%

$P = R \times B = 1.6 \times 525 = \underline{840}$ Gigabytes

20. Rate = 100% − 40% = 60%

$B = \dfrac{P}{R} = \dfrac{12}{.6} = \underline{20}$ Feet

22. $R = \dfrac{P}{B} = \dfrac{8}{20} = .4 = \underline{40\%}$ Increase in voters

19. Rate = 100% − 20% = 80%

$P = R \times B = .8 \times 650 = \underline{520}$ Miles per week

21. Rate = 100% + 20% = 120%

$B = \dfrac{P}{R} = \dfrac{90}{1.2} = \underline{75}$ Acres per day

---

CONCEPT REVIEW

1. A percent is a way of expressing a part of a(n) _____ . (6-1)

2. In previous chapters, we expressed these parts as _____ and _____ . (6-1)

3. Percent means "part per _____." The percent sign is written as _____ . (6-1)

4. To convert a percent to a decimal, we remove the percent sign and _____ by 100. (6-1)

5. To convert a decimal to a percent, we multiply by 100 and write a(n) _____ sign after the number. (6-1)

6. To convert a percent to a fraction, we remove the percent sign and place the number over _____ . (6-2)

7. List the steps for converting a fraction to a percent. (6-2)

8. The three basic parts of the percentage formula are the _____ , _____ , and _____ . (6-3)

9. The percentage formula is written as _____ . (6-3)

10. In the percentage formula, the _____ is the variable with the percent sign or the word *percent*. (6-4)

11. In the percentage formula, the _____ represents 100%, or the whole thing. In a sentence, it follows the word _____ . (6-5)

12. Write the formula for the rate of change. (6-6)

13. When calculating amounts in percent change situations, the rate of change is added to 100% if the change is a(n) _____ and subtracted from 100% if the change is a(n) _____ . (6-7)

14. Percentage _____ are a way of expressing a change from an original amount to a new amount without using a percent sign. (6-8)

CHAPTER

6

ASSESSMENT TEST

Convert the following percents to decimals.

1. 88%   **2.** $3\frac{3}{4}\%$ **3.** 59.68%   **4.** 422%   **5.** $\frac{9}{16}\%$

Convert the following decimals or whole numbers to percents.

6. 12.6   **7.** .681   **8.** 53   **9.** $24\frac{4}{5}$ **10.** .0929

CHAPTER

6

Convert the following percents to reduced fractions, mixed numbers, or whole numbers.

11. 19%   **12.** 217%   **13.** 7.44%   **14.** 126%   **15.** $25\frac{2}{5}\%$

Convert each of the following fractions or mixed numbers to percents.

16. $\frac{4}{5}$ **17.** $\frac{5}{9}$ **18.** $\frac{33}{4}$ **19.** $56\frac{3}{10}$ **20.** $\frac{745}{100}$

Solve the following for the portion, rate, or base, rounding decimals to hundredths and percents to the nearest tenth when necessary.

21. 24% of 1,700 =   **22.** 56 is _____ % of 125   **23.** 91 is 88% of _____

24. What number is 45% of 680?   **25.** $233.91 is what percent of $129.95?

26. 315 is 126% of _____   **27.** 60 increased by 15% = _____

28. If a number increases from 47 to 70.5, what is the rate of increase?

29. What is the base if the portion is 444 and the rate is 15%?

30. What is the portion if the base is 900 and the rate is $12\frac{3}{4}\%$?

31. What is 100% of 1,492?   **32.** 7,000 decreased by 62% = _____

Solve the following word problems for the unknown. Round decimals to hundredths and percents to the nearest tenth when necessary.

33. An ad for Target read, "This week only, all electronics 35% off!" If a television set normally sells for $349.95, what is the amount of the savings?

34. If 453 runners out of 620 completed a marathon, what percent of the runners finished the race?

35. Last year Keystone's corporate jet required $23,040 in maintenance and repairs.

   a. If this represents 32% of the total operating costs of the airplane, what was the total cost to fly the plane for the year?

b. If the plane flew 300,000 miles last year, what is the cost per mile to operate the plane?

c. Sky King Leasing offered a deal whereby it would operate the plane for Keystone for only $0.18 per mile. What is the percent decrease in operating expense per mile being offered by Sky King?

d. In 2009, the company began looking to buy another jet. Use the chart "More Jets for Sale" to calculate the rate of increase of jets available in 2009 compared with 1999. Round to the nearest whole percent.

More Jets for Sale

Number of used business Jets for sale worldwide:

Source: UBS Investment Research

36. A letter carrier can deliver mail to 112 homes per hour by walking and 168 homes per hour by driving.

a. By what percent is productivity increased by driving?

b. If a new ZIP Code system improves driving productivity by 12.5%, what is the new number of homes per hour for driving?

37. Last year the Tundra Corporation had sales of $343,500. If this year's sales are forecast to be $415,700, what is the percent increase in sales?

38. After a 15% pay raise, Scott Walker now earns $27,600. What was his salary before the raise?

39. According to Autodata research, in November 2008, Toyota sold 130,307 vehicles in the United States. In November 2009, sales increased 2.6% over the previous November.

a. How many vehicles did Toyota sell in November 2009?

b. The research also indicated that Toyota's November U.S. market share increased from 17.4% in 2008 to 17.9% in 2009, an increase of 0.5 percentage points. What percent does this increase represent?

40. Three of every seven sales transactions at Dollar Discount are on credit cards. What percent of the transactions are *not* credit card sales?

41. A pre-election survey shows that an independent presidential candidate has increased his popularity from 26.5 percent to 31.3 percent of the electorate, an increase of 4.8 percentage points. What percent does this increase represent?

42. By what percent is a 100-watt lightbulb brighter than a 60-watt bulb?

CHAPTER

6

43. In 1998, a 30-second television advertisement on the Super Bowl telecast cost $1.3 million. In 2010, the price of a 30-second ad had increased by 132% over the 1998 price. How much was a Super Bowl ad in 2010? Write your answer in numerical form.

44. Michael Reeves, an ice cream vendor, pays $17.50 for a five-gallon container of premium ice cream. From this quantity, he sells 80 scoops at $0.90 per scoop. If he sold smaller scoops, he could sell 98 scoops from the same container; however, he could charge only $0.80 per scoop. As his accountant, you are asked the following questions.

    a. If Michael switches to the smaller scoops, by how much will his profit per container go up or down? (Profit = Sales − Expenses)

    b. By what percent will the profit change? Round to the nearest tenth of a percent.

45. An insurance adjuster for UPS found that 12% of a shipment was damaged in transit. If the damaged goods amounted to $4,870, what was the total value of the shipment?

46. Morley Fast, a contractor, built a warehouse complex in Canmore for the following costs: land, $12,000; concrete and steel, $34,500; plumbing and electrical, $48,990; general carpentry and roof, $42,340; and other expenses, $34,220.

    a. What percent of the total cost is represented by each category of expenses?

    b. When the project was completed, Morley sold the entire complex for 185% of its cost. What was the selling price of the complex?

Education E-Books

Sales of digital textbooks for higher education

$300 million

250

200

150 — 106.5

100

50

0

'08 '09 '10 '11 '12 '13

——— Projections ———

275.0

Source: Albert N. Greco, Fordham Graduate School of Business Administration.

Use the chart "Education E-Books" for Exercises 47–49.

47. What is the projected rate of change in education e-book sales from 2008 to 2013? Round to the nearest tenth of a percent.

48. What were the sales of education e-books in 2009 if they were 10.3% higher than 2008? Round to the nearest tenth of a million.

49. If the 2013 projected figure represents a 19.6% increase from 2012, what are the projected education e-book sales for 2012? Round to the nearest tenth of a million.

BUSINESS DECISION: ALLOCATING OVERHEAD EXPENSES

50. You are the owner of a chain of three successful restaurants with the following number of seats in each location: airport, 340 seats; downtown, 218 seats; and suburban, 164 seats.

EXCEL 2

a. If the liability insurance premium is $16,000 per year, how much of that premium should be allocated to each of the restaurants based on percent of total seating capacity? Round each percent to the nearest tenth.

b. If you open a fourth location at the beach that has 150 seats and the liability insurance premium increases by 18%, what is the new allocation of insurance premium among the four locations?

c. (Optional) What other expenses could be allocated to the four restaurants?

d. (Optional) What other ways, besides seating capacity, could you use to allocate expenses?

COLLABORATIVE LEARNING ACTIVITY

Percents—The Language of Business

For emphasis and illustration, business percentage figures, when printed, are frequently presented in circle, bar, and line chart format. Charts add a compelling element to otherwise plain "numbers in the news."

As a team, search business publications, annual reports, and the Internet to find 10 interesting and varied examples of business percentage figures being presented in chart form. Share your findings with the class.

Business Math Times

GREEN NUMBERS – THE POWER OF ONE

According to Jim Hackler, theurbaneenvironmentalist.com, "the people of the United States represent less than 5 percent of the world's population—yet that 5 percent consumes more than a quarter of our planet's resources. If the rest of the world rose to the U.S. level of consumption, four additional planets would be needed to supply the resources and absorb the waste!"

Here's a look at some of Jim's intriguing findings, "how a single act can help (or hurt) the environment—especially when it's shared by millions."

IT'S TOO DARN HOT

If the thermostat in every house in America were lowered **1 degree Fahrenheit** during the winter, the nation would save **230 million barrels of crude oil**—enough to fill an oil tanker 400 times.

SHOWER POWER

If 40 million people were to spend **one minute less** each day in the shower over their lifetime, they would save **4 trillion gallons** of water—the total amount of snow and rain that falls over the entire lower 48 states in a day.

STRAIGHT FLUSH

If home builders had installed **one dual-flush toilet** instead of a standard low-flow toilet in every new house they built in 2008, they would have saved **1.65 billion gallons of water** a year.

IN THE CAN

One soft drink can recycled by each elementary school student in America would save **24.8 million cans**. That would be enough aluminum to create 21 Boeing 737 airplanes.

VIRTUAL PAYMENT

If every American switched to receiving just **one bill** as an electronic statement instead of a paper statement, the one-time savings would be **217,800,000 sheets**—enough to blanket the island of Key West in a single layer of paper.

WRAPACIOUS

One out of every 3 pounds of the waste that Americans generate is for packaging, which each year adds up to **77 million tons**—enough to fill the Louisiana Superdome 37 times.

"I'm updating the Wizard of Oz. In my version, the Tin Man is recycled into a Prius and they all drive home to Kansas on less than a half-tank of gas!"

© Randy Glasbergen www.glasbergen.com

BATH PARTY

If every American collected **1 gallon of water** once a week while waiting for the shower or bathwater to get hot and used it to water his or her houseplants, the total saved would be **15.8 billion gallons of water** a year—enough to fill the Reflecting Pool at the National Mall in Washington, D.C. 2,338 times.

Source: Green Numbers, "The Power of 1," Jim Hackler, *Sky Magazine*, March 2008, pages 48–51

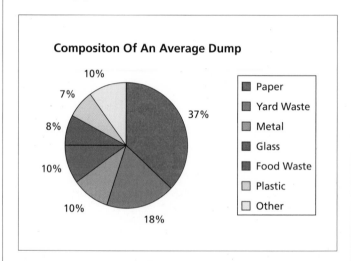

Compositon Of An Average Dump

- Paper — 37%
- Yard Waste — 18%
- Metal — 10%
- Glass — 10%
- Food Waste — 10%
- Plastic — 8%
- Other — 7%, 10%

ISSUES & ACTIVITIES

1. Assume that a dump received a total of 750,000 pounds of waste last week. Use the chart above to allocate the number of pounds of waste for each category.
2. If recycling one glass bottle or jar saves enough electricity to light a 100-watt bulb for four hours, how many bottles or jars will it take to light the bulb for a year?
3. Americans use 4 million plastic bottles every hour, but only 25% of plastic bottles are recycled. At that rate, how many plastic bottles are recycled in a week?
4. In teams, research the Internet to find current trends in "greening of America" statistics. List your sources and visually report your findings to the class.

BRAINTEASER – "BUY THE NUMBERS"

You recently purchased a 100-unit apartment building. As part of a fix-up project, you have decided to install new numbers on each front door. If the apartments are numbered from 1 to 100, how many nines will you need to buy?

See the end of Appendix A for the solution.

Dmitry Kalinovsky/Shutterstock.com

Invoices, Trade Discounts, and Cash Discounts

SECTION I　7　THE INVOICE

invoice A document detailing a sales transaction that contains a list of goods shipped or services rendered with an account of all costs.

In business, merchandise is bought and sold many times as it passes from the manufacturer through wholesalers and retailers to the final consumer. A bill of sale, or an **invoice**, is a business document used to keep track of these sales and purchases. From the seller's point of view, they are sales invoices; from the buyer's point of view, they are purchase invoices or purchase orders.

Invoices are a comprehensive record of a sales transaction. They show what merchandise or services have been sold, to whom, in what quantities, at what price, and under what conditions and terms. They vary in style and format from company to company, but most contain essentially the same information. Invoices are used extensively in business, and it is important to be able to read and understand them. In this chapter, you will learn how businesses use invoices and the math applications that relate to them.

7-1　READING AND UNDERSTANDING THE PARTS OF AN INVOICE

F.O.B. shipping point The buyer pays all transportation charges from the vendor's location.

F.O.B. destination The seller pays all the shipping changes to the buyer's store or warehouse and then bills the buyer for these charges on the invoice.

F.O.B. Term used in quoting shipping charges meaning "free on board" or "freight on board."

Exhibit 7-1 shows a typical format used in business for an invoice. The important parts have been labeled and are explained in Exhibit 7-2. Some of the terms have page references, which direct you to the sections in this chapter that further explain those terms and their business math applications. Exhibit 7-2 also presents some of the most commonly used invoice abbreviations. These pertain to merchandise quantities and measurements.

With some practice, these terms and abbreviations will become familiar to you. Take some time to look them over before you continue reading.

SHIPPING TERMS

Two frequently used shipping terms that you should become familiar with are **F.O.B. shipping point** and **F.O.B. destination**. **F.O.B.** means "free on board" or "freight on board." These terms define the shipping charges and when the title (ownership) of the goods is transferred from the seller to the buyer. Ownership becomes important when insurance claims must be filed due to problems in shipment.

F.O.B. Shipping Point　When the terms are F.O.B. shipping point, the buyer pays the shipping company directly. The merchandise title is transferred to the buyer at the manufacturer's factory or at a shipping point such as a railroad freight yard or air freight terminal. From this point, the buyer is responsible for the merchandise.

F.O.B. Destination　When the shipping terms are F.O.B. destination, the seller is responsible for prepaying the shipping charges to the destination. The destination is usually the buyer's store or warehouse. Unless prices are quoted as "delivered," the seller then bills the buyer on the invoice for the shipping charges.

Sometimes the freight terms are stated as F.O.B. with the name of a city. For example, if the seller is in Fort Worth and the buyer is in New York, F.O.B. Fort Worth means the title is transferred in Fort Worth and the buyer pays the shipping charges from Fort Worth to New York. If the terms are F.O.B. New York, the seller pays the shipping charges to New York and then bills the buyer for those charges on the invoice. Exhibit 7-3, Shipping Terms, on page 195, illustrates these transactions.

When companies ship and receive merchandise, invoices and purchase orders are used to record the details of the transaction.

istockphoto.com/endopack

EXHIBIT 7-1 Typical Invoice Format

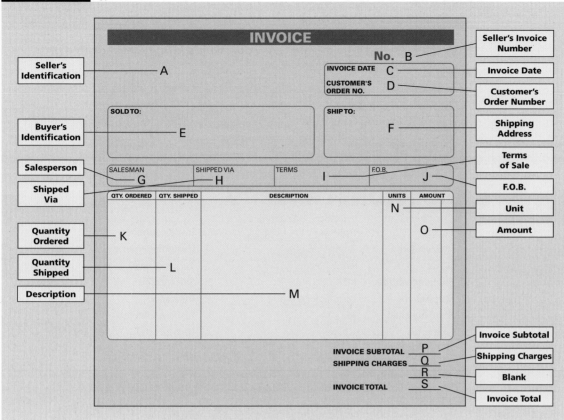

EXHIBIT 7-2 Invoice Terminology and Abbreviations

Invoice Terminology

A **Seller's Identification**—Name, address, and logo or corporate symbol of the seller

B **Seller's Invoice Number**—Seller's identification number of the transaction

C **Invoice Date**—Date the invoice was written

D **Customer's Order Number**—Buyer's identification number of the transaction

E **Buyer's Identification**—Name and mailing address of the buyer

F **Shipping Address**—Address where merchandise will be shipped

G **Salesperson**—Name of salesperson credited with the sale

H **Shipped Via**—Name of shipping company handling the shipment

I **Terms**—Terms of sale—Section detailing date of payment and cash discount (p. 210)

J **F.O.B.**—"Free on board"—Section detailing who pays the shipping company and when title is transferred. (p. 191)

K **Quantity Ordered**—Number of units ordered

L **Quantity Shipped**—Number of units shipped

M **Description**—Detailed description of the merchandise, including model numbers

N **Unit**—Price per unit of merchandise

O **Amount**—Extended total—Quantity in units times the unit price for each line (p. 195)

P **Invoice Subtotal**—Total of the Amount column—Merchandise total (p. 195)

Q **Shipping Charges**—Cost to physically transport the merchandise from the seller to the buyer (p. 192)

R **Blank Line**—Line used for other charges such as insurance or handling

S **Invoice Total**—Total amount of the invoice—Includes merchandise plus all other charges (p. 195)

Invoice Abbreviations

ea	each	pr	pair	in.	inch	oz	ounce
dz or doz	dozen	dm or drm	drum	ft	foot	g or gr	gram
gr or gro	gross	bbl	barrel	yd	yard	kg	kilogram
bx	box	sk	sack	mm	millimeter	pt	pint
cs	case	@	at	cm	centimeter	qt	quart
ct or crt	crate	C	100 items	m	meter	gal	gallon
ctn or cart	carton	M	1,000 items	lb	pound	cwt	hundred weight

EXAMPLE1 IDENTIFYING PARTS OF AN INVOICE

From the following Whole Grain Cereal Co. invoice, identify the indicated parts.

a. Seller	_____	b. Invoice number	_____
c. Invoice date	_____	d. Customer order #	_____
e. Buyer	_____	f. Terms of sale	_____
g. Shipping address	_____	h. Salesperson	_____
i. Shipped via	_____	j. Insurance	_____
k. Shipping charges	_____	l. Invoice subtotal	_____
m. Unit price—Fruit and Nut Flakes	_____	n. Invoice total	_____

SOLUTIONSTRATEGY

a. Seller	Organic Grain Cereal Co.	b. Invoice number	2112
c. Invoice date	August 19, 20XX	d. Customer order #	B-1623
e. Buyer	Kroger Supermarkets	f. Terms of sale	Net - 45 days
g. Shipping address	1424 Peachtree Rd	h. Salesperson	H. L. Mager
i. Shipped via	Terminal Transport	j. Insurance	$33.00
k. Shipping charges	$67.45	l. Invoice subtotal	$2,227.05
m. Unit price—Fruit and Nut Flakes	$19.34	n. Invoice total	$2,327.50

INVOICE

No. 2112

Organic Grain Cereal Co.
697 Canyon Road
Boulder, CO 80304

INVOICE DATE: August 19, 20XX
CUSTOMER'S ORDER NO.: B-1623

SOLD TO:
KROGER SUPERMARKETS
565 North Avenue
Atlanta, Georgia 30348

SHIP TO:
DISTRIBUTION CENTER
1424 Peachtree Road
Atlanta, Georgia 30341

SALESMAN	SHIPPED VIA	TERMS	F.O.B.
H. L. Mager	Terminal Transport	Net - 45 Days	Boulder, CO

QTY. ORDERED	QTY. SHIPPED	DESCRIPTION		UNIT	AMOUNT
55 cs.	55 cs.	Corn Crunchies	24 ounce	22.19	$1220 45
28 cs.	28 cs.	Fruit and Nut Flakes	24 ounce	19.34	541 52
41 cs.	22 cs.	Rice and Wheat Flakes	16 ounce	21.14	465 08

INVOICE SUBTOTAL	2,227.05
SHIPPING CHARGES	67.45
INSURANCE	33.00
INVOICE TOTAL	$2,327.50

TRYITEXERCISE1

From the following FotoFair invoice, identify the indicated parts.

a. Buyer	_____	b. Invoice number	_____
c. Invoice date	_____	d. Amount—Pocket Pro 55	_____
e. Seller	_____	f. Terms of sale	_____
g. Shipping address	_____	h. Salesperson	_____
i. Shipped via	_____	j. F.O.B.	_____
k. Shipping charges	_____	l. Invoice subtotal	_____
m. Unit price—Pocket Pro 75	_____	n. Invoice total	_____

CHECK YOUR ANSWERS WITH THE SOLUTIONS ON PAGE 225.

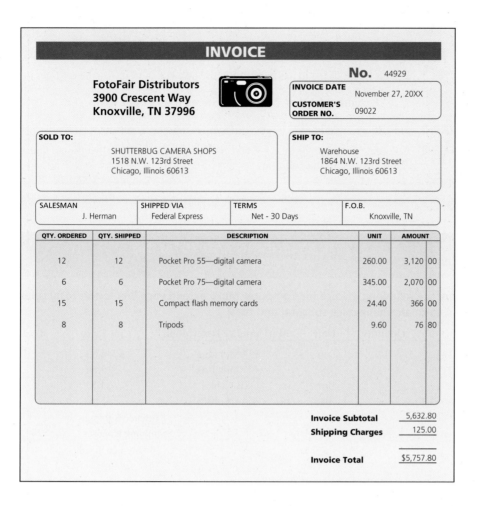

INVOICE

FotoFair Distributors
3900 Crescent Way
Knoxville, TN 37996

No. 44929

| INVOICE DATE | November 27, 20XX |
| CUSTOMER'S ORDER NO. | 09022 |

SOLD TO:
SHUTTERBUG CAMERA SHOPS
1518 N.W. 123rd Street
Chicago, Illinois 60613

SHIP TO:
Warehouse
1864 N.W. 123rd Street
Chicago, Illinois 60613

SALESMAN	SHIPPED VIA	TERMS	F.O.B.
J. Herman	Federal Express	Net - 30 Days	Knoxville, TN

QTY. ORDERED	QTY. SHIPPED	DESCRIPTION	UNIT	AMOUNT
12	12	Pocket Pro 55—digital camera	260.00	3,120 00
6	6	Pocket Pro 75—digital camera	345.00	2,070 00
15	15	Compact flash memory cards	24.40	366 00
8	8	Tripods	9.60	76 80

Invoice Subtotal	5,632.80
Shipping Charges	125.00
Invoice Total	$5,757.80

EXTENDING AND TOTALING AN INVOICE

7-2

Extending an invoice is the process of computing the value in the Total or Amount column for each line of the invoice. This number represents the total dollar amount of each type of merchandise or service being purchased. The **invoice subtotal** is the amount of all items on the invoice before shipping and handling charges; insurance; and other adjustments such as discounts, returns, and credits. The **invoice total** is the final amount due from the buyer to the seller.

invoice subtotal The amount of all merchandise or services on the invoice before adjustments.

invoice total The final amount due from the buyer to the seller.

EXHIBIT 7-3 Shipping Terms

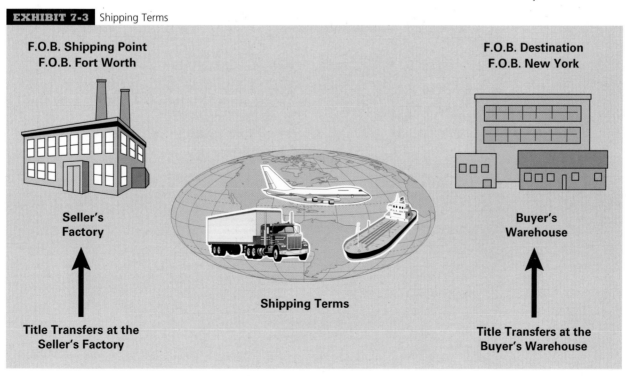

F.O.B. Shipping Point
F.O.B. Fort Worth

F.O.B. Destination
F.O.B. New York

Seller's Factory

Buyer's Warehouse

Shipping Terms

Title Transfers at the Seller's Factory

Title Transfers at the Buyer's Warehouse

STEPS TO EXTEND AND TOTAL AN INVOICE

STEP 1. For each line of the invoice, multiply the number of items by the cost per item.

Extended total = Number of items × Cost per item

STEP 2. Add all extended totals to get the invoice subtotal.

STEP 3. Calculate the invoice total by adding the freight charges, insurance, and any other charges to the subtotal.

EXAMPLE2 EXTENDING AND TOTALING AN INVOICE

From the following invoice for Computer Mart, extend each line to the Total column and calculate the invoice subtotal and total.

Stock #	Quantity	Unit	Merchandise Description	Unit Price	Total
4334	17	ea.	13" Monitors	$244.00	_____
1217	8	ea.	17" Monitors	525.80	_____
2192	2	doz.	USB Cables	24.50	_____
5606	1	bx.	Blu-ray discs	365.90	_____
				Invoice Subtotal	
				Shipping Charges	$244.75
				Invoice Total	_____

SOLUTIONSTRATEGY

					Total
13" Monitors	17	×	$244.00	=	$4,148.00
17" Monitors	8	×	525.80	=	4,206.40
USB Cables	2	×	24.50	=	49.00
Blu-ray discs	1	×	365.90	=	365.90
			Invoice Subtotal		$8,769.30
			Shipping Charges		+ 244.75
			Invoice Total		$9,014.05

TRYITEXERCISE2

From the following invoice for The Kitchen Connection, extend each line to the Total column and calculate the invoice subtotal and total.

Stock #	Quantity	Unit	Merchandise Description	Unit Price	Total
R443	125	ea.	Food Processors	$89.00	_____
B776	24	ea.	Microwave Ovens	225.40	_____
Z133	6	doz.	12" Mixers	54.12	_____
Z163	1	bx.	Mixer Covers	166.30	_____
				Invoice Subtotal	
				Shipping Charges	$194.20
				Invoice Total	_____

CHECK YOUR ANSWERS WITH THE SOLUTIONS ON PAGE 225.

REVIEW EXERCISES

What word is represented by each of the following abbreviations?

1. bx.   Box
2. pt _____
3. drm. _____
4. kg _____
5. gro.   Gross
6. oz _____
7. M. _____
8. cwt _____

Using the Panorama Products invoice below, extend each line to the Amount column and calculate the subtotal and total. Then answer Questions 9–22. (*Note:* Although 26 boxes of 2-inch reflective tape were ordered, only 11 boxes were shipped. Charge only for the boxes shipped.)

9. Seller   Panorama Products
10. Invoice number   R-7431
11. Invoice date _____
12. Cust. order # _____
13. Buyer _____
14. Terms of sale _____
15. Shipping address _____
16. Salesperson _____
17. Shipped via _____
18. Insurance _____
19. Shipping charges _____
20. Unit price—2" Tape _____
21. Invoice subtotal _____
22. Invoice total _____

INVOICE

No. R-7431

Panorama Products
486 5th Avenue
Eureka, CA 95501

INVOICE DATE	June 16, 20XX
CUSTOMER'S ORDER NO.	12144

SOLD TO:
J. M. Hardware Supply
2051 West Adams Blvd.
Lansing, MI 48901

SHIP TO:
SAME

SALESMAN	SHIPPED VIA	TERMS	F.O.B.
H. Marshall	Gilbert Trucking	Net 30 Days	Effingham, IL

QTY. ORDERED	QTY. SHIPPED	DESCRIPTION	UNIT	AMOUNT
16 cases	16 cases	Masking Tape ½" Standard	21.90	
12 cases	12 cases	Masking Tape 1½" Standard	26.79	
26 boxes	11 boxes	2" Reflective Tape	88.56	
37 cases	37 cases	Sandpaper Assorted	74.84	

INVOICE SUBTOTAL	_____
SHIPPING CHARGES	61.45
	_____
INVOICE TOTAL	_____

IN THE BUSINESS WORLD

Frequently, merchandise that is ordered from vendors is "out of stock" and goes into back-order status.

As a general rule, companies charge only for the merchandise that is shipped.

BUSINESS DECISION: MANAGING MERCHANDISE

23. You are the store manager for The Bedding Warehouse. The invoice below is due for payment to one of your vendors, Hamilton Mills.

a. Check the invoice for errors and correct any you find.

b. Your warehouse manager reports that there were three king-size sheets and five queen-size sheets returned, along with four packages of queen pillow cases. Calculate the revised total due.

c. The vendor has offered a 4% early payment discount that applies only to the merchandise, not the shipping or insurance. What is the amount of the discount?

d. What is the new balance due after the discount?

Retail store managers manage stores that specialize in selling a specific line of merchandise, such as groceries, meat, liquor, apparel, furniture, automobile parts, electronic items, or household appliances.

© Exactostock/SuperStock

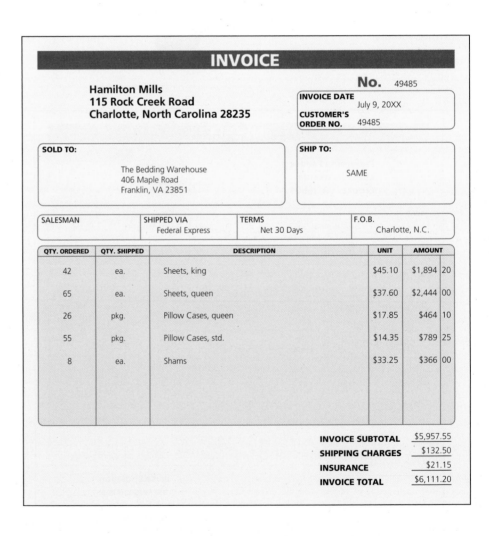

INVOICE

No. 49485

Hamilton Mills
115 Rock Creek Road
Charlotte, North Carolina 28235

| INVOICE DATE | July 9, 20XX |
| CUSTOMER'S ORDER NO. | 49485 |

SOLD TO:
The Bedding Warehouse
406 Maple Road
Franklin, VA 23851

SHIP TO:
SAME

SALESMAN	SHIPPED VIA	TERMS	F.O.B.
	Federal Express	Net 30 Days	Charlotte, N.C.

QTY. ORDERED	QTY. SHIPPED	DESCRIPTION	UNIT	AMOUNT
42	ea.	Sheets, king	$45.10	$1,894 20
65	ea.	Sheets, queen	$37.60	$2,444 00
26	pkg.	Pillow Cases, queen	$17.85	$464 10
55	pkg.	Pillow Cases, std.	$14.35	$789 25
8	ea.	Shams	$33.25	$366 00

INVOICE SUBTOTAL	$5,957.55
SHIPPING CHARGES	$132.50
INSURANCE	$21.15
INVOICE TOTAL	$6,111.20

TRADE DISCOUNTS—SINGLE

The path merchandise travels as it moves from the manufacturer through wholesalers and retailers to the ultimate consumer is known as a channel of distribution or trade channel. The businesses that form these channels are said to be "in the trade." In today's complex economy, a number of different trade channels are used to move goods and services efficiently.

Trade discounts are reductions from the manufacturer's suggested **list price**. They are given to businesses at various levels of the trade channel for the performance of marketing functions. These functions may include activities such as selling, advertising, storage, service, and display.

Manufacturers print catalogs showcasing their merchandise. Often these catalogs contain the manufacturer's suggested list or retail prices. Businesses in the trade receive price sheets from the manufacturer listing the trade discounts in percent form associated with each item in the catalog. By issuing updated price sheets of trade discounts, manufacturers have the flexibility of changing the prices of their merchandise without the expense of reprinting the entire catalog.

Trade discounts are sometimes quoted as a single discount and sometimes as a series or chain of discounts. The number of discounts is dependent on the extent of the marketing services performed by the channel member.

trade discounts Reductions from the manufacturer's list price given to businesses that are "in the trade" for performance of marketing functions.

list price Suggested retail selling price of an item set by the manufacturer or supplier. The original price from which discounts are taken.

CALCULATING THE AMOUNT OF A SINGLE TRADE DISCOUNT

7-3

The amount of a single trade discount is calculated by multiplying the list price by the trade discount rate.

> **Trade discount = List price × Trade discount rate**

EXAMPLE3 CALCULATING THE AMOUNT OF A SINGLE TRADE DISCOUNT

What is the amount of the trade discount on merchandise with a list price of $2,800 and a trade discount rate of 45%?

SOLUTIONSTRATEGY

Trade discount = List price × Trade discount rate
Trade discount = 2,800 × .45 = $1,260

TRYITEXERCISE3

Gifts Galore, a retail gift shop, buys merchandise with a list price of $7,600 from a wholesaler of novelty items and toys. The wholesaler extends a 30% trade discount rate to the retailer. What is the amount of the trade discount?

CHECK YOUR ANSWER WITH THE SOLUTION ON PAGE 225.

CALCULATING NET PRICE BY USING THE NET PRICE FACTOR, COMPLEMENT METHOD

7-4

The **net price** is the amount a business actually pays for the merchandise after the discount has been deducted. It may be calculated by subtracting the amount of the trade discount from the list price.

net price The amount a business actually pays for the merchandise after the discount has been deducted.

> **Net price = List price − Trade discount**

Frequently, merchants are more interested in knowing the net price of an item than the amount of the trade discount. In that case, the net price can be calculated directly from the list price without first finding the amount of the discount.

The list price of an item is considered to be 100%. If, for example, the trade discount on an item is 40% of the list price, the net price will be 60% because the two must equal 100%. This 60%, the complement of the trade discount rate (100% − 40%), is the portion of the list price that *is* paid. Known as the **net price factor**, it is usually written in decimal form.

net price factor The percent of the list price a business pays for merchandise. It is the multiplier used to calculate the net price.

STEPS TO CALCULATE NET PRICE BY USING THE NET PRICE FACTOR

STEP 1. Calculate the net price factor, complement of the trade discount rate.

$$\text{Net price factor} = 100\% - \text{Trade discount rate}$$

STEP 2. Calculate the net price.

$$\text{Net price} = \text{List price} \times \text{Net price factor}$$

Note: This procedure can be combined into one step by the formula.

$$\text{Net price} = \text{List price}(100\% - \text{Trade discount rate})$$

LEARNINGTIP

Complements are two numbers that add up to 100%. The trade discount rate and the net price factor are complements of each other. This means that if we know one of them, the other can be found by subtracting from 100%.

EXAMPLE4 CALCULATING THE NET PRICE

Calculate the net price of merchandise at Astana Imports listing for $900 less a trade discount rate of 45%.

SOLUTIONSTRATEGY

$$\text{Net price} = \text{List price}(100\% - \text{Trade discount rate})$$
$$\text{Net price} = 900(100\% - 45\%)$$
$$\text{Net price} = 900(.55) = \underline{\$495}$$

TRYITEXERCISE4

Central Hardware Store bought paint supplies listing for $2,100 with a single trade discount rate of 35%. What is the net price of the order?

CHECK YOUR ANSWER WITH THE SOLUTION ON PAGE 225.

7-5

CALCULATING TRADE DISCOUNT RATE WHEN LIST PRICE AND NET PRICE ARE KNOWN

The trade discount rate can be calculated by using the now-familiar percentage formula Rate = Portion ÷ Base. For this application, the amount of the trade discount is the portion, or numerator, and the list price is the base, or denominator.

$$\text{Trade discount rate} = \frac{\text{Trade discount}}{\text{List price}}$$

STEPS FOR CALCULATING TRADE DISCOUNT RATE

STEP 1. Calculate the amount of the trade discount.

$$\text{Trade discount} = \text{List price} - \text{Net price}$$

STEP 2. Calculate the trade discount rate.

$$\text{Trade discount rate} = \frac{\text{Trade discount}}{\text{List price}}$$

EXAMPLE5 CALCULATING THE SINGLE TRADE DISCOUNT AND RATE

Sterling Manufacturing sells tools to American Garden Supply. In a recent transaction, the list price of an order was $47,750 and the net price of the order was $32,100. Calculate the amount of the trade discount. What was the trade discount rate? Round your answer to the nearest tenth percent.

SOLUTIONSTRATEGY

Trade discount = List price − Net price
Trade discount = 47,750 − 32,100 = $15,650

$$\text{Trade discount rate} = \frac{\text{Trade discount}}{\text{List price}}$$

$$\text{Trade discount rate} = \frac{15,650}{47,750} = .3277 = 32.8\%$$

TRYITEXERCISE5

Wilson Sporting Goods recently sold tennis rackets listing for $109,500 to The Sports Authority. The net price of the order was $63,300. What was the amount of the trade discount? What was the trade discount rate? Round your answer to the nearest tenth percent.

CHECK YOUR ANSWERS WITH THE SOLUTION ON PAGE 225.

REVIEW EXERCISES   SECTION II   **7**

Calculate the following trade discounts. Round all answers to the nearest cent.

List Price	Trade Discount Rate	Trade Discount
1. $860.00	30%	$258.00

Trade discount = 860.00 × .30 = $258.00

2. 125.50	12%	_____
3. 41.75	19%	_____
4. 499.00	8%	_____
5. 88.25	50%	_____

Calculate the following trade discounts and net prices to the nearest cent.

	List Price	Trade Discount Rate	Trade Discount	Net Price
6.	$286.00	25%	$71.50	$214.50
7.	134.79	40%	_____	_____
8.	21.29	18%	_____	_____
9.	959.00	55%	_____	_____

Calculate the following net price factors and net prices by using the complement method. Round all answers to the nearest cent.

	List Price	Trade Discount Rate	Net Price Factor	Net Price
10.	$3,499.00	37%	63%	$2,204.37
11.	565.33	24%	_____	_____
12.	1,244.25	45.8%	_____	_____
13.	4.60	$12\frac{3}{4}\%$	_____	_____

Calculate the following trade discounts and trade discount rates. Round answers to the nearest tenth of a percent.

	List Price	Trade Discount	Trade Discount Rate	Net Price
14.	$4,500.00	$935.00	20.8%	$3,565.00
15.	345.50	_____	_____	225.00
16.	2.89	_____	_____	2.15

17. Find the amount of a trade discount of 30% on a television set that has a list price of $799.95.

18. Find the amount of a trade discount of 55% on a set of fine china that lists for $345.70.

19. What is the amount of a trade discount of 25% offered to a shoe store for merchandise purchased at a total list price of $7,800?

20. Whole Foods Market ordered 12 cases of organic vegetable soup with a list price of $18.90 per case and 8 cases of organic baked beans with a list price of $33.50 per case. The wholesaler offered Whole Foods a 39% trade discount.

  a. What is the total extended list price of the order?

  b. What is the total amount of the trade discount on this order?

  c. What is the total net amount Whole Foods owes the wholesaler for the order?

21. La Bella, a chain of clothing boutiques, purchased merchandise with a total list price of $25,450 from Sandy Sport, a manufacturer. The order has a trade discount of 34%.

  a. What is the amount of the trade discount?

  b. What is the net amount LaBella owes Sandy Sport for the merchandise?

22. An item with a trade discount of 41% has a list price of $289.50. What is the net price?

Whole Foods Market, with 284 stores and 52,500 employees, is the world's leading supermarket emphasizing natural and organic foods and America's first national "Certified Organic" grocer. In 2009, sales were $8.03 billion.

According to the Food Marketing Institute, in 2009, the 35,612 U.S. **supermarkets** generated sales of $557 billion. In addition, there were approximately 85,200 grocery stores, of which 25,900 were convenience stores.

Source: www.supermarketnews.com and www.wholefoodsmarket.com

Photo by Robert Brechner

23. Nathan and David Beauty Salon places an order for beauty supplies from a wholesaler. The list price of the order is $2,800. If the vendor offers a trade discount of 46%, what is the net price of the order?

24. A watch has a list price of $889 and can be bought by Sterling Jewelers for a net price of $545.75.

    a. What is the amount of the trade discount?

    b. What is the trade discount rate?

25. Nutrition Central pays $11.90 net price for a bottle of 60 multivitamins. The price represents a 30% trade discount from the manufacturer. What is the list price of the vitamins?

26. You are the buyer for the housewares department of the Galleria Department Store. A number of vendors in your area carry similar lines of merchandise. On sets of microwavable serving bowls, Kitchen Magic offers a list price of $400 per dozen less a 38% trade discount. Pro-Chef offers a similar set for a list price of $425 less a 45% trade discount.

    a. Which vendor is offering the lower net price?

    b. If you order 500 dozen sets of the bowls, how much money will be saved by using the lower-priced vendor?

General Nutrition Centers, Inc., a wholly owned subsidiary of GNC Corporation, consists of a worldwide network of over 6,600 locations and the www.gnc.com website. GNC, Inc., is the largest global specialty retailer of health and wellness products, including vitamins, minerals and herbal supplements, sports nutrition products, and diet products. As of December 31, 2009, GNC had a total of 5,271 full-time and 7,522 part-time employees. Revenues during this period were $1.7 billion.

The GNC website, www.gnc.com, provides an online library where consumers may research health-related topics.

BUSINESS DECISION: QUANTITY DISCOUNT

27. You are the purchasing manager for Tiger Electronics, a company that manufactures scanners and other computer peripherals. Your vendor for scanner motors, Enfield Industries, is now offering "quantity discounts" in the form of instant rebates and lower shipping charges as follows:

Quantity	Net Price	Rebate	Shipping
1–500 motors	$16	none	$1.30
501–1,000 motors	16	$1.20	.90
1,001–2,000 motors	16	1.80	.60

    a. Calculate the cost of the motors, including shipping charges, for each category.

    b. If you usually purchase 400 motors per month, what percent would be saved per motor by ordering 800 every two months? Round to the nearest tenth of a percent.

    c. What percent would be saved per motor by ordering 1,200 every three months? Round to the nearest tenth of a percent.

d. How much money can be saved in a year by purchasing the motors every three months instead of every month?

e. (Optional) What other factors besides price should be considered before changing your purchasing procedures?

SECTION III   7   TRADE DISCOUNTS—SERIES

Chain or **series trade discounts** Term used when a vendor offers a buyer more than one trade discount.

Trade discounts are frequently offered by manufacturers to wholesalers and retailers in a series of two or more, known as **chain** or **series trade discounts**. For example, a series of 25% and 10% is verbally stated as "25 and 10." It is written 25/10. A three-discount series is written 25/10/5. Multiple discounts are given for many reasons. Some of the more common ones follow.

Position or Level in the Channel of Distribution   A manufacturer might sell to a retailer at a 30% trade discount, whereas a wholesaler in the same channel might be quoted a 30% and a 15% trade discount.

Volume Buying   Many manufacturers and wholesalers grant an extra discount for buying a large volume of merchandise. For example, any purchase more than 5,000 units at one time may earn an extra 7% trade discount. Retailers with many stores or those with large storage capacity can enjoy a considerable savings (additional trade discounts) by purchasing in large quantities.

Advertising and Display   Additional discounts are often given to retailers and wholesalers who heavily advertise and aggressively promote a manufacturer's line of merchandise.

Competition   Competitive pressures often cause extra trade discounts to be offered. In certain industries such as household products and consumer electronics, price wars are not an uncommon occurrence.

LEARNING TIP

Remember, when calculating the net price by using a series of trade discounts, you *cannot* simply add the trade discounts together. Each discount must be applied to a successively lower base.

7-6   CALCULATING NET PRICE AND THE AMOUNT OF A TRADE DISCOUNT BY USING A SERIES OF TRADE DISCOUNTS

Finding net price with a series of trade discounts is accomplished by taking each trade discount, one at a time, from the previous net price until all discounts have been deducted. Note that you *cannot* simply add the trade discounts together. They must be calculated individually unless the net price factor method—a handy shortcut—is used. Trade discounts can be taken in any order, although they are usually listed and calculated in descending order.

For illustrative purposes, let's begin with an example of how to calculate a series of trade discounts one at a time; then we will try the shortcut method.

DOLLARS AND SENSE

An **industry trade group**, also known as a **trade association**, is an organization founded and funded by businesses that operate in a specific industry. An industry trade association participates in public relations activities such as advertising, education, political donations, lobbying, and publishing, but its main focus is collaboration between companies, or standardization.

Associations may offer other services, such as sponsoring conferences, providing networking, hosting charitable events, or offering classes or educational materials.

A directory of trade associations may be found at http://dir.yahoo.com/ Business_and_Economy/organizations/ trade_associations

EXAMPLE 6   CALCULATING NET PRICE AND THE AMOUNT OF A TRADE DISCOUNT

Calculate the net price and trade discount for merchandise with a list price of $2,000 less trade discounts of 30/20/15.

SOLUTION STRATEGY

$2,000	$2,000	$1,400	$1,400	$1,120	$1,120
× .30	− 600	× .20	− 280	× .15	− 168
$600	$1,400	$280	$1,120	$168	$952 = Net price

TRYITEXERCISE6

Northwest Publishers sold an order of books to The Bookworm, Inc., a chain of bookstores. The list price of the order was $25,000. The Bookworm buys in volume from Northwest. The Bookworm also prominently displays and heavily advertises Northwest's books. Northwest, in turn, gives The Bookworm a series of trade discounts amounting to 35/20/10. Calculate the net price of the order and the amount of the trade discount.

CHECK YOUR ANSWERS WITH THE SOLUTIONS ON PAGE 225.

CALCULATING THE NET PRICE OF A SERIES OF TRADE DISCOUNTS BY USING THE NET PRICE FACTOR, COMPLEMENT METHOD

7-7

As a shortcut, the net price can be calculated directly from the list price, bypassing the trade discount, by using the net price factor as before. Remember, the net price factor is the complement of the trade discount rate. With a series of discounts, we must find the complement of each trade discount to calculate the net price factor of the series.

The net price factor indicates to buyers what percent of the list price they actually *do* pay. For example, if the net price factor of a series of discounts is calculated to be .665, this means that the buyer is paying 66.5% of the list price.

STEPS FOR CALCULATING NET PRICE BY USING THE NET PRICE FACTOR

STEP 1. Find the complement of the trade discount rates in the series by subtracting each from 100% and converting them to decimal form.

STEP 2. Calculate the net price factor of the series by multiplying all the decimals together.

STEP 3. Calculate the net price by multiplying the list price by the net price factor.

Net price = List price × Net price factor

EXAMPLE7 CALCULATING NET PRICE FACTOR AND NET PRICE

The Crystal Gallery purchased merchandise from a manufacturer in Italy. The merchandise had a list price of $37,000 less trade discounts of 40/25/10. Calculate the net price factor and the net price of the order.

SOLUTIONSTRATEGY

Step 1. Subtract each trade discount from 100% and convert to decimals.

$$
\begin{array}{ccc}
100\% & 100\% & 100\% \\
-\,40\% & -\,25\% & -\,10\% \\
\hline
60\% = .6 & 75\% = .75 & 90\% = .9
\end{array}
$$

Step 2. Multiply all the complements together to get the net price factor.

Net price factor = .6 × .75 × .9

Net price factor = .405

Step 3. Net price = List price × Net price factor

Net price = 37,000 × .405

Net price = $14,985

TRYITEXERCISE7

Something's Fishy, a pet shop, always gets a 30/20/12 series of trade discounts from the Clearview Fish Tank Company. In June, the shop ordered merchandise with a list price of $3,500. In September, the shop placed an additional order listing for $5,800.

a. What is the net price factor for the series of trade discounts?

b. What is the net price of the merchandise purchased in June?

c. What is the net price of the merchandise purchased in September?

CHECK YOUR ANSWERS WITH THE SOLUTIONS ON PAGE 225.

7-8 CALCULATING THE AMOUNT OF A TRADE DISCOUNT BY USING A SINGLE EQUIVALENT DISCOUNT

single equivalent discount A single trade discount that equates to all the discounts in a series or chain.

Sometimes retailers and wholesalers want to know the one single discount rate that equates to a series of trade discounts. This is known as the **single equivalent discount**. We have already learned that the trade discounts *cannot* simply be added together.

Here is the logic: The list price of the merchandise is 100%. If the net price factor is the part of the list price that is paid, then 100% minus the net price factor is the part of the list price that is the trade discount. The single equivalent discount, therefore, is the complement of the net price factor (100% − Net price factor percent).

STEPS TO CALCULATE THE SINGLE EQUIVALENT DISCOUNT AND THE AMOUNT OF A TRADE DISCOUNT

STEP 1. Calculate the net price factor as before by subtracting each trade discount from 100% and multiplying them all together in decimal form.

STEP 2. Calculate the single equivalent discount by subtracting the net price factor in decimal form from 1.

Single equivalent discount = 1 − Net price factor

STEP 3. Find the amount of the trade discount by multiplying the list price by the single equivalent discount.

Trade discount = List price × Single equivalent discount

EXAMPLE8 CALCULATING THE SINGLE EQUIVALENT DISCOUNT AND THE AMOUNT OF A TRADE DISCOUNT

Calculate the single equivalent discount and amount of the trade discount on merchandise listing for $10,000 less trade discounts of 30/10/5.

SOLUTIONSTRATEGY

Step 1. Calculate the net price factor.

$$
\begin{array}{ccccc}
100\% & & 100\% & & 100\% \\
- 30\% & & - 10\% & & - 5\% \\
\hline
.70 & \times & .90 & \times & .95 & = .5985 = \text{Net price factor}
\end{array}
$$

Step 2. Calculate the single equivalent discount.

Single equivalent discount = 1 − Net price factor

Single equivalent discount = 1 − .5985 = <u>.4015</u>

Note: 40.15% is the single equivalent discount of the series 30%, 10%, and 5%.

Step 3. Calculate the amount of the trade discount.

Trade discount = List price × Single equivalent discount

Trade discount = 10,000 × .4015 = <u>$4,015</u>

TRYITEXERCISE8

The Rainbow Appliance Center purchased an order of dishwashers and ovens listing for $36,800. The manufacturer allows Rainbow a series of trade discounts of 25/15/10. What are the single equivalent discount and the amount of the trade discount?

CHECK YOUR ANSWERS WITH THE SOLUTIONS ON PAGE 225.

REVIEW EXERCISES

SECTION III   **7**

Calculate the following net price factors and net prices. For convenience, round net price factors to five decimal places when necessary.

	List Price	Trade Discount Rates	Net Price Factor	Net Price
1.	$360.00	12/10	.792	$285.12
2.	425.80	18/15/5	_____	_____
3.	81.75	20/10/10	_____	_____
4.	979.20	15/10/5	_____	_____
5.	7.25	25/15/10½	_____	_____
6.	.39	20/9/8	_____	_____

Calculate the following net price factors and single equivalent discounts. Round to five places when necessary.

Trade Discount Rates	Net Price Factor	Single Equivalent Discount
7. 15/10	.765	.235
8. 20/15/12	_____	_____
9. 25/15/7	_____	_____
10. 30/5/5	_____	_____
11. 35/15/7.5	_____	_____

Complete the following table. Round net price factors to five decimal places when necessary.

List Price	Trade Discount Rates	Net Price Factor	Single Equivalent Discount	Trade Discount	Net Price
12. $7,800.00	15/5/5	.76713	.23287	$1,816.39	$5,983.61
13. 1,200.00	20/15/7	_____	_____	_____	_____
14. 560.70	25/15/5	_____	_____	_____	_____
15. 883.50	18/12/9	_____	_____	_____	_____
16. 4.89	12/10/10	_____	_____	_____	_____
17. 2,874.95	30/20/5.5	_____	_____	_____	_____

18. What is the net price factor of a 25/10 series of trade discounts?

19. What is the net price factor of a 35/15/10 series of discounts?

20. Kidzstuff.com ordered toys, games, and videos from a vendor. The order had a list price of $10,300 less trade discounts of 25/15/12.

    a. What is the net price factor?

    b. What is the net price of the order?

21. Legacy Designs places an order for furniture listing for $90,500 less trade discounts of 25/20.

    a. What is the net price factor?

    b. What is the net price of the order?

Satellite radio, also called digital radio, receives radio signals broadcast from a network of satellites more than 22,000 miles above the earth. Sirius XM Radio, Inc., provides satellite radio services in the United States and Canada. In 2009, Sirius XM Radio had more than 19 million subscribers and revenues totaling $2.42 billion.

The company offers a programming lineup of 117 channels to subscribers, which include 63 channels of commercial-free music and 54 channels of sports, news, talk, entertainment, and traffic and weather.

Source: www.highspeedsat.com, www.siriusxm.com

22. Audio Giant received an order of Sirius XM satellite radios listing for $9,500 with trade discounts of 25/13/8.

    a. What is the net price factor?

    b. What is the single equivalent discount?

    c. What is the amount of the trade discount?

    d. What is the net price of the order?

23. The Speedy Auto Service Center can buy auto parts from Southeast Auto Supply at a series discount of 20/15/5 and from Northwest Auto Supply for 25/10/8.

    a. Which auto parts supplier offers a better discount to Speedy?

    b. If Speedy orders $15,000 in parts at list price per month, how much will it save in a year by choosing the lower-priced supplier?

24. La Fiesta Market buys merchandise from B. G. Distributors with a series discount of 35/15/7.

    a. What is the single equivalent discount?

    b. What is the amount of the trade discount on an order with a list price of $5,700?

25. Midtown Market received the following items at a discount of 25/20/10: 18 cases of canned peaches listing at $26.80 per case and 45 cases of canned pears listing at $22.50 per case.

    a. What is the total list price of this order?

    b. What is the amount of the trade discount?

    c. What is the net price of the order?

26. Shopper's Mart purchased the following items. Calculate the extended total after the trade discounts for each line, the invoice subtotal, and the invoice total.

The Pharmacy and Drug Store Industry in the United States retails a range of prescription and over-the-counter products. These include medicines; apothecaries; health and beauty items such as vitamin supplements, cosmetics, and toiletries; and photo processing services. According to the National Association of chain drugstores, in 2009, the drugstore industry generated revenue of over $200 billion.

Top U.S. drug retailers include Rite Aid, CVS, Target, Kmart, Kroger, Safeway, Duane Reade, Supervalu, Walgreens, and Walmart.

Quantity	Unit	Merchandise	Unit List	Trade Discounts	Extended Total
150	ea.	Blenders	$59.95	20/15/15	_____
400	ea.	Toasters	$39.88	20/10/10	_____
18	doz.	Coffee Mills	$244.30	30/9/7	_____
12	doz.	Juicers	$460.00	25/10/5	_____
				Invoice subtotal	_____
			Extra $5\frac{1}{2}$ % volume discount on total order		_____
				Invoice total	_____

27. Referring back to Exercise 26, you have just been hired as the buyer for the kitchen division of Shopper's Mart, a general merchandise retailer. After looking over the discounts offered to the previous buyer by the vendor, you decide to ask for better discounts.

    After negotiating with the vendor's salesperson, you now can buy blenders at trade discounts of 20/20/15 and juicers at 25/15/10. In addition, the vendor has increased the volume discount to $6\frac{1}{2}$%.

    a. How much would have been saved with your new discounts based on the quantities of the previous order (Exercise 26)?

    b. As a result of your negotiations, the vendor has offered an additional discount of 2% of the total amount due if the invoice is paid within 15 days instead of the usual 30 days. What would be the amount of this discount?

BUSINESS DECISION: THE ULTIMATE TRADE DISCOUNT

28. In 2009, as part of its bankruptcy reorganization, General Motors discontinued the Pontiac and Saturn models. One of the GM incentive programs designed to reduce inventory of these models was a $7,000 extra dealer incentive for each of these vehicles that the dealer moved into its rental or service fleets.

    As the accountant for a dealership with a number of these vehicles left in stock, your manager has asked you to calculate certain invoice figures. The normal trade discount from GM is 18%. If the average sticker price (list price) of these remaining vehicles at your dealership is $23,500, calculate the following.

    a. What is the amount of the trade discount, including the incentive?

    b. What is the trade discount rate? Round to the nearest tenth of a percent.

    c. What is the net price (invoice price) to your dealership?

    d. If the cars were then sold from the fleets at $1,000 over "invoice" (net price), what is the total percentage savings to the consumer based on the list price? Round to the nearest tenth of a percent.

    e. (Optional) Although these incentive prices reflect extraordinary discounts to the consumer, what other factors should a consumer consider before purchasing a "discontinued" brand of vehicle?

SECTION IV 7 CASH DISCOUNTS AND TERMS OF SALE

terms of sale The details of when an invoice must be paid and if a cash discount is being offered.

credit period The time period that the seller allows the buyer to pay an invoice.

net date, or **due date** The last day of the credit period.

cash discount An extra discount offered by the seller as an incentive for early payment of an invoice.

invoice date The date an invoice is written. The beginning of the discount and credit periods when ordinary dating is used.

cash discount period The time period in which a buyer can take advantage of the cash discount.

discount date The last day of the discount period.

As merchandise physically arrives at the buyer's back door, the invoice ordinarily arrives by mail through the front door. Today more and more arrive by e-mail. What happens next? The invoice has a section entitled **terms of sale**. The terms of sale are the details of when the invoice must be paid and whether any additional discounts will be offered.

Commonly, manufacturers allow wholesalers and retailers 30 days or even longer to pay the bill. In certain industries, the time period is as much as 60 or 90 days. This is known as the **credit period**. This gives the buyer time to unpack and check the order and, more important, begin selling the merchandise. This credit period clearly gives the wholesaler and retailer an advantage. They can generate revenue by selling merchandise that they have not paid for yet.

To encourage them to pay the bill earlier than the **net date**, or **due date**, sellers frequently offer buyers an optional extra discount over and above the trade discounts. This is known as a **cash discount**. Cash discounts are an extra few percent offered as an incentive for early payment of the invoice, usually within 10 to 15 days after the **invoice date**. This is known as the **cash discount period**. The last date for a buyer to take advantage of a cash discount is known as the **discount date**.

THE IMPORTANCE OF CASH DISCOUNTS

Both buyers and sellers benefit from cash discounts. Sellers get their money much sooner, which improves their cash flow, whereas buyers get an additional discount, which lowers their merchandise cost, thereby raising their margin or gross profit.

Cash discounts generally range from an extra 1% to 5% off the net price of the merchandise. A 1% to 5% discount may not seem significant, but it is. Let's say that an invoice is due in 30 days; however, a distributor would like payment sooner. It might offer the retailer a cash discount of 2% if the bill is paid within 10 days rather than 30 days. If the retailer chooses to take the cash discount, he or she must pay the bill by the 10th day after the date of the invoice. Note that this is *20 days* earlier than the due date. The retailer is therefore receiving a 2% discount for paying the bill 20 days early.

The logic: There are 18.25 twenty-day periods in a year (365 days divided by 20 days). By multiplying the 2% discount by the 18.25 periods, we see that on a yearly basis, 2% cash discounts can *theoretically* amount to 36.5%. Very significant!

DOLLARS AND SENSE

> Cash discounts are so important to wholesalers' and retailers' "profit picture" that frequently they borrow the money on a short-term basis to take advantage of the cash discount savings. This procedure is covered in Chapter 10, "Simple Interest."

CALCULATING CASH DISCOUNTS AND NET AMOUNT DUE

7-9

Cash discounts are offered in the terms of sale. A transaction with no cash discount would have terms of sale of net 30, for example. This means the **net amount** of the invoice is due in 30 days. If a cash discount is offered, the terms of sale would be written as 2/10, n/30. This means a 2% cash discount may be taken if the invoice is paid within 10 days; if not, the net amount is due in 30 days. (See Exhibit 7-4.)

Exhibit 7-5 shows a time line of the discount period and credit period on an invoice dated October 15. The 2/10, n/30 terms of sale stipulate a cash discount if the bill is paid within 10 days. If not, the balance is due in 30 days. As you can see, the cash discount period runs for 10 days from the invoice date, October 15 to October 25. The credit period, 30 days, extends from the invoice date through November 14.

Sometimes two cash discounts are offered, such as 3/15, 1/25, n/60. This means a 3% cash discount is offered if the invoice is paid within 15 days, a 1% cash discount if the invoice is paid within 25 days, with the net amount due in 60 days.

Cash discounts cannot be taken on shipping charges or returned goods, only on the net price of the merchandise. If shipping charges are included in the amount of an invoice, they must be subtracted before the cash discount is taken. After the cash discount has been deducted, the shipping charges are added back to get the invoice total.

net amount The amount of money due from the buyer to the seller.

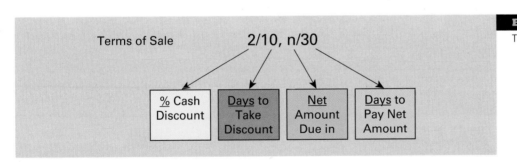

EXHIBIT 7-4

Terms of Sale

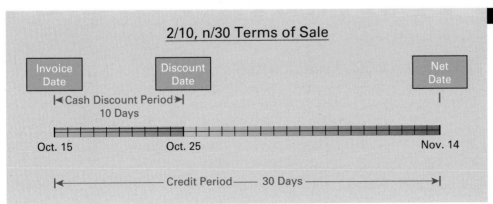

EXHIBIT 7-5

Terms of Sale Time Line

© Randy Glasbergen.
www.glasbergen.com

"Our terms are net 30 days. If you don't pay after 30 days, we come after you with a net!"

© 2002 by Randy Glasbergen. www.glasbergen.com

If arriving merchandise is damaged or is not what was ordered, those goods will be returned to the vendor. The amount of the returned goods must also be subtracted from the amount of the invoice. They are no longer a part of the transaction.

STEPS TO CALCULATE CASH DISCOUNT AND NET AMOUNT DUE

STEP 1. Calculate the amount of the cash discount by multiplying the cash discount rate by the net price of the merchandise.

$$\text{Cash discount} = \text{Net price} \times \text{Cash discount rate}$$

STEP 2. Calculate the net amount due by subtracting the amount of the cash discount from the net price.

$$\text{Net amount due} = \text{Net price} - \text{Cash discount}$$

Note: As with trade discounts, buyers are frequently more interested in the net amount due than the amount of the discount. When that is the case, we can simplify the calculation by using the complement method to determine the net amount due.

$$\text{Net amount due} = \text{Net price}(100\% - \text{Cash discount rate})$$

EXAMPLE 9 CALCULATING CASH DISCOUNT AND NET AMOUNT DUE

Rugs.com buys merchandise with an invoice amount of $16,000 from Karistan Carpet Mills. The terms of sale are 2/10, n/30. What is the amount of the cash discount? What is the net amount due on this order if the bill is paid by the 10th day?

SOLUTIONSTRATEGY

Cash discount = Net price × Cash discount rate

$$\text{Cash discount} = 16,000 \times .02 = \underline{\$320}$$

Net amount due = Net price − Cash discount

$$\text{Net amount due} = 16,000 - 320 = \underline{\$15,680}$$

TRYITEXERCISE9

Valiant Plumbing ordered sinks from a supplier. The sinks had a net price of $8,300 and terms of sale of 3/15, n/45. What is the amount of the cash discount? What is the net amount due if the bill is paid by the 15th day?

CHECK YOUR ANSWERS WITH THE SOLUTIONS ON PAGE 225.

CALCULATING NET AMOUNT DUE, WITH CREDIT GIVEN FOR PARTIAL PAYMENT

7-10

Sometimes buyers do not have all the money needed to take advantage of the cash discount. Manufacturers and suppliers usually allow them to pay part of the invoice by the discount date and the balance by the end of the credit period. This **partial payment** earns partial cash discount credit. In this situation, we must calculate how much **partial payment credit** is given.

Here is how it works: Assume a cash discount of 4/15, n/45 is offered to a retailer. A 4% cash discount means that the retailer will pay 96% of the bill (100% − 4%) and receive 100% credit. Another way to look at it is that every $0.96 paid toward the invoice earns $1.00 credit. We must determine how many $0.96s are in the partial payment. This will tell us how many $1.00s of credit we receive.

partial payment When a portion of the invoice is paid within the discount period.

partial payment credit The amount of the invoice paid off by the partial payment.

STEPS TO CALCULATE PARTIAL PAYMENT CREDIT AND NET AMOUNT DUE

STEP 1. Calculate the amount of credit given for a partial payment by dividing the partial payment by the complement of the cash discount rate.

$$\text{Partial payment credit} = \frac{\text{Partial payment}}{100\% - \text{Cash discount rate}}$$

STEP 2. Calculate the net amount due by subtracting the partial payment credit from the net price.

$$\text{Net amount due} = \text{Net price} - \text{Partial payment credit}$$

EXAMPLE10 CALCULATING NET AMOUNT DUE AFTER A PARTIAL PAYMENT

Happy Feet, a chain of children's shoe stores, receives an invoice from a tennis shoe manufacturer on September 3 with terms of 3/20, n/60. The net price of the order is $36,700. Happy Feet wants to send a partial payment of $10,000 by the discount date and the balance on the net date. How much credit does Happy Feet get for the partial payment? What is the remaining net amount due to the manufacturer?

SOLUTIONSTRATEGY

$$\text{Partial payment credit} = \frac{\text{Partial payment}}{100\% - \text{Case discount rate}}$$

$$\text{Partial payment credit} = \frac{10,000}{100\% - 3\%} = \frac{10,000}{.97} = \underline{\$10,309.28}$$

$$\text{Net amount due} = \text{Net price} - \text{Partial payment credit}$$

$$\text{Net amount due} = \$36,700.00 - \$10,309.28 = \underline{\$26,390.72}$$

TRYITEXERCISE10

All Pro Sports Center purchases $45,300 in baseball gloves from Spaulding on May 5. Spaulding allows 4/15, n/45. If All Pro sends a partial payment of $20,000 on the discount date, how much credit will be given for the partial payment? What is the net amount still due on the order?

CHECK YOUR ANSWERS WITH THE SOLUTIONS ON PAGE 226.

7-11

DETERMINING DISCOUNT DATE AND NET DATE BY USING VARIOUS TERMS OF SALE DATING METHODS

To determine the discount date and net date of an invoice, you must know how many days are in each month or use a calendar.

Following are two commonly used memory devices to help you remember how many days are in each month. Remember, in a leap year, February has 29 days. Leap years fall every four years. They are the only years evenly divisible by 4 and are the years of our next presidential elections (2012, 2016).

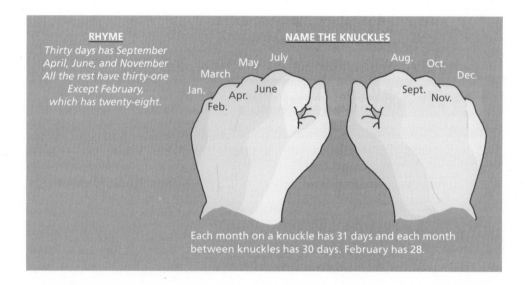

RHYME
Thirty days has September April, June, and November All the rest have thirty-one Except February, which has twenty-eight.

NAME THE KNUCKLES
Jan. Feb. March Apr. May June July Aug. Sept. Oct. Nov. Dec.

Each month on a knuckle has 31 days and each month between knuckles has 30 days. February has 28.

Another way to find these dates is to use the days-in-a-year calendar shown in Exhibit 7-6. In Chapter 10, you will be able to use this calendar again to find future dates and calculate the number of days of a loan.

STEPS TO FINDING A FUTURE DATE USING A DAYS-IN-A-YEAR CALENDAR

STEP 1. Find the "day number" of the starting date.

Note: In leap years, add 1 to the day numbers beginning with March 1.

STEP 2. Add the number of days of the discount or credit period to that day number.

Note: If the new day number is over 365, subtract 365. This means the future date is in the next year.

STEP 3. Find the date by looking up the new day number from Step 2.

EXAMPLE11 FINDING THE NET DATE

If an invoice dated April 14 is due in 75 days, what is the net date?

SOLUTIONSTRATEGY

Step 1. From the calendar, April 14 is day number 104.

Step 2. 104 + 75 = 179

Step 3. From the calendar, day number 179 is June 28.

TRYITEXERCISE11

If an invoice dated September 12 is due in 60 days, what is the net date?

CHECK YOUR ANSWER WITH THE SOLUTION ON PAGE 226.

EXHIBIT 7-6 Days-In-A-Year Calendar

Day of month	Jan.	Feb.	Mar.	Apr.	May	June	July	Aug.	Sept.	Oct.	Nov.	Dec.
1	1	32	60	91	121	152	182	213	244	274	305	335
2	2	33	61	92	122	153	183	214	245	275	306	336
3	3	34	62	93	123	154	184	215	246	276	307	337
4	4	35	63	94	124	155	185	216	247	277	308	338
5	5	36	64	95	125	156	186	217	248	278	309	339
6	6	37	65	96	126	157	187	218	249	279	310	340
7	7	38	66	97	127	158	188	219	250	280	311	341
8	8	39	67	98	128	159	189	220	251	281	312	342
9	9	40	68	99	129	160	190	221	252	282	313	343
10	10	41	69	100	130	161	191	222	253	283	314	344
11	11	42	70	101	131	162	192	223	254	284	315	345
12	12	43	71	102	132	163	193	224	255	285	316	346
13	13	44	72	103	133	164	194	225	256	286	317	347
14	14	45	73	104	134	165	195	226	257	287	318	348
15	15	46	74	105	135	166	196	227	258	288	319	349
16	16	47	75	106	136	167	197	228	259	289	320	350
17	17	48	76	107	137	168	198	229	260	290	321	351
18	18	49	77	108	138	169	199	230	261	291	322	352
19	19	50	78	109	139	170	200	231	262	292	323	353
20	20	51	79	110	140	171	201	232	263	293	324	354
21	21	52	80	111	141	172	202	233	264	294	325	355
22	22	53	81	112	142	173	203	234	265	295	326	356
23	23	54	82	113	143	174	204	235	266	296	327	357
24	24	55	83	114	144	175	205	236	267	297	328	358
25	25	56	84	115	145	176	206	237	268	298	329	359
26	26	57	85	116	146	177	207	238	269	299	330	360
27	27	58	86	117	147	178	208	239	270	300	331	361
28	28	59	87	118	148	179	209	240	271	301	332	362
29	29		88	119	149	180	210	241	272	302	333	363
30	30		89	120	150	181	211	242	273	303	334	364
31	31		90		151		212	243		304		365

During the next leap years, 2012 and 2016, add 1 to the day numbers beginning with March 1.

TERMS OF SALE—DATING METHODS

ORDINARY DATING

ordinary dating When the discount period and credit period start on the invoice date.

When the discount period and the credit period start on the date of the invoice, this is known as **ordinary dating**. It is the most common method of dating the terms of sale. The last day to take advantage of the cash discount, the discount date, is found by adding the number of days in the discount period to the date of the invoice. For example, to receive a cash discount, an invoice dated November 8 with terms of 2/10, n/30 should be paid no later than November 18 (November 8 + 10 days). The last day to pay the invoice, the net date, is found by adding the number of days in the credit period to the invoice date. With terms of 2/10, n/30, the net date would be December 8 (November 8 + 30 days). If the buyer does not pay the bill by the net date, the seller may impose a penalty charge for late payment.

EXAMPLE 12 USING ORDINARY DATING

AccuCare Pharmacy receives an invoice dated August 19 from Bristol Drug Wholesalers for merchandise. The terms of sale are 3/10, n/45. If AccuCare elects to take the cash discount, what is the discount date? If AccuCare does not take the cash discount, what is the net date?

SOLUTIONSTRATEGY

Find the discount date by adding the number of days in the discount period to the date of the invoice.

$$\text{Discount date} = \text{August 19} + 10 \text{ days} = \underline{\text{August 29}}$$

If the discount is not taken, find the net date by adding the number of days in the credit period to the invoice date.

$$\text{August 19} + 45 \text{ days} = \quad 12 \text{ days left in August (31} - 19)$$
$$+ \ 30 \text{ days in September}$$
$$\underline{+ \quad 3 \text{ days in October}}$$
$$45 \text{ days}$$

The net date, the 45th day, is <u>October 3</u>.

TRYITEXERCISE 12

Great Impressions Printing buys ink and paper from a supplier. The invoice date of the purchase is June 11. If the terms of sale are 4/10, n/60, what are the discount date and the net date of the invoice?

CHECK YOUR ANSWERS WITH THE SOLUTIONS ON PAGE 226.

EOM OR PROXIMO DATING

EOM dating End-of-month dating. Depending on invoice date, terms of sale start at the end of the month of the invoice or the end of the following month.

proximo, or **prox** Another name for EOM dating. Means "in the following month."

EOM dating, or end-of-month dating, means that the terms of sale start *after* the end of the month of the invoice. Another name for this dating method is **proximo**, or **prox**. Proximo means "in the following month." For example, 2/10 EOM, or 2/10 proximo, means that a 2% cash discount will be allowed if the bill is paid 10 days after the *end of the month* of the invoice. This is the case for any invoice dated from the 1st to the 25th of a month. If an invoice is dated after the 25th of the month, the terms of sale begin *after* the end of the *following* month. Unless otherwise specified, the net amount is due *20 days* after the discount date.

EXAMPLE13 USING EOM DATING

As the shipping manager for World Imports, answer the following questions.

a. What are the discount date and the net date of an invoice dated March 3 with terms of 3/15 EOM?

b. What are the discount date and the net date of an invoice dated March 27 with terms of 3/15 EOM?

SOLUTIONSTRATEGY

a. Because the invoice date is between the 1st and the 25th of the month, March 3, the discount date on terms of 3/15 EOM would be 15 days *after* the end of the month of the invoice. The net date would be 20 days later.

Discount date = 15 days after the end of March = April 15

Net date = April 15 + 20 days = May 5

b. Because the invoice date is after the 25th of the month, March 27, the discount date on terms of 3/15 EOM would be 15 days *after* the end of the month *following* the invoice month. The net date would be 20 days later.

Discount date = 15 days after the end of April = May 15

Net date = May 15 + 20 days = June 4

TRYITEXERCISE13

As the accounts receivable manager for River Bend Industries, answer the following questions.

a. What are the discount date and the net date of an invoice dated November 18 with terms of 3/15 EOM?

b. What are the discount date and the net date of an invoice dated November 27 with terms of 3/15 EOM?

CHECK YOUR ANSWERS WITH THE SOLUTIONS ON PAGE 226.

ROG DATING

Receipt of goods dating, or **ROG dating**, is a common method used when shipping times are long, such as with special or custom orders. When ROG dating is used, the terms of sale begin the day the goods are received at the buyer's location. With this method, the buyer does not have to pay for the merchandise before it arrives. An example would be 2/10 ROG. As usual, the net date is 20 days after the discount date.

ROG dating Receipt of goods dating. Terms of sale begin on the date the goods are received by the buyer.

EXAMPLE14 USING ROG DATING

What are the discount date and the net date for an invoice dated June 23 if the shipment arrives on August 16 and the terms are 3/15 ROG?

SOLUTIONSTRATEGY

In this case, the discount period starts on August 16, the date the shipment arrives. The net date will be 20 days after the discount date.

Discount date = August 16 + 15 days = August 31

Net date = August 31 + 20 days = September 20

TRYITEXERCISE14

What are the discount date and the net date of an invoice dated October 11 if the shipment arrives on December 29 and the terms are 2/20 ROG?

CHECK YOUR ANSWERS WITH THE SOLUTIONS ON PAGE 226.

EXTRA DATING

Extra, Ex, or X dating The buyer receives an extra discount period as an incentive to purchase slow-moving or out-of-season merchandise.

The last dating method commonly used in business today is called **Extra, Ex, or X dating**. With this dating method, the seller offers an extra discount period to the buyer as an incentive for purchasing slow-moving or out-of-season merchandise, such as Christmas goods in July and bathing suits in January. An example would be 3/10, 60 extra. This means the buyer gets a 3% cash discount in 10 days plus 60 *extra* days, or a total of 70 days. Once again, unless otherwise specified, the net date is 20 days after the discount date.

EXAMPLE15 USING EXTRA DATING

What are the discount date and the net date of an invoice dated February 9 with terms of 3/15, 40 Extra?

SOLUTIONSTRATEGY

These terms, 3/15, 40 Extra, give the retailer 55 days (15 + 40) from February 9 to take the cash discount. The net date will be 20 days after the discount date.

$$\text{Discount date} = \text{February 9} + 55 \text{ days} = \underline{\text{April 5}}$$

$$\text{Net date} = \text{April 5} + 20 \text{ days} = \underline{\text{April 25}}$$

LEARNINGTIP

Remember, when using extra dating, unless otherwise specified, the net date is 20 days after the discount date.

TRYITEXERCISE15

What are the discount date and the net date of an invoice dated February 22 with terms of 4/20, 60 Extra?

CHECK YOUR ANSWERS WITH THE SOLUTIONS ON PAGE 226.

SECTION IV · 7 · REVIEW EXERCISES

Calculate the cash discount and the net amount due for each of the following transactions.

	Amount of Invoice	Terms of Sale	Cash Discount	Net Amount Due
1.	$15,800.00	3/15, n/30	$474.00	$15,326.00
2.	12,660.00	2/10, n/45	_____	_____
3.	2,421.00	4/10, n/30	_____	_____
4.	6,940.20	2/10, n/30	_____	_____
5.	9,121.44	$3\frac{1}{2}$/15, n/60	_____	_____

For the following transactions, calculate the credit given for the partial payment and the net amount due on the invoice.

	Amount of Invoice	Terms of Sale	Partial Payment	Credit for Partial Payment	Net Amount Due
6.	$8,303.00	2/10, n/30	$2,500	$2,551.02	$5,751.98
7.	1,344.60	3/10, n/45	460	_____	_____
8.	5,998.20	4/15, n/60	3,200	_____	_____
9.	7,232.08	$4\frac{1}{2}$/20, n/45	5,500	_____	_____

Using the ordinary dating method, calculate the discount date and the net date for the following transactions.

	Date of Invoice	Terms of Sale	Discount Date(s)	Net Date
10.	November 4	2/10, n/45	Nov. 14	Dec. 19
11.	April 23	3/15, n/60	_____	_____
12.	August 11	3/20, n/45	_____	_____
13.	January 29	2/10, 1/20, n/60	_____	_____
14.	July 8	4/25, n/90	_____	_____

Using the EOM, ROG, and Extra dating methods, calculate the discount date and the net date for the following transactions. Unless otherwise specified, the net date is 20 days after the discount date.

	Date of Invoice	Terms of Sale	Discount Date	Net Date
15.	December 5	2/10, EOM	Jan. 10	Jan. 30
16.	June 27	3/15, EOM		
17.	September 1	3/20, ROG		
		Rec'd Oct. 3		
18.	February 11	2/10, 60 Extra		
19.	May 18	4/25, EOM		
20.	October 26	2/10, ROG		
		Rec'd Nov. 27		

21. The Apollo Company received an invoice from a vendor on April 12 in the amount of $1,420. The terms of sale were 2/15, n/45. The invoice included shipping charges of $108. The vendor sent $250 in merchandise that was not ordered. These goods will be returned by Apollo. (Remember, no discounts on shipping charges or returned goods.)

    a. What are the discount date and the net date?

    b. What is the amount of the cash discount?

    c. What is the net amount due?

"You'll have to be more careful, that's the second time this month you've paid an invoice on time."

22. An invoice is dated August 29 with terms of 4/15 EOM.

    a. What is the discount date?   b. What is the net date?

23. An invoice dated January 15 has terms of 3/20 ROG. The goods are delayed in shipment and arrive on March 2.

    a. What is the discount date?   b. What is the net date?

24. What payment should be made on an invoice in the amount of $3,400 dated August 7 if the terms of sale are 3/15, 2/30, n/45 and the bill is paid on

    a. August 19?

    b. September 3?

25. Red Tag Furniture received a SeaLand container of sofas from Thailand on April 14. The invoice, dated March 2, was for $46,230 in merchandise and $2,165 in shipping charges. The terms of sale were 3/15 ROG. Red Tag Furniture made a partial payment of $15,000 on April 27.

    a. What is the net amount due?

    b. What is the net date?

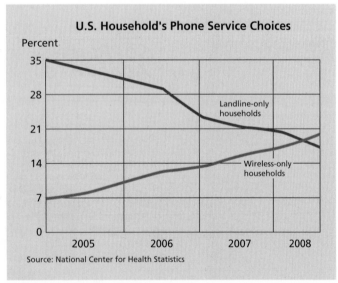

U.S. Household's Phone Service Choices

Source: National Center for Health Statistics

In 2008, for the first time, the number of U.S. households opting for only cell phones outnumbered those that had just traditional landlines in a high-tech shift accelerated by the recession.

About a third of people aged 18 to 24 live in households with only cell phones. The same is true of 4 in 10 people aged 25 to 29. Combined with wireless-only homes, that means that 35% of households are basically reachable only on cells. Six in 10 households have both landline and cell phones, while 1 in 50 have no phones at all.

Source: National Health Interview Survey, conducted by the CDC

26. City Cellular purchased $28,900 in cell phones on April 25. The terms of sale were 4/20, 3/30, n/60. Freight terms were F.O.B. destination. Returned goods amounted to $650.

    a. What is the net amount due if City Cellular sends the manufacturer a partial payment of $5,000 on May 20?

    b. What is the net date?

    c. If the manufacturer charges a $4\frac{1}{2}$ % late fee, how much would City Cellular owe if it did not pay the balance by the net date?

BUSINESS DECISION: THE EMPLOYMENT TEST

27. As part of the employment interview for an accounting job at Sound Design, you have
    been asked to answer the questions below, based on an invoice from one of Sound
    Design's vendors, Target Electronic Wholesalers.

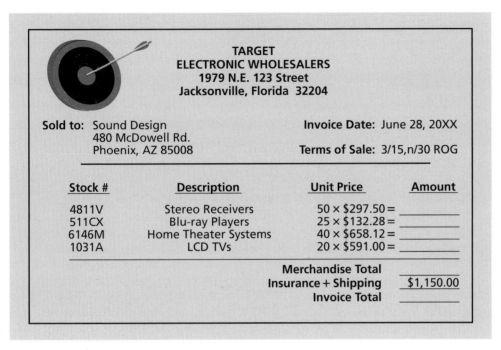

TARGET
ELECTRONIC WHOLESALERS
1979 N.E. 123 Street
Jacksonville, Florida 32204

Sold to: Sound Design
480 McDowell Rd.
Phoenix, AZ 85008

Invoice Date: June 28, 20XX

Terms of Sale: 3/15,n/30 ROG

Stock #	Description	Unit Price	Amount
4811V	Stereo Receivers	50 × $297.50 =	_____
511CX	Blu-ray Players	25 × $132.28 =	_____
6146M	Home Theater Systems	40 × $658.12 =	_____
1031A	LCD TVs	20 × $591.00 =	_____

Merchandise Total _____
Insurance + Shipping $1,150.00
Invoice Total _____

a. Extend each line and calculate the merchandise total and the total amount of the
   invoice, using the space provided on the invoice.

b. What are the discount date and the net date if the shipment arrived on July 16?

c. While in transit, five Blu-ray players and four LCD TVs were damaged and will be
   returned. What is the amount of the returned merchandise? What is the revised merchandise total?

d. What are the amount of the cash discount and the net amount due if the discount is
   taken?

e. If Sound Design sends in a partial payment of $20,000 within the discount period,
   what is the net balance still due?

CHAPTER
7

CHAPTER FORMULAS

The Invoice

Extended total = Number of items × Cost per item

Trade Discounts—Single

Trade discount = List price × Trade discount rate

Net price = List price − Trade discount

Net price = List price(100% − Trade discount rate)

$$\text{Trade discount rate} = \frac{\text{Trade discount}}{\text{List price}}$$

Trade Discounts—Series

Net price = List price × Net price factor

Single equivalent discount = 1 − Net price factor

Trade discount = List price × Single equivalent discount

Cash Discounts and Terms of Sale

Net amount due = Net price(100% − Cash discount rate)

$$\text{Partial payment credit} = \frac{\text{Partial payment}}{100\% - \text{Cash discount rate}}$$

Net amount due = Net price − Partial payment credit

CHAPTER SUMMARY

Section I: The Invoice

Topic	Important Concepts	Illustrative Examples
Reading and Understanding the Parts of an Invoice **Performance Objective 7-1, Page 192**	Refer to Exhibits 7-1, 7-2, and 7-3.	

Extending and Totaling an Invoice
 	
Performance Objective 7-2, Page 195
	Extended amount =
	   Number of items × Cost per item
	
	Invoice subtotal =
	   Total of extended amount column
	
	Invoice total =
	   Invoice subtotal + Other charges
		The Great Subversion, a sandwich shop, ordered 25 lb of ham at $3.69 per pound and 22 lb of cheese at $4.25 per pound. There is a $7.50 delivery charge. Extend each item and find the invoice subtotal and invoice total.
		
		25 × 3.69 = 92.25 Ham
		22 × 4.25 = 93.50 Cheese
		        185.75 Subtotal
		      + 7.50 Delivery
		   $193.25 Invoice total

Section II: Trade Discounts—Single

Topic	Important Concepts	Illustrative Examples
Calculating the Amount of a Single Trade Discount **Performance Objective 7-3, Page 199**	Trade discounts are reductions from the manufacturer's list price given to businesses in the trade for the performance of various marketing functions. Trade discount = List price × Trade discount rate	Sunglass King ordered merchandise with a list price of $12,700 from a manufacturer. Because it is in the trade, Sunglass King gets a 35% trade discount. What is the amount of the trade discount? Trade discount = 12,700 × .35 = $4,445

Section II (continued)

Topic	Important Concepts	Illustrative Examples

Calculating Net Price by Using the Net Price Factor, Complement Method
 	
Performance Objective 7-4, Page 199
	Net price factor =
	   $100\% -$ Trade discount rate
	
	Net price =
	   List price($100\% -$ Trade discount rate)
		From the previous problem, use the net price factor to find the net price of the order for Sunglass King.
		
		Net price = $12,700(100\% - 35\%)$
		
		Net price = $12,700 \times .65 = \underline{\$8,255}$

Calculating Trade Discount Rate When List Price and Net Price Are Known **Performance Objective 7-5, Page 200**	Trade discount rate = $\dfrac{\text{Trade discount}}{\text{List price}}$	Cycle World Bike Shop orders merchandise listing for $5,300 from Schwinn. The net price of the order is $3,200. What is the trade discount rate? Trade discount = $5,300 - 3,200 = \$2,100$ Trade discount rate = $\dfrac{2,100}{5,300} = \underline{39.6\%}$

Section III: Trade Discounts—Series

Topic	Important Concepts	Illustrative Examples
Calculating Net Price and the Amount of a Trade Discount by Using a Series of Trade Discounts **Performance Objective 7-6, Page 204**	Net price is found by taking each trade discount in the series from the succeeding net price until all discounts have been deducted. Trade discount = List price $-$ Net price	An invoice with merchandise listing for $4,700 was entitled to trade discounts of 20% and 15%. What is the net price and the amount of the trade discount? $4,700 \times .20 = 940$ $4,700 - 940 = 3,760$ $3,760 \times .15 = 564$ $3,760 - 564 = \underline{\$3,196}$ Net price Trade discount = $4,700 - 3,196 = \underline{\$1,504}$
Calculating Net Price of a Series of Trade Discounts by Using the Net Price Factor, Complement Method **Performance Objective 7-7, Page 205**	Net price factor is found by subtracting each trade discount rate from 100% (complement) and multiplying these complements together. Net price = List price $\times$ Net price factor	Use the net price factor method to verify your answer to the previous problem. $\begin{array}{ccc} 100\% & & 100\% \\ -\ 20\% & & -\ 15\% \\ \hline .80 & \times & .85 \end{array} = .68$ Net price factor Net price = $4,700 \times .68 = \underline{\$3,196}$

Calculating the Amount of a Trade Discount by Using a Single Equivalent Discount
 	
Performance Objective 7-8, Page 206
	Single equivalent discount =
	   $1 -$ Net price factor
	
	Trade discount =
	   List price $\times$ Single equivalent discount
		What is the single equivalent discount and the amount of the trade discount in the previous problem?
		
		Use this to verify your trade discount answer.
		
		Single equivalent discount = $1 - .68 = \underline{.32}$
		
		Trade discount = $4,700 \times .32 = \underline{\$1,504}$

Section IV: Cash Discounts and Terms of Sale

Topic	Important Concepts	Illustrative Examples

Calculating Cash Discounts and Net Amount Due
 	
Performance Objective 7-9, Page 211
	Terms of sale specify when an invoice must be paid and if a cash discount is offered. Cash discount is an extra discount offered by the seller as an incentive for early payment of an invoice.
	
	Cash discount =
	   Net price $\times$ Cash discount rate
	
	Net amount due =
	   Net price $-$ Cash discount
		Action Auto Parts orders merchandise for $1,800, including $100 in freight charges. Action gets a 3% cash discount. What is the amount of the cash discount and the net amount due?
		
		$1,800 - 100 = 1,700$ Net price
		
		Cash discount = $1,700 \times .03 = \underline{\$51}$
		
		$\begin{array}{r} 1,700 - 51 = 1.649 \\ +\ 100\ \text{Shipping} \\ \hline \underline{\$1,749}\ \text{Net amount due} \end{array}$

Section IV (continued)

Topic	Important Concepts	Illustrative Examples

Calculating Net Amount Due, with Credit Given for Partial Payment
 	
Performance Objective 7-10, Page 213
	$$\text{Partial payment credit} = \frac{\text{Partial payment}}{100\% - \text{Cash discount rate}}$$
	
	Net amount due =
	  Net price − Partial payment credit
		Elite Fashions makes a partial payment of $3,000 on an invoice of $7,900. The terms of sale are 3/15, n/30. What is the amount of the partial payment credit, and how much does Elite Fashions still owe on the invoice?
		
		$$\text{Part pmt credit} = \frac{3,000}{100\% - 3\%} = \$3,092.78$$
		
		Net amount due = 7,900.00
		              − 3,092.78
		              $4,807.22

Determining Discount Date and Net Date by Using Various Terms of Sale Dating Methods **Performance Objective 7-11, Page 214**	Discount date: last date to take advantage of a cash discount. Net date: last date to pay an invoice without incurring a penalty charge.	
Ordinary Dating Method **Performance Objective 7-11, Page 216**	Ordinary dating: discount period and the credit period start on the date of the invoice.	Galaxy Jewelers receives an invoice for merchandise on March 12 with terms of 3/15, n/30. What are the discount date and the net date? Disc date = March 12 + 15 days = March 27 Net date = March 12 + 30 days = April 11

EOM or Proximo Dating Method
 	
Performance Objective 7-11, Page 216
	EOM means end of month. It is a dating method in which the terms of sale start *after* the end of the month of the invoice.
	    If the invoice is dated after the 25th of the month, the terms of sale start *after* the end of the *following* month.
	    Unless otherwise specified, the net date is *20 days* after the discount date.
	    Proximo, or prox, is another name for EOM dating. It means "in the following month."
		Majestic Cleaning Service buys supplies with terms of sale of 2/10, EOM. What are the discount date and the net date if the invoice date is
		a. May 5?
		b. May 27?
		a. May 5 invoice terms start *after* the end of May:
		
		Discount date = June 10
		
		Net date = June 10 + 20 days = June 30
		
		b. May 27 invoice terms start *after* the end of the *following* month, June:
		
		Discount date = July 10
		
		Net date = July 10 + 20 days = July 30

ROG Dating Method **Performance Objective 7-11, Page 217**	ROG means receipt of goods. It is a dating method in which the terms of sale begin on the date the goods are received rather than the invoice date. This is used to accommodate long shipping times. Unless otherwise specified, the net date is *20 days* after the discount date.	An invoice dated August 24 has terms of 3/10 ROG. If the merchandise arrives on October 1, what are the discount date and the net date? Disc date = October 1 + 10 days = October 11 Net date = October 11 + 20 days = October 31
Extra Dating Method **Performance Objective 7-11, Page 218**	Extra, Ex, or X is a dating method in which the buyer receives an extra period of time before the terms of sale begin. Vendors use extra dating as an incentive to entice buyers to purchase out-of-season or slow-moving merchandise. Unless otherwise specified, the net date is *20 days* after the discount date.	Sugar Pine Candy Company buys merchandise from a vendor with terms of 3/15, 60 Extra. The invoice is dated December 11. What are the discount date and the net date? Disc date = December 11 + 75 days = February 24 Net date = February 24 + 20 = March 16

TRY IT: EXERCISE SOLUTIONS FOR CHAPTER 7

1. **a.** Shutterbug Camera Shops   **b.** 44929

     c. November 27, 20XX   **d.** $3,120.00

     e. FotoFair Distributors   **f.** Net - 30 days

     g. 1864 N.W. 123rd St., Chicago, IL 60613   **h.** J. Herman

     i. Federal Express   **j.** Knoxville, TN

     k. $125.00   **l.** $5,632.80

     m. $345.00   **n.** $5,757.80

2.

Stock #	Quantity	Unit	Merchandise Description	Unit Price	Total
R443	125	ea.	Food Processors	$89.00	$11,125.00
B776	24	ea.	Microwave Ovens	$225.40	$5,409.60
Z133	6	doz.	12" Mixers	$54.12	$324.72
Z163	1	bx.	Mixer Covers	$166.30	$166.30
				Invoice Subtotal	$17,025.62
				Shipping Charges	+ $194.20
				Invoice Total	$17,219.82

3. Trade discount = List price × Trade discount rate

     Trade discount = 7,600 × .30 = $2,280

4. Net price = List price(100% − Trade discount rate)

     Net price = 2,100(100% − 35%)

     Net price = 2,100 × .65 = $1,365

5. Trade discount = List price − Net price

     Trade discount = 109,500 − 63,300 = $46,200

     Trade discount rate = $\dfrac{\text{Trade discount}}{\text{List price}} = \dfrac{46,200}{109,500} = .4219 = 42.2\%$

6.

$$
\begin{array}{cccccc}
25{,}000 & 25{,}000 & 16{,}250 & 16{,}250 & 13{,}000 & 13{,}000 \\
\underline{\times\ \ .35} & \underline{-\ 8{,}750} & \underline{\times\ \ .20} & \underline{-\ 3{,}250} & \underline{\times\ \ .10} & \underline{-\ 1{,}300} \\
8{,}750 & 16{,}250 & 3{,}250 & 13{,}000 & 1{,}300 & \$11{,}700 = \text{Net price}
\end{array}
$$

     Trade discount = 25,000 − 11,700 = $13,300

7. **a.**

$$
\begin{array}{ccc}
100\% & 100\% & 100\% \\
\underline{-\ 30\%} & \underline{-\ 20\%} & \underline{-\ 12\%} \\
.7 \ \times & .8 \ \times & .88 \ = .4928 = \text{Net price factor}
\end{array}
$$

     b. Net price = List price × Net price factor

        Net price = 3,500 × .4928 = $1,724.80

     c. Net price = List price × Net price factor

        Net price = 5,800 × .4928 = $2,858.24

8.

$$
\begin{array}{ccc}
100\% & 100\% & 100\% \\
\underline{-\ 25\%} & \underline{-\ 15\%} & \underline{-\ 10\%} \\
.75 \ \times & .85 \ \times & .9 \ = .57375 = \text{Net price factor}
\end{array}
$$

     Single equivalent discount = 1 − Net price factor

     Single equivalent discount = 1 − .57375 = .42625

     Trade discount = List price × Single equivalent discount

     Trade discount = 36,800 × .42625 = $15,686

9. Cash discount = Net price × Cash discount rate

     Cash discount = 8,300 × .03 = $249

     Net amount due = Net price − Cash discount

     Net amount due = 8,300 − 249 = $8,051

10. Partial payment credit $= \dfrac{\text{Partial payment}}{100\% - \text{Cash discount rate}}$

Partial payment credit $= \dfrac{20{,}000}{100\% - 4\%} = \dfrac{20{,}000}{.96} = \underline{\$20{,}833.33}$

Net amount due $=$ Net price $-$ Partial payment credit

Net amount due $= 45{,}300.00 - 20{,}833.33 = \underline{\$24{,}466.67}$

11. From the calendar, September 12 is day number 255.

$255 + 60 = 315$

From the calendar, day number 315 is $\underline{\text{November 11}}$.

12. Discount date $=$ June 11 $+$ 10 days $= \underline{\text{June 21}}$

Net date $=$ June 11 $+$ 60 days

$$
\begin{array}{rl}
30 & \text{Days in June} \\
-\ 11 & \text{Discount date} \\
\hline
19 & \text{June} \\
31 & \text{July} \\
+\ 10 & \text{Aug} \longrightarrow \text{August 10}\\
\hline
60 & \text{Days}
\end{array}
$$

13. **a.** Discount date $=$ 15 days after end of November $= \underline{\text{December 15}}$

    Net date $=$ December 15 $+$ 20 days $= \underline{\text{January 4}}$

    b. Discount date $=$ 15 days after end of December $= \underline{\text{January 15}}$

    Net date $=$ January 15 $+$ 20 days $= \underline{\text{February 4}}$

14. Discount date $=$ December 29 $+$ 20 days $= \underline{\text{January 18}}$

    Net date $=$ January 18 $+$ 20 days $= \underline{\text{February 7}}$

15. Discount date $=$ February 22 $+$ 80 days $= \underline{\text{May 13}}$

    Net date $=$ May 13 $+$ 20 days $= \underline{\text{June 2}}$

CONCEPT REVIEW

1. The document detailing a sales transaction is known as a(n) _____ . (7-1)

2. F.O.B. shipping point and F.O.B. destination are shipping terms that specify where the merchandise _____ is transferred. (7-1)

3. To extend an invoice, for each line, we multiply the number of items by the _____ per item. (7-2)

4. To calculate the amount of a single trade discount, we multiply the _____ price by the trade discount rate. (7-3)

5. The _____ price is the amount a business actually pays for merchandise after the discount has been deducted. (7-4)

6. To calculate the net price factor, we subtract the trade discount rate from _____ . (7-4)

7. Write the formula for the trade discount rate. (7-5)

8. In a chain or _____ of trade discounts, we calculate the final net price by taking each discount one at a time from the previous net price. (7-6)

9. As a shortcut, we can use the net price _____ method to calculate the net price. (7-7)

10. To calculate the net price factor, we subtract each trade discount rate from 100% and then _____ all the complements together. (7-7)

11. A single trade discount that equates to all the discounts in a series or chain is called a single _____ discount. (7-8)

12. The "_____ of sale" specify when an invoice must be paid and if a(n) _____ discount is being offered. (7-9)

13. To calculate the credit given for a partial payment, we divide the amount of the partial payment by 100% _____ the cash discount rate. (7-10)

14. The most common method for dating an invoice is when the discount period and the credit period start on the date of the invoice. This method is known as _____ dating. (7-11)

ASSESSMENT TEST

Answer the following questions based on the Leisure Time Industries invoice on the following page.

1. Who is the vendor?

2. What is the date of the invoice?

3. What is the stock number of rockers?

4. What does dz. mean?

5. What is the unit price of plastic lounge covers?

6. What is the destination?

7. What is the extended total for chaise lounges with no armrest?

8. Who pays the freight if the terms are F.O.B. shipping point?

9. What is the invoice subtotal?   10.   What is the invoice total?

LEISURE TIME INDUSTRIES

LTI

Patio Furniture Manufacturers
1930 Main Street
Fort Worth, Texas 76102

DATE: November 2, 20XX

SOLD TO: Patio Magic Stores
3386 Fifth Avenue
Raleigh, NC 27613

INVOICE # B-112743

TERMS OF SALE: Net 30 days	SHIPPING INFO: FedEx Freight

STOCK #	QUANTITY	UNIT	MERCHANDISE DESCRIPTION	UNIT PRICE	TOTAL
1455	40	ea.	Chaise Lounges with armrest	$169.00	_____
1475	20	ea.	Chaise Lounges—no armrest	$127.90	_____
4387	24	ea.	Rocker Chairs	$87.70	_____
8100	3	dz.	Plastic Lounge Covers	$46.55	_____

INVOICE SUBTOTAL: _____
Packing and Handling: $125.00
Shipping Charges: $477.50

INVOICE TOTAL: _____

11. Picasso Art Supplies receives an invoice for the purchase of merchandise with a list price of $5,500. Because Picasso is in the trade, it receives a 27% trade discount. What is the amount of the trade discount?

12. Natureland Garden Center buys lawn mowers that list for $679.95 less a 30% trade discount.

   a. What is the amount of the trade discount?

   b. What is the net price of each lawn mower?

13. Shorty's BBQ Restaurant places an order listing for $1,250 with a meat and poultry supplier. Shorty's receives a trade discount of $422 on the order. What is the trade discount rate on this transaction?

14. Fantasia Florist Shop purchases an order of imported roses with a list price of $2,375 less trade discounts of 15/20/20.

   a. What is the amount of the trade discount?

   b. What is the net amount of the order?

15. All-American Sports can purchase sneakers for $450 per dozen less trade discounts of 14/12 from Ideal Shoes. Fancy Footwear is offering the same sneakers for $435 less trade discounts of 18/6. Which supplier offers a lower net price?

16. a. What is the net price factor for trade discounts of 25/15/10?

    b. Use that net price factor to find the net price of a couch listing for $800.

17. a. What is the net price factor of the trade discount series 20/15/11?

    b. What is the single equivalent discount?

18. The Empire Carpet Company orders merchandise for $17,700, including $550 in shipping charges, from Mohawk Carpet Mills on May 4. Carpets valued at $1,390 will be returned because they are damaged. The terms of sale are 2/10, n/30 ROG. The shipment arrives on May 26, and Empire wants to take advantage of the cash discount.

    a. By what date must Empire pay the invoice?

    b. As the bookkeeper for Empire, how much will you send to Mohawk?

Photo by Robert Brechner

The U.S. Carpet Industry

According to the Carpet and Rug Institute, carpet covers nearly 60% of all floors in the United States. In 2007, industry shipments totaled 1.6 billion square yards and generated more than $14 billion in revenue. Ninety percent of all domestic carpet is manufactured in Georgia, representing a significant economic impact to the state. Nationwide, the industry employs over 70,000 workers.

19. Lazy Days Laundry receives an invoice for detergent. The invoice is dated April 9 with terms of 3/15, n/30.

    a. What is the discount date?

    c. If the invoice terms are changed to 3/15 EOM, what is the new discount date?

    b. What is the net date?

    d. What is the new net date?

20. Ned's Sheds purchases building materials from Timbertown Lumber for $3,700 with terms of 4/15, n/30. The invoice is dated October 17. Ned's decides to send in a $2,000 partial payment.

    a. By what date must the partial payment be sent to take advantage of the cash discount?

    b. What is the net date?

    c. If partial payment was sent by the discount date, what is the balance still due on the order?

21. Club Z is in receipt of new electronics to control the lighting on its dance floor. The invoice, dated June 9, shows the total cost of the equipment as $14,350. Shipping charges amount to $428, and insurance is $72.80. Terms of sale are 2/10 prox. If the invoice is paid on July 9, what is the net amount due?

BUSINESS DECISION: THE BUSY EXECUTIVE

22. You are a salesperson for Victory Lane Wholesale Auto Parts. You have just taken a phone order from one of your best customers, Champion Motors. Because you were busy when the call came in, you recorded the details of the order on a notepad.

Phone Order Notes

- The invoice date is April 4, 20XX.
- The customer order no. is 443B.
- Champion Motors's warehouse is located at 7011 N.W. 4th Avenue, Columbus, Ohio 43205.
- Terms of sale—3/15, n/45.
- The order will be filled by D. Watson.
- The goods will be shipped by truck.
- Champion Motors's home office is located next to the warehouse at 7013 N.W. 4th Avenue.
- Champion ordered 44 car batteries, stock #394, listing for $69.95 each and 24 truck batteries, stock #395, listing for $89.95 each. These items get trade discounts of 20/15.
- Champion also ordered 36 cases of 10W/30 motor oil, stock #838-W, listing for $11.97 per case, and 48 cases of 10W/40 super-oil, stock #1621-S, listing for $14.97 per case. These items get trade discounts of 20/20/12.
- The shipping charges for the order amount to $67.50.
- Insurance charges amount to $27.68.

a. Transfer your notes to the invoice on the following page, extend each line, and calculate the total.

b. What is the discount date of the invoice?

c. If Champion sends a partial payment of $1,200 by the discount date, what is the balance due on the invoice?

d. What is the net date of the invoice?

e. Your company has a policy of charging a 5% late fee if invoice payments are more than five days late. What is the amount of the late fee that Champion will be charged if it fails to pay the balance due on time?

Founded in 1928, **Genuine Parts Company** is a service organization engaged in the distribution of automotive replacement parts, industrial replacement parts, office products, and electrical/electronic materials. The company serves customers from more than 1,900 locations with approximately 31,700 employees. Genuine Part's 2009 sales were $10.06 billion.

NAPA, representing the Automotive Parts Group at Genuine Parts, is the central hub of company activity. The group consists of 58 NAPA distribution centers serving approximately 5,800 NAPA Auto Parts Stores, of which 1,000 are company-owned.

Source: www.napaonline.com

INVOICE

Victory Lane
Wholesale Auto Parts
422 Riverfront Road
Cincinnati, Ohio 45244

Invoice #

Invoice Date:

Sold To:

Ship To:

Customer Order No.	Salesperson	Ship via	Terms of Sale	Filled By

Quantity Ordered	Stock Number	Description	Unit List Price	Trade Discounts	Extended Amount

Invoice Subtotal _____
Shipping Charges _____
Insurance _____
Invoice Total _____

COLLABORATIVE LEARNING ACTIVITY

Comparing Invoices and Discounts

1. As a team, collect invoices from a number of businesses in different industries in your area.
   a. How are they similar?
   b. How are they different?

2. Have each member of the team speak with a wholesaler or a retailer in your area.
   a. What are the typical trade discounts in that industry?
   b. What are the typical terms of sale in that industry?

© Najlah Feanny/Corbis

Markup and Markdown

Determining an appropriate selling price for a company's goods or services is an extremely important function in business. The price must be attractive to potential customers, yet sufficient to cover expenses and provide the company with a reasonable profit.

In business, expenses are separated into two major categories. The first is the **cost of goods sold**. To a manufacturer, this expense would be the cost of production; to a wholesaler or retailer, the expense is the price paid to a manufacturer or distributor for the merchandise. The second category includes all the other expenses required to operate the business, such as salaries, rent, utilities, taxes, insurance, advertising, and maintenance. These expenses are known as **operating expenses**, overhead expenses, or simply **overhead**.

The amount added to the cost of an item to cover the operating expenses and profit is known as the **markup, markon,** or **margin**. It is the difference between the cost and the selling price of an item. Markup is applied at all levels of the marketing channels of distribution. This chapter deals with the business math applications involved in the pricing of goods and services.

cost of goods sold The cost of the merchandise sold during an operating period. One of two major expense categories of a business.

operating expenses, or **overhead** All business expenses, other than cost of merchandise, required to operate a business, such as payroll, rent, utilities, and insurance.

markup, markon, or **margin** The amount added to the cost of an item to cover the operating expenses and profit. It is the difference between the cost and the selling price.

UNDERSTANDING AND USING THE RETAILING EQUATION TO FIND COST, AMOUNT OF MARKUP, AND SELLING PRICE OF AN ITEM

8-1

The fundamental principle on which business operates is to sell goods and services for a price high enough to cover all expenses and provide the owners with a reasonable profit. The formula that describes this principle is known as the **retailing equation**. The equation states that the selling price of an item is equal to the cost plus the markup.

retailing equation The selling price of an item is equal to the cost plus the markup.

Selling price = Cost + Markup

Using the abbreviations *C* for cost, *M* for markup, and *SP* for selling price, the formula is written as

$$SP = C + M$$

To illustrate, if a camera costs a retailer $60 and a $50 markup is added to cover operating expenses and profit, the selling price of the camera would be $110.

$60 (cost) + $50 (markup) = $110 (selling price)

In Chapter 5, we learned that equations are solved by isolating the unknowns on one side and the knowns on the other. Using this theory, when the amount of markup is the unknown, the equation can be rewritten as

Markup = Selling price − Cost $M = SP - C$

When the cost is the unknown, the equation becomes

Cost = Selling price − Markup $C = SP - M$

According to the retailing equation, the selling price of an item is equal to the cost plus the markup.

The following examples illustrate how these formulas are used to determine the dollar amount of cost, markup, and selling cost.

EXAMPLE 1 — FINDING THE SELLING PRICE

Mementos Gift Shop pays $8.00 for a picture frame. If a markup of $6.50 is added, what is the selling price of the frame?

SOLUTION STRATEGY

Because selling price is the unknown variable, we use the formula $SP = C + M$ as follows:

$$SP = C + M$$
$$SP = 8.00 + 6.50 = 14.50$$
$$\text{Selling price} = \underline{\$14.50}$$

TRY IT EXERCISE 1

For the following, use the basic retailing equation to solve for the unknown.

Hairbrushes cost the manufacturer $6.80 per unit to produce. If a markup of $9.40 each is added to the cost, what is the selling price per brush?

CHECK YOUR ANSWER WITH THE SOLUTION ON PAGE 259.

EXAMPLE 2 — FINDING THE AMOUNT OF MARKUP

Reliable Office Supply buys printing calculators from Taiwan for $22.50 each. If they are sold for $39.95, what is the amount of the markup?

SOLUTION STRATEGY

Because the markup is the unknown variable, we use the formula $M = SP - C$ as follows:

$$M = SP - C$$
$$M = 39.95 - 22.50 = 17.45$$
$$\text{Markup} = \underline{\$17.45}$$

TRY IT EXERCISE 2

For the following, use the basic retailing equation to solve for the unknown.

The 19th Hole sells a dozen golf balls for $28.50. If the distributor was paid $16.75, what is the amount of the markup?

CHECK YOUR ANSWER WITH THE SOLUTION ON PAGE 259.

EXAMPLE 3 — FINDING THE COST

Safeway Supermarkets sell Corn Crunchies for $3.29 per box. If the markup on this item is $2.12, how much did the store pay for the cereal?

SOLUTIONSTRATEGY

Because the cost is the unknown variable in this problem, we use the formula $C = SP - M$.

$$C = SP - M$$

$$C = 3.29 - 2.12 = 1.17$$

$$\text{Cost} = \underline{\$1.17}$$

TRYITEXERCISE3

For the following, use the basic retailing equation to solve for the unknown.

After a wholesaler adds a markup of $75 to a television set, it is sold to a retail store for $290. What is the wholesaler's cost?

CHECK YOUR ANSWER WITH THE SOLUTION ON PAGE 259.

CALCULATING PERCENT MARKUP BASED ON COST

8-2

In addition to being expressed in dollar amounts, markup is frequently expressed as a percent. There are two ways of representing markup as a percent: based on cost and based on selling price. Manufacturers and most wholesalers use cost as the base in calculating the percent markup because cost figures are readily available to them. When markup is based on cost, the cost is 100%, and the markup is expressed as a percent of that cost. Retailers, however, use selling price figures as the base of most calculations, including percent markup. In retailing, the selling price represents 100%, and the markup is expressed as a percent of that selling price.

markup based on cost When cost is 100% and the markup is expressed as a percent of that cost.

In Chapter 6, we used the percentage formula Portion = Rate × Base. To review these variables, portion is a *part* of a whole amount; base is the *whole amount*; and rate, as a percent, describes what part the portion is of the base. When we calculate markup as a percent, we are actually solving a rate problem using the formula Rate = Portion ÷ Base.

When the markup is based on cost, the percent markup is the rate; the dollar amount of markup is the portion; and the cost, representing 100%, is the base. The answer will describe what percent the markup is of the cost; therefore, it is called percent **markup based on cost**. We use the formula:

$$\text{Percent markup based on cost (rate)} = \frac{\text{Markup (portion)}}{\text{Cost (base)}} \quad \text{or} \quad \%M_{\text{COST}} = \frac{M}{C}$$

LEARNINGTIP

A shortcut for calculating the factors of the retailing equation is to use the markup table. The cells represent cost, markup, and selling price in both dollars and percents.

Markup Table

	$	%
C		
+ MU		
SP		

EXAMPLE4 — CALCULATING PERCENT MARKUP BASED ON COST

Blanco Industries produces stainless steel sinks at a cost of $56.00 each. If the sinks are sold to distributors for $89.60 each, what are the amount of the markup and the percent markup based on cost?

SOLUTIONSTRATEGY

$$M = SP - C$$

$$M = 89.60 - 56.00 = 33.60$$

$$\text{Markup} = \underline{\$33.60}$$

$$\%M_{\text{COST}} = \frac{M}{C}$$

LEARNINGTIP

Step 1. Fill in the given information using 100% for the base and X for this unknown. (orange)

Step 2. Calculate the figure for the remaining cell (red) in the column without the X.

$$\$89.60 - \$56.00 = \$33.60$$

	$	%
C	56.00	100
+ MU	33.60	X
SP	89.60	

Then form a box. (yellow)

(continue)

The figures in the box form a proportion.

$$\frac{56}{33.60} = \frac{100}{X}$$

Step 3. Solve the proportion for X by cross-multiplying the corner figures in the box.

$$56X = 33.60(100)$$

$$X = \frac{3,360}{56} = 60\%$$

$$\%M_{COST} = \frac{33.60}{56.00} = .6$$

Percent markup based on cost = <u>60%</u>

TRYITEXERCISE4

The Light Source buys lamps for $45 and sells them for $63. What are the amount of the markup and the percent markup based on cost?

CHECK YOUR ANSWERS WITH THE SOLUTIONS ON PAGE 259.

8-3

CALCULATING SELLING PRICE WHEN COST AND PERCENT MARKUP BASED ON COST ARE KNOWN

From the basic retailing equation, we know that the selling price is equal to the cost plus the markup. When the markup is based on cost, the cost equals 100%, and the selling price equals 100% plus the percent markup. If, for example, the percent markup is 30%, then

$$\text{Selling price} = \text{Cost} + \text{Markup}$$

$$\text{Selling price} = 100\% + 30\%$$

$$\text{Selling price} = 130\% \ of \text{ the cost}$$

Because *of* means multiply, we multiply the cost by (100% plus the percent markup).

Selling price = Cost(100% + Percent markup based on cost)

$$SP = C(100\% + \%M_{COST})$$

$100\% + 70\% = 170\%$

	$	%
C	50	100
+ *MU*		70
SP	*X*	170

Note: When the brown box has six cells, use the four corner figures to form the proportion.

$$100X = 50(170)$$

$$X = \underline{\$85}$$

EXAMPLE5 — CALCULATING THE SELLING PRICE

A wallet costs $50 to produce. If the manufacturer wants a 70% markup based on cost, what should be the selling price of the wallet?

SOLUTIONSTRATEGY

$$SP = C(100\% + \%M_{COST})$$

$$SP = 50(100\% + 70\%)$$

$$SP = 50(170\%) = 50(1.7) = 85$$

Selling price = <u>$85</u>

TRYITEXERCISE5

Superior Appliances buys toasters for $38. If a 65% markup based on cost is desired, what should be the selling price of the toaster?

CHECK YOUR ANSWER WITH THE SOLUTION ON PAGE 259.

CALCULATING COST WHEN SELLING PRICE AND PERCENT MARKUP BASED ON COST ARE KNOWN

8-4

To calculate cost when selling price and percent markup on cost are known, let's use our knowledge of solving equations from Chapter 5. Because we are dealing with the same three variables from the last section, simply solve the equation $SP = C(100\% + \%M_{COST})$ for the cost. Cost, the unknown, is isolated on one side of the equation by dividing both sides by (100% + Percent markup).

$$\text{Cost} = \frac{\text{Selling price}}{100\% + \text{Percent markup on cost}} \qquad C = \frac{SP}{100\% + \%M_{COST}}$$

EXAMPLE6 CALCULATING COST

American Eagle sells a blouse for $66. If a 50% markup based on cost is used, what is the cost of the blouse?

SOLUTIONSTRATEGY

$$\text{Cost} = \frac{\text{Selling price}}{100\% + \text{Percent markup on cost}}$$

$$\text{Cost} = \frac{66}{100\% + 50\%} = \frac{66}{150\%} = \frac{66}{1.5} = 44$$

$$\text{Cost} = \underline{\$44}$$

100% + 50% = 150%

	$	%
C	X	100
+ MU		50
SP	66	150

$$150X = 66(100)$$

$$X = \underline{\$44}$$

TRYITEXERCISE6

General Electric sells automatic coffeemakers to distributors for $39. If a 30% markup based on cost is used, how much did it cost to manufacture the coffee maker?

CHECK YOUR ANSWER WITH THE SOLUTION ON PAGE 259.

REVIEW EXERCISES

SECTION I

8

For the following items, calculate the missing information. Round dollars to the nearest cent and percents to the nearest tenth of a percent.

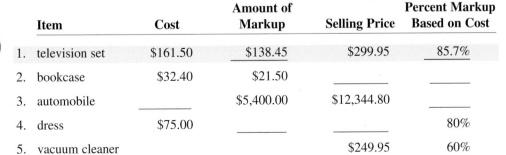

	Item	Cost	Amount of Markup	Selling Price	Percent Markup Based on Cost
1.	television set	$161.50	$138.45	$299.95	85.7%
2.	bookcase	$32.40	$21.50		
3.	automobile		$5,400.00	$12,344.80	
4.	dress	$75.00			80%
5.	vacuum cleaner			$249.95	60%

Item	Cost	Amount of Markup	Selling Price	Percent Markup Based on Cost
6. hat	$46.25	$50.00	$96.25	108.1%
7. computer	$1,350.00	_____	$3,499.00	_____
8. treadmill	_____	$880.00	$2,335.00	_____
9. 1 lb potatoes	$.58	_____	_____	130%
10. wallet	_____	_____	$44.95	75%

Solve the following word problems. Round dollars to the nearest cent and percents to the nearest tenth of a percent.

11. Alarm clocks cost the manufacturer $56.10 per unit to produce. If a markup of $29.80 is added to the cost, what is the selling price per clock?

12. En Vogue Boutique sells blouses for $22.88. If the cost per blouse is $15.50, what is the amount of the markup?

13. After a wholesaler adds a markup of $125 to a stereo, it is sold for $320. What is the cost of the stereo?

14. Amazon.com purchases flat-screen computer monitors from H.P. for $275.59 and sells them for $449.99.

    a. What is the amount of the markup?

    b. What is the percent markup based on cost?

Amazon.com, Inc., operates as an online retailer in North America and internationally. Its product categories include books, movies, music, and games; digital downloads; electronics and computers; home and garden; toys, kids, and baby; grocery; apparel, shoes, and jewelry; health and beauty; sports and outdoors; and tools, auto, and industrial products.

In 2009, Amazon.com generated sales of over $24.5 billion and had over 24,300 full- and part-time employees.

15. The Holiday Card Shop purchased stationery for $2.44 per box. A $1.75 markup is added to the stationery.

    a. What is the selling price?

    b. What is the percent markup based on cost?

16. Staples adds a $4.60 markup to calculators and sells them for $9.95.

    a. What is the cost of the calculators?

    b. What is the percent markup based on cost?

17. a. What is the amount of markup on a skateboard from Flying Wheels Skate Shop if the cost is $58.25 and the selling price is $118.88?

    b. What is the percent markup based on cost?

18. You are the manager of The Camera Connection. Use the advertisement for your store to answer the following questions.

    a. If the PowerShooter 1800 is marked up by $58.50, what is the cost and what is the percent markup on cost?

    b. If the CyberShooter 2400 has a cost of $88.00 what are the amount of the markup and the percent markup on cost?

    c. Which camera is more "profitable" to the store? Why?

    d. What other factors should be considered in determining profitability?

THE CAMERA CONNECTION

$109.99

PowerShooter **1800**

$199.99

CyberShooter **2400**

19. Crystal Auto Supply purchases water pumps from the distributor for $35.40 each. If Crystal adds a 120% markup based on cost, at what retail price should the pumps be sold?

20. Broadway Carpets sells designer rugs at retail for $875.88. If a 50% markup based on cost is added, what is the cost of the designer rugs?

21. What is the cost of a plasma TV that sells at retail for $1,750 with a 70% markup based on cost?

22. A real-wood filing cabinet from Office Solutions is marked up by $97.30 to $178.88.
    a.   What is the cost?

    b. What is the percent markup based on cost?

23. The Green Thumb Garden Shop purchases automatic lawn sprinklers for $12.50 from the manufacturer. If a 75% markup based on cost is added, at what retail price should the sprinklers be marked?

24. a. What is the cost of a desk lamp at Urban Accents if the selling price is $49.95 and the markup is 70% based on the cost?

    b. What is the amount of the markup?

BUSINESS DECISION: KEYSTONE MARKUP

25. In department and specialty store retailing, a common markup strategy is to double the cost of an item to arrive at a selling price. This strategy is known as **keystoning** the markup and is widely used in apparel, cosmetics, fashion accessories, shoes, and other categories of merchandise.

The reasoning for the high amount of markup is that these stores have particularly high operating expenses. In addition, they have a continuing need to update fixtures and remodel stores to attract customers.

You are the buyer in the women's shoe department of the Roma Grande Department Store. You normally keystone your markups on certain shoes and handbags. This amount of markup allows you enough gross margin so that you can lower prices when "sales" occur and still have a profitable department.

a. If you are looking for a line of handbags that will retail for $120, what is the most you can pay for the bags?

b. At a women's wear trade show, you find a line of handbags that you like with a suggested retail price of $130. The vendor has offered you trade discounts of 30/20/5. Will this series of trade discounts allow you to keystone the handbags?

c. (Challenge) The vendor tells you that the first two discounts, 30% and 20%, are fixed, but the 5% is negotiable. What trade discount, rounded to a whole percent, should you request in order to keystone the markup?

Top U.S. Shopping Centers
Gross Leasable Area (GLA) in sq ft

King of Prussia Mall King of Prussia, Pennsylvania	2,856,000
Mall of America Bloomington, Minnesota	2,777,918
South Coast Plaza Costa Mesa, California	2,700,000
Mill Creek Mall Erie, Pennsylvania	2,600,000
Del Amo Fashion Center Torrance, California	2,500,000
Grand Canyon Parkway Las Vagas, Nevada	2,500,000
Aventura Mall Aventura, FL	2,400,000
Sawgrass Mills Sunrise, Florida	2,383,906
The Galleria Houston, Texas	2,298,417

Source: www.shoppingcenters.com

Andre Blais /Shutterstock.com

SECTION II   8   MARKUP BASED ON SELLING PRICE

In Section I, we calculated markup as a percentage of the cost of an item. The cost was the base and represented 100%. As noted, this method is primarily used by manufacturers and wholesalers. In this section, the markup is calculated as a percentage of the selling price; therefore, the selling price will be the base and represent 100%. This practice is used by most retailers because most retail records and statistics are kept in sales dollars.

8-5   CALCULATING PERCENT MARKUP BASED ON SELLING PRICE

markup based on selling price When selling price is 100% and the markup is expressed as a percent of that selling price.

The calculation of percent **markup based on selling price** is the same as that for percent markup based on cost except that the base (the denominator) changes from cost to selling price. Remember, finding percent markup is a rate problem using the now familiar percentage formula Rate = Portion ÷ Base.

For this application of the formula, the percent markup based on selling price is the rate, the amount of the markup is the portion, and the selling price is the base. The formula is

$$\text{Percent markup based on selling price (rate)} = \frac{\text{Markup (portion)}}{\text{Selling price (base)}} \quad \text{or} \quad \%M_{SP} = \frac{M}{SP}$$

EXAMPLE7 CALCULATING THE PERCENT MARKUP BASED ON SELLING PRICE

Quality Hardware & Garden Supply purchases electric drills for $60 each. If it sells the drills for $125, what is the amount of the markup and what is the percent markup based on selling price?

SOLUTIONSTRATEGY

$$M = SP - C$$

$$M = 125 - 60 = 65$$

$$\text{Markup} = \underline{\$65}$$

$$\%M_{SP} = \frac{M}{SP}$$

$$\%M_{SP} = \frac{65}{125} = .52$$

Percent markup based on selling price = $\underline{52\%}$

$125 - $60 = $65

	$	%
C	60	
+ MU	65	X
SP	125	100

$$125X = 65(100)$$

$$X = \underline{52\%}$$

TRYITEXERCISE7

Deals on Wheels buys bicycles from the distributor for $94.50 each. If the bikes sell for $157.50, what is the amount of the markup and what is the percent markup based on selling price?

CHECK YOUR ANSWERS WITH THE SOLUTIONS ON PAGE 259.

CALCULATING SELLING PRICE WHEN COST AND PERCENT MARKUP BASED ON SELLING PRICE ARE KNOWN

8-6

When the percent markup is based on selling price, remember that the selling price is the base and represents 100%. This means the percent cost plus the percent markup must equal 100%. If, for example, the markup is 25% of the selling price, the cost must be 75% of the selling price.

$$\text{Cost} + \text{Markup} = \text{Selling price}$$

$$75\% + 25\% = 100\%$$

Because the percent markup is known, the percent cost will always be the complement, or

% Cost = 100% − Percent markup based on selling price

Because the selling price is the base, we can solve for the selling price by using the percentage formula Base = Portion ÷ Rate, where the cost is the portion and the percent cost or (100% − Percent markup on selling price) is the rate.

$$\text{Selling price} = \frac{\text{Cost}}{100\% - \text{Percent markup on selling price}} \quad \text{or} \quad SP = \frac{C}{100\% - \%M_{SP}}$$

EXAMPLE8 CALCULATING SELLING PRICE

High Point Furniture purchases wall units from the manufacturer for $550. If the store policy is to mark up all merchandise 60% based on the selling price, what is the retail selling price of the wall units?

SOLUTIONSTRATEGY

$$SP = \frac{C}{100\% - \%M_{SP}}$$

$$SP = \frac{550}{100\% - 60\%} = \frac{550}{40\%} = 1.375$$

Selling price = $\underline{\$1,375}$

$100\% - 60\% = 40\%$

	$	%
C	550	40
+ MU		60
SP	X	100

$$40X = 550(100)$$

$$X = \underline{\$1,375}$$

TRYITEXERCISE8

Grand Prix Menswear buys suits for $169 from the manufacturer. If a 35% markup based on selling price is the objective, what should be the selling price of the suit?

CHECK YOUR ANSWER WITH THE SOLUTION ON PAGE 259.

8-7 CALCULATING COST WHEN SELLING PRICE AND PERCENT MARKUP BASED ON SELLING PRICE ARE KNOWN

Often retailers know how much their customers are willing to pay for an item. The following procedure is used to determine the most a retailer can pay for an item and still get the intended markup.

To calculate the cost of an item when the selling price and percent markup based on selling price are known, we use a variation of the formula used in the last section. To solve for cost, we must isolate cost on one side of the equation by multiplying both sides of the equation by (100% − Percent markup). This yields the equation for cost:

LEARNINGTIP

The percent markup on cost is always *greater* than the corresponding percent markup on selling price because markup on cost uses cost as the base, which is *less* than the selling price. In the percentage formula, the lower the base, the greater the rate.

Cost = Selling price(100% − Percent markup on selling price)

$$C = SP(100\% - \%M_{SP})$$

EXAMPLE9 CALCULATING COST

A buyer for a chain of boutiques is looking for a line of dresses to retail for $120. If a 40% markup based on selling price is the objective, what is the most the buyer can pay for these dresses and still get the intended markup?

SOLUTIONSTRATEGY

$$C = SP(100\% - \%M_{SP})$$

$$C = 120(100\% - 40\%) = 120(.6) = 72$$

Cost = $\underline{\$72}$

$100 - 40 = 60$

	$	%
C	X	60
+ MU		40
SP	120	100

$$100X = 120(60)$$

$$X = \underline{\$72}$$

TRYITEXERCISE9

What is the most a gift shop buyer can pay for a set of wine glasses if he wants a 55% markup based on selling price and expects to sell the glasses for $79 at retail?

CHECK YOUR ANSWER WITH THE SOLUTION ON PAGE 259.

CONVERTING PERCENT MARKUP BASED ON COST TO PERCENT MARKUP BASED ON SELLING PRICE, AND VICE VERSA

8-8

CONVERTING PERCENT MARKUP BASED ON COST TO PERCENT MARKUP BASED ON SELLING PRICE

When percent markup is based on cost, it can be converted to percent markup based on selling price by using the following formula:

$$\text{Percent markup based on selling price} = \frac{\text{Percent markup based on cost}}{100\% + \text{Percent markup based on cost}}$$

EXAMPLE10 CONVERTING BETWEEN MARKUP TYPES

If a purse is marked up 60% based on cost, what is the corresponding percent markup based on selling price?

SOLUTIONSTRATEGY

$$\text{Percent markup based on selling price} = \frac{\text{Percent markup based on cost}}{100\% + \text{Percent markup based on cost}}$$

$$\text{Percent markup based on selling price} = \frac{60\%}{100\% + 60\%} = \frac{.6}{1.6} = .375$$

$$\text{Percent markup based on selling price} = \underline{37.5\%}$$

TRYITEXERCISE10

A suitcase is marked up 50% based on cost. What is the corresponding percent markup based on selling price?

CHECK YOUR ANSWER WITH THE SOLUTION ON PAGE 259.

LEARNINGTIP

This table provides a shortcut for converting between markup types. As before:

- Fill in the given information using 100% for the bases and X for the unknown. (orange)
- Calculate the figure for the remaining cell in the column without the X. (red)

$$100 + 60 = 160$$

- Form a proportion and solve for X.

	% C	% SP
C	100	
+ MU	60	X
SP	160	100

$$\frac{60}{160} = \frac{X}{100}$$

$$160X = 60(100)$$

$$X = \underline{37.5\%}$$

CONVERTING PERCENT MARKUP BASED ON SELLING PRICE TO PERCENT MARKUP BASED ON COST

When percent markup is based on selling price, it can be converted to percent markup based on cost by the formula:

$$\text{Percent markup based on cost} = \frac{\text{Percent markup based on selling price}}{100\% - \text{Percent markup based on selling price}}$$

EXAMPLE11 CONVERTING BETWEEN MARKUP TYPES

At Walmart, a Panasonic stereo is marked up 25% based on selling price. What is the corresponding percent markup based on cost? Round to the nearest tenth of a percent.

SOLUTIONSTRATEGY

$$\text{Percent markup based on cost} = \frac{\text{Percent markup based on selling price}}{100\% - \text{Percent markup based on selling price}}$$

$$\text{Percent markup based on cost} = \frac{25\%}{100\% - 25\%} = \frac{.25}{.75} = .3333$$

$$\text{Percent markup based on cost} = \underline{33.3\%}$$

$$100 - 25 = 75$$

	% C	% SP
C	100	75
+ MU	X	25
SP		100

$$75X = 25(100)$$
$$X = \underline{33.3\%}$$

TRYITEXERCISE11

At Video Outlet, a PlayStation video game is marked up 75% based on selling price. What is the corresponding percent markup based on cost? Round to the nearest tenth of a percent.

CHECK YOUR ANSWER WITH THE SOLUTION ON PAGE 259.

SECTION II 8 REVIEW EXERCISES

For the following items, calculate the missing information. Round dollars to the nearest cent and percents to the nearest tenth of a percent.

Item	Cost	Amount of Markup	Selling Price	Percent Markup Based on Cost	Percent Markup Based on Selling Price
1. sink	$65.00	$50.00	$115.00		43.5%
2. textbook	$34.44		$51.50		
3. telephone	$75.00				45%
4. bicycle			$133.50		60%
5. magazine				60%	
6. flashlight					35%
7. dollhouse	$71.25	$94.74	$165.99	133%	57.1%
8. bar of soap	$1.18	$.79			
9. truck	$15,449.00				38%
10. sofa			$1,299.00		55%
11. fan				150%	
12. drill					47%

Solve the following word problems. Round dollars to the nearest cent and percents to the nearest tenth of a percent.

13. You are the manager of Midtown Hardware. If the EnergyMax batteries in your advertisement have a cost of $3.25,

    a. What is the amount of the markup on these batteries?

    b. What is your percent markup based on selling price?

    c. If the vender reduces the cost to $2.90 as a promotional trade discount this week, what is your new amount of markup and what is percent markup based on selling price?

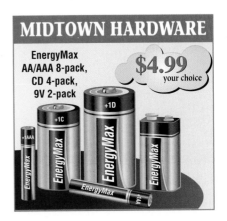

14. A distributor purchases tractors at a cost of $6,500 and sells them for $8,995.
    a. What is the amount of the markup?

    b. What is the percent markup based on selling price?

15. Waterbed City purchases beds from the manufacturer for $212.35. If the store policy is to mark up all merchandise 42% based on selling price, what is the retail selling price of the beds?

16. Video Depot uses a 40% markup based on selling price for its video game systems. On games and accessories, they use a 30% markup based on selling price.

    a. What is the cost and the amount of the markup of the game console system?

    b. What is the cost and the amount of the markup of the Sports Package game?

    c. As a promotion this month, the manufacturer is offering its dealers a rebate of $5.50 for each additional remote sold. What is the cost and percent markup based on selling price?

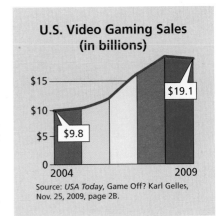

17. Galaxy Tools manufactures an 18-volt drill at a cost of $38.32. It imports rechargeable battery packs for $20.84 each. Galaxy offers its distributors a "package deal" that includes a drill and two battery packs. The markup is 36% based on selling price. What is the selling price of the package?

18. You are the buyer for The Shoe Outlet. You are looking for a line of men's shoes to retail for $79.95. If your objective is a 55% markup based on selling price, what is the most that you can pay for the shoes to still get the desired markup?

19. If the markup on a washing machine is 43% based on selling price, what is the corresponding percent markup based on cost?

20. If the markup on an oven is 200% based on cost, what is the corresponding percent markup based on selling price?

21. A purse has a cost of $21.50 and a selling price of $51.99.

   a. What is the amount of markup on the purse?

   b. What is the percent markup based on cost?

   c. What is the corresponding percent markup based on selling price?

Speedy Supermarket
Sale
4/$5

2 Liter Bubbly-Cola Products

SALE 3/$3

12 Pack Bubbly-Cola Products

22. As the manager of Speedy Supermarket, answer the following questions.

   a. If 2-liter Bubbly-Cola products cost Speedy $16.50 per case of 24 bottles, what are the amount of the markup and the percent markup on selling price per case?

   b. If 12-pack Bubbly-Cola products have a markup of $8.25 per case of six 12-packs at Speedy, what are the cost and the percent markup on selling price per case?

   c. Why has Speedy Supermarket chosen to use markup based on selling price?

BUSINESS DECISION: INCREASING THE MARGIN

23. If Costco pays $37.50 for the vacuum cleaner shown here,

   a. What is the percent markup based on selling price?

   b. If Costco pays $1.50 to the insurance company for each product replacement policy sold, what is the percent markup based on selling price of the vacuum cleaner and policy combination?

   c. If 6,000 vacuum cleaners are sold in a season and 40% are sold with the insurance policy, how many additional "markup dollars," the **gross margin**, was made by offering the policy?

   d. (Optional) As a housewares buyer for Costco, what is your opinion of such insurance policies, considering their effect on the "profit picture" of the department? How can you sell more policies?

12-AMP
POWERVAC PLUS
$89⁹⁹

• Microfiltration
• On-board tools

1-yr. Product
Replacement Policy, $7.99

MARKDOWNS, MULTIPLE OPERATIONS, AND PERISHABLE GOODS

SECTION III **8**

The original selling price of merchandise usually represents only a temporary situation based on customer and competitor reaction to that price. A price reduction from the original selling price of merchandise is known as a **markdown**. Markdowns are frequently used in retailing because of errors in initial pricing or merchandise selection. For example, the original price may have been set too high or the buyer ordered the wrong styles, sizes, or quantities of merchandise.

Most markdowns should not be regarded as losses but as sales promotion opportunities used to increase sales and profits. When a sale has been concluded, raising prices back to the original selling price is known as a **markdown cancellation**. This section deals with the mathematics of markdowns, a series of markups and markdowns, and the pricing of perishable merchandise.

markdown A price reduction from the original selling price of merchandise.

markdown cancellation Raising prices back to the original selling price after a sale is over.

DETERMINING THE AMOUNT OF MARKDOWN AND THE MARKDOWN PERCENT

8-9

A markdown is a reduction from the original selling price of an item to a new **sale price**. To determine the amount of a markdown, we use the formula:

sale price The promotional price of merchandise after a markdown.

$$\textbf{Markdown} = \textbf{Original selling price} - \textbf{Sale price}$$

For example, if a sweater was originally marked at $89.95 and then was sale-priced at $59.95, the amount of the markdown would be $30.00 ($89.95 − $59.95 = $30.00).

To find the markdown percent, we use the percentage formula once again, Rate = Portion ÷ Base, where the markdown percent is the rate, the amount of the markdown is the portion, and the original selling price is the base:

$$\textbf{Markdown percent} = \frac{\textbf{Markdown}}{\textbf{Original selling price}}$$

© 2010 Fuse/Jupiterimages Corporation

Prudent shoppers often spend time comparing products in order to make "informed" buying decisions.

EXAMPLE 12 DETERMINING THE MARKDOWN AND MARKDOWN PERCENT

A blender that originally sold for $60 was marked down and sold for $48. What is the amount of the markdown and the markdown percent?

SOLUTIONSTRATEGY

$$\text{Markdown} = \text{Original selling price} - \text{Sale price}$$

$$\text{Markdown} = 60 - 48 = 12$$

$$\text{Markdown} = \underline{\$12}$$

$$\text{Markdown percent} = \frac{\text{Markdown}}{\text{Original selling price}} = \frac{12}{60} = .2$$

$$\text{Markdown percent} = \underline{20\%}$$

LEARNINGTIP

Note that *markdown percent* calculations are an application of *rate of decrease*, covered in Chapter 6.

In the percentage formula, the markdown (portion) represents the amount of the decrease and the original selling price (base) represents the original amount.

TRYITEXERCISE 12

A tennis racquet that originally sold for $75 was marked down and sold for $56. What are the amount of the markdown and the markdown percent? Round your answer to the nearest tenth of a percent.

CHECK YOUR ANSWERS WITH THE SOLUTIONS ON PAGE 260.

8-10 DETERMINING THE SALE PRICE AFTER A MARKDOWN AND THE ORIGINAL PRICE BEFORE A MARKDOWN

DETERMINING SALE PRICE AFTER A MARKDOWN

In markdown calculations, the original selling price is the base, or 100%. After a markdown is subtracted from that price, the new price represents (100% − Markdown percent) *of* the original price. For example, if a chair is marked down 30%, the sale price would be 70% (100% − 30%) of the original price.

To find the new sale price after a markdown, we use the familiar percentage formula, Portion = Rate × Base, where the sale price is the portion, the original price is the base, and (100% − Markdown percent) is the rate.

Sale price = Original selling price(100% − Markdown percent)

EXAMPLE 13 DETERMINING THE SALE PRICE

Fernando's Hideaway, a men's clothing store, originally sold a line of ties for $55 each. If the manager decides to mark them down 40% for a clearance sale, what is the sale price of a tie?

SOLUTIONSTRATEGY

Remember, if the markdown is 40%, the sale price must be 60% (100% − 40%) *of* the original price.

$$\text{Sale price} = \text{Original selling price}(100\% - \text{Markdown percent})$$

$$\text{Sale price} = \$55(100\% - 40\%) = 55(.6) = 33$$

$$\text{Sale price} = \underline{\$33}$$

TRYITEXERCISE13

Craftsman's Village originally sold paneling for $27.50 per sheet. When the stock was almost depleted, the price was marked down 60% to make room for incoming merchandise. What was the sale price per sheet of paneling?

CHECK YOUR ANSWER WITH THE SOLUTION ON PAGE 260.

DETERMINING THE ORIGINAL PRICE BEFORE A MARKDOWN

To find the original selling price before a markdown, we use the sale price formula solved for the original selling price. The original selling price is isolated to one side by dividing both sides of the equation by (100% − Markdown percent). *Note*: This is actually the percentage formula Base = Portion ÷ Rate with the original selling price as the base.

$$\text{Original selling price} = \frac{\text{Sale price}}{100\% - \text{Markdown percent}}$$

EXAMPLE14 DETERMINING THE ORIGINAL SELLING PRICE

What was the original selling price of a backpack at Walmart that is currently on sale for $99 after a 25% markdown?

SOLUTIONSTRATEGY

Reasoning: $99 = 75% (100% − 25%) *of* the original price. Solve for the original price.

$$\text{Original selling price} = \frac{\text{Sale price}}{100\% - \text{Markdown percent}} = \frac{99}{100\% - 25\%} = \frac{99}{.75} = 132$$

Original selling price = $132

Wal-Mart Stores, Inc., serves customers and members more than 200 million times per week at more than 8,000 retail units under 53 different banners in 15 countries. In 2009, Walmart employed more than 2.1 million associates worldwide and generated sales of $401 billion.

Source: http://walmartstores.com

TRYITEXERCISE14

What was the original selling price of a necklace currently on sale for $79 after a 35% markdown? Round your answer to the nearest cent.

CHECK YOUR ANSWER WITH THE SOLUTION ON PAGE 260.

COMPUTING THE FINAL SELLING PRICE AFTER A SERIES OF MARKUPS AND MARKDOWNS

8-11

Products that do not undergo seasonal fluctuations in sales, such as food, tools, tires, and furniture, are known as **staple goods**. These products are usually marked up once and perhaps marked down occasionally, on sale. **Seasonal goods,** such as men's and women's fashion items, snow shovels, bathing suits, and holiday merchandise, may undergo many markups and markdowns during their selling season. Merchants must continually adjust prices as the season progresses. Getting caught with an excessive amount of out-of-season inventory can ruin an otherwise bright profit picture. Christmas decorations in January and snow tires in June are virtually useless profit-wise!

staple goods Products considered basic and routinely purchased that do not undergo seasonal fluctuations in sales, such as food, tools, and furniture.

seasonal goods Products that undergo seasonal fluctuations in sales, such as fashion apparel and holiday merchandise.

EXAMPLE 15 COMPUTING A SERIES OF MARKUPS AND MARKDOWNS

In March, Swim and Sport purchased designer bathing suits for $50 each. The original markup was 60% based on the selling price. In May, the shop took a 25% markdown by having a sale. After three weeks, the sale was over and all merchandise was marked up 15%. By July, many of the bathing suits were still in stock, so the shop took a 30% markdown to stimulate sales. At the end of August, the balance of the bathing suits were put on clearance sale with a final markdown of another 25%. Compute the intermediate prices and the final selling price of the bathing suits. Round to the nearest cent.

SOLUTIONSTRATEGY

When solving a series of markups and markdowns, remember that each should be based on the previous selling price. Use the formulas presented in this chapter and take each step one at a time.

Step 1. Find the original selling price, with markup based on the selling price.

$$\text{Selling price} = \frac{\text{Cost}}{100\% - \text{Percent markup}} = \frac{50}{100\% - 60\%} = \frac{50}{.4} = 125$$

Original selling price = $\underline{\$125}$

Step 2. Calculate the 25% markdown in May.

Sale price = Original selling price(100% − Markdown percent)

Sale price = 125(100% − 25%) = 125(.75) = 93.75

Sale price = $\underline{\$93.75}$

Step 3. Calculate the after-sale 15% markup.

Remember, the base is the previous selling price, $93.75.

Selling price = Sale price(100% + Percent markup)

Selling price = 93.75(100% + 15%) = 93.75(1.15) = 107.81

Selling price = $\underline{\$107.81}$

Step 4. Calculate the July 30% markdown.

Sale price = Previous selling price(100% − Markdown percent)

Sale price = 107.81(100% − 30%) = 107.81(.7) = 75.47

Sale price = $\underline{\$75.47}$

Step 5. Calculate the final 25% markdown.

Sale price = Previous selling price(100% − Markdown percent)

Sale price = 75.47(100% − 25%) = 75.47(.75) = 56.60

Final sale price = $\underline{\$56.60}$

TRYITEXERCISE 15

In September, Tire Depot in Chicago purchased snow tires from a distributor for $48.50 each. The original markup was 55% based on the selling price. In November, the tires were marked down 30% and put on sale. In December, they were marked up 20%. In February, the tires were again on sale at 30% off, and in March, they cleared out with a final 25% markdown. What was the final selling price of the tires? Round to the nearest cent.

CHECK YOUR ANSWERS WITH THE SOLUTIONS ON PAGE 260.

"STILL NO CUSTOMERS. WE'LL HAVE TO INVENT REBATES!"

© Henry Schwadron Reproduction rights obtainable from www.CartoonStock.com

CALCULATING THE SELLING PRICE OF PERISHABLE GOODS

8-12

Out-of-season merchandise still has some value, whereas **perishable goods** (such as fruits, vegetables, flowers, and dairy products) have a certain shelf life and then no value at all. For sellers of this type of merchandise to achieve their intended markups, the selling price must be based on the quantity of products sold at the original price. The quantity sold is calculated as total items less spoilage. For example, if a tomato vendor anticipates a 20% spoilage rate, the selling price of the tomatoes should be calculated based on 80% of the original stock. To calculate the selling price of perishables, use the formula:

perishable goods Products that have a certain shelf life and then no value at all, such as fruits, vegetables, flowers, and dairy products.

$$\text{Selling price of perishables} = \frac{\text{Total expected selling price}}{\text{Total quantity} - \text{Anticipated spoilage}}$$

EXAMPLE16 CALCULATING THE SELLING PRICE OF PERISHABLE GOODS

The Farmer's Market buys 1,500 pounds of fresh bananas at a cost of $0.60 a pound. If a 15% spoilage rate is anticipated, at what price per pound should the bananas be sold to achieve a 50% markup based on selling price? Round to the nearest cent.

SOLUTIONSTRATEGY

Step 1. Find the total expected selling price: The total expected selling price is found by applying the selling price formula, $SP = C \div (100\% - \%M_{SP})$. The cost will be the total pounds times the price per pound, $1,500 \times \$.60 = \$900$.

$$SP = \frac{\text{Cost}}{100\% - \%M_{SP}} = \frac{900}{100\% - 50\%} = \frac{900}{.5} = 1,800$$

Total expected selling price = $\underline{\$1,800}$

Step 2. Find the anticipated spoilage: To find the amount of anticipated spoilage, use the formula

Anticipated spoilage = Total quantity × Spoilage rate

Anticipated spoilage = $1,500 \times 15\% = 1,500(.15) = 225$

Anticipated spoilage = $\underline{225 \text{ pounds}}$

Step 3. Calculate the selling price of the perishables:

$$\text{Selling price of perishables} = \frac{\text{Total expected selling price}}{\text{Total quantity} - \text{Anticipated spoilage}}$$

$$\text{Selling price} = \frac{1,800}{1,500 - 225} = \frac{1,800}{1,275} = 1.411$$

Selling price of peaches = $\underline{\$1.41 \text{ per pound}}$

INTHE BUSINESSWORLD

Photo by Robert Brechner

Going Bananas!

Banana sales at 7-Eleven stores increased from 19 million in 2007 to an estimated 27.6 million in 2009. In October 2009, the chain tested a new plastic wrap developed by supplier Fresh Del Monte Produce to keep single bananas yellow and firm for five days—more than double the "perishable" shelf life for an unwrapped banana.

7-Eleven recognized that the wrapper could be an environmental issue and has asked supplier Fresh Del Monte to come up with a wrapper that is biodegradable.

Source: *USA Today*, Oct. 12, 2009, Page 1B.

TRYITEXERCISE16

Enchanted Gardens, a chain of flower shops, purchases 800 dozen roses for Valentine's Day at a cost of $6.50 per dozen. If a 10% spoilage rate is anticipated, at what price per dozen should the roses be sold to achieve a 60% markup based on selling price? Round to the nearest cent.

CHECK YOUR ANSWER WITH THE SOLUTION ON PAGE 260.

SECTION III **8** **REVIEW EXERCISES**

For the following items, calculate the missing information. Round dollars to the nearest cent and percents to the nearest tenth of a percent.

Item	Original Selling Price	Amount of Markdown	Sale Price	Markdown Percent
1. fish tank	$189.95	$28.50	$161.45	15%
2. sneakers	$53.88	_____	$37.50	_____
3. cantaloupe	_____	$.39	$1.29	_____
4. CD player	$264.95	_____	_____	30%
5. 1 yd carpet	_____	_____	$24.66	40%
6. suitcase	$68.00	$16.01	$51.99	23.5%
7. chess set	$115.77	$35.50	_____	_____
8. necklace	_____	$155.00	$235.00	_____
9. copier	$1,599.88	_____	_____	35%
10. pen	_____	_____	$15.90	25%

Solve the following word problems, rounding dollars to the nearest cent and percents to the nearest tenth of a percent.

11. A motorcycle that originally sold for $9,700 was marked down and sold for $7,950.

    a. What is the amount of the markdown?

    b. What is the markdown percent?

12. A Blu-ray disc that originally sold for $34.88 at Target was marked down by $12.11.

    a. What is the sale price?

    b. What is the markdown percent?

Target is an upscale discounter that provides high-quality, on-trend merchandise at attractive prices in spacious and guest-friendly stores. In addition, Target also operates an online business, Target.com.

In 2009, with 351,000 associates, Target operated 1,740 stores in 49 states. Revenue was $65.4 billion.

Source: www.target.com

Photo by Robert Brechner

13. a. A notebook that originally sold for $1.69 at Dollar General was marked down to $0.99. What is the amount of the markdown on these notebooks?

   b. What is the markdown percent?

   c. If the sale price is then marked up by 40%, what is the new selling price?

14. You are shopping for a headset and webcam at the Micro-Electronics Warehouse so that you can video-chat with your friends.

   a. Verify the "regular price" (original price) of each headset in the ad and calculate which headset offers the greater markdown percent, the BuddyChat 200 or BuddyChat 300.

MICRO-ELECTRONICS WAREHOUSE
Headset and Webcam SALE
See and say hello to your family and friends

BuddyChat 200 Headset
Reg. Price $29.99
Save $10
$19.99 After Savings

BuddyChat 300 Headset
Reg. price $41.99
Save $12
$29.99 After Savings

BuddyCam HD Webcam
Reg. Price $79.99
Save $20
$59.99 After Savings

   b. What is the markdown percent on the BuddyCam HD webcam?

   c. You have decided to purchase the headset with the greatest markdown percent and the BuddyCam HD webcam in order to take advantage of an "Extra $15 Rebate" offer when you purchase both. What is the markdown percent on your total purchase including the rebate?

15. Readers Delight, a bookstore, sells atlases for $75. If they are put on clearance sale at 60% off, what is the sale price?

16. Carousel Toys has Romper Buckaroos, wooden rocking horses for toddlers, on a 30% markdown sale for $72.09. What was the original price before they were marked down? Round to the nearest cent.

17. Lawn and Garden Galleria is having a 20% off sale on riding lawn mowers. The XL Deluxe model is on sale for $4,815. What was the original price of the mower?

18. From the Office Market coupon shown here,

    a. Calculate the markdown percent.

    b. If the offer was changed to "Buy 3, Get 2 Free," what would be the new markdown percent?

    c. Which offer is more profitable for the store? Explain.

19. In February, Golf World, a retail shop, purchased golf clubs for $453.50 per set. The original markup was 35% based on selling price. In April, the shop took a 20% markdown by having a special sale. After two weeks, the sale was over and the clubs were marked up 10%. In June, the shop offered a storewide sale of 15% off all merchandise, and in September, a final 10% markdown was taken on the clubs. What was the final selling price of the golf clubs?

20. Prestige Produce purchases 460 pounds of sweet potatoes at $0.76 per pound. If a 10% spoilage rate is anticipated, at what price per pound should the sweet potatoes be sold to achieve a 35% markup based on selling price?

21. A microwave oven cost The Appliance Warehouse $141.30 and was initially marked up by 55% based on selling price. In the next few months, the item was marked down 20%, marked up 15%, marked down 10%, and marked down a final 10%. What was the final selling price of the microwave oven?

22. The Flour Power Bakery makes 200 cherry cheesecakes at a cost of $2.45 each. If a spoilage rate of 5% is anticipated, at what price should the cakes be sold to achieve a 40% markup based on cost?

23. You have decided to purchase a set of four Good-Ride tires for your vehicle at the Tire Emporium.

    a. If the original price of these tires is $160.00 each, what are the amount of the Markdown with rebate per tire and the markdown percent if you get the rebate and pay cash?

    b. What are the amount of the markdown per tire and the markdown percent if you decide to put the purchase on your Good-Ride credit card and get the double rebate?

    c. When you purchased the set of four tires, you were offered an "Extra 5%" discount on the entire purchase if you also included wheel balancing at $5.75 per tire and a front-end alignment for $65.00. The sales tax in your state is 7.5%. What was the total amount of your purchase if you used your Good-Ride credit card?

    d. What are the advantages and disadvantages of using the credit card?

TIRE EMPORIUM

Good-Ride Raven GT – Tire Sale

Sale Price: $115 + $20 Rebate

Double rebate when you use your
Good-Ride Credit Card

BUSINESS DECISION: THE PERMANENT MARKDOWN

24. You are the manager of World Wide Athlete, a chain of six sporting goods shops in your area. The shops sell 12 racing bikes per week at a retail price of $679.99. Recently, you put the bikes on sale at $599.99. At the sale price, 15 bikes were sold during the one-week sale.

    a. What was your markdown percent on the bikes?

    b. What is the percent increase in number of bikes sold during the sale?

    c. How much more revenue would be earned in six months by permanently selling the bikes at the lower price rather than having a one-week sale each month? (6 sale weeks in 26 weeks)

    d. (Optional) As manager of World Wide, would you recommend this permanent price reduction? Explain.

World Wide Athlete

Racing Bike   Sale
$599⁹⁹

CHAPTER

8

CHAPTER FORMULAS

Markup

Selling price = Cost + Markup

Cost = Selling price − Markup

Markup = Selling price − Cost

$$\text{Percent markup}_{COST} = \frac{\text{Markup}}{\text{Cost}}$$

$$\text{Percent markup}_{SP} = \frac{\text{Markup}}{\text{Selling price}}$$

Selling price = Cost(100% + %Markup$_{COST}$)

$$\text{Cost} = \frac{\text{Selling price}}{100\% + \%\text{Markup}_{COST}}$$

$$\text{Selling price} = \frac{\text{Cost}}{100\% - \%\text{Markup}_{SP}}$$

Cost = Selling price(100% − %Markup$_{SP}$)

$$\%\text{Markup}_{SP} = \frac{\%\text{Markup}_{COST}}{100\% + \%\text{Markup}_{COST}}$$

$$\%\text{Markup}_{COST} = \frac{\%\text{Markup}_{SP}}{100\% - \%\text{Markup}_{SP}}$$

Markdown

Markdown = Original selling price − Sale price

$$\text{Markdown}\% = \frac{\text{Markdown}}{\text{Original price}}$$

Sale price = Original price(100% − Markdown%)

$$\text{Original price} = \frac{\text{Sale price}}{100\% - \text{Markdown}\%}$$

Perishables

$$\text{Selling price}_{Perishables} = \frac{\text{Expected selling price}}{\text{Total quantity} - \text{Spoilage}}$$

CHAPTER SUMMARY

Section I: Markup Based on Cost

Topic	Important Concepts	Illustrative Examples
Using the Basic Retailing Equation **Performance Objective 8-1, Page 233**	The basic retailing equation is used to solve for selling price (SP), cost (C), and amount of markup (M). Selling price = Cost + Markup $SP = C + M$ Cost = Selling price − Markup $C = SP - M$ Markup = Selling price − Cost $M = SP - C$	1. What is the selling price of a blender that costs $86.00 and has a $55.99 markup? $SP = 86.00 + 55.99$ Selling price = $141.99 2. What is the cost of a radio that sells for $125.50 and has a $37.29 markup? $C = 125.50 - 37.29$ Cost = $88.21 3. What is the markup on a set of dishes costing $53.54 and selling for $89.95? $M = 89.95 - 53.54$ Markup = $36.41

Section I (continued)

Topic	Important Concepts	Illustrative Examples
Calculating Percent Markup Based on Cost **Performance Objective 8-2, Page 235**	$\%\text{Markup}_{\text{COST}} = \dfrac{\text{Markup}}{\text{Cost}}$ $\%M_{\text{COST}} = \dfrac{M}{C}$	A calculator costs $25. If the markup is $10, what is the percent markup based on cost? $\%M_{\text{COST}} = \dfrac{10}{25} = .4$ $\%M_{\text{COST}} = \underline{40\%}$
Calculating Selling Price **Performance Objective 8-3, Page 236**	$\text{Selling price} = \text{Cost}(100\% + \%\text{Markup}_{\text{COST}})$ $SP = C(100\% + \%M_{\text{COST}})$	A desk costs $260 to manufacture. What should be the selling price if a 60% markup based on cost is desired? $SP = 260(100\% + 60\%)$ $SP = 260(1.6) = 416$ Selling price = $\underline{\$416}$
Calculating Cost **Performance Objective 8-4, Page 237**	$\text{Cost} = \dfrac{\text{Selling price}}{100\% + \%\text{Markup}_{\text{COST}}}$ $C = \dfrac{SP}{100\% + \%M_{\text{COST}}}$	What is the cost of a leather sofa with a selling price of $250 and a 45% markup based on cost? $C = \dfrac{250}{100\% + 45\%} = \dfrac{250}{1.45}$ Cost = $\underline{\$172.41}$

Section II: Markup Based on Selling Price

Topic	Important Concepts	Illustrative Examples
Calculating Percent Markup Based on Selling Price **Performance Objective 8-5, Page 240**	$\%\text{Markup}_{\text{SP}} = \dfrac{\text{Markup}}{\text{Selling price}}$ $\%M_{\text{SP}} = \dfrac{M}{SP}$	What is the percent markup on the selling price of a Hewlett Packard printer with a selling price of $400 and a markup of $188? $\%M_{\text{SP}} = \dfrac{188}{400} = .47$ $\%M_{\text{SP}} = \underline{47\%}$
Calculating Selling Price **Performance Objective 8-6, Page 241**	$\text{Selling price} = \dfrac{\text{Cost}}{100\% - \%\text{Markup}_{\text{SP}}}$ $SP = \dfrac{C}{100\% - \%M_{\text{SP}}}$	What is the selling price of a marker pen with a cost of $1.19 and a 43% markup based on selling price? $SP = \dfrac{1.19}{100\% - 43\%} = \dfrac{1.19}{.57}$ $SP = \underline{\$2.09}$
Calculating Cost **Performance Objective 8-7, Page 242**	$\text{Cost} = \text{Selling price}(100\% - \%\text{Markup}_{\text{SP}})$ $C = SP(100\% - \%M_{\text{SP}})$	What is the most a hardware store can pay for a drill if it will have a selling price of $65.50 and a 45% markup based on selling price? $C = 65.50(100\% - 45\%)$ $C = 65.50(.55)$ Cost = $\underline{\$36.03}$
Converting Percent Markup Based on Cost to Percent Markup Based on Selling Price **Performance Objective 8-8, Page 243**	$\%\text{Markup}_{\text{SP}} = \dfrac{\%\text{Markup}_{\text{COST}}}{100\% + \%\text{Markup}_{\text{COST}}}$ $\%M_{\text{SP}} = \dfrac{\%M_{\text{COST}}}{100\% + \%M_{\text{COST}}}$	If a hair dryer is marked up 70% based on cost, what is the corresponding percent markup based on selling price? $\%M_{\text{SP}} = \dfrac{70\%}{100\% + 70\%} = \dfrac{.7}{1.7}$ $\%M_{\text{SP}} = .4118 = \underline{41.2\%}$

Section II (continued)

Topic	Important Concepts	Illustrative Examples
Converting Percent Markup Based on Selling Price to Percent Markup Based on Cost **Performance Objective 8-8, Page 243**	$\%\text{Markup}_{\text{COST}} = \dfrac{\%\text{Markup}_{SP}}{100\% - \%\text{Markup}_{SP}}$ $\%M_{\text{COST}} = \dfrac{\%M_{SP}}{100\% - \%M_{SP}}$	If a toaster is marked up 35% based on selling price, what is the corresponding percent markup based on cost? $\%M_{\text{COST}} = \dfrac{35\%}{100\% - 35\%} = \dfrac{.35}{.65}$ $\%M_{\text{COST}} = .5384 = \underline{53.8\%}$

Section III: Markdowns, Multiple Operations, and Perishable Goods

Topic	Important Concepts	Illustrative Examples
Calculating Markdown and Markdown Percent **Performance Objective 8-9, Page 247**	Markdown = Original price − Sale price $MD = \text{Orig} - \text{Sale}$ $\text{Markdown}\% = \dfrac{\text{Markdown}}{\text{Original price}}$ $MD\% = \dfrac{MD}{\text{Orig}}$	Calculate the amount of markdown and the markdown percent of a television set that originally sold for $425.00 and was then put on sale for $299.95. Markdown = 425.00 − 299.95 Markdown = $\underline{\$125.05}$ $MD\% = \dfrac{125.05}{425.00} = .2942$ Markdown % = $\underline{29.4\%}$
Determining the Sale Price after a Markdown **Performance Objective 8-10, Page 248**	Sale price $= \text{Original price}\,(100\% - \text{Markdown}\%)$ $\text{Sale} = \text{Orig}(100\% - MD\%)$	What is the sale price of a computer that originally sold for $2,500 and was then marked down by 35%? Sale = 2,500(100% − 35%) Sale = 2,500(.65) = 1,625 Sale price = $\underline{\$1,625}$
Determining the Original Selling Price before a Markdown **Performance Objective 8-10, Page 249**	$\text{Original price} = \dfrac{\text{Sale price}}{100\% - \text{Markdown}\%}$ $\text{Orig} = \dfrac{\text{Sale}}{100\% - MD\%}$	What is the original selling price of an exercise bicycle, which is currently on sale at Sears for $235.88, after a 30% markdown? $\text{Original price} = \dfrac{235.88}{100\% - 30\%} = \dfrac{235.88}{.7}$ Original price = $\underline{\$336.97}$
Computing the Final Selling Price after a Series of Markups and Markdowns **Performance Objective 8-11, Page 249**	To solve for the final selling price after a series of markups and markdowns, calculate each step based on the previous selling price.	Compute the intermediate prices and the final selling price of an umbrella costing $27.50 with the following seasonal activity: a. Initial markup, 40% on cost b. 20% markdown c. 15% markdown d. 10% markup e. Final clearance, 25% markdown a. Initial 40% markup: $SP = C(100\% + \%M_{\text{COST}})$ $SP = 27.50(100\% + 40\%)$ $SP = 27.50(1.4) = 38.50$ Original price = $\underline{\$38.50}$ b. 20% markdown: $\text{Sale} = \text{Orig}(100\% - MD\%)$ $\text{Sale} = 38.50(100\% - 20\%)$ $\text{Sale} = 38.50(.8)$ Sale price = $\underline{\$30.80}$

Section III (continued)

Topic	Important Concepts	Illustrative Examples
		c. 15% markdown: $\quad$ Sale = Orig(100% − MD%) $\quad$ Sale = 30.80(100% − 15%) $\quad$ Sale = 30.80(.85) $\quad$ Sale price = $\underline{\$26.18}$ d. 10% markup: $\quad$ SP = sale price(100% + M%) $\quad$ SP = 26.18(100% + 10%) $\quad$ SP = 26.18(1.10) $\quad$ Selling price = $\underline{\$28.80}$ e. Final 25% markdown: $\quad$ Sale = Orig(100% − MD%) $\quad$ Sale = 28.80(100% − 25%) $\quad$ Sale = 28.80(.75) $\quad$ Final selling price = $\underline{\$21.60}$
Calculating the Selling Price of Perishable Goods **Performance Objective 8-12, Page 251**	$\text{Selling price}_{\text{Perishables}}$ $= \dfrac{\text{Total expected selling price}}{\text{Total quantity} - \text{Anticipated spoilage}}$ $SP_{\text{Perish.}} = \dfrac{\text{Exp. } SP}{\text{Quan.} - \text{Spoil.}}$	A grocery store purchases 250 pounds of apples from a wholesaler for $0.67 per pound. If a 10% spoilage rate is anticipated, what selling price per pound will yield a 45% markup based on cost? $\quad$ Total Cost = 250 lb @ .67 = $167.50 Exp $SP = C(100\% + M_{\text{COST}})$ Exp SP = 167.50(100% + 45%) Exp SP = 167.50(1.45) = $242.88 $SP_{\text{perish}} = \dfrac{242.88}{250 - 25} = \dfrac{242.88}{225}$ $SP_{\text{perish}} = \underline{\$1.08 \text{ per lb}}$

TRY IT: EXERCISE SOLUTIONS FOR CHAPTER 8

1. $SP = C + M = 6.80 + 9.40 = \underline{\$16.20}$

2. $M = SP - C = 28.50 - 16.75 = \underline{\$11.75}$

3. $C = SP - M = 290 - 75 = \underline{\$215}$

4. $M = SP - C = 63 - 45 = \underline{\$18}$

$\quad \%M_{\text{COST}} = \dfrac{M}{C} = \dfrac{18}{45} = .4 = 40\%$

5. $SP = C(100\% + \%M_{\text{COST}}) = 38(100\% + 65\%) = 38(1.65) = \underline{\$62.70}$

6. $C = \dfrac{SP}{100\% + \%M_{\text{COST}}} = \dfrac{39}{100\% + 30\%} = \dfrac{39}{1.3} = \underline{\$30}$

7. $M = SP - C = 157.50 - 94.50 = \underline{\$63}$

$\quad \%M_{SP} = \dfrac{M}{SP} = \dfrac{63.00}{157.50} = .40 = \underline{40\%}$

8. $SP = \dfrac{C}{100\% - \%M_{SP}} = \dfrac{169}{100\% - 35\%} = \dfrac{169}{.65} = \underline{\$260}$

9. $C = SP(100\% - \%M_{SP}) = 79(100\% - 55\%) = 79(.45) = \underline{\$35.55}$

10. $\%M_{SP} = \dfrac{\%M_{\text{COST}}}{100\% + \%M_{\text{COST}}} = \dfrac{50\%}{100\% + 50\%} = \dfrac{.5}{1.5} = .333 = \underline{33.3\%}$

11. $\%M_{\text{COST}} = \dfrac{\%M_{SP}}{100\% - \%M_{SP}} = \dfrac{75\%}{100\% - 75\%} = \dfrac{.75}{.25} = 3 = \underline{300\%}$

12. Markdown = Original price − Sale price = 75 − 56 = $\underline{\underline{\$19}}$

$$MD\% = \frac{MD}{\text{Original price}} = \frac{19}{75} = .2533 = \underline{\underline{25.3\%}}$$

13. Sale price = Original price(100% − MD%) = 27.50(100% − 60%) = 27.50(.4) = $\underline{\underline{\$11}}$

14. Original price = $\dfrac{\text{Sale price}}{100\% - MD\%} = \dfrac{79}{100\% - 35\%} = \dfrac{79}{.65} = \underline{\underline{\$121.54}}$

15. $SD = \dfrac{C}{100\% - \%M_{SP}} = \dfrac{48.50}{100\% - 55\%} = \dfrac{48.50}{.45} = \$107.78$

Markdown #1: Original price(100% − MD%) = 107.78(.7) = $75.45

20% markup: 75.45(100% + 20%) = 75.45(1.2) = $90.54

Markdown #2: Original price(100% − MD%) = 90.54(.7) = $63.38

Final markdown: Original price(100% − MD%) = 63.38(.75) = $\underline{\underline{\$47.54}}$

16. Total cost = 800 dozen @ $6.50 = $5,200

Expected selling price = $\dfrac{C}{100\% - \%M_{SP}} = \dfrac{5,200}{100\% - 60\%} = \dfrac{5,200}{.4} = \$13,000$

Selling price$_{\text{Perishables}}$ = $\dfrac{\text{Expected selling price}}{\text{Total quantity} - \text{Spoilage}} = \dfrac{13,000}{800 - 80} = \dfrac{13,000}{720} = \underline{\underline{\$18.06 \text{ per doz}}}$

CONCEPT REVIEW

1. The retailing equation states that the selling price is equal to the _____ plus the _____ . (8-1)

2. In business, expenses are separated into two major categories. The cost of _____ sold and _____ expenses. (8-1)

3. There are two ways of expressing markup as a percent: based on _____ and based on _____ _____ . (8-2)

4. Write the formula for calculating the selling price when markup is based on cost. (8-3)

5. To calculate cost, we divide the _____ price by 100% plus the percent markup on cost. (8-4)

6. The percent markup based on selling price is equal to the _____ divided by the selling price. (8-5)

7. When markup is based on selling price, the _____ price is the base and represents _____ percent. (8-6)

8. We use the formula for calculating _____ to find the most a retailer can pay for an item and still get the intended markup. (8-7)

9. To convert percent markup based on cost to percent markup based on selling price, we divide percent markup based on cost by 100% _____ the percent markup based on cost. (8-8)

10. To convert percent markup based on selling price to percent markup based on cost, we divide percent markup based on selling price by 100% _____ the percent markup based on selling price. (8-8)

11. A price reduction from the original selling price of merchandise is called a(n) _____. (8-9)

12. Write the formula for calculating the sale price after a markdown. (8-10)

13. In calculating a series of markups and markdowns, each calculation is based on the previous _____ price. (8-11)

14. Products that have a certain shelf life and then no value at all, such as fruit, vegetables, flowers, and dairy products, are known as _____ _____. (8-12)

ASSESSMENT TEST

Solve the following word problems. Round dollars to the nearest cent and percents to the nearest tenth of a percent.

1. Electric woks cost the manufacturer $83.22 to produce. If a markup of $69.38 is added to the cost, what is the selling price per unit?

2. Castle Mountain Furniture sells desks for $346.00. If the desks cost $212.66, what is the amount of the markup?

3. After Sunset Food Wholesalers adds a markup of $15.40 to a case of tomato sauce, it sells for $33.98. What is the wholesaler's cost per case?

4. Wyatt's Western Wear purchases shirts for $47.50 each. A $34.00 markup is added to the shirts.

    a. What is the selling price?

    b. What is the percent markup based on cost?

    c. What is the percent markup based on selling price?

5. As the manager of Dollar Depot, calculate the amount of the markup and the percent markup on selling price per case if these Softies products cost your store $5.60 per case of 12 boxes.

6. Bloomingdales purchases imported perfume for $24.30 per ounce. If the store policy is to mark up all merchandise in that department 39% based on selling price, what is the retail selling price of the perfume?

7. The Carpet Gallery is looking for a new line of nylon carpeting to retail at $39.88 per square yard. If management wants a 60% markup based on selling price, what is the most that can be paid for the carpeting to still get the desired markup?

8. a. At The Luminary, the markup on a halogen light fixture is 50% based on selling price. What is the corresponding percent markup based on cost?

    b. If the markup on a fluorescent light fixture transformer is 120% based on cost, what is the corresponding percent markup based on selling price?

9. A three-day cruise on the *Island Queen* originally selling for $988 was marked down by $210 at the end of the season.

   a. What is the sale price of the cruise?

   b. What is the markdown percent?

10. You are shopping for an executive desk chair at The Furniture Gallery

    a. Calculate the original price and markdown percent of each chair to determine which has the greater markdown percent.

    b. With the purchase of either chair, The Furniture Gallery is offering a 15% discount on plastic chair mats. You have chosen a mat with an original price of $29.00. You also purchase a two-year leather protection plan on the chair for $19.95. If you choose the chair with the greater markdown percent and the sales tax in your area is 6.3%, what is the total amount of your purchase?

The Furniture Gallery

Save $40 instantly
$79.99

OfficePro
Model 20
High Back
Leather Chair

Save $60 instantly
$89.99

OfficePro
Model 30
High Back
Leather Chair

11. Macy's originally sold designer jackets for $277. If they are put on sale at a markdown of 22%, what is the sale price?

12. What was the original selling price of a treadmill currently on sale for $2,484 after a 20% markdown?

EXCEL 2

13. Backyard Bonanza advertised a line of inflatable pools for the summer season. The store uses a 55% markup based on selling price.

    a. If they were originally priced at $124.99, what was the cost?

    b. As the summer progressed, they were marked down 25%, marked up 15%, marked down 20%, and cleared out in October at a final 25%-off sale. What was the final selling price of the pools?

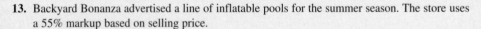
Photo by Robert Brechner

Macy's, Inc., is one of the nation's premier retailers, with fiscal 2009 sales of $23.5 billion. The company operates more than 800 Macy's department stores and furniture galleries in 45 states, the District of Columbia, Guam, and Puerto Rico, as well as 40 Bloomingdale's stores in 12 states.

Macy's, Inc.'s diverse workforce includes approximately 167,000 employees. The company also operates macys.com and bloomingdales.com.

Source: www.macysinc.com

14. Epicure Market prepares fresh gourmet entrees each day. On Wednesday, 80 baked chicken dinners were made at a cost of $3.50 each. A 10% spoilage rate is anticipated.

    a. At what price should the dinners be sold to achieve a 60% markup based on selling price?

    b. If Epicure offers a $1-off coupon in a newspaper advertisement, what markdown percent does the coupon represent?

EXCEL 3

15. a. What is the original selling price of the guitar on sale at Music Mania if the $1,999.99 sale price represents 20% off?

b. How much did the store pay for the guitar if the initial markup was 150% based on cost?

c. What is the percent markup based on selling price?

d. If next month the guitar is scheduled to be on sale for $1,599.99, what is the markdown percent?

BUSINESS DECISION: MAINTAINED MARKUP

16. The markup that a retail store actually realizes on the sale of its goods is called **maintained markup**. It is what is achieved after "retail reductions" (markdowns) have been subtracted from the initial markup. Maintained markup is one of the "keys to profitability" in retailing. It is the difference between the actual selling price and the cost and therefore has a direct effect on net profits.

$$\text{Maintained markup} = \frac{\text{Actual selling price} - \text{Cost}}{\text{Actual selling price}}$$

You are the buyer for Four Aces Menswear, a chain of men's clothing stores. For the spring season, you purchased a line of men's casual shirts with a manufacturer's suggested retail price of $29.50. Your cost was $16.00 per shirt.

a. What is the initial percent markup based on selling price?

b. The shirts did not sell as expected at the regular price, so you marked them down to $21.99 and sold them out. What is the maintained markup on the shirts?

c. When you complained to the manufacturer's sales representative about having to take excessive markdowns in order to sell the merchandise, she offered a $2 rebate per shirt. What is your new maintained markup?

COLLABORATIVE LEARNING ACTIVITY

Retailing and the Demographic Generations

Understanding the shopping and media habits of different age groups can help marketers optimize product assortment, pricing, promotion, and advertising decisions by creating targeted strategies and special offers. As an example, consider the following.

According to *USA Today*, in the book *Gen buY: How Tweens, Teens, and Twenty-Somethings Are Revolutionizing Retail*, authors Kit Yarrow and Jane O'Donnell say Generation Y—today's teens, tweens, and twenty-somethings—"were the least likely to cut back spending after the onset of the 2008 recession."

What's more, the authors point out that the 84 million Generation Y'ers, born from 1978 through 2000, are so influential, they've changed shopping for all consumers. They call Gen Y "the tastemakers, influencers, and most enthusiastic buyers of today" who will become "the mature, high-income purchasers of the future."

Because of Gen Y, we now have, among other things:

- More creative, technically advanced websites
- A wide availability of online customer reviews
- A faster stream of product introductions
- Bigger, more comfortable dressing rooms

Source: *USA Today*, "Generation Y forces retailers to keep up with technology, new stuff," by Richard Eisenberg, Sept. 14, 2009, page 6B.

As a team, divide up the four major demographic generations: the Silent Generation: the Baby Boomers, Generation X, and Generation Y (aka the Millennials) to research the following questions and report your findings to the class. Use visual presentations whenever possible and be sure to site your sources.

1. How did each generation get its distinctive name? List any "subgroups" that have been defined, such as Baby Boomers – Young and Baby Boomers – Old.
2. Define each generation in terms of years born, size, income and purchasing power, lifestyle preferences, and particularly consumer buying behavior.
3. How and to what extent does each generation use the Internet?
4. How do manufacturers, retailers, and shopping malls use these demographic distinctions to "target" their marketing efforts to the various generations? Give specific examples.

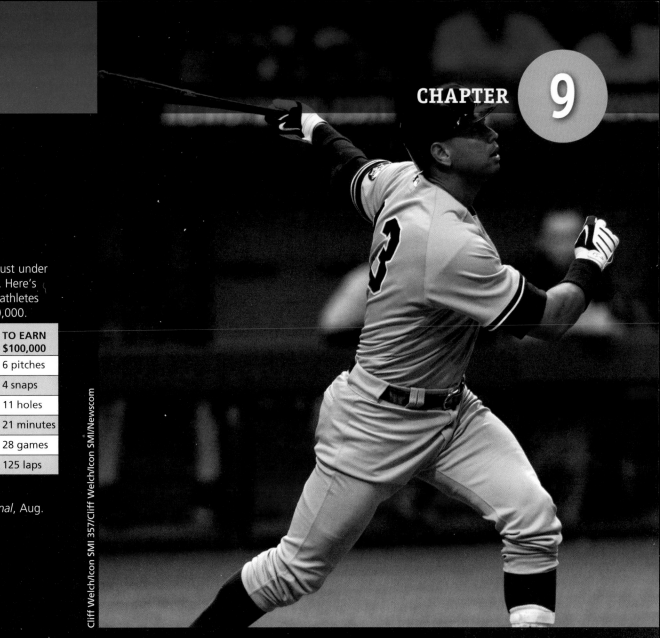

Cliff Welch/Icon SMI 357/Cliff Welch/Icon SMI/Newscom

MAJOR LEAGUE PAYDAY

It takes the average worker just under four years to earn $100,000. Here's how long it takes some star athletes to make approximately $100,000.

ATHLETE/SPORT 2009 Season	TO EARN $100,000
Alex Rodriguez, MLB	6 pitches
Ben Roethlisberger, NFL*	4 snaps
Tiger Woods, golf	11 holes
LeBron James, NBA*	21 minutes
Roger Federer, tennis	28 games
Tony Stewart, NASCAR	125 laps

*last full season

Source: *The Wall Street Journal*, Aug. 25, 2009, page D6.

Payroll

PERFORMANCE OBJECTIVES

SECTION I: Employee's Gross Earnings and Incentive Pay Plans

9-1: Prorating annual salary on the basis of weekly, biweekly, semimonthly, and monthly pay periods (p. 266)

9-2: Calculating gross pay by hourly wages, including regular and overtime rates (p. 267)

9-3: Calculating gross pay by straight and differential piecework schedules (p. 268)

9-4: Calculating gross pay by straight and incremental commission, salary plus commission, and drawing accounts (p. 270)

SECTION II: Employee's Payroll Deductions

9-5: Computing FICA taxes, both social security and Medicare, withheld from an employee's paycheck (p. 276)

9-6: Calculating an employee's federal income tax withholding (FIT) by the percentage method (p. 278)

9-7: Determining an employee's total withholding for federal income tax, social security, and Medicare using the combined wage bracket tables (p. 281)

SECTION III: Employer's Payroll Expenses and Self-Employed Person's Tax Responsibility

9-8: Computing FICA tax for employers and self-employment tax for self-employed persons (p. 286)

9-9: Computing the amount of state unemployment tax (SUTA) and federal unemployment tax (FUTA) (p. 288)

9-10: Calculating employer's fringe benefit expenses (p. 289)

9-11: Calculating quarterly estimated tax for self-employed persons (p. 290)

SECTION I   9   EMPLOYEE'S GROSS EARNINGS AND INCENTIVE PAY PLANS

Because payroll is frequently a company's largest operating expense, efficient payroll preparation and record keeping are extremely important functions in any business operation. Although today most businesses computerize their payroll functions, it is important for businesspeople to understand the processes and procedures involved.

Employers are responsible for paying employees for services rendered to the company over a period of time. In addition, the company is responsible for withholding certain taxes and other deductions from an employee's paycheck and depositing those taxes with the Internal Revenue Service (IRS) through authorized financial institutions. Other deductions, such as insurance premiums and charitable contributions, are also disbursed by the employer to the appropriate place.

In business, the term **gross pay** or **gross earnings** means the *total* amount of earnings due an employee for work performed before payroll deductions are withheld. The **net pay**, **net earnings**, or **take-home pay** is the actual amount of the employee's paycheck after all payroll deductions have been withheld. This concept is easily visualized by the formula

> **Net pay = Gross pay − Total deductions**

gross pay or **gross earnings** Total amount of earnings due an employee for work performed before payroll deductions are withheld.

net pay, **net earnings**, or **take-home pay** The actual amount of the employee's paycheck after all payroll deductions have been withheld.

This chapter deals with the business math involved in payroll management: the computation of employee gross earnings; the calculation of withholding taxes and other deductions; and the associated governmental deposits, regulations, and record keeping requirements.

9-1   PRORATING ANNUAL SALARY ON THE BASIS OF WEEKLY, BIWEEKLY, SEMIMONTHLY, AND MONTHLY PAY PERIODS

Employee compensation takes on many forms in the business world. Employees who hold managerial, administrative, or professional positions are paid a salary. A **salary** is a fixed gross amount of pay equally distributed over periodic payments without regard to the number of hours worked. Salaries are usually expressed as an annual, or yearly, amount. For example, a corporate accountant might receive an annual salary of $50,000.

Although salaries may be stated as annual amounts, they are usually distributed to employees on a more timely basis. A once-a-year paycheck would be a real trick to manage! Employees are most commonly paid in one of the following ways:

salary A fixed gross amount of pay equally distributed over periodic payments without regard to the number of hours worked.

Weekly	52 paychecks per year	Annual salary ÷ 52
Biweekly	26 paychecks per year	Annual salary ÷ 26
Semimonthly	24 paychecks per year	Annual salary ÷ 24
Monthly	12 paychecks per year	Annual salary ÷ 12

"In lieu of a bonus, here are some Instant Winner lottery scratch-off cards."

EXAMPLE1   PRORATING ANNUAL SALARY

What is the weekly, biweekly, semimonthly, and monthly amount of gross pay for a corporate accountant with an annual salary of $50,000?

SOLUTIONSTRATEGY

The amount of gross pay per period is determined by dividing the annual salary by the number of pay periods per year.

$$\text{Weekly pay} = \frac{50,000}{52} = \underline{\$961.54}$$

$$\text{Biweekly pay} = \frac{50,000}{26} = \underline{\$1,923.08}$$

$$\text{Semimonthly pay} = \frac{50,000}{24} = \underline{\$2,083.33}$$

$$\text{Monthly pay} = \frac{50,000}{12} = \underline{\$4,166.67}$$

TRYITEXERCISE1

An executive of a large manufacturing company earns a gross annual salary of $43,500. What is the weekly, biweekly, semimonthly, and monthly pay for this employee?

CHECK YOUR ANSWERS WITH THE SOLUTIONS ON PAGE 298.

CALCULATING GROSS PAY BY HOURLY WAGES, INCLUDING REGULAR AND OVERTIME RATES

9-2

Wages are earnings for routine or manual work, usually based on the number of hours worked. An **hourly wage** or **hourly rate** is the amount an employee is paid for each hour worked. The hourly wage is the most frequently used pay method and is designed to compensate employees for the amount of time spent on the job. The Fair Labor Standards Act of 1938, a federal law, specifies that a standard work week is 40 hours and **overtime**, amounting to at least $1\frac{1}{2}$ times the hourly rate, must be paid for all hours worked over 40 hours per week. Paying an employee $1\frac{1}{2}$ times the hourly rate is known as time-and-a-half.

Many companies have taken overtime a step farther than required by compensating employees at time-and-a-half for all hours over 8 hours per day instead of 40 hours per week. Another common payroll benefit is when companies pay double time, twice the hourly rate, for holidays, midnight shifts, and weekend hours.

wages Earnings for routine or manual work, usually based on the number of hours worked.

hourly wage or **hourly rate** The amount an employee is paid for each hour worked.

overtime According to federal law, the amount an employee is paid for each hour worked over 40 hours per week.

Minimum Wage Laws in the United States as of January 1, 2010

U. S. Department of Labor – Wage and Hour Division (WHD)

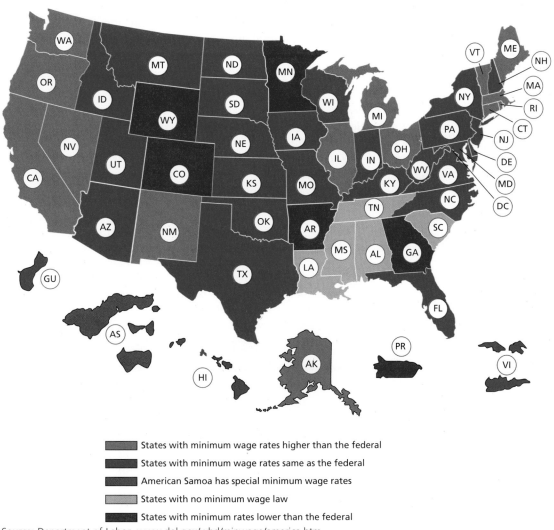

■ States with minimum wage rates higher than the federal
■ States with minimum wage rates same as the federal
■ American Samoa has special minimum wage rates
■ States with no minimum wage law
■ States with minimum rates lower than the federal

Source: Department of Labor, www.dol.gov/whd/minwage/america.htm

In May 2007, an amendment to the Fair Labor Standards Act became law. The amendment provided for a three-stage increase to the federal minimum wage for the first time in a decade. The $5.15 an-hour minimum wage was mandated to rise in three $0.70 increments to $7.25 an hour in July 2009.

According to the Department of Labor, as of January 2010, 14 states and Washington, D.C., had minimum wage rates higher than the federal minimum wage. Five states had minimum wage rates lower than the federal standard.

STEPS TO CALCULATE AN EMPLOYEE'S GROSS PAY BY HOURLY WAGES

STEP 1. Calculate an employee's regular gross pay for working 40 hours or less.

$$\text{Regular pay} = \text{Hourly rate} \times \text{Regular hours worked}$$

STEP 2. Calculate an employee's overtime pay by chain multiplying the hourly rate by the overtime factor by the number of overtime hours.

$$\text{Overtime pay} = \text{Hourly rate} \times \text{Overtime factor} \times \text{Overtime hours worked}$$

STEP 3. Calculate total gross pay.

$$\text{Total gross pay} = \text{Regular pay} + \text{Overtime pay}$$

EXAMPLE 2 CALCULATING HOURLY PAY

Karen Sullivan earns $8 per hour as a checker on an assembly line. If her overtime rate is time-and-a-half, what is her total gross pay for working 46 hours last week?

SOLUTION STRATEGY

To find Karen's total gross pay, compute her regular pay plus overtime pay.

Regular pay = Hourly rate × Regular hours worked
Regular pay = 8 × 40 = $320
Overtime pay = Hourly rate × Overtime factor × Overtime hours worked
Overtime pay = 8 × 1.5 × 6 = $72
Total gross pay = Regular pay + Overtime pay
Total gross pay = 320 + 72 = $392

TRY IT EXERCISE 2

Rick Morton works as a delivery truck driver for $10.50 per hour with time-and-a-half for overtime and double time on Sundays. What was his total gross pay last week if he worked 45 hours on Monday through Saturday in addition to a four-hour shift on Sunday?

CHECK YOUR ANSWER WITH THE SOLUTION ON PAGE 298.

9-3 CALCULATING GROSS PAY BY STRAIGHT AND DIFFERENTIAL PIECEWORK SCHEDULES

piecework Pay rate schedule based on an employee's production output, not hours worked.

A **piecework** pay rate schedule is based not on time but on production output. The incentive is that the more units the worker produces, the more money he or she makes. A straight piecework plan is when the worker receives a certain amount of pay per unit of output regardless of output quantity. A **differential piecework plan** gives workers a greater incentive to increase output because the rate per unit increases as output goes up. For example, a straight piecework plan might pay $3.15 per unit, whereas a differential plan might pay $3.05 for the first 50 units produced, $3.45 for units 51–100, and $3.90 for any units over 100.

straight piecework plan Pay per unit of output regardless of output quantity.

differential piecework plan Greater incentive method of compensation than straight piecework, where pay per unit increases as output goes up.

STEPS TO CALCULATE GROSS PAY BY PIECEWORK

Straight Piecework:

STEP 1. Multiply the number of pieces or output units by the rate per unit.

> **Total gross pay = Output quantity × Rate per unit**

Differential Piecework:

STEP 1. Multiply the number of output units at each level by the rate per unit at that level.

STEP 2. Find the total gross pay by adding the total from each level.

EXAMPLE3 CALCULATING PIECEWORK PAY

Barb Nelson works on a hat assembly line. Barb gets paid at a straight piecework rate of $0.35 per hat. What was Barb's total gross pay last week if she produced 1,655 hats?

SOLUTIONSTRATEGY

Total gross pay = Output quantity × Rate per unit
Total gross pay = 1,655 × .35 = $579.25

TRYITEXERCISE3

George Lopez works at a tire manufacturing plant. He is on a straight piecework rate of $0.41 per tire. What was George's total gross pay last week if he produced 950 tires?

CHECK YOUR ANSWER WITH THE SOLUTION ON PAGE 298.

EXAMPLE4 CALCULATING DIFFERENTIAL PIECEWORK PAY

Paula Duke assembled 190 watches last week. Calculate her total gross pay based on the following differential piecework schedule.

Pay Level	Watches Assembled	Rate per Watch
1	1–100	$2.45
2	101–150	$2.75
3	Over 150	$3.10

SOLUTIONSTRATEGY

To find Paula's total gross earnings, we calculate her earnings at each level of the pay schedule and add the totals. In this case, she will be paid for all of level 1, 100 watches; for all of level 2, 50 watches; and for 40 watches at level 3 (190 − 150 = 40).

Level pay = Output × Rate per piece
Level 1 = 100 × 2.45 = $245
Level 2 = 50 × 2.75 = $137.50
Level 3 = 40 × 3.10 = $124
Total gross pay = Level 1 + Level 2 + Level 3
Total gross pay = 245 + 137.50 + 124 = $506.50

TRYITEXERCISE4

You are the payroll manager for Trendy Toys, Inc., a manufacturer of small plastic toys. Your production workers are on a differential piecework schedule as follows.

Pay Level	Toys Produced	Rate per Toy
1	1–300	$0.68
2	301–500	$0.79
3	501–750	$0.86
4	Over 750	$0.94

Calculate last week's total gross pay for the following employees.

Name	Toys Produced	Total Gross Pay
C. Gomez	515	_____
L. Clifford	199	_____
M. Maken	448	_____
B. Nathan	804	_____

CHECK YOUR ANSWERS WITH THE SOLUTIONS ON PAGE 298.

9-4

CALCULATING GROSS PAY BY STRAIGHT AND INCREMENTAL COMMISSION, SALARY PLUS COMMISSION, AND DRAWING ACCOUNTS

STRAIGHT AND INCREMENTAL COMMISSION

commission Percentage method of compensation primarily used to pay employees who sell a company's goods and services.

straight commission Commission based on a specified percentage of the sales volume attained by an employee.

incremental commission Greater incentive method of compensation than straight commission whereby higher levels of sales earn increasing rates of commission.

Commission is a method of compensation primarily used to pay employees who sell a company's goods or services. **Straight commission** is based on a single specified percentage of the sales volume attained. For example, Delta Distributors pays its sales staff a commission of 8% on all sales. **Incremental commission** is much like the differential piecework rate whereby higher levels of sales earn increasing rates of commission. An example would be 5% commission on all sales up to $70,000, 6% on sales greater than $70,000 and up to $120,000, and 7% commission on any sales greater than $120,000.

STEPS TO CALCULATE GROSS PAY BY COMMISSION

Straight Commission:

STEP 1. Multiply the total sales by the commission rate.

$$\text{Total gross pay} = \text{Total sales} \times \text{Commission rate}$$

Incremental Commission:

STEP 1. Multiply the total sales at each level by the commission rate for that level.

STEP 2. Find the total gross pay by adding the total from each level.

EXAMPLE5 CALCULATING COMMISSIONS

Diamond Industries pays its sales force a commission rate of 6% of all sales. What was the total gross pay for an employee who sold $113,500 last month?

SOLUTIONSTRATEGY

$$\text{Total gross pay} = \text{Total sales} \times \text{Commission rate}$$
$$\text{Total gross pay} = 113,500 \times .06 = \underline{\$6,810}$$

TRYITEXERCISE5

Alexa Walsh sells for Supreme Designs, a manufacturer of women's clothing. Alexa is paid a straight commission of 2.4%. If her sales volume last month was $233,760, what was her total gross pay?

CHECK YOUR ANSWER WITH THE SOLUTION ON PAGE 298.

EXAMPLE6 CALCULATING INCREMENTAL COMMISSION

Vista Electronics pays its sales representatives on the following incremental commission schedule.

Level	Sales Volume	Commission Rate (%)
1	$1–$50,000	4
2	$50,001–$150,000	5
3	Over $150,000	6.5

What was the total gross pay for a sales rep who sold $162,400 last month?

SOLUTIONSTRATEGY

Using an incremental commission schedule, we find the pay for each level and then add the totals from each level. In this problem, the sales rep will be paid for all of level 1, $50,000; for all of level 2, $100,00; and for $12,400 of level 3 ($162,400 − $150,000 = $12,400).

Level pay = Sales per level × Commission rate

Level 1 pay = 50,000 × .04 = $\underline{\$2,000}$

Level 2 pay = 100,000 × .05 = $\underline{\$5,000}$

Level 3 pay = 12,400 × .065 = $\underline{\$806}$

Total gross pay = Level 1 + Level 2 + Level 3

Total gross pay = 2,000 + 5,000 + 806 = $\underline{\$7,806}$

TRYITEXERCISE6

Mike Lamb sells copiers for Royal Business Products. He is on an incremental commission schedule of 1.7% of sales up to $100,000 and 2.5% on sales greater than $100,000. What was Mike's total gross pay last month if his sales volume was $184,600?

CHECK YOUR ANSWER WITH THE SOLUTION ON PAGE 298.

INTHE BUSINESSWORLD

Companies often give sales managers *override* commissions. This is a small commission on the total sales of the manager's sales force.

Example: Jim and Diane sell for Apex Electronics. They each receive 15% commission on their sales. John, their sales manager, receives a 3% override on their total sales. If Jim sells $20,000 and Diane sells $30,000 in June, how much commission does each person receive?

- Jim: $20,000 × 15% = $3,000
- Diane: $30,000 × 15% = $4,500
- John: $50,000 × 3% = $1,500

SALARY PLUS COMMISSION

A variation of straight and incremental commission pay schedules is the **salary plus commission** whereby the employee is paid a guaranteed salary plus a commission on sales over a specified amount. To calculate the total gross pay, find the amount of commission and add it to the salary.

EXAMPLE7 CALCULATING SALARY PLUS COMMISSION

Karie Jabe works on a pay schedule of $1,500 per month salary plus a 3% commission on all sales greater than $40,000. If she sold $60,000 last month, what was her total gross pay?

SOLUTIONSTRATEGY

To solve for Karie's total gross pay, add her monthly salary to her commission for the month.

Commission = Commission rate $\times$ Sales subject to commission

Commission = 3%(60,000 − 40,000)

Commission = .03 $\times$ 20,000 = $600

Total gross pay = Salary + Commission

Total gross pay = 1,500 + 600 = $2,100

TRYITEXERCISE7

Ed Diamond is a sales representative for Jersey Shore Supply, Inc. He is paid a salary of $1,400 per month plus a commission of 4% on all sales greater than $20,000. If he sold $45,000 last month, what was his total gross earnings?

CHECK YOUR ANSWER WITH THE SOLUTION ON PAGE 298.

DRAW AGAINST COMMISSION

In certain industries and at certain times of the year, sales fluctuate significantly. To provide salespeople on commission with at least some income during slack periods of sales, a drawing account is used. A **drawing account**, or **draw against commission**, is a commission paid in advance of sales and later deducted from the commissions earned. If a period goes by when the salesperson does not earn enough commission to cover the draw, the unpaid balance carries over to the next period.

EXAMPLE8 CALCULATING DRAW AGAINST COMMISSION

Bill Carpenter is a salesperson for Power Electronics. The company pays 8% commission on all sales and gives Bill a $1,500 per month draw against commission. If he receives his draw at the beginning of the month and then sells $58,000 during the month, how much commission is owed to Bill?

SOLUTIONSTRATEGY

To find the amount of commission owed to Bill, find the total amount of commission he earned and subtract $1,500, the amount of his draw against commission.

Commission = Total sales $\times$ Commission rate

Commission = 58,000 $\times$ 8% = $4,640

Commission owed = Commission − Amount of draw

Commission owed = 4,640 − 1,500 = $3,140

TRYITEXERCISE8

Howard Lockwood sells for Catalina Designs, Inc. He is on a 3.5% straight commission with a $2,000 drawing account. If he is paid the draw at the beginning of the month and then sells $120,000 during the month, how much commission is owed to Howard?

CHECK YOUR ANSWER WITH THE SOLUTION ON PAGE 298.

SECTION I — 9 — REVIEW EXERCISES

Calculate the gross earnings per pay period for the following pay schedules.

	Annual Salary	Monthly	Semimonthly	Biweekly	Weekly
1.	$15,000	$1,250.00	$625.00	$576.92	$288.46
2.	$44,200	_____	_____	_____	_____
3.	$100,000	_____	_____	_____	_____
4.	$21,600	$1,800.00	$900.00	$830.77	$415.38
5.	_____	_____	$1,450.00	_____	_____
6.	_____	_____	_____	$875.00	_____
7.	_____	_____	_____	_____	$335.00

8. Mary Jo Prenaris is an office manager with gross earnings of $1,600 semimonthly. If her company switches pay schedules from semimonthly to biweekly, what are Mary Jo's new gross earnings?

9. Deb O'Connell is an accounting professional earning a salary of $58,000 at her firm. What is her equivalent weekly gross pay?

10. Jennifer Brunner works 40 hours per week as a chef's assistant. At the rate of $7.60 per hour, what are her gross weekly earnings?

11. Alan Kimball earns $22.34 per hour as a specialty chef at Le Bistro Restaurant. If he worked 53 hours last week and was paid time-and-a-half for weekly hours over 40, what was his gross pay?

12. Paul Curcio earns $8.25 per hour for regular time up to 40 hours, time-and-a-half for over-time, and double time for the midnight shift. Last week Paul worked 58 hours, including 6 on the midnight shift. What are his gross earnings?

MOONLIGHTING AMERICANS, 2009
Men and Women with Second Jobs

Men 3.3 million

Women 3.7 million

Source: Bureau of Labor Statistics, March 2010

By Anne R. Carey and Sam Ward, *USA TODAY*

As the payroll manager for Stargate Industries, your task is to complete the following weekly payroll record. The company pays overtime for all hours worked over 40 at the rate of time-and-a-half. Round to the nearest cent when necessary.

	Employee	M	T	W	T	F	S	S	Hourly Rate	Total Hours	Overtime Hours	Regular Pay	Overtime Pay	Total Pay
13.	Peters	7	8	5	8	8	0	0	$8.70	36	0	$313.20	0	$313.20
14.	Sands	6	5	9	8	10	7	0	$9.50	___	___	___	___	___
15.	Warner	8	6	11	7	12	0	4	$7.25	___	___	___	___	___
16.	Lee	9	7	7	7	9	0	8	$14.75	___	___	___	___	___

17. Larry Jefferson gets paid a straight piecework rate of $3.15 for each alternator he assembles for Allied Mechanical Corp. If he assembled 226 units last week, what was his gross pay?

You are the payroll manager for Euro Couture, a manufacturer of women's apparel. Your workers are paid per garment sewn on a differential piecework schedule as follows.

Pay Level	Garments Produced	Rate per Garment
1	1–50	$3.60
2	51–100	$4.25
3	101–150	$4.50
4	Over 150	$5.10

Calculate last week's total gross pay for each of the following employees.

Employee	Garments Produced	Total Gross Pay
18. Goodrich, P.	109	$433.00
19. Walker, A.	83	_____
20. Fox, B.	174	_____

21. Katrina Byrd assembles motor mounts for C-207 executive planes. Her company has established a differential piecework scale as an incentive to increase production due to backlogged orders. The pay scale is $11.50 for the first 40 mounts, $12.35 for the next 30 mounts, $13.00 for the next 20 mounts, and $13.40 for all remaining mounts assembled during the week. Katrina assembled 96 mounts last week. What was her total gross pay?

22. Bob Farrell works for a company that manufactures small appliances. Bob is paid $2.00 for each toaster, $4.60 for each microwave oven, and $1.55 for each food blender he assembles. If he produced 56 toasters, 31 microwave ovens, and 79 blenders, what were his total weekly gross earnings?

23. What is the total gross pay for a salesperson on a straight commission of 4.7% if his or her sales volume is $123,200?

24. Pamela Mello is paid on an incremental commission schedule. She is paid 2.6% on the first $60,000 and 3.4% on any sales over $60,000. If her weekly sales volume was $89,400, what was her total commission?

25. Dory Schrader is a buyer for Oceans of Notions. She is paid a weekly salary of $885 plus a 4% commission on sales over $45,000. If her sales were $62,000 last week, what was her total gross pay?

26. Thomas Rendell's company pays him a straight 6% commission with a $1,350 drawing account each month. If his sales last month totaled $152,480, how much commission is owed to Thomas?

27. Katie Jergens works for Dynamic Designs selling clothing. She is on a salary of $140 per week plus a commission of 7% of her sales. Last week she sold 19 dresses at $79.95 each, 26 skirts at $24.75 each, and 17 jackets at $51.50 each. What were her total gross earnings for the week?

28. Jerry King is a server in a restaurant that pays a salary of $22 per day. He also averages tips of 18% of his total gross food orders. Last week he worked 6 days and had total food orders of $2,766.50. What was his total gross pay for the week?

BUSINESS DECISION: MINIMUM WAGE TIED TO INFLATION

29. In an effort to keep low-wage workers' salaries commensurate with the cost of living, a number of states have amended their constitutions to allow the minimum wage to be adjusted with inflation. As of October 2009, 10 states—Arizona, Colorado, Florida, Missouri, Montana, Nevada, Ohio, Oregon, Vermont, and Washington—had tied their minimum wage to inflation.

You are the accountant for Delicious, Inc., a company that owns a chain of 18 fast-food restaurants in Florida. Each restaurant employs 35 workers, each averaging 20 hours per week at the current federal minimum wage, $7.25 per hour.

a. How many hours at minimum wage are paid out each week by Delicious?

b. At the current rate of $7.25 per hour, what is the amount of the weekly "minimum wage" portion of the restaurant's payroll?

"I think the best way for you to build the highest level of character is to work for me for the next 10 years at minimum wage."

c. If the inflation rate this year is .7%, calculate the "adjusted" minimum wage rate to be paid next year.

d. How much in "additional wages" will Delicious have to pay out next year at the adjusted rate?

e. (Optional) Go to www.dol.gov/whd/minwage/america.htm and click on your state to find the current minimum wage. Calculate the weekly "minimum wage" portion of the restaurant's payroll assuming the restaurant is located in your state.

f. (Optional) Suggest some ways that the restaurant chain or other small businesses can offset the increase in payroll and subsequent decrease in profit as a result of the minimum wage hike.

SECTION II 9 EMPLOYEE'S PAYROLL DEDUCTIONS

deductions or **withholdings** Funds withheld from an employee's paycheck.

mandatory deductions Deductions withheld from an employee's paycheck by law: social security, Medicare, and federal income tax.

voluntary deductions Deductions withheld from an employee's paycheck by request of the employee, such as insurance premiums, dues, loan payments, and charitable contributions.

"Hey! What happened to my paycheck?" This is the typical reaction of employees on seeing their paychecks for the first time after a raise or a promotion. As we will see, gross pay is by no means the amount of money the employee takes home.

Employers, by federal law, are required to deduct or withhold certain funds, known as **deductions** or **withholdings**, from an employee's paycheck. Employee payroll deductions fall into two categories: mandatory and voluntary. The three major **mandatory deductions** most workers in the United States are subject to are social security, Medicare, and federal income tax. Other mandatory deductions found only in some states are state income tax and state disability insurance.

In addition to the mandatory deductions, employees may also choose to have **voluntary deductions** taken out of their paychecks. Some examples include payments for life or health insurance premiums, union or professional organization dues, credit union savings deposits or loan payments, stock or bond purchases, and charitable contributions.

After all the deductions have been subtracted from the employee's gross earnings, the remaining amount is known as net, or take-home, pay.

> **Net pay = Gross pay − Total deductions**

9-5 COMPUTING FICA TAXES, BOTH SOCIAL SECURITY AND MEDICARE, WITHHELD FROM AN EMPLOYEE'S PAYCHECK

Federal Insurance Contribution Act (FICA) Federal legislation enacted in 1937 during the Great Depression to provide retirement funds and hospital insurance for retired and disabled workers. Today FICA is divided into two categories, social security and Medicare.

In 1937 during the Great Depression, Congress enacted legislation known as the **Federal Insurance Contribution Act (FICA)** with the purpose of providing monthly benefits to retired and disabled workers and to the families of deceased workers. This social security tax, which is assessed to virtually every worker in the United States, is based on a certain percent of the worker's income up to a specified limit or **wage base** per year. When the tax began in 1937, the tax rate was 1% up to a wage base of $3,000. At that time, the maximum a worker could be taxed per year for social security was $30 (3,000 × .01).

Today the FICA tax is divided into two categories. **Social security tax (OASDI,** which stands for Old Age, Survivors, and Disability Insurance) is a retirement plan, and **Medicare tax** is for health care and hospital insurance. The social security wage base changes every year. For the most current information, consult the Internal Revenue Service, *Circular E, Employer's Tax Guide*. In 2010, the following rates and wage base were in effect for the FICA tax and should be used for all exercises in this chapter:

	Tax Rate	Wage Base
Social Security (OASDI)	6.2%	$106,800
Medicare	1.45%	no limit

When an employee reaches the wage base for the year, he or she is no longer subject to the tax. In 2010, the maximum social security tax per year was $6,621.60 (106,800 × .062). There is no limit on the amount of Medicare tax. The 1.45% is in effect regardless of how much an employee earns.

wage base The amount of earnings up to which an employee must pay social security tax.

social security tax (OASDI) Old Age, Survivors, and Disability Insurance—a federal tax based on a percentage of a worker's income up to a specified limit or wage base for the purpose of providing monthly benefits to retired and disabled workers and to the families of deceased workers.

Medicare tax A federal tax used to provide health care benefits and hospital insurance to retired and disabled workers.

EXAMPLE9 CALCULATING SOCIAL SECURITY AND MEDICARE WITHHOLDINGS

What are the withholdings for social security and Medicare for an employee with gross earnings of $650 per week? Round to the nearest cent.

SOLUTIONSTRATEGY

To find the withholdings, we apply the tax rates for social security (6.2%) and Medicare (1.45%) to the gross earnings for the week:

Social security tax = Gross earnings × 6.2%

Social security tax = 650 × .062 = $40.30

Medicare tax = Gross earnings × 1.45%

Medicare tax = 650 × .0145 = 9.425 = $9.43

TRYITEXERCISE9

What are the withholdings for social security and Medicare for an employee with gross earnings of $5,000 per month?

CHECK YOUR ANSWERS WITH THE SOLUTIONS ON PAGE 299.

REACHING THE WAGE BASE LIMIT

In the pay period when an employee's year-to-date (YTD) earnings reach and surpass the wage base for social security, the tax is applied only to the portion of the earnings below the limit.

EXAMPLE10 CALCULATING SOCIAL SECURITY WITH WAGE BASE LIMIT

Vickie Hirsh has earned $104,900 so far this year. Her next paycheck, $5,000, will put her earnings over the wage base limit for social security. What is the amount of Vickie's social security withholdings for that paycheck?

SOLUTIONSTRATEGY

To calculate Vickie's social security deduction, first determine how much more she must earn to reach the wage base of $106,800.

IN THE BUSINESS WORLD

PAYROLL TAX HOLIDAY!
As part of the 2010 Tax Relief Act, the employee's portion of the Social Security tax was reduced from 6.2% to 4.2% for the tax year 2011. The wage base limit remained the same as in 2010, $106,800.

The current FICA deductions and wage base are listed in the IRS publication *Circular E, Employer's Tax Guide*.

This and other tax forms and publications can be obtained by calling the IRS at 1-800-TAX FORM or by accessing its website, www.irs.gov.

Photo by Robert Brechner

As a result of the historic healthcare reform package signed into law on March 23, 2010, the Medicare payroll tax will increase in 2013 for high-income individuals and couples.

Earnings subject to tax = Wage base − Year-to-date earnings

Earnings subject to tax = 106,800 − 104,900 = $1,900

Social security tax = Earnings subject to tax × 6.2%

Social security tax = 1,900 × .062 = $117.80

● TRYITEXERCISE10

Rick Nicotera has year-to-date earnings of $102,300. If his next paycheck is $6,000, what is the amount of his social security deduction?

CHECK YOUR ANSWER WITH THE SOLUTION ON PAGE 299.

9-6

CALCULATING AN EMPLOYEE'S FEDERAL INCOME TAX WITHHOLDING (FIT) BY THE PERCENTAGE METHOD

federal income tax (FIT) A graduated tax based on gross earnings, marital status, and number of exemptions that is paid by all workers earning over a certain amount in the United States.

withholding allowance, or **exemption** An amount that reduces an employee's taxable income. Employees are allowed one exemption for themselves, one for their spouse if the spouse does not work, and one for each dependent child or elderly parent living with the taxpayer but not working.

percentage method An alternative method to the wage bracket tables used to calculate the amount of an employee's federal income tax withholding.

In addition to social security and Medicare tax withholdings, an employer is also responsible, by federal law, for withholding an appropriate amount of **federal income tax (FIT)** from each employee's paycheck. This graduated tax allows the government a steady flow of tax revenues throughout the year. Self-employed persons must send quarterly tax payments based on estimated earnings to the Internal Revenue Service. By IRS rules, 90% of the income tax due for a given calendar year must be paid within that year to avoid penalties.

The amount of income tax withheld from an employee's paycheck is determined by his or her amount of gross earnings, marital status, and the number of **withholding allowances,** or **exemptions,** claimed. Employees are allowed one exemption for themselves, one for their spouse if the spouse does not work, and one for each dependent child or elderly parent living with the taxpayer but not working.

Each employee is required to complete a form called W-4, Employee's Withholding Allowance Certificate. The information provided on this form is used by the employer in calculating the amount of income tax withheld from the paycheck. Employees should keep track of their tax liability during the year and adjust the number of exemptions as their personal situations change (i.e., marriage, divorce, or birth of a child).

The **percentage method** for determining the amount of federal income tax withheld from an employee's paycheck is used by companies whose payroll processing is on a computerized system. The amount of tax withheld is based on the amount of gross earnings, the marital status of the employee, and the number of withholding allowances claimed.

The percentage method of calculating federal income tax requires the use of two tables. The first is the Percentage Method Amount for One Withholding Allowance Table, Exhibit 9-1. This table shows the dollar amount of one withholding allowance for the various payroll periods. The second, Exhibit 9-2, is the Tables for Percentage Method of Withholding.

EXHIBIT 9-1

Percentage Method Amount for One Withholding Allowance

Payroll Period	One Withholding Allowance
Weekly	$ 70.19
Biweekly	140.38
Semimonthly	152.08
Monthly	304.17
Quarterly	912.50
Semiannually	1,825.00
Annually	3,650.00
Daily or miscellaneous (each day of the payroll period)	14.04

EXHIBIT 9-2 Tables for Percentage Method of Withholding (For Wages Paid in 2010)

TABLE 1—WEEKLY Payroll Period

(a) SINGLE person (including head of household)—

If the amount of wages (after subtracting withholding allowances) is:		The amount of income tax to withhold is:	
Not over $116 ....$0			
Over—	**But not over—**		**of excess over—**
$116	—$200	......10%	—$116
$200	—$693	......$8.40 plus 15%	—$200
$693	—$1,302	......$82.35 plus 25%	—$693
$1,302	—$1,624	......$234.60 plus 27%	—$1,302
$1,624	—$1,687	......$321.54 plus 30%	—$1,624
$1,687	—$3,344	......$340.44 plus 28%	—$1,687
$3,344	—$7,225	......$804.40 plus 33%	—$3,344
$7,225	...............................$2,085.l3 plus 35%		—$7,225

(b) MARRIED person—

If the amount of wages (after subtracting withholding allowances) is:		The amount of income tax to withhold is:	
Not over $264 ....$0			
Over—	**But not over—**		**of excess over—**
$264	—$471	......10%	—$264
$471	—$1,457	......$20.70 plus 15%	—$471
$1,457	—$1,809	......$168.60 plus 25%	—$1,457
$1,809	—$2,386	......$256.60 plus 27%	—$1,809
$2,386	—$2,789	......$412.39 plus 25%	—$2,386
$2,789	—$4,173	......$513.14 plus 28%	—$2,789
$4,173	—$7,335	......$900.66 plus 33%	—$4,173
$7,335	...............................$1,944.12 plus 35%		—$7,335

TABLE 2—BIWEEKLY Payroll Period

(a) SINGLE person (including head of household)—

If the amount of wages (after subtracting withholding allowances) is:		The amount of income tax to withhold is:	
Not over $233 ....$0			
Over—	**But not over—**		**of excess over—**
$233	—$40l	......10%	—$233
$401	—$1,387	......$16.80 plus 15%	—$401
$1,387	—$2,604	......$164.70 plus 25%	—$1,387
$2,604	—$3,248	......$468.95 plus 27%	—$2,604
$3,248	—$3,373	......$642.83 plus 30%	—$3,248
$3,373	—$6,688	......$680.33 plus 28%	—$3,373
$6,688	—$14,450	......$1,608.53 plus 33%	—$6,688
$14,450	...............................$4,169.99 plus 35%		—$14,450

(b) MARRIED person—

If the amount of wages (after subtracting withholding allowances) is:		The amount of income tax to withhold is:	
Not over $529 ....$0			
Over—	**But not over—**		**of excess over—**
$529	—$942	......10%	—$529
$942	—$2,913	......$41.30 plus 15%	—$942
$2,913	—$3,617	......$336.95 plus 25%	—$2,913
$3,617	—$4,771	......$512.95 plus 27%	—$3,617
$4,771	—$5,579	......$824.53 plus 25%	—$4,771
$5,579	—$8,346	......$1,026.53 plus 28%	—$5,579
$8,346	—$14,669	......$1,801.29 plus 33%	—$8,346
$14,669	...............................$3,887.88 plus 35%		—$14,669

TABLE 3—SEMIMONTHLY Payroll Period

(a) SINGLE person (including head of household)—

If the amount of wages (after subtracting withholding allowances) is:		The amount of income tax to withhold is:	
Not over $252 ....$0			
Over—	**But not over—**		**of excess over—**
$252	—$434	......10%	—$252
$434	—$1,502	......$18.20 plus 15%	—$434
$1,502	—$2,821	......$178.40 plus 25%	—$1,502
$2,821	—$3,519	......$508.15 plus 27%	—$2,821
$3,519	—$3,654	......$696.61 plus 30%	—$3,519
$3,654	—$7,246	......$737.11 plus 28%	—$3,654
$7,246	—$15,654	......$1,742.87 plus 33%	—$7,246
$15,654	...............................$4,517.51 plus 35%		—$15,654

(b) MARRIED person—

If the amount of wages (after subtracting withholding allowances) is:		The amount of income tax to withhold is:	
Not over $573 ....$0			
Over—	**But not over—**		**of excess over—**
$573	—$1,021	......10%	—$573
$1,021	—$3,156	......$44.80 plus 15%	—$1,021
$3,156	—$3,919	......$365.05 plus 25%	—$3,156
$3,919	—$5,169	......$555.80 plus 27%	—$3,919
$5,169	—$6,044	......$893.30 plus 25%	—$5,169
$6,044	—$9,042	......$1,112.05 plus 28%	—$6,044
$9,042	—$15,892	......$1,951.49 plus 33%	—$9,042
$15,892	...............................$4,211.99 plus 35%		—$15,892

TABLE 4—MONTHLY Payroll Period

(a) SINGLE person (including head of household)—

If the amount of wages (after subtracting withholding allowances) is:		The amount of income tax to withhold is:	
Not over $504 ....$0			
Over—	**But not over—**		**of excess over—**
$504	—$869	......10%	—$504
$869	—$3,004	......$36.50 plus 15%	—$869
$3,004	—$5,642	......$356.75 plus 25%	—$3,004
$5,642	—$7,038	......$1,016.25 plus 27%	—$5,642
$7,038	—$7,308	......$1,393.17 plus 30%	—$7,038
$7,308	—$14,492	......$1,474.l7 plus 28%	—$7,308
$14,492	—$31,308	......$3,485.69 plus 33%	—$14,492
$31,308	...............................$9,034.97 plus 35%		—$31,308

(b) MARRIED person—

If the amount of wages (after subtracting withholding allowances) is:		The amount of income tax to withhold is:	
Not over $1,146 ....$0			
Over—	**But not over—**		**of excess over—**
$1,146	—$2,042	......10%	—$1,146
$2,042	—$6,313	......$89.60 plus 15%	—$2,042
$6,313	—$7,838	......$730.25 plus 25%	—$6,313
$7,838	—$10,338	......$1,111.50 plus 27%	—$7,838
$10,338	—$12,088	......$1,786.50 plus 25%	—$l0,338
$12,088	—$18,083	......$2,224.00 plus 28%	—$12,088
$18,083	—$31,783	......$3,902.60 plus 33%	—$18,083
$31,783	...............................$8,423.60 plus 35%		—$31,783

Catalog No. 21974B

STEPS TO CALCULATE THE INCOME TAX WITHHELD BY THE PERCENTAGE METHOD

STEP 1. Using the proper payroll period, multiply one withholding allowance, Exhibit 9-1, by the number of allowances claimed by the employee.

STEP 2. Subtract that amount from the employee's gross earnings to find the wages subject to federal income tax.

STEP 3. From Exhibit 9-2, locate the proper segment (Table 1, 2, 3, or 4) corresponding to the employee's payroll period. Within that segment, use the *left* side (a) for single employees and the *right* side (b) for married employees.

STEP 4. Locate the "Over—" and "But not over—" brackets containing the employee's taxable wages from Step 2. The tax is listed to the right as a percent or a dollar amount and a percent.

EXAMPLE 11 CALCULATING INCOME TAX WITHHOLDING

Lori Fast is a manager for Wayward Wind Travel. She is single and is paid $750 weekly. She claims two withholding allowances. Using the percentage method, calculate the amount of income tax that should be withheld from her paycheck each week.

SOLUTIONSTRATEGY

From Exhibit 9-1, the amount of one withholding allowance for an employee paid weekly is $70.19. Multiply this amount by the number of allowances claimed, two.

$$70.19 \times 2 = \$140.38$$

Subtract that amount from the gross earnings to get taxable income.

$$750.00 - 140.38 = \$609.62$$

From Exhibit 9-2, find the tax withheld from Lori's paycheck in Table 1(a), Weekly payroll period, Single person. Lori's taxable wages of $609.62 fall in the category "Over $200, but not over $693." The tax, therefore, is $8.40 plus 15% of the excess over $200.

Tax = 8.40 + .15(609.62 − 200.00)

Tax = 8.40 + .15(409.62)

Tax = 8.40 + 61.44 = $69.84

TRYITEXERCISE 11

Jan McMillan is married, claims five exemptions, and earns $3,670 per month. As the payroll manager of Jan's company, use the percentage method to calculate the amount of income tax that must be withheld from her paycheck.

CHECK YOUR ANSWER WITH THE SOLUTION ON PAGE 299.

DETERMINING AN EMPLOYEE'S TOTAL WITHHOLDING FOR FEDERAL INCOME TAX, SOCIAL SECURITY, AND MEDICARE USING THE COMBINED WAGE BRACKET TABLES

9-7

In 2001, the IRS introduced **combined wage bracket tables** that can be used to determine the combined amount of income tax, social security, and Medicare that must be withheld from an employee's gross earnings each pay period. These tables are found in *Publication 15-A, Employer's Supplemental Tax Guide*. This publication contains a complete set of tables for both single and married people, covering weekly, biweekly, semimonthly, monthly, and even daily pay periods.

Exhibit 9-3 shows a portion of the wage bracket tables for Married Persons—Weekly Payroll Period, and Exhibit 9-4 shows a portion of the wage bracket table for Single Persons—Monthly Payroll Period. Use these tables to solve wage bracket problems in this chapter.

combined wage bracket tables IRS tables used to determine the combined amount of income tax, social security, and Medicare that must be withheld from an employee's gross earnings each pay period.

STEPS TO FIND THE TOTAL INCOME TAX, SOCIAL SECURITY, AND MEDICARE WITHHELD USING THE COMBINED WAGE BRACKET TABLE

STEP 1. Based on the employee's marital status and period of payment, find the corresponding table (Exhibit 9-3 or 9-4).

STEP 2. Note that the two left-hand columns, labeled "At least" and "But less than," are the wage brackets. Scan down these columns until you find the bracket containing the gross pay of the employee.

STEP 3. Scan across the row of that wage bracket to the intersection of the column containing the number of withholding allowances claimed by the employee.

STEP 4. The number in that column on the wage bracket row is the amount of combined tax withheld.

EXAMPLE 12 USING THE COMBINED WAGE BRACKET TABLES

Use the combined wage bracket tables to determine the amount of income tax, social security, and Medicare withheld from the monthly paycheck of Erin Lane, a single employee claiming three withholding allowances and earning $2,975 per month.

SOLUTIONSTRATEGY

To find Erin Lane's monthly income tax withholding, choose the table for Single Persons—Monthly Payroll Period, Exhibit 9-4. Scanning down the "At least" and "But less than" columns, we find the wage bracket containing Erin's earnings: "At least 2,960—But less than 3,000."

Next, scan across that row from left to right to the "3" withholding allowances column. The number at that intersection, $443.97, is the total combined tax to be withheld from Erin's paycheck.

TRYITEXERCISE 12

Using the combined wage bracket tables, what is the total amount of income tax, social security, and Medicare that should be withheld from Brent Andrus's weekly paycheck of $835 if he is married and claims two withholding allowances?

CHECK YOUR ANSWER WITH THE SOLUTION ON PAGE 299.

EXHIBIT 9-3 Payroll Deductions—Married, Paid Weekly

MARRIED Persons—WEEKLY Payroll Period
(Far Wages Paid in 2010)

And the wages are—		And the number of withholding allowances claimed is—										
At least	But less than	0	1	2	3	4	5	6	7	8	9	10
		The amount of income, social security, and Medicare taxes to be withheld is—										
$790	$800	$129.82	$119.82	$108.82	$98.82	$87.82	$78.82	$71.82	$64.82	$60.82	$60.82	$60.82
800	810	132.58	121.58	111.58	100.58	90.58	80.58	73.58	66.88	61.58	61.58	61.58
810	820	134.35	124.35	113.35	103.35	92.35	82.35	75.35	68.35	62.35	62.35	62.35
820	830	137.11	126.11	116.11	105.11	95.11	84.11	77.11	70.11	63.11	63.11	63.11
830	840	138.88	125.88	117.88	107.88	96.88	86.88	78.88	71.88	64.88	63.88	63.88
840	850	141.64	130.64	120.64	109.64	99.64	88.64	80.64	73.64	66.64	64.64	64.64
850	860	143.41	133.41	122.41	112.41	101.41	91.41	82.41	75.41	68.41	65.41	65.41
860	870	146.17	135.17	125.17	114.17	104.17	93.17	84.17	77.17	70.17	66.17	66.17
870	880	147.94	137.94	126.94	116.94	105.94	95.94	85.94	78.94	71.94	66.94	66.94
880	890	150.70	139.70	129.70	118.70	108.70	97.70	87.70	80.70	73.70	67.70	67.70
890	900	152.47	142.47	131.47	121.47	110.47	100.47	89.47	82.47	75.47	68.47	68.47
900	910	155.23	144.23	134.23	123.23	113.23	102.23	92.23	84.23	77.23	70.23	69.23
910	920	157.00	147.00	136.00	126.00	115.00	105.00	94.00	86.00	79.00	72.00	70.00
920	930	159.76	148.76	138.76	127.76	117.76	106.76	96.76	87.76	80.76	73.76	70.76
930	940	161.53	151.53	140.53	130.53	119.53	109.53	98.53	89.53	82.53	75.53	71.53
940	950	164.29	153.29	143.29	132.29	122.29	111.29	101.29	91.29	84.29	77.29	72.29
950	960	166.06	156.06	145.06	135.06	124.06	114.06	103.06	93.06	86.06	79.06	73.06
960	970	168.82	157.82	147.82	136.82	126.82	115.82	105.82	94.82	87.82	80.82	73.82
970	980	170.59	160.59	149.59	139.59	128.59	118.59	107.59	91.59	89.59	82.59	75.59
980	990	173.35	162.35	152.35	141.35	131.35	120.35	110.35	99.35	91.35	84.35	77.35
990	1000	175.12	165.12	154.12	144.12	133.12	123.12	112.12	102.12	93.12	86.12	79.12
1000	1010	177.88	166.88	156.88	145.88	135.88	124.88	114.88	103.88	94.88	87.88	80.88
1010	1020	179.65	169.65	158.65	148.65	137.65	127.65	116.65	106.65	96.65	89.65	82.65
1020	1030	182.41	171.41	161.41	150.41	140.41	129.41	119.41	108.41	98.41	91.41	84.41
1030	1040	184.18	174.18	163.18	153.18	142.18	132.18	121.18	111.18	100.18	93.18	86.18
1040	1050	186.94	175.94	165.94	154.94	144.94	133.94	123.94	112.94	102.94	94.94	87.94
1050	1060	188.71	178.71	167.71	157.71	146.71	136.71	125.71	115.71	104.71	96.71	89.71
1060	1070	191.47	180.47	170.47	159.47	149.47	138.47	128.47	117.47	107.47	98.47	91.47
1070	1080	193.24	183.24	172.24	162.24	151.24	141.24	130.24	120.24	109.24	100.24	93.24
1080	1090	196.00	185.00	175.00	164.00	154.00	143.00	133.00	122.00	112.00	102.00	95.00
1090	1100	197.77	187.77	176.77	166.77	155.77	145.77	134.77	124.77	113.77	103.77	96.77
1100	1110	200.53	189.53	179.53	168.53	158.53	147.53	137.53	126.53	116.53	105.53	98.53
1110	1120	202.30	192.30	181.30	171.30	160.30	150.30	139.30	129.30	118.30	107.30	100.30
1120	1130	205.06	194.06	184.06	173.06	163.06	152.06	142.06	131.06	121.06	110.06	102.06
1130	1140	206.83	196.83	185.83	175.83	164.83	154.83	143.83	133.83	122.83	111.83	103.83
1140	1150	209.59	198.59	188.59	177.59	167.59	156.59	146.59	135.89	125.59	114.59	105.59
1150	1160	211.36	201.36	190.36	180.36	169.36	159.36	148.36	138.36	127.36	116.36	107.36
1160	1170	214.12	203.12	193.12	182.12	172.12	161.12	151.12	140.12	130.12	119.12	109.12
1170	1180	215.89	205.89	194.89	184.89	173.89	163.89	152.89	142.89	131.89	120.89	110.89
1180	1190	218.65	207.65	197.65	186.65	175.65	165.65	155.65	144.65	134.65	123.65	112.65
1190	1200	220.42	210.42	199.42	189.42	175.42	168.42	157.42	147.42	136.42	125.42	115.42
1200	1210	223.18	212.18	202.18	191.18	181.18	170.18	160.18	149.18	139.18	128.18	117.18
1210	1220	224.95	214.95	203.95	193.95	182.95	172.95	161.95	151.95	140.95	129.95	119.95
1220	1230	227.71	216.71	206.71	195.71	185.71	174.71	164.71	153.71	143.71	132.71	121.71
1230	1240	229.48	219.48	208.48	198.48	187.48	177.48	166.48	156.48	145.48	134.48	124.48
1240	1250	232.24	221.24	211.24	200.24	190.24	179.24	169.24	158.24	148.24	137.24	126.24
1250	1260	234.01	224.01	213.01	203.01	192.01	182.01	171.01	161.01	150.01	139.01	129.01
1260	1270	236.77	225.77	215.77	204.77	194.77	183.77	173.77	162.77	152.77	141.77	130.77
1270	1280	238.54	228.54	217.54	207.54	196.54	186.54	175.54	165.54	154.54	143.54	133.54
1280	1290	241.30	230.30	220.30	209.30	199.30	188.30	178.30	167.30	157.30	146.30	135.30
1290	1300	243.07	233.07	222.07	212.07	201.07	191.07	180.07	170.07	159.07	148.07	138.07
1300	1310	245.83	234.83	224.83	213.83	203.83	192.83	182.83	171.83	161.83	150.83	139.83
1310	1320	247.60	237.60	225.60	216.60	205.60	195.60	184.60	174.60	163.60	152.60	142.60
1320	1330	250.36	239.36	229.36	218.36	208.36	197.36	187.36	176.36	166.36	155.36	144.36
1330	1340	252.13	242.13	231.13	221.13	210.13	200.13	189.13	179.13	168.13	157.13	147.13
1340	1350	254.89	243.89	233.89	222.89	212.89	201.89	191.89	180.89	170.89	159.89	148.89
1350	1360	256.66	246.66	235.66	225.66	214.66	204.66	193.66	183.66	172.66	161.66	151.66
1360	1370	259.42	248.42	238.42	227.42	217.42	206.42	196.42	185.42	175.42	164.42	153.42
1370	1380	261.19	251.19	240.19	230.19	219.19	209.19	198.19	188.19	177.19	166.19	156.19
1380	1390	263.95	252.95	242.95	231.95	221.95	210.95	200.95	189.95	179.95	168.95	157.95

$1390 and over	Do not use this table. See page 46 for instructions.

EXHIBIT 9-4 Payroll Deductions—Single, Paid Monthly

SINGLE Persons—MONTHLY Payroll Period
(Far Wages Paid in 2010)

And the wages are—		And the number of withholding allowances claimed is—										
At least	But less than	0	1	2	3	4	5	6	7	8	9	10
		The amount of income, social security, and Medicare taxes to be withheld is—										
$2640	$2680	$508.49	$463.49	$417.49	$371.49	$326.49	$280.49	$236.49	$206.49	$203.49	$203.49	$203.49
2680	2720	517.55	472.55	426.55	380.55	335.55	289.55	243.55	213.55	206.55	206.55	206.55
2720	2760	526.61	481.61	435.61	389.61	344.61	298.61	252.61	220.61	209.61	209.61	209.61
2760	2800	535.67	490.67	444.67	398.67	353.67	307.67	261.67	227.67	212.67	212.67	212.67
2800	2840	544.73	499.73	453.73	407.73	362.73	316.73	270.73	234.73	215.73	215.73	215.73
2640	2880	553.79	508.79	462.79	416.79	371.79	325.79	279.79	241.79	218.79	218.79	218.79
2880	2920	562.85	517.85	471.85	425.85	380.85	334.85	288.85	248.85	221.85	221.85	221.85
2920	2960	571.91	526.91	480.91	434.91	389.91	343.91	297.91	255.91	224.91	224.91	224.91
2960	3000	580.97	535.97	489.97	443.97	398.97	352.97	306.97	262.97	231.97	227.97	227.97
3000	3040	592.03	545.03	499.03	453.03	408.03	362.03	316.03	271.03	239.03	231.03	231.03
3040	3080	605.09	554.09	508.09	462.09	417.09	371.09	325.09	280.09	246.09	234.09	234.09
3080	3120	618.15	563.15	517.15	471.15	426.15	380.15	334.15	289.15	253.15	237.15	237.15
3120	3160	631.21	572.21	526.21	480.21	435.21	389.21	343.21	298.21	260.21	240.21	240.21
3160	3200	644.27	581.27	535.27	489.27	444.27	398.27	352.27	307.27	267.27	243.27	243.27
3200	3240	657.33	590.33	544.33	498.33	453.33	407.33	361.33	316.33	274.33	246.33	246.33
3240	3280	670.39	599.39	553.39	507.39	462.39	416.39	370.39	325.39	281.39	251.39	249.39
3280	3320	683.45	608.45	562.45	516.45	471.45	425.45	379.45	334.45	288.45	258.45	252.45
3320	3360	696.51	620.51	571.51	525.51	480.51	434.51	388.51	343.51	297.51	265.51	255.51
3360	3400	709.57	633.57	580.57	534.57	489.57	443.57	397.57	352.57	306.57	272.57	258.57
3400	3440	722.63	646.63	589.63	543.63	498.63	452.63	406.63	361.63	315.63	279.63	261.63
3440	3480	735.69	659.69	598.69	552.69	507.69	461.69	415.69	370.69	324.69	286.69	264.69
3480	3520	748.75	672.75	607.75	561.75	516.75	470.75	424.75	379.75	333.75	295.75	267.75
3520	3560	761.81	685.81	616.81	570.81	525.81	479.81	433.81	388.81	342.81	300.81	270.81
3560	3600	774.87	698.87	625.87	579.87	534.87	488.87	442.87	397.87	351.87	307.87	276.87
3600	3640	787.93	711.93	635.93	588.93	543.93	497.93	451.93	406.93	360.93	315.93	283.93
3640	3680	800.99	724.99	648.99	597.99	552.99	506.99	460.99	415.99	369.99	324.99	290.99
3680	3720	814.05	738.05	662.05	607.05	562.05	516.05	470.05	425.05	379.05	334.05	298.05
3720	3760	827.11	751.11	675.11	616.11	571.11	525.11	479.11	434.11	388.11	343.11	305.11
3760	3800	840.17	764.17	688.17	625.17	580.17	534.17	488.17	443.17	397.17	352.17	312.17
3800	3840	853.23	777.23	701.23	634.23	589.23	543.23	497.23	452.23	406.23	361.23	319.23
3840	3880	866.29	790.29	714.29	643.29	598.29	552.29	506.29	461.29	415.29	370.29	326.29
3880	3920	879.35	803.35	727.35	652.35	607.35	561.35	515.35	470.35	424.35	379.35	333.35
3920	3960	892.41	816.41	740.41	664.41	616.41	570.41	524.41	479.41	433.41	388.41	342.41
3960	4000	905.47	829.47	753.47	677.47	625.47	579.47	533.47	488.47	442.47	397.47	351.47
4000	4040	918.53	842.53	766.53	690.53	634.53	588.53	542.53	497.53	451.53	406.53	360.53
4040	4080	931.59	855.59	779.59	703.59	643.59	597.59	551.59	506.59	460.59	415.59	369.59
4080	4120	944.65	868.65	792.65	716.65	652.65	606.65	560.65	515.65	469.65	424.65	378.65
4120	4160	957.71	881.71	805.71	729.71	661.71	615.71	569.71	524.71	478.71	433.71	387.71
4160	4200	970.77	894.77	818.77	742.77	670.77	624.77	578.77	533.77	487.77	442.77	396.77
4200	4240	983.83	907.83	831.83	755.83	679.83	633.83	587.83	542.83	496.83	451.83	405.83
4240	4280	996.89	920.89	844.89	768.89	692.89	642.89	596.89	551.89	505.89	460.89	414.89
4280	4320	1009.95	933.95	857.95	781.95	705.95	651.95	605.95	560.95	514.95	469.95	423.95
4320	4360	1023.01	947.01	871.01	795.01	719.01	661.01	615.01	570.01	524.01	479.01	433.01
4360	4400	1036.07	960.07	884.07	808.07	732.07	670.07	624.07	579.07	533.07	488.07	442.07
4400	4440	1049.13	973.13	897.13	821.13	745.13	679.13	633.13	588.13	542.13	497.13	451.13
4440	4480	1062.19	986.19	910.19	834.19	758.19	688.19	642.19	597.19	551.19	506.19	460.19
4480	4520	1075.25	999.25	923.25	847.25	771.25	697.25	651.25	606.25	560.25	515.25	469.25
4520	4560	1088.31	1012.31	936.31	860.31	784.31	708.31	660.31	615.31	569.31	524.31	478.31
4560	4600	1101.37	1025.37	949.37	873.37	797.37	721.37	669.37	624.37	578.37	533.37	487.37
4600	4640	1114.43	1038.43	962.43	886.43	810.43	734.43	678.43	633.43	587.43	542.43	496.43
4640	4680	1127.49	1051.49	975.49	899.49	823.49	747.49	687.49	642.49	596.49	551.49	505.49
4680	4720	1140.55	1064.55	988.55	912.55	836.55	760.55	696.55	651.55	605.55	560.55	514.55
4720	4760	1153.61	1077.61	1001.61	925.61	849.61	773.61	705.61	660.61	614.61	569.61	523.61
4760	4800	1166.67	1090.67	1014.67	938.67	862.67	786.67	714.67	669.67	623.67	578.67	532.67
4800	4840	1179.73	1103.73	1027.73	951.73	875.73	799.73	723.73	678.73	632.73	587.73	541.73
4840	4880	1192.79	1116.79	1040.79	964.79	888.79	812.79	735.79	687.79	641.79	596.79	550.79
4880	4920	1205.85	1129.85	1053.85	977.85	901.85	825.85	748.85	696.85	650.85	605.85	559.85
4920	4960	1218.91	1142.91	1066.91	990.91	914.91	838.91	761.91	705.91	659.91	614.91	568.91
4960	5000	1231.97	1155.97	1079.97	1003.97	927.97	851.97	774.97	714.97	668.97	623.97	577.97
5000	5040	1245.03	1169.03	1093.03	1017.03	941.03	865.03	788.03	724.03	678.03	633.03	587.03

$5040 and over	Do not use this table. See page 46 for instructions.

SECTION II · 9 · REVIEW EXERCISES

Solve the following problems using 6.2%, up to $106,800, for social security tax and 1.45%, no wage limit, for Medicare tax.

1. What are the withholdings for social security and Medicare for an employee with gross earnings of $825 per week?

    825 × .062 = <u>$51.15</u> Social security
    825 × .0145 = <u>$11.96</u> Medicare

2. What are the social security and Medicare withholdings for an executive whose annual gross earnings are $108,430?

3. Brian Hickman is an executive with Westco Distributors. His gross earnings are $9,800 per month.

    a. What are the withholdings for social security and Medicare for Brian in his January paycheck?

    b. In what month will Brian's salary reach the social security wage base limit?

    c. What are the social security and Medicare tax withholdings for Brian in the month named in part b?

4. Kristy Dunaway has biweekly gross earnings of $1,750. What are her total social security and Medicare tax withholdings for a whole year?

As payroll manager for Freeport Enterprises, it is your task to calculate the monthly social security and Medicare withholdings for the following employees.

Employee	Year-to-Date Earnings	Current Month	Social Security	Medicare
5. Perez, J.	$23,446	$3,422	$212.16	$49.62
6. Graham, C.	$14,800	$1,540	_____	_____
7. Jagger, R.	$105,200	$4,700	_____	_____
8. Andretti, K.	$145,000	$12,450	_____	_____

Use the percentage method of income tax calculation to complete the following payroll roster.

	Employee	Marital Status	Withholding Allowances	Pay Period	Gross Earnings	Income Tax Withholding
9.	Randolph, B.	M	2	Weekly	$594	$18.96
10.	White, W.	S	0	Semimonthly	$1,227	_____
11.	Milian, B.	S	1	Monthly	$4,150	_____
12.	Farley, D.	M	4	Biweekly	$1,849	_____

Use the combined wage bracket tables, Exhibits 9-3 and 9-4, to solve Exercises 13–19.

13. How much combined tax should be withheld from the paycheck of a married employee earning $1,075 per week and claiming four withholding allowances?

14. How much combined tax should be withheld from the paycheck of a single employee earning $3,185 per month and claiming zero withholding allowances?

15. Jeremy Dunn is single, claims two withholding allowances, and earns $4,025 per month. Calculate the amount of Jeremy's paycheck after his employer withholds social security, Medicare, and federal income tax.

I.R.S.
AUDITS DIVISION

"I sympathize with your wife having multiple personality disorder but you can't claim each one as a dependent."

	Employee	Marital Status	Withholding Allowances	Pay Period	Gross Earnings	Combined Withholding
16.	Alton, A.	S	3	Monthly	$4,633	$886.43
17.	Emerson, P.	M	5	Weekly	$937	_____
18.	Reese, S.	M	4	Weekly	$1,172	_____
19.	Benson, K.	S	1	Monthly	$3,128	_____

BUSINESS DECISION: TAKE HOME PAY

20. You are the payroll manager for the Canyon Ridge Resort. Mark Kelsch, the marketing director, earns a salary of $43,200 per year, payable monthly. He is married and claims four withholding allowances. His social security number is 444-44-4444.

In addition to federal income tax, social security, and Medicare, Mark pays 2.3% state income tax, $\frac{1}{2}$% for state disability insurance (both based on gross earnings), $23.74 for term life insurance, $122.14 to the credit union, and $40 to the United Way.

Fill out the following payroll voucher for Mark for the month of April.

Canyon Ridge Resort

Payroll Voucher

Employee: _____   Tax Filing Status: _____
SSN: _____   Withholding Allowances: ___

Full-time Pay Period From _____ To _____

Primary Withholdings: Additional Withholdings:

Federal income tax   _____   _____
Social security   _____   _____
Medicare   _____   _____
State income tax   _____   _____
State disability   _____

Gross Earnings: _____
− Total withholdings: _____

NET PAY   _____

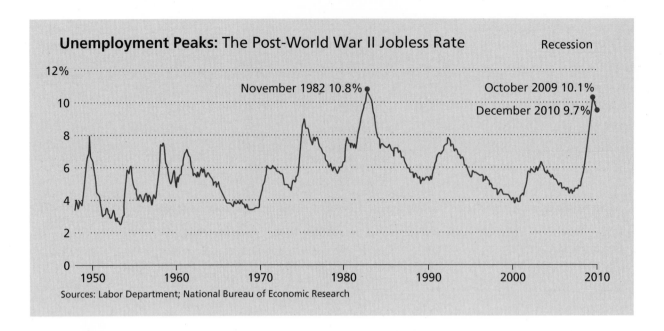

Unemployment Peaks: The Post-World War II Jobless Rate

Sources: Labor Department; National Bureau of Economic Research

SECTION III 9

EMPLOYER'S PAYROLL EXPENSES AND SELF-EMPLOYED PERSON'S TAX RESPONSIBILITY

To this point, we have discussed payroll deductions from the employee's point of view. Now let's take a look at the payroll expenses of the employer. According to the Fair Labor Standards Act, employers are required to maintain complete and up-to-date earnings records for each employee.

Employers are responsible for the payment of four payroll taxes: social security, Medicare, state unemployment tax (SUTA), and federal unemployment tax (FUTA). In addition, most employers are responsible for a variety of **fringe benefits** that are offered to their employees. These are benefits over and above an employee's normal earnings and can be a significant expense to the employer. Some typical examples are retirement plans, stock option plans, holiday leave, sick days, health and dental insurance, and tuition reimbursement. This section deals with the calculation of these employer taxes as well as the tax responsibility of self-employed persons.

fringe benefits Employer-provided benefits and service packages over and above an employee's paycheck, such as pension funds, paid vacations, sick leave, and health insurance.

9-8 COMPUTING FICA TAX FOR EMPLOYERS AND SELF-EMPLOYMENT TAX FOR SELF-EMPLOYED PERSONS

FICA TAX FOR EMPLOYERS

Employers are required to *match* all FICA tax payments, both social security and Medicare, made by each employee. For example, if a company withheld a total of $23,000 in FICA taxes from its employee paychecks this month, the company would be responsible for a matching share of $23,000.

EXAMPLE13 COMPUTING FICA TAX FOR EMPLOYEES AND THE EMPLOYER

Spectrum Engineering has 25 employees, each with gross earnings of $250 per week.

a. What are the total FICA (social security and Medicare) taxes that should be withheld from each employee's weekly paycheck?

b. At the end of the first quarter (13 weeks), what were the accumulated totals of the employee's share and the matching taxes for FICA that Spectrum had sent to the IRS?

SOLUTIONSTRATEGY

To solve for the total FICA tax due quarterly from the employees and the employer, calculate the tax due per employee per week, multiply by 25 to find the total weekly FICA for all employees, and multiply by 13 weeks to find the total quarterly amount withheld from all employees. The employer's share will be an equal amount.

a. Social security tax = Gross earnings × 6.2% = 250 × .062 = $15.50
    Medicare tax = Gross earnings × 1.45% = 250 × .0145 = $3.63
    Total FICA tax per employee per week = 15.50 + 3.63 = $19.13

b. Total FICA tax per week = FICA tax per employee × 25 employees
    Total FICA tax per week = 19.13 × 25 = $478.25

    Total FICA tax first quarter = Total FICA tax per week × 13 weeks
    Total FICA tax first quarter = 478.25 × 13 = 6,217.25

    Total FICA tax first quarter—Employee's share = $6,217.25
    Total FICA tax first quarter—Employer's share = $6,217.25

TRYITEXERCISE13

Big Pine Tree Service has 18 employees, 12 with gross earnings of $350 per week and 6 with gross earnings of $425 per week. What are the employee's share and the employer's share of the social security and Medicare tax for the first quarter of the year?

CHECK YOUR ANSWERS WITH THE SOLUTIONS ON PAGE 299.

SELF-EMPLOYMENT TAX

The self-employment tax, officially known as the Self-Employment Contributions Act (SECA) tax, is the self-employed person's version of the FICA tax. It is due on the net earnings from self-employment.

Self-employed persons are responsible for social security and Medicare taxes at twice the rate deducted for employees. Technically, they are the employee and the employer and therefore must pay both shares. For a self-employed person, the social security and Medicare tax rates are twice the normal rates, as follows:

	Tax Rate	Wage Base
Social Security	12.4% (6.2% × 2)	$106,800
Medicare	2.9% (1.45% × 2)	No limit

EXAMPLE14 CALCULATING SELF-EMPLOYMENT TAX

What are the social security and Medicare taxes of a self-employed landscaper with net earnings of $43,800 per year?

SOLUTIONSTRATEGY

To find the amount of self-employment tax due, we apply the self-employed tax rates, 12.4% for social security and 2.9% for Medicare, to the net earnings.

Social security tax = Net earnings × Tax rate

Social security tax = 43,800 × .124 = $5,431.20

Medicare tax = Net earnings × Tax rate

Medicare tax = 43,800 × .029 = $1,270.20

● TRYITEXERCISE14

Les Roberts, a self-employed commercial artist, had total net earnings of $60,000 last year. What was the amount of the social security and Medicare taxes Les was required to send the IRS last year?

CHECK YOUR ANSWERS WITH THE SOLUTIONS ON PAGE 299.

9-9 COMPUTING THE AMOUNT OF STATE UNEMPLOYMENT TAX (SUTA) AND FEDERAL UNEMPLOYMENT TAX (FUTA)

Federal Unemployment Tax Act (FUTA) A federal tax that is paid by employers for each employee to provide unemployment compensation to workers who have lost their jobs.

State Unemployment Tax Act (SUTA) A state tax that is paid by employers for each employee to provide unemployment compensation to workers who have lost their jobs.

The **Federal Unemployment Tax Act (FUTA)**, together with state unemployment systems, provides for payments of unemployment compensation to workers who have lost their jobs. Most employers are responsible for both a federal and a state unemployment tax.

In 2010, the FUTA tax was 6.2% of the first $7,000 of wages paid to each employee during the year. Generally, an employer can take a credit against the FUTA tax for amounts paid into state unemployment funds. These state taxes are commonly known as the **State Unemployment Tax Act (SUTA)**. This credit cannot be more than 5.4% of the first $7,000 of employees' taxable wages.

SUTA tax rates vary from state to state according to the employment record of the company. These merit-rating systems found in many states provide significant SUTA tax savings to companies with good employment records.

For companies with full and timely payments to the state unemployment system, the FUTA tax rate used in this chapter will be .8% (6.2% FUTA rate − 5.4% SUTA credit).

● EXAMPLE15 CALCULATING SUTA AND FUTA TAXES

Uniphase Industries, Inc., had a total payroll of $50,000 last month. Uniphase pays a SUTA tax rate of 5.4% and a FUTA rate of 6.2% less the SUTA credit. If none of the employees had reached the $7,000 wage base, what is the amount of SUTA and FUTA tax the company must pay?

● SOLUTIONSTRATEGY

To calculate the SUTA and FUTA taxes, apply the appropriate tax rates to the gross earnings subject to the tax, in this case, all the gross earnings.

$$\text{SUTA tax} = \text{Gross earnings} \times 5.4\%$$
$$\text{SUTA tax} = 50,000 \times .054 = \underline{\$2,700}$$

The FUTA tax rate will be .8%. Remember, it is actually 6.2% less the 5.4% credit.

$$\text{FUTA tax} = \text{Gross earnings} \times .8\%$$
$$\text{FUTA tax} = 50,000 \times .008 = \underline{\$400}$$

● TRYITEXERCISE15

Sunshine Catering had a total payroll of $10,000 last month. Sunshine pays a SUTA tax rate of 5.4% and a FUTA rate of 6.2% less the SUTA credit. If none of the employees had reached the $7,000 wage base, what is the amount of SUTA and FUTA tax the company must pay?

CHECK YOUR ANSWERS WITH THE SOLUTIONS ON PAGE 299.

CALCULATING EMPLOYER'S FRINGE BENEFIT EXPENSES

9-10

In addition to compensating employees with a paycheck, most companies today offer employee fringe benefit and services packages. These packages include a wide variety of benefits such as pension plans, paid vacations and sick leave, day-care centers, tuition assistance, and health insurance. Corporate executives may receive benefits such as company cars, first-class airline travel, and country club memberships. At the executive level of business, these benefits are known as **perquisites**, or **perks**.

Over the past decade, employee benefits have become increasingly important to workers. They have grown in size to the point where today total benefits may cost a company as much as 40% to 50% of payroll. Frequently, employees are given a *menu* of fringe benefits from which to choose up to a specified dollar amount. These plans are known as **cafeteria-style** or **flexible benefit programs**.

perquisites, or **perks** Executive-level fringe benefits such as first-class airline travel, company cars, and country club membership.

cafeteria-style or **flexible benefit program** A plan whereby employees are given a menu of fringe benefits from which to choose up to a specified dollar amount.

STEPS TO CALCULATE EMPLOYER'S FRINGE BENEFITS EXPENSE

STEP 1. If the fringe benefit is a percent of gross payroll, multiply that percent by the amount of the gross payroll. If the fringe benefit is a dollar amount per employee, multiply that amount by the number of employees.

STEP 2. Find the total fringe benefits by adding all the individual fringe benefit amounts.

STEP 3. Calculate the fringe benefit percent by using the percentage formula Rate = Portion ÷ Base with total fringe benefits as the portion and gross payroll as the base (remember to convert your answer to a percent).

$$\text{Fringe benefit percent} = \frac{\text{Total fringe benefits}}{\text{Gross payroll}}$$

EXAMPLE 16 CALCULATING FRINGE BENEFITS

In addition to its gross payroll of $150,000 per month, Premier Distributors, Inc., with 75 employees, pays 7% of payroll to a retirement fund, 9% for health insurance, and $25 per employee for a stock purchase plan.

a. What are the company's monthly fringe benefit expenses?

b. What percent of payroll does this represent?

SOLUTION STRATEGY

a. To solve for monthly fringe benefits, compute the amount of each benefit and add them to find the total.

Retirement fund expense = Gross payroll × 7%
Retirement fund expense = 150,000 × .07 = $10,500

Health insurance expense = Gross payroll × 9%
Health insurance expense = 150,000 × .09 = $13,500

Stock plan expense = Number of employees × $25
Stock plan expense = 75 × 25 = $1,875

Total fringe benefits = Retirement + Health + Stock
Total fringe benefits = 10,500 + 13,500 + 1,875 = $25,875

b. $\text{Fringe benefit percent} = \dfrac{\text{Total fringe benefits}}{\text{Gross payroll}} = \dfrac{25,875}{150,000} = .1725 = \underline{17.25\%}$

Photo by Robert Brechner

Paid vacation time is one of the many fringe benefits offered by employers today.

● TRYITEXERCISE16

Dynamo Productions employs 250 workers with a gross payroll of $123,400 per week. Fringe benefits are 5% of gross payroll for sick days and holiday leave, 8% for health insurance, and $12.40 per employee for dental insurance.

a. What is the total weekly cost of fringe benefits for Dynamo?

b. What percent of payroll does this represent?

c. What is the cost of these fringe benefits to the company for a year?

CHECK YOUR ANSWERS WITH THE SOLUTIONS ON PAGE 299.

9-11 CALCULATING QUARTERLY ESTIMATED TAX FOR SELF-EMPLOYED PERSONS

By IRS rules, you must pay self-employment tax if you had net earnings of $400 or more as a self-employed person. This is income that is not subject to withholding tax. Quarterly estimated tax is the method used to pay tax on these earnings. You may pay all of your estimated tax by April or in four equal amounts: in April, June, September, and January of the following year.

To calculate the quarterly estimated tax of a self-employed person, we divide the total of social security, Medicare, and income tax by 4. (There are 4 quarters in a year.) Internal Revenue Service form 1040 ES, Quarterly Estimated Tax Payment Voucher, Exhibit 9-5, is used to file this tax with the IRS each quarter.

$$\text{Quarterly estimated tax} = \frac{\text{Social security} + \text{Medicare} + \text{Income tax}}{4}$$

EXHIBIT 9-5 Quarterly Estimated Tax Payment Voucher

Form 1040-ES	**20XX** Payment Voucher **4**		OMB No. 1545-0087
Department of the Treasury Internal Revenue Service			

File only if you are making a payment of estimated tax by check or money order. Mail this voucher with your check or money order payable to the **"United States Treasury."** Write your social security number and "20XX Form 1040-ES" on your check or money order. Do not send cash. Enclose, but do not staple or attach, your payment with this voucher.

Calendar year—Due Jan. 15,

Amount of estimated tax you are paying by check or money order. $

Type or print	Your first name and initial	Your last name	Your social security number
	If joint payment, complete for spouse		
	Spouse's first name and initial	Spouse's last name	Spouse's social security number
	Address (number, street, and apt. no.)		
	City, state, and ZIP code (If a foreign address, enter city, province or state, postal code, and country.)		

For Privacy Act and Paperwork Reduction Act Notice, see instructions on page 5.

Page 6

EXAMPLE 17   CALCULATING QUARTERLY ESTIMATED TAX FOR SELF-EMPLOYED PERSONS

Ben Qualls is a self-employed marketing consultant. His estimated annual earnings this year are $110,000. His social security tax rate is 12.4% up to the wage base, Medicare is 2.9%, and his estimated federal income tax rate is 18%. How much estimated tax must he send to the IRS each quarter?

SOLUTIONSTRATEGY

Note that Ben's salary is above the social security wage base limit.

Social security $= 106,800 \times .124 = \$13,243.20$

Medicare $= 110,000 \times .029 = \$3,190.00$

Income tax $= 110,000 \times .18 = \$19,800.00$

$$\text{Quarterly estimated tax} = \frac{\text{Social security} + \text{Medicare} + \text{Income tax}}{4}$$

$$\text{Quarterly estimated tax} = \frac{13,243.20 + 3,190.00 + 19,800.00}{4} = \frac{36,233.20}{4} = \underline{\$9,058.30}$$

TRYITEXERCISE 17

Howard Lockwood is a self-employed freelance editor and project director for a large publishing company. His annual salary this year is estimated to be $120,000 with a federal income tax rate of 20%. What is the amount of estimated tax Howard must send to the IRS each quarter?

CHECK YOUR ANSWER WITH THE SOLUTION ON PAGE 299.

REVIEW EXERCISES   SECTION III   9

1. Westside Auto Supply has 8 delivery truck drivers, each with gross earnings of $570 per week.

   a. What are the total social security and Medicare taxes that should be withheld from these employees' paychecks each week?

   $570 \times 8 = \$4,560$ Gross earnings per week

   $4,560 \times .062 = \underline{\$282.72}$ Total social security

   $4,560 \times .0145 = \underline{\$66.12}$ Total Medicare

   b. What is the employer's share of these taxes for these employees for the first quarter of the year?

   $282.72 \times 13 = \underline{\$3,675.36}$ Social security for the first quarter

   $66.12 \times 13 = \underline{\$859.56}$ Medicare for the first quarter

2. Fandango Furniture Manufacturing, Inc., has 40 employees on the assembly line, each with gross earnings of $325 per week.

   a. What are the total social security and Medicare taxes that should be withheld from the employees' paychecks each week?

   b. What is the employer's share of these taxes for the first quarter of the year for these employees?

3. Arrow Asphalt & Paving Company has 24 employees, 15 with gross earnings of $345 per week and nine with gross earnings of $385 per week. What is the total social security and Medicare tax the company must send to the Internal Revenue Service for the first quarter of the year?

4. What are the social security and Medicare taxes due on gross earnings of $53,200 per year for Tricia Marvel, a self-employed commercial artist?

   $53,200 \times .124 = \underline{\$6,596.80}$ Social security

   $53,200 \times .029 = \underline{\$1,542.80}$ Medicare

5. What are the social security and Medicare taxes due on gross earnings of $42,600 per year for a self-employed person?

6. Lee Sutherlin is a self-employed electrical consultant. He estimates his annual net earnings at $38,700. How much social security and Medicare must he pay this year?

7. Barry Michaels earns $36,500 per year as the housewares manager at the Home Design Center.

   a. If the SUTA tax rate is 5.4% of the first $7,000 earned each year, how much SUTA tax must the company pay each year for Barry?

      $7,000 \times .054 = \underline{\$378}$ SUTA annually

   b. If the FUTA tax rate is 6.2% of the first $7,000 earned in a year minus the SUTA tax paid, how much FUTA tax must the company pay each year for Barry?

      $7,000 \times .008 = \underline{\$56}$ FUTA annually

8. Dave O'Bannon earns $41,450 annually as a line supervisor for Redwood Manufacturers.

   a. If the SUTA tax rate is 5.4% of the first $7,000 earned in a year, how much SUTA tax must Redwood pay each year for Dave?

   b. If the FUTA tax rate is 6.2% of the first $7,000 earned in a year minus the SUTA tax paid, how much FUTA tax must the company pay each year for Dave?

9. Tanya Willis worked part time last year as a cashier in a Safeway Supermarket. Her total gross earnings were $6,443.

   a. How much SUTA tax must the supermarket pay to the state for Tanya?

   b. How much FUTA tax must be paid for her?

10. Amazon Appliance Company has three installers. Larry earns $355 per week, Curly earns $460 per week, and Moe earns $585 per week. The company's SUTA rate is 5.4%, and the FUTA rate is 6.2% minus the SUTA. As usual, these taxes are paid on the first $7,000 of each employee's earnings.

    a. How much SUTA and FUTA tax does Amazon owe for the first quarter of the year?

    b. How much SUTA and FUTA tax does Amazon owe for the second quarter of the year?

11. Jiffy Janitorial Service employs 48 workers and has a gross payroll of $25,200 per week. Fringe benefits are 6.4% for sick days and holiday leave, 5.8% for health and hospital insurance, and $14.50 per employee per week for uniform allowance.

    a. What is the total weekly cost of fringe benefits for Jiffy?

$$25,200 \times .064 = \$1,612.80$$
$$25,200 \times .058 = 1,461.60$$
$$48 \times 14.50 = \underline{696.00}$$
$$\underline{\$3,770.40}$$

    b. What percent of payroll does this represent?

$$R = \frac{P}{B} = \frac{3,770.40}{25,200.00} = .1496 = \underline{\underline{15\%}}$$

    c. What is Jiffy's annual cost of fringe benefits?

$$3,770.40 \times 52 = \underline{\$196,060.80} \text{ Annual cost of fringe benefits}$$

12. North Beach Limousine Service employs 166 workers and has a gross payroll of $154,330 per week. Fringe benefits are $4\frac{1}{2}\%$ of gross payroll for sick days and maternity leave, 7.4% for health insurance, 3.1% for the retirement fund, and $26.70 per employee per week for a stock purchase plan.

    a. What is the total weekly cost of fringe benefits for the company?

    b. What percent of payroll does this represent? Round to the nearest tenth of a percent.

    c. What is the company's annual cost of fringe benefits?

"IT CONTAINS QUARTERLY ESTIMATED TAX FORMS FROM THE I.R.S."

Harley Schwadron/Cartoon Stock

13. Marc Batchelor, a self-employed sales consultant, has estimated annual earnings of $300,000 this year. His social security tax rate is 12.4% up to the wage base, Medicare is 2.9%, and his federal income tax rate is 24%.

   a. How much estimated tax must Marc send to the IRS each quarter?

   b. What form should he use?

BUSINESS DECISION: NEW FRINGE BENEFITS

14. You are the Human Resource Manager for Sunlink International, a cellular phone company with 800 employees. Top management has asked you to implement three additional fringe benefits that were negotiated with employee representatives and agreed upon by a majority of the employees. These include group term life insurance, a group legal services plan, and a wellness center.

   The life insurance is estimated to cost $260 per employee per quarter. The legal plan will cost $156 semiannually per employee. The company will contribute 40% to the life insurance premium and 75% to the cost of the legal services plan. The employees will pay the balance through payroll deductions from their biweekly paychecks. In addition, they will be charged $\frac{1}{4}$% of their gross earnings per paycheck for maintaining the wellness center. The company will pay the initial cost of $500,000 to build the center. This expense will be spread over 5 years.

   a. What total amount should be deducted *per paycheck* for these new fringe benefits for an employee earning $41,600 per year?

   b. What is the total *annual* cost of the new fringe benefits to Sunlink?

© moodboard/Alamy

Human Resource managers handle or oversee all aspects of human resources work. Typical areas of responsibility include unemployment compensation, fringe benefits, training, and employee relations. They held about 904,900 jobs in 2008, with median annual earnings of $96,130. The middle 50% earned between $73,480 and $126,050.

CHAPTER FORMULAS

Hourly Wages

Regular pay = Hourly rate × Regular hours worked

Overtime pay = Hourly rate × Overtime factor × Overtime hours worked

Total gross pay = Regular pay + Overtime pay

Piecework

Total gross pay = Output quantity × Rate per unit

Commission

Total gross pay = Total sales × Commission rate

Payroll Deductions

Total deductions = Social security + Medicare + Income tax + Voluntary deductions

Net pay = Gross pay − Total deductions

Fringe Benefits

$$\text{Fringe benefit percent} = \frac{\text{Total fringe benefits}}{\text{Gross payroll}}$$

Quarterly Estimated Tax

$$\text{Quarterly estimated tax} = \frac{\text{Social security} + \text{Medicare} + \text{Income tax}}{4}$$

CHAPTER SUMMARY

Section I: Employee's Gross Earnings and Incentive Pay Plans

Topic	Important Concepts	Illustrative Examples
Prorating Annual Salary to Various Pay Periods **Performance Objective 9-1, Page 266**	Salaried employees are most commonly paid based on one of the following pay schedules: *Weekly:* 52 paychecks per year Annual salary ÷ 52 *Biweekly:* 26 paychecks per year Annual salary ÷ 26 *Semimonthly:* 24 paychecks per year Annual salary ÷ 24 *Monthly:* 12 paychecks per year Annual salary ÷ 12	What are the gross earnings of an employee with an annual salary of $40,000 based on weekly, biweekly, semimonthly, and monthly pay schedules? Weekly = $\frac{40,000}{52}$ = $769.233 Biweekly = $\frac{40,000}{26}$ = $1,538.46 Semimonthly = $\frac{40,000}{24}$ = $1,666.67 Monthly = $\frac{40,000}{12}$ = $3,333.33
Calculating Gross Pay by Regular Hourly Wages and Overtime **Performance Objective 9-2, Page 267**	An hourly wage is the amount an employee is paid for each hour worked. Regular time specifies that a standard work week is 40 hours. Overtime amounting to at least time-and-a-half must be paid for all hours over 40. Some employers pay double time for weekend, holiday, and midnight shifts. Regular pay = Hourly rate × Hours worked Overtime pay = Hourly rate × Overtime factor × Hours worked Total gross pay = Regular pay + Overtime pay	Sami Brady earns $9.50 per hour as a supervisor in a plant. If her overtime rate is time-and-a-half and holidays are double time, what is Sami's total gross pay for working 49 hours last week, including 4 holiday hours? Regular pay = 9.50 × 40 = $380.00 Time-and-a-half pay = 9.50 × 1.5 × 5 = $71.25 Double-time pay = 9.50 × 2 × 4 = $76.00 Total gross pay = 380.00 + 71.25 + 76.00 = $527.25

Section I (continued)

Topic	Important Concepts	Illustrative Examples
Calculating Gross Pay by Straight and Differential Piecework Schedules **Performance Objective 9-3, Page 268**	A piecework pay rate schedule is based on production output, not time. Straight piecework pays the worker a certain amount of pay per unit regardless of quantity. In differential piecework, the rate per unit increases as output quantity goes up. Total gross pay = Output quantity × Rate per unit	Chemical Labs pays its workers $2.50 per unit of production. What is the gross pay of a worker producing 233 units? Gross pay = 233 × 2.50 = $582.50 Fortune Manufacturing pays its production workers $0.54 per unit up to 5,000 units and $0.67 per unit above 5,000 units. What is the gross pay of an employee who produces 6,500 units? 5,000 × .54 = 2,700 1,500 × .67 = 1,005 Total gross pay $3,705
Calculating Gross Pay by Straight and Incremental Commission **Performance Objective 9-4, Page 270**	Commission is a method of compensation primarily used to pay employees who sell goods and services. Straight commission is based on a single specified percentage of the sales volume attained. Incremental commission, like differential piecework, is when various levels of sales earn increasing rates of commission. Total gross pay = Total sales × Commission rate	Horizon Products pays 4% straight commission on all sales. What is the gross pay of an employee who sells $135,000? Gross pay = 135,000 × .04 = $5,400 Discovery Imports pays incremental commissions of 3.5% on sales up to $100,000 and 4.5% on all sales greater than $100,000. What is the gross pay of an employee selling $164,000? 100,000 × .035 = 3,500 64,000 × .045 = 2,880 Gross pay $6,380
Calculating Gross Pay by Salary Plus Commission **Performance Objective 9-4, Page 270**	Salary plus commission is a pay schedule whereby the employee receives a guaranteed salary in addition to a commission on sales over a specified amount.	An employee is paid a salary of $350 per week plus a 2% commission on sales greater than $8,000. If he sold $13,400 last week, how much did he earn? 350 + 2%(13,400 − 8,000) 350 + .02 × 5,400 350 + 108 = $458
Calculating Gross Pay with Drawing Accounts **Performance Objective 9-4, Page 270**	A drawing account, or draw against commission, is a commission paid in advance of sales and later deducted from the commission earned.	Steve Korb sells for a company that pays $6\frac{1}{2}\%$ commission with a $600 per month drawing account. If Steve takes the draw and then sells $16,400 in goods, how much commission is he owed? (16,400 × .065) − 600 1,066 − 600 = $466

Section II: Employee's Payroll Deductions

Topic	Important Concepts	Illustrative Examples
Computing FICA Taxes, Both Social Security and Medicare **Performance Objective 9-5, Page 276**	FICA taxes are divided into two categories: social security and Medicare. When employees reach the wage base for the year, they are no longer subject to the tax. 		Tax Rate	Wage Base
Social Security	6.2%	$106,800
Medicare	1.45%	no limit		What are the FICA tax withholdings for social security and Medicare for an employee with gross earnings of $760 per week? Social security = $760 × 6.2% = $47.12 Medicare = $760 × 1.45% = $11.02
Calculating Federal Income Tax Using Percentage Method	1. Multiply one withholding allowance, in Exhibit 9-1, by the number of allowances the employee claims.	Michelle Wolf is single, earns $1,800 per week as a loan officer for Bank of America, and claims three withholding allowances.

Section II (continued)

Topic	Important Concepts	Illustrative Examples
Performance Objective 9-6, Page 278	2. Subtract that amount from the employee's gross earnings to find the income subject to income tax. 3. Determine the amount of tax withheld from the appropriate section of Exhibit 9-2.	Calculate the amount of federal income tax withheld from Michelle's weekly paycheck. From Exhibit 9-1: $70.19 \times 3 = \$210.57$ Taxable income $=$ $1,800 - 210.57 = \$1,589.43$ From Exhibit 9-2: Withholding tax $=$ $234.60 + 27\%(1,589.43 - 1,302.00)$ $234.60 + .27(287.43)$ $234.60 + 77.61 = \underline{\$312.21}$
Determining an Employee's Total Withholding for Federal Income Tax, Social Security, and Medicare Using the Combined Wage Bracket Tables **Performance Objective 9-7, Page 281**	1. Based on marital status and payroll period, choose either Exhibit 9-3 or 9-4. 2. Scan down the left-hand columns until you find the bracket containing the gross pay of the employee. 3. Scan across the row of that wage bracket to the intersection of that employee's "withholding allowances claimed" column. 4. The number in that column on the wage bracket row is the amount of combined withholding tax.	What amount of combined tax should be withheld from the monthly paycheck of a single employee claiming two withholding allowances and earning \$3,495 per month? Use Exhibit 9-4. Scan down the wage brackets to \$3,480–\$3,520. Scan across to "2" withholding allowances to find the tax, $\underline{\$607.75}$.

Section III: Employer's Payroll Expenses and Self-Employed Person's Tax Responsibility

Topic	Important Concepts	Illustrative Examples
Computing FICA Tax for Employers **Performance Objective 9-8, Page 286**	Employers are required to match all FICA tax payments made by each employee.	Last month Midland Services withheld a total of \$3,400 in FICA taxes from employee paychecks. What is the company's FICA liability? The company is responsible for a matching amount withheld from the employees, $\underline{\$3,400}$.
Computing Self-Employment Tax **Performance Objective 9-8, Page 287**	Self-employed persons are responsible for social security and Medicare taxes at twice the rate deducted for employees. Technically, they are the employee and the employer; therefore, they must pay both shares, as follows: *Social Security* 12.4% (6.2% × 2), wage base \$106,800 *Medicare* 2.9% (1.45% × 2), no limit	What are the social security and Medicare taxes due on gross earnings of \$4,260 per month for a self-employed person? *Social security* Gross earnings × 12.4% = $4,260 \times .124 = \underline{\$528.24}$ *Medicare* Gross earnings × 2.9% = $4,260 \times .029 = \underline{123.54}$
Computing the Amount of State Unemployment Tax (SUTA) and Federal Unemployment Tax (FUTA) **Performance Objective 9-9, Page 288**	SUTA and FUTA taxes provide for unemployment compensation to workers who have lost their jobs. These taxes are paid by the employer. The SUTA tax rate is 5.4% of the first \$7,000 of earnings per year by each employee. The FUTA tax rate used in this chapter is 6.2% of the first \$7,000 minus the SUTA tax paid (6.2% − 5.4% = .8%).	Trans Lux, Inc., had a total payroll of \$40,000 last month. If none of the employees has reached the \$7,000 wage base, what is the amount of SUTA and FUTA tax due? $SUTA = 40,000 \times 5.4\% = \underline{\$2,160}$ $FUTA = 40,000 \times .8\% = \underline{\$320}$

Section III (continued)

Topic	Important Concepts	Illustrative Examples
Calculating Employer's Fringe Benefit Expenses **Performance Objective 9-10, Page 289**	In addition to compensating employees with a paycheck, most companies offer benefit packages that may include pensions, paid sick days, tuition assistance, and health insurance. Fringe benefits represent a significant expense to employers. $$\text{Fringe benefit percent} = \frac{\text{Total fringe benefits}}{\text{Gross payroll}}$$	Linear Industries employs 48 workers and has a monthly gross payroll of \$120,000. In addition, the company pays 6.8% to a pension fund, 8.7% for health insurance, and \$30 per employee for a stock purchase plan. What are Linear's monthly fringe benefit expenses? What percent of payroll does this represent? $120,000 \times 6.8\% = 8,160$ $120,000 \times 8.7\% = 10,440$ $48 \times \$30 = +1,440$ Total fringe benefits $\underline{\$20,040}$ $$\text{Fringe benefit \%} = \frac{20,040}{120,000} = \underline{16.7\%}$$
Calculating Quarterly Estimated Tax for Self-Employed Persons **Performance Objective 9-11, Page 290**	Each quarter self-employed persons must send to the IRS Form 1040-ES along with a tax payment for social security, Medicare, and income tax. Quarterly estimated tax $$= \frac{\text{Social security} + \text{Medicare} + \text{Income tax}}{4}$$	Amanda Turner is a self-employed decorator. She estimates her annual net earnings at \$44,000 for the year. Her income tax rate is 10%. What is the amount of her quarterly estimated tax? $44,000 \times .124 = \$5,456$ Social security $44,000 \times .029 = \$1,276$ Medicare $44,000 \times .10 = \$4,400$ Income tax $\text{Quarterly estimated tax} = \dfrac{5,456 + 1,276 + 4,400}{4}$ $= \dfrac{11,132}{4} = \underline{2,783}$

TRY IT: EXERCISE SOLUTIONS FOR CHAPTER 9

1. Weekly pay $= \dfrac{\text{Annual salary}}{50} = \dfrac{43,500}{52} = \underline{\$836.54}$

Biweekly pay $= \dfrac{\text{Annual salary}}{26} = \dfrac{43,500}{26} = \underline{\$1,673.08}$

Semimonthly pay $= \dfrac{\text{Annual salary}}{24} = \dfrac{43,500}{24} = \underline{1,812.50}$

Monthly pay $= \dfrac{\text{Annual salary}}{12} = \dfrac{43,500}{12} = \underline{\$3,625.00}$

2. Regular pay = Hourly rate × Regular hours worked

Regular pay $= 10.50 \times 40 = \underline{\$420}$

Time-and-a-half pay
   = Hourly rate × Overtime factor × Hours worked

Time-and-a-half pay $= 10.50 \times 1.5 \times 5 = \underline{\$78.75}$

Double time pay
   = Hourly rate × Overtime factor × Hours worked
Double time pay $= 10.50 \times 2 \times 4 = \underline{\$84}$

Total gross pay = Regular pay + Overtime pay
Total gross pay $= 420.00 + 78.75 + 84.00 = \underline{\$582.75}$

3. Total gross pay = Output quantity × Rate per unit

Total gross pay $= 950 \times .41 = \underline{\$389.50}$

4. Level pay = Output rate per piece
   Gomez: $300 \times .68 = \$204.00$
   $200 \times .79 = 158.00$
   $15 \times .86 = + 12.90$
   $\underline{\$374.90}$ Total gross pay

Clifford: $199 \times .68 = \underline{\$135.32}$ Total gross pay

Maken: $300 \times .68 = \$204.00$
   $148 \times .79 = +116.92$
   $\underline{\$320.92}$ Total gross pay

Nathan: $300 \times .68 = \$204.00$
   $200 \times .79 = 158.00$
   $250 \times .86 = 215.00$
   $54 \times .94 = + 50.76$
   $\underline{\$627.76}$ Total gross pay

5. Total gross pay = Total sales × Commission rate

Total gross pay $= 233,760 \times .024 = \underline{\$5,610.24}$

6. Level pay = Sales per level × Commission rate

Level pay $= 100,000 \times .017 = \$1,700$
   $84,600 \times .025 = +2,115$
   $\underline{\$,3815}$

7. Commission = Commission rate × Sales subject to commission

Commission $= 4\%(45,000 - 20,000)$

Commission $= .04 \times 25,000 = \$1,000$

Total gross pay = Salary + Commission
Total gross pay $= 1,400 + 1,000 = \underline{\$2,400}$

8. Commission = Total sales × Commission rate

Commission $= 120,000 \times 3.5\% = \$4,200$

Commission owed = Commission − Amount of draw
Commission owed $= 4,200 - 2,000 = \underline{\$2,200}$

9. Social security tax = Gross earnings × 6.2%

    Social security tax = 5,000 × .062 = $310

    Medicare tax = Gross earnings × 1.45%

    Medicare tax = 5,000 × .0145 = $72.50

10. Earnings subject to tax = Wage base − Year-to-date earnings

    Earnings subject to tax = 106,800 − 102,300 = $4,500

    Social security tax = Earnings subject to tax × 6.2%

    Social security tax = 4,500 × .062 = $279.00

11. From Exhibit 9-1

    Withholding allowance = 1 allowance × Exemptions

    Withholding allowance = $304.17 × 5 = $1,520.85

    Taxable income = Gross pay − Withholding allowance

    Taxable income = 3,670.00 − 1,520.85 = $2,149.15

    From Exhibit 9-2, Table 4(b):

    Category $2,042 to $6,313

    Withholding Tax = 89.60 + 15% of amount greater than $2,042

    Withholding Tax = 89.60 + .15(2,149.15 − 2,042.00)

    Withholding Tax = 89.60 + .15(107.15)

    Withholding Tax = 89.60 + 16.07 = $105.67

12. From Exhibit 9-3

    $835 Weekly, married, 2 allowances = $117.88

13. *12 employees @ $350*

    Social security = 350 × .062 = 21.70

    Medicare = 350 × .0145 = 5.08

    Total FICA per employee = 21.70 + 5.08 = $26.78

    Total FICA per week = 26.78 × 12 employees = $321.36

    Total FICA per quarter = 321.36 × 13 weeks = $4,177.68

    6 employees @ $425

    Social security = 425 × .062 = 26.35

    Medicare = 425 × .0145 = 6.16

    Total FICA per employee = 26.35 + 6.16 = $32.51

Total FICA per week = 32.51 × 6 employees = $195.06

Total FICA per quarter = 195.06 × 13 weeks = $2,535.78

Total FICA per quarter:

   Employees' share = 4,177.68 + 2,535.78 = $6,713.46
   Employer's share = 4,177.68 + 2,535.78 = $6,713.46

14. Social security = 60,000 × .124 = $7,440

    Medicare = 60,000 × .029 = $1,740

15. SUTA tax = Gross earnings × 5.4%
    SUTA tax = 10,000 × .054 = $540

    FUTA tax = Gross earnings × .8%
    FUTA tax = 10,000 × .008 = $80

16. **a.** Fringe benefits
    Sick days = Gross payroll × 5%
    Sick days = 123,400 × .05 = $6,170

    Health insurance = Gross payroll × 8%
    Health insurance = 123,400 × .08 = $9,872

    Dental insurance = Number of employees × 12.40
    Dental insurance = 250 × 12.40 = $3,100

    Total fringe benefits = 6,170 + 9,872 + 3,100 = $19,142

    b. Fringe benefit percent = $\dfrac{\text{Total fringe benefit}}{\text{Gross payroll}}$

    Fringe benefit percent = $\dfrac{19,142}{123,400}$ = .155 = 15.5%

    c. Yearly fringe benefits = Weekly total × 52
    Yearly fringe benefits = 19,142 × 52 = $995,384

17. Social security = 106,800 × .124 = $13,243.20
    Medicare = 120,000 × .029 = $3,480.00
    Income tax = 120,000 × .2 = $24,000.00

    Quarterly estimated tax = $\dfrac{\text{Social security} + \text{Medicare} + \text{Income tax}}{4}$

    Quarterly estimated tax = $\dfrac{13,243.20 + 3,480.00 + 24,000.00}{4}$

    $= \dfrac{40,723.20}{4} = \$10,180.80$

CONCEPT REVIEW

1. Gross pay is the amount of earnings before payroll _____ are withheld; net pay is the actual amount of the _____. (9.1)

2. Annual salaries are commonly prorated to be paid weekly, biweekly, _____ and _____. (9-1)

3. Total gross pay includes regular pay and _____ pay, which according to federal law is for hours worked over _____ hours per week. (9-2)

4. When employees are paid on their production output, not hours worked, this is called _____. (9-3)

5. To calculate total gross pay for an employee paid on commission, we multiply the total _____ by the commission rate. (9-4)

6. A draw against commission is commission paid in _____ of sales and later _____ from the commission earned. (9-4)

7. The current employee tax rate for social security is _____ percent of gross earnings; the current tax rate for Medicare is _____ percent of gross earnings. (9-5)

8. The 2010 wage base limit for social security was _____. (9-5)

9. In addition to social security and Medicare tax withholdings, an employer is also responsible, by federal law, for withholding an appropriate amount of federal _____ tax from each employee's paycheck. (9-6)

10. The combined wage bracket table is based on the _____ status of the employee and the _____ period used. The columns list the combined taxes to be withheld based on the number of withholding _____ claimed. (9-7)

11. Self-employed persons are responsible for social security and Medicare taxes at _____ the rate deducted for employees. This amounts to _____ percent for social security and _____ percent for Medicare. (9-8)

12. For companies with full and timely payments to the state unemployment system, the SUTA tax rate is _____ percent of gross earnings and the FUTA tax rate is _____ percent of gross earnings. (9-9)

13. A plan whereby employees are given a menu of fringe benefits from which to choose is known as the _____ style or _____ benefit program. (9-10)

14. Write the formula for quarterly estimated tax for self-employed persons. (9-11)

ASSESSMENT TEST

1. Bill Pearson earns $2,800 semimonthly as a congressional aide for a senator in the state legislature.

   a. How much are his annual gross earnings?

   b. If the senator switches pay schedules from semimonthly to biweekly, what will Bill's new gross earnings be per payroll period?

2. Barbara Sultan works 40 hours per week as a registered nurse. At the rate of $31.50 per hour, what are her gross weekly earnings?

3. Eric Shotwell's company pays him $18.92 per hour for regular time up to 40 hours and time-and-a-half for overtime. His time card for Monday through Friday last week had 8.3, 8.8, 7.9, 9.4, and 10.6 hours. What was Eric's total gross pay?

4. Mitch Anderson is a security guard. He earns $7.45 per hour for regular time up to 40 hours, time-and-a-half for overtime, and double time for the midnight shift. If Mitch worked 56 hours last week, including 4 on the midnight shift, how much were his gross earnings?

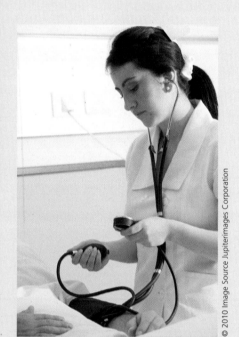

© 2010 Image Source/Jupiterimages Corporation

Registered nurses (RNs) treat patients, educate patients and the public about various medical conditions, and provide advice and emotional support to patients' family members. RNs record patients' per_____ _____stic tests and analyze results, operate medical machinery, administer treatment and medications, and help with patient follow-up and rehabilitation.

Overall job opportunities for registered nurses are excellent. Employment of registered nurses is expected to grow by 22 percent from 2008 to 2018, much faster than the average for all other occupations. According to the Bureau of Labor Statistics, in 2008, the median annual wages of registered nurses was $62,450.

5. Fergie Nelson assembles toasters for the Gold Coast Corporation. She is paid on a differential piecework rate of $2.70 per toaster for the first 160 toasters and $3.25 for each toaster over 160.

EXCEL

6. You work in the payroll department of Universal Manufacturing. The following piece rate schedule is used for computing earnings for assembly line workers. As an overtime bonus, on Saturdays, each unit produced counts as $1\frac{1}{2}$ units.

1–100	$2.30
101–150	2.60
151–200	2.80
over 200	3.20

Calculate the gross earnings for the following Universal Manufacturing employees.

Employee	Mon.	Tues.	Wed.	Thurs.	Fri.	Sat.	Total Units	Gross Earnings
a. Shane	0	32	16	36	27	12	_____	_____
b. Gonzales	18	26	24	10	13	0	_____	_____
c. Bethards	26	42	49	51	34	20	_____	_____

7. Kate Fitzgerald's company pays differential piecework for electronic product manufacturing. Production pay rates for a particular circuit board assembly and soldering are $18.20 per board for the first 14 boards, $19.55 each for boards 15–30, $20.05 each for boards 31–45, and $20.48 each for boards 46 and up. If Kate assembled and soldered 52 boards last week, what was her total gross pay?

8. Foremost Fish Market pays a straight commission of 18% on gross sales, divided equally among the three employees working the counter. If Foremost sold $22,350 in seafood last week, how much was each counter employee's total gross pay?

9. Bryan Vincent booked $431,000 in new sales last month. Commission rates are 1% for the first $150,000, 1.8% for the next $200,000, and 2.3% for amounts over $350,000. What was Bryan's total gross pay?

10. Spencer Morris works in the telemarketing division for a company that pays a salary of $735 per month plus a commission of $3\frac{1}{2}$% of all sales greater than $15,500. If he sold $45,900 last month, what was his total gross pay?

11. Bonnie Woodruff is on a 2.1% straight commission with a $700 drawing account. If she is paid the draw at the beginning of the month and then sells $142,100 during the month, how much commission is owed to Bonnie?

12. Arturo Muina is the captain on a charter fishing boat. He is paid a salary of $140 per day. He also averages tips amounting to 12% of the $475 daily charter rate. Last month during a fishing tournament, Arturo worked 22 days. What were his total gross earnings for the month?

Regardless of what they sell, **telemarketers** are responsible for initiating telephone sales calls to potential clients, using a prepared selling script. They are usually paid on a commission based on the amount of their sales volume or number of new "leads" they generate.

Wavebreakmedia Ltd/Shutterstock.com

CHAPTER 9

Solve the following problems using 6.2% up to $106,800 for social security withholding and 1.45% for Medicare.

13. What are the withholdings for social security and Medicare for an employee with gross earnings of $725 per week?

14. Dan Dietrich is an executive with Coronado Distributors. His gross earnings are $9,850 per month.

   a. What are the withholdings for social security and Medicare for Dan's January paycheck?

   b. In what month will his salary reach the social security wage base limit?

   c. What are the social security and Medicare tax withholdings for Dan in the month named in part b?

Use the *percentage method* to solve the following.

15. Larry Alison is single, claims one withholding allowance, and earns $2,450 per month.

   a. What is the amount of Larry's paycheck after his employer withholds social security, Medicare, and income tax?

IN THE BUSINESS WORLD

Consider the tax implications of a pay raise. In part c, Larry got a 15% raise, but his total deductions increased by 25.9%! His net pay raise, after taxes, was 13.4%

   b. If Larry gets married and changes to two withholding allowances, what will be the new amount of his paycheck?

   c. If he then gets a 15% raise, what is the new amount of his paycheck?

Use the *combined wage bracket tables*, Exhibits 9-3 and 9-4, for Exercises 16 and 17.

16. How much combined tax should be withheld from the paycheck of a married employee earning $910 per week and claiming three withholding allowances?

17. How much combined tax should be withheld from the paycheck of a single employee earning $4,458 per month and claiming zero withholding allowances?

18. Fran Mallory is married, claims five withholding allowances, and earns $3,500 per month. In addition to social security, Medicare, and FIT, Fran pays 2.1% state income tax, $\frac{1}{2}$% for state disability insurance (both based on gross income), $43.11 for life insurance, and $72.30 to the credit union. As payroll manager for Fran's company, calculate her net take-home pay per month.

19. Vanguard Fabricators has 83 employees on the assembly line, each with gross earnings of $329 per week.

    a. What are the total social security and Medicare taxes that should be withheld from the employee paychecks each week?

    b. At the end of the first quarter (13 weeks), what are the accumulated totals of the employee's share and the *matching* taxes for FICA that Vanguard had sent to the IRS?

20. Paul Warren is a self-employed mechanic. Last year he had total gross earnings of $44,260. What are Paul's quarterly social security and Medicare payments due to the IRS?

21. Tim Ries earns $48,320 annually as a supervisor for the Lakeside Bank.

    a. If the SUTA tax rate is 5.4% of the first $7,000 earned in a year, how much SUTA tax must the bank pay each year for Tim?

    b. If the FUTA tax rate is 6.2% of the first $7,000 earned in a year minus the SUTA tax paid, how much FUTA tax must the bank pay each year for Tim?

22. Universal Exporting has three warehouse employees: John Abner earns $422 per week, Anne Clark earns $510 per week, and Todd Corbin earns $695 per week. The company's SUTA tax rate is 5.4%, and the FUTA rate is 6.2% minus the SUTA. As usual, these taxes are paid on the first $7,000 of each employee's earnings.

    a. How much SUTA and FUTA tax did the company pay on these employees in the first quarter of the year?

    b. How much SUTA and FUTA tax did Universal pay in the second quarter of the year?

23. Sky High Crane Company employs 150 workers and has a gross payroll of $282,100 per week. Fringe benefits are $6\frac{1}{2}$% of gross payroll for sick days and holiday leave, 9.1% for health and hospital insurance, 4.6% for the retirement fund, and $10.70 per employee per week for a stock purchase plan.

   a. What is the total weekly cost of fringe benefits for the company?

   b. What percent of payroll does this represent?

   c. What is the company's annual cost of fringe benefits?

24. Ransford Alda is a self-employed security consultant with estimated annual earnings of $90,000. His social security tax rate is 12.4%, Medicare is 2.9%, and his federal income tax rate is 14%.

   a. How much estimated tax must Ransford send to the IRS each quarter?

   b. What form should he use?

BUSINESS DECISION: THE BRIDE, THE GROOM, AND THE TAX MAN

25. Two of your friends, Chuck and Joan, have been dating for a year. Chuck earns $3,000 per month as the manager of an Aeropostale store. Joan is a sophomore in college and is not currently working. They plan to marry but cannot decide whether to get married now or wait a year or two.

After studying the payroll chapter in your business math class, you inform Chuck that married couples generally pay less income taxes and that if they got married now instead of waiting, he would have less income tax withheld from his paychecks. Chuck's current tax filing status is single, one exemption. If he and Joan got married, he could file as married, two exemptions. Use the percentage method and Exhibits 9-1 and 9-2 to calculate the following:

   a. How much income tax is withheld from Chuck's paycheck each month now?

   b. How much income tax would be withheld from Chuck's check if he and Joan got married?

c. Assuming Joan has three more years of full-time college before going to work and Chuck expects a 10% raise in one year and a 15% raise the year after, what is the total three-year tax advantage of their getting married now?

COLLABORATIVE LEARNING ACTIVITY

Researching the Job Market

1. As a team, collect "Help Wanted" ads from the classified section of your local newspaper. (Note: Weekend editions are usually the most comprehensive.) Find examples of various jobs that are paid by salary, hourly rate, piece rate, and commission. Answer the following for similar jobs.

    a. How much do they pay?

    b. What pay periods are used?

    c. What fringe benefits are being offered?

2. As a team, research the Internet or library for the following payroll information. Present your findings to the class. List your sources for the answers.

    a. Starting salaries of employees in various industries and in government occupations.

    b. Personal and household income by area of the country or by state. How does your area or state compare?

    c. Starting salaries by amount of education for various professions.

THE ALPHABET OF INTERNET COMMERCE

E-COMMERCE

Electronic commerce, commonly known as e-commerce or e-business, consists of the buying and selling of products and services over the Internet. Electronic commerce that is conducted between businesses is referred to as business-to-business, or B2B. Electronic commerce that is conducted between businesses and consumers, on the other hand, is referred to as business-to-consumer, or B2C.

Online retailers are sometimes known as e-tailers, and online retail is referred to as e-tail. Today most big retailers have an electronic commerce presence on the Internet.

According to Forrester Research, in 2009,

- 154 million people in the United States bought something online, 4% more than in 2008.
- Three product categories—computers, apparel, and consumer electronics—represented more than 44 percent of online sales, amounting to $67.6 billion.
- While consumer goods worth $155 billion were bought online in 2009, $917 billion of in-store retail sales were generated by "Web-influenced" research.

Sources: www.wikipedia.org; http://techcrunch.com, Erick Schonfeld, Forrester Forecast, "Online Retail Sales Will Grow to $250 Billion by 2014," March 8, 2010.

U.S. Online Retail Sales Estimates ($ billions)

	2009	2010	2011	2012	2013	2014
Sales	$155.2	$172.9	$191.7	$210.0	$229.8	$248.7
% of total US retail sales	6%	7%	7%	7%	8%	8%

Source: Forrester Research

"Yes, I did the book report myself. I found it on eBay myself, I bid on it myself, I paid for it myself, I printed it myself..."

© Randy Glasbergen www.glasbergen.com

M-COMMERCE

Mobile commerce, also known as m-commerce, is the ability to conduct commerce using a mobile device, such as a mobile phone, a personal digital assistant (PDA), or a smartphone.

Mobile commerce began in 1997 when the first two mobile-phone-enabled Coca Cola vending machines were installed in the Helsinki area in Finland. The machines accepted payment via SMS text messages. The first banking service based on mobile phones was launched in 1997 by Merita Bank of Finland, also using SMS.

Sources: www.wikipedia.org; www.internetretailer.com, Paul Demery, "Big Retailers See Big Impact of Mobile on Web and Store Sales," Oct. 10, 2010.

TOP M-COMMERCE SITES
(by traffic)

Retailer	Unique Monthly Visitors (000)	Average Monthly Visits (per person)	Average Time per Visit (minutes)
eBay	6,400	7.5	10
Amazon	5,824	5.6	10
Walmart	2,299	4.2	10
Target	2,156	3.5	8
Barnes & Noble	1,253	4.6	10
Macy's	1,070	3.7	11

Source: The Nielsen Company, June 2010

ISSUES & ACTIVITIES

1. Use the chart at the left to respond to the following:
   a. Calculate the percent increase in sales from year to year to determine which year is estimated to have the greatest increase.
   b. In 2014, online retail sales of $248.7 billion are estimated to represent 8% of total retail sales. Using these figures, calculate the estimated total retail sales in 2014.
2. Use the chart above to answer the following questions:
   a. What percent of Amazon's monthly visitors is eBay's?
   b. What percent of Target's unique monthly visitors is Macy's?
3. In teams, research the Internet to find current trends in "Internet Commerce" statistics. List your sources and visually report your findings to the class.

BRAINTEASER – "WORK, DON'T WORK"

You have agreed to work under the conditions that you are to be paid $55 for every day you work and you must pay back $66 for every day you don't work. If after 30 days you have earned $924, how many days did you work?

See the end of Appendix A for the solution.

Simple Interest and Promissory Notes

UNDERSTANDING AND COMPUTING SIMPLE INTEREST

The practice of borrowing and lending money dates back in history for thousands of years. Today institutions such as banks, savings and loans, and credit unions are specifically in business to borrow and lend money. They constitute a significant portion of the service sector of the American economy.

Interest is the rental fee charged by a lender to a business or an individual for the use of money. The amount of interest charged is determined by three factors: the amount of money being borrowed or invested, known as the **principal**; the percent of interest charged on the money per year, known as the **rate**; and the length of time of the loan, known as **time**. The manner in which the interest is computed is an additional factor that influences the amount of interest. The two most commonly used methods in business today for computing interest are simple and compound.

Simple interest means that the interest is calculated *only once* for the entire time period of the loan. At the end of the time period, the borrower repays the principal plus the interest. Simple interest loans are usually made for short periods of time, such as a few days, weeks, or months. **Compound interest** means that the interest is calculated *more than once* during the time period of the loan. When compound interest is applied to a loan, each succeeding time period accumulates interest on the previous interest in addition to interest on the principal. Compound interest loans are generally for time periods of a year or longer.

This chapter discusses the concepts of simple interest; simple discount, which is a variation of a simple interest loan; and promissory notes. Chapter 11 covers the concepts and calculations related to compound interest and present value.

interest The price or rental fee charged by a lender to a borrower for the use of money.

principal A sum of money, either invested or borrowed, on which interest is calculated.

rate The percent that is charged or earned for the use of money per year.

time Length of time, expressed in days, months, or years, of an investment or loan.

simple interest Interest calculated solely on the principal amount borrowed or invested. It is calculated only once for the entire time period of the loan.

compound interest Interest calculated at regular intervals on the principal and previously earned interest. Covered in Chapter 11.

10-1   COMPUTING SIMPLE INTEREST FOR LOANS WITH TERMS OF YEARS OR MONTHS

Simple interest is calculated by using a formula known as the simple interest formula. It is stated as

$$\text{Interest} = \text{Principal} \times \text{Rate} \times \text{Time}$$
$$I = PRT$$

When using the simple interest formula, the time factor, T, must be expressed in years or a fraction of a year.

SIMPLE INTEREST FORMULA—YEARS OR MONTHS

Years

When the time period of a loan is a year or longer, use the number of years as the time factor, converting fractional parts to decimals. For example, the time factor for a 2-year loan is 2, 3 years is 3, $1\frac{1}{2}$ years is 1.5, $4\frac{3}{4}$ years is 4.75, and so on.

Months

When the time period of a loan is for a specified number of months, express the time factor as a fraction of a year. The number of months is the numerator, and 12 months (1 year) is the denominator. A loan for 1 month would have a time factor of $\frac{1}{12}$; a loan for 2 months would have a factor of $\frac{2}{12}$, or $\frac{1}{6}$; a 5-month loan would use $\frac{5}{12}$ as the factor; a loan for 18 months would use $\frac{18}{12}$, or $1\frac{1}{2}$, written as 1.5.

Banking institutions all over the world are in business specifically to borrow and lend money at a profitable rate of interest.

© dbimages/Alamy

EXAMPLE1 CALCULATING SIMPLE INTEREST

a. What is the amount of interest for a loan of $8,000 at 9% interest for 1 year?

SOLUTIONSTRATEGY

To solve this problem, we apply the simple interest formula:

$$\text{Interest} = \text{Principal} \times \text{Rate} \times \text{Time}$$
$$\text{Interest} = 8,000 \times 9\% \times 1$$
$$\text{Interest} = 8,000 \times .09 \times 1$$
$$\text{Interest} = \underline{\$720}$$

b. What is the amount of interest for a loan of $16,500 at $12\frac{1}{2}\%$ interest for 7 months?

SOLUTIONSTRATEGY

In this example, the rate is converted to .125 and the time factor is expressed as a fraction of a year, $\frac{7}{12}$.

$$\text{Interest} = \text{Principal} \times \text{Rate} \times \text{Time}$$
$$\text{Interest} = 16,500 \times .125 \times \frac{7}{12}$$
$$\text{Interest} = \underline{\$1,203.13}$$

Calculator Sequence: 16500 $\times$ .125 $\times$ 7 $\div$ 12 $=$ $\underline{\$1,203.13}$

TRYITEXERCISE1

Find the amount of interest on each of the following loans.

	Principal	Rate (%)	Time
a.	$4,000	7	$2\frac{1}{4}$ years
b.	$45,000	$9\frac{3}{4}$	3 months
c.	$130,000	10.4	42 months

CHECK YOUR ANSWERS WITH THE SOLUTIONS ON PAGE 337.

CALCULATING SIMPLE INTEREST FOR LOANS WITH TERMS OF DAYS BY USING THE EXACT INTEREST AND ORDINARY INTEREST METHODS

10-2

There are two methods for calculating the time factor, T, when applying the simple interest formula using days. Because time must be expressed in years, loans whose terms are given in days must be made into a fractional part of a year. This is done by dividing the days of a loan by the number of days in a year.

SIMPLE INTEREST FORMULA—DAYS

Exact Interest

The first method for calculating the time factor is known as **exact interest**. Exact interest uses *365 days* as the time factor denominator. This method is used by government agencies, the Federal Reserve Bank, and most credit unions.

$$\text{Time} = \frac{\text{Number of days of a loan}}{365}$$

exact interest Interest calculation method using 365 days (366 in leap year) as the time factor denominator.

ordinary interest, or **banker's rule**
Interest calculation method using 360 days as the time factor denominator.

Ordinary Interest

The second method for calculating the time factor is known as **ordinary interest**. Ordinary interest uses *360 days* as the denominator of the time factor. This method dates back to the time before electronic calculators and computers. In the past, when calculating the time factor manually, a denominator of 360 was easier to use than 365.

Regardless of today's electronic sophistication, banks and most other lending institutions still use ordinary interest because it yields a somewhat higher amount of interest than does the exact interest method. Over the years, ordinary interest has become known as the **banker's rule**.

$$\text{Time} = \frac{\text{Number of days of a loan}}{360}$$

EXAMPLE2 CALCULATING EXACT INTEREST

Using the exact interest method, what is the amount of interest on a loan of $4,000 at 7% interest for 88 days?

SOLUTIONSTRATEGY

Because we are looking for exact interest, we will use 365 days as the denominator of the time factor in the simple interest formula:

$$\text{Interest} = \text{Principal} \times \text{Rate} \times \text{Time}$$

$$\text{Interest} = 4,000 \times .07 \times \frac{88}{365}$$

$$\text{Interest} = 67.506849$$

$$\text{Interest} = \underline{\$67.51}$$

Calculator Sequence: 4000 × .07 × 88 ÷ 365 = $67.51

TRYITEXERCISE2

Joe Hale goes to a credit union and borrows $23,000 at 8% for 119 days. If the credit union calculates interest by the exact interest method, what is the amount of interest on the loan?

CHECK YOUR ANSWER WITH THE SOLUTION ON PAGE 337.

EXAMPLE3 CALCULATING ORDINARY INTEREST

Using the ordinary interest method, what is the amount of interest on a loan of $19,500 at 12% interest for 160 days?

SOLUTIONSTRATEGY

Because we are looking for ordinary interest, we will use 360 days as the denominator of the time factor in the simple interest formula:

$$\text{Interest} = \text{Principal} \times \text{Rate} \times \text{Time}$$

$$\text{Interest} = 19,500 \times .12 \times \frac{160}{360}$$

$$\text{Interest} = \underline{\$1,040}$$

Calculator Sequence: 19500 × .12 × 160 ÷ 360 = $1,040

TRYITEXERCISE3

Karen Mitroff goes to the bank and borrows $15,000 at $9\frac{1}{2}\%$ for 250 days. If the bank uses the ordinary interest method, how much interest will Karen have to pay?

CHECK YOUR ANSWER WITH THE SOLUTION ON PAGE 337.

CALCULATING THE MATURITY VALUE OF A LOAN

When the time period of a loan is over, the loan is said to mature. At that time, the borrower repays the original principal plus the interest. The total payback of principal and interest is known as the **maturity value** of a loan. Once the interest has been calculated, the maturity value can be found by using the formula:

> **Maturity value = Principal + Interest**
>
> $MV = P + I$

For example, if a loan for $50,000 had interest of $8,600, the maturity value would be found by adding the principal and the interest: 50,000 + 8,600 = $58,600.

Maturity value can also be calculated directly without first calculating the interest by using the following formula:

> **Maturity value = Principal(1 + Rate × Time)**
>
> $MV = P(1 + RT)$

10-3

maturity value The total payback of principal and interest of an investment or a loan.

LEARNINGTIP

When using the maturity value formula, $MV = P(1 + RT)$, the order of operation is

- Multiply Rate by Time
- Add the 1
- Multiply by the Principal

EXAMPLE4 CALCULATING MATURITY VALUE

What is the maturity value of a loan for $25,000 at 11% for $2\frac{1}{2}$ years?

SOLUTIONSTRATEGY

Because this example asks for the maturity value, not the amount of interest, we will use the formula for finding maturity value directly, $MV = P(1 + RT)$. Remember to multiply the rate and time first, then add the 1. Note that the time, $2\frac{1}{2}$ years, should be converted to the decimal equivalent 2.5 for ease in calculation.

Maturity value = Principal(1 + Rate × Time)
Maturity value = 25,000(1 + .11 × 2.5)
Maturity value = 25,000(1 + .275)
Maturity value = 25,000(1.275)
Maturity value = $31,875

TRYITEXERCISE4

a. What is the amount of interest and the maturity value of a loan for $15,400 at $6\frac{1}{2}$ % simple interest for 24 months? (Use the formula $MV = P + I$.)

b. Apollo Air Taxi Service borrowed $450,000 at 8% simple interest for 9 months to purchase a new airplane. Use the formula $MV = P(1 + RT)$ to find the maturity value of the loan.

CHECK YOUR ANSWERS WITH THE SOLUTIONS ON PAGE 337.

10-4

CALCULATING THE NUMBER OF DAYS OF A LOAN

loan date The first day of a loan.

due date or **maturity date** The last day of a loan.

The first day of a loan is known as the **loan date**, and the last day is known as the **due date** or **maturity date**. When these dates are known, the number of days of the loan can be calculated by using the "Days in Each Month" chart and the steps that follow.

Days in Each Month

28 Days	30 Days	31 Days
February (29 leap year)	April	January
	June	March
	September	May
	November	July
		August
		October
		December

STEPS FOR DETERMINING THE NUMBER OF DAYS OF A LOAN

STEP 1. Determine the number of days remaining in the first month by subtracting the loan date from the number of days in that month.

STEP 2. List the number of days for each succeeding whole month.

STEP 3. List the number of loan days in the last month.

STEP 4. Add the days from Steps 1, 2, and 3.

LEARNINGTIP

An alternative method for calculating the number of days of a loan is to use the Days-in-a-Year Calendar, Exhibit 7-6, page 215.

- Subtract the "day number" of the loan date from the "day number" of the maturity date.
- If the maturity date is in the next year, add 365 to that day number, then subtract. *Note:* In leap years, add 1 to the day numbers beginning with March 1.

EXAMPLE5 CALCULATING DAYS OF A LOAN

Kevin Krease borrowed money from the Charter Bank on August 18 and repaid the loan on November 27. What was the number of days of the loan?

SOLUTIONSTRATEGY

The number of days from August 18 to November 27 would be calculated as follows:

Step 1. Days remaining in first month

Aug. 31
Aug. −18
—————
13 ——→ August   13 days

Step 2. Days in succeeding whole months ——→ September   30 days
——→ October   31 days

Step 3. Days of loan in last month ——————→ November   +27 days

Step 4. Add the days   Total 101 days

TRYITEXERCISE5

a. A loan was made on April 4 and had a due date of July 18. What was the number of days of the loan?

b. Ryan McPherson borrowed $3,500 on June 15 at 11% interest. If the loan was due on October 9, what was the amount of interest on Ryan's loan using the exact interest method?

CHECK YOUR ANSWERS WITH THE SOLUTIONS ON PAGE 337.

DETERMINING THE MATURITY DATE OF A LOAN

10-5

When the loan date and number of days of the loan are known, the maturity date can be found as follows:

STEPS FOR DETERMINING THE MATURITY DATE OF A LOAN

STEP 1. Find the number of days remaining in the first month by subtracting the loan date from the number of days in that month.

STEP 2. Subtract the days remaining in the first month (Step 1) from the number of days of the loan.

STEP 3. Continue subtracting days in each succeeding whole month until you reach a month with a difference less than the total days in that month. At that point, the maturity date will be the day that corresponds to the difference.

EXAMPLE 6 — DETERMINING MATURITY DATE OF A LOAN

What is the maturity date of a loan taken out on April 14 for 85 days?

SOLUTION STRATEGY

Step 1. Days remaining in first month

	30 Days in April
	-14 Loan date April 14
Days remaining in April	16

Step 2. Subtract remaining days in first month from days of the loan

	85 Days of the loan
	-16 Days remaining in April
Difference	69

Step 3. Subtract succeeding whole months

	69 Difference
	-31 Days in May
Difference	38
	38 Difference
	-30 Days in June
Difference	8

At this point, the difference, 8, is less than the number of days in the next month, July; therefore, the maturity date is July 8.

TRY IT EXERCISE 6

a. What is the maturity date of a loan taken out on September 9 for 125 days?

b. On October 21, Jill Voorhis went to the Regal National Bank and took out a loan for $9,000 at 10% ordinary interest for 80 days. What is the maturity value and maturity date of this loan?

CHECK YOUR ANSWERS WITH THE SOLUTIONS ON PAGE 337.

REVIEW EXERCISES

SECTION I

10

Find the amount of interest on each of the following loans.

	Principal	Rate (%)	Time	Interest
1.	$5,000	8	2 years	$800.00
2.	$75,000	$10\frac{3}{4}$	6 months	_____
3.	$100,000	12.7	18 months	_____

	Principal	Rate (%)	Time	Interest
4.	$80,000	15	$3\frac{1}{2}$ years	_____
5.	$6,440	$5\frac{1}{2}$	7 months	_____
6.	$13,200	9.2	$4\frac{3}{4}$ years	_____

Use the exact interest method (365 days) and the ordinary interest method (360 days) to compare the amount of interest for the following loans.

	Principal	Rate (%)	Time (days)	Exact Interest	Ordinary Interest
7.	$45,000	13	100	$1,602.74	$1,625.00
8.	$184,500	$15\frac{1}{2}$	58	_____	_____
9.	$32,400	8.6	241	_____	_____
10.	$7,230	9	18	_____	_____
11.	$900	$10\frac{1}{4}$	60	_____	_____
12.	$100,000	10	1	_____	_____
13.	$2,500	12	74	_____	_____
14.	$350	14.1	230	_____	_____
15.	$50,490	$9\frac{1}{4}$	69	_____	_____
16.	$486,000	$13\frac{1}{2}$	127	_____	_____

Find the amount of interest and the maturity value of the following loans. Use the formula $MV = P + I$ to find the maturity values.

	Principal	Rate (%)	Time	Interest	Maturity Value
17.	$54,000	11.9	2 years	$12,852.00	$66,852.00
18.	$125,000	$12\frac{1}{2}$	5 months	_____	_____
19.	$33,750	8.4	10 months	_____	_____
20.	$91,000	$9\frac{1}{4}$	$2\frac{1}{2}$ years	_____	_____
21.	$56,200	10.2	4 years	_____	_____
22.	$135,000	7.7	18 months	_____	_____

Find the maturity value of the following loans. Use $MV = P(1 + RT)$ to find the maturity values.

	Principal	Rate (%)	Time	Maturity Value
23.	$1,500	9	2 years	$1,770.00
24.	$18,620	$10\frac{1}{2}$	30 months	_____
25.	$1,000,000	11	3 years	_____
26.	$750,000	13.35	11 months	_____
27.	$128,400	8.3	2.5 years	_____
28.	$5,200	14.8	16 months	_____

From the following information, determine the number of days of each loan.

	Loan Date	Due Date	Number of Days
29.	September 5	December 12	98
30.	June 27	October 15	_____
31.	January 23	November 8	_____
32.	March 9	July 30	_____
33.	August 3	September 27	_____
34.	November 18	March 2	_____

From the following information, determine the maturity date of each loan.

	Loan Date	Time of Loan (days)	Maturity Date
35.	October 19	45	December 3
36.	February 5	110	_____
37.	May 26	29	_____
38.	July 21	200	_____
39.	December 6	79	_____
40.	January 13	87	_____
41.	April 27	158	_____

Solve the following word problems. Round to the nearest cent when necessary.

42. On April 12, Michelle Lizaro borrowed $5,000 from her credit union at 9% for 80 days. The credit union uses the ordinary interest method.

   a. What is the amount of interest on the loan?

   b. What is the maturity value of the loan?

   c. What is the maturity date of the loan?

43. What is the maturity value of a $60,000 loan for 100 days at 12.2% interest using the exact interest method?

44. Central Auto Parts borrowed $350,000 at 9% interest on July 19 for 120 days.

   a. If the bank uses the ordinary interest method, what is the amount of interest on the loan?

   b. What is the maturity date?

45. Emil Benson missed an income tax payment of $9,000. The Internal Revenue Service charges a 13% simple interest penalty calculated by the exact interest method. If the tax was due on April 15 but was paid on August 19, what was the amount of the penalty charge?

46. At the City National Credit Union, a 7%, $8,000 loan for 180 days had interest charges of $276.16. What type of interest did City National use, ordinary or exact?

47. Kyle Rohrs borrowed $1,080 on June 16 at 9.2% exact interest from the Wells Fargo Bank. On August 10, Kyle repaid the loan. How much interest did he pay?

Credit unions differ from banks and other financial institutions in that the members who are account holders are the owners of the credit union. Credit unions serve groups that share something in common, such as where they work or where they live. The largest credit union in the United States is Navy Federal Credit Union in Vienna, Virginia, with $36.4 billion in assets and 3.2 million members.

According to the National Credit Union Administration, in 2010, there were over 7,950 federally insured credit unions in the United States with assets of over $679 billion and over 89.8 million members. As with banks, deposits are insured up to $250,000 per account.

BUSINESS DECISION: COMPETING BANKS

48. You are the accounting manager for Kool Ragz, Inc., a manufacturer of men's and women's clothing. The company needs to borrow $1,800,000 for 90 days in order to purchase a large quantity of material at "closeout" prices. The interest rate for such loans at your bank, Rimrock Bank, is 11% using ordinary interest.
    a. What is the amount of interest on this loan?

    b. After making a few "shopping" calls, you find that Southside National Bank will lend at 11% using exact interest. What is the amount of interest on this offer?

    c. So that you can keep your business, Rimrock Bank has offered a loan at 10.5% using ordinary interest. What is the amount of interest on this offer?

    d. (Challenge) If Southside National wants to beat Rimrock's last offer (part c) by charging $1,250 less interest, what rate, rounded to the nearest hundredths of a percent, must it quote using exact interest?

Banks are financial institutions that accept deposits and channel the money into lending activities such as business and personal loans, automobile loans, and mortgages.

Top banks in the United States based on assets in 2009 were Bank of America, $2.8 trillion; JP Morgan Chase, $2.175 trillion; Citigroup Inc., $1.9 trillion; Wells Fargo, $1.3 billion; PNC Financial Services, $291 billion; and U.S. Bancorp, $266 billion.

Losevsky Pavel/Shutterstock.com

SECTION II   **10**   USING THE SIMPLE INTEREST FORMULA

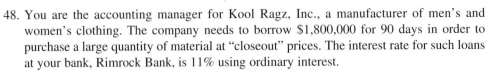

In Section I, we used the simple interest formula, $I = PRT$, to solve for the interest. Frequently in business, however, the principal, rate, or time might be the unknown factor. Remember from Chapter 5 that an equation can be solved for any of the variables by isolating that variable to one side of the equation. In this section, we convert the simple interest formula to equations that solve for each of the other variable factors.

If you find this procedure difficult to remember, use the magic triangle, as we did in Chapter 6, to calculate the portion, rate, and base. Remember, to use the Magic Triangle, cover the variable you are solving for and the new formula will "magically" appear!

Magic Triangle
Simple Interest Formula

$$I = PRT$$

10-6   ### SOLVING FOR THE PRINCIPAL

When using the simple interest formula to solve for principal, P, we isolate the P on one side of the equation by dividing both sides of the equation by RT. This yields the new equation:

$$\text{Principal} = \frac{\text{Interest}}{\text{Rate} \times \text{Time}} \qquad P = \frac{I}{RT}$$

We can also find the formula in the Magic Triangle by covering the unknown variable, P, as follows:

**Magic Triangle
Solving for Principal**

$$P = \frac{I}{RT}$$

EXAMPLE7 FINDING THE PRINCIPAL OF A LOAN

Allied Bank loaned Checkpoint Industries money at 8% interest for 90 days. If the amount of interest was $4,000, use the ordinary interest method to find the amount of principal borrowed.

SOLUTIONSTRATEGY

To solve for the principal, we use the formula $P = \frac{I}{RT}$.

$P = \frac{I}{RT}$ Substitute the known variables into the equation.

$P = \frac{4,000}{.08 \times \frac{90}{360}}$ Calculate the denominator first.
Calculator sequence: .08 [×] 90 [÷] 360 [=] [M+]

$P = \frac{4,000}{.02}$ Next, divide the numerator by the denominator.
Calculator sequence: 4000 [÷] [MR] [=] 200,000

Principal = $200,000   The company borrowed $200,000 from the bank.

TRYITEXERCISE7

Telex Electronics borrowed money at 9% interest for 125 days. If the interest charge was $560, use the ordinary interest method to calculate the amount of principal of the loan.

CHECK YOUR ANSWER WITH THE SOLUTION ON PAGE 337.

SOLVING FOR THE RATE

10-7

When we solve the simple formula for rate, the answer will be a decimal that must be converted to a percent. In business, interest rates are always expressed as a percent.

When the rate is the unknown variable, we isolate the R on one side of the equation by dividing both sides of the equation by PT. This yields the new equation:

$$\text{Rate} = \frac{\text{Interest}}{\text{Principal} \times \text{Time}} \qquad R = \frac{I}{PT}$$

We can also find the formula in the Magic Triangle by covering the unknown variable, R, as follows:

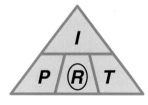

**Magic Triangle
Solving for Rate**

$$R = \frac{I}{PT}$$

EXAMPLE8 FINDING THE RATE OF A LOAN

Using the ordinary interest method, what is the rate of interest on a loan of $5,000 for 125 days if the amount of interest is $166? Round your answer to the nearest hundredth of a percent.

SOLUTIONSTRATEGY

To solve for the rate, we use the formula $R = \dfrac{I}{PT}$.

$R = \dfrac{I}{PT}$ Substitute the known variables into the equation.

$R = \dfrac{166}{5,000 \times \dfrac{125}{360}}$ Calculate the denominator first.

Calculator sequence: 5000 ⨯ 125 ÷ 360 = M+

Next, divide the numerator by the denominator.

$R = \dfrac{166}{1,736.111111}$ *Note:* Don't round the denominator.

Calculator sequence: 166 ÷ MR = .095616

$R = .095616$ Round the answer to the nearest hundredth percent.

Rate = 9.56%   The bank charged 9.56% interest.

TRYITEXERCISE8

Using the ordinary interest method, what is the rate of interest on a loan of $25,000 for 245 days if the amount of interest is $1,960? Round your answer to the nearest hundredth of a percent.

CHECK YOUR ANSWER WITH THE SOLUTION ON PAGE 337.

10-8

SOLVING FOR THE TIME

When solving the simple interest formula for time, a whole number in the answer represents years and a decimal represents a portion of a year. The decimal should be converted to days by multiplying it by 360 for ordinary interest or by 365 for exact interest. Lending institutions consider any part of a day to be a full day. Therefore, any fraction of a day is rounded up to the next higher day even if it is less than .5.

For example, an answer of 3 means 3 years. An answer of 3.22 means 3 years and .22 of the next year. Assuming ordinary interest, multiply the decimal portion of the answer, .22, by 360. This gives 79.2, which represents the number of days. The total time of the loan would be 3 years and 80 days. Remember to always round up any fraction of a day.

When using the simple interest formula to solve for time, T, we isolate the T on one side of the equation by dividing both sides of the equation by PR. This yields the new equation:

$$\text{Time} = \frac{\text{Interest}}{\text{Principal} \times \text{Rate}} \qquad T = \frac{I}{PR}$$

We can also find the formula in the Magic Triangle by covering the unknown variable, T, as follows:

LEARNINGTIP

Remember, when time, T, is calculated, any fraction of a day is rounded up to the next higher day even if it is less than .5.

For example, 25.1 days would round up to 26 days.

Magic Triangle Solving for Time

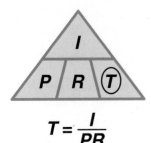

$$T = \frac{I}{PR}$$

EXAMPLE9 FINDING THE TIME PERIOD OF A LOAN

What would be the time period of a loan for $7,600 at 11% ordinary interest if the amount of interest is $290?

SOLUTIONSTRATEGY

To solve for the time, we use the formula $T = \dfrac{I}{PR}$.

$T = \dfrac{I}{PR}$ Substitute the known variables into the equation.

$T = \dfrac{290}{7,600 \times .11}$ Calculate the denominator first.
Calculator sequence: 7600 ☒ .11 ═ M+

$T = \dfrac{290}{836}$ Next, divide the numerator by the denominator.
Calculator sequence: 290 ÷ MR ═ .3468899

$T = .3468899$ years Because the answer is a decimal, the time is less than 1 year. Using ordinary interest, we multiply the entire decimal by 360 to find the number of days of the loan.

$T = .3468899 \times 360$ Calculator Sequence: .3468899 ☒ 360 ═ 124.8 or <u>125 days</u>

Time = 124.8 days, or <u>125 days</u>

TRYITEXERCISE9

What is the time period of a loan for $15,000 at 9.5% ordinary interest if the amount of interest is $650?

CHECK YOUR ANSWER WITH THE SOLUTION ON PAGE 337.

CALCULATING LOANS INVOLVING PARTIAL PAYMENTS BEFORE MATURITY

10-9

Frequently, businesses and individuals who have borrowed money for a specified length of time find that they want to save some interest by making one or more partial payments on the loan before the maturity date. The most commonly used method for this calculation is known as the **U.S. rule**. The rule states that when a partial payment is made on a loan, the payment is first used to pay off the accumulated interest to date and the balance is used to reduce the principal. In this application, the ordinary interest method (360 days) will be used for all calculations.

U.S. rule Method for distributing early partial payments of a loan whereby the payment is first used to pay off the accumulated interest to date, with the balance used to reduce the principal.

STEPS FOR CALCULATING MATURITY VALUE OF A LOAN AFTER ONE OR MORE PARTIAL PAYMENTS

STEP 1. Using the simple interest formula with *ordinary* interest, compute the amount of interest due from the date of the loan to the date of the partial payment.

STEP 2. Subtract the interest from Step 1 from the partial payment. This pays the interest to date.

STEP 3. Subtract the balance of the partial payment after Step 2 from the original principal of the loan. This gives the adjusted principal.

STEP 4. If another partial payment is made, repeat Steps 1, 2, and 3 using the adjusted principal and the number of days since the last partial payment.

STEP 5. The maturity value is computed by adding the interest since the last partial payment to the adjusted principal.

LEARNINGTIP

Remember to use *ordinary interest*, 360 days, for all calculations involving partial payments.

To help you visualize the details of a loan with partial payments, construct a timeline such as the one illustrated in Exhibit 10-1.

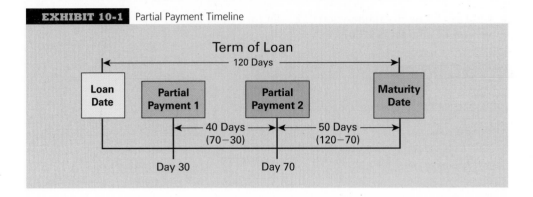

EXHIBIT 10-1 Partial Payment Timeline

EXAMPLE 10 CALCULATING LOANS INVOLVING PARTIAL PAYMENTS

Ray Windsor borrowed $10,000 at 9% interest for 120 days. On day 30, Ray made a partial payment of $2,000. On day 70, he made a second partial payment of $3,000. What is the maturity value of the loan after the partial payments?

SOLUTIONSTRATEGY

Step 1. Compute the interest from the date of the loan to the partial payment. In this problem, the first partial payment was made on day 30.

$$I = PRT$$
$$I = 10,000 \times .09 \times \frac{30}{360} = 75$$
$$I = \$75$$

Step 2. Subtract the interest from the partial payment.

$2,000 Partial payment
− 75 Accumulated interest
$1,925 Amount of partial payment left to reduce the principal

Step 3. Reduce the principal.

$10,000 Original principal
− 1,925 Amount of partial payment used to reduce principal
$8,075 Adjusted principal

Step 4. A second partial payment of $3,000 was made on day 70. We now repeat Steps 1, 2, and 3 to credit the second partial payment properly. Remember, use the adjusted principal and 40 days (70 − 30 = 40) for this calculation.

Step 1.

$$I = PRT$$
$$I = \$8,075 \times .09 \times \frac{40}{360}$$
$$I = \$80.75 \quad \text{Accumulated interest since last partial payment}$$

Step 2.

$3,000.00 Partial payment
− 80.75 Accumulated interest
$2,919.25 Amount of partial payment left to reduce principal

Step 3.

$8,075.00 Principal
−2,919.25 Amount of partial payment used to reduce principal
$5,155.75 Adjusted principal

Step 5. Once all partial payments have been credited, we find the maturity value of the loan by calculating the interest due from the last partial payment to the maturity date and adding it to the last adjusted principal.

Note: The last partial payment was made on day 70 of the loan; therefore, 50 days remain on the loan (120 − 70 = 50 days).

$$I = PRT$$

$$I = \$5{,}155.75 \times .09 \times \frac{50}{360}$$

$$I = \$64.45 \text{ Interest from last partial payment to maturity date}$$

Maturity Value = Principal + Interest

Maturity Value = $5,155.75 + $64.45

Maturity Value = $5,220.20

TRYITEXERCISE10

Rita Peterson borrowed $15,000 at 12% ordinary interest for 100 days. On day 20 of the loan, she made a partial payment of $4,000. On day 60, she made another partial payment of $5,000. What is the maturity value of the loan after the partial payments?

CHECK YOUR ANSWER WITH THE SOLUTION ON PAGE 337.

REVIEW EXERCISES

SECTION II **10**

Compute the principal for the following loans. Use ordinary interest when time is stated in days.

	Principal	Rate (%)	Time	Interest
1.	$1,250	12	2 years	$300
2.	_____	9	$1\frac{1}{2}$ years	$675
3.	_____	8	9 months	$3,000
4.	_____	10.7	90 days	$5,350
5.	_____	13.1	210 days	$917
6.	_____	6	6 months	$2,250
7.	_____	10.5	3 years	$8,190

Compute the rate for the following loans. Round answers to the nearest tenth of a percent; use ordinary interest when time is stated in days.

	Principal	Rate (%)	Time	Interest
8.	$5,000	8	3 years	$1,200
9.	$1,800	_____	5 months	$105
10.	$48,000	_____	60 days	$728
11.	$4,600	_____	168 days	$275
12.	$125,000	_____	2 years	$18,750
13.	$36,700	_____	190 days	$2,000
14.	$295,500	_____	14 months	$39,800

DOLLARS AND SENSE

Collateral is a borrower's pledge of specific property, such as a car, a boat, or a home, to a lender to secure repayment of a loan. Collateral serves as protection for a lender against a borrower's risk of default.

If a borrower defaults on a loan, that borrower forfeits (gives up) the property pledged as collateral—and the lender then becomes the owner of the collateral. In a typical mortgage loan transaction, for instance, the real estate that is acquired with the help of the loan serves as collateral.

"Where I come from it's called collateral."

© Vahan Shirvanian Reproduction rights obtainable from www.CartoonStock.com

Use the ordinary interest method to compute the time for the following loans. Round answers to the next higher day when necessary.

	Principal	Rate (%)	Time	Interest
15.	$18,000	12	158 days	$948
16.	$7,900	10.4	_____	$228
17.	$4,500	$9\frac{3}{4}$	_____	$375
18.	$25,000	8.9	_____	$4,450
19.	$680	15	_____	$51
20.	$41,000	6.4	_____	$3,936
21.	$3,600	14.3	_____	$125

Calculate the missing information for the following loans. Round percents to the nearest tenth and days to the next higher day when necessary.

	Principal	Rate (%)	Time (days)	Interest Method	Interest	Maturity Value
22.	$16,000	13	_____	Ordinary	$760	_____
23.	_____	9.5	100	Exact	$340	_____
24.	$3,600	_____	160	Exact	$225	_____
25.	$25,500	$11\frac{1}{4}$	300	Ordinary	_____	_____
26.	_____	10.4	_____	Exact	$4,000	$59,000

Solve the following word problems. Round answers to the nearest cent when necessary.

27. Kendall Motors, a Buick dealership, borrowed $225,000 on April 16 to purchase a shipment of new cars. The interest rate was 9.3% using the ordinary interest method. The amount of interest was $9,600.

   a. For how many days was the loan?

b. What was the maturity date of the loan?

28. Mike Drago took out a loan for $3,500 at the Gold Coast Bank for 270 days. If the bank uses the ordinary interest method, what rate of interest was charged if the amount of interest was $269? Round your answer to the nearest tenth of a percent.

29. Tiffany Francis borrowed money from her credit union to buy a car at 13.5% simple interest. If the loan was repaid in 2 years and the amount of interest was $2,700, how much did Tiffany borrow?

30. What is the maturity date of a loan for $5,000 at 15% exact interest taken out on June 3? The amount of interest on the loan was $150.

31. You are the owner of a Supercuts Hair Salon. What rate of interest were you charged on an ordinary interest loan for $135,000 in equipment if the interest was $4,400 and the time period was from January 16 to April 27? Round your answer to the nearest tenth of a percent.

32. Michelle Payne deposited $8,000 in a savings account paying 6.25% simple interest. How long will it take for her investment to amount to $10,000?

33. The Actor's Playhouse theater borrowed $100,000 at 8% ordinary interest for 90 days to purchase new stage lighting equipment. On day 40 of the loan, the theater made a partial payment of $35,000. What is the new maturity value of the loan?

$$I = PRT = 100,000 \times .08 \times \frac{40}{360} = \$888.89$$

$35,000.00 Paid	$100,000.00
− 888.89 Interest	− 34,111.11
$34,111.11	$65,888.89
	Adjusted Principal

$$MV = P(1 + RT) = 65,888.89\left(1 + .08 \times \frac{50}{360}\right) = \underline{\$66,620.99}$$

34. Steve Perry borrowed $10,000 at 12% ordinary interest for 60 days. On day 20 of the loan, Steve made a partial payment of $4,000. What is the new maturity value of the loan?

Supercuts, with over 2,300 locations, has been ranked the number one hair care franchise in the United States and the fifth best franchise opportunity overall in *Entrepreneur* magazine's annual "Franchise 500" issue.

Initial investment to franchise a Supercuts salon is $111,000–$239,700. Financial requirements are $100,000 liquid assets and $300,000 net worth. The franchise fee is $22,500 for the first salon and $12,500 for each additional salon.

Supercuts is owned by **Regis Corporation**, global leader in salon and hair care services.

Since its inception in 1922, Regis has grown to over 60 distinct brands of salons, education centers, and specialized hair service centers, serving 160 million customers annually through 12,800 worldwide locations. In 2009, Regis Corporation had revenue of $2.41 billion with 59,000 full-time employees.

35. Pamela Boyd borrowed $20,000 at 6.5% ordinary interest for 150 days. On day 30 of the loan, she made a partial payment of $8,000. What is the new maturity value of the loan?

36. The Mutt Hut Pet Shop borrowed $60,000 on March 15 for 90 days. The rate was 13% using the ordinary interest method. On day 25 of the loan, The Mutt Hut made a partial payment of $16,000, and on day 55 of the loan, The Mutt Hut made a second partial payment of $12,000.

    a. What is the new maturity value of the loan?

    b. What is the maturity date of the loan?

37. a. How many years will it take $5,000 invested at 8% simple interest to double to $10,000?

    b. How long will it take if the interest rate is increased to 10%?

Taco Bell serves more than 2 billion consumers each year in more than 5,800 restaurants in the United States In 2009, Taco Bell generated sales of $1.9 billion in company restaurants and $4.8 billion in franchise restaurants. The initial investment to franchise a Taco Bell is $1.3 million–$2.3 million. Franchise fees are $45,000 initial fee, then 5.5% monthly royalty fees and 4.5% monthly advertising fees.

Yum! Brands, Inc., based in Louisville, Kentucky, is the world's largest restaurant company in terms of system restaurants, with more than 37,000 restaurants in over 110 countries and territories and more than 1 million associates. Yum! is ranked #239 on the *Fortune* 500 List, with nearly $11 billion in revenue in 2009. Four of the restaurant brands—KFC, Pizza Hut, Taco Bell, and Long John Silver's—are the global leaders of the chicken, pizza, Mexican-style food, and quick-service seafood categories, respectively.

BUSINESS DECISION: THE OPPORTUNITY COST

38. You are the owner of four Taco Bell restaurant locations. You have a business loan with Citizens Bank taken out 60 days ago that is due in 90 days. The amount of the loan is $40,000, and the rate is 9.5% using ordinary interest.

    You currently have some excess cash. You have the choice of sending Citizens $25,000 now as a partial payment on your loan or purchasing an additional $25,000 of serving supplies such as food containers, cups, and plastic dinnerware for your inventory at a special discount price that is "10% off" your normal cost of these items.

    a. How much interest will you save on this loan if you make the partial payment and don't purchase the additional serving supplies?

b. How much will you save by purchasing the discounted serving supplies and not making the partial payment?

c. (Optional) What other factors should you consider before making this decision?

UNDERSTANDING PROMISSORY NOTES AND DISCOUNTING

SECTION III

10

Technically, the document that states the details of a loan and is signed by the borrower is known as a **promissory note**. *Promissory* means it is a promise to pay the principal back to the lender on a certain date. *Note* means that the document is a negotiable instrument and can be transferred or sold to others not involved in the original loan. Much like a check, with proper endorsement by the payee, the note can be transferred to another person, company, or lending institution.

Promissory notes are either noninterest-bearing or interest-bearing. When a note is noninterest-bearing, the maturity value equals the principal because there is no interest being charged. With interest-bearing notes, the maturity value equals the principal plus the interest.

Exhibit 10-2 is an example of a typical promissory note with its parts labeled. Notice the similarity between a note and a check. A list explaining the labels follows.

Maker: The person or company borrowing the money and issuing the note.

Payee: The person or institution lending the money and receiving the payment.

Term: The time period of the note, usually stated in days. (Use ordinary interest.)

Date: The date that the note is issued.

Face Value or Principal: The amount of money borrowed.

Interest Rate: The annual rate of interest being charged.

Maturity Date or Due Date: The date when maturity value is due the payee.

promissory note A debt instrument in which one party agrees to repay money to another within a specified period of time. Promissory notes may be noninterest-bearing at no interest or interest-bearing at a specified rate of interest.

EXHIBIT 10-2 Interest-Bearing Promissory Note

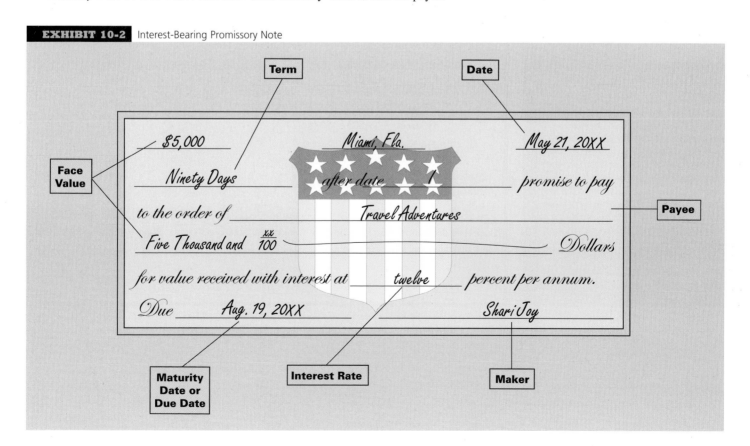

10-10 CALCULATING BANK DISCOUNT AND PROCEEDS FOR A SIMPLE DISCOUNT NOTE

simple discount notes Promissory notes in which the interest is deducted from the principal at the beginning of the loan.

bank discount The amount of interest charged (deducted from principal) on a discounted promissory note.

proceeds The amount of money that the borrower receives at the time a discounted note is made.

To this point, we have been dealing with *simple interest notes* in which the interest was added to the principal to determine the maturity value. Another way of lending money is to deduct the interest from the principal at the beginning of the loan and give the borrower the difference. These are known as **simple discount notes**. When this method is used, the amount of interest charged is known as the **bank discount** and the amount that the borrower receives is known as the **proceeds**. When the term of the note is over, the borrower will repay the entire principal, or face value, of the note as the maturity value.

For example, Julie goes to a bank and signs a simple interest note for $5,000. If the interest charge amounts to $500, she will receive $5,000 at the beginning of the note and repay $5,500 on maturity of the note. If the bank used a simple discount note for Julie's loan, the bank discount (interest) would be deducted from the face value (principal). Julie's proceeds on the loan would be $4,500, and on maturity she would pay $5,000.

BANK DISCOUNT

Because bank discount is the same as interest, we use the formula $I = PRT$ as before, substituting bank discount for interest, face value for principal, and discount rate for interest rate. *Note:* Use ordinary interest, 360 days, for simple discount notes whose terms are stated in days.

> **Bank discount = Face value × Discount rate × Time**

PROCEEDS

The proceeds of a note are calculated using the following formula:

> **Proceeds = Face value − Bank discount**

EXAMPLE11 CALCULATING BANK DISCOUNT AND PROCEEDS

What are the bank discount and proceeds of a $7,000 note at a 14% discount rate for 270 days?

SOLUTIONSTRATEGY

Bank discount = Face value × Discount rate × Time

Bank discount = $7,000 × .14 × $\frac{270}{360}$

Bank discount = $\underline{\$735}$

Proceeds = Face value − Bank discount

Proceeds = $7,000 − $735

Proceeds = $\underline{\$6,265}$

TRYITEXERCISE11

Erin Lang signed a $20,000 simple discount promissory note at the Sovereign Bank for a student loan. The discount rate is 13%, and the term of the note is 330 days. What is the amount of the bank discount, and what are Erin's proceeds on the loan?

CHECK YOUR ANSWERS WITH THE SOLUTIONS ON PAGE 337.

DOLLARS ANDSENSE

Student Aid
The U.S. Department of Education student aid programs are the largest source of student aid in America. The Free Application for Federal Student Aid (FAFSA) is the form used by virtually all two- and four-year colleges, universities, and career schools for federal, state, and college aid.

In March 2010, President Obama signed historic student loan legislation into law. The bill ties the annual Pell Grant increase to the consumer price index and expands the Income-Based Repayment program. For more information, visit www.fafsa.ed.gov and http://ibrinfo.org.

CALCULATING TRUE, OR EFFECTIVE, RATE OF INTEREST FOR A SIMPLE DISCOUNT NOTE

10-11

In a simple interest note, the borrower receives the full face value, whereas with a simple discount note, the borrower receives only the proceeds. Because the proceeds are less than the face value, the stated discount rate is not the true or actual interest rate of the note.

To protect the consumer, the U.S. Congress has passed legislation requiring all lending institutions to quote the **true, or effective, interest rate** for all loans. Effective interest rate is calculated by substituting the bank discount for interest and the proceeds for principal in the rate formula,

true, or effective, interest rate The actual interest rate charged on a discounted note. Takes into account the fact that the borrower does not receive the full amount of the principal.

$$\text{Effective interest rate} = \frac{\text{Bank discount}}{\text{Proceeds} \times \text{Time}}$$

EXAMPLE 12 CALCULATING EFFECTIVE INTEREST RATE

What is the effective interest rate of a simple discount note for $10,000 at a bank discount rate of 14% for a period of 90 days? Round to the nearest tenth of a percent.

SOLUTIONSTRATEGY

To find the effective interest rate, we must first calculate the amount of the bank discount and the proceeds of the note, then substitute these numbers in the effective interest rate formula.

Step 1. Bank Discount

Bank discount = Face value × Discount rate × Time

Bank discount = $10,000 × .14 × $\frac{90}{360}$

Bank discount = $350

Step 2. Proceeds

Proceeds = Face value − Bank discount

Proceeds = 10,000 − 350

Proceeds = $9,650

Step 3. Effective Interest Rate

Effective interest rate = $\frac{\text{Bank discount}}{\text{Proceeds} \times \text{Time}}$

Effective interest rate = $\frac{350}{9,650 \times \frac{90}{360}}$

Effective interest rate = $\frac{350}{2,412.50}$

Effective interest rate = .14507, or 14.5%

TRYITEXERCISE 12

What is the effective interest rate of a simple discount note for $40,000 at a bank discount rate of 11% for a period of 270 days? Round your answer to the nearest hundredth of a percent.

CHECK YOUR ANSWER WITH THE SOLUTION ON PAGE 337.

DISCOUNTING NOTES BEFORE MATURITY

10-12

Frequently in business, companies extend credit to their customers by accepting short-term promissory notes as payment for goods or services. These notes are simple interest and are usually for less than one year. Prior to the maturity date of these notes, the payee (lender)

discounting a note A process whereby a company or an individual can cash in or sell a promissory note at a discount at any time before maturity.

discount period The time period between the date a note is discounted and the maturity date. Used to calculate the proceeds of a discounted note.

may take the note to a bank and sell it. This is a convenient way for a company or individual to *cash in* a note at any time before maturity. This process is known as **discounting a note**.

When a note is discounted at a bank, the original payee receives the proceeds of the discounted note and the bank (the new payee) receives the maturity value of the note when it matures. The time period used to calculate the proceeds is from the date the note is discounted to the maturity date. This is known as the **discount period**.

Exhibit 10-3 illustrates the timeline for a 90-day simple interest note discounted on the 60th day.

EXHIBIT 10-3

Timeline for Discounted Note

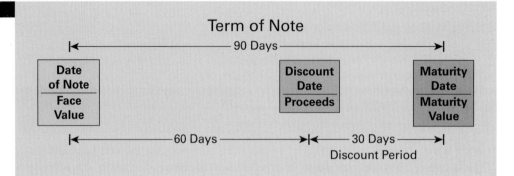

 STEPS FOR DISCOUNTING A NOTE BEFORE MATURITY

STEP 1. Calculate the maturity value of the note. If the original note was noninterest-bearing, the maturity value will be the same as the face value. If the original note was interest-bearing, the maturity value should be calculated as usual:

Maturity value = Principal(1 + Rate × Time)

STEP 2. Determine the number of days or months of the discount period. The discount period is used as the numerator of the time in Step 3.

STEP 3. Calculate the amount of the bank discount by using the following formula. *Note*: Use ordinary interest, 360 days, for discounting a note before maturity, when the terms are stated in days.

Bank discount = Maturity value × Discount rate × Time

STEP 4. Calculate the proceeds of the note by using the formula:

Proceeds = Maturity value − Bank discount

EXAMPLE13 CALCULATING PROCEEDS OF A DISCOUNTED NOTE

Continental Industries received a $15,000 promissory note for 150 days at 12% simple interest from one of its customers. After 90 days, Continental needed cash, so it discounted the note at the InterAmerican Bank at a discount rate of 14%. What are the proceeds Continental will receive from the discounted note?

SOLUTIONSTRATEGY

Step 1. Calculate the maturity value of the original note:

$$\text{Maturity value} = \text{Principal}(1 + \text{Rate} \times \text{Time})$$

$$\text{Maturity value} = 15,000\left(1 + .12 \times \frac{150}{360}\right)$$

$$\text{Maturity value} = 15,000(1 + .05) = 15,000(1.05)$$

$$\text{Maturity value} = \$15,750$$

Step 2. Find the number of days of the discount period: In this example, the note was discounted after 90 days of a 150-day note; therefore, the discount period is 60 days (150 − 90 = 60).

Step 3. Calculate the amount of the bank discount:

Bank discount = Maturity value × Discount rate × Time

Bank discount = $15,750 × .14 × $\frac{60}{360}$

Bank discount = $367.50

Step 4. Calculate the proceeds of the discounted note:

Proceeds = Maturity value − Bank discount

Proceeds = $15,750.00 − $367.50

Proceeds = $15,382.50

● TRYITEXERCISE13

Legacy Lumber received a $35,000 promissory note at 10% simple interest for 6 months from one of its customers. After 4 months, the note was discounted at the Keystone Bank at a discount rate of 14%. What are the proceeds Legacy will receive from the discounted note?

CHECK YOUR ANSWER WITH THE SOLUTION ON PAGE 338.

PURCHASING U.S. TREASURY BILLS

10-13

U.S. Treasury bills, or T-bills, are short-term government securities with maturities of 4 weeks, 13 weeks, and 26 weeks. Sold by banks, brokers, and dealers in increments of $1,000, these securities represent loans to the U.S. government and are considered to be among the safest of investments. Just like discounted bank notes, T-bills are sold at a discount from their face value.

U.S. Treasury bills, or **T-bills** Short-term government securities that represent loans to the U.S. government.

For example, you might pay $970 for a T-bill with a face value of $1,000. When the bill matures, you would be paid its face value, $1,000. Your interest is the difference between the face value and the purchase price—in this example, $30. The interest is determined by the discount rate, which is set when the bills are initially auctioned by the U.S. Treasury.

When comparing T-bills to discounted bank notes, the interest of a T-bill is the equivalent of the bank discount of a note; the face value of a T-bill is the equivalent of the proceeds of a note. Use the following formulas for T-bill calculations:

> **Interest = Face value × Discount rate × Time**
>
> **Purchase price = Face value − Interest**
>
> **Effective interest rate = $\dfrac{\text{Interest}}{\text{Purchase price} \times \text{Time}}$**

● EXAMPLE14 PURCHASING U.S. TREASURY BILLS

Peggy Estes purchased $5,000 in U.S. Treasury bills with a discount rate of 4% for a period of 13 weeks.

a. How much interest did Peggy earn on the T-bill investment?
b. How much was the purchase price of Peggy's T-bills?
c. What was the effective interest rate of Peggy's T-bill investment? Round to the nearest hundredth of a percent.

● SOLUTIONSTRATEGY

a. Interest = Face value × Discount rate × Time

Interest = $5,000 × .04 × $\frac{13}{52}$ = $50

(continued)

DOLLARS AND SENSE

For more information about Treasury bills, go to www.ustreas.gov, and click on "Bonds and Securities." For daily Treasury bill rates, click on "Interest Rate Statistics" in the "Direct Links" column.

b.   Purchase price = Face value − Interest

    Purchase price = 5,000 − 50 = <u>$4,950</u>

c.   Effective interest rate = $\dfrac{\text{Interest}}{\text{Purchase price} \times \text{Time}}$

    Effective interest rate = $\dfrac{50}{4{,}950 \times \frac{13}{52}}$ = .040404 = <u>4.04%</u>

TRY IT EXERCISE 14

Bob Schaller purchased $10,000 in U.S. Treasury bills with a discount rate of 4.6% for a period of 26 weeks.

a.   How much interest did Bob earn on the T-bill investment?
b.   How much was the purchase price of Bob's T-bills?
c.   What was the effective interest rate of Bob's T-bill investment? Round to the nearest hundredth of a percent.

CHECK YOUR ANSWERS WITH THE SOLUTIONS ON PAGE 338.

SECTION III   10   REVIEW EXERCISES

Calculate the bank discount and proceeds for the following simple discount notes. Use the ordinary interest method, 360 days, when applicable.

	Face Value	Discount Rate (%)	Term	Bank Discount	Proceeds
1.	$4,500	13	6 months	$292.50	$4,207.50
2.	$235	11.3	50 days	_____	_____
3.	$1,850	$12\frac{1}{2}$	1 year	_____	_____
4.	$35,000	9.65	11 months	_____	_____
5.	$7,800	$8\frac{1}{4}$	130 days	_____	_____

Using ordinary interest, 360 days, calculate the missing information for the following simple discount notes.

	Face Value	Discount Rate (%)	Date of Note	Term (days)	Maturity Date	Bank Discount	Proceeds
6.	$16,800	10	June 3	80	Aug. 22	$373.33	$16,426.67
7.	$5,000	14.7	April 16	_____	July 9	_____	_____
8.	$800	12.1	Sept. 3	109	_____	_____	_____
9.	$1,300	$9\frac{1}{2}$	Aug. 19	_____	Nov. 27	_____	_____
10.	$75,000	15	May 7	53	_____	_____	_____

Using ordinary interest, 360 days, calculate the bank discount, proceeds, and effective rate for the following simple discount notes. Round effective rate to the nearest hundredth of a percent.

	Face Value	Discount Rate (%)	Term (days)	Bank Discount	Proceeds	Effective Rate (%)
11.	$2,700	14	126	$132.30	$2,567.70	14.72
12.	$6,505	10.39	73	_____	_____	_____

	Face Value	Discount Rate (%)	Term (days)	Bank Discount	Proceeds	Effective Rate (%)
13.	$3,800	$14\frac{1}{2}$	140	_____	_____	_____
14.	$95,000	9.7	45	_____	_____	_____
15.	$57,500	$12\frac{3}{4}$	230	_____	_____	_____

The following interest-bearing promissory notes were discounted at a bank by the payee before maturity. Use the ordinary interest method, 360 days, to calculate the missing information.

	Face Value	Interest Rate (%)	Date of Note	Term of Note (days)	Maturity Date	Maturity Value	Date of Discount	Discount Period (days)	Discount Rate (%)	Proceeds
16.	$2,500	12	Mar. 4	70	May 13	$2,558.33	Apr. 15	28	13	$2,532.46
17.	$4,000	10.4	Dec. 12	50	_____	_____	Jan. 19	_____	15	_____
18.	$850	$13\frac{1}{2}$	June 7	125	_____	_____	Sept. 3	_____	16.5	_____
19.	$8,000	9	May 10	90	_____	_____	July 5	_____	10.2	_____
20.	$1,240	7.6	Sept. 12	140	_____	_____	Dec. 5	_____	11.8	_____

Calculate the interest, purchase price, and effective interest rate of the following Treasury bill (T-bill) purchases. Round effective interest rate to the nearest hundredth of a percent.

	Face Value	Discount Rate (%)	Term (weeks)	Interest	Purchase Price	Effective Rate (%)
21.	$15,000	5.20	13	$195	$14,805	5.27
22.	$50,000	4.40	26	_____	_____	___
23.	$80,000	4.82	13	_____	_____	___
24.	$35,000	3.80	4	_____	_____	___
25.	$100,000	4.15	26	_____	_____	___

Use the ordinary interest method, 360 days, to solve the following word problems. Round to the nearest cent when necessary.

26. Roni Lockard signed a $24,000 simple discount promissory note at the Pacific National Bank. The discount rate was 14%, and the note was made on February 19 for 50 days.

   a. What proceeds will Roni receive on the note?

   b. What is the maturity date of the note?

27. Chris Gill signed a $10,000 simple discount promissory note at a bank discount rate of 13%. If the term of the note was 125 days, what was the effective interest rate of the note? Round your answer to the nearest hundredth of a percent.

28. Pinnacle Manufacturing received a $40,000 promissory note at 12% simple interest for 95 days from one of its customers. On day 70, Pinnacle discounted the note at the Berryville Bank at a discount rate of 15%. The note was made on September 12.

    a.   What was the maturity date of the note?

    b.   What was the maturity value of the note?

    c.   What was the discount date of the note?

    d.   What proceeds did Pinnacle receive after discounting the note?

29. Christy Thomas purchased $150,000 in U.S. Treasury bills with a discount rate of 4.2% for a period of 4 weeks.

    a.   How much interest did Christy earn on the T-bill investment?

    b.   How much was the purchase price of Christy's T-bills?

    c.   What was the effective interest rate of Christy's T-bill investment? Round to the nearest hundredth of a percent.

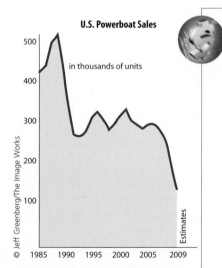

U.S. Powerboat Sales

in thousands of units

Estimates

1985   1990   1995   2000   2005   2009

© Jeff Greenberg/The Image Works

According to the National Marine Manufacturers Association, in 2008, there were about 17 million boats in use, with over 70 million enthusiasts. Sales and service expenditures for boats amounted to $33.6 billion. Top manufacturers include Sea Ray, Bayliner, Boston Whaler, Chaparral, and Robalo.

BUSINESS DECISION: FINANCING THE DEALERS

30. Richie Powers is the owner of American Eagle Boats, a manufacturer of custom pleasure boats. Because of the economic recession and slow boat sales recently, American Eagle has begun accepting promissory notes from its dealers to help finance large orders. This morning American Eagle accepted a 90-day, 9.5% promissory note for $600,000 from Champion Marine, one of its sales dealers.

    You are a manager for Atlantic Bank, and Richie is one of your clients. Atlantic's discount rate is currently 16%. Richie's goal is to discount the note as soon as possible, but not until the proceeds are at least equal to the face value of the note, $600,000.

    a.   As his banker, Richie has asked you to "run the numbers" at ten-day intervals starting with day 20 and advise him as to when he can discount the note and still receive his $600,000.

b. (Challenge) Calculate the exact day the note should be discounted to meet Richie's goal.

CHAPTER FORMULAS

Simple Interest

Interest = Principal × Rate × Time

$$\text{Time (exact interest)} = \frac{\text{Number of days of a loan}}{365}$$

$$\text{Time (ordinary interest)} = \frac{\text{Number of days of a loan}}{360}$$

Maturity value = Principal + Interest

Maturity value = Principal(1 + Rate × Time)

The Simple Interest Formula

$$\text{Principal} = \frac{\text{Interest}}{\text{Rate} \times \text{Time}}$$

$$\text{Rate} = \frac{\text{Interest}}{\text{Principal} \times \text{Time}}$$

$$\text{Time} = \frac{\text{Interest}}{\text{Principal} \times \text{Rate}}$$

Simple Discount Notes

Bank discount = Face value × Discount rate × Time

Proceeds = Face value − Bank discount

$$\text{Effective interest rate} = \frac{\text{Bank discount}}{\text{Proceeds} \times \text{Time}}$$

Discounting a Note before Maturity

Bank discount = Maturity value × Discount rate × Time

Proceeds = Maturity value − Bank discount

Purchasing U.S. Treasury Bills

Interest = Face value × Discount rate × Time

Purchase price = Face value − Interest

$$\text{Effective interest rate} = \frac{\text{Interest}}{\text{Purchase price} \times \text{Time}}$$

CHAPTER SUMMARY

Section I: Understanding and Computing Simple Interest

Topic	Important Concepts	Illustrative Examples
Computing Simple Interest for Loans with Terms of Years or Months **Performance Objective 10-1, Page 308**	Simple interest is calculated by using the formula $I = PRT$. $\qquad$ Interest = Principal × Rate × Time *Note*: Time is always expressed in years or fractions of a year.	What is the amount of interest for a loan of $20,000 at 12% simple interest for 9 months? $I = 20{,}000 \times .12 \times \dfrac{9}{12}$ Interest = $1,800
Calculating Simple Interest for Loans with Terms of Days by Using the Exact Interest Method **Performance Objective 10-2, Page 309**	Exact interest uses *365 days* as the time factor denominator. $\text{Time (exact)} = \dfrac{\text{Number of days of a loan}}{365}$	Using the exact interest method, what is the amount of interest on a loan of $5,000 at 8% for 95 days? $I = PRT$ $I = 5{,}000 \times .08 \times \dfrac{95}{365}$ Interest = $104.11
Calculating Simple Interest for Loans with Terms of Days by Using the Ordinary Interest Method **Performance Objective 10-2, Page 310**	Ordinary interest uses *360 days* as the time factor denominator. $\text{Time (ordinary)} = \dfrac{\text{Number of days of a loan}}{360}$	Using the ordinary interest method, what is the amount of interest on a loan of $8,000 at 9% for 120 days? $I = PRT$ $I = 8{,}000 \times .09 \times \dfrac{120}{360}$ Interest = $240
Calculating the Maturity Value of a Loan **Performance Objective 10-3, Page 311**	When the time period of a loan is over, the loan is said to mature. The total payback of principal and interest is known as the maturity value of a loan. $\qquad$ Maturity value = Principal + Interest Maturity value = Principal(1 + Rate × Time)	What is the maturity value of a loan for $50,000 at 12% interest for 3 years? $MV = 50{,}000(1 + .12 \times 3)$ $MV = 50{,}000(1.36)$ Maturity value = $68,000
Calculating the Number of Days of a Loan **Performance Objective 10-4, Page 312**	1. Determine the number of days remaining in the first month by subtracting the loan date from the number of days in that month. 2. List the number of days for each succeeding whole month. 3. List the number of loan days in the last month. 4. Add the days from Steps 1, 2, and 3.	Steve Adams borrowed money from the Republic Bank on May 5 and repaid the loan on August 19. For how many days was this loan? $\qquad$ May 31 $\qquad$ − May $\;$ 5 $\qquad\qquad$ 26 Days in May $\qquad\qquad$ 61 June–July $\qquad$ +19 August $\qquad\qquad$ 106 Days
Determining the Maturity Date of a Loan **Performance Objective 10-5, Page 313**	1. Determine the number of days remaining in the first month. 2. Subtract days from Step 1 from number of days in the loan. 3. Subtract days in each succeeding whole month until you reach a month in which the difference is less than the days in that month. The maturity date will be the day of that month that corresponds to the difference.	What is the maturity date of a loan taken out on June 9 for 100 days? June $\;$ 30 $\qquad\qquad\quad$ 100 Days of the loan June −9 $\qquad\qquad$ − 21 Days in June $\quad$ 21 Days in June $\qquad$ 79 $\qquad\qquad\qquad\qquad$ − 31 Days in July $\qquad\qquad\qquad\qquad\quad$ 48 $\qquad\qquad\qquad\qquad$ − 31 Days in August $\qquad\qquad\qquad\qquad\quad$ 17 At this point, the difference, 17, is less than the days in September; therefore, the maturity date is September 17.

Section II: Using the Simple Interest Formula

Topic	Important Concepts	Illustrative Examples
Solving for the Principal **Performance Objective 10-6, Page 316**	$\text{Principal} = \dfrac{\text{Interest}}{\text{Rate} \times \text{Time}}$	Kye Morrow borrowed money at 10% interest for 2 years. If the interest charge was $800, how much principal did Kye borrow? $\text{Principal} = \dfrac{800}{.10 \times 2} = \dfrac{800}{.2}$ $\text{Principal} = \underline{\$4,000}$
Solving for the Rate **Performance Objective 10-7, Page 317**	$\text{Rate} = \dfrac{\text{Interest}}{\text{Principal} \times \text{Time}}$	Arnold Parker borrowed $3,000 for 75 days. If the interest was $90 using ordinary interest, what was the rate on Arnold's loan? $\text{Rate} = \dfrac{90}{3,000 \times \frac{75}{360}} = \dfrac{90}{625}$ $\text{Rate} = .144 = \underline{14.4\%}$
Solving for the Time **Performance Objective 10-8, Page 318**	When solving for time, whole numbers are years and decimals are multiplied by 360 or 365 to get days. Any fraction of a day should be rounded up to the next higher day because lending institutions consider any portion of a day to be another day. $\text{Time} = \dfrac{\text{Interest}}{\text{Principal} \times \text{Rate}}$	What is the time period of a loan for $20,000 at 9% ordinary interest if the amount of interest is $1,000? $\text{Time} = \dfrac{1,000}{20,000 \times .09} = \dfrac{1,000}{1,800} = .555555$ $\text{Time} = .555555 \times 360 = 199.99 = \underline{200 \text{ Days}}$
Calculating Loans Involving Partial Payments before Maturity **Performance Objective 10-9, Page 319**	1. Using the simple interest formula with *ordinary* interest, compute the amount of interest due from the date of the loan to the date of the partial payment. 2. Subtract the interest from Step 1 from the partial payment. This pays the interest to date. 3. Subtract the balance of the partial payment after Step 2 from the original principal of the loan. This gives the adjusted principal. 4. If another partial payment is made, repeat Steps 1, 2, and 3 using the adjusted principal and the number of days since the last partial payment. 5. The maturity value is computed by adding the interest since the last partial payment to the adjusted principal.	Sue Williams borrowed $7,000 at 10% ordinary interest for 120 days. On day 90, Sue made a partial payment of $3,000. What was the new maturity value of the loan? $I = PRT$ $I = 7,000 \times .10 \times \dfrac{90}{360} = \$175$ $\begin{array}{rl} \$3,000 & \text{Partial payment} \\ -\ 175 & \text{Accumulated interest} \\ \hline \$2,825 & \text{Reduces principal} \\ \$7,000 & \text{Original principal} \\ -\ 2,825 & \\ \hline \$4,175 & \text{Adjusted principal} \end{array}$ Days remaining $= 120 - 90 = 30$ $I = PRT$ $I = 4,175 \times .10 \times \dfrac{30}{360} = \$34.79$ Maturity value $= P + I$ $MV = 4,175 + 34.79$ Maturity value $= \underline{\$4,209.79}$

Section III: Understanding Promissory Notes and Discounting

Topic	Important Concepts	Illustrative Examples
Calculating Bank Discount and Proceeds for a Simple Discount Note **Performance Objective 10-10, Page 326**	With discounting, the interest, known as the bank discount, is deducted from the face value of the loan. The borrower gets the difference, known as the proceeds. Bank discount = Face value × Discount rate × Time Proceeds = Face value − Bank discount	What are the bank discount and proceeds of a $10,000 note discounted at 12% for 6 months? Bank discount = $10,000 \times .12 \times \frac{6}{12}$ Bank discount = \$600 Proceeds = $10,000 - 600 = \underline{\$9,400}$
Calculating True, or Effective, Rate of Interest for a Simple Discount Note **Performance Objective 10-11, Page 327**	Because the proceeds are less than the face value of a loan, the true, or effective, interest rate is higher than the stated bank discount rate. Effective interest rate = $\dfrac{\text{Bank discount}}{\text{Proceeds} \times \text{Time}}$	What is the effective rate of a simple discount note for $20,000 at a bank discount of 15% for a period of 9 months? Bank discount = $FV \times R \times T$ Bank discount = $20,000 \times .15 \times \frac{9}{12}$ Bank discount = \$2,250 Proceeds = Face value − Bank discount Proceeds = $20,000 - 2,250$ Proceeds = \$17,750 Effective interest rate = $\dfrac{2,250}{17,750 \times \frac{9}{12}}$ Effective interest rate = $\underline{16.9\%}$
Discounting Notes before Maturity **Performance Objective 10-12, Page 327**	Frequently, companies extend credit to their customers by accepting short-term promissory notes as payment for goods or services. These notes can be cashed in early by discounting them at a bank and receiving the proceeds. 1. Calculate the maturity value. $MV = P(1 + RT)$ 2. Determine the discount period. 3. Calculate the bank discount. Bank discount = $MV \times R \times T$ 4. Calculate the proceeds. Proceeds = MV − Bank discount	Reliable Food Wholesalers received a $100,000 promissory note for 6 months at 11% interest from SuperSaver Supermarkets. If Reliable discounts the note after 4 months at a discount rate of 15%, what proceeds will it receive? $MV = 100,000\left(1 + .11 \times \frac{6}{12}\right)$ $MV = \$105,500$ Discount period = 2 months (6 − 4) Bank discount = $105,500 \times .15 \times \frac{2}{12}$ Bank discount = \$2,637.50 Proceeds = $105,500.00 - 2,637.50$ Proceeds = $\underline{\$102,862.50}$
Purchasing U.S. Treasury Bills **Performance Objective 10-13, Page 329**	U.S. Treasury bills, or T-bills, are short-term government securities with maturities of 4 weeks, 13 weeks, and 26 weeks. Sold by banks, brokers, and dealers in increments of $1,000, these securities represent loans to the U.S. government. Just like discounted bank notes, T-bills are sold at a discount from their face value. Interest = Face value × Discount rate × Time Purchase price = Face value − Interest Effective interest rate = $\dfrac{\text{Interest}}{\text{Purchase price} \times \text{Time}}$	Cindy Lane purchased $3,000 in U.S. Treasury bills with a discount rate of 5% for a period of 26 weeks. a. How much interest did Cindy earn on the T-bill investment? Interest = $3,000 \times .05 \times \frac{26}{52} = \underline{\$75}$ b. How much was the purchase price of Cindy's T-bills? Purchase price = $3,000 - 75 = \underline{\$2,925}$ c. What was the effective interest rate of Cindy's T-bill investment? Round to the nearest hundredth of a percent. Effective interest rate = $\dfrac{75}{2,925 \times \frac{26}{52}}$ = $.05128 = \underline{5.13\%}$

TRY IT: EXERCISE SOLUTIONS FOR CHAPTER 10

1a. $I = PRT = 4{,}000 \times .07 \times 2.25 = \underline{\$630}$

1b. $I = PRT = 45{,}000 \times .0975 \times \frac{3}{12} = \underline{\$1{,}096.88}$

1c. $I = PRT = 130{,}000 \times .104 \times \frac{42}{12} = \underline{\$47{,}320}$

2. $I = PRT = 23{,}000 \times .08 \times \frac{119}{365} = \underline{\$599.89}$

3. $I = PRT = 15{,}000 \times .095 \times \frac{250}{360} = \underline{\$989.58}$

4a. $I = PRT = 15{,}400 \times .065 \times \frac{24}{12} = \underline{\$2{,}002}$

$MV = P + I = 15{,}400 + 2{,}002 = \underline{\$17{,}402}$

4b. $MV = P(1 + RT) = 450{,}000\left(1 + .08 \times \frac{9}{12}\right) = \underline{\$477{,}000}$

5a.
```
   30              26 April
  −4              61 May–June
  ───             ─────
  26 Days         +18 July
                  ─────
                  105 Days
```

5b.
```
   30              15 June
  −15             92 July–Sept.
  ───             ─────
  15 Days         +9 Oct.
                  ─────
                  116 Days
```

$I = PRT = 3{,}500 \times .11 \times \frac{116}{365} = \underline{\$122.36}$

6a.
```
Days in Sept.  30        125 Days of loan
Loan date     −9        −21 Days of Sept.
Days of Sept.  21        ───
                         104
                        −31 October
                         ───
                         73
                        −30 November
                         ───
                         43
                        −31 December
                         ───
                         12 ──→ January 12
```

6b. $MV = P(1 + RT) = 9{,}000\left(1 + .10 \times \frac{80}{360}\right) = \underline{\$9{,}200}$

```
   31              10 Oct.
  −21             61 Nov.–Dec.
  ───             ─────
  10 Days         +9 Jan. ──→ January 9
                  ─────
                  80 Days
```

7. $P = \dfrac{I}{RT} = \dfrac{560}{.09 \times \frac{125}{360}} = \underline{\$17{,}920}$

8. $R = \dfrac{I}{PT} = \dfrac{1{,}960}{25{,}000 \times \frac{245}{360}} = .1152 = \underline{11.52\%}$

9. $I = \dfrac{I}{PR} = \dfrac{650}{15{,}000 \times .095} = .4561404$

$\phantom{I = \dfrac{I}{PR} = } \times 360$

$\phantom{I = \dfrac{I}{PR} = } 164.2 = \underline{165 \text{ Days}}$

10. $I = PRT = 15{,}000 \times .12 \times \frac{20}{360} = \$100$ ⠀⠀⠀ 1st partial payment = 20 days

```
  4,000 Payment      15,000
 − 100 Interest     − 3,900
 ─────              ──────
  3,900             11,100 Adjustment Principal
```

$I = PRT = 11{,}100 \times .12 \times \frac{40}{360} = \$148$ ⠀⠀⠀ 2nd partial payment = 40 days (60 − 20)

```
  5,000 Payment      11,100
 − 148 Interest     − 4,852
 ─────              ──────
  4,852              6,248 Adjustment Principal
```
⠀⠀⠀⠀⠀⠀⠀⠀⠀⠀⠀⠀⠀⠀⠀ Days remaining = 40 (100 − 60)

$I = PRT = 6{,}248 \times .12 \times \frac{40}{360} = \$83.31$

Final due = $P + I = 6{,}248.00 + 83.31 = \underline{\$6{,}331.31}$

11. Bank discount = $FV \times R \times T = 20{,}000 \times .13 \times \frac{330}{360} = \underline{\$2{,}383.33}$

Proceeds = Face value − Bank discount = $20{,}000.00 − 2{,}383.33 = \underline{\$17{,}616.67}$

12. Bank discount = $FV \times R \times T = 40{,}000 \times .11 \times \frac{270}{360} = \underline{\$3{,}300}$

Proceeds = Face value − Bank discount = $40{,}000 − 3{,}300 = \$36{,}700$

Effective interest rate = $\dfrac{\text{Bank discount}}{\text{Proceeds} \times \text{Time}} = \dfrac{3{,}300}{36{,}700 \times \frac{270}{360}} = 11.99\%$

13. $MV = P(1 + RT) = 35,000\left(1 + .10 \times \frac{6}{12}\right) = \underline{\$36,750}$

$$\begin{array}{r} 6 \text{ months} \\ - \ 4 \text{ months} \\ \hline \text{Discount period} = \ \ 2 \text{ months} \end{array}$$

Bank discount $= MV \times R \times T = 36,750 \times .14 \times \frac{2}{12} = \$857.50$

Proceeds = Maturity value − Bank discount = $36,750.00 − 857.50 = \underline{\$35,892.50}$

14. a. Interest = Face value × Discount rate × Time = $10,000 \times .046 \times \frac{26}{52} = \underline{\$230}$

b. Purchase price = Face value − Interest = $10,000 − 230 = \underline{\$9,770}$

c. Effective interest rate $= \dfrac{\text{Interest}}{\text{Purchase price} \times \text{Time}} = \dfrac{230}{9,770 \times \frac{26}{52}} = .04708 = \underline{4.71\%}$

CONCEPT REVIEW

1. The price or rental fee charged by a lender to a borrower for the use of money is known as _____. (10.1)

2. List the three factors that determine the amount of interest charged on a loan. (10-1)

3. Interest calculated solely on the principal amount borrowed is known as _____ interest, while interest calculated at regular intervals on the principal and previously earned interest is known as _____ interest. (10-1)

4. The interest calculation method that uses 365 days (366 in leap year) as the time factor denominator is known as _____ interest. (10-2)

5. The interest calculation method that uses 360 days as the time factor denominator is known as _____ interest. (10-2)

6. Maturity value is the total payback of principal and interest of a loan. List the two formulas for calculating maturity value. (10-3)

7. The first day of a loan is known as the _____ date; the last day of a loan is known as the _____ date. (10-4, 10-5)

8. Write the formula for calculating simple interest. (10-6)

9. When solving the simple interest formula for principal, rate, or time, the _____ is always the numerator. (10-6, 10-7, 10-8)

10. The U.S. rule states that when a partial payment is made on a loan, the payment is first used to pay off the accumulated _____ to date and the balance is used to reduce the _____. (10-9)

11. The amount of money that the borrower receives at the time a discounted note is made is known as the _____. (10-10)

12. The actual interest rate charged on a discounted note is known as the _____, or _____, interest rate. (10-11)

13. When a note is discounted before maturity, the proceeds are calculated by substracting the amount of the bank discount from the _____ value of the loan. (10-12)

14. Discounted short term loans made to the U.S. government are known as U.S. Treasury _____. (10-13)

ASSESSMENT TEST

Using the exact interest method (365 days), find the amount of interest on the following loans.

Principal	Rate (%)	Time (days)	Exact Interest
1. $15,000	13	120	_____
2. $1,700	$12\frac{1}{2}$	33	_____

Using the ordinary interest method (360 days), find the amount of interest on the following loans.

Principal	Rate (%)	Time (days)	Ordinary Interest
3. $20,600	12	98	_____
4. $286,000	$13\frac{1}{2}$	224	_____

What is the maturity value of the following loans? Use $MV = P(1 + RT)$ to find the maturity values.

Principal	Rate (%)	Time	Maturity Value
5. $15,800	14	4 years	_____
6. $120,740	$11\frac{3}{4}$	7 months	_____

© Jack Corbett. Reproduction rights obtainable from www.CartoonStock.com

"WE OFFER 35% INTEREST ON ALL MONEY YOU NEVER WITHDRAW!"

From the following information, determine the number of days of each loan.

	Loan Date	Due Date	Number of Days
7.	April 16	August 1	_____
8.	October 20	December 18	_____

From the following information, determine the maturity date of each loan.

	Loan Date	Time Loan (days)	Maturity Date
9.	November 30	55	_____
10.	May 15	111	_____

Compute the principal for the following loans. Round answers to the nearest cent.

	Principal	Rate (%)	Time	Interest
11.	_____	12	2 years	$2,800
12.	_____	$10\frac{1}{2}$	10 months	$5,900

Compute the rate for the following loans. Round answers to the nearest tenth of a percent.

	Principal	Rate (%)	Time	Interest
13.	$2,200	_____	4 years	$800
14.	$50,000	_____	9 months	$4,500

Use the ordinary interest method to compute the time for the following loans. Round answers to the next higher day when necessary.

	Principal	Rate (%)	Time (days)	Interest
15.	$13,500	13	_____	$350
16.	$7,900	10.4	_____	$625

Calculate the missing information for the following loans. Round percents to the nearest tenth and days to the next higher day when necessary.

	Principal	Rate (%)	Time (days)	Interest Method	Interest	Maturity Value
17.	$13,000	14	_____	Ordinary	$960	_____
18.	_____	12.2	133	Exact	$1,790	_____
19.	$2,500	_____	280	Ordinary	$295	_____

CHAPTER

10

Using ordinary interest, calculate the missing information for the following simple discount notes.

	Face Value	Discount Rate (%)	Date of Note	Term (days)	Maturity Date	Bank Discount	Proceeds
20.	$50,000	13	Apr. 5	_____	Aug. 14	_____	_____
21.	$875,000	$9\frac{1}{2}$	Oct. 25	87	_____	_____	_____

Using ordinary interest (360 days), calculate the bank discount, proceeds, and effective rate for the following simple discount notes. Round effective rate to the nearest hundredth of a percent.

	Face Value	Discount Rate (%)	Term (days)	Bank Discount	Proceeds	Effective Rate (%)
22.	$22,500	$10\frac{1}{2}$	60	_____	_____	_____
23.	$290,000	11.9	110	_____	_____	_____

The following interest-bearing promissory notes were discounted at a bank by the payee before maturity. Use the ordinary interest method (360 days) to solve for the missing information.

	Face Value	Interest Rate (%)	Date of Note	Term of Note (days)	Maturity Date	Maturity Value	Date Note Discounted	Discount Period (days)	Discount Rate (%)	Proceeds
24.	$8,000	11	Jan. 12	83	_____	_____	Mar. 1	_____	15	_____
25.	$5,500	$13\frac{1}{2}$	June 17	69	_____	_____	July 22	_____	13.7	_____

Calculate the interest, purchase price, and effective interest rate of the following Treasury bill (T-bill) purchases. Round effective interest rate to the nearest hundredth of a percent.

	Face Value	Discount Rate (%)	Term (weeks)	Interest	Purchase Price	Effective Rate (%)
26.	$75,000	5.15	4	_____	_____	_____
27.	$28,000	4.90	26	_____	_____	_____

Solve the following word problems. Round to the nearest cent when necessary.

28. On May 23, Samantha Best borrowed $4,000 from the Tri City Credit Union at 13% for 160 days. The credit union uses the exact interest method.

a. What was the amount of interest on the loan?

b. What was the maturity value of the loan?

c. What is the maturity date of the loan?

29. Ronald Brown missed an income tax payment of $2,600. The Internal Revenue Service charges a 15% simple interest penalty calculated by the exact interest method. If the tax was due on April 15 but was paid on July 17, what was the amount of the penalty charge?

30. Katie Chalmers borrowed money from her credit union at 13.2% simple interest to buy furniture. If the loan was repaid in $2\frac{1}{2}$ years and the amount of interest was $1,320, how much did Katie borrow?

31. Mickey Sporn took out a loan for $5,880 at the Linville Ridge Bank for 110 days. The bank uses the ordinary method for calculating interest. What rate of interest was charged if the amount of interest was $275? Round to the nearest tenth of a percent.

32. Alicia Eastman deposited $2,000 in a savings account at the Biltmone Bank paying 6% ordinary interest. How long will it take for her investment to amount to $2,600?

33. Laurie Carron borrowed $16,000 at 14% ordinary interest for 88 days. On day 30 of the loan, she made a partial payment of $7,000. What was the new maturity value of the loan?

34. Euromart Tile Company borrowed $40,000 on April 6 for 66 days. The rate was 14% using the ordinary interest method. On day 25 of the loan, Euromart made a partial payment of $15,000, and on day 45 of the loan, Euromart made a second partial payment of $10,000.

   a. What was the new maturity value of the loan?

   b. What was the maturity date of the loan?

35. Brandi Lee signed a $30,000 simple discount promissory note at the Signature Bank. The discount rate was 13% ordinary interest, and the note was made on August 9 for 95 days.

   a. What proceeds did Brandi receive on the note?

   b. What was the maturity date of the note?

   c. What was the effective interest rate of the note? Round the answer to the nearest hundredth of a percent.

36. Varsity Press, a publisher of college textbooks, received a $70,000 promissory note at 12% ordinary interest for 60 days from one of its customers, Reader's Choice Bookstores. After 20 days, Varsity Press discounted the note at the Grove Isle Bank at a discount rate of 14.5%. The note was made on March 21.

a. What was the maturity date of the note?

b. What was the maturity value of the note?

c. What was the discount date of the note?

d. What proceeds did Varsity Press receive after discounting the note?

On-campus and online **bookstores** are the main sources of textbooks for college students. According to the National Association of College Stores, the 4,500 college bookstores in the United States had sales of $9.8 billion for the 2007–2008 fiscal year.

In 2009, new book sales were 68.5% of course material sales, while used books were 30.5% of all course materials.

37. Fernando Rodriguez purchased $64,000 in U.S. Treasury bills with a discount rate of 4.7% for a period of 13 weeks.

a. How much interest did Fernando earn on the T-bill investment?

b. How much was the purchase price of Fernando's T-bills?

c. What was the effective interest rate of Fernando's T-bill investment? Round to the nearest hundredth of a percent.

BUSINESS DECISION: BORROWING TO TAKE ADVANTAGE OF A CASH DISCOUNT

38. You are the accountant for Suite Dreams, a retail furniture store. Recently, an order of sofas and chairs was received from a manufacturer with terms of 3/15, n/45. The order amounted to $230,000, and Suite Dreams can borrow money at 13% ordinary interest.

a. How much can be saved by borrowing the funds for 30 days to take advantage of the cash discount? (Remember, Suite Dreams must borrow only the net amount due after the cash discount is taken.)

DOLLARS AND SENSE

This Business Decision illustrates an important business concept—borrowing money to take advantage of a cash discount.

Note how much can be saved by taking the cash discount even if the money is borrowed.

For a review of cash discounts, see Section IV, Chapter 7.

b. What would you recommend?

COLLABORATIVE LEARNING ACTIVITY

The Automobile Loan

As a team, choose a particular type of automobile category that you want to research (such as sport utility vehicle, sports car, hybrid, or luxury sedan). Then have each member of the team choose a different manufacturer's model within that category.

For example, if the team picked sport utility vehicle, individual choices might include Chevy Equinox, Mazda CX-7, Ford Escape, or Honda CRV.

a. From your local newspaper and the Internet, collect advertisments and offers for the purchase of the model you have chosen.

b. Visit or call a dealership for the vehicle you picked. Speak with a salesperson about the types of "deals" currently being offered on that model.

- What loan rates and terms are available from the dealer?
- Who is the actual lender?

c. Contact various lending institutions (banks, finance companies, credit unions) and inquire about vehicle loans.

- What loan rates and terms are being offered?
- Which lending institution is offering the best deal? Why?
- How do these rates and terms compare with those from the dealership?

THE DIME SAVINGS BANK OF NEW Y
FSB

Product | Rate% | eld %

THE PREFERRED ACCOUNT
Checking with high-rate savings.

Savings
Minimum deposit of $100

4.26 **4.35**

24-MONTH CD · **5.12** **5.25**

© Robert Brenner/Photo Edit

Compound Interest and Present Value

PERFORMANCE OBJECTIVES

SECTION I: Compound Interest—The Time Value of Money

11-1: Manually calculating compound amount (future value) and compound interest (p. 346)

11-2: Computing compound amount (future value) and compound interest by using compound interest tables (p. 347)

11-3: Creating compound interest table factors for periods beyond the table (p. 350)

11-4: Calculating annual percentage yield (APY) or effective interest rate (p. 351)

11-5: (Optional) Calculating compound amount (future value) by using the compound interest formula (p. 352)

SECTION II: Present Value

11-6: Calculating the present value of a future amount by using present value tables (p. 357)

11-7: Creating present value table factors for periods beyond the table (p. 359)

11-8: (Optional) Calculating present value of a future amount by using the present value formula (p. 360)

COMPOUND INTEREST—THE TIME VALUE OF MONEY   SECTION I   11

In Chapter 10, we studied simple interest in which the formula $I = PRT$ was applied once during the term of a loan or an investment to find the amount of interest. In business, another common way of calculating interest is by using a method known as *compounding*, or **compound interest**, in which the interest calculation is applied a number of times during the term of the loan or investment.

Compound interest yields considerably higher interest than simple interest does because the investor is earning interest on the interest. With compound interest, the interest earned for each period is reinvested or added to the previous principal before the next calculation or compounding. The previous principal plus interest then becomes the new principal for the next period. For example, $100 invested at 8% interest is worth $108 after the first year ($100 principal + $8 interest). If the interest is not withdrawn, the interest for the next period will be calculated based on $108 principal.

As this compounding process repeats itself each period, the principal keeps growing by the amount of the previous interest. As the number of compounding periods increases, the amount of interest earned grows dramatically, especially when compared with simple interest, as illustrated in Exhibit 11-1.

compound interest Interest that is applied a number of times during the term of a loan or an investment. Interest paid on principal and previously earned interest.

EXHIBIT 11-1 The Time Value of Money

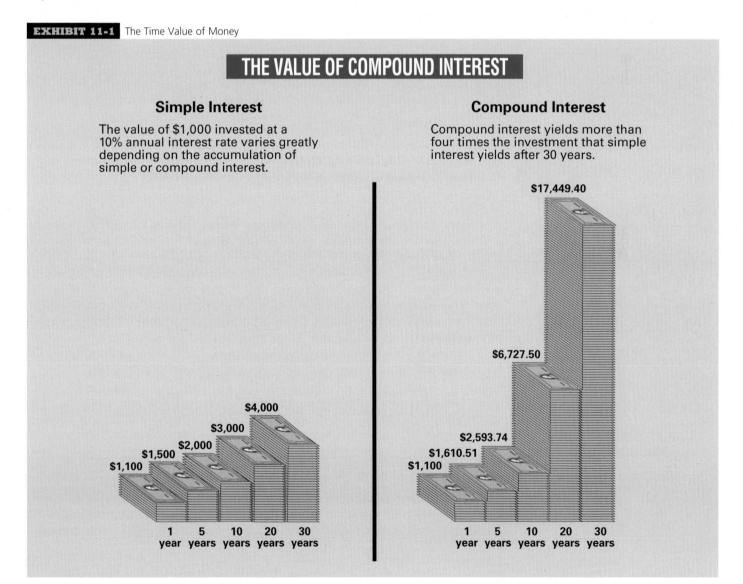

THE VALUE OF COMPOUND INTEREST

Simple Interest

The value of $1,000 invested at a 10% annual interest rate varies greatly depending on the accumulation of simple or compound interest.

$1,100
$1,500
$2,000
$3,000
$4,000

1 year   5 years   10 years   20 years   30 years

Compound Interest

Compound interest yields more than four times the investment that simple interest yields after 30 years.

$17,449.40
$6,727.50
$2,593.74
$1,610.51
$1,100

1 year   5 years   10 years   20 years   30 years

This chapter introduces you to an all-important business concept, the **time value of money**. Consider this: If you were owed $1,000, would you rather have it now or one year from now? If you answered "now," you already have a feeling for the concept. Money "now,"

time value of money The idea that money "now," or in the present, is more desirable than the same amount of money in the future because it can be invested and earn interest as time goes by.

compound amount, or **future value (FV)** The total amount of principal and accumulated interest at the end of a loan or an investment.

present amount, or **present value (PV)** An amount of money that must be deposited today at compound interest to provide a specified lump sum of money in the future.

or in the *present*, is more desirable than the same amount of money in the *future* because it can be invested and earn interest as time goes by.

In this chapter, you learn to calculate the **compound amount (future value)** of an investment at compound interest when the **present amount (present value)** is known. You also learn to calculate the present value that must be deposited now at compound interest to yield a known future amount. (See Exhibit 11-2.)

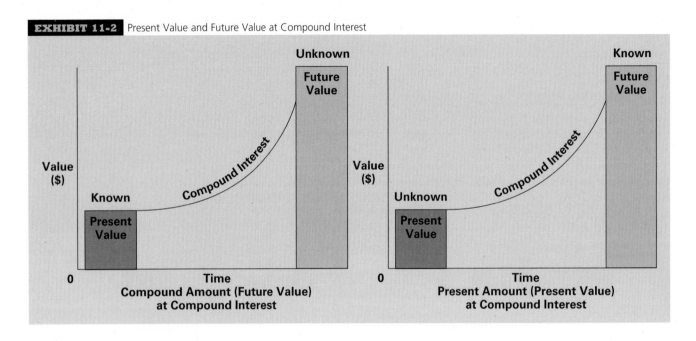

EXHIBIT 11-2 Present Value and Future Value at Compound Interest

11-1 MANUALLY CALCULATING COMPOUND AMOUNT (FUTURE VALUE) AND COMPOUND INTEREST

The Time Value of Money

Compounding divides the time of a loan or an investment into compounding periods or simply periods. To manually calculate the compound amount or future value of an investment, we must compound or calculate the interest as many times as there are compounding periods at the interest rate per period.

For example, an investment made for 5 years at 12% compounded annually (once per year) would have five compounding periods (5 years × 1 period per year), each at 12%. If the same investment was compounded semiannually (two times per year), there would be 10 compounding periods (5 years × 2 periods per year), each at 6% (12% annual rate ÷ 2 periods per year).

The amount of compound interest is calculated by subtracting the principal from the compound amount.

$$\text{Compound interest} = \text{Compound amount} - \text{Principal}$$

EXAMPLE1 MANUALLY CALCULATING COMPOUND INTEREST

a. Katie Trotta invested $5,000 in a passbook savings account at 10% interest compounded annually for 2 years. Manually calculate the compound amount of the investment and the total amount of compound interest Katie earned.

SOLUTIONSTRATEGY

To solve this compound interest problem manually, we must apply the simple interest formula twice because there are two compounding periods (2 years × 1 period per year). Note how the interest from the first period is reinvested or added to the original principal to earn interest in the second period.

Original principal	$5,000.00	
Interest—period 1	+ 500.00	($I = PRT = 5,000.00 \times .10 \times 1$)
Principal—period 2	5,500.00	
Interest—period 2	+ 550.00	($I = PRT = 5,500.00 \times .10 \times 1$)
Compound Amount	$6,050.00	

Compound Amount	$6,050.00
Principal	− 5,000.00
Compound Interest Earned	$1,050.00

b. Manually recalculate the compound amount and compound interest from the previous example by using semiannual compounding (two times per year). How much more interest would Katie earn if the bank offered semiannual compounding?

SOLUTIONSTRATEGY

To solve this compound interest problem, we must apply the simple interest formula four times because there are four compounding periods (2 years × 2 periods per year). Note that the time factor is now $\frac{6}{12}$, or $\frac{1}{2}$, because semiannual compounding means every 6 months.

Original principal	$5,000.00	
Interest—period 1	+ 250.00	($I = PRT = 5,000.00 \times .10 \times \frac{1}{2}$)
Principal—period 2	5,250.00	
Interest—period 2	+ 262.50	($I = PRT = 5,250.00 \times .10 \times \frac{1}{2}$)
Principal—period 3	5,512.50	
Interest—period 3	+ 275.63	($I = PRT = 5,512.50 \times .10 \times \frac{1}{2}$)
Principal—period 4	5,788.13	
Interest—period 4	+ 289.41	($I = PRT = 5,788.13 \times .10 \times \frac{1}{2}$)
Compound Amount	$6,077.54	

Compound Amount	$6,077.54
Principal	− 5,000.00
Compound Interest	$1,077.54

For the same investment values, semiannual compounding yields $27.54 more than annual compounding:

Interest with semiannual compounding	$1,077.54
Interest with annual compounding	− 1,050.00
	$27.54

"You're not getting any younger, Harvey...Ageing improves wine, compound interest...and nothing else."

TRYITEXERCISE1

Gail Parker invested $10,000 at 12% interest compounded semiannually for 3 years. Manually calculate the compound amount and the compound interest of Gail's investment.

CHECK YOUR ANSWERS WITH THE SOLUTIONS ON PAGE 366.

COMPUTING COMPOUND AMOUNT (FUTURE VALUE) AND COMPOUND INTEREST BY USING COMPOUND INTEREST TABLES

11-2

You do not have to work many compound interest problems manually, particularly those with numerous compounding periods, before you start wishing for an easier way! In actuality, there are two other methods for solving compound interest problems. The first uses a compound interest formula, and the second uses compound interest tables.

The compound interest formula, $A = P(1 + i)^n$, contains an exponent and therefore requires the use of a calculator with an exponential function key. The use of the compound interest formula is covered in Performance Objective 11-5.

A compound interest table, such as Table 11-1 on page 348, is a useful set of factors that represent the future values of $1 at various interest rates for a number of compounding

TABLE 11-1 Compound Interest Table (Future Value of $1 at Compound Interest)

Periods	$\frac{1}{2}\%$	1%	$1\frac{1}{2}\%$	2%	3%	4%	5%	6%	7%	8%	Periods
1	1.00500	1.01000	1.01500	1.02000	1.03000	1.04000	1.05000	1.06000	1.07000	1.08000	1
2	1.01003	1.02010	1.03023	1.04040	1.06090	1.08160	1.10250	1.12360	1.14490	1.16640	2
3	1.01508	1.03030	1.04568	1.06121	1.09273	1.12486	1.15763	1.19102	1.22504	1.25971	3
4	1.02015	1.04060	1.06136	1.08243	1.12551	1.16986	1.21551	1.26248	1.31080	1.36049	4
5	1.02525	1.05101	1.07728	1.10408	1.15927	1.21665	1.27628	1.33823	1.40255	1.46933	5
6	1.03038	1.06152	1.09344	1.12616	1.19405	1.26532	1.34010	1.41852	1.50073	1.58687	6
7	1.03553	1.07214	1.10984	1.14869	1.22987	1.31593	1.40710	1.50363	1.60578	1.71382	7
8	1.04071	1.08286	1.12649	1.17166	1.26677	1.36857	1.47746	1.59385	1.71819	1.85093	8
9	1.04591	1.09369	1.14339	1.19509	1.30477	1.42331	1.55133	1.68948	1.83846	1.99900	9
10	1.05114	1.10462	1.16054	1.21899	1.34392	1.48024	1.62889	1.79085	1.96715	2.15892	10
11	1.05640	1.11567	1.17795	1.24337	1.38423	1.53945	1.71034	1.89830	2.10485	2.33164	11
12	1.06168	1.12683	1.19562	1.26824	1.42576	1.60103	1.79586	2.01220	2.25219	2.51817	12
13	1.06699	1.13809	1.21355	1.29361	1.46853	1.66507	1.88565	2.13293	2.40985	2.71962	13
14	1.07232	1.14947	1.23176	1.31948	1.51259	1.73168	1.97993	2.26090	2.57853	2.93719	14
15	1.07768	1.16097	1.25023	1.34587	1.55797	1.80094	2.07893	2.39656	2.75903	3.17217	15
16	1.08307	1.17258	1.26899	1.37279	1.60471	1.87298	2.18287	2.54035	2.95216	3.42594	16
17	1.08849	1.18430	1.28802	1.40024	1.65285	1.94790	2.29202	2.69277	3.15882	3.70002	17
18	1.09393	1.19615	1.30734	1.42825	1.70243	2.02582	2.40662	2.85434	3.37993	3.99602	18
19	1.09940	1.20811	1.32695	1.45681	1.75351	2.10685	2.52695	3.02560	3.61653	4.31570	19
20	1.10490	1.22019	1.34686	1.48595	1.80611	2.19112	2.65330	3.20714	3.86968	4.66096	20
21	1.11042	1.23239	1.36706	1.51567	1.86029	2.27877	2.78596	3.39956	4.14056	5.03383	21
22	1.11597	1.24472	1.38756	1.54598	1.91610	2.36992	2.92526	3.60354	4.43040	5.43654	22
23	1.12155	1.25716	1.40838	1.57690	1.97359	2.46472	3.07152	3.81975	4.74053	5.87146	23
24	1.12716	1.26973	1.42950	1.60844	2.03279	2.56330	3.22510	4.04893	5.07237	6.34118	24
25	1.13280	1.28243	1.45095	1.64061	2.09378	2.66584	3.38635	4.29187	5.42743	6.84848	25

Periods	9%	10%	11%	12%	13%	14%	15%	16%	17%	18%	Periods
1	1.09000	1.10000	1.11000	1.12000	1.13000	1.14000	1.15000	1.16000	1.17000	1.18000	1
2	1.18810	1.21000	1.23210	1.25440	1.27690	1.29960	1.32250	1.34560	1.36890	1.39240	2
3	1.29503	1.33100	1.36763	1.40493	1.44290	1.48154	1.52088	1.56090	1.60161	1.64303	3
4	1.41158	1.46410	1.51807	1.57352	1.63047	1.68896	1.74901	1.81064	1.87389	1.93878	4
5	1.53862	1.61051	1.68506	1.76234	1.84244	1.92541	2.01136	2.10034	2.19245	2.28776	5
6	1.67710	1.77156	1.87041	1.97382	2.08195	2.19497	2.31306	2.43640	2.56516	2.69955	6
7	1.82804	1.94872	2.07616	2.21068	2.35261	2.50227	2.66002	2.82622	3.00124	3.18547	7
8	1.99256	2.14359	2.30454	2.47596	2.65844	2.85259	3.05902	3.27841	3.51145	3.75886	8
9	2.17189	2.35795	2.55804	2.77308	3.00404	3.25195	3.51788	3.80296	4.10840	4.43545	9
10	2736	2.59374	2.83942	3.10585	3.39457	3.70722	4.04556	4.41144	4.80683	5.23384	10
11	2.58043	2.85312	3.15176	3.47855	3.83586	4.22623	4.65239	5.11726	5.62399	6.17593	11
12	2.81266	3.13843	3.49845	3.89598	4.33452	4.81790	5.35025	5.93603	6.58007	7.28759	12
13	3.06580	3.45227	3.88328	4.36349	4.89801	5.49241	6.15279	6.88579	7.69868	8.59936	13
14	3.34173	3.79750	4.31044	4.88711	5.53475	6.26135	7.07571	7.98752	9.00745	10.14724	14
15	3.64248	4.17725	4.78459	5.47357	6.25427	7.13794	8.13706	9.26552	10.53872	11.97375	15
16	3.97031	4.59497	5.31089	6.13039	7.06733	8.13725	9.35762	10.74800	12.33030	14.12902	16
17	4.32763	5.05447	5.89509	6.86604	7.98608	9.27646	10.76126	12.46768	14.42646	16.67225	17
18	4.71712	5.55992	6.54355	7.68997	9.02427	10.57517	12.37545	14.46251	16.87895	19.67325	18
19	5.14166	6.11591	7.26334	8.61276	10.19742	12.05569	14.23177	16.77652	19.74838	23.21444	19
20	5.60441	6.72750	8.06231	9.64629	11.52309	13.74349	16.36654	19.46076	23.10560	27.39303	20
21	6.10881	7.40025	8.94917	10.80385	13.02109	15.66758	18.82152	22.57448	27.03355	32.32378	21
22	6.65860	8.14027	9.93357	12.10031	14.71383	17.86104	21.64475	26.18640	31.62925	38.14206	22
23	7.25787	8.95430	11.02627	13.55235	16.62663	20.36158	24.89146	30.37622	37.00623	45.00763	23
24	7.91108	9.84973	12.23916	15.17863	18.78809	23.21221	28.62518	35.23642	43.29729	53.10901	24
25	8.62308	10.83471	13.58546	17.00006	21.23054	26.46192	32.91895	40.87424	50.65783	62.66863	25

The values in Table 11-1 were generated by the formula $FV = (1 + i)^n$ rounded to five decimal places, where i is the interest rate per period and n is the total number of periods.

Interest Compounded		Compounding Periods per Year
Annually	Every year	1
Semiannually	Every 6 months	2
Quarterly	Every 3 months	4
Monthly	Every month	12
Daily	Every day	365
Continuously		Infinite

EXHIBIT 11-3
Compounding Periods per Year

periods. Because these factors are based on $1, the future values of other principal amounts are found by multiplying the appropriate table factor by the number of dollars of principal.

Compound amount (future value) = Table factor × Principal

To use the compound interest tables, we must know the number of compounding periods and the interest rate per period. Exhibit 11-3 above shows the various compounding options and the corresponding number of periods per year. *Note:* The greater the number of compounding periods per year, the higher the interest earned on the investment. Today interest can actually be calculated on a continuous basis—that is, up to the minute. In competitive markets, many banks offer continuous compounding as an incentive to attract new deposits.

To find the number of compounding periods of an investment, multiply the number of years by the number of periods per year.

Compounding periods = Years × Periods per year

To find the interest rate per period, divide the annual, or nominal, rate by the number of periods per year.

$$\text{Interest rate per period} = \frac{\text{Nominal rate}}{\text{Periods per year}}$$

STEPS FOR USING COMPOUND INTEREST TABLES

STEP 1. Scan across the top row to find the interest rate per period.

STEP 2. Look down that column to the row corresponding to the number of periods.

STEP 3. The table factor at the intersection of the rate-per-period column and the number-of-periods row is the future value of $1 at compound interest. Multiply the table factor by the principal to determine the compound amount.

Compound amount = Table factor × Principal

EXAMPLE2 USING COMPOUND INTEREST TABLES

John Anderson invested $1,200 in a certificate of deposit (CD) at 8% interest compounded quarterly for 5 years. Use Table 11-1 to find the compound amount of John's investment. What is the amount of the compound interest?

SOLUTIONSTRATEGY

To solve this compound interest problem, we must first find the interest rate per period and the number of compounding periods.

$$\text{Interest rate per period} = \frac{\text{Nominal rate}}{\text{Periods per year}}$$

$$\text{Interest rate per period} = \frac{8\%}{4} = 2\%$$

Compounding periods = Years × Periods per year

Compounding periods = 5 × 4 = 20

Now find the table factor by scanning across the top row of the compound interest table to 2% and down the 2% column to 20 periods. The table factor at that intersection is 1.48595. The compound amount is found by multiplying the table factor by the principal:

$$\text{Compound amount} = \text{Table factor} \times \text{Principal}$$
$$\text{Compound amount} = 1.48595 \times 1,200 = \underline{\$1,783.14}$$

The amount of interest is found by subtracting the principal from the compound amount.

$$\text{Compound interest} = \text{Compound amount} - \text{Principal}$$
$$\text{Compound interest} = 1,783.14 - 1,200.00 = \underline{\$583.14}$$

TRYITEXERCISE2

Jenny Chao invested $20,000 at 14% interest compounded semiannually for 8 years. Use Table 11-1 to find the compound amount of her investment. What is the amount of compound interest Jenny earned?

CHECK YOUR ANSWERS WITH THE SOLUTIONS ON PAGE 366.

11-3

CREATING COMPOUND INTEREST TABLE FACTORS FOR PERIODS BEYOND THE TABLE

When the number of periods of an investment is greater than the number of periods provided by the compound interest table, you can compute a new table factor by multiplying the factors for any two periods that add up to the number of periods required. For answer consistency in this chapter, use the two table factors that represent *half*, or values as close as possible to half, of the periods required. For example,

20 periods ⟍
           → 40 periods
20 periods ⟋

20 periods ⟍
           → 41 periods
21 periods ⟋

STEPS FOR CREATING NEW COMPOUND INTEREST TABLE FACTORS

STEP 1. For the stated interest rate per period, find the two table factors that represent *half*, or values as close as possible to half, of the periods required.

STEP 2. Multiply the two table factors from Step 1 to form the new factor.

STEP 3. Round the new factor to five decimal places.

EXAMPLE3 CALCULATING COMPOUND AMOUNT FOR PERIODS BEYOND THE TABLE

Calculate a new table factor and find the compound amount of $10,000 invested at 12% compounded monthly for 3 years.

SOLUTIONSTRATEGY

This investment requires a table factor for 36 periods (12 periods per year for 3 years). Because Table 11-1 provides factors only up to 25 periods, we must create one using the steps above.

Step 1. At 12% interest compounded monthly, the rate per period is 1%. Because we are looking for 36 periods, we will use the factors for 18 and 18 periods at 1%.

Table factor for 18 periods, 1% = 1.19615
Table factor for 18 periods, 1% = 1.19615

Step 2. Multiply the factors for 18 and 18 periods.

$$1.19615 \times 1.19615 = 1.4307748$$

Step 3. Round to five decimal places.

The new table factor for 36 periods is 1.43077.

The compound amount of the $10,000 investment is

Compound amount = Table factor × Principal
Compound amount = 1.43077 × 10,000 = $14,307.70

TRYITEXERCISE3

Stan Gray invests $3,500 at 16% interest compounded quarterly for 7 years. Calculate a new table factor and find the compound amount of Stan's investment.

CHECK YOUR ANSWERS WITH THE SOLUTIONS ON PAGE 366.

Source: www.hetemeel.com
© INTERFOTO/Alamy

CALCULATING ANNUAL PERCENTAGE YIELD (APY) OR EFFECTIVE INTEREST RATE

11-4

In describing investments and loans, the advertised or stated interest rate is known as the **annual**, or **nominal**, **rate**. It is also the rate used to calculate the compound interest. Consider, however, what happens to an investment of $100 at 12% nominal interest.

As we learned in Performance Objective 11-2, the greater the number of compounding periods per year, the higher the amount of interest earned. (See Exhibit 11-4.) Although the nominal interest rate is 12%, with monthly compounding, the $100 earns more than 12%. This is why many investment offers today advertise daily or continuous compounding. How much are these investments really earning?

annual, or **nominal**, **rate** The advertised or stated interest rate of an investment or loan. The rate used to calculate the compound interest.

Compounding	Interest Earned
Annually	$12.00
Semiannually	$12.36
Quarterly	$12.55
Monthly	$12.68

EXHIBIT 11-4
Compound Interest Earned on $100 at 12%

annual percentage yield (APY),
or **effective rate** The real or true rate
of return on an investment. It is the total
compound interest earned in 1 year divided
by the principal. The more compounding
periods per year, the higher the APY.

The **annual percentage yield (APY)**, or **effective rate**, reflects the real rate of return on an investment. APY is calculated by finding the total compound interest earned in 1 year and dividing by the principal. *Note*: This is actually the simple interest formula (from Chapter 10) solved for rate $R = I \div PT$, where T is equal to 1.

$$\text{Annual percentage (APY)} = \frac{\text{Total compound interest earned in 1 year}}{\text{Principal}}$$

From Exhibit 11-4, on page 351, we can see that the annual percentage yield is the same as the nominal rate when interest is compounded annually; however, it jumps to 12.36% ($12.36) when the compounding is changed to semiannually and to 12.68% ($12.68) when compounded monthly.

EXAMPLE 4   CALCULATING APY

What is the compound amount, compound interest, and annual percentage yield of $4,000 invested for 1 year at 8% compounded semiannually?

SOLUTION STRATEGY

First, we must find the total compound interest earned in 1 year. We can find the compound amount using the factor for 4%, two periods, from Table 11-1.

Compound amount = Table factor × Principal

Compound amount = 1.08160 × 4,000 = $4,326.40

Compound interest = Compound amount − Principal

Compound interest = 4,326.40 − 4,000 = $326.40

$$\text{Annual percentage yield} = \frac{\text{Total compound interest earned in 1 year}}{\text{Principal}}$$

$$\text{Annual percentage yield} = \frac{326.40}{4,000.00} = 8.16\%$$

TRY IT EXERCISE 4

Jill Quinn invested $7,000 in a certificate of deposit for 1 year at 6% interest compounded quarterly. What is the compound amount, compound interest, and annual percentage yield of Jill's investment? Round the APY to the nearest hundredth of a percent.

CHECK YOUR ANSWERS WITH THE SOLUTIONS ON PAGE 366.

11-5   (OPTIONAL) CALCULATING COMPOUND AMOUNT (FUTURE VALUE) BY USING THE COMPOUND INTEREST FORMULA

If your calculator has an exponential function key, y^x, you can calculate the compound amount of an investment by using the compound interest formula.

The compound interest formula states:

$$A = P(1 + i)^n$$

where:

A = Compound amount
P = Principal
i = Interest rate per period (expressed as a decimal)
n = Total compounding periods (years × periods per year)

STEPS FOR SOLVING THE COMPOUND INTEREST FORMULA

STEP 1. Add the 1 and the interest rate per period, i.

STEP 2. Raise the sum from Step 1 to the nth (number of compounding periods) power by using the y^x key on your calculator.

STEP 3. Multiply the principal, P, by the answer from Step 2.

Calculator Sequence: 1 $+$ i $=$ y^x n $\times$ P $=$ A

EXAMPLE5 USING THE COMPOUND INTEREST FORMULA

Use the compound interest formula to calculate the compound amount of $5,000 invested at 10% interest compounded semiannually for 3 years.

SOLUTIONSTRATEGY

This problem is solved by substituting the investment information into the compound interest formula. It is important to solve the formula using the sequence of steps outlined above. Note that the rate per period, i, is 5% (10% ÷ 2 periods per year). The total number of periods, the exponent n, is 6 (3 years × 2 periods per year).

$$A = P(1 + i)^n$$

$$A = 5,000(1 + .05)^6$$

$$A = 5,000(1.05)^6$$

$$A = 5,000(1.3400956) = 6,700.4782 = \underline{\$6,700.48}$$

Calculator Sequence: 1 $+$ .05 $=$ y^x 6 $\times$ 5000 $=$ $6,700.4782 = \underline{\$6,700.48}$

TRYITEXERCISE5

Use the compound interest formula to calculate the compound amount of $3,000 invested at 8% interest compounded quarterly for 5 years.

CHECK YOUR ANSWER WITH THE SOLUTION ON PAGE 366.

REVIEW EXERCISES

SECTION I **11**

For the following investments, find the total number of compounding periods and the interest rate per period.

JUMP START
WWW

	Term of Investment	Nominal (Annual) Rate (%)	Interest Compounded	Compounding Periods	Rate per Period (%)
1.	3 years	13	annually	3	13
2.	5 years	16	quarterly		
3.	12 years	8	semiannually		
4.	6 years	18	monthly		
5.	4 years	14	quarterly		
6.	9 years	10.5	semiannually		
7.	9 months	12	quarterly		

Manually calculate the compound amount and compound interest for the following investments.

	Principal	Time Period (years)	Nominal Rate (%)	Interest Compounded	Compound Amount	Compound Interest
8.	$4,000	2	10	annually	$4,840.00	$840.00
9.	$10,000	1	12	quarterly	_____	_____
10.	$8,000	3	8	semiannually	_____	_____
11.	$2,000	4	6	annually	_____	_____

Using Table 11-1, calculate the compound amount and compound interest for the following investments.

	Principal	Time Period (years)	Nominal Rate (%)	Interest Compounded	Compound Amount	Compound Interest
12.	$7,000	4	13	annually	$11,413.29	$4,413.29
13.	$11,000	6	14	semiannually	_____	_____
14.	$5,300	3	8	quarterly	_____	_____
15.	$67,000	2	18	monthly	_____	_____
16.	$25,000	15	11	annually	_____	_____
17.	$400	2	6	monthly	_____	_____
18.	$8,800	$12\frac{1}{2}$	10	semiannually	_____	_____

The following investments require table factors for periods beyond the table. Create the new table factor, rounded to five places, and calculate the compound amount for each.

	Principal	Time Period (years)	Nominal Rate (%)	Interest Compounded	New Table Factor	Compound Amount
19.	$13,000	3	12	monthly	1.43077	$18,600.01
20.	$19,000	29	9	annually	_____	_____
21.	$34,700	11	16	quarterly	_____	_____
22.	$10,000	40	13	annually	_____	_____
23.	$1,000	16	14	semiannually	_____	_____

For the following investments, compute the amount of compound interest earned in 1 year and the annual percentage yield (APY).

	Principal	Nominal Rate (%)	Interest Compounded	Compound Interest Earned in 1 Year	Annual Percentage Yield (APY)
24.	$5,000	10	semiannually	$512.50	10.25%
25.	$2,000	13	annually	_____	_____
26.	$36,000	12	monthly	_____	_____
27.	$1,000	8	quarterly	_____	_____
28.	$8,000	6	semiannually	_____	_____

Solve the following word problems by using Table 11-1.

29. Sherry Smith invested $3,000 at the Horizon Bank at 6% interest compounded quarterly.

   a. What is the annual percentage yield of this investment?

    b.   What will Sherry's investment be worth after 6 years?

30. As a savings plan for college, when their son Bob was born, the Wilburs deposited $10,000 in an account paying 8% compounded annually. How much will the account be worth when Bob is 18 years old?

31. You are owner of a UPS Store franchise. You have just deposited $12,000 in an investment account earning 12% compounded monthly. This account is intended to pay for store improvements in $2\frac{1}{2}$ years. At that rate, how much will be available in the account for the project?

32. The First National Bank is offering a 6-year certificate of deposit (CD) at 4% interest compounded quarterly; Second National Bank is offering a 6-year CD at 5% interest compounded annually.

    a.   If you were interested in investing $8,000 in one of these CDs, calculate the compound amount of each offer.

    b.   What is the annual percentage yield of each CD?

    c.   (Optional) If Third National Bank has a 6-year CD at 4.5% interest compounded monthly, use the compound interest formula to calculate the compound amount of this offer.

UPS Store franchises were voted #20 among all 500 U.S. franchise concepts by *Entrepreneur Magazine* in 2010, the #1 franchise opportunity in the Postal and Business Services category for 20 consecutive years, and the #1 franchise among veterans in the VetFran Program in 2008. With 4,300 locations, the minimum requirements are $60,000–$100,000 in cash or liquid assets.

Some of the products and services UPS Stores provide include packing and shipping services, mailbox and postal services, copying, faxing, notary services, finishing and printing services, and packaging and moving supplies.

33. A certain animal husbandry program has a flock of sheep that increases in size by 15% every year. If there are currently 48 sheep, how many sheep are expected to be in the flock in 5 years? Round to the nearest whole sheep.

LEARNINGTIP

Compounding Sheep!
The concept of compounding may also be used to compound "other variables" besides money. Use the compound interest table or formula for Exercises 33 and 34.

34. The rate of bacteria growth in a laboratory experiment was measured at 16% per hour. If this experiment is repeated and begins with 5 grams of bacteria, how much bacteria should be expected after 12 hours? Round to the nearest tenth of a gram.

(Optional) Solve the following exercises and word problems by using the compound interest formula.

	Principal	Time Period (years)	Nominal Rate (%)	Interest Compounded	Compound Amount	Compound Interest
35.	$5,000	4	4.2	semiannually	$5,904.40	$904.40
36.	$700	8	1.5	monthly	_____	_____
37.	$2,800	$2\frac{1}{2}$	3.1	quarterly	_____	_____
38.	$12,450	10	2.6	annually	_____	_____

39. Gabriel Hopen, a 32-year-old commercial artist, has just signed a contract with an advertising agency. Gabriel's starting salary is $47,800. The agency has agreed to increase his salary by 8.5% annually. How much will Gabriel's salary be after 5 years? Round to the nearest whole dollar.

40. The FernRod Motorcycle Company invested $250,000 at 4.5% compounded monthly to be used for the expansion of their manufacturing facilities. How much money will be available for the project in $3\frac{1}{2}$ years?

BUSINESS DECISION: DAILY COMPOUNDING

41. As an incentive to attract savings deposits, most financial institutions today offer **daily** and even **continuous compounding**. This means that savings, or passbook, accounts, as well as CDs, earn interest compounded each day or even more frequently—continuously, such as every hour or even every minute. Let's take a look at daily compounding.

    To calculate the compound amount, A, of an investment with daily compounding, use the compound interest formula modified as follows:

    • Rate per period (daily) $= \frac{i}{365}$ (nominal interest rate, i, divided by 365)

    • Number of periods (days), n, = number of days of the investment.

    $$A = P\left(1 + \frac{i}{365}\right)^n$$

    Calculator Sequence: 1 [+] [(] i [÷] 365 [)] [y^x] n [×] P [=] A

    a. On April 19, Thomas Ash deposited $2,700 in a passbook savings account at 3.5% interest compounded daily. What is the compound amount of his account on August 5?

    b. Using daily compounding, recalculate the compound amount for each of the three certificates of deposit in Exercise 32.

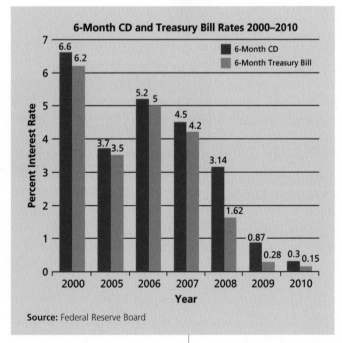

6-Month CD and Treasury Bill Rates 2000–2010

- 6-Month CD
- 6-Month Treasury Bill

2000: 6.6, 6.2
2005: 3.7, 3.5
2006: 5.2, 5
2007: 4.5, 4.2
2008: 3.14
2009: 1.62, 0.87
2010: 0.28, 0.3, 0.15

Percent Interest Rate / Year

PRESENT VALUE

In Section I, we learned how to find a future value when the present value was known. Let's take a look at the reverse situation, also commonly found in business. When a future value (an amount needed in the future) is known, the present value is the amount that must be invested today to accumulate with compound interest to that future value. For example, if a corporation wants $100,000 in 5 years (future value—known) to replace its fleet of trucks, what amount must be invested today (present value—unknown) at 8% compounded quarterly to achieve this goal? (See Exhibit 11-5.)

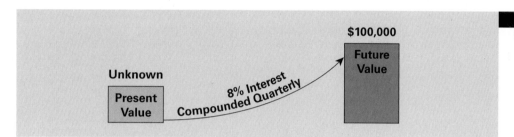

EXHIBIT 11-5

Present Value to Future Value

CALCULATING THE PRESENT VALUE OF A FUTURE AMOUNT BY USING PRESENT VALUE TABLES

11-6

Just as there are compound interest tables to aid in the calculation of compound amounts, present value tables help calculate the present value of a known future amount. Table 11-2 is such a table. Note that this table is similar to the compound interest table in that the table factors are based on the interest rate per period and the number of compounding periods.

STEPS FOR USING PRESENT VALUE TABLES

STEP 1. Scan across the top row to find the interest rate per period.

STEP 2. Look down that column to the row corresponding to the number of periods.

STEP 3. The table factor found at the intersection of the rate-per-period column and the number-of-periods row is the present value of $1 at compound interest. Multiply the table factor by the compound amount to determine the present value.

Present value = Table factor × Compound amount (future value)

EXAMPLE6 CALCULATING PRESENT VALUE

Charlie Watson will need $5,000 in 8 years. Use Table 11-2 to find how much he must invest now at 6% interest compounded semiannually to have $5,000, 8 years from now.

SOLUTIONSTRATEGY

To solve this present value problem, we will use 3% per period (6% nominal rate ÷ 2 periods per year) and 16 periods (8 years × 2 periods per year).

Step 1. Scan the top row of the present value table to 3%.

Step 2. Look down that column to the row corresponding to 16 periods.

TABLE 11-2   Present Value Table (Present Value of $1 at Compound Interest)

Periods	$\frac{1}{2}$%	1%	$1\frac{1}{2}$%	2%	3%	4%	5%	6%	7%	8%	Periods
1	0.99502	0.99010	0.98522	0.98039	0.97087	0.96154	0.95238	0.94340	0.93458	0.92593	1
2	0.99007	0.98030	0.97066	0.96117	0.94260	0.92456	0.90703	0.89000	0.87344	0.85734	2
3	0.98515	0.97059	0.95632	0.94232	0.91514	0.88900	0.86384	0.83962	0.81630	0.79383	3
4	0.98025	0.96098	0.94218	0.92385	0.88849	0.85480	0.82270	0.79209	0.76290	0.73503	4
5	0.97537	0.95147	0.92826	0.90573	0.86261	0.82193	0.78353	0.74726	0.71299	0.68058	5
6	0.97052	0.94205	0.91454	0.88797	0.83748	0.79031	0.74622	0.70496	0.66634	0.63017	6
7	0.96569	0.93272	0.90103	0.87056	0.81309	0.75992	0.71068	0.66506	0.62275	0.58349	7
8	0.96089	0.92348	0.88771	0.85349	0.78941	0.73069	0.67684	0.62741	0.58201	0.54027	8
9	0.95610	0.91434	0.87459	0.83676	0.76642	0.70259	0.64461	0.59190	0.54393	0.50025	9
10	0.95135	0.90529	0.86167	0.82035	0.74409	0.67556	0.61391	0.55839	0.50835	0.46319	10
11	0.94661	0.89632	0.84893	0.80426	0.72242	0.64958	0.58468	0.52679	0.47509	0.42888	11
12	0.94191	0.88745	0.83639	0.78849	0.70138	0.62460	0.55684	0.49697	0.44401	0.39711	12
13	0.93722	0.87866	0.82403	0.77303	0.68095	0.60057	0.53032	0.46884	0.41496	0.36770	13
14	0.93256	0.86996	0.81185	0.75788	0.66112	0.57748	0.50507	0.44230	0.38782	0.34046	14
15	0.92792	0.86135	0.79985	0.74301	0.64186	0.55526	0.48102	0.41727	0.36245	0.31524	15
16	0.92330	0.85282	0.78803	0.72845	0.62317	0.53391	0.45811	0.39365	0.33873	0.29189	16
17	0.91871	0.84438	0.77639	0.71416	0.60502	0.51337	0.43630	0.37136	0.31657	0.27027	17
18	0.91414	0.83602	0.76491	0.70016	0.58739	0.49363	0.41552	0.35034	0.29586	0.25025	18
19	0.90959	0.82774	0.75361	0.68643	0.57029	0.47464	0.39573	0.33051	0.27651	0.23171	19
20	0.90506	0.81954	0.74247	0.67297	0.55368	0.45639	0.37689	0.31180	0.25842	0.21455	20
21	0.90056	0.81143	0.73150	0.65978	0.53755	0.43883	0.35894	0.29416	0.24151	0.19866	21
22	0.89608	0.80340	0.72069	0.64684	0.52189	0.42196	0.34185	0.27751	0.22571	0.18394	22
23	0.89162	0.79544	0.71004	0.63416	0.50669	0.40573	0.32557	0.26180	0.21095	0.17032	23
24	0.88719	0.78757	0.69954	0.62172	0.49193	0.39012	0.31007	0.24698	0.19715	0.15770	24
25	0.88277	0.77977	0.68921	0.60953	0.47761	0.37512	0.29530	0.23300	0.18425	0.14602	25

Periods	9%	10%	11%	12%	13%	14%	15%	16%	17%	18%	Periods
1	0.91743	0.90909	0.90090	0.89286	0.88496	0.87719	0.86957	0.86207	0.85470	0.84746	1
2	0.84168	0.82645	0.81162	0.79719	0.78315	0.76947	0.75614	0.74316	0.73051	0.71818	2
3	0.77218	0.75131	0.73119	0.71178	0.69305	0.67497	0.65752	0.64066	0.62437	0.60863	3
4	0.70843	0.68301	0.65873	0.63552	0.61332	0.59208	0.57175	0.55229	0.53365	0.51579	4
5	0.64993	0.62092	0.59345	0.56743	0.54276	0.51937	0.49718	0.47611	0.45611	0.43711	5
6	0.59627	0.56447	0.53464	0.50663	0.48032	0.45559	0.43233	0.41044	0.38984	0.37043	6
7	0.54703	0.51316	0.48166	0.45235	0.42506	0.39964	0.37594	0.35383	0.33320	0.31393	7
8	0.50187	0.46651	0.43393	0.40388	0.37616	0.35056	0.32690	0.30503	0.28478	0.26604	8
9	0.46043	0.42410	0.39092	0.36061	0.33288	0.30751	0.28426	0.26295	0.24340	0.22546	9
10	0.42241	0.38554	0.35218	0.32197	0.29459	0.26974	0.24718	0.22668	0.20804	0.19106	10
11	0.38753	0.35049	0.31728	0.28748	0.26070	0.23662	0.21494	0.19542	0.17781	0.16192	11
12	0.35553	0.31863	0.28584	0.25668	0.23071	0.20756	0.18691	0.16846	0.15197	0.13722	12
13	0.32618	0.28966	0.25751	0.22917	0.20416	0.18207	0.16253	0.14523	0.12989	0.11629	13
14	0.29925	0.26333	0.23199	0.20462	0.18068	0.15971	0.14133	0.12520	0.11102	0.09855	14
15	0.27454	0.23939	0.20900	0.18270	0.15989	0.14010	0.12289	0.10793	0.09489	0.08352	15
16	0.25187	0.21763	0.18829	0.16312	0.14150	0.12289	0.10686	0.09304	0.08110	0.07078	16
17	0.23107	0.19784	0.16963	0.14564	0.12522	0.10780	0.09293	0.08021	0.06932	0.05998	17
18	0.21199	0.17986	0.15282	0.13004	0.11081	0.09456	0.08081	0.06914	0.05925	0.05083	18
19	0.19449	0.16351	0.13768	0.11611	0.09806	0.08295	0.07027	0.05961	0.05064	0.04308	19
20	0.17843	0.14864	0.12403	0.10367	0.08678	0.07276	0.06110	0.05139	0.04328	0.03651	20
21	0.16370	0.13513	0.11174	0.09256	0.07680	0.06383	0.05313	0.04430	0.03699	0.03094	21
22	0.15018	0.12285	0.10067	0.08264	0.06796	0.05599	0.04620	0.03819	0.03162	0.02622	22
23	0.13778	0.11168	0.09069	0.07379	0.06014	0.04911	0.04017	0.03292	0.02702	0.02222	23
24	0.12640	0.10153	0.08170	0.06588	0.05323	0.04308	0.03493	0.02838	0.02310	0.01883	24
25	0.11597	0.09230	0.07361	0.05882	0.04710	0.03779	0.03038	0.02447	0.01974	0.01596	25

The values in Table 11-2 were generated by the formula $PV = \dfrac{1}{(1 + i)^n}$ rounded to five decimal places, where i is the interest rate per period and n is the total number of periods.

Step 3. Find the table factor at the intersection of Steps 1 and 2 and multiply it by the compound amount to find the present value. Table factor = .62317.

$$\text{Present value} = \text{Table factor} \times \text{Compound amount}$$

$$\text{Present value} = .62317 \times 5,000 = \underline{\$3,115.85}$$

● TRYITEXERCISE6

Count Gustav wants to renovate his castle in Boulogne in 3 years. He estimates the cost to be $3,000,000. Use Table 11-2 to find how much the count must invest now at 8% interest compounded quarterly to have $3,000,000, 3 years from now.

CHECK YOUR ANSWER WITH THE SOLUTION ON PAGE 366.

CREATING PRESENT VALUE TABLE FACTORS FOR PERIODS BEYOND THE TABLE

11-7

Just as with the compound interest tables, there may be times when the number of periods of an investment or a loan is greater than the number of periods provided by the present value tables. When this occurs, you can create a new table factor by multiplying the table factors for any two periods that add up to the number of periods required.

For answer consistency in this chapter, use the two table factors that represent *half*, or values as close as possible to half, of the periods required. For example,

20 periods			20 periods		
	→ 40 periods			→ 41 periods	
20 periods			21 periods		

STEPS FOR CREATING NEW TABLE FACTORS

STEP 1. For the stated interest rate per period, find the two table factors that represent *half*, or values as close as possible to half, of the periods required.

STEP 2. Multiply the two table factors from Step 1 to form the new factor.

STEP 3. Round the new factor to five decimal places.

● EXAMPLE7 CREATING PRESENT VALUE TABLE FACTORS

Calculate a new table factor and find the present value of $2,000 if the interest rate is 12% compounded quarterly for 8 years.

● SOLUTIONSTRATEGY

This investment requires a table factor for 32 periods, four periods per year for 8 years. Because Table 11-2 provides factors only up to 25 periods, we must create one by using the steps above.

Step 1. At 12% interest compounded quarterly, the rate per period is 3%. Because we are looking for 32 periods, we will use the factors for 16 and 16 periods at 3%.

$$\text{Table factor for 16 periods, 3\%} = .62317$$

$$\text{Table factor for 16 periods, 3\%} = .62317$$

Step 2. Multiply the factors for 16 and 16 periods:

$$.62317 \times .62317 = .3883408$$

Step 3. Rounding to five decimal places, the new table factor for 32 periods is .38834. The present value of the $2,000 investment is

$$\text{Present value} = \text{Table factor} \times \text{Compound amount}$$
$$\text{Present value} = .38834 \times 2{,}000 = \underline{\$776.68}$$

TRYITEXERCISE7

Calculate a new table factor and find the present value of $8,500 if the interest rate is 6% compounded quarterly for 10 years.

CHECK YOUR ANSWERS WITH THE SOLUTIONS ON PAGE 366.

11-8 **(OPTIONAL) CALCULATING PRESENT VALUE OF A FUTURE AMOUNT BY USING THE PRESENT VALUE FORMULA**

If your calculator has an exponential function key, y^x, you can calculate the present value of an investment by using the present value formula.

The present value formula states:

$$PV = \frac{A}{(1+i)^n}$$

where:

      PV = **Present value**
       A = **Compound amount**
       i = **Interest rate per period (expressed as a decimal)**
      n = **Total compounding periods (years × periods per year)**

 STEPS **FOR SOLVING THE PRESENT VALUE FORMULA**

STEP 1. Add the 1 and the interest rate per period, i.

STEP 2. Raise the sum from Step 1 to the nth power by using the y^x key on your calculator.

STEP 3. Divide the compound amount, A, by the answer from Step 2.

 Calculator sequence 1 $\boxed{+}$ i $\boxed{=}$ $\boxed{y^x}$ n $\boxed{=}$ $\boxed{M+}$ A $\boxed{\div}$ $\boxed{MR}$ $\boxed{=}$ PV

EXAMPLE8 USING THE PRESENT VALUE FORMULA

Use the present value formula to calculate the present value of $3,000 if the interest rate is 16% compounded quarterly for 6 years.

SOLUTIONSTRATEGY

This problem is solved by substituting the investment information into the present value formula. It is important to solve the formula using the sequence of steps outlined. Note the rate per period, i, is 4% (16% ÷ 4 periods per year). The total number of periods, the exponent n, is 24 (6 years × 4 periods per year).

$$\text{Present value} = \frac{A}{(1+i)^n}$$
$$\text{Present value} = \frac{3{,}000}{(1+.04)^{24}}$$
$$\text{Present value} = \frac{3{,}000}{(1.04)^{24}}$$
$$\text{Present value} = \frac{3{,}000}{2.5633041} = \underline{\$1{,}170.36}$$

 Calculator Sequence: 1 $\boxed{+}$ .04 $\boxed{=}$ $\boxed{y^x}$ 24 $\boxed{=}$ $\boxed{M+}$ 3000 $\boxed{\div}$ $\boxed{MR}$ $\boxed{=}$ $\underline{\$1{,}170.36}$

● TRYITEXERCISE8

Sam and Rosa Alonso want to accumulate $30,000, 17 years from now as a college fund for their baby son, Michael. Use the present value formula to calculate how much they must invest now at an interest rate of 8% compounded semiannually to have $30,000 in 17 years.

CHECK YOUR ANSWER WITH THE SOLUTION ON PAGE 366.

REVIEW EXERCISES   SECTION II 11

For the following investments, calculate the present value (principal) and the compound interest. Use Table 11-2. Round your answers to the nearest cent.

	Compound Amount	Term of Investment	Nominal Rate (%)	Interest Compounded	Present Value	Compound Interest
1.	$6,000	3 years	9	annually	$4,633.08	$1,366.92
2.	$24,000	6 years	14	semiannually	_____	_____
3.	$650	5 years	8	quarterly	_____	_____
4.	$2,000	12 years	6	semiannually	_____	_____
5.	$50,000	25 years	11	annually	_____	_____
6.	$14,500	18 months	10	semiannually	_____	_____
7.	$9,800	4 years	12	quarterly	_____	_____
8.	$100,000	10 years	9	annually	_____	_____
9.	$250	1 year	18	monthly	_____	_____
10.	$4,000	27 months	8	quarterly	_____	_____

The following investments require table factors for periods beyond the table. Create the new table factor rounded to five places and calculate the present value for each.

	Compound Amount	Term of Investment (years)	Nominal Rate (%)	Interest Compounded	New Table Factor	Present Value
11.	$12,000	10	16	quarterly	.20829	$2,499.48
12.	$33,000	38	7	annually	_____	_____
13.	$1,400	12	12	quarterly	_____	_____
14.	$1,000	45	13	annually	_____	_____
15.	$110,000	17	8	semiannually	_____	_____

Solve the following word problems by using Table 11-2.

16. How much must be invested today at 6% compounded quarterly to have $8,000 in 3 years?

Ken Mellott/Shutterstock.com

Corporate bonds are debt obligations, or IOUs, issued by private and public corporations. They are typically issued in multiples of $1,000. Bonds are commonly used to finance company modernization and expansion programs.

When you buy a bond, you are lending money to the corporation that issued it. The corporation promises to return your money (or principal) on a specified maturity date. Until that time, it also pays you a stated rate of interest. The average daily trading volume in the U.S. Bond Market in 2010 was $853 billion, and in 2009, the outstanding U.S. bond market debt was $31.2 trillion.

LEARNINGTIP

Present Value of a Songbird!
Just as with compounding, the concept of present value of a future amount may also be applied to "other variables" besides money. Use the present value table or formula for Exercises 21 and 22.

17. Samantha Wimberly is planning a vacation in Europe in 4 years, after graduation. She estimates that she will need $3,500 for the trip.

   a. If her bank is offering 4-year certificates of deposit with 8% interest compounded quarterly, how much must Samantha invest now to have the money for the trip?

   b. How much compound interest will be earned on the investment?

18. Pinnacle Homes, a real estate development company, is planning to build five homes, each costing $125,000, in $2\frac{1}{2}$ years. The Galaxy Bank pays 6% interest compounded semiannually. How much should the company invest now to have sufficient funds to build the homes in the future?

19. Tri-Star Airlines intends to pay off a $20,000,000 corporate bond issue that comes due in 4 years. How much must the company set aside now at 6% interest compounded monthly to accumulate the required amount of money?

20. Stuart Daniels estimates that he will need $25,000 to set up a small business in 7 years.

   a. How much must Stuart invest now at 12% interest compounded quarterly to achieve his goal?

   b. How much compound interest will he earn on the investment?

21. Summertime songbird population within the Mid-America flyway is predicted to increase over the next 8 years at the rate of 2% per year. If the songbird population is predicted to reach 55 million in 8 years, how many songbirds are there today? Round to the nearest million.

22. The requirement for computer server capacity at Acme Industries is expected to increase at a rate of 15% per year for the next 5 years. If the server capacity is expected to be 1,400 gigabytes in 5 years, how many gigabytes of capacity are there today? Round to the nearest whole gigabyte.

(Optional) Solve the following exercises and word problems by using the present value formula

	Principal	Term of Investment	Nominal Rate (%)	Interest Compounded	Present Value	Compound Interest
23.	$4,500	7 years	3.8	annually	$3,466.02	$1,033.98
24.	$15,000	8 years	4.5	monthly	_____	_____
25.	$18,900	10 years	1.9	semiannually	_____	_____
26.	$675	15 months	2.7	quarterly	_____	_____

27. Alana and Eva Rodriguez are planning a cross-country road trip in 3 years. They estimate $6,000 will be needed to cover expenses. The National Bank of Pinecrest is offering a 3-year CD paying 3.62% interest compounded quarterly.

    a. How much should they set aside now to achieve their goal? Round to the nearest whole dollar.

    b. How much interest will Alana and Eva earn on the CD?

28. Mike Gioulis would like to have $25,000 in 4 years to pay off a balloon payment on his business mortgage. His money market account is paying 1.825% compounded daily. Disregarding leap years, how much money must Mike put in his account now to achieve his goal? Round to the nearest whole dollar.

BUSINESS DECISION: THE INFLATION FACTOR

29. You are the finance manager for Olympia Industries. The company plans to purchase $1,000,000 in new assembly line machinery in 5 years.

    a. How much must be set aside now at 6% interest compounded semiannually to accumulate the $1,000,000 in 5 years?

    b. If the inflation rate on this type of equipment is 4% per year, what will be the cost of the equipment in 5 years, adjusted for inflation?

    c. Use the inflation-adjusted cost of the equipment to calculate how much must be set aside now.

    d. (Optional) Use the present value formula to calculate how much would be required now if you found a bank that offered 6% interest compounded daily.

Inflation should be taken into account when making financial plans that cover time periods longer than a year.

CHAPTER

11

CHAPTER FORMULAS

Compound Interest

Compound interest = Compound amount − Principal

Compounding periods = Years × Periods per year

$$\text{Interest rate per period} = \frac{\text{Nominal rate}}{\text{Periods per year}}$$

Compound amount = Table factor × Principal

$$\text{Annual percentage yield (APY)} = \frac{\text{Total compound interest earned in 1 year}}{\text{Principal}}$$

Compound amount = Principal(1 + Interest rate per period)^{periods}

Present Value

Present value = Table factor × Compound amount

$$\text{Present value} = \frac{\text{Compound amount}}{(1 + \text{Interest rate per period})^{\text{periods}}}$$

CHAPTER SUMMARY

Section I: Compound Interest—The Time Value of Money

Topic	Important Concepts	Illustrative Examples
Manually Calculating Compound Amount (Future Value) **Performance Objective 11-1, Page 346**	In compound interest, the interest is applied a number of times during the term of an investment. Compound interest yields considerably higher interest than simple interest does because the investor is earning interest on the interest. Interest can be compounded annually, semi-annually, quarterly, monthly, daily, and continuously. 1. Determine number of compounding periods (years × periods per year). 2. Apply the simple interest formula, $I = PRT$, as many times as there are compounding periods, adding interest to principal before each succeeding calculation.	Manually calculate the compound amount of a $1,000 investment at 8% interest compounded annually for 2 years. Original principal 1,000.00 Interest—period 1 + 80.00 Principal—period 2 1,080.00 Interest—period 2 + 86.40 Compound amount $1,166.40
Calculating Amount of Compound Interest **Performance Objective 11-1, Page 346**	Amount of compound interest is calculated by subtracting the original principal from the compound amount. Compound interest = Compound amount − Principal	What is the amount of compound interest earned in the problem above? 1,166.40 − 1,000.00 = $166.40
Computing Compound Amount (Future Value) by Using Compound Interest Tables **Performance Objective 11-2, Page 347**	1. Scan across the top row of Table 11-1 to find the interest rate per period. 2. Look down that column to the row corresponding to the number of compounding periods. 3. The table factor found at the intersection of the rate-per-period column and the periods row is the future value of $1.00 at compound interest. Compound amount = Table factor × Principal	Use Table 11-1 to find the compound amount of an investment of $2,000 at 12% interest compounded quarterly for 6 years. Rate = 3% per period (12% ÷ 4) Periods = 24 (6 years × 4) Table factor = 2.03279 Compound amount = 2.03279 × 2,000 = $4,065.58

Creating Compound Interest Table Factors for Periods beyond the Table
 	
Performance Objective 11-3, Page 350
	1. For the stated interest rate per period, find the two table factors that represent *half*, or values as close as possible to half, of the periods required.
	2. Multiply the two table factors from Step 1 to form the new factor.
	3. Round the new factor to five decimal places.
		Create a new table factor for 5% interest for 30 periods.
		     Multiply the 5% factors for 15 and 15 periods from Table 11-1.
		5%, 15 periods = 2.07893
		5%, 15 periods = × 2.07893
		    30 4.3219499
		
		New factor rounded = 4.32195

Section I (continued)

Topic	Important Concepts	Illustrative Examples
Calculating Annual Percentage Yield (APY) or Effective Interest Rate **Performance Objective 11-4, Page 351**	To calculate annual percentage yield, divide total compound interest earned in 1 year by the principal. $$\text{Annual percentage yield (APY)} = \frac{1 \text{ year compound interest}}{\text{Principal}}$$	What is the annual percentage yield of $5,000 invested for 1 year at 12% compounded monthly? From Table 11-1, we use the table factor for 12 periods, 1%, to find the compound amount: $$1.12683 \times 5,000 = 5,634.15$$ Interest = Cmp. amt. − Principal Interest = 5,634.15 − 5,000.00 = 634.15 $$\text{APY} = \frac{634.15}{5,000} = \underline{12.68\%}$$
(Optional) Calculating Compound Amount (Future Value) by Using the Compound Interest Formula **Performance Objective 11-5, Page 352**	In addition to the compound interest tables, another method for calculating compound amount is by using the compound interest formula. $A = P(1 + i)^n$ where: A = Compound amount P = Principal i = Interest rate per period (decimal form) n = Number of compounding periods	What is the compound amount of $3,000 invested at 8% interest compounded quarterly for 10 years? $A = P(1 + i)^n$ $A = 3,000(1 + .02)^{40}$ $A = 3,000(1.02)^{40}$ $A = 3,000(2.2080396)$ $A = \underline{\$6,624.12}$

Section II: Present Value

Topic	Important Concepts	Illustrative Examples
Calculating the Present Value of a Future Amount by Using Present Value Tables **Performance Objective 11-6, Page 357**	When the future value, an amount needed in the future, is known, the present value is the amount that must be invested today to accumulate, with compound interest, to that future value. 1. Scan across the top row of Table 11-2 to find the rate per period. 2. Look down that column to the row corresponding to the number of periods. 3. The table factor found at the intersection of the rate-per-period column and the periods row is the present value of $1 at compound interest. Present value = Table factor × Compound amount	How much must be invested now at 10% interest compounded semiannually to have $8,000, 9 years from now? Rate = 5% (10% ÷ 2) Periods = 18 (9 years × 2) Table factor = .41552 Present value = .41552 × 8,000 Present value = $\underline{\$3,324.16}$
Creating Present Value Table Factors for Periods beyond the Table **Performance Objective 11-7, Page 359**	1. For the stated interest rate per period, find the two table factors that represent *half*, or values as close as possible to half, of the periods required. 2. Multiply the two table factors from Step 1 for the new factor. 3. Round the new factor to five decimal places.	Create a new table factor for 6% interest for 41 periods. Multiply the 6% factors for 21 and 20 periods from Table 11-2. 6%, 21 periods = .29416 6%, 20 periods = × .31180 41 .0917191 New factor rounded = $\underline{.09172}$
(Optional) Calculating Present Value of a Future Amount by Using the Present Value Formula **Performance Objective 11-8, Page 360**	If your calculator has an exponential function key, y^x, you can calculate the present value of an investment by using the present value formula. $$PV = \frac{A}{(1 + i)^n}$$ where: PV = Present value A = Compound amount i = Interest rate per period (decimal form) n = Total compounding periods	How much must be invested now to have $12,000 in 10 years if the interest rate is 12% compounded quarterly? $$\text{Present value} = \frac{12,000}{(1 + .03)^{40}}$$ $$PV = \frac{12,000}{(1.03)^{40}} = \frac{12,000}{3.2620378}$$ Present value = $\underline{\$3,678.68}$

TRY IT EXERCISE SOLUTIONS FOR CHAPTER 11

1.

10,000.00	Original principal
+ 600.00	$(I = PRT = 10,000 \times .12 \times \frac{1}{2} = 600)$
10,600.00	Principal period 2
+ 636.00	$(I = PRT = 10,600 \times .12 \times \frac{1}{2} = 636)$
11,236.00	Principal period 3
+ 674.16	$(I = PRT = 11,236 \times .12 \times \frac{1}{2} = 674.16)$
11,910.16	Principal period 4
+ 714.61	$(I = PRT = 11,910.16 \times .12 \times \frac{1}{2} = 714.61)$
12,624.77	Principal period 5
+ 757.49	$(I = PRT = 12,624.77 \times .12 \times \frac{1}{2} = 757.49)$
13,382.26	Principal period 6
+ 802.94	$(I = PRT = 13,382.26 \times .12 \times \frac{1}{2} = 802.94)$
$14,185.20	Compound amount

Compound Interest = 14,185.20 − 10,000.00 = $4,185.20

2. 7%, 16 periods

Compound amount = Table factor × Principal

Compound amount = 2.95216 × 20,000 = $59,043.20

Compound interest = Compound amount − Principal

Compound interest = 59,043.20 − 20,000.00 = $39,043.20

3. Table factor required = 4%, 28 periods

4%, 14 periods: 1.73168
4%, 14 periods: × 1.73168
28 periods   2.9987156 = 2.99872 New table factor
               4%, 28 periods

Compound amount = 2.99872 × 3,500 = $10,495.52

4. $1\frac{1}{2}$%, 4 periods

Compound amount = 1.06136 × 7,000 = $7,429.52

Compound interest = 7,429.52 − 7,000.00 = $429.52

$$\frac{\text{Annual}}{\text{percentage yield}} = \frac{\text{1 year interest}}{\text{Principal}} = \frac{429.52}{7,000.00} = 6.14\%$$

5. $A = P(1 + i)^n$ $P = \$3,000$

$$i = \frac{8\%}{4} = .02$$

$$n = 5 \times 4 = 20$$

$A = 3,000(1 + .02)^{20}$

$A = 3,000(1.02)^{20}$

$A = 3,000(1.4859474)$

$A = \$4,457.84$

6. 2%, 12 periods

Present value = Table factor × Compound amount

Present value = .78849 × 3,000,000 = $2,365,470

7. Table factor required = $1\frac{1}{2}$%, 40 Periods

$1\frac{1}{2}$%, 20 periods: .74247

$1\frac{1}{2}$%, 20 periods: × .74247
40 periods = .5512617 = .55126 New table factor
                     $1\frac{1}{2}$%, 40 periods

Present value = .55126 × 8,500 = $4,685.71

8. $PV = \dfrac{A}{(1 + i)^n}$ $A = 30,000$

$$i = \frac{8\%}{2} = .04$$

$$n = 17 \times 2 = 34$$

$$PV = \frac{30,000}{(1 + .04)^{34}}$$

$$PV = \frac{30,000}{(1.04)^{34}}$$

$$PV = \frac{30,000}{3.7943163} = \$7,906.56$$

CONCEPT REVIEW

1. Interest calculated solely on the principal is known as _____ interest, whereas interest calculated on the principal and previously earned interest is known as _____ interest. (11-1)

2. The concept that money "now," or in the present, is more desirable than the same amount of money in the future because it can be invested and earn interest as time goes by is known as the _____ of money. (11-1)

3. The total amount of principal and accumulated interest at the end of a loan or an investment is known as the _____ amount or _____ value. (11-1)

4. An amount of money that must be deposited today at compound interest to provide a specified lump sum of money in the future is known as the _____ amount or _____ value. (11-1, 11-6)

5. The amount of compound interest is calculated by subtracting the _____ from the compound amount. (11-1)

6. Compound interest is actually the _____ interest formula applied a number of times. (11-1)

7. A compound interest table is a useful set of factors that represent the future value of _____ at various interest rates for a number of compounding periods. (11-2)

8. A shortcut method for calculating approximately how long it takes money to double in value at compound interest is called the Rule of _____. (11-3)

9. Write the formula for calculating the number of compounding periods of a loan or an investment. (11-2)

10. Write the formula for calculating the interest rate per period of a loan or an investment. (11-2)

11. Newly created table factors for compound interest and present value should be rounded to _____ decimal places. (11-3, 11-7)

12. The annual percentage yield (APY) is equal to the total compound interest earned in _____ year divided by the _____. (11-4)

13. When using the compound interest table or the present value table, the factor is found at the intersection of the rate-per-_____ column and the number-of-_____ row. (11-2, 11-6)

14. To use the compound interest formula and the present value formula, you need a calculator with a(n) _____ function (y^x) key. (11-5, 11-8)

ASSESSMENT TEST

CHAPTER 11

Note: Round to the nearest cent when necessary.

Using Table 11-1, calculate the compound amount and compound interest for the following investments.

	Principal	Time Period (years)	Nominal Rate (%)	Interest Compounded	Compound Amount	Compound Interest
1.	$14,000	6	14	semiannually	_____	_____
2.	$7,700	5	6	quarterly	_____	_____
3.	$3,000	1	18	monthly	_____	_____
4.	$42,000	19	11	annually	_____	_____

The following investments require table factors for periods beyond the table. Create the new table factor and calculate the compound amount for each.

	Principal	Time Period (years)	Nominal Rate (%)	Interest Compounded	New Table Factor	Compound Amount
5.	$20,000	11	16	quarterly	_____	_____
6.	$10,000	4	6	monthly	_____	_____

For the following investments, compute the amount of compound interest earned in 1 year and the annual percentage yield. Round APY to the nearest hundredth of a percent.

	Principal	Nominal Rate (%)	Interest Compounded	Compound Interest Earned in 1 Year	Annual Percentage Yield (APY)
7.	$8,500	12	monthly	_____	_____
8.	$1,000,000	8	quarterly	_____	_____

Calculate the present value (principal) and the compound interest for the following investments. Use Table 11-2. Round answers to the nearest cent.

	Compound Amount	Term of Investment	Nominal Rate (%)	Interest Compounded	Present Value	Compound Interest
9.	$150,000	22 years	15	annually	_____	_____
10.	$20,000	30 months	14	semiannually	_____	_____
11.	$900	$1\frac{3}{4}$ years	18	monthly	_____	_____
12.	$5,500	15 months	8	quarterly	_____	_____

CHAPTER

11

The following investments require table factors for periods beyond the table. Create the new table factor and the present value for each.

	Compound Amount	Time Period (years)	Nominal Rate (%)	Interest Compounded	New Table Factor	Present Value
13.	$1,300	4	12	monthly	_____	_____
14.	$100,000	50	5	annually	_____	_____

Solve the following word problems by using Table 11-1 or 11-2. When necessary, create new table factors. Round dollars to the nearest cent and percents to the nearest hundredth of a percent.

15. What is the compound amount and compound interest of $36,000 invested at 12% compounded semiannually for 7 years?

16. What is the present value of $73,000 in 11 years if the interest rate is 8% compounded semiannually?

17. What is the compound amount and compound interest of $15,000 invested at 6% compounded quarterly for 27 months?

18. What is the annual percentage yield of a $10,000 investment for 1 year at 12% interest compounded monthly?

19. City Wide Delivery Service uses vans costing $24,800 each. How much will the company have to invest today to accumulate enough money to buy six new vans at the end of 4 years? City Wide's bank is currently paying 12% interest compounded quarterly.

20. You are the owner of a Jani-King cleaning service franchise. Your accountant has determined that the business will need $27,500 in new equipment in 3 years. If your bank is paying 6% interest compounded monthly, how much must you invest today to meet this financial goal? Round to the nearest whole dollar.

istockphoto.com/LL28 Photography

Jani-King is the world's largest commercial cleaning franchise company with over 12,000 owners worldwide. Jani-King contracts commercial cleaning services for many different facilities including healthcare, office, hotel/resort, manufacturing, restaurant, and sporting venues.

Jani-King has been rated the #1 Commercial Cleaning Franchise Company for 23 years in a row by *Entrepreneur Magazine*. In most regions, one may start a Jani-King franchise for as little as $3,000. Cleaning services is a $100 billion industry and is projected to grow to more than $155 billion. The U.S. Bureau of Labor Statistics reports that professional cleaning specialists will be the fastest-growing occupation in this decade.

21. Valerie Walton invested $8,800 at the Northern Trust Credit Union at 12% interest compounded quarterly.

a. What is the annual percentage yield of this investment?

b. What will Valerie's investment be worth after 6 years?

22. Bob and Joy Salkind want to save $50,000 in $5\frac{1}{2}$ years for home improvement projects. If the Bank of Aventura is paying 8% interest compounded quarterly, how much must they deposit now to have the money for the project?

23. While rummaging through the attic, you discover a savings account left to you by a relative. When you were 5 years old, he invested $20,000 in your name at 6% interest compounded semiannually. If you are now 20 years old, how much is the account worth?

"That's it then - Time is money."

24. Applegate Industries is planning to expand its production facility in a few years. New plant construction costs are estimated to be $4.50 per square foot. The company invests $850,000 today at 8% interest compounded quarterly.

   a. How many square feet of new facility could be built after $3\frac{1}{2}$ years? Round to the nearest whole square foot.

   b. If the company waits 5 years and construction costs increase to $5.25 per square foot, how many square feet could be built? Round to the nearest whole square foot. What do you recommend?

25. Over the past 10 years, you've made the following investments:

   1. Deposited $10,000 at 8% compounded semiannually in a 3-year certificate of deposit.
   2. After the 3 years, you took the maturity value (principal and interest) of that CD and added another $5,000 to buy a 4-year, 6% certificate compounded quarterly.
   3. When that certificate matured, you added another $8,000 and bought a 3-year, 7% certificate compounded annually.

   a. What was the total worth of your investment when the last certificate matured?

   b. What is the total amount of compound interest earned over the 10-year period?

26. Fred North owns Redlands Farms, a successful strawberry farm. The strawberry plants increase at a compound rate of 12% per year. Each year Fred brings new land under cultivation for the new strawberry plants. If the farm has 50 acres of strawberry plants today, how many acres of strawberry plants will the farm have in 8 years? Round to the nearest whole acre.

LEARNINGTIP

Use tables or formulas to solve Exercises 26 and 27.

27. At Reliable Trucking, Inc., annual sales are predicted to increase over the next 3 years at a rate of 6% per year. Sales equate to "fleet miles." If Reliable's fleet miles are predicted to reach 4.4 million in 3 years, what is the number of fleet miles today? Round to the nearest tenth of a million.

CHAPTER

11

(Optional) Solve the following exercises and word problems using formulas.

	Principal	Time Period (years)	Nominal Rate (%)	Interest Compounded	Compound Amount	Compound Interest
28.	$3,425	11	6.6	monthly	_____	_____
29.	$21,800	6	2.9	semiannually	_____	_____
30.	$400	$2\frac{1}{2}$	4.2	quarterly	_____	_____
31.	$9,630	5	3.1	annually	_____	_____

	Principal	Term of Investment	Nominal Rate (%)	Interest Compounded	Present Value	Compound Interest
32.	$6,300	14 years	6.3	annually	_____	_____
33.	$80,200	9 months	4.8	quarterly	_____	_____
34.	$27,500	10 years	3.6	semiannually	_____	_____
35.	$2,440	5 years	1.5	monthly	_____	_____

36. What is the compound amount and compound interest of a $73,000 investment earning 2.9% interest compounded semiannually for 4 years? Round to the nearest whole dollar.

37. Jorge Rodriguez would like to pay off his condo when he retires. How much must he invest now at 2.3% interest compounded quarterly to have $125,000 in 11 years? Round to the nearest whole dollar.

38. Quinn and Julius inherited $50,000 each from their great-grandmother's estate. Quinn invested her money in a 5-year CD paying 1.6% interest compounded semiannually. Julius deposited his money in a money market account paying 1.05% compounded monthly.
    a. How much money will each have in 5 years? Round to the nearest whole dollar.

    b. How much compound interest will they each have earned at the end of the 5 years?

39. Greg and Verena Sava need $20,000 in 3 years to expand their goat cheese business. The Bank of Sutton is offering a 3-year CD paying 3.9% compounded monthly. How much should they invest now to achieve their goal? Round to the nearest whole dollar.

BUSINESS DECISION: PAY ME NOW, PAY ME LATER

40. You are the owner of an apartment building that is being offered for sale for $1,500,000. You receive an offer from a prospective buyer who wants to pay you $500,000 now, $500,000 in 6 months, and $500,000 in 1 year.

a. What is the actual present value of this offer considering you can earn 12% interest compounded monthly on your money?

b. If another buyer offers to pay you $1,425,000 cash now, which is a better deal?

c. Because you understand the "time value of money" concept, you have negotiated a deal with the original buyer from part a whereby you will accept the three-payment offer but will charge 12% interest compounded monthly on the two delayed payments. Calculate the total purchase price under this new arrangement.

d. Now calculate the present value of the new deal to verify that you will receive the original asking price of $1,500,000 for your apartment building.

DOLLARS AND SENSE

Pay Me Now, Pay Me Later **is a good example of how the "time value of money" concept can be applied in business.**
Remember:
When interest can be earned, money today is more desirable than the same amount of money in the future.

COLLABORATIVE LEARNING ACTIVITY

Putting Your Money To Work

As a team, research financial institutions in your area (brick-and-mortar banks), as well as Internet-only institutions (virtual banks and eBanks), to find and list various certificates of deposit currently being offered. Assume that you want to invest $10,000 for 12 months.

a. What interest rates do these CDs pay? How often is interest compounded?
b. What is the early withdrawal penalty?
c. Are these CDs insured? If so, by whom? What is the limit per account?
d. Overall, which institution offers the CD that would earn the most interest after 12 months?

GO ONLINE FOR MORE ACTIVITIES • www.cengagebrain.com

istockphoto.com/Ken Mellott

CHAPTER **12**

Annuities

PERFORMANCE OBJECTIVES

FUTURE VALUE OF AN ANNUITY:
ORDINARY AND ANNUITY DUE

SECTION I

12

The concepts relating to compound interest in Chapter 11 were mainly concerned with lump sum investments or payments. Frequently in business, situations involve a series of equal periodic payments or receipts rather than lump sums. These are known as annuities. An **annuity** is the payment or receipt of *equal* cash amounts per period for a specified amount of time. Some common applications are insurance and retirement plan premiums and payouts; loan payments; and savings plans for future events such as starting a business, going to college, or purchasing expensive items (e.g., real estate or business equipment).

annuity Payment or receipt of equal amounts of money per period for a specified amount of time.

In this chapter, you learn to calculate the future value of an annuity, the amount accumulated at compound interest from a series of equal periodic payments. You also learn to calculate the present value of an annuity, the amount that must be deposited now at compound interest to yield a series of equal periodic payments. Exhibit 12-1 graphically shows the difference between the future value of an annuity and the present value of an annuity.

All the exercises in this chapter are of the type known as **simple annuities**. This means that the number of compounding periods per year coincides with the number of annuity payments per year. For example, if the annuity payments are monthly, the interest is compounded monthly; if the annuity payments are made every six months, the interest is compounded semiannually. **Complex annuities** are those in which the annuity payments and compounding periods do not coincide.

simple annuities Annuities in which the number of compounding periods per year coincides with the number of annuity payments per year.

complex annuities Annuities in which the annuity payments and compounding periods do not coincide.

As with compound interest, annuities can be calculated manually, by tables, and by formulas. Manual computation is useful for illustrative purposes; however, it is too tedious because it requires a calculation for each period. The table method is the easiest and most widely used and is the basis for this chapter's exercises. As in Chapter 11, there are formulas to calculate annuities; however, they require calculators with the exponential function key, y^x, and the change-of-sign key, $+/-$. These optional Performance Objectives are for students with business, financial, or scientific calculators.

CALCULATING THE FUTURE VALUE OF AN
ORDINARY ANNUITY BY USING TABLES

12-1

Annuities are categorized into annuities certain and contingent annuities. **Annuities certain** are annuities that have a specified number of periods, such as $200 per month for 5 years or $500 semiannually for 10 years. **Contingent annuities** are based on an uncertain time period, such as a retirement plan that is payable only for the lifetime of the retiree. This chapter is concerned only with annuities certain.

annuities certain Annuities that have a specified number of time periods.

contingent annuities Annuities based on an uncertain time period, such as the life of a person.

EXHIBIT 12-1 Timeline Illustrating Present and Future Value of an Annuity

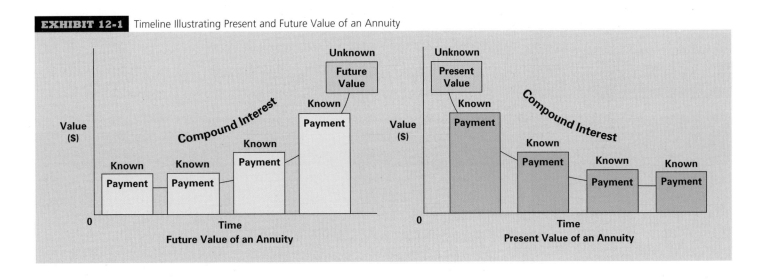

ordinary annuity Annuity that is paid or received at the end of each time period.

annuity due Annuity that is paid or received at the beginning of each time period.

future value of an annuity, or **amount of an annuity** The total amount of the annuity payments and the accumulated interest on those payments.

When the annuity payment is made at the end of each period, it is known as an **ordinary annuity**. When the payment is made at the beginning of each period, it is called an **annuity due**. A salary paid at the end of each month is an example of an ordinary annuity. A mortgage payment or rent paid at the beginning of each month is an example of an annuity due.

The **future value of an annuity** is also known as the **amount of an annuity**. It is the total of the annuity payments plus the accumulated compound interest on those payments.

For illustrative purposes, consider the following annuity calculated manually.

What is the future value of an ordinary annuity of $10,000 per year for 4 years at 6% interest compounded annually?

Because this is an ordinary annuity, the payment is made at the *end* of each period (in this case, years). Each interest calculation uses $I = PRT$, with $R = .06$ and $T = 1$ year.

Time	Balance	
Beginning of period 1	0	
	+ 10,000.00	First annuity payment (end of period 1)
End of period 1	10,000.00	
Beginning of period 2	10,000.00	
	600.00	Interest earned, period 2 ($10,000.00 \times .06 \times 1$)
	+ 10,000.00	Second annuity payment (end of period 2)
End of period 2	20,600.00	
Beginning of period 3	20,600.00	
	1,236.00	Interest earned, period 3 ($20,600.00 \times .06 \times 1$)
	+ 10,000.00	Third annuity payment (end of period 3)
End of period 3	31,836.00	
Beginning of period 4	31,836.00	
	1,910.16	Interest earned, period 4 ($31,836.00 \times .06 \times 1$)
	+ 10,000.00	Fourth annuity payment (end of period 4)
End of period 4	$43,746.16	Future value of the ordinary annuity

As you can see, calculating annuities this way is tedious. An annuity of 10 years with payments made monthly would require 120 calculations. As with compound interest, we will use tables to calculate the future value (amount) of an annuity.

"We could both avoid this daily annoyance, sir, if you'd buy me an *annuity!*"

STEPS FOR CALCULATING FUTURE VALUE (AMOUNT) OF AN ORDINARY ANNUITY

STEP 1. Calculate the interest rate per period for the annuity (nominal rate ÷ periods per year).

STEP 2. Determine the number of periods of the annuity (years × periods per year).

STEP 3. From Table 12-1 on pages 375–376, locate the ordinary annuity table factor at the intersection of the rate-per-period column and the number-of-periods row.

STEP 4. Calculate the future value of the ordinary annuity.

$$\text{Future value (ordinary annuity)} = \text{Ordinary annuity table factor} \times \text{Annuity payment}$$

LEARNINGTIP

The procedure for using the annuity tables, Tables 12-1 and 12-2, is the same as we used with the compound interest and present value tables in Chapter 11.

Table factors are found at the intersection of the rate-per-period column and the number-of-periods row.

TABLE 12-1 Future Value (Amount) of an Ordinary Annuity of $1

Periods	$\frac{1}{2}\%$	1%	$1\frac{1}{2}\%$	2%	3%	4%	5%	6%	7%	8%	Periods
1	1.00000	1.00000	1.00000	1.00000	1.00000	1.00000	1.00000	1.00000	1.00000	1.00000	1
2	2.00500	2.01000	2.01500	2.02000	2.03000	2.04000	2.05000	2.06000	2.07000	2.08000	2
3	3.01502	3.03010	3.04522	3.06040	3.09090	3.12160	3.15250	3.18360	3.21490	3.24640	3
4	4.03010	4.06040	4.09090	4.12161	4.18363	4.24646	4.31013	4.37462	4.43994	4.50611	4
5	5.05025	5.10101	5.15227	5.20404	5.30914	5.41632	5.52563	5.63709	5.75074	5.86660	5
6	6.07550	6.15202	6.22955	6.30812	6.46841	6.63298	6.80191	6.97532	7.15329	7.33593	6
7	7.10588	7.21354	7.32299	7.43428	7.66246	7.89829	8.14201	8.39384	8.65402	8.92280	7
8	8.14141	8.28567	8.43284	8.58297	8.89234	9.21423	9.54911	9.89747	10.25980	10.63663	8
9	9.18212	9.36853	9.55933	9.75463	10.15911	10.58280	11.02656	11.49132	11.97799	12.48756	9
10	10.22803	10.46221	10.70272	10.94972	11.46388	12.00611	12.57789	13.18079	13.81645	14.48656	10
11	11.27917	11.56683	11.86326	12.16872	12.80780	13.48635	14.20679	14.97164	15.78360	16.64549	11
12	12.33556	12.68250	13.04121	13.41209	14.19203	15.02581	15.91713	16.86994	17.88845	18.97713	12
13	13.39724	13.80933	14.23683	14.68033	15.61779	16.62684	17.71298	18.88214	20.14064	21.49530	13
14	14.46423	14.94742	15.45038	15.97394	17.08632	18.29191	19.59863	21.01507	22.55049	24.21492	14
15	15.53655	16.09690	16.68214	17.29342	18.59891	20.02359	21.57856	23.27597	25.12902	27.15211	15
16	16.61423	17.25786	17.93237	18.63929	20.15688	21.82453	23.65749	25.67253	27.88805	30.32428	16
17	17.69730	18.43044	19.20136	20.01207	21.76159	23.69751	25.84037	28.21288	30.84022	33.75023	17
18	18.78579	19.61475	20.48938	21.41231	23.41444	25.64541	28.13238	30.90565	33.99903	37.45024	18
19	19.87972	20.81090	21.79672	22.84056	25.11687	27.67123	30.53900	33.75999	37.37896	41.44626	19
20	20.97912	22.01900	23.12367	24.29737	26.87037	29.77808	33.06595	36.78559	40.99549	45.76196	20
21	22.08401	23.23919	24.47052	25.78332	28.67649	31.96920	35.71925	39.99273	44.86518	50.42292	21
22	23.19443	24.47159	25.83758	27.29898	30.53678	34.24797	38.50521	43.39229	49.00574	55.45676	22
23	24.31040	25.71630	27.22514	28.84496	32.45288	36.61789	41.43048	46.99583	53.43614	60.89330	23
24	25.43196	26.97346	28.63352	30.42186	34.42647	39.08260	44.50200	50.81558	58.17667	66.76476	24
25	26.55912	28.24320	30.06302	32.03030	36.45926	41.64591	47.72710	54.86451	63.24904	73.10594	25
26	27.69191	29.52563	31.51397	33.67091	38.55304	44.31174	51.11345	59.15638	68.67647	79.95442	26
27	28.83037	30.82089	32.98668	35.34432	40.70963	47.08421	54.66913	63.70577	74.48382	87.35077	27
28	29.97452	32.12910	34.48148	37.05121	42.93092	49.96758	58.40258	68.52811	80.69769	95.33883	28
29	31.12439	33.45039	35.99870	38.79223	45.21885	52.96629	62.32271	73.63980	87.34653	103.96594	29
30	32.28002	34.78489	37.53868	40.56808	47.57542	56.08494	66.43885	79.05819	94.46079	113.28321	30
31	33.44142	36.13274	39.10176	42.37944	50.00268	59.32834	70.76079	84.80168	102.07304	123.34587	31
32	34.60862	37.49407	40.68829	44.22703	52.50276	62.70147	75.29883	90.88978	110.21815	134.21354	32
33	35.78167	38.86901	42.29861	46.11157	55.07784	66.20953	80.06377	97.34316	118.93343	145.95062	33
34	36.96058	40.25770	43.93309	48.03380	57.73018	69.85791	85.06696	104.18375	128.25876	158.62667	34
35	38.14538	41.66028	45.59209	49.99448	60.46208	73.65222	90.32031	111.43478	138.23688	172.31680	35
36	39.33610	43.07688	47.27597	51.99437	63.27594	77.59831	95.83632	119.12087	148.91346	187.10215	36

The values in Table 12-1 were generated by the formula $\dfrac{(1+i)^n - 1}{i}$ and rounded to five decimal places, where i is the interest rate per period and n is the total number of periods.

(Continued)

TABLE 12-1 Future Value (Amount) of an Ordinary Annuity of $1   (*Continued*)

Periods	9%	10%	11%	12%	13%	14%	15%	16%	17%	18%	Periods
1	1.00000	1.00000	1.00000	1.00000	1.00000	1.00000	1.00000	1.00000	1.00000	1.00000	1
2	2.09000	2.10000	2.11000	2.12000	2.13000	2.14000	2.15000	2.16000	2.17000	2.18000	2
3	3.27810	3.31000	3.34210	3.37440	3.40690	3.43960	3.47250	3.50560	3.53890	3.57240	3
4	4.57313	4.64100	4.70973	4.77933	4.84980	4.92114	4.99338	5.06650	5.14051	5.21543	4
5	5.98471	6.10510	6.22780	6.35285	6.48027	6.61010	6.74238	6.87714	7.01440	7.15421	5
6	7.52333	7.71561	7.91286	8.11519	8.32271	8.53552	8.75374	8.97748	9.20685	9.44197	6
7	9.20043	9.48717	9.78327	10.08901	10.40466	10.73049	11.06680	11.41387	11.77201	12.14152	7
8	11.02847	11.43589	11.85943	12.29969	12.75726	13.23276	13.72682	14.24009	14.77325	15.32700	8
9	13.02104	13.57948	14.16397	14.77566	15.41571	16.08535	16.78584	17.51851	18.28471	19.08585	9
10	15.19293	15.93742	16.72201	17.54874	18.41975	19.33730	20.30372	21.32147	22.39311	23.52131	10
11	17.56029	18.53117	19.56143	20.65458	21.81432	23.04452	24.34928	25.73290	27.19994	28.75514	11
12	20.14072	21.38428	22.71319	24.13313	25.65018	27.27075	29.00167	30.85017	32.82393	34.93107	12
13	22.95338	24.52271	26.21164	28.02911	29.98470	32.08865	34.35192	36.78620	39.40399	42.21866	13
14	26.01919	27.97498	30.09492	32.39260	34.88271	37.58107	40.50471	43.67199	47.10267	50.81802	14
15	29.36092	31.77248	34.40536	37.27971	40.41746	43.84241	47.58041	51.65951	56.11013	60.96527	15
16	33.00340	35.94973	39.18995	42.75328	46.67173	50.98035	55.71747	60.92503	66.64885	72.93901	16
17	36.97370	40.54470	44.50084	48.88367	53.73906	59.11760	65.07509	71.67303	78.97915	87.06804	17
18	41.30134	45.59917	50.39594	55.74971	61.72514	68.39407	75.83636	84.14072	93.40561	103.74028	18
19	46.01846	51.15909	56.93949	63.43968	70.74941	78.96923	88.21181	98.60323	110.28456	123.41353	19
20	51.16012	57.27500	64.20283	72.05244	80.94683	91.02493	102.44358	115.37975	130.03294	146.62797	20
21	56.76453	64.00250	72.26514	81.69874	92.46992	104.76842	118.81012	134.84051	153.13854	174.02100	21
22	62.87334	71.40275	81.21431	92.50258	105.49101	120.43600	137.63164	157.41499	180.17209	206.34479	22
23	69.53194	79.54302	91.14788	104.60289	120.20484	138.29704	159.27638	183.60138	211.80134	244.48685	23
24	76.78981	88.49733	102.17415	118.15524	136.83147	158.65862	184.16784	213.97761	248.80757	289.49448	24
25	84.70090	98.34706	114.41331	133.33387	155.61956	181.87083	212.79302	249.21402	292.10486	342.60349	25
26	93.32398	109.18177	127.99877	150.33393	176.85010	208.33274	245.71197	290.08827	342.76268	405.27211	26
27	102.72313	121.09994	143.07864	169.37401	200.84061	238.49933	283.56877	337.50239	402.03234	479.22109	27
28	112.96822	134.20994	159.81729	190.69889	227.94989	272.88923	327.10408	392.50277	471.37783	566.48089	28
29	124.13536	148.63093	178.39719	214.58275	258.58338	312.09373	377.16969	456.30322	552.51207	669.44745	29
30	136.30754	164.49402	199.02088	241.33268	293.19922	356.78685	434.74515	530.31173	647.43912	790.94799	30
31	149.57522	181.94342	221.91317	271.29261	332.31511	407.73701	500.95692	616.16161	758.50377	934.31863	31
32	164.03699	201.13777	247.32362	304.84772	376.51608	465.82019	577.10046	715.74746	888.44941	1103.49598	32
33	179.80032	222.25154	275.52922	342.42945	426.46317	532.03501	664.66552	831.26706	1040.48581	1303.12526	33
34	196.98234	245.47670	306.83744	384.52098	482.90338	607.51991	765.36535	965.26979	1218.36839	1538.68781	34
35	215.71075	271.02437	341.58955	431.66350	546.68082	693.57270	881.17016	1120.71295	1426.49102	1816.65161	35
36	236.12472	299.12681	380.16441	484.46312	618.74933	791.67288	1014.34568	1301.02703	1669.99450	2144.64890	36

The values in Table 12-1 were generated by the formula $\dfrac{(1 + i)^n - 1}{i}$ and rounded to five decimal places, where i is the interest rate per period and n is the total number of periods.

EXAMPLE1 CALCULATING THE FUTURE VALUE OF AN ORDINARY ANNUITY

Stuart Daniels deposited $3,000 at the *end* of each year for 8 years in his savings account. If his bank paid 5% interest compounded annually, use Table 12-1 to find the future value of Stuart's account.

SOLUTIONSTRATEGY

Step 1. The rate period is 5% (5% ÷ 1 period per year).

Step 2. The number of periods is eight (8 years × 1 period per year).

Step 3. From Table 12-1, the table factor for 5%, eight periods is 9.54911.

Step 4. Future value = Ordinary annuity table factor × Annuity payment

Future value = 9.54911 × 3,000 = $28,647.33

TRYITEXERCISE1

Freeport Bank is paying 8% interest compounded quarterly. Use Table 12-1 to find the future value of $1,000 deposited at the *end* of every 3 months for 6 years.

CHECK YOUR ANSWER WITH THE SOLUTION ON PAGE 401.

DOLLARS AND SENSE

According to CNNmoney.com, as of March 2010, about 43% of Americans have saved less than $10,000 for retirement!

CALCULATING THE FUTURE VALUE OF AN ANNUITY DUE BY USING TABLES

12-2

Once again, for illustrative purposes, let's manually calculate the future value of the annuity. This time, however, it is an annuity due.

What is the amount of an annuity due of $10,000 per year for 4 years at 6% interest compounded annually?

Because this is an annuity due, the payment is made at the *beginning* of each period. Each interest calculation uses $I = PRT$, with $R = .06$ and $T = 1$ year.

Time	Balance	
Beginning of period 1	10,000.00	First annuity payment (beginning of period 1)
	+ 600.00	Interest earned, period 1 (10,000.00 × .06 × 1)
End of period 1	10,600.00	
Beginning of period 2	10,600.00	
	10,000.00	Second annuity payment (beginning of period 2)
	+ 1,236.00	Interest earned, period 2 (20,600.00 × .06 × 1)
End of period 2	21,836.00	
Beginning of period 3	21,836.00	
	10,000.00	Third annuity payment (beginning of period 3)
	+ 1,910.16	Interest earned, period 3 (31,836.00 × .06 × 1)
End of period 3	33,746.16	
Beginning of period 4	33,746.16	
	10,000.00	Fourth annuity payment (beginning of period 4)
	+ 2,624.77	Interest earned, period 4 (43,746.16 × .06 × 1)
End of period 4	$46,370.93	Future value of the annuity due

Saving for College

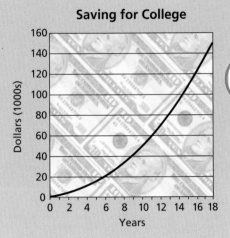

If parents save and invest $10 per workday at 12% interest from the birth date of their child, when the child is 18 and ready for college, the parents would have $150,000 accumulated—through the power of compounding.

When the future value of an annuity due is calculated, the table factor is found by using the same table as ordinary annuities (Table 12-1), with some modifications in the steps. With annuities due, you must *add* one period to the number of periods and *subtract* 1.00000 from the table factor.

STEPS FOR CALCULATING FUTURE VALUE (AMOUNT) OF AN ANNUITY DUE

STEP 1. Calculate the number of periods of the annuity (years × periods per year) and *add* one period to the total.

STEP 2. Calculate the interest rate per period (nominal rate ÷ periods per year).

STEP 3. From Table 12-1, locate the table factor at the intersection of the rate-per-period column and the number-of-periods row.

STEP 4. *Subtract* 1.00000 from the ordinary annuity table factor to get the annuity due table factor.

STEP 5. Calculate the future value of the annuity due.

Future value (annuity due) = Annuity due table factor × Annuity payment

EXAMPLE2 CALCULATING THE FUTURE VALUE OF AN ANNUITY DUE

Chris Manning deposited $60 at the *beginning* of each month for 2 years at his credit union. If the interest rate was 12% compounded monthly, use Table 12-1 to calculate the future value of Chris's account.

SOLUTIONSTRATEGY

Step 1. Number of periods of the annuity due is 24 (2 × 12) + 1 for a total of 25.

Step 2. Interest rate per period is 1% (12% ÷ 12).

Step 3. The ordinary annuity table factor at the intersection of the rate column and the periods row is 28.24320.

Step 4. Subtract 1.00000 from the table factor:

$$\begin{array}{ll} 28.24320 & \text{ordinary annuity table factor} \\ -\ 1.00000 & \\ \hline 27.24320 & \text{annuity due table factor} \end{array}$$

Step 5. Future value = Annuity due table factor × Annuity payment

Future value = 27.24320 × 60 = $1,634.59

TRYITEXERCISE2

Vista Savings & Loan is paying 6% interest compounded quarterly. Use Table 12-1 to calculate the future value of $1,000 deposited at the *beginning* of every 3 months for 5 years.

CHECK YOUR ANSWER WITH THE SOLUTION ON PAGE 401.

12-3 (OPTIONAL) CALCULATING THE FUTURE VALUE OF AN ORDINARY ANNUITY AND AN ANNUITY DUE BY FORMULA

Students with financial, business, or scientific calculators may use the following formulas to solve for the future value of an ordinary annuity and the future value of an annuity due.

LEARNINGTIP

Note that the annuity due formula is the same as the ordinary annuity formula except that it is multiplied by (1 + *i*). This is to account for the additional period of the annuity due.

Future value of an ordinary annuity	Future value of an annuity due
$FV = Pmt \times \dfrac{(1 + i)^n - 1}{i}$	$FV = Pmt \times \dfrac{(1 + i)^n - 1}{i} \times (1 + i)$

where:

> FV = future value
> Pmt = annuity payment
> i = interest rate per period (nominal rate ÷ periods per year)
> n = number of periods (years × periods per year)

Ordinary Annuity
Calculator Sequence: 1 $+$ i $=$ y^x n $-$ 1 $=$ $\div$ i $\times$ Pmt $=$ $FV_{\text{ordinary annuity}}$

Annuity Due
Calculator Sequence: 1 $+$ i $=$ $\times$ $FV_{\text{ordinary annuity}}$ $=$ $FV_{\text{annuity due}}$

EXAMPLE3 USING FORMULAS TO CALCULATE ANNUITIES

a. What is the future value of an ordinary annuity of $100 per month for 3 years at 12% interest compounded monthly?

b. What is the future value of this investment if it is an annuity due?

SOLUTIONSTRATEGY

a. For this future value of an ordinary annuity problem, we use i = 1% (12% ÷ 12) and n = 36 periods (3 years × 12 periods per year).

$$FV = Pmt \times \frac{(1+i)^n - 1}{i}$$

$$FV = 100 \times \frac{(1 + .01)^{36} - 1}{.01}$$

$$FV = 100 \times \frac{(1.01)^{36} - 1}{.01}$$

$$FV = 100 \times \frac{1.4307688 - 1}{.01}$$

$$FV = 100 \times \frac{.4307688}{.01}$$

$$FV = 100 \times 43.07688 = \underline{\$4,307.69}$$

Calculator Sequence: 1 $+$ .01 $=$ y^x 36 $-$ 1 $=$ $\div$ .01 $\times$ 100 $=$ $\underline{\$4,307.69}$

b. To solve the problem as an annuity due rather than an ordinary annuity, multiply $(1 + i)$, for one extra compounding period, by the future value of the ordinary annuity.

$$FV_{\text{annuity due}} = (1 + i) \times FV_{\text{ordinary annuity}}$$

$$FV_{\text{annuity due}} = (1 + .01) \times 4,307.69$$

$$FV_{\text{annuity due}} = (1.01) \times 4,307.69 = \underline{\$4,350.77}$$

Calculator Sequence: 1 $+$ .01 $=$ $\times$ 4,307.69 $=$ $\underline{\$4,350.77}$

TRYITEXERCISE3

Katrina Byrd invested $250 at the *end* of every 3-month period for 5 years at 8% interest compounded quarterly.

a. How much is Katrina's investment worth after 5 years?

b. If Katrina had invested the money at the *beginning* of each 3-month period rather than at the end, how much would be in the account?

CHECK YOUR ANSWERS WITH THE SOLUTIONS ON PAGE 401.

Note: Round to the nearest cent when necessary.

Use Table 12-1 to calculate the future value of the following ordinary annuities.

	Annuity Payment	Payment Frequency	Time Period (years)	Nominal Rate (%)	Interest Compounded	Future Value of the Annuity
1.	$1,000	every 3 months	4	8	quarterly	$18,639.29
2.	$2,500	every 6 months	5	10	semiannually	_____
3.	$10,000	every year	10	9	annually	_____
4.	$200	every month	2	12	monthly	_____
5.	$1,500	every 3 months	7	16	quarterly	_____

Use Table 12-1 to calculate the future value of the following annuities due.

	Annuity Payment	Payment Frequency	Time Period (years)	Nominal Rate (%)	Interest Compounded	Future Value of the Annuity
6.	$400	every 6 months	12	10	semiannually	$18,690.84
7.	$1,000	every 3 months	3	8	quarterly	_____
8.	$50	every month	$2\frac{1}{2}$	18	monthly	_____
9.	$2,000	every year	25	5	annually	_____
10.	$4,400	every 6 months	8	6	semiannually	_____

Solve the following exercises by using Table 12-1.

11. Paragon Savings & Loan is paying 6% interest compounded monthly. How much will $100 deposited at the *end* of each month be worth after 2 years?

12. Suntech Distributors, Inc., deposits $5,000 at the *beginning* of each 3-month period for 6 years in an account paying 8% interest compounded quarterly.

  a. How much will be in the account at the end of the 6-year period?

  b. What is the total amount of interest earned in this account?

13. Dana Phipps deposits $85 each payday into an account at 12% interest compounded monthly. She gets paid on the last day of each month. How much will her account be worth at the end of 30 months?

14. Jorge Otero has set up an annuity due with the United Credit Union. Each month $170 is electronically debited from his checking account and placed into a savings account earning 6% interest compounded monthly. What is the value of Jorge's account after 18 months?

15. When Ben Taylor was born, his parents began depositing $500 at the *beginning* of every year into an annuity to save for his college education. If the account paid 7% interest compounded annually for the first 10 years and then dropped to 5% for the next 8 years, how much is the account worth now that Ben is 18 years old and ready for college?

LEARNINGTIP

Exercise 15, Solution Hint
Once you have determined the account value after the first 10 years, don't forget to apply 5% compound interest to that value for the remaining 8 years.

(Optional) Solve the following exercises by using formulas.

Ordinary Annuities

	Annuity Payment	Payment Frequency	Time Period (years)	Nominal Rate (%)	Interest Compounded	Future Value of the Annuity
16.	$2,000	every 6 months	3	3.0	semiannually	$12,459.10
17.	$300	every month	8	6.0	monthly	_____
18.	$1,800	every 3 months	$3\frac{1}{2}$	4.0	quarterly	_____

Annuities Due

	Annuity Payment	Payment Frequency	Time Period (years)	Nominal Rate (%)	Interest Compounded	Future Value of the Annuity
19.	$675	every month	5	1.5	monthly	$42,082.72
20.	$4,800	every 3 months	3	6.0	quarterly	_____
21.	$7,000	every year	10	3.2	annually	_____

22. To establish a "rainy day" cash reserve account, Bonanza Industries deposits $10,000 of its profit at the end of each quarter into a money market account that pays 1.75% interest compounded quarterly.

    a. How much will the account be worth in 3 years?

    b. How much will the account be worth in $4\frac{1}{2}$ years?

23. As a part of his retirement planning strategy, Mark Woodson deposits $125 each payday into an investment account at 3% interest compounded monthly. Mark gets paid on the first day of each month.

    a. How much will his account be worth in 5 years?

    b. How much will his account be worth in 15 years?

24. Hi-Tech Hardware has been in business for a few years and is doing well. The owner has decided to save for a future expansion to a second location. He invests $1,000 at the *end* of every month at 12% interest compounded monthly.

   a. How much will be available for the second store after $2\frac{1}{2}$ years?

   b. How much would be in the account if the owner saved for 5 years?

   c. How much would be in the account after 5 years if it had been an annuity due?

BUSINESS DECISION: PLANNING YOUR NEST EGG

25. As part of your retirement plan, you have decided to deposit $3,000 at the *beginning* of each year into an account paying 5% interest compounded annually.

   a. How much would the account be worth after 10 years?

   b. How much would the account be worth after 20 years?

   c. When you retire in 30 years, what will be the total worth of the account?

   d. If you found a bank that paid 6% interest compounded annually rather than 5%, how much would you have in the account after 30 years?

   e. (Optional) Use the future value of an annuity due formula to calculate how much you would have in the account after 30 years if the bank in part d switched from annual compounding to monthly compounding and you deposited $250 at the *beginning* of each month instead of $3,000 at the *beginning* of each year.

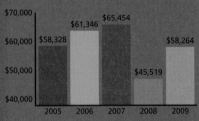

DOLLARS AND SENSE

70.5 is the new 65
For millions of American workers, the dream of retiring at age 65 has disappeared thanks to the Great Recession of 2008–2009. During this time, the average 401(k) retirement plan lost over 10% of its value. Most will have to work an extra 5.5 years to regain lost ground!

Average 401(k) Balances

Year	Balance
2005	$58,328
2006	$61,346
2007	$65,454
2008	$45,519
2009	$58,264

Source: *New York Post*, Feb. 28, 2010, page 35, Gregory Bresiger.

SECTION II

12

PRESENT VALUE OF AN ANNUITY: ORDINARY AND ANNUITY DUE

In Section I of this chapter, we learned to calculate the future value of an annuity. This business situation requires that a series of equal payments be made into an account, such as a savings account. The annuity starts with nothing and accumulates at compound interest to a future amount. Now consider the opposite situation. What if we wanted an account from which we could withdraw a series of equal payments over a period of time? This business situation requires that a lump sum amount be deposited at compound interest now to yield the specified annuity payments. The lump sum that is required up front is known as the **present value of an annuity.**

Let's look at a business situation using this type of annuity. A company owes $10,000 interest to bondholders at the end of each month for the next 3 years. The company decides to set up an account with a lump sum deposit now, which at compound interest will yield the $10,000 monthly payments for 3 years. After 3 years, the debt will have been paid and the account will be zero.

Just as in Section I, these annuities can be ordinary, whereby withdrawals from the account are made at the *end* of each period, or annuity due, in which the withdrawals are made at the *beginning*. As with the future value of an annuity, we will use tables to calculate the present value of an annuity. Once again, in addition to tables, these annuities can be solved by using formulas requiring a calculator with a y^x key.

present value of an annuity Lump sum amount of money that must be deposited now to provide a specified series of equal payments (annuity) in the future.

CALCULATING THE PRESENT VALUE OF AN ORDINARY ANNUITY BY USING TABLES

12-4

Table 12-2 on pages 385 and 386 is used to calculate the lump sum required to be deposited now to yield the specified annuity payment.

STEPS FOR CALCULATING PRESENT VALUE OF AN ORDINARY ANNUITY

STEP 1. Calculate the interest rate per period for the annuity (nominal rate ÷ periods per year).

STEP 2. Determine the number of periods of the annuity (years × periods per year).

STEP 3. From Table 12-2, locate the present value table factor at the intersection of the rate-per-period column and the number-of-periods row.

STEP 4. Calculate the present value of the ordinary annuity.

$$\text{Present value (ordinary annuity)} = \text{Ordinary annuity table factor} \times \text{Annuity payment}$$

EXAMPLE 4 CALCULATING THE PRESENT VALUE OF AN ORDINARY ANNUITY

How much must be deposited now at 9% compounded annually to yield an annuity payment of $5,000 at the end of each year for 10 years?

SOLUTIONSTRATEGY

Step 1. The rate per period is 9% (9% ÷ 1 period per year).

Step 2. The number of periods is 10 (10 years × 1 period per year).

Step 3. From Table 12-2, the table factor for 9%, 10 periods is 6.41766.

Step 4. Present value = Ordinary annuity table factor × Annuity payment
Present value = 6.41766 × 5,000 = $32,088.30

TRYITEXERCISE 4

The Broadway Movieplex needs $20,000 at the end of each 6-month movie season for renovations and new projection equipment. How much must be deposited now at 8% compounded semiannually to yield this annuity payment for the next 6 years?

CHECK YOUR ANSWER WITH THE SOLUTION ON PAGE 401.

12-5

CALCULATING THE PRESENT VALUE OF AN ANNUITY DUE BY USING TABLES

The present value of an annuity due is calculated by using the same table as ordinary annuities, with some modifications in the steps.

STEPS FOR CALCULATING PRESENT VALUE OF AN ANNUITY DUE

STEP 1. Calculate the number of periods of the annuity (years × periods per year) and *subtract* one period from the total.

STEP 2. Calculate the interest rate per period (nominal rate ÷ periods per year).

STEP 3. From Table 12-2, locate the table factor at the intersection of the rate-per-period column and the number-of-periods row.

STEP 4. *Add* 1.00000 to the ordinary annuity table factor to get the annuity due table factor.

STEP 5. Calculate the present value of the annuity due.

$$\text{Present value (annuity due)} = \text{Annuity due table factor} \times \text{Annuity payment}$$

EXAMPLE5 CALCULATING THE PRESENT VALUE OF AN ANNUITY DUE

How much must be deposited now at 10% compounded semiannually to yield an annuity payment of $2,000 at the beginning of each 6-month period for 7 years?

SOLUTIONSTRATEGY

Step 1. The number of periods for the annuity due is 14 (7 years × 2 periods per year) less 1 period = 13.

Step 2. The rate per period is 5% (10% ÷ 2 periods per year).

Step 3. From Table 12-2, the ordinary annuity table factor for 5%, 13 periods is 9.39357.

Step 4. Add 1 to the table factor from Step 3 to get 10.39357, the annuity due table factor.

Step 5. Present value (annuity due) = Annuity due table factor × Annuity payment
Present value = 10.39357 × 2,000 = $20,787.14

TRYITEXERCISE5

You are the accountant at Supreme Lumber, Inc. Based on sales and expense forecasts, you have estimated that $10,000 must be sent to the Internal Revenue Service for income tax payments at the *beginning* of each 3-month period for the next 3 years. How much must be deposited now at 6% compounded quarterly to yield the annuity payment needed?

CHECK YOUR ANSWER WITH THE SOLUTION ON PAGE 401.

| TABLE 12-2 | Present Value (Amount) of an Ordinary Annuity of $1 |

Periods	$\frac{1}{2}\%$	1%	$1\frac{1}{2}\%$	2%	3%	4%	5%	6%	7%	8%	Periods
1	0.99502	0.99010	0.98522	0.98039	0.97087	0.96154	0.95238	0.94340	0.93458	0.92593	1
2	1.98510	1.97040	1.95588	1.94156	1.91347	1.88609	1.85941	1.83339	1.80802	1.78326	2
3	2.97025	2.94099	2.91220	2.88388	2.82861	2.77509	2.72325	2.67301	2.62432	2.57710	3
4	3.95050	3.90197	3.85438	3.80773	3.71710	3.62990	3.54595	3.46511	3.38721	3.31213	4
5	4.92587	4.85343	4.78264	4.71346	4.57971	4.45182	4.32948	4.21236	4.10020	3.99271	5
6	5.89638	5.79548	5.69719	5.60143	5.41719	5.24214	5.07569	4.91732	4.76654	4.62288	6
7	6.86207	6.72819	6.59821	6.47199	6.23028	6.00205	5.78637	5.58238	5.38929	5.20637	7
8	7.82296	7.65168	7.48593	7.32548	7.01969	6.73274	6.46321	6.20979	5.97130	5.74664	8
9	8.77906	8.56602	8.36052	8.16224	7.78611	7.43533	7.10782	6.80169	6.51523	6.24689	9
10	9.73041	9.47130	9.22218	8.98259	8.53020	8.11090	7.72173	7.36009	7.02358	6.71008	10
11	10.67703	10.36763	10.07112	9.78685	9.25262	8.76048	8.30641	7.88687	7.49867	7.13896	11
12	11.61893	11.25508	10.90751	10.57534	9.95400	9.38507	8.86325	8.38384	7.94269	7.53608	12
13	12.55615	12.13374	11.73153	11.34837	10.63496	9.98565	9.39357	8.85268	8.35765	7.90378	13
14	13.48871	13.00370	12.54338	12.10625	11.29607	10.56312	9.89864	9.29498	8.74547	8.24424	14
15	14.41662	13.86505	13.34323	12.84926	11.93794	11.11839	10.37966	9.71225	9.10791	8.55948	15
16	15.33993	14.71787	14.13126	13.57771	12.56110	11.65230	10.83777	10.10590	9.44665	8.85137	16
17	16.25863	15.56225	14.90765	14.29187	13.16612	12.16567	11.27407	10.47726	9.76322	9.12164	17
18	17.17277	16.39827	15.67256	14.99203	13.75351	12.65930	11.68959	10.82760	10.05909	9.37189	18
19	18.08236	17.22601	16.42617	15.67846	14.32380	13.13394	12.08532	11.15812	10.33560	9.60360	19
20	18.98742	18.04555	17.16864	16.35143	14.87747	13.59033	12.46221	11.46992	10.59401	9.81815	20
21	19.88798	18.85698	17.90014	17.01121	15.41502	14.02916	12.82115	11.76408	10.83553	10.01680	21
22	20.78406	19.66038	18.62082	17.65805	15.93692	14.45112	13.16300	12.04158	11.06124	10.20074	22
23	21.67568	20.45582	19.33086	18.29220	16.44361	14.85684	13.48857	12.30338	11.27219	10.37106	23
24	22.56287	21.24339	20.03041	18.91393	16.93554	15.24696	13.79864	12.55036	11.46933	10.52876	24
25	23.44564	22.02316	20.71961	19.52346	17.41315	15.62208	14.09394	12.78336	11.65358	10.67478	25
26	24.32402	22.79520	21.39863	20.12104	17.87684	15.98277	14.37519	13.00317	11.82578	10.80998	26
27	25.19803	23.55961	22.06762	20.70690	18.32703	16.32959	14.64303	13.21053	11.98671	10.93516	27
28	26.06769	24.31644	22.72672	21.28127	18.76411	16.66306	14.89813	13.40616	12.13711	11.05108	28
29	26.93302	25.06579	23.37608	21.84438	19.18845	16.98371	15.14107	13.59072	12.27767	11.15841	29
30	27.79405	25.80771	24.01584	22.39646	19.60044	17.29203	15.37245	13.76483	12.40904	11.25778	30
31	28.65080	26.54229	24.64615	22.93770	20.00043	17.58849	15.59281	13.92909	12.53181	11.34980	31
32	29.50328	27.26959	25.26714	23.46833	20.38877	17.87355	15.80268	14.08404	12.64656	11.43500	32
33	30.35153	27.98969	25.87895	23.98856	20.76579	18.14765	16.00255	14.23023	12.75379	11.51389	33
34	31.19555	28.70267	26.48173	24.49859	21.13184	18.41120	16.19290	14.36814	12.85401	11.58693	34
35	32.03537	29.40858	27.07559	24.99862	21.48722	18.66461	16.37419	14.49825	12.94767	11.65457	35
36	32.87102	30.10751	27.66068	25.48884	21.83225	18.90828	16.54685	14.62099	13.03521	11.71719	36

The values in Table 12-2 were generated by the formula $\dfrac{(1 + i)^n - 1}{i(1 + i)^n}$ and rounded to five decimal places, where i is the interest rate per period and n is the total number of periods.

(Continued)

TABLE 12-2 Present Value (Amount) of an Ordinary Annuity of $1 *(Continued)*

Periods	9%	10%	11%	12%	13%	14%	15%	16%	17%	18%	Periods
1	0.91743	0.90909	0.90090	0.89286	0.88496	0.87719	0.86957	0.86207	0.85470	0.84746	1
2	1.75911	1.73554	1.71252	1.69005	1.66810	1.64666	1.62571	1.60523	1.58521	1.56564	2
3	2.53129	2.48685	2.44371	2.40183	2.36115	2.32163	2.28323	2.24589	2.20958	2.17427	3
4	3.23972	3.16987	3.10245	3.03735	2.97447	2.91371	2.85498	2.79818	2.74324	2.69006	4
5	3.88965	3.79079	3.69590	3.60478	3.51723	3.43308	3.35216	3.27429	3.19935	3.12717	5
6	4.48592	4.35526	4.23054	4.11141	3.99755	3.88867	3.78448	3.68474	3.58918	3.49760	6
7	5.03295	4.86842	4.71220	4.56376	4.42261	4.28830	4.16042	4.03857	3.92238	3.81153	7
8	5.53482	5.33493	5.14612	4.96764	4.79877	4.63886	4.48732	4.34359	4.20716	4.07757	8
9	5.99525	5.75902	5.53705	5.32825	5.13166	4.94637	4.77158	4.60654	4.45057	4.30302	9
10	6.41766	6.14457	5.88923	5.65022	5.42624	5.21612	5.01877	4.83323	4.65860	4.49409	10
11	6.80519	6.49506	6.20652	5.93770	5.68694	5.45273	5.23371	5.02864	4.83641	4.65601	11
12	7.16073	6.81369	6.49236	6.19437	5.91765	5.66029	5.42062	5.19711	4.98839	4.79322	12
13	7.48690	7.10336	6.74987	6.42355	6.12181	5.84236	5.58315	5.34233	5.11828	4.90951	13
14	7.78615	7.36669	6.98187	6.62817	6.30249	6.00207	5.72448	5.46753	5.22930	5.00806	14
15	8.06069	7.60608	7.19087	6.81086	6.46238	6.14217	5.84737	5.57546	5.32419	5.09158	15
16	8.31256	7.82371	7.37916	6.97399	6.60388	6.26506	5.95423	5.66850	5.40529	5.16235	16
17	8.54363	8.02155	7.54879	7.11963	6.72909	6.37286	6.04716	5.74870	5.47461	5.22233	17
18	8.75563	8.20141	7.70162	7.24967	6.83991	6.46742	6.12797	5.81785	5.53385	5.27316	18
19	8.95011	8.36492	7.83929	7.36578	6.93797	6.55037	6.19823	5.87746	5.58449	5.31624	19
20	9.12855	8.51356	7.96333	7.46944	7.02475	6.62313	6.25933	5.92884	5.62777	5.35275	20
21	9.29224	8.64869	8.07507	7.56200	7.10155	6.68696	6.31246	5.97314	5.66476	5.38368	21
22	9.44243	8.77154	8.17574	7.64465	7.16951	6.74294	6.35866	6.01133	5.69637	5.40990	22
23	9.58021	8.88322	8.26643	7.71843	7.22966	6.79206	6.39884	6.04425	5.72340	5.43212	23
24	9.70661	8.98474	8.34814	7.78432	7.28288	6.83514	6.43377	6.07263	5.74649	5.45095	24
25	9.82258	9.07704	8.42174	7.84314	7.32998	6.87293	6.46415	6.09709	5.76623	5.46691	25
26	9.92897	9.16095	8.48806	7.89566	7.37167	6.90608	6.49056	6.11818	5.78311	5.48043	26
27	10.02658	9.23722	8.54780	7.94255	7.40856	6.93515	6.51353	6.13636	5.79753	5.49189	27
28	10.11613	9.30657	8.60162	7.98442	7.44120	6.96066	6.53351	6.15204	5.80985	5.50160	28
29	10.19828	9.36961	8.65011	8.02181	7.47009	6.98304	6.55088	6.16555	5.82039	5.50983	29
30	10.27365	9.42691	8.69379	8.05518	7.49565	7.00266	6.56598	6.17720	5.82939	5.51681	30
31	10.34280	9.47901	8.73315	8.08499	7.51828	7.01988	6.57911	6.18724	5.83709	5.52272	31
32	10.40624	9.52638	8.76860	8.11159	7.53830	7.03498	6.59053	6.19590	5.84366	5.52773	32
33	10.46444	9.56943	8.80054	8.13535	7.55602	7.04823	6.60046	6.20336	5.84928	5.53197	33
34	10.51784	9.60857	8.82932	8.15656	7.57170	7.05985	6.60910	6.20979	5.85409	5.53557	34
35	10.56682	9.64416	8.85524	8.17550	7.58557	7.07005	6.61661	6.21534	5.85820	5.53862	35
36	10.61176	9.67651	8.87859	8.19241	7.59785	7.07899	6.62314	6.22012	5.86171	5.54120	36

The values in Table 12-2 were generated by the formula $\dfrac{(1 + i)^n - 1}{i(1 + i)^n}$ and rounded to five decimal places, where i is the interest rate per period and n is the total number of periods.

(OPTIONAL) CALCULATING THE PRESENT VALUE OF AN ORDINARY ANNUITY AND AN ANNUITY DUE BY FORMULA

12-6

Students with financial, business, or scientific calculators may use the following formulas to solve for the present value of an ordinary annuity and the present value of an annuity due. Note that the annuity due formula is the same as the ordinary annuity formula except that it is multiplied by $(1 + i)$. This is to account for the fact that with an annuity due, each payment earns interest for one additional period because payments are made at the beginning of each period, not the end.

Present value of an ordinary annuity	Present value of an annuity due
$PV = Pmt \times \dfrac{1 - (1 + i)^{-n}}{i}$	$PV = Pmt \times \dfrac{1 - (1 + i)^{-n}}{i} \times (1 + i)$

where:

PV = present value (lump sum)
Pmt = annuity payment
i = interest rate per period (nominal rate ÷ periods per year)
n = number of periods (years × periods per year)

Ordinary Annuity
Calculator Sequence: 1 [+] i [=] [y^x] n [+/−] [=] [M+] 1 [−] [MR] [=] [÷] i [×] Pmt [=] PV

Annuity Due
Calculator Sequence: 1 [+] i [=] [×] $PV_{\text{ordinary annuity}}$ [=] $PV_{\text{annuity due}}$

EXAMPLE6 CALCULATING PRESENT VALUE OF AN ANNUITY BY FORMULA

a. What is the present value of an ordinary annuity of $100 per month for 4 years at 12% interest compounded monthly?

b. What is the present value of this investment if it is an annuity due?

SOLUTIONSTRATEGY

a. For this present value of an ordinary annuity problem, we use $i = 1\%$ (12% ÷ 12) and $n = 48$ periods (4 years × 12 periods per year).

$$PV = Pmt \times \frac{1 - (1 + i)^{-n}}{i}$$

$$PV = 100 \times \frac{1 - (1 + .01)^{-48}}{.01}$$

$$PV = 100 \times \frac{1 - (1.01)^{-48}}{.01}$$

$$PV = 100 \times \frac{1 - .6202604}{.01}$$

$$PV = 100 \times \frac{.3797396}{.01}$$

$$PV = 100 \times 37.97396 = \underline{\$3,797.40}$$

Calculator Sequence:

1 [+] .01 [=] [y^x] 48 [+/−] [=] [M+] 1 [−] [MR] [=] [÷] .01 [×] 100 [=] $3,797.40

b. To solve as an annuity due rather than an ordinary annuity, multiply the present value of the ordinary annuity by $(1 + i)$ for one extra compounding period.

$$PV_{\text{annuity due}} = (1 + i) \times PV_{\text{ordinary annuity}}$$

$$PV_{\text{annuity due}} = (1 + .01) \times 3,797.40$$

$$PV_{\text{annuity due}} = (1.01) \times 3,797.40 = \underline{\$3,835.37}$$

Calculator Sequence: 1 [+] .01 [=] [×] 3,797.40 [=] $3,835.37

TRYITEXERCISE6

Use the present value of an annuity formula to solve the following.

a. Angus McDonald wants $500 at the *end* of each 3-month period for the next 6 years. If Angus's bank is paying 8% interest compounded quarterly, how much must he deposit now to receive the desired ordinary annuity?

b. If Angus wants the payments at the *beginning* of each 3-month period rather than at the end, how much should he deposit?

CHECK YOUR ANSWERS WITH THE SOLUTIONS ON PAGE 401.

SECTION II 12 REVIEW EXERCISES

Note: Round to the nearest cent when necessary.

Use Table 12-2 to calculate the present value of the following ordinary annuities.

	Annuity Payment	Payment Frequency	Time Period (years)	Nominal Rate (%)	Interest Compounded	Present Value of the Annuity
1.	$300	every 6 months	7	10	semiannually	$2,969.59
2.	$2,000	every year	20	7	annually	_____
3.	$1,600	every 3 months	6	12	quarterly	_____
4.	$1,000	every month	$1\frac{3}{4}$	6	monthly	_____
5.	$8,500	every 3 months	3	16	quarterly	_____

Use Table 12-2 to calculate the present value of the following annuities due.

	Annuity Payment	Payment Frequency	Time Period (years)	Nominal Rate (%)	Interest Compounded	Present Value of the Annuity
6.	$1,400	every year	10	11	annually	$9,151.87
7.	$1,300	every 3 months	4	12	quarterly	_____
8.	$500	every month	$2\frac{1}{4}$	18	monthly	_____
9.	$7,000	every 6 months	12	8	semiannually	_____
10.	$4,000	every year	18	7	annually	_____

Solve the following exercises by using Table 12-2.

11. Diamond Savings & Loan is paying 6% interest compounded monthly. How much must be deposited now to withdraw an annuity of $400 at the end of each month for 2 years?

12. Jami Minard wants to receive an annuity of $2,000 at the beginning of each year for the next 10 years. How much should be deposited now at 6% compounded annually to accomplish this goal?

13. As the chief accountant for Proline Industries, you have estimated that the company must pay $100,000 income tax to the IRS at the end of each quarter this year. How much should be deposited now at 8% interest compounded quarterly to meet this tax obligation?

14. Ron Sample is the grand prize winner in a college tuition essay contest awarded through a local organization's scholarship fund. The winner receives $2,000 at the beginning of each year for the next 4 years. How much should be invested at 7% interest compounded annually to award the prize?

15. Silver Tip Golf Course management has contracted to pay a golf green maintenance specialist a $680 monthly fee at the end of each month to provide advice on improving the quality of the greens on its 18-hole course. How much should be deposited now into an account that earns 6% compounded monthly to be able to make monthly payments to the consultant for the next year?

16. Analysts at Sky West Airlines did a 3-year projection of expenses. They calculated that the company will need $15,800 at the *beginning* of each 6-month period to buy fuel, oil, lube, and parts for aircraft operations and maintenance. Sky West can get 6% interest compounded semiannually from its bank. How much should Sky West deposit now to support the next 3 years of operations and maintenance expenses?

(Optional) Solve the following exercises by using formulas.

Present value of an ordinary annuity

	Annuity Payment	Payment Frequency	Time Period (yrs)	Nominal Rate (%)	Interest Compounded	Present Value of the Annuity
17.	$500	every 3 months	$3\frac{1}{4}$	6.0	quarterly	$5,865.77
18.	$280	every month	5	3.0	monthly	_____
19.	$950	every year	8	2.9	annually	_____

Present value of an annuity due

	Annuity Payment	Payment Frequency	Time Period (yrs)	Nominal Rate (%)	Interest Compounded	Present Value of the Annuity
20.	$1,100	every year	5	5.8	annually	$4,929.14
21.	$425	every month	$4\frac{3}{4}$	4.5	monthly	_____
22.	$700	every 6 months	7	3.6	semiannually	_____

23. As part of an inheritance, Joan Townsend will receive an annuity of $1,500 at the *end* of each month for the next 6 years. What is the present value of this inheritance at a rate of 2.4% interest compounded monthly?

24. Norm Legend has been awarded a scholarship from Canmore College. For the next 4 years, he will receive $3,500 for tuition and books at the *beginning* of each quarter. How much must the school set aside now in an account earning 3% interest compounded quarterly to pay Norm's scholarship?

BUSINESS DECISION: THE INSURANCE SETTLEMENT

25. Apollo Enterprises has been awarded an insurance settlement of $5,000 at the end of each 6-month period for the next 10 years.

   a. As the accountant, calculate how much the insurance company must set aside now at 6% interest compounded semiannually to pay this obligation to Apollo.

   b. How much would the insurance company have to invest now if the Apollo settlement was changed to $2,500 at the end of each 3-month period for 10 years and the insurance company earned 8% interest compounded quarterly?

   c. How much would the insurance company have to invest now if the Apollo settlement was paid at the beginning of each 3-month period rather than at the end?

SECTION III 12 SINKING FUNDS AND AMORTIZATION

sinking funds Accounts used to set aside equal amounts of money at the end of each period at compound interest for the purpose of saving for a future obligation.

amortization A financial arrangement whereby a lump-sum obligation is incurred at compound interest now, such as a loan, and is paid off or liquidated by a series of equal periodic payments for a specified amount of time.

IN THE BUSINESS WORLD

Mortgages, which are real estate loans, are a common example of amortization. More detailed coverage, including the preparation of amortization schedules, is found in Chapter 14.

Sinking funds and amortization are two common applications of annuities. In the previous sections of this chapter, the amount of the annuity payment was known and you were asked to calculate the future or present value (lump sum) of the annuity. In this section, the future or present value of the annuity is known and the amount of the payments is calculated.

A sinking fund situation occurs when the future value of an annuity is known and the payment required each period to amount to that future value is the unknown. **Sinking funds** are accounts used to set aside equal amounts of money at the end of each period at compound interest for the purpose of saving for a future obligation. Businesses use sinking funds to accumulate money for such things as new equipment, facility expansion, and other expensive items needed in the future. Another common use is to retire financial obligations such as bond issues that come due at a future date. Individuals can use sinking funds to save for a college education, a car, the down payment on a house, or a vacation.

Amortization is the opposite of a sinking fund. **Amortization** is a financial arrangement whereby a lump-sum obligation is incurred at compound interest now (present value) and is paid off or liquidated by a series of equal periodic payments for a specified amount of time. With amortization, the amount of the loan or obligation is given and the equal payments that will amortize, or pay off, the obligation must be calculated. Some business uses of amortization include paying off loans and liquidating insurance or retirement funds.

In this section, you learn to calculate the sinking fund payment required to save for a future amount and the amortization payment required to liquidate a present amount. We assume that all annuities are ordinary, with payments made at the *end* of each period. As in previous sections, these exercises can be calculated by tables or by formulas.

12-7 CALCULATING THE AMOUNT OF A SINKING FUND PAYMENT BY TABLE

In a sinking fund, the future value is known; therefore, we use the future value of an annuity table (Table 12-1) to calculate the amount of the payment.

STEPS FOR CALCULATING THE AMOUNT OF A SINKING FUND PAYMENT

STEP 1. Using the appropriate rate per period and number of periods of the sinking fund, find the future value table factor from Table 12-1.

STEP 2. Calculate the amount of the sinking fund payment.

$$\text{Sinking fund payment} = \frac{\text{Future value of the sinking fund}}{\text{Future value table factor}}$$

EXAMPLE7 CALCULATING THE AMOUNT OF A SINKING FUND PAYMENT

What sinking fund payment is required at the end of each 6-month period at 6% interest compounded semiannually to amount to $12,000 in 4 years?

SOLUTIONSTRATEGY

Step 1. This sinking fund is for eight periods (4 years × 2 periods per year) at 3% per period (6% ÷ 2 periods per year). From Table 12-1, eight periods, 3% per period gives a future value table factor of 8.89234.

Step 2. Sinking fund payment = $\dfrac{\text{Future value of the sinking fund}}{\text{Future value table factor}}$

Sinking fund payment = $\dfrac{12,000}{8.89234}$ = $\underline{\$1,349.48}$

TRYITEXERCISE7

Magi Khoo wants to accumulate $8,000 in 5 years for a trip to Europe. If Magi's bank is paying 12% interest compounded quarterly, how much must she deposit at the end of each 3-month period in a sinking fund to reach her desired goal?

CHECK YOUR ANSWER WITH THE SOLUTION ON PAGE 402.

Sinking funds enable businesses to plan for future purchases of expensive equipment.

Liz Van Steenburgh/Shutterstock.com

12-8 CALCULATING THE AMOUNT OF AN AMORTIZATION PAYMENT BY TABLE

Amortization is the process of "paying off" a financial obligation with a series of equal and regular payments over a period of time. With amortization, the original amount of the loan or obligation is known (present value); therefore, we use the present value table (Table 12-2) to calculate the amount of the payment.

STEPS FOR CALCULATING THE AMOUNT OF AN AMORTIZATION PAYMENT

STEP 1. Using the appropriate rate per period and number of periods of the amortization, find the present value table factor from Table 12-2.

STEP 2. Calculate the amount of the amortization payment.

$$\text{Amortization payment} = \frac{\text{Original amount of obligation}}{\text{Present value table factor}}$$

EXAMPLE8 CALCULATING THE AMOUNT OF AN AMORTIZATION PAYMENT

What amortization payments are required each month at 12% interest to pay off a $10,000 loan in 2 years?

SOLUTIONSTRATEGY

Step 1. This amortization is for 24 periods (2 years × 12 periods per year) at 1% per period (12% ÷ 12 periods per year). From Table 12-2, 24 periods, 1% per period gives a present value table factor of 21.24339.

Step 2. $\text{Amortization payment} = \dfrac{\text{Original amount of obligation}}{\text{Present value table factor}}$

$\text{Amortization payment} = \dfrac{10,000}{21.24339} = \underline{\$470.73}$

TRYITEXERCISE8

Captain Bob Albrecht purchased a new fishing boat for $130,000. He made a $20,000 down payment and financed the balance at his bank for 7 years. What amortization payments are required every 3 months at 16% interest to pay off the boat loan?

CHECK YOUR ANSWER WITH THE SOLUTION ON PAGE 402.

12-9 (OPTIONAL) CALCULATING SINKING FUND PAYMENTS BY FORMULA

In addition to using Table 12-1, sinking fund payments may be calculated by using the formula

$$\text{Sinking fund payment} = FV \times \frac{i}{(1+i)^n - 1}$$

where:

FV = amount needed in the future

i = interest rate per period (nominal rate ÷ periods per year)

n = number of periods (years × periods per year)

Calculator Sequence:

1 $+$ i $=$ y^x n $-$ 1 $=$ M+ i $÷$ MR $×$ FV $=$ Sinking fund payment

EXAMPLE9 CALCULATING SINKING FUND PAYMENTS BY FORMULA

Ocean Air Corporation needs $100,000 in 5 years to pay off a bond issue. What sinking fund payment is required at the end of each month at 12% interest compounded monthly to meet this financial obligation?

SOLUTIONSTRATEGY

To solve this sinking fund problem, we use 1% interest rate per period (12% ÷ 12) and 60 periods (5 years × 12 periods per year).

Sinking fund payment = Future value $\times \dfrac{i}{(1 + i)^n - 1}$

Sinking fund payment = $10,000 \times \dfrac{.01}{(1 + .01)^{60} - 1}$

Sinking fund payment = $100,000 \times \dfrac{.01}{.8166967}$

Sinking fund payment = $100,000 \times .0122444 = \underline{\$1,224.44}$

Calculator Sequence:

1 $+$ .01 $=$ y^x 60 $-$ 1 $=$ M+ .01 $÷$ MR $×$ 100,000 $=$ $\underline{\$1,224.44}$

TRYITEXERCISE9

Lake Louise Ski Rental Center will need $40,000 in 6 years to replace aging equipment. What sinking fund payment is required at the end of each month at 6% interest compounded monthly to amount to the $40,000 in 6 years?

CHECK YOUR ANSWER WITH THE SOLUTION ON PAGE 402.

(OPTIONAL) CALCULATING AMORTIZATION PAYMENTS BY FORMULA

12-10

In addition to using Table 12-2, amortization payments may be calculated by using the formula

$$\text{Amortization payment} = PV \times \frac{i}{1 - (1 + i)^{-n}}$$

where:

PV = amount of the loan or obligation

i = interest rate per period (nominal rate ÷ periods per year)

n = number of periods (years × periods per year)

Calculator Sequence:

1 $+$ i $=$ y^x n $+/-$ $=$ M+ 1 $-$ MR $=$ MC M+ i $÷$ MR $×$ PV $=$ Amortization payment

EXAMPLE 10 CALCULATING AMORTIZATION PAYMENTS BY FORMULA

What amortization payment is required each month at 18% interest to pay off $5,000 in 3 years?

SOLUTIONSTRATEGY

To solve this amortization problem, we use 1.5% interest rate per period (18% ÷ 12) and 36 periods (3 years × 12 periods per year).

$$\text{Amortization payment} = \text{Present value} \times \frac{i}{1-(1+i)^{-n}}$$

$$\text{Amortization payment} = 5,000 \times \frac{.015}{1-(1+.015)^{-36}}$$

$$\text{Amortization payment} = 5,000 \times \frac{.015}{.4149103}$$

$$\text{Amortization payment} = 5,000 \times .0361524 = \underline{\$180.76}$$

Calculator Sequence:

1 + .015 = y^x 36 +/− = M+ 1 − MR = MC M+ .015 ÷ MR × 5,000 =

$$\underline{\$180.76}$$

TRYITEXERCISE 10

Apex Manufacturing recently purchased a new computer system for $150,000. What amortization payment is required each month at 12% interest to pay off this obligation in 8 years?

CHECK YOUR ANSWER WITH THE SOLUTION ON PAGE 402.

SECTION III **12** REVIEW EXERCISES

Note: Round to the nearest cent when necessary.

For the following sinking funds, use Table 12-1 to calculate the amount of the periodic payments needed to amount to the financial objective (future value of the annuity).

	Sinking Fund Payment	Payment Frequency	Time Period (years)	Nominal Rate (%)	Interest Compounded	Future Value (Objective)
1.	$2,113.50	every 6 months	8	10	semiannually	$50,000
2.	_____	every year	14	9	annually	$250,000
3.	_____	every 3 months	5	12	quarterly	$1,500
4.	_____	every month	$1\frac{1}{2}$	12	monthly	$4,000
5.	_____	every 3 months	4	16	quarterly	$18,750

You have just been hired as a loan officer at the Eagle National Bank. Your first assignment is to calculate the amount of the periodic payment required to amortize (pay off) the following loans being considered by the bank (use Table 12-2).

	Loan Payment	Payment Period	Term of Loan (years)	Nominal Rate (%)	Present Value (Amount of Loan)
6.	$4,189.52	every year	12	9	$30,000
7.	_____	every 3 months	5	8	$5,500

	Loan Payment	Payment Period	Term of Loan (years)	Nominal Rate (%)	Present Value (Amount of Loan)
8.	_____	every month	$1\frac{3}{4}$	18	$10,000
9.	_____	every 6 months	8	6	$13,660
10.	_____	every month	1.5	12	$850

Solve the following exercises by using tables.

11. Everest Industries established a sinking fund to pay off a $10,000,000 loan that comes due in 8 years for a corporate yacht.

   a. What equal payments must be deposited into the fund every 3 months at 6% interest compounded quarterly for Everest to meet this financial obligation?

   b. What is the total amount of interest earned in this sinking fund account?

Corporate yachts provide companies with ways to recognize employees; secure the undivided attention of valued clients; perform product launches; hold meetings, conferences, and presentations; and serve as handsome tax write-offs.
   The 130-foot *Daedalus*, built in 1997 by Delta Marine Industries, is presently owned by The Boeing Company.

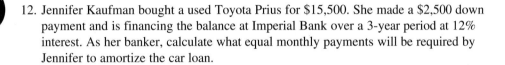

12. Jennifer Kaufman bought a used Toyota Prius for $15,500. She made a $2,500 down payment and is financing the balance at Imperial Bank over a 3-year period at 12% interest. As her banker, calculate what equal monthly payments will be required by Jennifer to amortize the car loan.

13. Green Thumb Landscaping buys new lawn equipment every 3 years. It is estimated that $25,000 will be needed for the next purchase. The company sets up a sinking fund to save for this obligation.

   a. What equal payments must be deposited every 6 months if interest is 8% compounded semiannually?

   b. What is the total amount of interest earned by the sinking fund?

14. Paul and Donna Kelsch are planning a Mediterranean cruise in 4 years and will need $7,500 for the trip. They decide to set up a "sinking fund" savings account for the vacation. They intend to make regular payments at the end of each 3-month period into the account that pays 6% interest compounded quarterly. What periodic sinking fund payment will allow them to achieve their vacation goal?

15. Valerie Ross is ready to retire and has saved $200,000 for that purpose. She wants to amortize (liquidate) that amount in a retirement fund so that she will receive equal annual payments over the next 25 years. At the end of the 25 years, no funds will be left in the account. If the fund earns 4% interest, how much will Valerie receive each year?

(Optional) Solve the following exercises by using the sinking fund or amortization formula.

Sinking fund payment

	Sinking Fund Payment	Payment Frequency	Time Period (yrs)	Nominal Rate (%)	Interest Compounded	Future Value (Objective)
16.	$345.97	every 3 months	5	6.0	quarterly	$8,000
17.	_____	every month	8	1.5	monthly	$5,500
18.	_____	every 6 months	$3\frac{1}{2}$	4.0	semiannually	$1,900

Amortization payment

	Loan Payment	Payment Frequency	Time Period (yrs)	Nominal Rate (%)	Present Value (Amount of Loan)
19.	$3,756.68	every year	10	10.6	$22,500
20.	_____	every 3 months	4	8.8	$9,000
21.	_____	every month	6	9.0	$4,380

22. Turnberry Manufacturing has determined that it will need $500,000 in 8 years for a new roof on its southeastern regional warehouse. A sinking fund is established for the roof at 3.4% compounded semiannually. What equal payments are required every 6 months to accumulate the needed funds for the roof?

23. Randy Scott purchased a motorcycle for $8,500 with a loan amortized over 5 years at 7.2% interest. What equal monthly payments are required to amortize this loan?

24. Betty Price purchased a new home for $225,000 with a 20% down payment and the remainder amortized over a 15-year period at 9% interest.

   a.   What amount did Betty finance?

   b.   What equal monthly payments are required to amortize this loan over 15 years?

   c.   What equal monthly payments are required if Betty decides to take a 20-year loan rather than a 15-year loan?

How Long Does $1 Million Last?

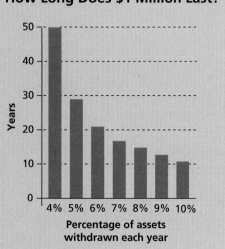

This chart shows the number of years a $1 million portfolio with an annual return of 8.7% can last based on percentage of assets withdrawn each year.

25. The Shangri-La Hotel has a financial obligation of $1,000,000 due in 5 years for kitchen equipment. A sinking fund is established to meet this obligation at 7.5% interest compounded monthly.

    a. What equal monthly sinking fund payments are required to accumulate the needed amount?

    b. What is the total amount of interest earned in the account?

BUSINESS DECISION: DON'T FORGET INFLATION!

26. You are the vice president of finance for Neptune Enterprises, Inc., a manufacturer of scuba diving gear. The company is planning a major plant expansion in 5 years. You have decided to start a sinking fund to accumulate the funds necessary for the project. Current bank rates are 8% compounded quarterly. It is estimated that $2,000,000 in today's dollars will be required; however, the inflation rate on construction costs and plant equipment is expected to average 5% per year for the next 5 years.

    a. Use the compound interest concept from Chapter 11 to determine how much will be required for the project, taking inflation into account.

    b. What sinking fund payments will be required at the end of every 3-month period to accumulate the necessary funds?

DOLLARS AND SENSE

This Business Decision, "Don't Forget Inflation," illustrates how inflation can affect long-range financial planning in business. Notice how much more the project will cost in 5 years because of rising prices.

At www.bls.gov, the Bureau of Labor Statistics provides an inflation calculator that you can use to enter a year and a dollar amount of buying power and then calculate how much buying power would be required for the same amount of goods or services in a subsequent year after inflation.

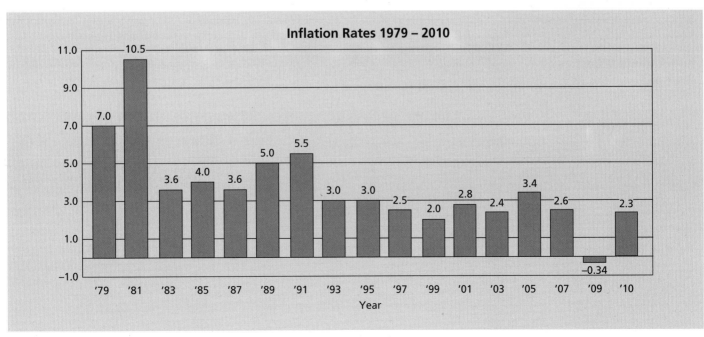

Source: Bureau of Labor Statistics, March 2010.

CHAPTER

12

CHAPTER FORMULAS

Future value of an annuity

Future value (ordinary annuity) = Ordinary annuity table factor × Annuity payment

$$FV \text{ (ordinary annuity)} = \text{Payment} \times \frac{(1+i)^n - 1}{i}$$

Future value (annuity due) = Annuity due table factor × Annuity payment

$$FV \text{ (annuity due)} = \text{Payment} \times \frac{(1+i)^n - 1}{i} \times (1+i)$$

Present value of an annuity

Present value (ordinary annuity) = Ordinary annuity table factor × Annuity payment

$$PV \text{ (ordinary annuity)} = \text{Payment} \times \frac{1 - (1+i)^{-n}}{i}$$

Present value (annuity due) = Annuity due table factor × Annuity payment

$$PV \text{ (annuity due)} = \text{Payment} \times \frac{1 - (1+i)^{-n}}{i} \times (1+i)$$

Sinking Fund

$$\text{Sinking fund payment} = \frac{\text{Future value of the sinking fund}}{\text{Future value table factor}}$$

$$\text{Sinking fund payment} = \text{Future value} \times \frac{i}{(1+i)^n - 1}$$

Amortization

$$\text{Amortization payment} = \frac{\text{Original amount of obligation}}{\text{Present value table factor}}$$

$$\text{Amortization payment} = \text{Present value} \times \frac{i}{1 - (1+i)^{-n}}$$

CHAPTER SUMMARY

Section I: Future Value of an Annuity: Ordinary and Annuity Due

Topic	Important Concepts	Illustrative Examples
Calculating the Future Value of an Ordinary Annuity by Using Tables **Performance Objective 12-1, Page 373**	An annuity is the payment or receipt of *equal* cash amounts per period for a specified amount of time. 1. Calculate the interest rate per period for the annuity (nominal rate ÷ periods per year). 2. Determine the number of periods of the annuity (years × periods per year). 3. From Table 12-1, locate the ordinary annuity table factor at the intersection of the rate column and the periods row. 4. Calculate the future value of an ordinary annuity by Future value (ordinary annuity) = Table factor × Annuity payment	Calculate the future value of an ordinary annuity of $500 every 6 months for 5 years at 12% interest compounded semiannually. Rate per period = 6% (12% ÷ 2 periods per year) Periods = 10 (5 years × 2 periods per year) Table factor 6%, 10 periods = 13.18079 Future value = 13.18079 × 500 Future value = $6,590.40

Section I (continued)

Topic	Important Concepts	Illustrative Examples
Calculating the Future Value of an Annuity Due by Using Tables **Performance Objective 12-2, Page 377**	1. Calculate the number of periods of the annuity (years × periods per year) and add one period to the total. 2. Calculate the interest rate per period (nominal rate ÷ periods per year). 3. Locate the table factor at the intersection of the rate column and the periods row. 4. Subtract 1 from the ordinary annuity table factor to get the annuity due table factor. 5. Calculate the future value of an annuity due by Future value (annuity due) = Table factor × Annuity payment	Calculate the future value of an annuity due to $100 per month for 2 years at 12% interest compounded monthly. Periods = 24, (2 × 12) + 1 for a total of 25 Rate per period = 1%, (12% ÷ 12) Table factor 1%, 25 periods = 28.24320 28.24320 − 1 = 27.24320 Future value = 27.24320 × 100 Future value = $2,724.32
(Optional) Calculating the Future Value of an Ordinary Annuity and an Annuity Due by Formula **Performance Objective 12-3, Page 378**	*Future Value: Ordinary Annuity* $FV = Pmt \times \dfrac{(1+i)^n - 1}{i}$ *Future Value: Annuity Due* $FV = Pmt \times \dfrac{(1+i)^n - 1}{i} \times (1+i)$ where: FV = future value Pmt = annuity payment i = interest rate per period (nominal rate ÷ periods per year) n = number of periods (years × periods per year)	a. What is the future value of an *ordinary annuity* of $200 per month for 4 years at 12% interest compounded monthly? $FV = 200 \times \dfrac{(1+.01)^{48} - 1}{.01}$ $FV = 200 \times 61.222608$ $FV = \$12,244.52$ b. What is the future value of this investment if it is an *annuity due*? $FV = 12,244.52 \times (1 + .01)$ $FV = 12,244.52 \times 1.01$ $FV = \$12,366.97$

Section II: Present Value of an Annuity: Ordinary and Annuity Due

Topic	Important Concepts	Illustrative Examples
Calculating the Present Value of an Ordinary Annuity by Using Tables **Performance Objective 12-4, Page 383**	1. Calculate the interest rate per period for the annuity (nominal rate ÷ periods per year). 2. Determine the number of periods of the annuity (years × periods per year). 3. From Table 12-2, locate the present value table factor at the intersection of the rate column and the periods row. 4. Calculate the present value of an ordinary annuity by Present value (ordinary annuity) = Table factor × Annuity payment	How much must be deposited now at 5% compounded annually to yield an annuity payment of $1,000 at the end of each year for 11 years? Rate per period = 5% (5% ÷ 1 period per year) Number of periods = 11 (11 years × 1 period per year) Table factor 5%, 11 periods is 8.30641 Present value = 8.30641 × 1,000 Present value = $8,306.41
Calculating the Present Value of an Annuity Due by Using Tables **Performance Objective 12-5, Page 384**	1. Calculate the number of periods (years × periods per year) and subtract 1 from the total. 2. Calculate rate per period (nominal rate ÷ periods per year). 3. Locate the table factor at the intersection of the rate column and the periods row. 4. Add 1 to the ordinary annuity table factor to get the annuity due table factor. 5. Calculate the present value of an annuity due by Present value (annuity due) = Table factor × Annuity payment	How much must be deposited now at 8% compounded semiannually to yield an annuity payment of $1,000 at the beginning of each 6-month period for 5 years? Number of periods = 10 (5 × 2) less 1 period = 9 Rate per period = 4% (8% ÷ 2) Table factor 4%, 9 periods = 7.43533 7.43533 + 1 = 8.43533 Present value = 8.43533 × 1,000 Present value = $8,435.33

Section II (continued)

Topic	Important Concepts	Illustrative Examples
(Optional) Calculating the Present Value of an Ordinary Annuity and an Annuity Due by Formula **Performance Objective 12-6, Page 387**	*Present Value: Ordinary Annuity* $PV = Pmt \times \dfrac{1-(1+i)^{-n}}{i}$ *Present Value: Annuity Due* $PV = Pmt \times \dfrac{1-(1+i)^{-n}}{i} \times (1+i)$ where: PV = present value Pmt = annuity payment i = interest rate per period (nominal rate ÷ periods per year) n = number of periods (years × periods per year)	a. What is the present value of an ordinary annuity of \$100 per month for 5 years at 12% interest compounded monthly? $PV = 100 \times \dfrac{1-(1+.01)^{-60}}{.01}$ $PV = 100 \times 44.955038$ $PV = \underline{\$4,495.50}$ b. What is the present value of this investment if it is an annuity due? $PV_{\text{annuity due}} = PV_{\text{ordinary annuity}} \times (1+i)$ $PV = 4,495.50 \times (1+.01)$ $PV = 4,495.50 \times 1.01$ $PV = \underline{\$4,540.46}$

Section III: Sinking Funds and Amortization

Topic	Important Concepts	Illustrative Examples
Calculating the Amount of a Sinking Fund Payment by Table **Performance Objective 12-7, Page 390**	Sinking funds are accounts used to set aside equal amounts of money at the end of each period at compound interest for the purpose of saving for a known future financial obligation. 1. Using the appropriate rate per period and number of periods, find the future value table factor from Table 12-1. 2. Calculate the amount of the sinking fund payment by Sinking fund payment = $\dfrac{\text{Future value of sinking fund}}{\text{Future value table factor}}$	What sinking fund payment is required at the end of each 6-month period at 10% interest compounded semiannually to amount to \$10,000 in 7 years? Number of periods = 14(7 years × 2 periods per year) Rate per period = 5%(10% ÷ 2 periods per year) Table factor 14 periods, 5% = 19.59863 Payment = $\dfrac{10,000}{19.59863}$ Payment = $\underline{\$510.24}$
Calculating the Amount of an Amortization Payment by Table **Performance Objective 12-8, Page 392**	Amortization is a financial arrangement whereby a lump-sum obligation is incurred now (present value) and is paid off or liquidated by a series of equal periodic payments for a specified amount of time. 1. Using the appropriate rate per period and number of periods of the amortization, find the present value table factor from Table 12-2. 2. Calculate the amount of the amortization payment by Amortization payment = $\dfrac{\text{Original amount obligation}}{\text{Present value table factor}}$	What amortization payments are required at the end of each month at 18% interest to pay off a \$15,000 loan in 3 years? Number of periods = 36 (3 years × 12 periods per year) Rate per period = 1.5% (18% ÷ 12 periods per year) Table factor 36 periods, 1.5% = 27.66068 Amortization payment = $\dfrac{15,000}{27.66068}$ Amortization payment = $\underline{\$542.29}$

Section III (continued)

Topic	Important Concepts	Illustrative Examples
(Optional) Calculating Sinking Fund Payments by Formula **Performance Objective 12-9, Page 392**	Sinking fund payments can be calculated by using the following formula $Pmt = FV \times \dfrac{i}{(1+i)^n - 1}$ where: Pmt = sinking fund payment FV = future value, amount needed in the future i = interest rate per period (nominal rate ÷ periods per year) n = number of periods (years × periods per year)	What sinking fund payment is required at the end of each month at 12% interest compounded monthly to amount to $10,000 in 4 years? Rate per period = 1% (12% ÷ 12) Periods = 48 (4 × 12) $Pmt = 10,000 \times \dfrac{.01}{(1+.01)^{48} - 1}$ $Pmt = 10,000 \times \dfrac{.01}{.6122261}$ $Pmt = 10,000 \times .0163338$ Sinking fund payment = $163.34
(Optional) Calculating Amortization Payments by Formula **Performance Objective 12-10, Page 393**	Amortization payments are calculated by using the following formula: $Pmt = PV \times \dfrac{i}{1 - (1+i)^{-n}}$ where: Pmt = amortization payment PV = present value, amount of the loan or obligation i = interest rate per period (nominal rate ÷ periods per year) n = number of periods (years × periods per year)	What amortization payment is required each month at 18% interest to pay off $3,000 in 2 years? Rate = 1.5% (18% ÷ 12) Periods = 24 (2 × 12) $Pmt = 3,000 \times \dfrac{.015}{1 - (1+.015)^{-24}}$ $Pmt = 3,000 \times \dfrac{.015}{.3004561}$ $Pmt = 3,000 \times .0499241$ Amortization payment = $149.77

TRY IT: EXERCISE SOLUTIONS FOR CHAPTER 12

1. 2%, 24 periods

Future value = Table factor × Annuity payment

Future value = 30.42186 × 1,000 = $30,421.86

2. Periods = 20 (5 × 4) + 1 = 21

Rate = $\dfrac{6\%}{4} = 1\frac{1}{2}\%$

Table factor = 24.47052

$\underline{\qquad - 1.00000}$

23.47052

Future value = Table factor × Annuity payment

Future value = 23.47052 × 1,000 = $23,470.52

3. a. 2%, 20 periods

$FV = Pmt \times \dfrac{(1+i)^n - 1}{i}$

$FV = 250 \times \dfrac{(1+.02)^{20} - 1}{.02} = 250 \times \dfrac{(1.02)^{20} - 1}{.02}$

$FV = 250 \times 24.297369 = \underline{\$6,074.34}$

b. $FV_{\text{annuity due}} = (1 + i) \times FV_{\text{ordinary annuity}}$

$FV_{\text{annuity due}} = (1 + .02) \times 6,074.34 = \underline{\$6,195.83}$

4. 4%, 12 periods

Present value = Table factor × Annuity payment

Present value = 9.38507 × 20,000 = $187,701.40

5. Periods = 12 (3 × 4) − 1 = 11

Rate = $\dfrac{6\%}{4} = 1\frac{1}{2}\%$

Table factor = 10.07112

$\underline{\qquad + 1.00000}$

11.07112

Present value = Table factor × Annuity payment

Present value = 11.07112 × 10,000 = $110,711.20

6. a. 2%, 24 periods

$PV = Pmt \times \dfrac{1 - (1+i)^{-n}}{i}$

$PV = 500 \times \dfrac{1 - (1+.02)^{-24}}{.02} = 500 \times \dfrac{1 - .6217215}{.02}$

$PV = 500 \times 18.913925 = \underline{\$9,456.96}$

b. $PV_{\text{annuity due}} = (1 + i) \times PV_{\text{ordinary annuity}}$

$PV_{\text{annuity due}} = (1 + .02) \times 9,456.96 = \underline{\$9,646.10}$

7. 3%, 20 periods

$$\text{Sinking fund payment} = \frac{\text{Future value of sinking fund}}{\text{Future value table factor}}$$

$$\text{Sinking fund payment} = \frac{8,000}{26.87037} = \underline{\$297.73}$$

8. Amount financed = 130,000 − 20,000 = $110,000
4%, 28 periods

$$\text{Amortization payment} = \frac{\text{Original amount of obligation}}{\text{Present value table factor}}$$

$$\text{Amortization payment} = \frac{110,000}{16.66306} = \underline{\$6,601.43}$$

9. .5%, 72 periods

$$\text{Sinking fund payment} = FV \times \frac{i}{(1 + i)^n - 1}$$

$$\text{Sinking fund payment} = 40,000 \times \frac{.005}{(1 + .005)^{72} - 1}$$

$$\text{Sinking fund payment} = 40,000 \times .0115729 = \underline{\$462.92}$$

10. 1%, 96 periods

$$\text{Amortization payment} = PV \times \frac{i}{1 - (1 + i)^{-n}}$$

$$\text{Amortization payment} = 150,000 \times \frac{.01}{1 - (1 + .01)^{-96}}$$

$$\text{Amortization payment} = 150,000 \times .0162528 = \underline{\$2,437.93}$$

CONCEPT REVIEW

1. Payment or receipt of equal amounts of money per period for a specified amount of time is known as a(n) _____. (12-1)

2. In a simple annuity, the number of compounding _____ per year coincides with the number of annuity _____ per year. (12-1)

3. An ordinary annuity is paid or received at the _____ of each time period. (12-1, 12-2)

4. An annuity due is paid or received at the _____ of each time period. (12-1, 12-2)

5. The total amount of the annuity payments and the accumulated interest on those payments is known as the _____ value of an annuity. (12-1)

6. The table factor for an annuity due is found by _____ one period to the number of periods of the annuity and then subtracting _____ from the resulting table factor. (12-2)

7. Write the formula for calculating the future value of an ordinary annuity when using a calculator with an exponential function, y^x, key. (12-3)

8. Write the formula for calculating the future value of an annuity due when using a calculator with an exponential function, (y^x), key. (12-3)

9. The lump sum amount of money that must be deposited today to provide a specified series of equal payments (annuity) in the future is known as the _____ value of an annuity. (12-4)

10. The table factor for the present value of an annuity due is found by _____ one period from the number of periods of the annuity and then adding _____ to the resulting table factor. (12-5)

11. A(n) _____ fund is an account used to set aside equal amounts of money at compound interest for the purpose of saving for a future obligation. (12-7)

12. _____ is a financial arrangement whereby a lump-sum obligation is incurred at compound interest now, such as a loan, and is then paid off by a series of equal periodic payments. (12-7, 12-8)

13. Write the formula for calculating a sinking fund payment by table. (12-7)

14. Write the formula for calculating an amortization payment by table. (12-8)

ASSESSMENT TEST

Note: Round to the nearest cent when necessary.

Use Table 12-1 to calculate the future value of the following ordinary annuities.

	Annuity Payment	Payment Frequency	Time Period (years)	Nominal Rate (%)	Interest Compounded	Future Value of the Annuity
1.	$4,000	every 3 months	6	8	quarterly	_____
2.	$10,000	every year	20	5	annually	_____

Use Table 12-1 to calculate the future value of the following annuities due.

	Annuity Payment	Payment Frequency	Time Period (years)	Nominal Rate (%)	Interest Compounded	Future Value of the Annuity
3.	$1,850	every 6 months	12	10	semiannually	_____
4.	$200	every month	$1\frac{3}{4}$	12	monthly	_____

Use Table 12-2 to calculate the present value of the following ordinary annuities.

	Annuity Payment	Payment Frequency	Time Period (years)	Nominal Rate (%)	Interest Compounded	Present Value of the Annuity
5.	$6,000	every year	9	5	annually	_____
6.	$125,000	every 3 months	3	6	quarterly	_____

Use Table 12-2 to calculate the present value of the following annuities due.

	Annuity Payment	Payment Frequency	Time Period (years)	Nominal Rate (%)	Interest Compounded	Present Value of the Annuity
7.	$700	every month	$1\frac{1}{2}$	12	monthly	_____
8.	$2,000	every 6 months	6	4	semiannually	_____

Use Table 12-1 to calculate the amount of the periodic payments needed to amount to the financial objective (future value of the annuity) for the following sinking funds.

	Sinking Fund Payment	Payment Frequency	Time Period (years)	Nominal Rate (%)	Interest Compounded	Future Value (Objective)
9.	_____	every year	13	7	annually	$20,000
10.	_____	every month	$2\frac{1}{4}$	12	monthly	$7,000

Use Table 12-2 to calculate the amount of the periodic payment required to amortize (pay off) the following loans.

	Loan Payment	Payment Period	Term of Loan (years)	Nominal Rate (%)	Interest Compounded	Present Value (Amount of Loan)
11.	_____	every 3 months	8	8	quarterly	$6,000
12.	_____	every month	$2\frac{1}{2}$	18	monthly	$20,000

Solve the following exercises by using tables.

13. How much will $800 deposited into a savings account at the *end* of each month be worth after 2 years at 6% interest compounded monthly?

14. How much will $3,500 deposited at the *beginning* of each 3-month period be worth after 7 years at 12% interest compounded quarterly?

CHAPTER

12

15. What amount must be deposited now to withdraw $200 at the *beginning* of each month for 3 years if interest is 12% compounded monthly?

16. How much must be deposited now to withdraw $4,000 at the *end* of each year for 20 years if interest is 7% compounded annually?

17. Mary Evans plans to buy a used car when she starts college three years from now. She can make deposits at the end of each month into a 6% sinking fund account compounded monthly. If she wants to have $14,500 available to buy the car, what should be the amount of her monthly sinking fund payments?

18. A sinking fund is established by Alliance Industries at 8% interest compounded semiannually to meet a financial obligation of $1,800,000 in 4 years.

    a. What periodic sinking fund payment is required every 6 months to reach the company's goal?

    b. How much greater would the payment be if the interest rate was 6% compounded semiannually rather than 8%?

19. Lucky Strike, a bowling alley, purchased new equipment from Brunswick in the amount of $850,000. Brunswick is allowing Lucky Strike to amortize the cost of the equipment with monthly payments over 2 years at 12% interest. What equal monthly payments will be required to amortize this loan?

20. Aaron Grider buys a home for $120,500. After a 15% down payment, the balance is financed at 8% interest for 9 years.

    a. What equal quarterly payments will be required to amortize this mortgage loan?

    b. What is the total amount of interest Aaron will pay on the loan?

(Optional) Solve the following exercises by using formulas.

Ordinary annuity

	Annuity Payment	Payment Frequency	Time Period (yrs)	Nominal Rate (%)	Interest Compounded	Future Value of the Annuity
21.	$150	every month	4	3.0	monthly	_____
22.	$5,600	every year	9	1.8	annually	_____

Annuity due

	Annuity Payment	Payment Frequency	Time Period (yrs)	Nominal Rate (%)	Interest Compounded	Future Value of the Annuity
23.	$500	every 6 months	5	3.0	semiannually	_____
24.	$185	every month	$1\frac{1}{2}$	6.0	monthly	_____

Present value of an ordinary annuity

	Annuity Payment	Payment Frequency	Time Period (yrs)	Nominal Rate (%)	Interest Compounded	Present Value of the Annuity
25.	$1,500	every month	4	1.5	monthly	_____
26.	$375	every 6 months	2	3	semiannually	_____

Present value of an annuity due

	Annuity Payment	Payment Frequency	Time Period (yrs)	Nominal Rate (%)	Interest Compounded	Present Value of the Annuity
27.	$2,400	every 3 months	4	10	quarterly	_____
28.	$600	every year	20	4.3	annually	_____

Sinking fund payment

	Sinking Fund Payment	Payment Frequency	Time Period (yrs)	Nominal Rate (%)	Interest Compounded	Future Value (Objective)
29.	_____	every year	4	3.7	annually	$25,000
30.	_____	every 3 months	3	2	quarterly	$3,600

Amortization payment

	Loan Payment	Payment Frequency	Time Period (yrs)	Nominal Rate (%)	Present Value (Amount of Loan)
31.	_____	every 6 months	$2\frac{1}{2}$	12.0	$10,400
32.	_____	every month	4	13.5	$2,200

33. The town of Bay Harbor is planning to buy five new hybrid police cars in 4 years. The cars are expected to cost $38,500 each.

    a. What equal quarterly payments must the city deposit into a sinking fund at 3.5% interest compounded quarterly to achieve its goal?

    b. What is the total amount of interest earned in the account?

Hybrid vehicles run off a rechargeable battery and gasoline. With each hybrid burning 20%–30% less gasoline than comparably sized conventional models, they are in great demand by consumers.

  As of December 2009, more than 1.6 million hybrids were registered in the United States. According to forecasts by J.D. Power and Associates, sales of hybrid and diesel-powered vehicles will more than triple by 2015. In 2010, The Coca-Cola Company had the largest heavy-duty diesel-electric hybrid truck fleet in North America.

CHAPTER

12

34. The Mesa Grande Bank is paying 9% interest compounded monthly.

   a. If you deposit $100 into a savings plan at the beginning of each month, how much will it be worth in 10 years?

   b. How much would the account be worth if the payments were made at the end of each month rather than at the beginning?

35. Sandpiper Savings & Loan is offering mortgages at 7.32% interest. What monthly payments would be required to amortize a loan of $200,000 for 25 years?

BUSINESS DECISION: TIME IS MONEY!

36. You are one of the retirement counselors at the Valley View Bank. You have been asked to give a presentation to a class of high school seniors about the importance of saving for retirement. Your boss, the vice president of the trust division, has designed an example for you to use in your presentation. The students are shown five retirement scenarios and are asked to guess which yields the most money. *Note*: All annuities are *ordinary*. Although some people stop investing, the money remains in the account at 10% interest compounded annually.

   a. Look over each scenario and make an educated guess as to which investor will have the largest accumulation of money invested at 10% over the next 40 years. Then for your presentation, calculate the final value for each scenario.

     • Venus invests $1,200 per year and stops after 15 years.

     • Kevin waits 15 years, invests $1,200 per year for 15 years, and stops.

     • Rafael waits 15 years, then invests $1,200 per year for 25 years.

     • Magda waits 10 years, invests $1,500 per year for 15 years, and stops.

     • Heather waits 10 years, then invests $1,500 per year for 30 years.

   b. Based on the results, what message will this presentation convey to the students?

   c. Recalculate each scenario as an annuity due.

   d. How can the results be used in your presentation?

Saving for your child's college education

There are many ways to "grow" money—tax free—for your child's college education using annuities. Here are three popular options:

• **529 Savings Plans**—A 529 plan is a tax-advantaged savings plan designed to encourage saving for future college costs. These "qualified tuition plans" are sponsored by states, state agencies, or educational institutions. – www. sec.gov/investor/pubs/intro529.htm

• **Coverdell Education Savings Accounts**—Coverdell accounts work like IRAs: you make annual contributions to an investment account, and the investment grows free of federal taxes. – www. savingforcollege.com

• **Zero Coupon Bonds**—Municipal bonds (also known as "munis") represent investments in state and local government projects such as schools, highways, hospitals, and other important public projects. – www.investinginbonds.com

Source: Adapted from: *The Miami Herald*, Oct. 25, 2009, page 1E, "5 Ways to Save for College."

© Randy Glasbergen / glasbergen.com

NINE MONTHS OLD AND I STILL HAVEN'T SAVED A CENT FOR MY RETIREMENT. WELL, IT'S TOO LATE TO START NOW!

GLASBERGEN

© Randy Glasbergen. www.glasbergen.com

COLLABORATIVE LEARNING ACTIVITY

The "Personal" Sinking Fund

1. As a team, design a "personal" sinking fund for something to save for in the future.

    a. What are the amount and the purpose of the fund?
    b. What savings account interest rates are currently being offered at banks and credit unions in your area?
    c. Choose the best rate and calculate what monthly payments would be required to accumulate the desired amount in 1 year, 2 years, and 5 years.

2. As a team, research the annual reports or speak with accountants of corporations in your area that use sinking funds to accumulate money for future obligations. Answer the following questions about those sinking funds.

    a. What is the name of the corporation?
    b. What is the purpose and the amount of the sinking fund?
    c. For how many years is the fund?
    d. How much are the periodic payments?
    e. At what interest rate are these funds growing?

Growing Money

Refer to the "Dollars and Sense" tip on the previous page that discusses how to save for a child's college education. Divide into teams to further research and report to the class on the following.

a. What is the current status of the three tax-free savings plans?

    *   529 plans
    *   Coverdell Education Savings Accounts
    *   zero coupon bonds

b. What are the current interest rates and contribution limits of the various plans?

c. Speak with a certified financial planner to research other alternatives, such as custodial accounts and IRAs, that are available to those who want to save for their child's college education.

MANAGING YOUR MONEY

7 NEW RULES TO LIVE BY

Why is there so much month left at the end of the money? In recent years, our economy has undergone some dramatic changes. The "Great Recession" has significantly altered the financial planning parameters for individuals and families seeking financial freedom.

Here are some new planning guidelines from the editors of *Money* magazine and Bank of America to help you attain your long-term financial goals.

- **Savings** – Save at least 15% (and ideally 20%) of your income for long-term goals. The old rule was 10%, but that was when you could count on pension plans, shorter retirement periods, and better market returns.
- **Debt** – Keep your debt-to-income ratio under 30%. That's down from 36% so that you can direct more cash flow toward emergency and retirement savings. As a cushion, keep a six-month reserve of cash in a high-yield savings account and any additional emergency money in a short-term bond index fund.
- **Home** – Look at refinancing when rates are one percentage point lower than your current rate, not two as in years past when closing costs were higher. You should plan to live in the house for at least as long as it will take to pay off the closing costs and fees with the reduction in payment. (See the Mortgage Refinancing Worksheet on page 476 in Chapter 14.)
- **Spending** – Keep discretionary spending (clothes, dining out, movies) under 20% of your take-home pay. Before the recession, you could play with up to 30%, but average debt obligations have risen.
- **Investments** – Invest no more than 5% of your portfolio in your company stock or any single stock. The old yardstick was 10%, but you'll be safer with more diversification.
- **Allocation** – To determine how much of your portfolio should be in stocks, subtract your age from 110. The old formula subtracted your age from 100, but rising medical costs and increasing life spans necessitate being more aggressive. If you are comfortable with even more risk, subtract your age from 120.
- **Retirement** – To figure out how big a nest egg you'll need, multiply your ideal annual income by 30. (First, subtract any pension and Social Security income you will receive). That's up from the previous rule of 25 because of increased longevity.

Source: *Make Peace With Your Money,* "Money & Main St." guidebook series. Bank of America, *Money* Magazine, 7 New Rules to Live By, page 6.

Copyright by Matt Wuerker

HELPFUL WEBSITES

The Internet can be a valuable source of money management information. Some helpful websites are www.bankrate.com, www.creditinfocenter.com, www.moneymanagement.org, www.betterbudgeting.com, and http://moneycentral.msn.com.

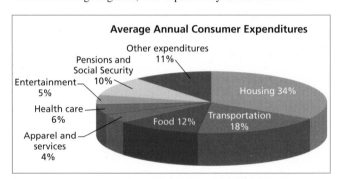

Average Annual Consumer Expenditures

- Other expenditures 11%
- Pensions and Social Security 10%
- Entertainment 5%
- Health care 6%
- Apparel and services 4%
- Food 12%
- Housing 34%
- Transportation 18%

Source: U.S. Department of Commerce, *Statistical Abstract of the United States 2010.* Consumer Expenditures in 2007, Table 668, page 440.

ISSUES & ACTIVITIES

1. Use the chart above to:
   a. Distribute the various expenditure categories for a family with annual earnings of $55,000.
   b. Distribute your annual earnings for each expenditure category.
   c. Determine which of your expenditure categories are higher than average and which are lower than average.
   d. List some ways you can save on your annual expenditures.
2. For a family with annual earnings of $64,000, use the "7 New Rules to Live By" to answer the following questions.
   a. Ideally, how much should the family save?
   b. What should the family's debt limit be?
   c. If the family's portfolio amounts to $93,000, what should their limit be on any single stock?
   d. If the family's ideal annual income is $45,000 after pensions and Social Security, how big of a nest egg will they need?
3. In teams, use the websites listed above and other Internet sites to find current trends in "financial planning." List your sources and visually report your findings to the class.

BRAINTEASER – "SKY-HIGH DEBT!"

If a stack of 1,000 thousand dollar bills ($1 million) is 4 inches thick, how high would the stack be if it was equal to $13.72 trillion, the national debt as of December 2010?

See the end of Appendix A for the solution.

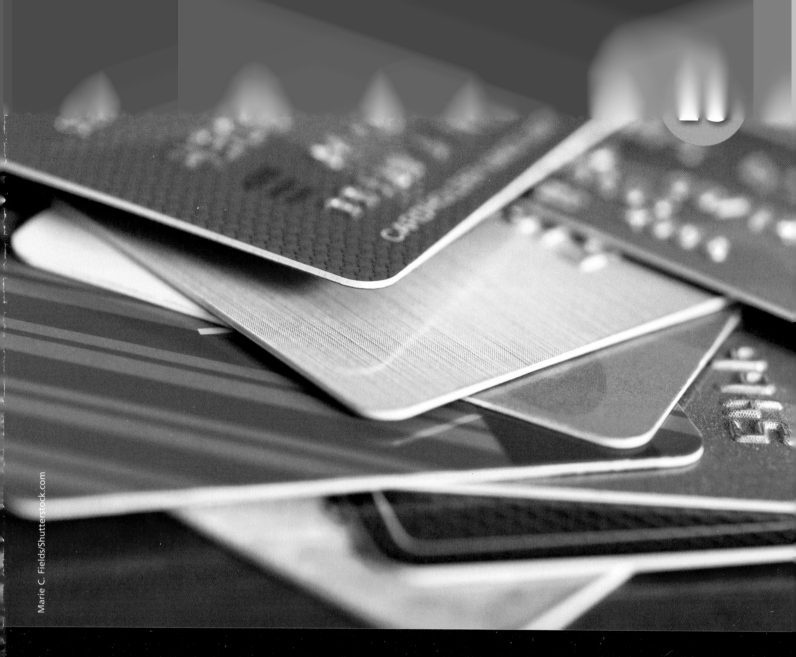

Marie C. Fields/Shutterstock.com

Consumer and Business Credit

SECTION I 13 OPEN-END CREDIT—CHARGE ACCOUNTS, CREDIT CARDS, AND LINES OF CREDIT

"Buy now, pay later" is a concept that has become an everyday part of the way individuals and businesses purchase goods and services. Merchants in all categories, as well as lending institutions, encourage us to just say "charge it!" Consumers are offered a wide variety of charge accounts with many extra services and incentives attached. Many businesses have charge accounts in the company name. These accounts may be used to facilitate employee travel and entertainment expenses or to fill up the company delivery truck with gasoline without having to deal with cash. Exhibit 13-1 shows a sample credit card and its parts.

Lending and borrowing money comprise a huge portion of the U.S. economic system. Over the years, as the practice became more prevalent, the federal government enacted various legislation to protect the consumer from being misled about credit and finance charges. One of the most important and comprehensive pieces of legislation, known as Regulation Z, covers both installment credit and **open-end credit**.

Regulation Z of the Consumer Credit Protection Act, also known as the Truth in Lending Act, as well as the Fair Credit and Charge Card Disclosure Act require that lenders fully disclose to the customer, in writing, the cost of the credit and detailed information about their terms. Features such as finance charge, annual percentage rate (APR), cash advances, and annual fees must be disclosed in writing at the time you apply. The **finance charge** is the dollar amount that is paid for the credit. The **annual percentage rate (APR)** is the effective or true annual interest rate being charged. If a card company offers you a written "preapproved" credit solicitation, the offer must include these terms. Also, card issuers must inform customers if they make certain changes in rates or coverage for credit insurance.

open-end credit A loan arrangement in which there is no set number of payments. As the balance of the loan is reduced, the borrower can renew the amount of the loan up to a pre-approved credit limit. A form of revolving credit.

finance charge Dollar amount that is paid for credit. Total of installment payments for an item less the cost of that item.

annual percentage rate (APR) Effective or true annual interest rate being charged for credit. Must be revealed to borrowers under the Truth in Lending Act.

EXHIBIT 13-1 Parts of a Credit Card

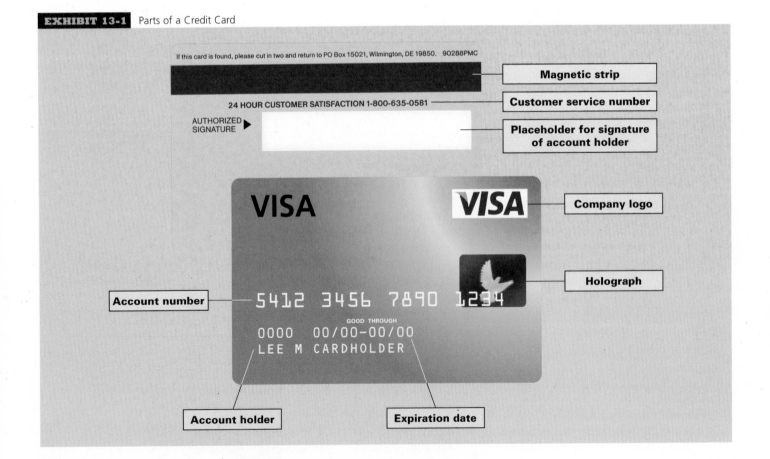

In 2010, the Federal Reserve implemented a series of amendments to Regulation Z, known as the Credit Card Accountability, Responsibility, and Disclosure Act (the Credit Card Act). These amendments were designed to further protect consumers who use credit cards from a number of costly and undisclosed bank practices. Exhibit 13-2 outlines the major provisions of these new credit card reforms. Exhibits 13-3 and 13-5 illustrate how these reforms now appear on your monthly credit card statement and bank credit card offer disclosures.

When loans are backed by a simple promise to repay, they are known as **unsecured loans**. Most open-end credit accounts are unsecured. Loans that are backed by tangible assets, such as car and boat loans and home mortgage loans, are known as **secured loans**. These loans are backed, or secured, by an asset that can be repossessed and sold by the lender if the borrower fails to comply with the rules of the loan. Secured loans are covered in Section II of this chapter and in Chapter 14.

Revolving credit is the most popular type of open-end credit. Under this agreement, the consumer has a prearranged credit limit and two payment options. The first option is to use the account as a regular charge account, whereby the balance is paid off at the end of the month with no finance charge. The second option is to make a minimum payment or portion of the payment but less than the full balance. This option leaves a carryover balance, which accrues finance charges by using the simple interest formula

$$\text{Interest} = \text{Principal} \times \text{Rate} \times \text{Time}$$

The name *revolving credit* comes from the fact that there is no set number of payments as with installment credit. The account revolves month to month, year to year—technically never being paid off as long as minimum monthly payments are made. Exhibit 13-3 illustrates a typical revolving credit monthly statement.

unsecured loans Loans that are backed simply by the borrower's "promise" to repay, without any tangible asset pledged as collateral. These loans carry more risk for the lender and therefore have higher interest rates than secured loans.

secured loans Loans that are backed by a tangible asset, such as a car, boat, or home, which can be repossessed and sold if the borrower fails to pay back the loan. These loans carry less risk for the lender and therefore have lower interest rates than do unsecured loans.

revolving credit Loans made on a continuous basis and billed periodically. Borrower makes minimum monthly payments or more and pays interest on the outstanding balance. This is a form of open-end credit extended by many retail stores and credit card companies.

EXHIBIT 13-2 How Credit Card Reforms Affect You

How Credit Card Reforms Affect You

What your credit card company has to tell you
- When they plan to increase your rate or other fees
- How long it will take to pay off your balance

New rules regarding rates, fees, and limits
- No interest rate increases for the first year
- Increased rates apply only to new charges
- Restrictions on over-the-limit transactions
- Caps on high-fee cards
- Protection for underage consumers

Changes to billing and payments
- Standard payment dates and times
- Payments directed to highest interest balances first
- No two-cycle (double-cycle) billing

Reasonable penalty fees and protections
- No fees of more than $25 ($35 in specialcases)
- No inactivity fees
- One fee limit for a single transaction
- Explanation of rate increases
- Re-evaluation of increases every six months

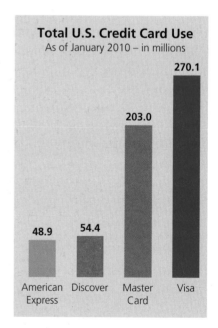

Total U.S. Credit Card Use
As of January 2010 – in millions

American Express	Discover	Master Card	Visa
48.9	54.4	203.0	270.1

CALCULATING THE FINANCE CHARGE AND NEW BALANCE BY USING THE UNPAID OR PREVIOUS MONTH'S BALANCE METHOD

13-1

Open-end credit transactions are divided into time periods known as **billing cycles**. These cycles are commonly between 28 and 31 days. At the end of a billing cycle, a statement is sent to the account holder much like the one in Exhibit 13-3.

billing cycles Time periods, usually 28 to 31 days, used in billing revolving credit accounts. Account statements are sent to the borrower after each billing cycle.

EXHIBIT 13-3   Reformed Bank Credit Card Account Statement

XXX Bank Credit Card Account Statement
Account Number XXXX XXXX XXXX XXXX
February 21, 2012 to March 22, 2012

Summary of Account Activity

Previous Balance	$535.07
Payments	−$450.00
Other Credits	−$13.45
Purchases	+$529.57
Balance Transfers	+$785.00
Cash Advances	+$318.
Past Due Amount	+$0.
Fees Charged	+$69.4
Interest Charged	+$10.89
New Balance	$1,784.53
Credit limit	$2,000.00
Available credit	$215.47
Statement closing date	3/22/2012
Days in billing cycle	30

Questions?

Call Customer Service	1-XXX-XXX-XXXX
Lost or Stolen Credit Card	1-XXX-XXX-XXXX

Payment Information

New Balance	$1,784.53
Minimum Payment Due	$53.00
Payment Due Date	4/20/12

Late Payment Warning: If we do not receive your minimum payment by the date listed above, you may have to pay a $35 late fee and your APRs may be increased up to the Penalty APR of 28.99%

Minimum Payment Warning: If you make only the minimum payment each period, you will pay more in interest and take you longer to pay off your balance. For example:

If you make no additional charges using this card and each month you pay...	You will pay off the balance shown on this statement in about...	And you will end up paying an estimated total of...
Only the minimum payment	10 years	$3,284
$62	3 years	$2,232 (Savings=$1,052)

If you would like information about credit counseling services, call 1-800-XXX-XXXX.

Please send billing inquiries and correspondence to:
PO Box XXXX, Anytown, Anystate XXXXX

Notice of Changes to Your Interest Rates

You have triggered the Penalty APR of 28.99%. ...hange will impact your account as follows:

Transactions made on or after 4/9/12: As of 5/10/12, the Penalty APR will apply to these transactions. We may keep the APR at this level indefinitely.

Transactions made before 4/9/12: Current rates will continue to apply to these transactions. However, if you are more than 60 days late on your account, the Penalty APR will apply to those transactions as well.

1) Summary of account activity

A summary of the transactions on your account—your payments, credits, purchases, balance transfers, cash advances, fees, interest charges, and amounts past due. It will also show your new balance, your available credit, and the last day of the billing period.

2) Payment information

Your total new balance, the minimum payment amount, and the date your payment is due.

3) Late payment warning

This section states any additional fees and the higher interest rate that may be charged if your payment is late.

4) Minimum payment warning

This is an estimate of how long it can take to pay off your credit card balance if you make only the minimum payment each month and an estimate of how much you likely will pay, including interest, in order to pay off your bill in three years.

5) Notice of changes to your interest rates

If you trigger the penalty rate, your credit card company may notify you that your rates will be increasing. The credit card company must tell you at least 45 days before your rates change.

Source: Federal Reserve

EXHIBIT 13-3   Reformed Bank Credit Card Account Statement

Important Changes to Your Account Terms   ⑥

The following is a summary of changes that are being made to your account terms. For more detailed information, please refer to the booklet enclosed with this statement.

These changes will impact your account as follows:

Transactions made on or after 4/9/12: As of 5/10/12, any changes to APRs described below will apply to these transactions.

Transactions made before 4/9/12: Current APRs will continue to apply to these transactions.

If you are already being charged a higher Penalty APR for purchases: In this case, any changes to APRs described below will not go into effect at this time. These changes will go into effect when the Penalty APR no longer applies to your account.

Revised Terms, as of 5/10/12	
APR for Purchases	16.99%

Transactions   ⑦

Reference Number	Trans Date	Post Date	Description of Transaction or Credit	Amount
5884186PS0388W6YM	2/22	2/23	Store #1	$133.74
854338203FS8OO0Z5	2/25	2/25	Pymt Thank You	$450.00
564891561545KOSHD	2/25	2/26	Store #2	$247.36
1542202074TWWZV48	2/26	2/26	Cash Advance	$318.00
4545754784KOHUIOS	2/27	3/1	Balance Transfer	$785.00
2564561023184102315	2/28	3/1	Store #3	$34.32
045148714518979874	3/4	3/5	Store #4	$29.45
0547810544898718AF	3/15	3/17	Store #5	$72.25
			Fees ⑧	
9525156489SFD4545Q	2/23	2/23	Late Fee	$35.00
84151564SADS8745H	2/27	2/27	Balance Transfer Fee	$23.55
256489156189451516L	2/28	2/28	Cash Advance Fee	$10.90
			TOTAL FEES FOR THIS PERIOD	**$69.45**
			Interest Charged	
			Interest Charge on Purchases	$6.31
			Interest Charge on Cash Advances	$4.58
			TOTAL INTEREST FOR THIS PERIOD	**$10.89**

2012 Totals Year-to-Date	
Total fees charged in 2012 ⑨	$90.14
Total interest charged in 2012	$18.27

Interest Charge Calculation   ⑩

Your **Annual Percentage Rate (APR)** is the   interest rate on your account.

Type of Balance	Annual Percentage Rate (APR)	Balance Subject to Interest Rate	Interest Charge
Purchases	14.99% (v)	$512.14	$6.31
Cash Advances	21.99% (v)	$253.50	$4.58
Balance Transfers	0.00%	$637.50	$0.00

(v) = Variable Rate

6) Other changes to your account terms

If your credit card company is going to raise interest rates or fees or make other significant changes to your account, it must notify you at least 45 days before the changes take effect.

7) Transactions

A list of all the transactions that have occurred since your last statement (purchases, payments, credits, cash advances, and balance transfers).

8) Fees and interest charges

Credit card companies must list the fees and interest charges separately on your monthly bill. Interest charges must be listed by type of transaction.

9) Year-to-date totals

This is the total that you have paid in fees and interest charges for the current year. You can avoid some fees, such as over-the-limit fees, by managing how much you charge and by paying on time to avoid late payment fees.

10) Interest charge calculation

A summary of the interest rates on the different types of transactions, account balances, the amount of each, and the interest charged for each type of transaction.

STEPS TO CALCULATE THE FINANCE CHARGE AND NEW BALANCE BY USING THE UNPAID BALANCE METHOD

STEP 1. Divide the annual percentage rate by 12 to find the monthly or periodic interest rate. (Round to the nearest hundredth percent when necessary.)

$$\text{Periodic rate} = \frac{\text{Annual percentage rate}}{12}$$

STEP 2. Calculate the finance charge by multiplying the previous month's balance by the periodic interest rate from Step 1.

$$\textbf{Finance charge} = \textbf{Previous month's balance} \times \textbf{Periodic rate}$$

STEP 3. Total all the purchases and cash advances for the month.

STEP 4. Total all the payments and credits for the month.

STEP 5. Use the following formula to determine the new balance:

$$\begin{array}{ccccccc} \textbf{New} & & \textbf{Previous} & & \textbf{Finance} & & \textbf{Purchases and} & & \textbf{Payments and} \\ \textbf{balance} & = & \textbf{balance} & + & \textbf{charge} & + & \textbf{cash advances} & - & \textbf{credits} \end{array}$$

EXAMPLE 1   CALCULATING THE FINANCE CHARGE AND NEW BALANCE BY USING THE UNPAID BALANCE METHOD

Jake Morrison has a revolving department store credit account with an annual percentage rate of 18%. His balance from last month is $322.40. During the month, he purchased shirts for $65.60 and a baseball bat for $43.25. He returned a tie for a credit of $22.95 and made a $50 payment. If the department store uses the unpaid balance method, what is the finance charge on the account and what is Jake's new balance?

SOLUTIONSTRATEGY

Step 1. Periodic rate $= \dfrac{\text{Annual percentage rate}}{12}$

Periodic rate $= \dfrac{18\%}{12} = 1.5\%$

Step 2. Finance charge = Previous month's balance × Periodic rate
Finance charge = 322.40 × .015
Finance charge = 4.836 = $4.84

Step 3. Total the purchases for the month:

$$\$65.60 + \$43.25 = \$108.85$$

Step 4. Total the payments and credits for the month:

$$\$50.00 + \$22.95 = \$72.95$$

Step 5. Find the new balance for Jake's account by using the formula

$$\begin{array}{ccccccc} \text{New} & & \text{Previous} & & \text{Finance} & & \text{Purchases and} & & \text{Payments and} \\ \text{balance} & = & \text{balance} & + & \text{charge} & + & \text{cash advances} & - & \text{credits} \end{array}$$

$$\begin{array}{ccccccc} \text{New} & & & & & & & & \\ \text{balance} & = & \$322.40 & + & \$4.84 & + & \$108.85 & - & \$72.95 \end{array}$$

New balance = $363.14

TRYITEXERCISE1

Mike Dennis has a Bank of America account with an annual percentage rate of 15%. His previous month's balance is $214.90. During July, Mike's account showed the following activity.

Statement of Account Bank of America.

NAME	DATE	DESCRIPTION OF TRANSACTIONS	CHARGES
MIKE DENNIS	07/06	**Royal Cleaners**	**$35.50**
	07/09	**Payment**	**40.00**
ACCOUNT NUMBER	07/15	**Macy's**	**133.25**
097440	07/16	**Antonio's Restaurant**	**41.10**
BILLING CYCLE	07/21	**CVS Pharmacy**	**29.00**
JULY 1–31	07/27	**CVS Pharmacy (credit)**	**9.12**

What is the finance charge for July, and what is Mike's new balance?

CHECK YOUR ANSWERS WITH THE SOLUTIONS ON PAGE 446.

CALCULATING THE FINANCE CHARGE AND NEW BALANCE BY USING THE AVERAGE DAILY BALANCE METHOD

13-2

In business today, the method most widely used to calculate the finance charge on a revolving credit account is known as the **average daily balance**. This method precisely tracks the activity in an account on a daily basis. Each day's balance of a billing cycle is totaled and then divided by the number of days in that cycle. This gives an average of all the daily balances.

For accounts in which many charges are made each month, the average daily balance method results in much higher interest than the unpaid balance method because interest starts accruing on the day purchases are made or cash advances are taken.

average daily balance In revolving credit, the most commonly used method for determining the finance charge for a billing cycle. It is the total of the daily balances divided by the number of days in the cycle.

 STEPS TO CALCULATE THE FINANCE CHARGE AND NEW BALANCE BY USING THE AVERAGE DAILY BALANCE

STEP 1. Starting with the previous month's balance as the first unpaid balance, multiply each by the number of days that balance existed until the next account transaction.

STEP 2. At the end of the billing cycle, find the sum of all the daily balance figures.

STEP 3. Find the average daily balance.

$$\text{Average daily balance} = \frac{\text{Sum of the daily balances}}{\text{Days in billing cycle}}$$

STEP 4. Calculate the finance charge.

$$\text{Finance charge} = \text{Average daily balance} \times \text{Periodic rate}$$

STEP 5. Compute the new balance as before.

$$\frac{\text{New}}{\text{balance}} = \frac{\text{Previous}}{\text{balance}} + \frac{\text{Finance}}{\text{charge}} + \frac{\text{Purchases and}}{\text{cash advances}} - \frac{\text{Payments and}}{\text{credits}}$$

EXAMPLE2 USING THE AVERAGE DAILY BALANCE METHOD

Morgan Patrick has a Bank of America revolving credit account with a 15% annual percentage rate. The finance charge is calculated by using the average daily balance method. The billing date is the first day of each month, and the billing cycle is the number of days in that month. During the month of March, Morgan's account showed the following activity.

Statement of Account   Bank of America

NAME		
MORGAN PATRICK		

ACCOUNT NUMBER
1229-3390-0038

BILLING CYCLE
MARCH 1–31

DATE	DESCRIPTION OF TRANSACTIONS	CHARGES
03/01	Previous month's balance	$215.60
03/07	Sports Authority	125.11
03/10	Texaco	23.25
03/12	Payment	75.00
03/17	Amazon.com (credit)	54.10
03/23	H.L. Mager, DDS	79.00
03/23	Texaco	19.43
03/24	Dollar General	94.19

What is the finance charge for March, and what is Morgan's new balance?

SOLUTIONSTRATEGY

Steps 1 and 2. To calculate the daily balances and their sum, set up a chart like the one below that lists the activity in the account by dates and number of days.

Dates	Number of Days	Activity/Amount		Unpaid Balance	Daily Balances (unpaid bal. × days)
March 1–6	6	Previous balance		$215.60	$1,293.60
March 7–9	3	Charge	+$125.11	340.71	1,022.13
March 10–11	2	Charge	+23.25	363.96	727.92
March 12–16	5	Payment	−75.00	288.96	1,444.80
March 17–22	6	Credit	−54.10	234.86	1,409.16
March 23	1	Charges	+79.00		
			+19.43	333.29	333.29
March 24–31	8	Charge	+94.19	427.48	3,419.84
	31 days in cycle				Total $9,650.74

Step 3. Average daily balance $= \dfrac{\text{Sum of the daily balances}}{\text{Days in billing cycle}} = \dfrac{9{,}650.74}{31} = \$311.31$

Step 4. The periodic rate is 1.25% (15% ÷ 12).

Finance charge = Average daily balance × Periodic rate

Finance charge = 311.31 × .0125 = $3.89

Step 5.

$$\underset{\text{balance}}{\text{New}} = \underset{\text{balance}}{\text{Previous}} + \underset{\text{charge}}{\text{Finance}} + \underset{\text{cash advances}}{\text{Purchases and}} - \underset{\text{credits}}{\text{Payments and}}$$

$$\underset{\text{balance}}{\text{New}} = \$215.60 + \$3.89 + \$340.98 - \$129.10$$

$$\underset{\text{balance}}{\text{New}} = \underline{\$431.37}$$

LEARNINGTIP

Shortcut
"New Balance" can be calculated by adding the finance charge to the last "Unpaid Balance" of the month.

$427.48 + $3.89 = $431.37

TRYITEXERCISE2

Kendra Wolf has a Bank of America revolving credit account with an 18% annual percentage rate. The finance charge is calculated by using the average daily balance method. The billing date is the first day of each month, and the billing cycle is the number of days in that month. During the month of August, Kendra's account showed the following activity.

Statement of Account — Bank of America

NAME	DATE	DESCRIPTION OF TRANSACTIONS	CHARGES
KENDRA WOLF	08/01	**Previous month's balance**	**$158.69**
	08/05	**Nathan's Beauty Salon**	55.00
ACCOUNT NUMBER	08/11	**Payment**	100.00
2967-39460-0098	08/15	**Walmart**	43.22
	08/17	**Saks Fifth Avenue**	54.10
BILLING CYCLE	08/20	**eBay.com**	224.50
AUGUST 1–31	08/26	**Cash Advance**	75.00

What is the finance charge for August, and what is Kendra's new balance?

CHECK YOUR ANSWERS WITH THE SOLUTIONS ON PAGE 446.

CALCULATING THE FINANCE CHARGE AND NEW BALANCE OF BUSINESS AND PERSONAL LINES OF CREDIT

13-3

One of the most useful types of open-end credit is the business or personal **line of credit**. In this section, we investigate the unsecured credit line, which is based on your own merit. In Chapter 14, we discuss the home equity line of credit, which is secured by a home or another piece of real estate property.

line of credit Pre-approved amount of open-end credit based on borrower's ability to pay.

A line of credit is an important tool for ongoing businesses and responsible individuals. For those who qualify, unsecured lines of credit generally range from $2,500 to $250,000. The amount is based on your ability to pay as well as your financial and credit history. This pre-approved borrowing power essentially gives you the ability to become your own private banker. Once the line has been established, you can borrow money by simply writing a check. Lines of credit usually have an annual usage fee of between $50 and $100, and most lenders require that you update your financial information each year.

With credit lines, you pay interest only on the outstanding average daily balance of your loan. For most lines and some credit cards, the interest rate is variable and is based on, or indexed to, the prime rate. The **U.S. prime rate** is the lending rate at which the largest and most creditworthy corporations in the country borrow money from banks. The current prime rate is published daily in *The Wall Street Journal* in a chart entitled "Consumer Rates and Returns to Investors." Exhibit 13-4 shows an example of this chart.

U.S. prime rate Lending rate at which the largest and most creditworthy corporations borrow money from banks. The interest rate of most lines of credit is tied to the movement of the prime rate.

A typical line of credit quotes interest as the prime rate plus a fixed percent, such as "prime + 3%" or "prime + 6.8%." Some lenders have a minimum rate regardless of the prime rate, such as "prime + 3%, minimum 10%." In this case, when the prime is greater than 7%, the rate varies up and down. When the prime falls to less than 7%, the minimum 10% rate applies. This guarantees the lender at least a 10% return on funds loaned. Exhibit 13-5 is an example of a credit card rate disclosure indexed to the prime rate.

Like the calculation of finance charges and new balances on credit cards (see the steps on page 415), the finance charge on a line of credit is based on average daily balance and is calculated by

Finance charge = Average daily balance × Periodic rate

This means that interest begins as soon as you write a check for a loan. Typically, the loan is paid back on a flexible schedule. In most cases, balances of $100 or less must be paid in full. Larger balances require minimum monthly payments of $100 or 2% of the outstanding balance, whichever is greater. As you repay, the line of credit renews itself. The new balance of the line of credit is calculated by

New balance = Previous balance + Finance charge + Loans − Payments

EXHIBIT 13-4

Consumer Rates and Returns
to Investors – July 3, 2010

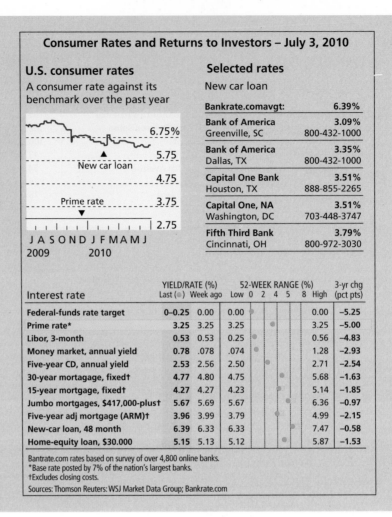

Consumer Rates and Returns to Investors – July 3, 2010

U.S. consumer rates

A consumer rate against its benchmark over the past year

6.75%
5.75
New car loan
4.75
Prime rate
3.75
2.75

J A S O N D J F M A M J
2009   2010

Selected rates

New car loan

Bankrate.comavgt:	**6.39%**
Bank of America Greenville, SC	**3.09%** 800-432-1000
Bank of America Dallas, TX	**3.35%** 800-432-1000
Capital One Bank Houston, TX	**3.51%** 888-855-2265
Capital One, NA Washington, DC	**3.51%** 703-448-3747
Fifth Third Bank Cincinnati, OH	**3.79%** 800-972-3030

Interest rate	YIELD/RATE (%) Last (●)	Week ago	52-WEEK RANGE (%) Low 0 2 4 5 8 High	3-yr chg (pct pts)
Federal-funds rate target	0–0.25	0.00	0.00 ● — — — — 0.00	–5.25
Prime rate*	3.25	3.25	3.25 — — ● — — 3.25	–5.00
Libor, 3-month	0.53	0.53	0.25 ● — — — — 0.56	–4.83
Money market, annual yield	0.78	.078	.074 ● — — — — 1.28	–2.93
Five-year CD, annual yield	2.53	2.56	2.50 — ● — — — 2.71	–2.54
30-year mortagage, fixed†	4.77	4.80	4.75 — — — ● — 5.68	–1.63
15-year mortgage, fixed†	4.27	4.27	4.23 — — — ● — 5.14	–1.85
Jumbo mortgages, $417,000-plus†	5.67	5.69	5.67 — — — — ● 6.36	–0.97
Five-year adj mortgage (ARM)†	3.96	3.99	3.79 — — — ● — 4.99	–2.15
New-car loan, 48 month	6.39	6.33	6.33 — — — — ● 7.47	–0.58
Home-equity loan, $30.000	5.15	5.13	5.12 — — — ● — 5.87	–1.53

Bantrate.com rates based on survey of over 4,800 online banks.
*Base rate posted by 7% of the nation's largest banks.
†Excludes closing costs.

Sources: Thomson Reuters; WSJ Market Data Group; Bankrate.com

EXAMPLE3 CALCULATING FINANCE CHARGES ON A LINE OF CREDIT

Shari's Chocolate Shop has a $20,000 line of credit with the Shangri-La National Bank. The annual percentage rate charged on the account is the current prime rate plus 4%. There is a minimum APR on the account of 10%. The starting balance on April 1 was $2,350. On April 9, Shari borrowed $1,500 to pay for a shipment of assorted gift items. On April 20, she made a $3,000 payment on the account. On April 26, she borrowed another $2,500 to pay for air conditioning repairs. The billing cycle for April has 30 days. If the current prime rate is 8%, what is the finance charge on the account and what is Shari's new balance?

SOLUTIONSTRATEGY

To solve this problem, we must find the annual percentage rate, the periodic rate, the average daily balance, the finance charge, and the new balance.

Annual percentage rate: The annual percentage rate is prime plus 4%, with a minimum of 10%. Because the current prime is 8%, the APR on this line of credit is 12% (8% + 4%).

Periodic rate:

$$\text{Periodic rate} = \frac{\text{Annual percentage rate}}{12 \text{ months}} = \frac{12\%}{12} = 1\%$$

Average daily balance: From the information given, we construct the following chart showing the account activity.

Dates	Number of Days	Activity/Amount	Unpaid Balance	Daily Balances (unpaid balance × days)
April 1–8	8	Previous balance	$2,350	$18,800
April 9–19	11	Borrowed $1,500	3,850	42,350
April 20–25	6	Payment $3,000	850	5,100
April 26–30	5	Borrowed $2,500	3,350	16,750
	30 days in cycle			Total $83,000

$$\text{Average daily balance} = \frac{\text{Sum of the daily balances}}{\text{Days in billing cycle}} = \frac{83{,}000}{30} = \$2{,}766.67$$

Finance charge:

Finance charge = Average daily balance × Periodic rate

Finance charge = 2,766.67 × .01 = $27.67

New balance:

$$\text{New balance} = \frac{\text{Previous}}{\text{balance}} + \frac{\text{Finance}}{\text{charge}} + \frac{\text{Loan}}{\text{amounts}} - \text{Payments}$$

New balance = $2,350 + $27.67 + $4,000 − $3,000

New balance = $3,377.67

● TRYITEXERCISE3

Angler Marine has a $75,000 line of credit with Harborside Bank. The annual percentage rate is the current prime rate plus 4.5%. The balance on November 1 was $12,300. On November 7, Angler borrowed $16,700 to pay for a shipment of fishing equipment, and on November 21, it borrowed another $8,800. On November 26, a $20,000 payment was made on the account. The billing cycle for November has 30 days. If the current prime rate is 8.5%, what is the finance charge on the account and what is Angler's new balance?

CHECK YOUR ANSWERS WITH THE SOLUTIONS ON PAGES 446–447.

EXHIBIT 13-5 Reformed Credit Card Rate Disclosure

Interest Rates and Interest Charges	
Annual Percentage Rate (APR) for Purchases ①	**8.99%, 10.99%, or 12.99%** introductory APR for one year, based on your creditworthiness After that, your APR will be **14.99%**. This APR will vary with the market based on the Prime Rate.
APR for Balance Transfers ②	**15.99%** This APR will vary with the market based on the Prime Rate.
APR for Cash Advances ③	**21.99%** This APR will vary with the market based on the Prime Rate.
Penalty APR and When it Applies ④	**28.99%** This APR may be applied to your account if you: 1) Make a late payment. 2) Go over your credit limit. 3) Make a payment that is returned. 4) Do any of the above on another account that you have with us. **How Long Will the Penalty APR Apply?** If your APRs are increased for any of these reasons, the Penalty APR will apply until you make six consecutive minimum payments when due.
How to Avoid Paying Interest on Purchases ⑤	Your due date is at least 25 days after the close of each billing cycle. We will not charge you any interest on purchases if you pay your entire balance by the due date each month.
Minimum Interest Charge ⑥	If you are charged interest, the charge will be no less than $1.50.
For Credit Card Tips from the Federal Reserve Board	To learn more about factors to consider when applying for or using a credit card, visit the website of the Federal Reserve Board at **http://www.federalreserve.gov/creditcard**.

1) APR for purchases

The interest rate you pay on an annual basis if you carry over balances on purchases from one billing cycle to the next.

2) APR for balance transfers

The interest rate you pay if you transfer a balance from another card. Balance transfer fees may also apply.

3) APR for cash advances

The interest rate you pay if you withdraw a cash advance from your credit card account. Cash advance fees may also apply.

4) Penalty APR and when it applies

Your credit card company may increase your interest rate (with 45 days' advance notice) if you pay your bill late, go over your credit limit, or make a payment that is returned.

How long will the penalty APR apply?

Credit card companies must tell you how long the penalty rates will be in effect. You may be able to go back to regular rates if you pay your bills on time for a period of time.

5) How to avoid paying interest on purchases

You can avoid interest charges on purchases by paying your bill in full by the due date.

6) Minimum interest charge

Credit card companies often have a minimum interest amount. These charges typically range from $0.50 to $2.00 per month.

EXHIBIT 13-5   Reformed Credit Card Rate Disclosure

Fees	
Set-up and Maintenance Fees ⑦	NOTICE: Some of these set-up and maintenance fees will be assessed before you begin using your card and will reduce the amount of credit you initially have available. For example, if you are assigned the minimum credit limit of $250, your initial available credit will be only about $209 (or about $204 if you choose to have an additional card).
• Annual Fee	**$20**
• Account Set-up Fee	**$20** (one-time fee)
• Participation Fee	**$12** annually (**$1** per month)
• Additional Card Fee	**$5** annually (if applicable)
Transaction Fees ⑧	
• Balance Transfer	Either **$5** or **3%** of the amount of each transfer, whichever is greater (maximum fee: $100).
• Cash Advance	Either **$5** or **3%** of the amount of each cash advance, whichever is greater.
• Foreign Transaction	**2%** of each transaction in U.S. dollars.
Penalty Fees ⑨	
• Late Payment	**$29** if balance is less than or equal to $1,000; **$35** if balance is more than $1,000
• Over-the Credit Limit	**$29**
• Returned Payment	**$35** ⑩

⑪

How We Will Calculate Your Balance: We use a method called "average daily balance (including new purchases)."

⑫

Loss of Introductory APR: We may end your introductory APR and apply the Penalty APR if you become more than 60 days late in paying your bill.

7) Set-up and maintenance fees

Some credit cards offered to people with lower, or subprime, credit scores may charge a variety of fees.

8) Transaction Fees

Credit card companies may charge you a fee (either a fixed dollar amount or a percentage of the transaction) for transferring a balance, getting a cash advance, or making a transaction in a foreign country.

9) Penalty fees

Fee if you pay your bill late, your balance goes over your credit limit, or you make a payment but you don't have enough money in your account to cover the payment.

10) Other fees

Some cards require other fees (known as "account protection") for credit insurance, debt cancellation, or debt suspension coverage.

11) How we will calculate your balance

Credit card companies can use one of several methods to calculate your outstanding balance.
- Adjusted balance method
- Average daily balance method, including new purchases
- Average daily balance method, excluding new purchases
- Previous balance method

12) Loss of introductory APR

If your card has a special lower rate that is called an "introductory rate," this area will list the ways you can lose this lower rate.

SECTION I **13** **REVIEW EXERCISES**

Calculate the missing information on the following revolving credit accounts. Interest is calculated on the unpaid or previous month's balance.

	Previous Balance	Annual Percentage Rate (APR)	Monthly Periodic Rate	Finance Charge	Purchases and Cash Advances	Payments and Credits	New Balance
1.	$167.88	18%	1.5%	$2.52	$215.50	$50.00	$335.90
2.	$35.00	12%	___	___	$186.40	$75.00	___
3.	$455.12	___	1.75%	___	$206.24	$125.00	___
4.	$2,390.00	___	$1\frac{1}{4}\%$	___	$1,233.38	$300.00	___
5.	$3,418.50	9%	___	___	$329.00	$1,200.00	___
6.	$857.25	___	2%	___	$166.70	$195.00	___

7. Anny Winslow has a Bank of America revolving credit account with an annual percentage rate of 12% calculated on the previous month's balance. Answer the questions that follow using the monthly statement below.

Statement of Account　　Bank of America

NAME		
ANNY WINSLOW		

ACCOUNT NUMBER		
2290-0090-4959		

BILLING CYCLE		
SEPTEMBER 1–30		

DATE	DESCRIPTION OF TRANSACTIONS	CHARGES
09/01	Previous month's balance	$120.00
09/08	Radio Shack	65.52
09/11	Payment	70.00
09/14	Union Oil	23.25
09/22	Cash Advance	60.00
09/26	Safeway Supermarket	59.16

a. What is the finance charge?

b. What is Anny's new balance?

Kathy Hansen has a revolving credit account. The finance charge is calculated on the previous month's balance, and the annual percentage rate is 21%. Complete the following five-month account activity table for Kathy.

Month	Previous Month's Balance	Finance Charge	Purchases and Cash Advances	Payments and Credits	New Balance End of Month
8. March	$560.00	___	$121.37	$55.00	___
9. April	___	___	$46.45	$65.00	___
10. May	___	___	$282.33	$105.00	___
11. June	___	___	$253.38	$400.00	___
12. July	___	___	$70.59	$100.00	___

13. Calculate the average daily balance for November for a revolving credit account with a previous month's balance of $550 and the following activity.

Date	Activity	Amount
November 6	Purchase	$83.20
November 13	Payment	$150.00
November 19	Purchase	$348.50
November 24	Credit	$75.25
November 27	Cash advance	$200.00

$$\text{Average daily balance} = \frac{20{,}335.25}{30} = \underline{\underline{\$677.84}}$$

14. Calculate the average daily balance for October for a revolving credit account with a previous month's balance of $140 and the following activity.

Date	Activity	Amount
October 3	Cash advance	$50.00
October 7	Payment	$75.00
October 10	Purchase	$26.69
October 16	Credit	$40.00
October 25	Purchase	$122.70

15. Calculate the average daily balance for February for a revolving credit account with a previous month's balance of $69.50 and the following activity.

Date	Activity	Amount
February 6	Payment	$58.00
February 9	Purchase	$95.88
February 15	Purchase	$129.60
February 24	Credit	$21.15
February 27	Cash advance	$100.00

16. Carolyn Salkind has a Bank of America revolving credit account with a 15% annual percentage rate. The finance charge is calculated by using the average daily balance method. The billing date is the first day of each month, and the billing cycle is the number of days in that month. During March, Carolyn's account showed the following activity.

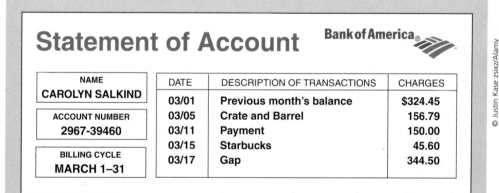

Statement of Account — Bank of America

NAME CAROLYN SALKIND

ACCOUNT NUMBER 2967-39460

BILLING CYCLE MARCH 1–31

DATE	DESCRIPTION OF TRANSACTIONS	CHARGES
03/01	Previous month's balance	$324.45
03/05	Crate and Barrel	156.79
03/11	Payment	150.00
03/15	Starbucks	45.60
03/17	Gap	344.50

a. What is the finance charge for March?

b. What is Carolyn's new balance?

Gap Inc. operates as a specialty retailer. The company offers clothing, accessories, and personal care products for men, women, children, and babies under the Gap, Old Navy, Banana Republic, Piperlime, and Athleta brand names.

The company offers its products through retail stores and catalogs as well as brand name websites. The Gap also franchises agreements with unaffiliated franchisees to operate Gap and Banana Republic stores worldwide. As of March 2010, the company operated approximately 3,100 stores worldwide. In 2009, sales were over $3.3 billion, with 135,000 full-time employees.

© Justin Kase zsixz/Alamy

17. The Freemont Bank offers a business line of credit that has an annual percentage rate of prime rate plus 5.4%, with a minimum of 11%. What is the APR if the prime rate is

   a. 7%   b. 10.1%   c. 9.25%   d. 5 %

     7 + 5.4
     = 12.4%

EXCEL 1

18. The Jewelry Exchange has a $30,000 line of credit with Nations Bank. The annual percentage rate is the current prime rate plus 4.7%. The balance on March 1 was $8,400. On March 6, the company borrowed $6,900 to pay for a shipment of supplies, and on March 17, it borrowed another $4,500 for equipment repairs. On March 24, a $10,000 payment was made on the account. The billing cycle for March has 31 days. The current prime rate is 9%.

   a. What is the finance charge on the account?

   b. What is the company's new balance?

   c. On April 1, how much credit does the Jewelry Exchange have left on the account?

BUSINESS DECISION: PICK THE RIGHT PLASTIC

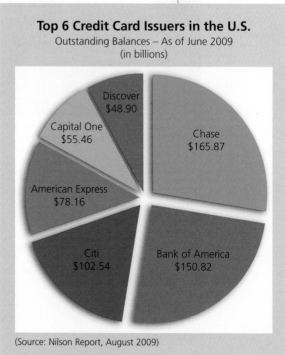

Top 6 Credit Card Issuers in the U.S.
Outstanding Balances – As of June 2009
(in billions)

Discover $48.90

Capital One $55.46

Chase $165.87

American Express $78.16

Citi $102.54

Bank of America $150.82

(Source: Nilson Report, August 2009)

19. On October 22, you plan to purchase a $3,000 computer by using one of your two credit cards. The Silver Card charges 18% interest and calculates interest on the previous month's balance; however, you are not charged interest for the month of the purchase. The Gold Card charges 18% interest and calculates interest based on the average daily balance. Both cards have a $0 balance as of October 1.

   Your plan is to make a $1,000 payment in November, make a $1,000 payment in December, and pay off the remaining balance in January. All your payments will be received and posted on the 10th of each month. No other charges will be made on the account.

   a. Based on this information, calculate the interest charged by each card for this purchase.

   b. Which card is the better deal and by how much?

CLOSED-END CREDIT—INSTALLMENT LOANS

SECTION II

13

Closed-end credit in the form of installment loans is used extensively today for the purchase of durable goods such as cars, boats, electronic equipment, furniture, and appliances, as well as services such as vacations and home improvements. An **installment loan** is a lump-sum loan whereby the borrower repays the principal plus interest in a specified number of equal monthly payments. These loans generally range from 6 months to 10 years depending on what is being financed.

When a home or another real estate property is financed, the installment loan is known as a **mortgage**. A mortgage may be for as long as 30 years on a home and even longer on commercial property such as an office building or a factory. These loans, along with home equity loans, are discussed in Chapter 14.

Many installment loans are secured by the asset for which the loan was made. For example, when a bank makes a car loan for three years, the consumer gets the car to use and monthly payments to make, but the lender still owns the car. Only after the final payment is made on the loan does the lender turn over the title (the proof of ownership document) to the borrower. An additional form of security for the lending institution is that borrowers are often asked to make a down payment as part of the loan agreement.

A **down payment** is a percentage of the purchase price that the buyer must pay in a lump sum at the time of purchase. Down payments on installment loans vary by category of merchandise and generally range from between 0% to 30% of the price of the item. Sometimes the amount of the down payment is based on the credit rating of the borrower. Usually, the better the credit, the lower the down payment.

installment loan Loan made for a specified number of equal monthly payments. A form of closed-end credit used for purchasing durable goods such as cars, boats, and furniture and services such as vacations and home improvements.

mortgage An installment loan made for homes and other real estate property.

down payment Portion of the purchase price that the buyer must pay in a lump sum at the time of purchase.

Until the loan on this vehicle is repaid, the lending institution is technically the owner.

© 2010 Polka Dot Images/Jupiterimages Corporation

CALCULATING THE TOTAL DEFERRED PAYMENT PRICE AND THE AMOUNT OF THE FINANCE CHARGE OF AN INSTALLMENT LOAN

13-4

Let's take a look at some of the terminology of installment loans. When a consumer buys goods or services without any financing, the price paid is known as the **cash price** or **purchase price**. When financing is involved, the **amount financed** is found by subtracting the down payment from the cash or purchase price. Sometimes the down payment will be listed as a dollar amount, and other times it will be expressed as a percent of the purchase price.

cash or **purchase price** Price paid for goods and services without the use of financing.

amount financed After the down payment, the amount of money that is borrowed to complete a sale.

> **Amount financed = Purchase price − Down payment**

When the down payment is listed as a percent of the purchase price, it can be found by using

> **Down payment = Purchase price × Down payment percent**

A finance charge, which includes simple interest and any loan origination fees, is then added to the amount financed to give the total amount of installment payments.

> **Total amount of installment payments = Amount financed + Finance charge**

The finance charge can be found by subtracting the amount financed from the total amount of installment payments.

> **Finance charge = Total amount of installment payments − Amount financed**

When the amount of the monthly payments is known, the total amount of installment payments can be found by multiplying the monthly payment amount by the number of payments.

> **Total amount of installment payments = Monthly payment amount × Number of monthly payments**

The total deferred payment price is the total amount of installment payments plus the down payment. This represents the total out-of-pocket expenses incurred by the buyer for an installment purchase.

> **Total deferred payment price = Total of installment payments + Down payment**

EXAMPLE 4 CALCULATING INSTALLMENT LOAN VARIABLES

Tracy Hall is interested in buying a computer. At Radio Shack, she picks out a computer and a printer for a total cash price of $2,550. The salesperson informs her that if she qualifies for an installment loan, she may pay 20% now as a down payment and finance the balance with payments of $110 per month for 24 months.

a. What is the finance charge on this loan?
b. What is the total deferred payment price of Tracy's computer?

SOLUTIONSTRATEGY

a. Finance charge:
To calculate the finance charge on this loan, we must first find the amount of the down payment, the amount financed, and the total amount of the installment payments.

Down payment = Purchase price × Down payment percent

Down payment = 2,550 × 20% = 2,550 × .2 = $510

Amount financed = Purchase price − Down payment

Amount financed = 2,550 − 510 = $2,040

Total amount of installment payments = Monthly payment amount × Number of monthly payments

Total amount of installment payments = 110 × 24 = $2,640

Finance charge = Total amount of installment payments − Amount financed

Finance charge = 2,640 − 2,040

Finance charge = $600

b. Total deferred payment price:

Total deferred payment price = Total of installment payments + Down payment

Total deferred payment price = 2,640 + 510

Total deferred payment price = $3,150

● TRYITEXERCISE4

Bob Johnson found a car he wanted to buy at Autorama Auto Sales. He had the option of paying $12,500 in cash or financing the car with a 4-year installment loan. The loan required a 15% down payment and equal monthly payments of $309.90 for 48 months.

a. What is the finance charge on the loan?

b. What is the total deferred payment price of Bob's car?

CHECK YOUR ANSWERS WITH THE SOLUTIONS ON PAGE 447.

CALCULATING THE REGULAR MONTHLY PAYMENTS OF AN INSTALLMENT LOAN BY THE ADD-ON INTEREST METHOD

13-5

One of the most common methods of calculating the finance charge on an installment loan is known as **add-on interest**. Add-on interest is essentially the simple interest that we studied in Chapter 10. The term gets its name from the fact that the simple interest is computed and then added to the amount financed to get the total of installment payments. The interest or finance charge is computed by using the simple interest formula

add-on interest Popular method of calculating the interest on an installment loan. Found by adding the simple interest ($I = PRT$) to the amount financed.

| **Interest** | **=** | **Principal** | **×** | **Rate** | **×** | **Time** |
| (*finance charge*) | | (*amount financed*) | | | | |

STEPS TO CALCULATE THE REGULAR MONTHLY PAYMENT OF AN INSTALLMENT LOAN USING ADD-ON INTEREST

STEP 1. Calculate the amount to be financed by subtracting the down payment from the purchase price. *Note:* When the down payment is expressed as a percent, the amount financed can be found by the complement method because the percent financed is 100% minus the down payment percent.

Amount financed = Purchase price(100% − Down payment percent)

STEP 2. Compute the add-on interest finance charge by using $I = PRT$, with the amount financed as the principal.

STEP 3. Find the total of installment payments by adding the finance charge to the amount financed.

Total of installment payments = Amount financed + Finance charge

STEP 4. Find the regular monthly payments by dividing the total of installment payments by the number of months of the loan.

$$\text{Regular monthly payments} = \frac{\text{Total of installment payments}}{\text{Number of months of the loan}}$$

EXAMPLE5 CALCULATING MONTHLY PAYMENTS

David Kendall bought a new boat with a 7% add-on interest installment loan from his credit union. The purchase price of the boat was $19,500. The credit union required a 20% down payment and equal monthly payments for 5 years (60 months). What are David's monthly payments?

SOLUTIONSTRATEGY

Step 1. Amount financed = Purchase price(100% − Down payment percent)

Amount financed = 19,500(100% − 20%) = 19,500 × .8

Amount financed = $15,600

Step 2.
$$\underset{(finance\ charge)}{\text{Interest}} = \underset{(amount\ financed)}{\text{Principal}} \times \text{Rate} \times \text{Time}$$

Finance charge = 15,600 × .07 × 5

Finance charge = $5,460

Step 3. Total of installment payments = Amount financed + Finance charge

Total of installment payments = 15,600 + 5,460

Total of installment payments = $21,060

Step 4. Regular monthly payments = $\dfrac{\text{Total of installment payments}}{\text{Number of months of the loan}}$

Regular monthly payments = $\dfrac{21,060}{60}$

Regular monthly payments = $351

TRYITEXERCISE5

Eileen Townsend bought a bedroom set from El Dorado Furniture with a 6% add-on interest installment loan from her bank. The purchase price of the furniture was $1,500. The bank required a 10% down payment and equal monthly payments for 2 years. What are Eileen's monthly payments?

CHECK YOUR ANSWER WITH THE SOLUTION ON PAGE 447.

13-6 CALCULATING THE ANNUAL PERCENTAGE RATE OF AN INSTALLMENT LOAN BY APR TABLES AND BY FORMULA

As we learned in Objective 13-5, the add-on interest calculation for an installment loan is the same as the procedure we used on the simple interest promissory note. Although the interest is calculated the same way, the manner in which the loans are repaid is different. With promissory notes, the principal plus interest is repaid at the end of the loan period. The borrower has the use of the principal for the full time period of the loan. With an installment loan, the principal plus interest is repaid in equal regular payments. Each month in which a payment is made, the borrower has less and less use of the principal.

For this reason, the effective or true interest rate on an installment loan is considerably higher than the simple add-on rate. As we learned in Section I of this chapter, the effective or true annual interest rate being charged on open- and closed-end credit is known as the APR.

The Federal Reserve Board has published APR tables that can be used to find the APR of an installment loan. APR tables, such as Table 13-1, have values representing the finance charge per $100 of the amount financed. To look up the APR of a loan, we must first calculate the finance charge per $100.

TABLE 13-1 Annual Percentage Rate (APR) Finance Charge per $100

ANNUAL PERCENTAGE RATE TABLE FOR MONTHLY PAYMENT PLANS
SEE INSTRUCTIONS FOR USE OF TABLES

FRB-103-M

ANNUAL PERCENTAGE RATE

(FINANCE CHARGE PER $100 OF AMOUNT FINANCED)

NUMBER OF PAYMENTS	10.00%	10.25%	10.50%	10.75%	11.00%	11.25%	11.50%	11.75%	12.00%	12.25%	12.50%	12.75%	13.00%	13.25%	13.50%	13.75%
1	0.83	0.85	0.87	0.90	0.92	0.94	0.96	0.98	1.00	1.02	1.04	1.06	1.08	1.10	1.12	1.15
2	1.25	1.28	1.31	1.35	1.38	1.41	1.44	1.47	1.50	1.53	1.57	1.60	1.63	1.66	1.69	1.72
3	1.67	1.71	1.76	1.80	1.84	1.88	1.92	1.96	2.01	2.05	2.09	2.13	2.17	2.22	2.26	2.30
4	2.09	2.14	2.20	2.25	2.30	2.35	2.41	2.46	2.51	2.57	2.62	2.67	2.72	2.78	2.83	2.88
5	2.51	2.58	2.64	2.70	2.77	2.83	2.89	2.96	3.02	3.08	3.15	3.21	3.27	3.34	3.40	3.46
6	2.94	3.01	3.08	3.16	3.23	3.31	3.38	3.45	3.53	3.60	3.68	3.75	3.83	3.90	3.97	4.05
7	3.36	3.45	3.53	3.62	3.70	3.78	3.87	3.95	4.04	4.12	4.21	4.29	4.38	4.47	4.55	4.64
8	3.79	3.88	3.98	4.07	4.17	4.26	4.36	4.46	4.55	4.65	4.74	4.84	4.94	5.03	5.13	5.22
9	4.21	4.32	4.43	4.53	4.64	4.75	4.85	4.96	5.07	5.17	5.28	5.39	5.49	5.60	5.71	5.82
10	4.64	4.76	4.88	4.99	5.11	5.23	5.35	5.46	5.58	5.70	5.82	5.94	6.05	6.17	6.29	6.41
11	5.07	5.20	5.33	5.45	5.58	5.71	5.84	5.97	6.10	6.23	6.36	6.49	6.62	6.75	6.88	7.01
12	5.50	5.64	5.78	5.92	6.06	6.20	6.34	6.48	6.62	6.76	6.90	7.04	7.18	7.32	7.46	7.60
13	5.93	6.08	6.23	6.38	6.53	6.68	6.84	6.99	7.14	7.29	7.44	7.59	7.75	7.90	8.05	8.20
14	6.36	6.52	6.69	6.85	7.01	7.17	7.34	7.50	7.66	7.82	7.99	8.15	8.31	8.48	8.64	8.81
15	6.80	6.97	7.14	7.32	7.49	7.66	7.84	8.01	8.19	8.36	8.53	8.71	8.88	9.06	9.23	9.41
16	7.23	7.41	7.60	7.78	7.97	8.15	8.34	8.53	8.71	8.90	9.08	9.27	9.46	9.64	9.83	10.02
17	7.67	7.86	8.06	8.25	8.45	8.65	8.84	9.04	9.24	9.44	9.63	9.83	10.03	10.23	10.43	10.63
18	8.10	8.31	8.52	8.73	8.93	9.14	9.35	9.56	9.77	9.98	10.19	10.40	10.61	10.82	11.03	11.24
19	8.54	8.76	8.98	9.20	9.42	9.64	9.86	10.08	10.30	10.52	10.74	10.96	11.18	11.41	11.63	11.85
20	8.98	9.21	9.44	9.67	9.90	10.13	10.37	10.60	10.83	11.06	11.30	11.53	11.76	12.00	12.23	12.46
21	9.42	9.66	9.90	10.15	10.39	10.63	10.88	11.12	11.36	11.61	11.85	12.10	12.34	12.59	12.84	13.08
22	9.86	10.12	10.37	10.62	10.88	11.13	11.39	11.64	11.90	12.16	12.41	12.67	12.93	13.19	13.44	13.70
23	10.30	10.57	10.84	11.10	11.37	11.63	11.90	12.17	12.44	12.71	12.97	13.24	13.51	13.78	14.05	14.32
24	10.75	11.02	11.30	11.58	11.86	12.14	12.42	12.70	12.98	13.26	13.54	13.82	14.10	14.38	14.66	14.95
25	11.19	11.48	11.77	12.06	12.35	12.64	12.93	13.22	13.52	13.81	14.10	14.40	14.69	14.98	15.28	15.57
26	11.64	11.94	12.24	12.54	12.85	13.15	13.45	13.75	14.06	14.36	14.67	14.97	15.28	15.59	15.89	16.20
27	12.09	12.40	12.71	13.03	13.34	13.66	13.97	14.29	14.60	14.92	15.24	15.56	15.87	16.19	16.51	16.83
28	12.53	12.86	13.18	13.51	13.84	14.16	14.49	14.82	15.15	15.48	15.81	16.14	16.47	16.80	17.13	17.46
29	12.98	13.32	13.66	14.00	14.33	14.67	15.01	15.35	15.70	16.04	16.38	16.72	17.07	17.41	17.75	18.10
30	13.43	13.78	14.13	14.48	14.83	15.19	15.54	15.89	16.24	16.60	16.95	17.31	17.66	18.02	18.38	18.74
31	13.89	14.25	14.61	14.97	15.33	15.70	16.06	16.43	16.79	17.16	17.53	17.90	18.27	18.63	19.00	19.38
32	14.34	14.71	15.09	15.46	15.84	16.21	16.59	16.97	17.35	17.73	18.11	18.49	18.87	19.25	19.63	20.02
33	14.79	15.18	15.57	15.95	16.34	16.73	17.12	17.51	17.90	18.29	18.69	19.08	19.47	19.87	20.26	20.66
34	15.25	15.65	16.05	16.44	16.85	17.25	17.65	18.05	18.46	18.86	19.27	19.67	20.08	20.49	20.90	21.31
35	15.70	16.11	16.53	16.94	17.35	17.77	18.18	18.60	19.01	19.43	19.85	20.27	20.69	21.11	21.53	21.95
36	16.16	16.58	17.01	17.43	17.86	18.29	18.71	19.14	19.57	20.00	20.43	20.87	21.30	21.73	22.17	22.60
37	16.62	17.06	17.49	17.93	18.37	18.81	19.25	19.69	20.13	20.58	21.02	21.46	21.91	22.36	22.81	23.25
38	17.08	17.53	17.98	18.43	18.88	19.33	19.78	20.24	20.69	21.15	21.61	22.07	22.52	22.99	23.45	23.91
39	17.54	18.00	18.46	18.93	19.39	19.86	20.32	20.79	21.26	21.73	22.20	22.67	23.14	23.61	24.09	24.56
40	18.00	18.48	18.95	19.43	19.90	20.38	20.86	21.34	21.82	22.30	22.79	23.27	23.76	24.25	24.73	25.22
41	18.47	18.95	19.44	19.93	20.42	20.91	21.40	21.89	22.39	22.88	23.38	23.88	24.38	24.88	25.38	25.88
42	18.93	19.43	19.93	20.43	20.93	21.44	21.94	22.45	22.96	23.47	23.98	24.49	25.00	25.51	26.03	26.55
43	19.40	19.91	20.42	20.94	21.45	21.97	22.49	23.01	23.53	24.05	24.57	25.10	25.62	26.15	26.68	27.21
44	19.86	20.39	20.91	21.44	21.97	22.50	23.03	23.57	24.10	24.64	25.17	25.71	26.25	26.79	27.33	27.88
45	20.33	20.87	21.41	21.95	22.49	23.03	23.58	24.12	24.67	25.22	25.77	26.32	26.88	27.43	27.99	28.55
46	20.80	21.35	21.90	22.46	23.01	23.57	24.13	24.69	25.25	25.81	26.37	26.94	27.51	28.08	28.65	29.22
47	21.27	21.83	22.40	22.97	23.53	24.10	24.68	25.25	25.82	26.40	26.98	27.56	28.14	28.72	29.31	29.89
48	21.74	22.32	22.90	23.48	24.06	24.64	25.23	25.81	26.40	26.99	27.58	28.18	28.77	29.37	29.97	30.57
49	22.21	22.80	23.39	23.99	24.58	25.18	25.78	26.38	26.98	27.59	28.19	28.80	29.41	30.02	30.63	31.24
50	22.69	23.29	23.89	24.50	25.11	25.72	26.33	26.95	27.56	28.18	28.80	29.42	30.04	30.67	31.29	31.92
51	23.16	23.78	24.40	25.02	25.64	26.26	26.89	27.52	28.15	28.78	29.41	30.05	30.68	31.32	31.96	32.60
52	23.64	24.27	24.90	25.53	26.17	26.81	27.45	28.09	28.73	29.38	30.02	30.67	31.32	31.98	32.63	33.29
53	24.11	24.76	25.40	26.05	26.70	27.35	28.00	28.66	29.32	29.98	30.64	31.30	31.97	32.63	33.30	33.97
54	24.59	25.25	25.91	26.57	27.23	27.90	28.56	29.23	29.91	30.58	31.25	31.93	32.61	33.29	33.98	34.66
55	25.07	25.74	26.41	27.09	27.77	28.44	29.13	29.81	30.50	31.18	31.87	32.56	33.26	33.95	34.65	35.35
56	25.55	26.23	26.92	27.61	28.30	28.99	29.69	30.39	31.09	31.79	32.49	33.20	33.91	34.62	35.33	36.04
57	26.03	26.73	27.43	28.13	28.84	29.54	30.25	30.97	31.68	32.39	33.11	33.83	34.56	35.28	36.01	36.74
58	26.51	27.23	27.94	28.66	29.37	30.10	30.82	31.55	32.27	33.00	33.74	34.47	35.21	35.95	36.69	37.43
59	27.00	27.72	28.45	29.18	29.91	30.65	31.39	32.13	32.87	33.61	34.36	35.11	35.86	36.62	37.37	38.13
60	27.48	28.22	28.96	29.71	30.45	31.20	31.96	32.71	33.47	34.23	34.99	35.75	36.52	37.29	38.06	38.83

continued

TABLE 13-1 Annual Percentage Rate (APR) Finance Charge per $100

ANNUAL PERCENTAGE RATE TABLE FOR MONTHLY PAYMENT PLANS
SEE INSTRUCTIONS FOR USE OF TABLES   FRB-104-M

ANNUAL PERCENTAGE RATE

(FINANCE CHARGE PER $100 OF AMOUNT FINANCED)

NUMBER OF PAYMENTS	14.00%	14.25%	14.50%	14.75%	15.00%	15.25%	15.50%	15.75%	16.00%	16.25%	16.50%	16.75%	17.00%	17.25%	17.50%	17.75%
1	1.17	1.19	1.21	1.23	1.25	1.27	1.29	1.31	1.33	1.35	1.37	1.40	1.42	1.44	1.46	1.48
2	1.75	1.78	1.82	1.85	1.88	1.91	1.94	1.97	2.00	2.04	2.07	2.10	2.13	2.16	2.19	2.22
3	2.34	2.38	2.43	2.47	2.51	2.55	2.59	2.64	2.68	2.72	2.76	2.80	2.85	2.89	2.93	2.97
4	2.93	2.99	3.04	3.09	3.14	3.20	3.25	3.30	3.36	3.41	3.46	3.51	3.57	3.62	3.67	3.73
5	3.53	3.59	3.65	3.72	3.78	3.84	3.91	3.97	4.04	4.10	4.16	4.23	4.29	4.35	4.42	4.48
6	4.12	4.20	4.27	4.35	4.42	4.49	4.57	4.64	4.72	4.79	4.87	4.94	5.02	5.09	5.17	5.24
7	4.72	4.81	4.89	4.98	5.06	5.15	5.23	5.32	5.40	5.49	5.58	5.66	5.75	5.83	5.92	6.00
8	5.32	5.42	5.51	5.61	5.71	5.80	5.90	6.00	6.09	6.19	6.29	6.38	6.48	6.58	6.67	6.77
9	5.92	6.03	6.14	6.25	6.35	6.46	6.57	6.68	6.78	6.89	7.00	7.11	7.22	7.32	7.43	7.54
10	6.53	6.65	6.77	6.88	7.00	7.12	7.24	7.36	7.48	7.60	7.72	7.84	7.96	8.08	8.19	8.31
11	7.14	7.27	7.40	7.53	7.66	7.79	7.92	8.05	8.18	8.31	8.44	8.57	8.70	8.83	8.96	9.09
12	7.74	7.89	8.03	8.17	8.31	8.45	8.59	8.74	8.88	9.02	9.16	9.30	9.45	9.59	9.73	9.87
13	8.36	8.51	8.66	8.81	8.97	9.12	9.27	9.43	9.58	9.73	9.89	10.04	10.20	10.35	10.50	10.66
14	8.97	9.13	9.30	9.46	9.63	9.79	9.96	10.12	10.29	10.45	10.62	10.78	10.95	11.11	11.28	11.45
15	9.59	9.76	9.94	10.11	10.29	10.47	10.64	10.82	11.00	11.17	11.35	11.53	11.71	11.88	12.06	12.24
16	10.20	10.39	10.58	10.77	10.95	11.14	11.33	11.52	11.71	11.90	12.09	12.28	12.46	12.65	12.84	13.03
17	10.82	11.02	11.22	11.42	11.62	11.82	12.02	12.22	12.42	12.62	12.83	13.03	13.23	13.43	13.63	13.83
18	11.45	11.66	11.87	12.08	12.29	12.50	12.72	12.93	13.14	13.35	13.57	13.78	13.99	14.21	14.42	14.64
19	12.07	12.30	12.52	12.74	12.97	13.19	13.41	13.64	13.86	14.09	14.31	14.54	14.76	14.99	15.22	15.44
20	12.70	12.93	13.17	13.41	13.64	13.88	14.11	14.35	14.59	14.82	15.06	15.30	15.54	15.77	16.01	16.25
21	13.33	13.58	13.82	14.07	14.32	14.57	14.82	15.06	15.31	15.56	15.81	16.06	16.31	16.56	16.81	17.07
22	13.96	14.22	14.48	14.74	15.00	15.26	15.52	15.78	16.04	16.30	16.57	16.83	17.09	17.36	17.62	17.88
23	14.59	14.87	15.14	15.41	15.68	15.96	16.23	16.50	16.78	17.05	17.32	17.60	17.88	18.15	18.43	18.70
24	15.23	15.51	15.80	16.08	16.37	16.65	16.94	17.22	17.51	17.80	18.09	18.37	18.66	18.95	19.24	19.53
25	15.87	16.17	16.46	16.76	17.06	17.35	17.65	17.95	18.25	18.55	18.85	19.15	19.45	19.75	20.05	20.36
26	16.51	16.82	17.13	17.44	17.75	18.06	18.37	18.68	18.99	19.30	19.62	19.93	20.24	20.56	20.87	21.19
27	17.15	17.47	17.80	18.12	18.44	18.76	19.09	19.41	19.74	20.06	20.39	20.71	21.04	21.37	21.69	22.02
28	17.80	18.13	18.47	18.80	19.14	19.47	19.81	20.15	20.48	20.82	21.16	21.50	21.84	22.18	22.52	22.86
29	18.45	18.79	19.14	19.49	19.83	20.18	20.53	20.88	21.23	21.58	21.94	22.29	22.64	22.99	23.35	23.70
30	19.10	19.45	19.81	20.17	20.54	20.90	21.26	21.62	21.99	22.35	22.72	23.08	23.45	23.81	24.18	24.55
31	19.75	20.12	20.49	20.87	21.24	21.61	21.99	22.37	22.74	23.12	23.50	23.88	24.26	24.64	25.02	25.40
32	20.40	20.79	21.17	21.56	21.95	22.33	22.72	23.11	23.50	23.89	24.28	24.68	25.07	25.46	25.86	26.25
33	21.06	21.46	21.85	22.25	22.65	23.06	23.46	23.86	24.26	24.67	25.07	25.48	25.88	26.29	26.70	27.11
34	21.72	22.13	22.54	22.95	23.37	23.78	24.19	24.61	25.03	25.44	25.86	26.28	26.70	27.12	27.54	27.97
35	22.38	22.80	23.23	23.65	24.08	24.51	24.94	25.36	25.79	26.23	26.66	27.09	27.52	27.96	28.39	28.83
36	23.04	23.48	23.92	24.35	24.80	25.24	25.68	26.12	26.57	27.01	27.46	27.90	28.35	28.80	29.25	29.70
37	23.70	24.16	24.61	25.06	25.51	25.97	26.42	26.88	27.34	27.80	28.26	28.72	29.18	29.64	30.10	30.57
38	24.37	24.84	25.30	25.77	26.24	26.70	27.17	27.64	28.11	28.59	29.06	29.53	30.01	30.49	30.96	31.44
39	25.04	25.52	26.00	26.48	26.96	27.44	27.92	28.41	28.89	29.38	29.87	30.36	30.85	31.34	31.83	32.32
40	25.71	26.20	26.70	27.19	27.69	28.18	28.68	29.18	29.68	30.18	30.68	31.18	31.68	32.19	32.69	33.20
41	26.39	26.89	27.40	27.91	28.41	28.92	29.44	29.95	30.46	30.97	31.49	32.01	32.52	33.04	33.56	34.08
42	27.06	27.58	28.10	28.62	29.15	29.67	30.19	30.72	31.25	31.78	32.31	32.84	33.37	33.90	34.44	34.97
43	27.74	28.27	28.81	29.34	29.88	30.42	30.96	31.50	32.04	32.58	33.13	33.67	34.22	34.76	35.31	35.86
44	28.42	28.97	29.52	30.07	30.62	31.17	31.72	32.28	32.83	33.39	33.95	34.51	35.07	35.63	36.19	36.76
45	29.11	29.67	30.23	30.79	31.36	31.92	32.49	33.06	33.63	34.20	34.77	35.35	35.92	36.50	37.08	37.66
46	29.79	30.36	30.94	31.52	32.10	32.68	33.26	33.84	34.43	35.01	35.60	36.19	36.78	37.37	37.96	38.56
47	30.48	31.07	31.66	32.25	32.84	33.44	34.03	34.63	35.23	35.83	36.43	37.04	37.64	38.25	38.86	39.46
48	31.17	31.77	32.37	32.98	33.59	34.20	34.81	35.42	36.03	36.65	37.27	37.88	38.50	39.13	39.75	40.37
49	31.86	32.48	33.09	33.71	34.34	34.96	35.59	36.21	36.84	37.47	38.10	38.74	39.37	40.01	40.65	41.29
50	32.55	33.18	33.82	34.45	35.09	35.73	36.37	37.01	37.65	38.30	38.94	39.59	40.24	40.89	41.55	42.20
51	33.25	33.89	34.54	35.19	35.84	36.49	37.15	37.81	38.46	39.12	39.79	40.45	41.11	41.78	42.45	43.12
52	33.95	34.61	35.27	35.93	36.60	37.27	37.94	38.61	39.28	39.96	40.63	41.31	41.99	42.67	43.36	44.04
53	34.65	35.32	36.00	36.68	37.36	38.04	38.72	39.41	40.10	40.79	41.48	42.17	42.87	43.57	44.27	44.97
54	35.35	36.04	36.73	37.42	38.12	38.82	39.52	40.22	40.92	41.63	42.33	43.04	43.75	44.47	45.18	45.90
55	36.05	36.76	37.46	38.17	38.88	39.60	40.31	41.03	41.74	42.47	43.19	43.91	44.64	45.37	46.10	46.83
56	36.76	37.48	38.20	38.92	39.65	40.38	41.11	41.84	42.57	43.31	44.05	44.79	45.53	46.27	47.02	47.77
57	37.47	38.20	38.94	39.68	40.42	41.16	41.91	42.65	43.40	44.15	44.91	45.66	46.42	47.18	47.94	48.71
58	38.18	38.93	39.68	40.43	41.19	41.95	42.71	43.47	44.23	45.00	45.77	46.54	47.32	48.09	48.87	49.65
59	38.89	39.66	40.42	41.19	41.96	42.74	43.51	44.29	45.07	45.85	46.64	47.42	48.21	49.01	49.80	50.60
60	39.61	40.39	41.17	41.95	42.74	43.53	44.32	45.11	45.91	46.71	47.51	48.31	49.12	49.92	50.73	51.55

continued

TABLE 13-1 Annual Percentage Rate (APR) Finance Charge per $100

ANNUAL PERCENTAGE RATE TABLE FOR MONTHLY PAYMENT PLANS
SEE INSTRUCTIONS FOR USE OF TABLES

FRB-105-M

ANNUAL PERCENTAGE RATE

NUMBER OF PAYMENTS	18.00%	18.25%	18.50%	18.75%	19.00%	19.25%	19.50%	19.75%	20.00%	20.25%	20.50%	20.75%	21.00%	21.25%	21.50%	21.75%
	(FINANCE CHARGE PER $100 OF AMOUNT FINANCED)															
1	1.50	1.52	1.54	1.56	1.58	1.60	1.62	1.65	1.67	1.69	1.71	1.73	1.75	1.77	1.79	1.81
2	2.26	2.29	2.32	2.35	2.38	2.41	2.44	2.48	2.51	2.54	2.57	2.60	2.63	2.66	2.70	2.73
3	3.01	3.06	3.10	3.14	3.18	3.23	3.27	3.31	3.35	3.39	3.44	3.48	3.52	3.56	3.60	3.65
4	3.78	3.83	3.88	3.94	3.99	4.04	4.10	4.15	4.20	4.25	4.31	4.36	4.41	4.47	4.52	4.57
5	4.54	4.61	4.67	4.74	4.80	4.86	4.93	4.99	5.06	5.12	5.18	5.25	5.31	5.37	5.44	5.50
6	5.32	5.39	5.46	5.54	5.61	5.69	5.76	5.84	5.91	5.99	6.06	6.14	6.21	6.29	6.36	6.44
7	6.09	6.18	6.26	6.35	6.43	6.52	6.60	6.69	6.78	6.86	6.95	7.04	7.12	7.21	7.29	7.38
8	6.87	6.96	7.06	7.16	7.26	7.35	7.45	7.55	7.64	7.74	7.84	7.94	8.03	8.13	8.23	8.33
9	7.65	7.76	7.87	7.97	8.08	8.19	8.30	8.41	8.52	8.63	8.73	8.84	8.95	9.06	9.17	9.28
10	8.43	8.55	8.67	8.79	8.91	9.03	9.15	9.27	9.39	9.51	9.63	9.75	9.88	10.00	10.12	10.24
11	9.22	9.35	9.49	9.62	9.75	9.88	10.01	10.14	10.28	10.41	10.54	10.67	10.80	10.94	11.07	11.20
12	10.02	10.16	10.30	10.44	10.59	10.73	10.87	11.02	11.16	11.31	11.45	11.59	11.74	11.88	12.02	12.17
13	10.81	10.97	11.12	11.28	11.43	11.59	11.74	11.90	12.05	12.21	12.36	12.52	12.67	12.83	12.99	13.14
14	11.61	11.78	11.95	12.11	12.28	12.45	12.61	12.78	12.95	13.11	13.28	13.45	13.67	13.79	13.95	14.12
15	12.42	12.59	12.77	12.95	13.13	13.31	13.49	13.67	13.85	14.03	14.21	14.39	14.57	14.75	14.93	15.11
16	13.22	13.41	13.60	13.80	13.99	14.18	14.37	14.56	14.75	14.94	15.13	15.33	15.52	15.71	15.90	16.10
17	14.04	14.24	14.44	14.64	14.85	15.05	15.25	15.46	15.66	15.86	16.07	16.27	16.48	16.68	16.89	17.09
18	14.85	15.07	15.28	15.49	15.71	15.93	16.14	16.36	16.57	16.79	17.01	17.22	17.44	17.66	17.88	18.09
19	15.67	15.90	16.12	16.35	16.58	16.81	17.03	17.26	17.49	17.72	17.95	18.18	18.41	18.64	18.87	19.10
20	16.49	16.73	16.97	17.21	17.45	17.69	17.93	18.17	18.41	18.66	18.90	19.14	19.38	19.63	19.87	20.11
21	17.32	17.57	17.82	18.07	18.33	18.58	18.83	19.09	19.34	19.60	19.85	20.11	20.36	20.62	20.87	21.13
22	18.15	18.41	18.68	18.94	19.21	19.47	19.74	20.01	20.27	20.54	20.81	21.08	21.34	21.61	21.88	22.15
23	18.98	19.26	19.54	19.81	20.09	20.37	20.65	20.93	21.21	21.49	21.77	22.05	22.33	22.61	22.90	23.18
24	19.82	20.11	20.40	20.69	20.98	21.27	21.56	21.86	22.15	22.44	22.74	23.03	23.33	23.62	23.92	24.21
25	20.66	20.96	21.27	21.57	21.87	22.18	22.48	22.79	23.10	23.40	23.71	24.02	24.32	24.63	24.94	25.25
26	21.50	21.82	22.14	22.45	22.77	23.09	23.41	23.73	24.04	24.36	24.68	25.01	25.33	25.65	25.97	26.29
27	22.35	22.68	23.01	23.34	23.67	24.00	24.33	24.67	25.00	25.33	25.67	26.00	26.34	26.67	27.01	27.34
28	23.20	23.55	23.89	24.23	24.58	24.92	25.27	25.61	25.96	26.30	26.65	27.00	27.35	27.70	28.05	28.40
29	24.06	24.41	24.77	25.13	25.49	25.84	26.20	26.56	26.92	27.28	27.64	28.00	28.37	28.73	29.09	29.46
30	24.92	25.29	25.66	26.03	26.40	26.77	27.14	27.52	27.89	28.26	28.64	29.01	29.39	29.77	30.14	30.52
31	25.78	26.16	26.55	26.93	27.32	27.70	28.09	28.47	28.86	29.25	29.64	30.03	30.42	30.81	31.20	31.59
32	26.65	27.04	27.44	27.84	28.24	28.64	29.04	29.44	29.84	30.24	30.64	31.05	31.45	31.85	32.26	32.67
33	27.52	27.93	28.34	28.75	29.16	29.57	29.99	30.40	30.82	31.23	31.65	32.07	32.49	32.91	33.33	33.75
34	28.39	28.81	29.24	29.66	30.09	30.52	30.95	31.37	31.80	32.23	32.67	33.10	33.53	33.96	34.40	34.83
35	29.27	29.71	30.14	30.58	31.02	31.47	31.91	32.35	32.79	33.24	33.68	34.13	34.58	35.03	35.47	35.92
36	30.15	30.60	31.05	31.51	31.96	32.42	32.87	33.33	33.79	34.25	34.71	35.17	35.63	36.09	36.56	37.02
37	31.03	31.50	31.97	32.43	32.90	33.37	33.84	34.32	34.79	35.26	35.74	36.21	36.69	37.16	37.64	38.12
38	31.92	32.40	32.88	33.37	33.85	34.33	34.82	35.30	35.79	36.28	36.77	37.26	37.75	38.24	38.73	39.23
39	32.81	33.31	33.80	34.30	34.80	35.30	35.80	36.30	36.80	37.30	37.81	38.31	38.82	39.32	39.83	40.34
40	33.71	34.22	34.73	35.24	35.75	36.26	36.78	37.29	37.81	38.33	38.85	39.37	39.89	40.41	40.93	41.46
41	34.61	35.13	35.66	36.18	36.71	37.24	37.77	38.30	38.83	39.36	39.89	40.43	40.96	41.50	42.04	42.58
42	35.51	36.05	36.59	37.13	37.67	38.21	38.76	39.30	39.85	40.40	40.95	41.50	42.05	42.60	43.15	43.71
43	36.42	36.97	37.52	38.08	38.63	39.19	39.75	40.31	40.87	41.44	42.00	42.57	43.13	43.70	44.27	44.84
44	37.33	37.89	38.46	39.03	39.60	40.18	40.75	41.33	41.90	42.48	43.06	43.64	44.22	44.81	45.39	45.98
45	38.24	38.82	39.41	39.99	40.58	41.17	41.75	42.35	42.94	43.53	44.13	44.72	45.32	45.92	46.52	47.12
46	39.16	39.75	40.35	40.95	41.55	42.16	42.76	43.37	43.98	44.58	45.20	45.81	46.42	47.03	47.65	48.27
47	40.08	40.69	41.30	41.92	42.54	43.15	43.77	44.40	45.02	45.64	46.27	46.90	47.53	48.16	48.79	49.42
48	41.00	41.63	42.26	42.89	43.52	44.15	44.79	45.43	46.07	46.71	47.35	47.99	48.64	49.28	49.93	50.58
49	41.93	42.57	43.22	43.86	44.51	45.16	45.81	46.46	47.12	47.77	48.43	49.09	49.75	50.41	51.08	51.74
50	42.86	43.52	44.18	44.84	45.50	46.17	46.83	47.50	48.17	48.84	49.52	50.19	50.87	51.55	52.23	52.91
51	43.79	44.47	45.14	45.82	46.50	47.18	47.86	48.55	49.23	49.92	50.61	51.30	51.99	52.69	53.38	54.08
52	44.73	45.42	46.11	46.80	47.50	48.20	48.89	49.59	50.30	51.00	51.71	52.41	53.12	53.83	54.55	55.26
53	45.67	46.38	47.08	47.79	48.50	49.22	49.93	50.65	51.37	52.09	52.81	53.53	54.26	54.98	55.71	56.44
54	46.62	47.34	48.06	48.79	49.51	50.24	50.97	51.70	52.44	53.17	53.91	54.65	55.39	56.14	56.88	57.63
55	47.57	48.30	49.04	49.78	50.52	51.27	52.02	52.76	53.52	54.27	55.02	55.78	56.54	57.30	58.06	58.82
56	48.52	49.27	50.03	50.78	51.54	52.30	53.06	53.83	54.60	55.37	56.14	56.91	57.68	58.46	59.24	60.02
57	49.47	50.24	51.01	51.79	52.56	53.34	54.12	54.90	55.68	56.47	57.25	58.04	58.84	59.63	60.43	61.22
58	50.43	51.22	52.00	52.79	53.58	54.38	55.17	55.97	56.77	57.57	58.38	59.18	59.99	60.80	61.62	62.43
59	51.39	52.20	53.00	53.80	54.61	55.42	56.23	57.05	57.87	58.68	59.51	60.33	61.15	61.98	62.81	63.64
60	52.36	53.18	54.00	54.82	55.64	56.47	57.30	58.13	58.96	59.80	60.64	61.48	62.32	63.17	64.01	64.86

STEPS TO FIND THE ANNUAL PERCENTAGE RATE OF AN INSTALLMENT LOAN BY USING APR TABLES

STEP 1. Calculate the finance charge per $100.

$$\text{Finance charge per \$100} = \frac{\text{Finance charge} \times 100}{\text{Amount financed}}$$

STEP 2. From Table 13-1, scan down the Number of Payments column to the number of payments for the loan in question.

STEP 3. Scan to the right in that Number of Payments row to the table factor that most closely corresponds to the finance charge per $100 calculated in Step 1.

STEP 4. Look to the top of the column containing the finance charge per $100 to find the APR of the loan.

EXAMPLE6 CALCULATING APR BY TABLES

Gary Robbins purchased a used motorcycle for $7,000. He made a down payment of $1,000 and financed the remaining $6,000 for 36 months. With monthly payments of $200 each, the total finance charge on the loan was $1,200 ($200 × 36 = $7,200 − $6,000 = $1,200). Use Table 13-1 to find what annual percentage rate was charged on Gary's loan.

SOLUTIONSTRATEGY

Step 1. $$\text{Finance charge per \$100} = \frac{\text{Finance charge} \times 100}{\text{Amount financed}}$$

$$\text{Finance charge per \$100} = \frac{1,200 \times 100}{6,000} = \frac{120,000}{6,000}$$

$$\text{Finance charge per \$100} = \$20$$

Step 2.   Using Table 13-1, scan down the Number of Payments column to 36 payments.

Step 3.   Scan to the right in that Number of Payments row until you find $20, the finance charge per $100.

Step 4.   Looking at the top of the column containing the $20, you will find the annual percentage rate for the loan to be 12.25%.

TRYITEXERCISE6

Erica Larsen purchased a living room set for $4,500 from Century Designs. She made a $500 down payment and financed the balance with an installment loan for 24 months. If her payments are $190 per month, what APR is she paying on the loan?

CHECK YOUR ANSWER WITH THE SOLUTION ON PAGE 447.

CALCULATING APR BY FORMULA

When APR tables are not available, the annual percentage rate can be closely approximated by the formula

$$\text{APR} = \frac{72I}{3P(n + 1) + I(n - 1)}$$

where:

I = finance charge on the loan
P = principal, or amount financed
n = number of months of the loan

EXAMPLE 7 CALCULATING APR BY FORMULA

Refer to Example 6, Gary Robbins' motorcycle purchase. This time use the APR formula to find the annual percentage rate. How does it compare with the APR from the table?

SOLUTIONSTRATEGY

$$APR = \frac{72I}{3P(n + 1) + I(n - 1)}$$

$$APR = \frac{72(1,200)}{3(6,000)(36 + 1) + 1,200(36 - 1)} = \frac{86,400}{666,000 + 42,000} = \frac{86,400}{708,000}$$

$$APR = .1220338 = \underline{12.20\%}$$

Note: In comparing the two answers, we can see that using the formula gives a close approximation of the Federal Reserve Board's APR table value of 12.25%.

TRYITEXERCISE 7

Christina Pitt repaid a $2,200 installment loan with 18 monthly payments of $140 each. Use the APR formula to determine the annual percentage rate of Christina's loan.

CHECK YOUR ANSWER WITH THE SOLUTION ON PAGE 447.

CALCULATING THE FINANCE CHARGE AND MONTHLY PAYMENT OF AN INSTALLMENT LOAN BY USING THE APR TABLES

13-7

When the annual percentage rate and number of months of an installment loan are known, the APR tables can be used in reverse to find the amount of the finance charge. Once the finance charge is known, the monthly payment required to amortize the loan can be calculated as before.

STEPS TO FIND THE FINANCE CHARGE AND THE MONTHLY PAYMENT OF AN INSTALLMENT LOAN BY USING THE APR TABLES

STEP 1. Using the APR and the number of payments of the loan, locate the table factor at the intersection of the APR column and the Number of Payments row. This factor represents the finance charge per $100 financed.

STEP 2. Calculate the total finance charge of the loan.

$$\text{Finance charge} = \frac{\text{Amount financed} \times \text{Table factor}}{100}$$

STEP 3. Calculate the monthly payment.

$$\text{Monthly payment} = \frac{\text{Amount financed} + \text{Finance charge}}{\text{Number of months of the loan}}$$

EXAMPLE 8 CALCULATING FINANCE CHARGE BY APR TABLES

Classic Motors uses Regal Bank to finance automobile and truck sales. This month Regal is offering up to 48-month installment loans with an APR of 15.5%. For qualified buyers, no down payment is required. If Todd Martin wants to finance a new truck for $17,500, what are the finance charge and the monthly payment on Todd's loan?

SOLUTION STRATEGY

Step 1. The table factor at the intersection of the 15.5% APR column and the 48 Payments row is $34.81.

Step 2. $\text{Finance charge} = \dfrac{\text{Amount financed} \times \text{Table factor}}{100}$

$\text{Finance charge} = \dfrac{17,500 \times 34.81}{100} = \dfrac{609,175}{100}$

$\text{Finance charge} = \$6,091.75$

Step 3. $\text{Monthly payment} = \dfrac{\text{Amount financed} + \text{Finance charge}}{\text{Number of months of the loan}}$

$\text{Monthly payment} = \dfrac{17,500 + 6,091.75}{48} = \dfrac{23,591.75}{48}$

$\text{Monthly payment} = \$491.49$

TRY IT EXERCISE 8

Computer Mart uses a finance company that is offering up to 24-month installment loans with an APR of 13.25%. For qualified buyers, no down payment is required. If Randy Salazar wants to finance a computer and printer for $3,550, what are the finance charge and the monthly payment on Randy's loan?

CHECK YOUR ANSWERS WITH THE SOLUTIONS ON PAGE 447.

13-8

CALCULATING THE FINANCE CHARGE REBATE AND THE PAYOFF FOR LOANS PAID OFF EARLY BY USING THE SUM-OF-THE-DIGITS METHOD

finance charge rebate Unearned portion of the finance charge that the lender returns to the borrower when an installment loan is paid off early.

sum-of-the-digits method or **Rule of 78** Widely accepted method for calculating the finance charge rebate. Based on the assumption that more interest is paid in the early months of a loan, when a greater portion of the principal is available to the borrower.

Frequently, borrowers choose to repay installment loans before the full time period of the loan has elapsed. When loans are paid off early, the borrower is entitled to a **finance charge rebate** because the principal was not kept for the full amount of time on which the finance charge was calculated. At payoff, the lender must return, or rebate, to the borrower any unearned portion of the finance charge.

A widely accepted method for calculating the finance charge rebate is known as the **sum-of-the-digits method** or the **Rule of 78**. This method is based on the assumption that the lender earns more interest in the early months of a loan, when the borrower has the use of much of the principal, than in the later months, when most of the principal has already been paid back.

When using this method, the finance charge is assumed to be divided in parts equal to the sum of the digits of the months of the loan. Because the sum of the digits of a 12-month loan is 78, the technique has become known as the Rule of 78.

$$\text{Sum of the digits of } 12 = 1 + 2 + 3 + 4 + 5 + 6 + 7 + 8 + 9 + 10 + 11 + 12 = 78$$

The amount of finance charge in any given month is represented by a fraction whose numerator is the number of payments remaining, and the denominator is the sum of the digits of the number of months in the loan.

For a 12-month loan, for example, the fraction of the finance charge in the first month would be $\frac{12}{78}$. The numerator is 12 because in the first month, no payments have been made; therefore, 12 payments remain. The denominator is 78 because the sum of the digits of 12 payments is 78. In the second month, the lender earns $\frac{11}{78}$; in the third month, $\frac{10}{78}$. This decline continues until the last month when only $\frac{1}{78}$ remains. Exhibit 13-6 illustrates the distribution of a $1,000 finance charge by using the sum-of-the-digits method.

With the sum-of-the-digits method, a **rebate fraction** is established based on when a loan is paid off. The numerator of the rebate fraction is the sum of the digits of the number of remaining payments, and the denominator is the sum of the digits of the total number of payments.

$$\text{Rebate fraction} = \frac{\text{Sum of the digits of the number of remaining payments}}{\text{Sum of the digits of the total number of payments}}$$

Although the sum of the digits is easily calculated by addition, it can become tedious for loans of 24, 36, or 48 months. For this reason, we will use the sum-of-the-digits formula to find the numerator and denominator of the rebate fraction. In the formula, *n* represents the number of payments.

$$\text{Sum of digits} = \frac{n(n+1)}{2}$$

rebate fraction Fraction used to calculate the finance charge rebate. The numerator is the sum of the digits of the number of payments remaining at the time the loan is paid off; the denominator is the sum of the digits of the total number of payments of the loan.

© Glowimages RM/Alamy

Installment financing is frequently used when consumers purchase big-ticket items such as appliances and electronic equipment.

EXHIBIT 13-6 Distribution of a $1,000 Finance Charge over 12 Months

Month Number	Finance Charge Fraction	×	$1,000	=	Finance Charge
1	$\frac{12}{78}$	×	$1,000	=	$153.85
2	$\frac{11}{78}$	×	$1,000	=	$141.03
3	$\frac{10}{78}$	×	$1,000	=	$128.21
4	$\frac{9}{78}$	×	$1,000	=	$115.38
5	$\frac{8}{78}$	×	$1,000	=	$102.56
6	$\frac{7}{78}$	×	$1,000	=	$89.74
7	$\frac{6}{78}$	×	$1,000	=	$76.92
8	$\frac{5}{78}$	×	$1,000	=	$64.10
9	$\frac{4}{78}$	×	$1,000	=	$51.28
10	$\frac{3}{78}$	×	$1,000	=	$38.46
11	$\frac{2}{78}$	×	$1,000	=	$25.64
12	$\frac{1}{78}$	×	$1,000	=	$12.82

INTHE BUSINESSWORLD

This table clearly illustrates that the majority of the finance charge on an installment loan is incurred in the first half of the loan.

STEPS TO CALCULATE THE FINANCE CHARGE REBATE AND LOAN PAYOFF

STEP 1. Calculate the rebate fraction.

$$\text{Rebate fraction} = \frac{\text{Sum of the digits of the number of remaining payments}}{\text{Sum of the digits of the total number of payments}}$$

STEP 2. Determine the finance charge rebate.

$$\text{Finance charge rebate} = \text{Rebate fraction} \times \text{Total finance charge}$$

STEP 3. Find the loan payoff.

$$\begin{array}{c}\text{Loan}\\\text{payoff}\end{array} = \left(\begin{array}{c}\text{Payment}\\\text{remaining}\end{array} \times \begin{array}{c}\text{Payments}\\\text{amount}\end{array}\right) - \begin{array}{c}\text{Finance charge}\\\text{rebate}\end{array}$$

EXAMPLE9 CALCULATING EARLY LOAN PAYOFF FIGURES

Suzie Starr financed a $1,500 health club membership with an installment loan for 12 months. The payments were $145 per month, and the total finance charge was $240. After 8 months, she decided to pay off the loan. What is the finance charge rebate, and what is her loan payoff?

SOLUTIONSTRATEGY

Step 1. Rebate fraction:

Set up the rebate fraction by using the sum-of-the-digits formula. Because Suzie already made eight payments, she has four payments remaining ($12 - 8 = 4$).

The *numerator* will be the sum of the digits of the number of remaining payments, 4.

$$\text{Sum of the digits of } 4 = \frac{n(n+1)}{2} = \frac{4(4+1)}{2} = \frac{4(5)}{2} = \frac{20}{2} = \underline{10}$$

The *denominator* will be the sum of the digits of the number of payments, 12.

$$\text{Sum of the digits of } 12 = \frac{n(n+1)}{2} = \frac{12(12+1)}{2} = \frac{12(13)}{2} = \frac{156}{2} = \underline{78}$$

The rebate fraction is therefore $\frac{10}{78}$.

Step 2. Finance charge rebate:

Finance charge rebate = Rebate fraction × Total finance charge

Finance charge rebate $= \frac{10}{78} \times 240$

Finance charge rebate $= 30.7692 = \underline{\$30.77}$

Step 3. Loan payoff:

Loan payoff = (Payments remaining × Payment amount) − Finance charge rebate

Loan payoff $= (4 \times 145) - 30.77$

Loan payoff $= 580.00 - 30.77$

Loan payoff $= \underline{\$549.23}$

TRYITEXERCISE9

Mark Sanchez financed a $4,000 piano with an installment loan for 36 months. The payments were $141 per month, and the total finance charge was $1,076. After 20 months, Mark decided to pay off the loan. What is the finance charge rebate, and what is his loan payoff?

CHECK YOUR ANSWERS WITH THE SOLUTIONS ON PAGES 447–448.

SECTION II 13 REVIEW EXERCISES

Note: Round all answers to the nearest cent when necessary.

Calculate the amount financed, the finance charge, and the total deferred payment price for the following installment loans.

	Purchase (Cash) Price	Down Payment	Amount Financed	Monthly Payment	Number of Payments	Finance Charge	Total Deferred Payment Price
1.	$1,400	$350	$1,050.00	$68.00	24	$582.00	$1,982.00
2.	$3,500	20%	_____	$257.00	12	_____	_____

	Purchase (Cash) Price	Down Payment	Amount Financed	Monthly Payment	Number of Payments	Finance Charge	Total Deferred Payment Price
3.	$12,000	10%	_____	$375.00	36	_____	_____
4.	$2,900	0	_____	$187.69	18	_____	_____
5.	$8,750	15%	_____	$198.33	48	_____	_____
6.	$5,400	$1,500	_____	$427.50	12	_____	_____
7.	$20,000	25%	_____	$682.70	36	_____	_____

Calculate the amount financed, the finance charge, and the monthly payments for the following add-on interest loans.

	Purchase (Cash) Price	Down Payment	Amount Financed	Add-on Interest	Number of Payments	Finance Charge	Monthly Payment
8.	$788	10%	$709.20	8%	12	$56.74	$63.83
9.	$1,600	$250	_____	10%	24	_____	_____
10.	$4,000	15%	_____	$11\frac{1}{2}\%$	30	_____	_____
11.	$17,450	$2,000	_____	14%	48	_____	_____
12.	$50,300	25%	_____	12.4%	60	_____	_____
13.	$12,300	5%	_____	9%	36	_____	_____
14.	$5,225	$1,600	_____	7.8%	18	_____	_____

Calculate the finance charge, the finance charge per $100, and the annual percentage rate for the following installment loans by using the APR table, Table 13-1.

	Amount Financed	Number of Payments	Monthly Payment	Finance Charge	Finance Charge per $100	APR
15.	$2,300	24	$109.25	$322.00	$14.00	13%
16.	$14,000	36	$495.00	_____	_____	_____
17.	$1,860	18	$115.75	_____	_____	_____
18.	$35,000	60	$875.00	_____	_____	_____
19.	$6,550	24	$307.30	_____	_____	_____
20.	$17,930	48	$540.47	_____	_____	_____

Calculate the finance charge and the annual percentage rate for the following installment loans by using the APR formula.

	Amount Financed	Number of Payments	Monthly Payment	Finance Charge	APR
21.	$500	12	$44.25	$31.00	11.25%
22.	$2,450	36	$90.52	_____	_____
23.	$13,000	48	$373.75	_____	_____
24.	$100,000	72	$2,055.50	_____	_____
25.	$35,600	60	$845.50	_____	_____
26.	$8,850	30	$333.35	_____	_____

Calculate the finance charge and the monthly payment for the following loans by using the APR table, Table 13-1.

	Amount Financed	Number of Payments	APR	Table Factor	Finance Charge	Monthly Payment
27.	$5,000	48	13.5%	$29.97	$1,498.50	$135.39
28.	$7,500	36	12%	____	____	____
29.	$1,800	12	11.25%	____	____	____
30.	$900	18	14%	____	____	____
31.	$12,200	24	12.75%	____	____	____
32.	$3,875	30	16.5%	____	____	____

Calculate the missing information for the following installment loans that are being paid off early.

	Number of Payments	Payments Made	Payments Remaining	Sum-of-the-Digits Payments Remaining	Sum-of-the-Digits Number of Payments	Rebate Fraction
33.	12	4	8	36	78	36/78
34.	36	22	____	____	____	____
35.	24	9	____	____	____	____
36.	60	40	____	____	____	____
37.	48	8	____	____	____	____
38.	18	5	____	____	____	____

You are the loan department supervisor for the Pacific National Bank. The following installment loans are being paid off early, and it is your task to calculate the rebate fraction, the finance charge rebate, and the payoff for each loan.

	Amount Financed	Number of Payments	Monthly Payment	Payments Made	Rebate Fraction	Finance Charge Rebate	Loan Payoff
39.	$3,000	24	$162.50	9	120/300	$360.00	$2,077.50
40.	$1,600	18	$104.88	11	____	____	____
41.	$9,500	48	$267.00	36	____	____	____
42.	$4,800	36	$169.33	27	____	____	____
43.	$11,000	30	$440.00	20	____	____	____
44.	$6,200	12	$585.50	8	____	____	____

45. Belinda Raven is interested in buying a solar energy system for her home. At Sun-Catchers Inc., she picks out a system for a total cash price of $1,899. The salesperson informs her that if she qualifies for an installment loan, she may pay 10% now as a down payment and finance the balance with payments of $88.35 per month for 24 months.

   a.   What is the finance charge on this loan?

   b.   What is the total deferred payment price of the system?

46. Meghan Pease purchased a small sailboat for $8,350. She made a down payment of $1,400 and financed the balance with monthly payments of $239.38 for 36 months.

   a.   What is the finance charge on the loan?

Solar Energy

Although solar energy is a relatively new energy source, it may become the most important energy source of the future. Presently, available tax credits and incentives greatly reduce startup costs for solar power systems. Some of the major advantages of solar power include the fact that it is renewable, is nonpolluting, does not emit greenhouse gases, and provides free energy and heat from the sun.

According to www.sunworkssolar.com, by 2016, the U.S. solar industry is expected to support more than 440,000 permanent full-time jobs.

b. Use Table 13-1 to find what annual percentage rate was charged on Meghan's loan.

47. Valerie Ross financed a cruise to the Bahamas with a 5% add-on interest installment loan from her bank. The total price of the trip was $1,500. The bank required equal monthly payments for 2 years. What are Valerie's monthly payments?

48. Doug Black bought a jet ski with a 9% add-on interest installment loan from his credit union. The purchase price was $1,450. The credit union required a 15% down payment and equal monthly payments for 48 months. What are Doug's monthly payments?

Photo by Robert Brechner

Timeshare is a form of holiday ownership or right to the use of a property either directly or through a "points club." Each time sharer is allotted a period of time, typically a week or longer, for a great many years or in perpetuity. The timeshare industry is more than 30 years old and generates revenues of over $9.4 billion per annum. Today there are 6.7 million timeshare owners worldwide.

According to the American Resort Development Association, there were 1,548 timeshare resorts in the United States in 2009, representing approximately 170,200 units. Major companies now involved in timeshare include Hilton, Hyatt, Four Seasons, Marriott, Sheraton, Ramada, and De Vere.

49. Olivia Fast found a timeshare offer entitling her to 3 weeks per year in a Rocky Mountain townhouse. She had the option of paying $7,600 in cash or financing the timeshare with a 2-year installment loan. The loan required a 20% down payment and equal monthly payments of $283.73.

a. What is the finance charge on Olivia's loan?

b. What is the total deferred payment price of the timeshare contract?

50. Tim Houston purchased a wall unit for $2,400. He made a $700 down payment and financed the balance with an installment loan for 48 months. If Tim's payments are $42.50 per month, use the APR formula to calculate what annual percentage rate he is paying on the loan.

51. Stereo Central uses the Second National Bank to finance customer purchases. This month the bank is offering 24-month installment loans with an APR of 15.25%. For qualified buyers, no down payment is required. If Nathan David wants to finance a complete stereo system for $1,300, use the APR tables to calculate the finance charge and the monthly payment on his loan.

52. At a recent boat show, Nautica Bank was offering boat loans for up to 5 years with APRs of 13.5%. On new boats, a 20% down payment was required. Scott Vaughn wanted to finance a $55,000 boat for 5 years.

a. What would be the finance charge on the loan?

b. What would be the monthly payment?

53. Find the sum of the digits of

a. 24

b. 30

54. a. What is the rebate fraction of a 36-month loan paid off after the 14th payment?

b. What is the rebate fraction of a 42-month loan paid off after the 19th payment?

55. Charlie Allen financed a $3,500 Nautilus home gym with an 8% add-on interest installment loan for 24 months. The loan required a 10% down payment.

a. What is the finance charge on the loan?

b. What are Charlie's monthly payments?

Home Gym

Nautilus, Inc., is a fitness products company headquartered in Vancouver, Washington. Its principal business activities include designing, developing, sourcing, and marketing high-quality cardiovascular and strength fitness products and related accessories.

Nautilus products are sold under the brand names Nautilus, Bowflex, Universal, and Schwinn Fitness. Products offered include home gyms, free weight equipment, treadmills, indoor cycling equipment, ellipticals, and fitness accessories and apparel. In 2009, Nautilus, Inc., had 640 full-time employees and generated revenue of $189.3 million.

c. What annual percentage rate is being charged on the loan?

d. If Charlie decides to pay off the loan after 16 months, what is his loan payoff?

56. Chuck Wells is planning to buy a Winnebago motor home. The listed price is $165,000. Chuck can get a secured loan from his bank at 7.25% for as long as 60 months if he pays 15% down. Chuck's goal is to keep his payments below $3,800 per month and amortize the loan in 42 months.

a. Can he pay off the loan in 42 months and keep his payments under $3,800?

b. What are Chuck's options to get his payments closer to his goal?

c. Chuck spoke with his bank's loan officer, who has agreed to finance the deal with a 6.95% loan if Chuck can pay 20% down. Will these conditions meet Chuck's goal?

Winnebago Industries, Inc., founded in 1958 and headquartered in Forest City, Iowa, manufactures motor homes, which are self-contained recreation vehicles used primarily in leisure travel and outdoor recreation activities.

The company markets its motor homes through independent dealers under the Winnebago, Itasca, and ERA brand names in the United States and Canada. In 2009, Winnebago employed 1,630 workers and generated sales of $211.5 million through more than 245 dealer locations.

d. Chuck has told the seller he cannot buy the motor home at the listed price. If the seller agrees to reduce the listed price by $4,600 and Chuck pays the 20% down, will Chuck meet his goal?

BUSINESS DECISION: READING THE FINE PRINT

The advertisement for the 3-D TV at the Electronic Boutique shown below appeared in your local newspaper this morning. Answer the questions that follow based on the information in the ad.

57. a. If you purchased the TV on January 24 of this year and the billing date of the installment loan is the 15th of each month, when would your first payment be due?

b. What is the required amount of that payment?

c. If that payment is late or less than required, what happens and how much does that amount to?

d. If that payment is more than 30 days late, what happens and how much does that amount to?

e. Explain the advantages and disadvantages of this offer.

Electronic Boutique

NO INTEREST & NO PAYMENTS*
FOR 12 MONTHS
on all 3-D TVs

*Offer is subject to credit approval. No finance charges assessed and no monthly payment required on the promotional purchase if you pay this amount in full by the payment due date as shown on the twelfth (12th) billing statement after purchase date. If you do not, finance charges will be assessed on the promotional purchase amount from the purchase date and minimum monthly payment will be required on balance of amount. Standard account terms apply to non-promotional balances and, after the promotion ends, to promotional purchases. APR = 22.73%. APR of 24.75% applies if payment is more than 30 days late. Sales tax will be paid at the time of purchase.

$3,499 **Optimax Plus**
46" 3-D TV with Built-In Guide for an instant summary of your favorite shows & 2-Tuner Picture-in-Picture for watching two shows at once features 3-line digital comb filter for optimized color detail and sharpness. Component and S-Video inputs will keep you connected to the latest in digital technology.

spaxiax/Shutterstock.com

CHAPTER FORMULAS

Open-End Credit

$$\text{Periodic rate} = \frac{\text{Annual percentage rate}}{12}$$

$$\text{Finance charge} = \text{Previous month's balance} \times \text{Periodic rate}$$

$$\text{Average daily balance} = \frac{\text{Sum of the daily balances}}{\text{Days in billing cycle}}$$

$$\text{Finance charge} = \text{Average daily balance} \times \text{Periodic rate}$$

$$\begin{array}{c}\text{New}\\\text{balance}\end{array} = \begin{array}{c}\text{Previous}\\\text{balance}\end{array} + \begin{array}{c}\text{Finance}\\\text{charge}\end{array} + \begin{array}{c}\text{Purchases and}\\\text{cash advances}\end{array} - \begin{array}{c}\text{Payments and}\\\text{credits}\end{array}$$

Closed-End Credit

$$\text{Amount financed} = \text{Purchase price} - \text{Down payment}$$

$$\text{Down payment} = \text{Purchase price} \times \text{Down payment percent}$$

$$\text{Amount financed} = \text{Purchase price}(100\% - \text{Down payment percent})$$

$$\text{Total amount of installment payments} = \text{Amount financed} + \text{Finance charge}$$

$$\text{Finance charge} = \text{Total amount of installment payments} - \text{Amount financed}$$

$$\begin{array}{c}\text{Total amount of}\\\text{installment payments}\end{array} = \begin{array}{c}\text{Monthly payment}\\\text{amount}\end{array} \times \begin{array}{c}\text{Number of}\\\text{monthly payments}\end{array}$$

$$\text{Total deferred payment price} = \text{Total of installment payments} + \text{Down payment}$$

$$\begin{array}{c}\text{Interest}\\(\textit{finance charge})\end{array} = \begin{array}{c}\text{Principal}\\(\textit{amount financed})\end{array} \times \text{Rate} \times \text{Time}$$

$$\text{Regular monthly payments} = \frac{\text{Total of installment payments}}{\text{Number of months of loan}}$$

$$\text{APR} = \frac{72I}{3P(n + 1) + I(n - 1)}$$

$$\text{Finance charge} = \frac{\text{Amount financed} \times \text{APR table factor}}{100}$$

$$\text{Sum of digits} = \frac{n(n + 1)}{2}$$

$$\text{Rebate fraction} = \frac{\text{Sum of the digits of remaining payments}}{\text{Sum of the digits of total payment}}$$

$$\text{Finance charge rebate} = \text{Rebate fraction} \times \text{Total finance charge}$$

$$\text{Loan payoff} = (\text{Payments remaining} \times \text{Payment amount}) - \text{Finance charge rebate}$$

CHAPTER SUMMARY

Section I: Open-End Credit—Charge Accounts, Credit Cards, and Lines of Credit

Topic	Important Concepts	Illustrative Examples
Calculating the Finance Charge and New Balance by Using the Previous Month's Balance Method **Performance Objective 13-1, Page 411**	1. Divide the annual percentage rate by 12 to find the monthly or periodic interest rate. 2. Calculate the finance charge by multiplying the previous month's balance by the periodic interest rate from Step 1. 3. Total all the purchases and cash advances for the month. 4. Total all the payments and credits for the month. 5. Use the following formula to determine the new balance: $$\text{New bal} = \text{Prev bal} + \text{Fin chg} + \text{Purch \& csh} - \text{Pmts \& crd}$$	Calculate the finance charge and the new balance of an account with an annual percentage rate of 15%. Previous month's balance = $186.11 Purchases = $365.77 Payments = $200 Periodic rate = $\frac{15}{12}$ = 1.25% Finance charge = 186.11 × .0125 = $2.33 New balance $\quad$ = 186.11 + 2.33 + 365.77 − 200.00 $\quad$ = $354.21
Calculating the Finance Charge and New Balance by Using the Average Daily Balance Method **Performance Objective 13-2, Page 415**	1. Starting with the previous month's balance, multiply each by the number of days that balance existed until the next account transaction. 2. At the end of the billing cycle, add all the daily balances × days figures. 3. $\text{Average daily balance} = \dfrac{\text{Sum of the daily balances}}{\text{Number of days of billing cycle}}$ 4. $\text{Finance charge} = \text{Periodic rate} \times \text{Average daily balance}$ 5. $\text{New bal} = \text{Prev bal} + \text{Fin chg} + \text{Purch \& csh} - \text{Pmts \& crd}$	Calculate the finance charge and the new balance of an account with a periodic rate of 1%, a previous balance of $132.26, and the following activity. May 5 Purchase $45.60 May 9 Cash advance 100.00 May 15 Credit 65.70 May 23 Purchase 75.62 May 26 Payment 175.00 $132.26 × 4 days = $529.04 177.86 × 4 days = 711.44 277.86 × 6 days = 1,667.16 212.16 × 8 days = 1,697.28 287.78 × 3 days = 863.34 112.78 × 6 days = 676.68 $\overline{}$31 days $\quad$ $6,144.94 Average daily balance = $\dfrac{6,144.94}{31}$ = $198.22 Finance charge = 1% × 198.22 = $1.98 New balance = 132.26 + 1.98 + 221.22 − 240.70 $\quad$ = $114.76
Calculating the Finance Charge and New Balance of Business and Personal Lines of Credit **Performance Objective 13-3, Page 415**	With business and personal lines of credit, the annual percentage rate is quoted as the current prime rate plus a fixed percent. $\quad$ Once the APR rate is determined, the finance charge and new balance are calculated as before using the average daily balance method. $$\text{New bal} = \text{Previous balance} + \text{Finance charge} + \text{Loans} - \text{Payments}$$	What are the finance charge and new balance of a line of credit with an APR of the current prime rate plus 4.6%? Previous balance = $2,000 Average daily balance = $3,200 Payments = $1,500 Loans = $3,600 Current prime rate = 7% $\quad\quad$ APR = 7% + 4.6% = 11.6% $\quad\quad$ Periodic rate = $\frac{11.6}{12}$ = .97% Finance charge = 3,200 × .0097 = $31.04 New balance = 2,000 + 31.04 + 3,600 − 1,500 $\quad\quad$ = $4,131.04

Section II: Closed-End Credit—Installment Loans

Topic	Important Concepts	Illustrative Examples
Calculating the Total Deferred Payment Price and the Amount of the Finance Charge of an Installment Loan **Performance Objective 13-4, Page 425**	$$\text{Finance charge} = \begin{array}{c}\text{Total amount}\\\text{of installment}\\\text{payments}\end{array} - \begin{array}{c}\text{Amount}\\\text{financed}\end{array}$$ $$\begin{array}{c}\text{Total deferred}\\\text{payment price}\end{array} = \begin{array}{c}\text{Total of}\\\text{installment}\\\text{payments}\end{array} + \begin{array}{c}\text{Down}\\\text{payment}\end{array}$$	Value City Furniture sold a $1,900 bedroom set to Jeremy Jackson. Jeremy put down $400 and financed the balance with an installation loan of 24 monthly payments of $68.75 each. What are the finance charge and total deferred payment price of the bedroom set? Total amount of payments = $68.75 × 24 = $1,650 Finance charge = 1,650 − 1,500 = $150 Total deferred payment price = 1,650 + 400 = $2,050
Calculating the Regular Monthly Payments of an Installment Loan by the Add-on Interest Method **Performance Objective 13-5, Page 427**	1. Calculate the amount financed by subtracting the down payment from the purchase price. 2. Compute the add-on interest finance charge by using $I = PRT$, with the amount financed as the principal. 3. Find the total of the installment payments by adding the interest to the amount financed. 4. Calculate the monthly payment by dividing the total of the installment payments by the number of months of the loan.	Diane Barber financed a new car with an 8% add-on interest loan. The purchase price of the car was $13,540. The bank required a $1,500 down payment and equal monthly payments for 48 months. What are Diane's monthly payments? Amount financed = 13,540 − 1,500 = $12,040 Interest = 12,040 × .08 × 4 = $3,852.80 Total of installment payments = 12,040.00 + 3,852.80 = $15,892.80 Monthly payment = $\dfrac{15,892.80}{48}$ = $331.10
Calculating the Annual Percentage Rate by APR Tables **Performance Objective 13-6, Page 428**	1. Calculate the finance charge per $100 by $$\frac{\text{Finance charge} \times 100}{\text{Amount financed}}$$ 2. From Table 13-1, scan down the Payments column to the number of payments of the loan. 3. Scan to the right in that row to the table factor that most closely corresponds to the finance charge per $100. 4. Look to the top of the column containing the finance charge per $100 to find the APR of the loan.	Steve Moran purchased a home gym for $8,000. He made a $1,500 down payment and financed the remaining $6,500 for 30 months. If Steve's total finance charge is $1,858, what APR is he paying on the loan? Finance charge per $100 = $\dfrac{1,858 \times 100}{6,500}$ = $28.58 From Table 13-1, scan down the Payments column to 30. Then scan right to the table factor closest to 28.58, which is 28.64. The top of that column shows the APR to be 20.5%.
Calculating the Annual Percentage Rate of an Installment Loan by Formula **Performance Objective 13-6, Page 432**	When APR tables are not available, the annual percentage rate can be approximated by the formula $$APR = \frac{72I}{3P(n+1) + I(n-1)}$$ where I = finance charge on the loan P = principal; amount financed n = number of months of the loan	Using the APR formula, verify the 20.5% found in the table in the previous example. $APR = \dfrac{72(1,858)}{3(6,500)(30+1) + 1,858(30-1)}$ $= \dfrac{133,776}{658,382}$ = .2031 = 20.3%
Calculating the Finance Charge and Monthly Payment of an Installment Loan by Using the APR Tables **Performance Objective 13-7, Page 433**	1. From Table 13-1, locate the table factor at the intersection of the APR and number of payments of the loan. This table factor is the finance charge per $100. 2. Total finance charge $$= \frac{\text{Amount financed} \times \text{Table factor}}{100}$$ 3. Monthly payment $$= \frac{\text{Amount financed} + \text{Finance charge}}{\text{Number of months of the loan}}$$	Appliance Mart uses Galaxy Bank to finance customer purchases. This month Galaxy is offering loans up to 36 months with an APR of 13.25%. For qualified buyers, no down payment is required. If Clark Shaw wants to purchase a $2,350 stove using a 36-month loan, what are the finance charge and monthly payment of the loan? From Table 13-1, the table factor for 36 payments, 13.25% = 21.73 Total finance charge = $\dfrac{2,350 \times 21.73}{100}$ = $510.66 Monthly payment = $\dfrac{2,350.00 + 510.66}{36}$ = $79.46

Section II (continued)

Topic	Important Concepts	Illustrative Examples
Calculating the Finance Charge Rebate and the Payoff for Loans Paid Off Early by Using the Sum-of-the-Digits, or Rule of 78, Method **Performance Objective 13-8, Page 434**	1. Calculate the rebate fraction by $$\text{Rebate fraction} = \frac{\text{Sum of the digits of the number of remaining payments}}{\text{Sum of the digits of the total number of payments}}$$ 2. Determine the finance charge rebate by Finance charge rebate $$= \text{Rebate fraction} \times \text{Total finance charge}$$ 3. Find the loan payoff by Loan payoff $$= \left(\begin{array}{c}\text{Payments}\\\text{remaining}\end{array} \times \begin{array}{c}\text{Payments}\\\text{amount}\end{array} - \begin{array}{c}\text{Finance charge}\\\text{rebate}\end{array}\right)$$	Jill Otis financed a $2,000 riding lawn mower with an installment loan for 24 months. The payments are $98 per month, and the total finance charge is $352. After 18 months, Jill decides to pay off the loan. What is the finance charge rebate, and what is the loan payoff? $$\text{Rebate fraction} = \frac{\text{Sum of the digits of 6}}{\text{Sum of the digits of 24}}$$ $$\text{Sum of the digits 6} = \frac{6(7)}{2} = 21$$ $$\text{Sum of the digits 24} = \frac{24(25)}{2} = 300$$ $$\text{Rebate fraction} = \frac{21}{300}$$ $$\text{Finance charge rebate} = \frac{21}{300} \times 352 = \underline{\$24.64}$$ $$\text{Loan payoff} = (6 \times 98) - 24.64$$ $$= 588.00 - 24.64 = \underline{\$563.36}$$

TRY IT: EXERCISE SOLUTIONS FOR CHAPTER 13

1. Periodic rate $= \dfrac{\text{APR}}{12} = \dfrac{15\%}{12} = 1.25\%$

Finance charge = Previous balance × Periodic rate

Finance charge $= 214.90 \times .0125 = \underline{\$2.69}$

New balance = Previous balance + Finance charge + Purchases and cash advance − Payments and credits

New balance $= 214.90 + 2.69 + 238.85 - 49.12 = \underline{\$407.32}$

2. Periodic rate $= \dfrac{\text{APR}}{12} = \dfrac{18\%}{12} = 1.5\%$

Dates	Days	Activity/Amount		Unpaid Balance	Daily Balances
Aug. 1–4	4	Previous balance	$158.69	$158.69	$ 634.76
Aug. 5–10	6	Charge	55.00	213.69	1,282.14
Aug. 11–14	4	Payment	−100.00	113.69	454.76
Aug. 15–16	2	Charge	43.22	156.91	313.82
Aug. 17–19	3	Charge	54.10	211.01	633.03
Aug. 20–25	6	Charge	224.50	435.51	2,613.06
Aug. 26–31	6	Cash advance	75.00	510.51	3,063.06
	31				$8,994.63

Average daily balance $= \dfrac{\text{Sum of the daily balances}}{\text{Days in billing cycle}} = \dfrac{8,994.63}{31} = \$290.15$

Finance charge = Average daily balance × Periodic rate

Finance charge $= \$290.15 \times .015 = \underline{\$4.35}$

New balance = Previous balance + Finance charge + Purchases and cash advance − Payments and credits

New balance $= 158.69 + 4.35 + 451.82 - 100.00 = \underline{\$514.86}$

3. APR = Prime rate + 4.5%

APR $= 8.5 + 4.5 = 13\%$

Periodic rate $= \dfrac{13\%}{12} = 1.08\%$

Dates	Days	Activity/Amount		Unpaid Balance	Daily Balances
Nov. 1–6	6	Previous balance	$12,300	$12,300	$73,800
Nov. 7–20	14	Borrowed	16,700	29,000	406,000
Nov. 21–25	5	Borrowed	8,800	37,800	189,000
Nov. 26–30	5	Payment	−20,000	17,800	89,000
	30				$757,800

Average daily balance $= \dfrac{757,800}{30} = \$25,260$

Finance charge $= 25,260 \times .0108 = \underline{\$272.81}$

New balance $=$ Previous balance $+$ Finance charge $+$ Loan amounts $-$ Payments

New balance $= 12,300.00 + 272.81 + 25,500.00 - 20,000.00 = \underline{\$18,072.81}$

4. **a.** Down payment $=$ Purchase price $\times$ Down payment percent

   Down payment $= 12,500 \times .15 = \$1,875$

   Amount financed $=$ Purchase price $-$ Down payment

   Amount financed $= 12,500 - 1,875 = \$10,625$

   Total amount of installment payments $=$ Monthly payment $\times$ Number of payments

   Total amount of installment payments $= 309.90 \times 48 = \$14,875.20$

   Finance charge $=$ Total amount of installment payments $-$ Amount financed

   Finance charge $= 14,875.20 - 10,625.00 = \underline{\$4,250.20}$

   b. Total deferred payment price $=$ Total amount of installment payments $+$ Down payment

   Total deferred payment price $= 14,875.20 + 1,875.00 = \underline{\$16,750.20}$

5. Amount financed $=$ Purchase price$(100\% -$ Down payment $\%)$

   Amount financed $= 1,500 \times .9 = \$1,350$

   Finance charge $=$ Amount financed $\times$ Rate $\times$ Time

   Finance charge $= 1,350 \times .06 \times 2 = \$162$

   Total of installment payments $=$ Amount financed $+$ Finance charge

   Total of installment payments $= 1,350 + 162 = \$1,512$

   Monthly payments $= \dfrac{\text{Total of installment payments}}{\text{Number of months of loan}}$

   Monthly payments $= \dfrac{1,512}{24} = \underline{\$63}$

6. Amount financed $= 4,500 - 500 = \$4,000$

   Total payments $= 190 \times 24 = 4,560$

   Finance charge $= 4,560 - 4,000 = \$560$

   Finance charge per $100 = \dfrac{\text{Finance charge} \times 100}{\text{Amount financed}} = \dfrac{560 \times 100}{4,000} = \$14$

   From Table 13-1 APR for $\$14 = \underline{13\%}$

7. Total payments $= 140 \times 18 = 2,520$

   Finance charge $= 2,520 - 2,200 = \$320$

   $\text{APR} = \dfrac{72I}{3P(n + 1) + I(n - 1)}$

   $\text{APR} = \dfrac{72(320)}{3(2,200)(18 + 1) + 320(18 - 1)} = \dfrac{23,040}{125,400 + 5,440}$

   $\text{APR} = \dfrac{23,040}{130,840} = .17609 = \underline{17.6\%}$

8. 13.25%, 24-month table factor $= \$14.38$

   Finance charge $= \dfrac{\text{Amount financed} \times \text{Table factor}}{100}$

   Finance charge $= \dfrac{3,550.00 \times 14.38}{100} = \dfrac{51,049}{100} = \underline{\$510.49}$

   Monthly payment $= \dfrac{\text{Amount financed} + \text{Finance charge}}{\text{Number of months of loan}}$

   Monthly payment $= \dfrac{3,550.00 + 510.49}{24} = \dfrac{4,060.49}{24}$

   Monthly payment $= \underline{\$169.19}$

9. 16 months remaining; total of 36 months

   Sum of the digits $16 = \dfrac{n(n + 1)}{2} = \dfrac{16(16 + 1)}{2} = \dfrac{272}{2} = 136$

   Sum of the digits $36 = \dfrac{n(n + 1)}{2} = \dfrac{36(36 + 1)}{2} = \dfrac{1,332}{2} = 666$

CHAPTER

13

$$\text{Rebate fraction} = \frac{136}{666}$$

$$\text{Finance charge rebate} = \text{Rebate fraction} \times \text{Total finance charge} = \frac{136}{666} \times 1,076$$

$$\text{Finance charge rebate} = \underline{\$219.72}$$

$$\text{Loan payoff} = (\text{Payments remaining} \times \text{Payment amount}) - \text{Finance charge rebate}$$

$$\text{Loan payoff} = (16 \times 141) - 219.72 = 2,256.00 - 219.72$$

$$\text{Loan payoff} = \underline{\$2,036.28}$$

CONCEPT REVIEW

1. _____ credit is a loan arrangement in which there is no set number of payments. (13-1)

2. The effective or true annual interest rate being charged for credit is known as the _____ _____ _____ and is abbreviated _____. (13-1)

3. Loans that are backed by the borrower's "promise" to repay are known as _____ loans, whereas loans that are backed by a tangible asset are known as _____ loans. (13-1)

4. Loans made on a continuous basis and billed periodically are known as _____ credit. (13-1)

5. Name the two most common methods used to calculate the finance charge of a revolving credit account. (13-1, 13-2)

6. Write the formula for calculating the average daily balance of a revolving credit account. (13-2)

7. A pre-approved amount of open-end credit is known as a(n) _____ of credit. (13-3)

8. The interest rate of most lines of credit is tied to the movement of the _____ rate. (13-3)

9. A loan made for a specified number of equal monthly payments is known as a(n) _____ loan. (13-4)

10. The portion of the purchase price of an asset paid in a lump sum at the time of purchase is known as the _____ payment. (13-4)

11. A popular method for calculating the interest on an installment loan is known as _____ interest. (13-5)

12. Write the formula for calculating the APR of an installment loan. (13-6)

13. The finance charge _____ is the unearned portion of the finance charge that is returned to a borrower when an installment loan is paid off early. (13-8)

14. The most common method for calculating the finance charge rebate of an installment loan is known as the sum-of-the-_____ method or the Rule of _____. (13-8)

ASSESSMENT TEST

1. Heather MacMaster's revolving credit account has an annual percentage rate of 16%. The previous month's balance was $345.40. During the current month, Heather's purchases and cash advances amounted to $215.39 and her payments and credits totaled $125.00.

   a. What is the monthly periodic rate of the account?

   b. What is the finance charge?

   c. What is Heather's new balance?

2. Daniel Noguera has a Bank of America revolving credit account with an annual percentage rate of 12% calculated on the previous month's balance. In April, the account had the following activity.

Statement of Account — Bank of America

NAME			
DANIEL NOGUERA			

DATE	DESCRIPTION OF TRANSACTIONS	CHARGES
04/01	Previous month's balance	$301.98
04/08	Mason Gym & Health Club	250.00
04/09	Payment	75.00
04/15	Nordstrom	124.80
04/25	Cash Advance	100.00
04/28	Rimrock Hotel	178.90

ACCOUNT NUMBER
9595-55-607

BILLING CYCLE
APRIL 1–30

   a. What is the finance charge?

   b. What is Daniel's new balance?

3. Charlotte Williams has a Visa account. The finance charge is calculated on the previous month's balance, and the annual percentage rate is 20%. Complete the following three-month account activity table for Charlotte.

	Month	Previous Month's Balance	Finance Charge	Purchases and Cash Advances	Payments and Credits	New Balance End of Month
a.	December	$267.00	_____	$547.66	$95.00	_____
b.	January	_____	_____	$213.43	$110.00	_____
c.	February	_____	_____	$89.95	$84.00	_____

4. Calculate the average daily balance for January of a charge account with a previous month's balance of $480.94 and the following activity.

Date	Activity	Amount
January 7	Cash advance	$80.00
January 12	Payment	$125.00
January 18	Purchase	$97.64
January 24	Credit	$72.00
January 29	Purchase	$109.70
January 30	Purchase	$55.78

5. Mel Arrandt has a Bank of America account with a 13% annual percentage rate calculated on the average daily balance. The billing date is the first day of each month, and the billing cycle is the number of days in that month.

Statement of Account — Bank of America

NAME			
MEL ARRANDT			

DATE	DESCRIPTION OF TRANSACTIONS	CHARGES
09/01	Previous month's balance	$686.97
09/04	eBay.com	223.49
09/08	Payment	350.00
09/12	Staples	85.66
09/21	Delta Air Lines (credit)	200.00
09/24	Barnes and Noble Books	347.12
09/28	Milam's Supermarket	64.00

ACCOUNT NUMBER
4495-5607

BILLING CYCLE
SEPTEMBER 1–30

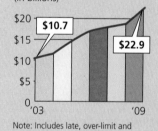

Credit card fees rise
Penalty fee income collected by credit card issuers more than doubled from 2003 to 2009.
Penalty fee income:
(in billions)

$20
$10.7
$15
$22.9
$10
$5
0
'03   '09

Note: Includes late, over-limit and non-sufficient-funds fees
Source: R.K. Hammer Investment Bankers

CHAPTER

13

a. What is the average daily balance for September?

b. What is the finance charge for September?

c. What is Mel's new balance?

6. Alpine Construction, Inc., has a $100,000 line of credit with the Bow Valley Bank. The annual percentage rate is the current prime rate plus $3\frac{1}{4}\%$. The balance on June 1 was $52,900. On June 8, Alpine borrowed $30,600 to pay for a shipment of lumber and roofing materials and on June 18 borrowed another $12,300 for equipment repairs. On June 28, a $35,000 payment was made on the account. The billing cycle for June has 30 days. The current prime rate is $7\frac{3}{4}\%$.

a. What is the finance charge on the account?

b. What is Alpine's new balance?

7. George Bergeman bought an ultralight airplane for $29,200. He made a 15% down payment and financed the balance with payments of $579 per month for 60 months.

a. What is the finance charge on George's loan?

b. What is the total deferred payment price of the airplane?

8. David Sporn bought a saddle from Linville Western Gear with a 9.3% add-on interest installment loan. The purchase price of the saddle was $1,290. The loan required a 15% down payment and equal monthly payments for 24 months.

a. What is the total deferred payment price of the saddle?

b. What are David's monthly payments?

iStockphoto.com/Nancy Nehring

Up, Up, and Away!
Ultralight aircraft provide an exciting and affordable flying solution for many people. They allow you to own an aircraft that doesn't require an expensive hangar or a special pilot license; and, best of all, you can haul it with your car or truck.

Ultralights are defined by the U.S. FAA as a single-seat vehicle of less than 5 U.S. gallons of fuel capacity, empty weight of less than 254 pounds, and a top speed of 64 mph. Restrictions include flying only during daylight hours over unpopulated areas. Quicksilver and Buckeye Corporations are the industry leaders in ultralight and powered parachute-type aircraft.

9. Sound Blaster Recording Studio purchased a new digital recording console for $28,600. A down payment of $5,000 was made and the balance financed with monthly payments of $708 for 48 months.

a. What is the finance charge on the loan?

b. Use Table 13-1 to find what annual percentage rate was charged on the equipment loan.

10. Chris Manning purchased a $7,590 motorcycle with a 36-month installment loan. The monthly payments are $261.44 per month.

   a. Use the APR formula to calculate the annual percentage rate of the loan. Round to the nearest hundredth of a percent.

   b. Use the APR tables to verify your answer from part a.

11. SkyHigh Aircraft Sales uses the Executive National Bank to finance customer aircraft purchases. This month Executive National is offering 60-month installment loans with an APR of 11.25%. A 15% down payment is required. The president of Vista Industries wants to finance the purchase of a company airplane for $250,000.

   a. Use the APR tables to calculate the finance charge.

   b. What are the monthly payments on Vista's aircraft loan?

12. After making 11 payments on a 36-month loan, you pay it off.

   a. What is your rebate fraction?

   b. If the finance charge was $1,300, what is your finance charge rebate?

13. An Auntie Anne's franchise financed a $68,000 pretzel oven with a $6\frac{1}{2}$% add-on interest installment loan for 48 months. The loan required a 20% down payment.

   a. What is the finance charge on the loan?

   b. What are the monthly payments?

   c. What annual percentage rate is being charged on the loan?

   d. If the company decides to pay off the loan after 22 months, what is the loan payoff?

© Jeff Greenberg/Alamy

Auntie Anne's, Inc., Is a leading franchisor of snack outlets, with over 1,050 pretzel stores located in some 45 states and 23 other countries. The stores are found primarily in high-traffic areas such as malls, airports, train stations, and stadiums.

In June 2006, Auntie Anne's sold its billionth pretzel! In 2009, Auntie Anne's sales exceeded $300 million. Total initial investment to purchase a franchise ranges from $197,875 to $439,100.

14. You are a salesperson for Mega Marine Boat Sales. A customer is interested in purchasing the Donzi Classic shown in the accompanying ad and has asked you the following questions.

    a. What is the APR of the loan? (Use the formula.)

    b. What is the total deferred payment price of the boat?

    c. If the loan is paid off after 7 years, what would be the payoff?

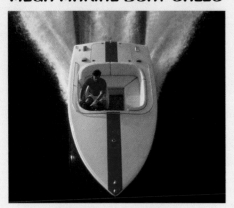

MEGA MARINE BOAT SALES

Donzi Classic
Sale price $29,000
Now $379 per month
$6,000 Down – 120 Months

© Transtock Inc./Alamy

15. Joe Keener found the accompanying ad for a Ford Mustang in his local newspaper. If the sales tax in his state is 7% and the tag and title fees are $165, calculate the following information for Joe.

    a. The total cost of the car, including tax, tag, and title

    b. The amount financed

    c. The finance charge

    d. The total deferred price of the car

    e. The annual percentage rate of the loan rounded to the nearest hundredth

FORD MUSTANG

$6,000 DOWN - PLUS TAX, TAG, TITLE
60-MONTHS WITH APPROVED
CREDIT

INCLUDES: AUTO TRANS., AIR
COND., 2-DOOR, AM/FM WITH CD &
SIRIUS XM RADIO, POWER WINDOWS AND
LOCKS, POWER STEERING

$28,525

$557 PER MO.

© izmostock/Alamy

BUSINESS DECISION: PURCHASE VS. LEASE

16. You are interested in getting a Nissan Rogue. You have decided to look into leasing to see how it compares with buying. In recent years, you have noticed that advertised lease payments are considerably lower than those advertised for financing a purchase. It always seemed as if you would be getting "more car for the money!"

In your research, you have found that a closed-end vehicle lease is an agreement in which you make equal monthly payments based on your estimated usage for a set period of time. Then you turn the vehicle back in to the leasing dealer. No equity, no ownership, no asset at the end! You also have the option of purchasing the vehicle at an agreed-upon price. Leasing terminology is different from that of purchasing, but they are related.

Purchase		**Lease**
Purchase price	=	Capitalized cost
Down payment	=	Capitalized cost reduction
Interest rate	=	Money factor
End-of-lease market price	=	Residual value

Use the advertisement below and the Purchase vs. Lease Worksheet on page 454 to compare the total cost of each option. The residual value of the car is estimated to be $13,650. The lease has no termination fees or charges. If you decide to purchase, your bank requires a down payment of $3,800 and will finance the balance with a 10.25% APR loan for 36 months. The sales tax in your state is 6.5%, and the tag and title charges are $75. The *opportunity cost* is the interest your down payment could have earned if you didn't purchase the vehicle. Currently, your money earns 4.5% in a savings account.

a. What is the total purchase price of the vehicle, including tax, tag, and title?

b. What are the monthly payments on the loan?

c. What is the total cost of purchasing?

d. What is the total cost of leasing?

e. In your own words, explain which of these financing choices is a better deal and why.

Nissan Rogue

$19,995

$249

LEASE PER MO.

36 mos.
No security deposit.
$2,500 at signing.
Plus tax, tag & title
with approved
credit.

© Car Culture/Corbis

f. (Optional) Choose an ad from your local newspaper for a lease offer on a vehicle you would like to have. Gather the necessary information needed to complete a Purchase vs. Lease Worksheet. Use local dealers and banks to find the information you need or do some research on the Internet. Report your findings and conclusions to the class.

CHAPTER
13

Purchase vs. Lease Worksheet

Cost of Purchasing

1. Total purchase price, including tax, tag, and title   _____
2. Down payment   _____
3. Total of loan payments (monthly payment _____ × _____ months)   _____
4. Opportunity cost on down payment (_____% × _____ years × line 2)   _____
5. Less: Expected market value of vehicle at the end of the loan   _____
6. **Total cost of purchasing (lines 2 + 3 + 4 − 5)**   _____

Cost of Leasing

1. Capitalized cost, including tax, tag, and title.   _____
2. Down payment (capitalized cost reduction
   _____ + security deposit _____)   _____
3. Total of lease payments (monthly payments _____ × _____ months)   _____
4. Opportunity cost on down payment (_____% × _____ years × line 2)   _____
5. End-of-lease termination fees and charges (excess mileage or damage)   _____
6. Less: Refund of security deposit   _____
7. **Total cost of leasing (lines 2 + 3 + 4 + 5 − 6)**   _____

Lockhorns © 2010 Wm Hoest Enterprises, Inc. King Features Syndicate

"WHEN DID I BUY THIS CAR? IN ABOUT 60 MONTHS."

COLLABORATIVE LEARNING ACTIVITY

Plastic Choices

1. Have each member of the team contact a bank, credit union, or retail store in your area that offers a credit card. Get a brochure and/or a copy of the credit agreement.

   a. For each card, determine the following:
      • Annual interest rate
      • Method used for computing interest
      • Credit limit
      • Annual fee
      • "Fine-print" features

   b. Based on your research, which cards are the best and worst deals?

2. Go to www.cardtrak.com or www.bankrate.com.

   a. Research and list the best credit card deals being offered around the country.
   b. Compare your local banks' offers with those found on the Internet.

3. Research the Internet for recent changes to the following:

   a. The Credit Card Accountability, Responsibility, and Disclosure Act (the Credit Card Act)
   b. Other financial regulations relating to consumer credit and credit cards
   c. Laws in your state relating to consumer credit and credit cards

AP Photo/Robert F. Bukaty

Check out our great rates – they're among Maine's best!

4.875
4.944 A.P.R.

30-Year Fixed Rate Mortgage

Mortgages

SECTION I 14 MORTGAGES—FIXED-RATE AND ADJUSTABLE-RATE

real estate Land, including any permanent improvements such as homes, apartment buildings, factories, hotels, shopping centers, or any other "real" structures.

mortgage A loan in which real property is used as security for a debt.

Federal Housing Administration (FHA) A government agency within the U.S. Department of Housing and Urban Development (HUD) that sets construction standards and insures residential mortgage loans made by approved lenders.

VA mortgages or **GI Loans** Long-term, low-down-payment home loans made by private lenders to eligible veterans, the payment of which is guaranteed by the Veterans Administration in the event of a default.

conventional loans Real estate loans made by private lenders that are not FHA-insured or VA-guaranteed.

private mortgage insurance (PMI) A special form of insurance primarily on mortgages for single-family homes, allowing the buyer to borrow more by putting down a smaller down payment.

adjustable-rate mortgage (ARM) A mortgage loan in which the interest rate changes periodically, usually in relation to a predetermined economic index.

Real estate is defined as "land, including the air above and the earth below, plus any permanent improvements to the land, such as homes, apartment buildings, factories, hotels, shopping centers, or any other 'real' property." Whether for commercial or residential property, practically all real estate transactions today involve some type of financing. The mortgage loan is the most popular method of financing real estate purchases.

A **mortgage** is any loan in which real property is used as security for a debt. During the term of the loan, the property becomes security, or collateral, for the lender, sufficient to ensure recovery of the amount loaned.

Mortgages today fall into one of three categories: FHA-insured, VA-guaranteed, and conventional. The National Housing Act of 1934 created the **Federal Housing Administration (FHA)** to encourage reluctant lenders to invest their money in the mortgage market, thereby stimulating the depressed construction industry. Today the FHA is a government agency within the Department of Housing and Urban Development (HUD). The FHA insures private mortgage loans made by approved lenders.

In 1944, the Servicemen's Readjustment Act (GI Bill of Rights) was passed to help returning World War II veterans purchase homes. Special mortgages were established known as **Veterans Affairs (VA) mortgages** or **GI Loans**. Under this and subsequent legislation, the government guarantees payment of a mortgage loan made by a private lender to a veteran/buyer should the veteran default on the loan.

VA loans may be used by eligible veterans, surviving spouses, and active service members to buy, construct, or refinance homes, farm residences, or condominiums. Down payments by veterans are not required but are left to the discretion of lenders, whereas FHA and conventional loans require a down payment from all buyers.

Conventional loans are made by private lenders and generally have a higher interest rate than either an FHA or VA loan. Most conventional lenders are restricted to loaning 80% of the appraised value of a property, thus requiring a 20% down payment. If the borrower agrees to pay the premium for **private mortgage insurance (PMI)**, the conventional lender can lend up to 95% of the appraised value of the property.

Historically, high interest rates in the early 1980s caused mortgage payments to skyrocket beyond the financial reach of the average home buyer. To revitalize the slumping mortgage industry, the **adjustable-rate mortgage (ARM)** was created. These are mortgage loans under which the interest rate is periodically adjusted to more closely

Mortgage loans are the most common form of loan made for real estate property purchases.

Photo by Robert Brechner

coincide with changing economic conditions. ARMs are very attractive, particularly to first-time buyers, because a low teaser rate may be offered for the first few years and then adjusted upward to a higher rate later in the loan. Today the adjustable-rate mortgage has become the most widely accepted option to the traditional 15- and 30-year fixed-rate mortgages.

Extra charges known as **mortgage discount points** are frequently added to the cost of a loan as a rate adjustment factor. This allows lenders to increase their yield without showing an increase in the mortgage interest rate. Each discount point is equal to 1% of the amount of the loan.

By their nature, mortgage loans involve large amounts of money and long periods of time. Consequently, the monthly payments and the amount of interest paid over the years can be considerable. Exhibit 14-1 illustrates the 30-year mortgage rates in the United States from 1974 to 2010 and the monthly payment on a $100,000 mortgage at various interest rate levels.

In reality, the higher interest mortgages would have been refinanced as rates declined, but consider the "housing affordability" factor. In 1982, payments on a $100,000 mortgage were $1,548 per month, compared with $457 in 2010!

In this section, you learn to calculate the monthly payments of a mortgage and prepare a partial amortization schedule of that loan. You also calculate the amount of property tax and insurance required as part of each monthly payment. In addition, you learn about the **closing**, the all-important final step in a real estate transaction, and the calculation of the closing costs. Finally, you learn about the important components of an adjustable-rate mortgage: the index, the lender's margin, the interest rate, and the cost caps.

mortgage discount points Extra charges frequently added to the cost of a mortgage, allowing lenders to increase their yield without showing an increase in the mortgage interest rate.

closing A meeting at which the buyer and seller of real estate conclude all matters pertaining to the transaction. At the closing, the funds are transferred to the seller and the ownership or title is transferred to the buyer.

DOLLARS AND SENSE

As a result of declining mortgage rates in recent years, a record 68.8% of families own their own homes today. That amounts to nearly 76 million households.

Purchasing and financing a home is one of the most important financial decisions a person will ever make. Substantial research should be done and much care taken in choosing the correct time to buy, the right property to buy, and the best financial offer to accept. (See Exhibit 14-2, "Mortgage Shopping Worksheet," pages 463–464.)

CALCULATING THE MONTHLY PAYMENT AND TOTAL INTEREST PAID ON A FIXED-RATE MORTGAGE

14-1

In Chapter 12, we learned that amortization is the process of paying off a financial obligation in a series of equal, regular payments over a period of time. We calculated the amount of an amortization payment by using the present value of an annuity table or the optional amortization formula.

Because mortgages run for relatively long periods of time, we can also use a special present-value table in which the periods are listed in years. The table factors represent the monthly payment required per $1,000 of debt to amortize a mortgage. The monthly payment includes mortgage interest and an amount to reduce the principal. (See Table 14-1.)

EXHIBIT 14-1 Historical Mortgage Rates and Monthly Payments

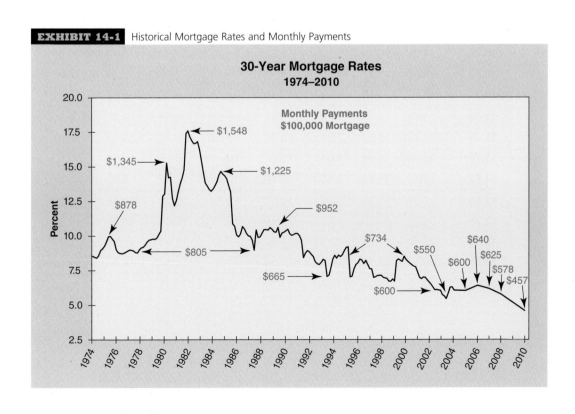

30-Year Mortgage Rates
1974–2010

Monthly Payments
$100,000 Mortgage

TABLE 14-1
Monthly Payments to Amortize Principal and Interest per $1,000 Financed

Monthly Payments
(Necessary to amortize a loan of $1,000)

Interest Rate (%)	5 Years	10 Years	15 Years	20 Years	25 Years	30 Years	35 Years	40 Years
3.50	$18.19	$9.89	$7.15	$5.80	$5.01	$4.49	$4.13	$3.87
3.75	18.30	10.01	7.27	5.93	5.14	4.63	4.28	4.03
4.00	18.42	10.12	7.40	6.06	5.28	4.77	4.43	4.18
4.25	18.53	10.24	7.52	6.19	5.42	4.92	4.58	4.34
4.50	18.64	10.36	7.65	6.33	5.56	5.07	4.73	4.50
4.75	18.76	10.48	7.78	6.46	5.70	5.22	4.89	4.66
5.00	18.88	10.61	7.91	6.60	5.85	5.37	5.05	4.83
5.25	18.99	10.73	8.04	6.74	6.00	5.53	5.21	4.99
5.50	19.11	10.86	8.18	6.88	6.15	5.68	5.38	5.16
5.75	19.22	10.98	8.31	7.03	6.30	5.84	5.54	5.33
6.00	19.34	11.11	8.44	7.17	6.45	6.00	5.71	5.51
6.25	19.45	11.23	8.58	7.31	6.60	6.16	5.88	5.68
6.50	19.57	11.36	8.72	7.46	6.76	6.33	6.05	5.86
6.75	19.69	11.49	8.85	7.61	6.91	6.49	6.22	6.04
7.00	19.81	11.62	8.99	7.76	7.07	6.66	6.39	6.22
7.25	19.92	11.75	9.13	7.91	7.23	6.83	6.57	6.40
7.50	20.04	11.88	9.28	8.06	7.39	7.00	6.75	6.59
7.75	20.16	12.01	9.42	8.21	7.56	7.17	6.93	6.77
8.00	20.28	12.14	9.56	8.37	7.72	7.34	7.11	6.96
8.25	20.40	12.27	9.71	8.53	7.89	7.52	7.29	7.15
8.50	20.52	12.40	9.85	8.68	8.06	7.69	7.47	7.34
8.75	20.64	12.54	10.00	8.84	8.23	7.87	7.66	7.53
9.00	20.76	12.67	10.15	9.00	8.40	8.05	7.84	7.72
9.25	20.88	12.81	10.30	9.16	8.57	8.23	8.03	7.91
9.50	21.01	12.94	10.45	9.33	8.74	8.41	8.22	8.11
9.75	21.13	13.08	10.60	9.49	8.92	8.60	8.41	8.30
10.00	21.25	13.22	10.75	9.66	9.09	8.78	8.60	8.50
10.25	21.38	13.36	10.90	9.82	9.27	8.97	8.79	8.69
10.50	21.50	13.50	11.06	9.99	9.45	9.15	8.99	8.89
10.75	21.62	13.64	11.21	10.16	9.63	9.34	9.18	9.09
11.00	21.75	13.78	11.37	10.33	9.81	9.53	9.37	9.29
11.25	21.87	13.92	11.53	10.50	9.99	9.72	9.57	9.49
11.50	22.00	14.06	11.69	10.67	10.17	9.91	9.77	9.69
11.75	22.12	14.21	11.85	10.84	10.35	10.10	9.96	9.89
12.00	22.25	14.35	12.01	11.02	10.54	10.29	10.16	10.09
12.25	22.38	14.50	12.17	11.19	10.72	10.48	10.36	10.29
12.50	22.50	14.64	12.33	11.37	10.91	10.68	10.56	10.49
12.75	22.63	14.79	12.49	11.54	11.10	10.87	10.76	10.70
13.00	22.76	14.94	12.66	11.72	11.28	11.07	10.96	10.90

LEARNINGTIP

Remember that the table values represent monthly payments "per $1,000" financed. When calculating the amount of the monthly payment, you must first determine the number of $1,000s being financed, then multiply that figure by the table factor.

STEPS TO FIND THE MONTHLY MORTGAGE PAYMENT BY USING AN AMORTIZATION TABLE AND TO FIND TOTAL INTEREST

STEP 1. Find the number of $1,000s financed.

$$\text{Number of \$1,000s financed} = \frac{\text{Amount financed}}{1,000}$$

STEP 2. Using Table 14-1, locate the table factor, monthly payment per $1,000 financed, at the intersection of the number-of-years column and the interest-rate row.

STEP 3. Calculate the monthly payment.

$$\text{Monthly payment} = \text{Number of \$1,000s financed} \times \text{Table factor}$$

STEP 4. Find the total interest of the loan.

$$\text{Total interest} = (\text{Monthly payment} \times \text{Number of payments}) - \text{Amount financed}$$

EXAMPLE1 CALCULATING MONTHLY PAYMENT AND TOTAL INTEREST

What is the monthly payment and total interest on a $50,000 mortgage at 8% for 30 years?

SOLUTIONSTRATEGY

Step 1. Number of $1,000s financed $= \dfrac{\text{Amount financed}}{1,000} = \dfrac{50,000}{1,000} = 50$

Step 2. Table factor for 8%, 30 years is 7.34.

Step 3. Monthly payment = Number of $1,000s financed × Table factor

Monthly payment = 50 × 7.34

Monthly payment = $367

Step 4. Total interest = (Monthly payment × Number of payments) − Amount financed

Total interest = (367 × 360) − 50,000

Total interest = 132,120 − 50,000

Total interest = $82,120

TRYITEXERCISE1

What is the monthly payment and total interest on an $85,500 mortgage at 7% for 25 years?

CHECK YOUR ANSWERS WITH THE SOLUTIONS ON PAGE 479.

PREPARING A PARTIAL AMORTIZATION SCHEDULE OF A MORTGAGE

14-2

Mortgages used to purchase residential property generally require regular, equal payments. A portion of the payment is used to pay interest on the loan; the balance of the payment is used to reduce the principal. This type of mortgage is called a **level-payment plan** because the amount of the payment remains the same for the duration of the loan. The amount of the payment that is interest gradually decreases, while the amount that reduces the debt gradually increases.

level-payment plan Mortgages with regular, equal payments over a specified period of time.

amortization schedule A chart that shows the month-by-month breakdown of each mortage payment into interest and principal and the outstanding balance of the loan.

An **amortization schedule** is a chart that shows the status of the mortgage loan after each payment. The schedule illustrates month by month how much of the mortgage payment is interest and how much is left to reduce to principal. The schedule also shows the outstanding balance of the loan after each payment.

In reality, amortization schedules are long because they show the loan status for each month. A 30-year mortgage, for example, would require a schedule with 360 lines (12 months $\times$ 30 years = 360 payments).

STEPS TO CREATE AN AMORTIZATION SCHEDULE FOR A LOAN

STEP 1. Use Table 14-1 to calculate the amount of the monthly payment.

STEP 2. Calculate the amount of interest for the current month using $I = PRT$, where P is the current outstanding balance of the loan, R is the annual interest rate, and T is $\frac{1}{12}$.

STEP 3. Find the portion of the payment used to reduce principal.

Portion of payment reducing principal = Monthly payment − Interest

STEP 4. Calculate the outstanding balance of the mortgage loan.

Outstanding balance = Previous balance − Portion of payment reducing principal

STEP 5. Repeat Steps 2, 3, and 4 for each succeeding month and enter the values on a schedule with columns labeled as follows.

Payment Number	Monthly Payment	Monthly Interest	Portion Used to Reduce Principal	Loan Balance

EXAMPLE2 PREPARING A PARTIAL AMORTIZATION SCHEDULE

Prepare an amortization schedule for the first three months of the $50,000 mortgage at 8% for 30 years from Example 1. Remember, you have already calculated the monthly payment to be $367.

SOLUTIONSTRATEGY

Step 1. $367 (from Example 1, page 459)

Step 2. Month 1:

Interest = Principal $\times$ Rate $\times$ Time

Interest = $50,000 \times .08 \times \frac{1}{12}$

Interest = $333.33

Step 3. Portion of payment reducing principal = Monthly payment − Interest

Portion of payment reducing principal = $367.00 − $333.33

Portion of payment reducing principal = $33.67

Step 4. Outstanding balance = Previous balance − Portion of payment reducing principal

Outstanding balance = 50,000.00 − 33.67

Outstanding balance after one payment = $49,966.33

Step 5. Repeat Steps 2, 3, and 4, for two more payments and enter the values on the schedule.

Month 2:

Interest = $49,966.33 \times .08 \times \frac{1}{12} = $333.11

(*Note:* Although very slightly, interest decreased.)

Portion reducing principal = 367.00 − 333.11 = $33.89

Outstanding balance after two payments = 49,966.33 − 33.89 = $49,932.44

Month 3:

Interest = $49,932.44 \times .08 \times \frac{1}{12} = \$332.88$

Portion reducing principal = 367.00 − 332.88 = $34.12

Outstanding balance after three payments = 49,932.44 − 34.12 = $49,898.32

Amortization Schedule
$50,000 Loan, 8%, 30 years

Payment Number	Monthly Payment	Monthly Interest	Portion Used to Reduce Principal	Loan Balance
0				$50,000.00
1	$367	$333.33	$33.67	$49,966.33
2	$367	$333.11	$33.89	$49,932.44
3	$367	$332.88	$34.12	$49,898.32

● TRYITEXERCISE2

Prepare an amortization schedule of the first four payments of a $75,000 mortgage at 9% for 15 years. Use Table 14-1 to calculate the amount of the monthly payment.

CHECK YOUR ANSWERS WITH THE SOLUTIONS ON PAGES 479–480.

CALCULATING THE MONTHLY PITI OF A MORTGAGE LOAN

14-3

In reality, mortgage payments include four parts: principal, interest, taxes, and insurance—thus the abbreviation **PITI**. VA, FHA, and most conventional loans require borrowers to pay $\frac{1}{12}$ of the estimated annual property taxes and hazard insurance with each month's mortgage payment. Each month the taxes and insurance portions of the payment are placed in a type of savings account for safekeeping known as an **escrow account**. Each year when the property taxes and hazard insurance premiums are due, the lender disburses those payments from the borrower's escrow account. During the next 12 months, the account again builds up to pay the next year's taxes and insurance.

PITI An abbreviation for the total amount of a mortgage payment; includes principal, interest, property taxes, and hazard insurance.

escrow account Bank account used by mortgage lenders for the safekeeping of the funds accumulating to pay next year's property taxes and hazard insurance.

STEPS TO CALCULATE THE PITI OF A MORTGAGE

STEP 1. Calculate the principal and interest portion, PI, of the payment as before, using the amortization table, Table 14-1.

STEP 2. Calculate the monthly tax and insurance portion, TI.

$$\text{Monthly TI} = \frac{\text{Estimated property tax + Hazard insurance}}{12}$$

STEP 3. Calculate the total monthly PITI.

$$\text{Monthly PITI} = \text{Monthly PI} + \text{Monthly TI}$$

EXAMPLE 3 CALCULATING THE MONTHLY PITI OF A MORTGAGE

Lorie Kojian purchased a home with a mortgage of $87,500 at 7.5% for 30 years. The property taxes are $2,350 per year, and the hazard insurance premium is $567.48. What is the monthly PITI payment of Lorie's loan?

SOLUTION STRATEGY

Step 1. From the amortization table, Table 14-1, the factor for 7.5%, 30 years is 7.00. When we divide the amount of Lorie's loan by 1,000, we get 87.5 as the number of 1,000s financed. The principal and interest portion, PI, is therefore $87.5 \times 7.00 = \$612.50$.

Step 2. $\text{Monthly TI} = \dfrac{\text{Estimated property tax} + \text{Hazard insurance}}{12}$

$\text{Monthly TI} = \dfrac{2,350.00 + 567.48}{12} = \dfrac{2,917.48}{12} = \$243.12$

Step 3. Monthly PITI = PI + TI

Monthly PITI = 612.50 + 243.12

Monthly PITI = $\underline{\$855.62}$

TRY IT EXERCISE 3

Michael Veteramo purchased a home with a mortgage of $125,600 at 9.25% for 20 years. The property taxes are $3,250 per year, and the hazard insurance premium is $765. What is the monthly PITI payment of Michael's loan?

CHECK YOUR ANSWER WITH THE SOLUTION ON PAGE 480.

14-4 UNDERSTANDING CLOSING COSTS AND CALCULATING THE AMOUNT DUE AT CLOSING

title or **deed** The official document representing the right of ownership of real property.

closing costs Expenses incurred in conjunction with the sale of real estate, including loan origination fees, credit reports, appraisal fees, title search, title insurance, inspections, attorney's fees, recording fees, and broker's commission.

settlement or **closing statement** A document that provides a detailed accounting of payments, credits, and closing costs of a real estate transaction.

The term *closing* or *settlement* is used to describe the final step in a real estate transaction. This is a meeting at which time documents are signed; the buyer pays the agreed-upon purchase price; and the seller delivers the **title**, or right of ownership, to the buyer. The official document conveying ownership is known as the **deed**.

Closing costs are the expenses incurred in conjunction with the sale of real estate. In the typical real estate transaction, both the buyer and the seller are responsible for a number of costs that are paid for at the time of closing. The party obligated for paying a particular closing cost is often determined by local custom or by negotiation. Some closing costs are expressed as dollar amounts, whereas others are a percent of the amount financed or amount of the purchase price.

At closing, the buyer is responsible for the purchase price (mortgage + down payment) plus closing costs. The amount received by the seller after all expenses have been paid is known as the proceeds. The **settlement statement** or **closing statement** is a document, usually prepared by an attorney, that provides a detailed breakdown of the real estate transaction. This document itemizes closing costs and indicates how they are allocated between the buyer and the seller.

Exhibit 14-2, "Mortgage Shopping Worksheet," can be used to compare mortgage offers from various lenders. It provides a comprehensive checklist of important loan information, typical fees, closing and settlement costs, and other questions and considerations people should be aware of when shopping for a mortgage loan.

EXHIBIT 14-2 Mortgage Shopping Worksheet

Mortgage Shopping Worksheet

	Lender 1	Lender 2
Name of Lender		
Name of Contact		
Date of Contact		
Mortgage Amount		

Basic Information on the Loans

	Lender 1	Lender 2
Type of mortgage: fixed rate, adjustable rate, conventional, FHA, other? If adjustable, see page 464		
Minimum down payment required		
Loan term (length of loan)		
Contract interest rate		
Annual percentage rate (APR)		
Points (may be called loan discount points)		
Monthly private mortgage insurance (PMI) premiums		
How long must you keep PMI?		
Estimated monthly escrow for taxes and hazard insurance		
Estimated monthly payment (principal, interest, taxes, insurance, PMI)		

Fees

Different institutions may have different names for some fees and may charge different fees. We have listed some typical fees you may see on loan documents.

	Lender 1	Lender 2
Appraisal fee or loan processing fee		
Origination fee or underwriting fee		
Lender fee or funding fee		
Appraisal fee		
Attorney's fees		
Document preparation and recording fees		
Broker's fees (may be quoted as points, origination fees, or interest rate add-on)		
Credit report fee		
Other fees		

Name of Lender		

Other Costs at Closing/Settlement

	Lender 1	Lender 2
Title search/title insurance		
For lender		
For you		
Estimated prepaid amounts for interest, taxes, hazard insurance, payments to escrow		
State and local taxes, stamp taxes, transfer taxes		
Flood determination		
Prepaid private mortgage insurance (PMI)		
Surveys and home inspections		

Total Fees and Other Closing/Settlement Cost Estimates		

Other Questions and Considerations about the Loan

	Lender 1	Lender 2
Are any of the fees or costs waivable?		

Prepayment penalties

	Lender 1	Lender 2
Is there a prepayment penalty?		
If so, how much is it?		
How long does the penalty period last? (for example, three years? five years?)		
Are extra principal payments allowed?		

continued

EXHIBIT 14-2 Mortgage Shopping Worksheet (continued)

Mortgage Shopping Worksheet

	Lender 1	Lender 2
Lock-ins		
Is the lock-in agreement in writing?	_____	_____
Is there a fee to lock in?	_____	_____
When does the lock-in occur—at application, approval, or another time?	_____	_____
How long will the lock-in last?	_____	_____
If the rate drops before closing, can you lock in at a lower rate?	_____	_____
If the loan is an adjustable rate mortgage:		
What is the initial rate?	_____	_____
What is the maximum the rate could be next year?	_____	_____
What are the rate and payment caps for each year and over the life of the loan?	_____	_____
What is the frequency of rate change and of any changes to the monthly payment?	_____	_____
What index will the lender use?	_____	_____
What margin will the lender add to the index?	_____	_____
Credit life insurance		
Does the monthly amount quoted to you include a charge for credit life insurance?	_____	_____
If so, does the lender require credit life insurance as a condition of the loan?	_____	_____
How much does the credit life insurance cost?	_____	_____
How much lower would your monthly payment be without the credit life insurance?	_____	_____
If the lender does not require credit life insurance and you still want to buy it, what rates can you get from other insurance providers?	_____	_____

DOLLARS AND SENSE

The amount of interest paid and the length of a mortgage can be dramatically reduced by making **biweekly payments** (every two weeks) instead of monthly. By choosing this mortgage payment option, you are taking advantage of the all-important "time value of money" concept.

Here's an example. A 30-year, 7% mortgage for $100,000 has monthly payments of $666. The total interest you will pay on the loan is $139,509. If, instead, you make biweekly payments of $333, you would pay off the loan in 23 years and the total interest would be $103,959. The biweekly option saves you $35,550 in interest and seven years of payments!

To see how this option can be applied to your mortgage, go to www.bankrate.com and type *biweekly mortgage calculator* in the search box.

EXAMPLE 4 CALCULATING MORTGAGE CLOSING COSTS

Barry and Donna Rae Schwartz are purchasing a $180,000 home. The down payment is 25%, and the balance will be financed with a 25-year fixed-rate mortgage at 6.5% and 2 discount points (each point is 1% of the amount financed). When Barry and Donna Rae signed the sales contract, they put down a deposit of $15,000, which will be credited to their down payment at the time of the closing. In addition, they must pay the following expenses: credit report, $80; appraisal fee, $150; title insurance premium, $\frac{1}{2}$% of amount financed; title search, $200; and attorney's fees, $450.

a. Calculate the amount due from Barry and Donna Rae at the closing.

b. If the sellers are responsible for the broker's commission, which is 6% of the purchase price, $900 in other closing costs, and the existing mortgage with a balance of $50,000, what proceeds will they receive on the sale of the property?

SOLUTION STRATEGY

a. Down payment = 180,000 × 25% = $45,000

Amount financed = 180,000 − 45,000 = $135,000

Closing Costs, Buyer

Discount points (135,000 × 2%)	$ 2,700
Down payment (45,000 − 15,000 deposit)	30,000
Credit report	80
Appraisal fee	150
Title insurance (135,000 × $\frac{1}{2}$%)	675
Title search	200
Attorney's fees	450
Due at closing	$34,255

b.

Proceeds, Seller

Sale price		$180,000
Less: Broker's commission:		
180,000 × 6%	$10,800	
Closing costs	900	
Mortgage payoff	50,000	
		− 61,700
Proceeds to seller		$118,300

● TRYITEXERCISE4

Jonathan Monahan is purchasing a townhouse for $120,000. The down payment is 20%, and the balance will be financed with a 15-year fixed-rate mortgage at 9% and 3 discount points (each point is 1% of the amount financed). When Jonathan signed the sales contract, he put down a deposit of $10,000, which will be credited to his down payment at the time of the closing. In addition, he must pay the following expenses: loan application fee, $100; property transfer fee, $190; title insurance premium, $\frac{3}{4}$% of amount financed; hazard insurance premium, $420; prepaid taxes, $310; and attorney's fees, $500.

a. Calculate the amount due from Jonathan at the closing.

b. If the seller is responsible for the broker's commission, which is $5\frac{1}{2}$% of the purchase price, $670 in other closing costs, and the existing mortgage balance of $65,000, what proceeds will the seller receive on the sale of the property?

CHECK YOUR ANSWERS WITH THE SOLUTIONS ON PAGE 480.

CALCULATING THE INTEREST RATE OF AN ADJUSTABLE-RATE MORTGAGE (ARM)

With a fixed-rate mortgage, the interest rate stays the same during the life of the loan. With an adjustable-rate mortgage (ARM), the interest rate changes periodically, usually in relation to an index, and payments may go up or down accordingly. In recent years, the ARM has become the most widely accepted alternative to the traditional 30-year fixed-rate mortgage.

The primary components of an ARM are the index, lender's margin, calculated interest rate, initial interest rate, and cost caps. With most ARMs, the interest rate and monthly payment change every year, every three years, or every five years. The period between one rate change and the next is known as the **adjustment period**. A loan with an adjustment period of one year, for example, is called a one-year ARM.

Most lenders tie ARM interest rate changes to changes in an **index rate**. These indexes usually go up and down with the general movement of interest rates in the nation's economy. When the index goes up, so does the mortgage rate, resulting in higher monthly payments. When the index goes down, the mortgage rate may or may not go down.

adjustment period The amount of time between one rate change and the next on an adjustable-rate mortgage; generally one, two, or three years.

index rate The economic index to which the interest rate on an adjustable-rate mortgage is tied.

lender's margin or **spread** The percentage points added to an index rate to get the interest rate of an adjustable-rate mortgage.

calculated or **initial ARM interest rate** The interest rate of an adjustable-rate mortgage to which all future adjustments and caps apply.

teaser rate A discounted interest rate for the first adjustment period of an adjustable-rate mortgage that is below the current market rate of interest.

interest-rate caps Limits on the amount the interest rate can increase on an ARM.

periodic rate caps Limits on the amount the interest rate of an ARM can increase per adjustment period.

overall rate caps Limits on the amount the interest rate of an ARM can increase over the life of the loan.

To calculate the interest rate on an ARM, lenders add a few points called the **lender's margin** or **spread** to the index rate. The amount of the margin can differ among lenders and can make a significant difference in the amount of interest paid over the life of a loan.

> **Calculated ARM interest rate = Index rate + Lender's margin**

The **calculated** or **initial ARM interest rate** is usually the rate to which all future adjustments and caps apply, although this rate may be discounted by the lender during the first payment period to attract and qualify more potential borrowers. This low initial interest rate, sometimes known as a **teaser rate**, is one of the main appeals of the ARM; however, without some protection from rapidly rising interest rates, borrowers might be put in a position of not being able to afford the rising mortgage payments. To prevent this situation, standards have been established requiring limits or caps on increases.

Interest-rate caps place a limit on the amount the interest rate can increase. These may come in the form of **periodic rate caps**, which limit the increase from one adjustment period to the next, and **overall rate caps**, which limit the increase over the life of the mortgage. The following formulas can be used to find the maximum interest rates of an ARM:

> **Maximum rate per adjustment period = Previous rate + Periodic rate cap**
>
> **Maximum overall ARM rate = Initial rate + Overall rate cap**

EXAMPLE5 CALCULATING ARM RATES

Florence Powers bought a home with an adjustable-rate mortgage. The lender's margin on the loan is 2.5%, and the overall rate cap is 6% over the life of the loan.

a. If the current index rate is 4.9%, what is the calculated interest rate of the ARM?

b. What is the maximum overall rate of the loan?

SOLUTIONSTRATEGY

a. Because the loan interest rate is tied to an index, we use the formula

        Calculated ARM interest rate = Index rate + Lender's margin

        Calculated ARM interest rate = 4.9% + 2.5%

        Calculated ARM interest rate = <u>7.4%</u>

b.   Maximum overall rate = Calculated rate + Overall rate cap

        Maximum overall rate = 7.4% + 6%

        Maximum overall rate = <u>13.4%</u>

TRYITEXERCISE5

Kate Fitzgerald bought a home with an adjustable-rate mortgage. The lender's margin on the loan is 3.4%, and the overall rate cap is 7% over the life of the loan. The current index rate is 3.2%.

a. What is the initial interest rate of the ARM?

b. What is the maximum overall rate of the loan?

CHECK YOUR ANSWERS WITH THE SOLUTIONS ON PAGE 480.

REVIEW EXERCISES

Using Table 14-1 as needed, calculate the required information for the following mortgages.

	Amount Financed	Interest Rate	Term of Loan (years)	Number of $1,000s Financed	Table Factor	Monthly Payment	Total Interest
1.	$80,000	9.00%	20	80	9.00	$720.00	$92,800.00
2.	$72,500	6.00%	30				
3.	$130,900	8.50%	25				
4.	$154,300	9.25%	15				
5.	$96,800	7.75%	30				
6.	$422,100	5.50%	20				
7.	$184,300	6.25%	15				

8. Marc Bove purchased a home with a $78,500 mortgage at 9% for 15 years. Calculate the monthly payment and prepare an amortization schedule for the first four months of Marc's loan.

Payment Number	Monthly Payment	Monthly Interest	Portion Used to Reduce Principal	Loan Balance
0				$78,500.00
1				
2				
3				
4				

As one of the loan officers for Grove Gate Bank, calculate the monthly principal and interest, PI, using Table 14-1 and the monthly PITI for the following mortgages.

	Amount Financed	Interest Rate	Term of Loan (years)	Monthly PI	Annual Property Tax	Annual Insurance	Monthly PITI
9.	$76,400	8.00%	20	$639.47	$1,317	$866	$821.39
10.	$128,800	4.75%	15		$2,440	$1,215	
11.	$174,200	7.25%	30		$3,505	$1,432	
12.	$250,000	9.50%	25		$6,553	$2,196	
13.	$164,500	6.75%	30		$3,125	$1,569	
14.	$98,200	7.50%	10		$1,688	$935	

15. Ben and Mal Scott plan to buy a home for $272,900. They will make a 10% down payment and qualify for a 25-year, 7% mortgage loan.

   a. What is the amount of their monthly payment?

   b. How much interest will they pay over the life of the loan?

16. Michael Sanchez purchased a condominium for $88,000. He made a 20% down payment and financed the balance with a 30-year, 9% fixed-rate mortgage.

    a. What is the amount of the monthly principal and interest portion, PI, of Michael's loan?

    b. Construct an amortization schedule for the first four months of Michael's mortgage.

Payment Number	Monthly Payment	Monthly Interest	Portion Used to Reduce Principal	Loan Balance
0				_____
1	_____	_____	_____	_____
2	_____	_____	_____	_____
3	_____	_____	_____	_____
4	_____	_____	_____	_____

    c. If the annual property taxes are $1,650 and the hazard insurance premium is $780 per year, what is the total monthly PITI of Michael's loan?

17. Luis Schambach is shopping for a 15-year mortgage for $150,000. Currently, the Fortune Bank is offering an 8.5% mortgage with 4 discount points and the Northern Trust Bank is offering an 8.75% mortgage with no points. Luis is unsure which mortgage is a better deal and has asked you to help him decide. (Remember, each discount point is equal to 1% of the amount financed.)

    a. What is the total interest paid on each loan?

    b. Taking into account the closing points, which bank is offering a better deal and by how much?

18. Phil Pittman is interested in a fixed-rate mortgage for $100,000. He is undecided whether to choose a 15- or 30-year mortgage. The current mortgage rate is 5.5% for the 15-year mortgage and 6.5% for the 30-year mortgage.

    a. What are the monthly principal and interest payments for each loan?

    b. What is the total amount of interest paid on each loan?

c. Overall, how much more interest is paid by choosing the 30-year mortgage?

19. Larry and Cindy Lynden purchased a townhome in Alison Estates with an adjustable-rate mortgage. The lender's margin on the loan is 4.1%, and the overall rate cap is 5% over the life of the loan. The current index rate is the prime rate, 3.25%.

a. What is the calculated interest rate of the ARM?

Calculated ARM interest rate = Index rate + Lender's margin

Calculated ARM interest rate = 3.25 + 4.1 = 7.35%

b. What is the maximum overall rate of the loan?

Maximum overall ARM rate = Initial rate + Overall rate cap

Maximum overall ARM rate = 7.35 + 5.0 = 12.35%

20. Heather Gott bought a home with an adjustable-rate mortgage. The lender's margin on the loan is 3.5%, and the overall rate cap is 8% over the life of the loan.

a. If the current index rate is 3.75%, what is the calculated interest rate of the ARM?

b. What is the maximum overall ARM rate of Heather's loan?

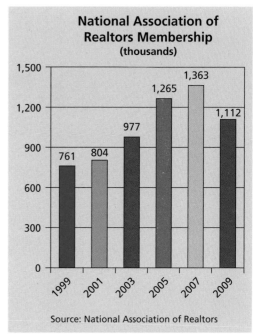

21. Joe and Gloria Moutran are purchasing a house in Winter Springs financed with an adjustable-rate mortgage. The lender's margin on the loan is 2.75%, and the overall rate cap is 6.2% over the life of the loan. The current index rate is 5.8%.

a. What is the calculated interest rate of the ARM?

b. What is the maximum overall ARM rate of the loan?

22. You are a real estate broker for Aurora Realty. One of your clients, Erica Heston, has agreed to purchase one of the homes your office has listed for sale for a negotiated price of $235,000. The down payment is 20%, and the balance will be financed with a 15-year fixed-rate mortgage at 8.75% and $3\frac{1}{2}$ discount points. The annual property tax is $5,475, and the hazard insurance premium is $2,110. When Erica signed the original contract, she put down a deposit of $5,000, which will be credited to her down payment. In addition, at the time of closing, Dawn must pay the following expenses:

Appraisal fee	$215
Credit report	$65
Roof inspection	$50
Mortgage insurance premium	$\frac{1}{2}$% of amount financed
Title search	$125
Attorney's fees	$680
Escrow fee	$210
Prepaid interest	$630

As Erica's real estate broker, she has asked you the following questions:

a. What is the total monthly PITI of the mortgage loan?

b. What is the total amount of interest that will be paid on the loan?

c. How much is due from Erica at the time of the closing?

d. If your real estate office is entitled to a commission from the seller of $6\frac{1}{2}\%$ of the price of the home, how much commission is made on the sale?

BUSINESS DECISION: BUYING DOWN THE MORTGAGE

23. The buyer of a piece of real estate is often given the option of buying down the loan. This option gives the buyer a choice of loan terms in which various combinations of interest rates and discount points are offered. The choice of how many points and what rate is optimal is often a matter of how long the buyer intends to keep the property.

Darrell Frye is planning to buy an office building at a cost of $988,000. He must pay 10% down and has a choice of financing terms. He can select from a 7% 30-year loan and pay 4 discount points, a 7.25% 30-year loan and pay 3 discount points, or a 7.5% 30-year loan and pay 2 discount points. Darrell expects to hold the building for four years and then sell it. Except for the three rate and discount point combinations, all other costs of purchasing and selling are fixed and identical.

a. What is the amount being financed?

b. If Darrell chooses the 4-point 7% loan, what will be his total outlay in points and payments after 48 months?

c. If Darrell chooses the 3-point 7.25% loan, what will be his total outlay in points and payments after 48 months?

d. If Darrell chooses the 2-point 7.5% loan, what will be his total outlay in points and payments after 48 months?

e. Of the three choices for a loan, which gives Darrell the fewest payments?

SECOND MORTGAGES—HOME EQUITY LOANS AND LINES OF CREDIT

SECTION II

14

In recent years, the "housing crisis" brought on by the economic recession has taken a toll on homeowners. In 2010, the Mortgage Bankers Association reported that more than 1 in 10 home-owners with a mortgage were in foreclosure or were behind in their payments. (See Exhibit 14-3.)

Despite these statistics, homeowners today may use the *equity* in their homes to qualify for a sizable amount of credit at interest rates that are historically low. In addition, under existing law, the interest may be tax-deductible because the debt is secured by the home.

A **home equity loan** is a lump-sum second mortgage loan based on the available equity in a home. A **home equity line of credit** is a form of revolving credit also based on the available equity. Because the home is likely to be a consumer's largest asset, many homeowners use these loans and credit lines only for major expenditures such as debt consolidation, education, home improvements, business expansion, medical bills, and vacations.

With home equity lines of credit, the borrower will be approved for a specific amount of credit known as the **credit limit**. This is the maximum amount that can be borrowed at any one time on that line of credit.

home equity loan A lump-sum second mortgage loan based on the available equity in a home.

home equity line of credit A revolving credit second mortgage loan made on the available equity in a home.

credit limit A pre-approved limit on the amount of a home equity line of credit.

CALCULATING THE POTENTIAL AMOUNT OF CREDIT AVAILABLE TO A BORROWER

14-6

Most lenders set the credit limit on a home equity loan or line by taking a percentage of the appraised value of the house and subtracting the balance owed on the existing mortgage. In determining your actual credit limit, the lender also will consider your ability to repay by looking at your income, debts, and other financial obligations as well as your credit history.

STEPS **TO CALCULATE THE POTENTIAL AMOUNT OF CREDIT AVAILABLE TO A BORROWER**

STEP 1. Calculate the percentage of appraised value.

> **Percentage of appraised value = Appraised value × Lender's percentage**

STEP 2. Find the potential amount of credit available.

> **Potential credit = Percentage of appraised value − First mortgage balance**

EXAMPLE 6 **CALCULATING POTENTIAL CREDIT OF A HOME EQUITY LOAN**

Terri Alexander owns a house that was recently appraised for $115,700. The balance on her existing mortgage is $67,875. If her bank is willing to loan up to 75% of the appraised value, what is the potential amount of credit available to Terri on a home equity loan?

SOLUTIONSTRATEGY

Step 1. Percentage of appraised value = Appraised value × Lender's percentage
Percentage of appraised value = 115,700 × .75
Percentage of appraised value = $86,775

Step 2. Potential credit = Percentage of appraised value − First mortgage balance
Potential credit = 86,775 − 67,875
Potential credit = $18,900

TRYITEXERCISE6

Justin Schaefer owns a home that was recently appraised for $92,900. The balance on his existing first mortgage is $32,440. If his credit union is willing to loan up to 80% of the appraised value, what is the potential amount of credit available to Justin on a home equity line of credit?

CHECK YOUR ANSWER WITH THE SOLUTION ON PAGE 480.

EXHIBIT 14-3

Home Equity Lending

Foreclosure Filings and Repossessions 2006–2010 (in thousands)

Year	Repossessions	Foreclosure Filings
2010	1,100	3,500
2009	918	2,800
2008	850	2,300
2007	404	1,250
2006	269	885

■ Repossessions   ■ Foreclosure Filings

Sources: Bloomberg, MSNBC, CNN, Reuters

By permission of Gary Varvel and Creators Syndicate, Inc

DOLLARS ANDSENSE

In 2010, the signing of the financial reform bill into law meant real financial reform had finally become a reality. Almost two years after the near collapse of the financial system, Congress put new rules in place to prevent the abusive lending practices responsible for the crisis. Highlights of the new law include:

- A Consumer Financial Protection Bureau (CFPB) to stop unfair lending practices
- Governmental authority to step in and safely shut down failing financial firms
- Prohibitions on abusive mortgage lending practices such as kickbacks for steering people into high-rate loans when they qualify for lower rates
- Stronger foreclosure prevention, including an emergency loan fund to help families at risk of losing their home because of unemployment or illness

Source: www.responsiblelending.org

14-7

CALCULATING THE HOUSING EXPENSE RATIO AND THE TOTAL OBLIGATIONS RATIO OF A BORROWER

qualifying ratios Ratios used by lenders to determine whether borrowers have the economic ability to repay loans.

Mortgage lenders use ratios to determine whether borrowers have the economic ability to repay the loan. FHA, VA, and conventional lenders all use monthly gross income as the base for calculating these **qualifying ratios**. Two important ratios used for this purpose are the **housing expense ratio** and the **total obligations ratio**. These ratios are expressed as percents and are calculated by using the following formulas:

$$\text{Housing expense ratio} = \frac{\text{Monthly housing expense (PITI)}}{\text{Monthly gross income}}$$

$$\text{Total obligations ratio} = \frac{\text{Total monthly financial obligations}}{\text{Monthly gross income}}$$

housing expense ratio The ratio of a borrower's monthly housing expense (PITI) to monthly gross income.

total obligations ratio The ratio of a borrower's total monthly financial obligations to monthly gross income.

The mortgage business uses widely accepted guidelines for these ratios that should not be exceeded. The ratio guidelines are shown in Exhibit 14-4.

EXHIBIT 14-4 Lending Ratio Guidelines

Mortgage Type	Housing Expense Ratio	Total Obligations Ratio
FHA	29%	41%
Conventional	28%	36%

Note that the ratio formulas are an application of the percentage formula; the ratio is the rate, the PITI or total obligations are the portion, and the monthly gross income is the base. With this in mind, we are able to solve for any of the variables.

EXAMPLE7 CALCULATING MORTGAGE LENDING RATIOS

Sue Harper earns a gross income of $2,490 per month. She has applied for a mortgage with a monthly PITI of $556. Sue has other financial obligations totaling $387.50 per month.

a. What is Sue's housing expense ratio?

b. What is Sue's total obligations ratio?

c. According to the Lending Ratio Guidelines in Exhibit 14-4, for what type of mortgage would she qualify, if any?

SOLUTIONSTRATEGY

a. $\text{Housing expense ratio} = \dfrac{\text{Monthly housing expense (PITI)}}{\text{Monthly gross income}}$

   $\text{Housing expense ratio} = \dfrac{556}{2,490}$

   $\text{Housing expense ratio} = .2232 = 22.3\%$

b. $\text{Total obligations ratio} = \dfrac{\text{Total monthly financial obligations}}{\text{Monthly gross income}}$

   $\text{Total obligations ratio} = \dfrac{556.00 + 387.50}{2,490} = \dfrac{943.50}{2,490}$

   $\text{Total obligations ratio} = .3789 = 37.9\%$

c. According to the Lending Ratio Guidelines, Sue would qualify for an FHA mortgage but not a conventional mortgage; her total obligations ratio is 37.9%, which is above the limit for conventional mortgages.

TRYITEXERCISE7

Roman Bass earns a gross income of $3,100 per month. He has made application at the Golden Gables Bank for a mortgage with a monthly PITI of $669. Roman has other financial obligations totaling $375 per month.

a. What is Roman's housing expense ratio?

b. What is Roman's total obligations ratio?

c. According to the Lending Ratio Guidelines in Exhibit 14-4, for what type of mortgage would he qualify, if any?

CHECK YOUR ANSWERS WITH THE SOLUTIONS ON PAGE 481.

Note: Round all answers to the nearest cent when necessary.

For the following second mortgage applications, calculate the percentage of appraised value and the potential credit.

	Appraised Value	Lender's Percentage	Percentage of Appraised Value	Balance of First Mortgage	Potential Credit
1.	$118,700	75%	$89,025	$67,900	$21,125
2.	$89,400	65%	_____	$37,800	_____
3.	$141,200	80%	_____	$99,100	_____
4.	$324,600	75%	_____	$197,500	_____
5.	$98,000	65%	_____	$66,000	_____
6.	$243,800	60%	_____	$101,340	_____
7.	$1,329,000	70%	_____	$514,180	_____

Calculate the housing expense ratio and the total obligations ratio for the following mortgage applications.

Applicant	Monthly Gross Income	Monthly PITI Expense	Other Monthly Financial Obligations	Housing Expense Ratio (%)	Total Obligations Ratio (%)
8. Parker	$2,000	$455	$380	22.75	41.75
9. Forman	$3,700	$530	$360		
10. Martin	$3,100	$705	$720		
11. Panko	$4,800	$1,250	$430		
12. Emerson	$2,900	$644	$290		
13. Jameson	$4,250	$1,150	$475		
14. Renquest	$6,725	$1,648	$580		

15. Use Exhibit 14-4, Lending Ratio Guidelines, on page 473 to answer the following questions:

   a. Which of the applicants in Exercises 8–14 would *not* qualify for a conventional mortgage?

   b. Which of the applicants in Exercises 8–14 would *not* qualify for any mortgage?

16. Ronald and Samantha Brady recently had their condominium in Port Isaac appraised for $324,600. The balance on their existing first mortgage is $145,920. If their bank is willing to loan up to 75% of the appraised value, what is the amount of credit available to the Bradys on a home equity line of credit?

   324,600 × .75 = $243,450
                   − 145,920
   Available credit $97,530

17. The Barclays own a home that was recently appraised for $219,000. The balance on their existing first mortgage is $143,250. If their bank is willing to loan up to 65% of the appraised value, what is the potential amount of credit available to the Barclays on a home equity loan?

18. Ransford and Alda Mariano own a home recently appraised for $418,500. The balance on their existing mortgage is $123,872. If their bank is willing to loan up to 80% of the appraised value, what is the amount of credit available to them?

19. Michelle Heaster is thinking about building an addition on her home. The house was recently appraised at $154,000, and the balance on her existing first mortgage is $88,600. If Michelle's bank is willing to loan 70% of the appraised value, does she have enough equity in the house to finance a $25,000 addition?

20. Jamie and Alice Newmark have a combined monthly gross income of $9,702 and monthly expenses totaling $2,811. They plan to buy a home with a mortgage whose monthly PITI will be $2,002.

   a. What is Jamie and Alice's combined housing expense ratio?

   b. What is their total obligations ratio?

   c. For what kind of mortgage can they qualify, if any?

   d. (Optional challenge) By how much would they need to reduce their monthly expenses in order to qualify for an FHA mortgage?

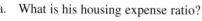

© 2010 Masterfile/Radius Images/JupiterImages

21. You are a mortgage broker at Interamerican Bank. One of your clients, Bill Cramer, has submitted an application for a mortgage with a monthly PITI of $1,259. His other financial obligations total $654.50 per month. Bill earns a gross income of $4,890 per month.

   a. What is his housing expense ratio?

   b. What is his total obligations ratio?

Mortgage brokers are real estate financing professionals acting as the intermediary between consumers and lenders during mortgage transactions. A mortgage broker works with consumers to help them through the complex mortgage origination process.

Brokers earn commissions in exchange for bringing borrowers and lenders together and receive payment when the mortgage loan is closed.

c. According to the Lending Ratio Guidelines on page 473, for what type of mortgage would Bill qualify, if any?

d. If Bill decided to get a part-time job so that he could qualify for a conventional mortgage, how much additional monthly income would he need?

BUSINESS DECISION: DOES IT PAY TO REFINANCE YOUR MORTGAGE?

22. According to CNNMoney.com, with mortgage rates near 35-year lows, you may be able to cut your payments sharply by refinancing your loan. To qualify for the best rates, you need a credit score of 740 or higher and usually at least 20% equity.

Even if you have to settle for a higher rate, a new loan may save you money. The main consideration is whether you will live in your home long enough to offset the refinance closing costs.

Your current mortgage payment is $1,458.50 per month, with a balance of $214,800. You have a chance to refinance at the Biltmore Bank with a 30-year, 5.5% mortgage. The closing costs of the loan are application fee, $90; credit report, $165; title insurance, .4% of the amount financed; title search, $360; and attorney's fees, $580.

You plan to live in your home for at least four more years. Use the Mortgage Refinancing Worksheet below to see if it makes sense to refinance your mortgage.

MORTGAGE REFINANCING WORKSHEET

STEP 1. Current monthly mortgage payment...................................... ☐

STEP 2. New monthly mortgage payment if you refinance..................... ☐

New rate _____   Current mortgage balance _____

| Table 14-1 factor _____ | × | # of 1,000s to borrow _____ |

STEP 3. Monthly savings.. ☐

| Step 1. _____ | – | Step 2. _____ |

STEP 4. Total refinance closing costs (appraisal, title search, etc.)............. ☐

STEP 5. Total months needed to recoup your costs............................. ☐

| Step 4 result | ÷ | Step 3 result |

STEP 6. Total months you plan to live in your home........................... ☐

The Bottom Line – If you plan to live in your home longer than the result in Step 5, it makes sense to refinance.

CHAPTER FORMULAS

Fixed-Rate Mortgages

Monthly payment = Number of $1,000s financed × Table 14-1 factor

Total interest = (Monthly payment × Number of payments) − Amount financed

$$\text{Monthly taxes and Insurance (TI)} = \frac{\text{Estimated property tax} + \text{Hazard insurance}}{12}$$

Monthly PITI = Monthly PI + Monthly TI

Adjustable-Rate Mortgages

Calculated interest rate = Index rate + Lender's margin

Maximum rate per adjustment period = Previous rate + Periodic rate cap

Maximum overall rate = Initial rate + Overall rate cap

Home Equity Loans and Lines of Credit

Percentage of appraised value = Appraised value × Lender's percentage

Second mortgage potential credit = Percentage of appraised value − First mortgage balance

$$\text{Housing expense ratio} = \frac{\text{Monthly housing expense (PITI)}}{\text{Monthly gross income}}$$

$$\text{Total obligations ratio} = \frac{\text{Total monthly financial obligations}}{\text{Monthly gross income}}$$

CHAPTER SUMMARY

Section I: Mortgages—Fixed-Rate and Adjustable-Rate

Topic	Important Concepts	Illustrative Examples
Calculating the Monthly Payment and Total Interest Paid on a Fixed-Rate Mortgage **Performance Objective 14-1, Page 457**	1. Find the number of $1,000s financed by $$\text{Number of }\$1{,}000s = \frac{\text{Amount financed}}{1{,}000}$$ 2. From Table 14-1, locate the table factor, monthly payment per $1,000 financed, at the intersection of the number-of-years column and the interest-rate row. 3. Calculate the monthly payment by Monthly payment = Number of 1,000s financed × Table factor 4. Find the total interest of the loan by $$\underset{\text{interest}}{\text{Total}} = \left(\underset{\text{payments}}{\text{Monthly}} \times \underset{\text{payments}}{\text{Number of}}\right) - \underset{\text{financed}}{\text{Amount}}$$	What is the monthly payment and total interest on a $100,000 mortgage at 9.5% for 30 years? $$\text{Number of 1,000s} = \frac{100{,}000}{1{,}000} = 100$$ Table factor: $9\frac{1}{2}$%, 30 years = 8.41 Monthly payment = 100 × 8.41 = $841 Total interest of the loan = (841 × 360) − 100,000 = 302,760 − 100,000 = $202,760
Preparing a Partial Amortization Schedule of a Mortgage **Performance Objective 14-2, Page 459**	1. Calculate the monthly payment of the loan as before. 2. Calculate the amount of interest for the current month using $I = PRT$, where P is the current outstanding balance of the loan, R is the annual interest rate, and T is $\frac{1}{12}$. 3. Find the portion of the payment used to reduce principal by $$\underset{\text{principal}}{\underset{\text{payment reducing}}{\text{Portion of}}} = \underset{\text{payment}}{\text{Monthly}} - \text{Interest}$$ 4. Calculate outstanding balance of the loan by $$\underset{\text{balance}}{\text{Outstanding}} = \underset{\text{balance}}{\text{Previous}} - \underset{\text{reducing principal}}{\text{Portion of payment}}$$ 5. Repeat Steps 2, 3, and 4 for each succeeding month and enter the values on a schedule labeled appropriately.	Prepare an amortization schedule for the first month of a $70,000 mortgage at 9% for 20 years. Using Table 14-1, we find the monthly payment of the mortgage to be $630. *Month 1:* Interest = Principal × Rate × Time Interest = 70,000 × .09 × $\frac{1}{12}$ Interest = $525 Portion of payment reducing principal 630 − 525 = $105 Outstanding balance after one payment 70,000 − 105 = $69,895 An amortization schedule can now be prepared from these data.

Section I (continued)

Topic	Important Concepts	Illustrative Examples
Calculating the Monthly PITI of a Mortgage Loan **Performance Objective 14-3, Page 461**	In reality, mortgage payments include four elements: principal, interest, taxes, and insurance—thus the abbreviation PITI. *Monthly PITI of a mortgage:* 1. Calculate the principal and interest portion (PI) of the payment as before using Table 14-1. 2. Calculate the monthly tax and insurance portion (TI) by $$\text{Monthly TI} = \frac{\text{Estimated property tax} + \text{Hazard Insurance}}{12}$$ 3. Calculate the total monthly PITI by Monthly PITI = Monthly PI + Monthly TI	Maureen Cassidy purchased a home for \$97,500 with a mortgage at 8.5% for 15 years. The property taxes are \$1,950 per year, and the hazard insurance premium is \$466. What is the monthly PITI payment of Maureen's loan? Using a table factor of 9.85 from Table 14-1, we find the monthly PI for this 8.5%, 15-year mortgage to be \$960.38. $$\text{Monthly T1} = \frac{1,950 + 466}{12}$$ $$= \frac{2,416}{12} = \$201.33$$ Monthly PITI = PI + TI $= 960.38 + 201.33 = \underline{\$1,161.71}$

Calculating the Amount Due at Closing
 	
Performance Objective 14-4, Page 462
	Closing costs are the expenses incurred in conjunction with the sale of real estate. Both buyer and seller are responsible for specific costs.
	    The party responsible for paying a particular closing cost is often determined by local custom or by negotiation.
	    Some closing costs are expressed as dollar amounts, whereas others are a percent of the amount financed or amount of the purchase price.
	    At closing, the buyer is responsible for the purchase price (mortgage and down payment) plus closing costs.
	    The amount received by the seller after all expenses have been paid is known as the proceeds.
		Typical Closing Costs
		Buyer: Attorney's fee, inspections, credit report, appraisal fee, hazard insurance premium, title exam and insurance premium, escrow fee, prepaid taxes and interest
		Seller: Attorney's fee, broker's commission, survey expense, inspections, abstract of title, certificate of title, escrow fee, prepayment penalty—existing loan, documentary stamps

Calculating the Interest Rate of an Adjustable-Rate Mortgage (ARM) **Performance Objective 14-5, Page 465**	Use the following formulas to find the various components of an ARM: $$\frac{\text{Calculated interest rate}} {} = \text{Index rate} + \text{Lender's margin}$$ $$\frac{\text{Max rate per period}}{} = \text{Previous rate} + \text{Periodic cap}$$ $$\frac{\text{Maximum overall rate of ARM}}{} = \text{Initial rate} + \text{Overall cap}$$	Howard Gold bought a home with an adjustable-rate mortgage. The margin on the loan is 3.5%, and the rate cap is 8% over the life of the loan. If the current index rate is 3.6%, what is the calculated interest rate and the maximum overall rate of the loan? Calculated interest rate = 3.6% + 3.5% = <u>7.1%</u> Maximum overall rate = 7.1% + 8% = <u>15.1%</u>

Section II: Second Mortgages—Home Equity Loans and Lines of Credit

Topic	Important Concepts	Illustrative Examples
Calculating the Potential Amount of Credit Available to a Borrower **Performance Objective 14-6, Page 471**	Most lenders set the credit limit on a home equity loan or line by taking a percentage of the appraised value of the home and subtracting the balance owed on the existing first mortgage. In determining your actual credit limit, the lender also will consider your ability to repay by looking at your income, debts, and other financial obligations, as well as your credit history. *Potential amount of credit available to borrower:* 1. Calculate the percentage of appraised value by $$\frac{\text{Percentage of appraised value}}{} = \frac{\text{Appraised value}}{} \times \frac{\text{Lender's percentage}}{}$$ 2. Find the potential amount of credit available by $$\frac{\text{Potential credit}}{} = \frac{\text{Percentage of appraised value}}{} - \frac{\text{First mortgage debt}}{}$$	The McCartneys own a home that was recently appraised for \$134,800. The balance on their existing first mortgage is \$76,550. If their bank is willing to loan up to 70% of the appraised value, what is the amount of credit available to the McCartneys on a home equity loan? Percentage of appraised value = 134,800 × .70 $= \$94,360$ Available credit = 94,360 − 76,550 = <u>\$17,810</u>

Section II (continued)

Topic	Important Concepts	Illustrative Examples
Calculating the Housing Expense Ratio and the Total Obligations Ratio of a Borrower **Performance Objective 14-7, Page 472**	Mortgage lenders use ratios to determine whether borrowers have the economic ability to repay the loan. Two important ratios used for this purpose are the housing expense ratio and the total obligations ratio. These ratios are expressed as percents and are calculated by using the following formulas: Housing expense ratio $= \dfrac{\text{Monthly housing expense (PITI)}}{\text{Monthly gross income}}$ Total obligations ratio $= \dfrac{\text{Total monthly financial obligations}}{\text{Monthly gross income}}$	Vickie Howard earns a gross income of $3,750 per month. She has made application for a mortgage with a monthly PITI of $956. Vickie has other financial obligations totaling $447 per month. a. What is her housing expense ratio? b. What is her total obligations ratio? c. According to the Lending Ratio Guidelines on page 473, for what type of mortgage would Vickie qualify, if any? Housing expense ratio $= \dfrac{956}{3,750} = 25.5\%$ Total obligation ratio $= \dfrac{1,403}{3,750} = 37.4\%$ According to the Lending Ratio Guidelines, Vickie would qualify for an FHA mortgage but not a conventional mortgage; her total obligations ratio is 37.4%, which is above the limit for conventional mortgages.

TRY IT: EXERCISE SOLUTIONS FOR CHAPTER 14

1. Number of 1,000s financed $= \dfrac{\text{Amount financed}}{1,000}$

   Number of 1,000s financed $= \dfrac{85,500}{1,000} = 85.5$

   Table factor 7%, 25 years $= 7.07$

   Monthly payment $=$ Number of 1,000s financed $\times$ Table factor
   Monthly payment $= 85.5 \times 7.07 = \underline{\$604.49}$

   Total interest $=$ (Monthly payment $\times$ Number of payments) $-$ Amount financed
   Total interest $= (604.49 \times 300) - 85,500$
   Total interest $= 181,347 - 85,500 = \underline{\$95,847}$

2. Number of 1,000s financed $= \dfrac{75,000}{1,000} = 75$

   Table factor 9%, 15 years $= 10.15$
   Monthly payment $= 75 \times 10.15 = 761.25$

   Month 1

   $I = PRT = 75,000 \times .09 \times \dfrac{1}{12} = \$562.50$

   Portion of payment reducing principal $= 761.25 - 562.50 = \$198.75$
   Outstanding balance $= 75,000 - 198.75 = \$74,801.25$

   Month 2

   $I = PRT = 74,801.25 \times .09 \times \dfrac{1}{12} = \$561.01$

   Portion of payment reducing principal $= 761.25 - 561.01 = \$200.24$
   Outstanding balance $= 74,801.25 - 200.24 = \$74,601.01$

   Month 3

   $I = PRT = 74,601.01 \times .09 \times \dfrac{1}{12} = \$559.51$

   Portion of payment reducing principal $= 761.25 - 559.51 = \$201.74$
   Outstanding balance $= 74,601.01 - 201.74 = \$74,399.27$

Month 4

$$I = PRT = 74{,}399.27 \times .09 \times \frac{1}{12} = \$557.99$$

Portion of payment reducing principal $= 761.25 - 557.99 = \$203.26$

Outstanding balance $= 74{,}399.27 - 203.26 = \$74{,}196.01$

<u>Amortization Schedule</u>
$75,000, 9%, 15 years

Payment Number	Monthly Payment	Monthly Interest	Portion Used to Reduce Principal	Loan Balance
0				$75,000.00
1	$761.25	$562.50	$198.75	$74,801.25
2	$761.25	$561.01	$200.24	$74,601.01
3	$761.25	$559.51	$201.74	$74,399.27
4	$761.25	$557.99	$203.26	$74,196.01

3. Number of 1,000s $= \dfrac{125{,}600}{1{,}000} = 125.6$

Table factor 9.25%, 20 years $= 9.16$

Monthly payment (PI) $= 125.6 \times 9.16 = \$1{,}150.50$

Monthly TI $= \dfrac{\text{Property tax} + \text{Hazard insurance}}{12}$

Monthly TI $= \dfrac{3{,}250 + 765}{12} = \dfrac{4{,}015}{12} = \$334.58$

Monthly PITI $= \text{PI} + \text{TI} = 1{,}150.50 + 334.58 = \underline{\underline{\$1{,}485.08}}$

4. a. Down payment $= 120{,}000 \times 20\% = \$24{,}000$

Amount financed $= 120{,}000 - 24{,}000 = \$96{,}000$

Closing Costs, Buyer:

Discount points (96,000 × 3%)	$ 2,880
Down payment (24,000 − 10,000)	14,000
Application fee........................	100
Condominium transfer fee...............	190
Title insurance (96,000 × $\frac{3}{4}$%)	720
Hazard insurance	420
Prepaid taxes	310
Attorney's fees.......................	500
Due at closing	$19,120

b. *Proceeds, Seller:*

Purchase price		$120,000
Less: Broker's commission		
120,000 × $5\frac{1}{2}$%.........	$ 6,600	
Closing costs..........	670	
Mortgage payoff........	65,000	
		− 72,270
Proceeds to seller		$47,730

5. a. Calculated ARM rate $=$ Index rate $+$ Lender's margin

Calculated ARM rate $= 3.2 + 3.4 = \underline{6.6\%}$

b. Maximum overall rate $=$ Calculated ARM rate $+$ Overall rate cap

Maximum overall rate $= 6.6 + 7.0 = \underline{13.6\%}$

6. Percentage of appraised value $=$ Appraised value $\times$ Lender's percentage

Percentage of appraised value $= 92{,}900 \times 80\% = \$74{,}320$

Potential credit $=$ Percentage of appraised value $-$ First mortgage balance

Potential credit $= 74{,}320 - 32{,}440 = \underline{\$41{,}880}$

7. a. Housing expense ratio $= \dfrac{\text{Monthly housing expense (PITI)}}{\text{Monthly gross income}}$

Housing expense ratio $= \dfrac{669}{3,100} = 21.6\%$

b. Total obligations ratio $= \dfrac{\text{Total monthly financial obligation}}{\text{Monthly gross income}}$

Total obligations ratio $= \dfrac{669 + 375}{3,100} = \dfrac{1,044}{3,100} = 33.7\%$

c. According to the guidelines, Roman qualifies for both FHA and conventional mortgages.

CONCEPT REVIEW

1. Land, including permanent improvements on that land, is known as ____ ____. (14-1)

2. A(n) ____ is a loan in which real property is used as security for a debt. (14-1)

3. Mortgage ____ points are an extra charge frequently added to the cost of a mortgage. (14-1, 14-4)

4. A chart that shows the month-by-month breakdown of each mortgage payment into interest and principal is known as a(n) ____ schedule. (14-2)

5. A(n) ____ account is a bank account used by mortgage lenders to accumulate next year's property taxes and hazard insurance. (14-3)

6. Today most mortgage payments include four parts, abbreviated PITI. Name these parts. (14-3)

7. The final step in a real estate transaction is a meeting at which time the buyer pays the agreed-upon purchase price and the seller delivers the ownership documents. This meeting is known as the ____. (14-4)

8. The official document representing the right of ownership of real property is known as the ____ or the ____. (14-4)

9. List four mortgage loan closing costs. (14-4)

10. A mortgage in which the interest rate changes periodically, usually in relation to a predetermined economic index, is known as a(n) ____ rate mortgage. (14-5)

11. A home equity ____ is a lump-sum second mortgage based on the available equity in a home. (14-6)

12. A home equity ____ of credit is a revolving credit second mortgage loan on the equity in a home. (14-6)

13. Write the formula for the housing expense ratio. (14-7)

14. Write the formula for the total obligations ratio. (14-7)

ASSESSMENT TEST

You are one of the branch managers of the Insignia Bank. Today two loan applications were submitted to your office. Calculate the requested information for each loan.

	Amount Financed	Interest Rate	Term of Loan	Number of $1,000s Financed	Table Factor	Monthly Payment	Total Interest
1.	$134,900	7.75%	25 years	____	____	____	____
2.	$79,500	8.25%	20 years	____	____	____	____

DOLLARS AND SENSE

Here are some popular real estate websites that buyers, sellers, and renters can use to research locations in which they are interested.
- Realtor.com
- Zillow.com
- Redfin.com
- HotPads.com
- PropertyShark.com

3. Suzanne Arthurs purchased a home with a $146,100 mortgage at 6.5% for 30 years. Calculate the monthly payment and prepare an amortization schedule for the first three months of Suzanne's loan.

Payment Number	Monthly Payment	Monthly Interest	Portion Used to Reduce Principal	Loan Balance
0				$146,100.00
1	____	____	____	____
2	____	____	____	____
3	____	____	____	____

Use Table 14-1 to calculate the monthly principal and interest and calculate the monthly PITI for the following mortgages.

	Amount Financed	Interest Rate	Term of Loan	Monthly PI	Annual Property Tax	Annual Insurance	Monthly PITI
4.	$54,200	9.00%	25 years	____	$719	$459	____
5.	$132,100	8.75%	15 years	____	$2,275	$1,033	____

For the following second mortgage applications, calculate the percentage of appraised value and the potential credit.

	Appraised Value	Lender's Percentage	Percentage of Appraised Value	Balance of First Mortgage	Potential Credit
6.	$114,500	65%	____	$77,900	____
7.	$51,500	80%	____	$27,400	____
8.	$81,200	70%	____	$36,000	____

For the following mortgage applications, calculate the housing expense ratio and the total expense ratio.

	Applicant	Monthly Gross Income	Monthly PITI Expense	Other Monthly Financial Obligations	Housing Expense Ratio (%)	Total Obligations Ratio (%)
9.	Morton	$5,300	$1,288	$840	____	____
10.	Hauser	$3,750	$952	$329	____	____

11. As a loan officer using the Lending Ratio Guidelines on page 473, what type of mortgage can you offer Morton and Hauser from Exercises 9 and 10?

12. Dale Evans bought the Lazy D Ranch with an adjustable-rate mortgage. The lender's margin on the loan is 3.9%, and the overall rate cap is 6% over the life of the loan.

   a. If the current index rate is 4.45%, what is the calculated interest rate of the ARM?

   b. What is the maximum overall rate of Dale's loan?

13. Diversified Investments purchased a 24-unit apartment building for $650,000. After a 20% down payment, the balance was financed with a 20-year, 7.75% fixed-rate mortgage.

   a. What is the amount of the monthly principal and interest portion of the loan?

b. As Diversified's loan officer, construct an amortization schedule for the first two months of the mortgage.

Payment Number	Monthly Payment	Monthly Interest	Portion Used to Reduce Principal	Loan Balance
0				_____
1	_____	_____	_____	_____
2	_____	_____	_____	_____

c. If the annual property taxes are $9,177 and the hazard insurance premium is $2,253 per year, what is the total monthly PITI of the loan?

d. If each apartment rents for $825 per month, how much income will Diversified make per month after the PITI is paid on the building?

14. Larry Mager purchased a ski lodge in Telluride for $850,000. His bank is willing to finance 70% of the purchase price. As part of the mortgage closing costs, Larry had to pay $4\frac{1}{4}$ discount points. How much did this amount to?

15. A Denny's Restaurant franchisee is looking for a 20-year mortgage with 90% financing to build a new location costing $775,000. The Spring Creek Bank is offering an 8% mortgage with $1\frac{1}{2}$ discount points; Foremost Savings & Loan is offering a 7.5% mortgage with 4 discount points. The franchisee is unsure which mortgage is the better deal and has asked for your help.

a. What is the total interest paid on each loan?

p77/ZUMA Press/Newscom

Denny's Corporation, through its subsidiaries, engages in the ownership and operation of a chain of family-style restaurants primarily in the United States. Its restaurants offer traditional American-style food. The company owns and operates its restaurants under the Denny's brand name.

As of December 30, 2009, Denny's Corporation operated 1,551 restaurants, including 1,318 franchised/licensed restaurants and 233 company-owned and operated restaurants; employed 11,000 full-time workers; and had sales of over $608 million.

Source: http://finance.yahoo.com

b. Taking into account the discount points, which lender is offering a better deal and by how much?

16. How much more total interest will be paid on a 30-year fixed-rate mortgage for $100,000 at 9.25% compared with a 15-year mortgage at 8.5%?

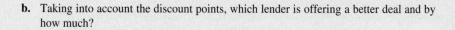

CHAPTER 14

17. Adam Marsh is purchasing a $134,000 condominium apartment. The down payment is 20%, and the balance will be financed with a 20-year fixed-rate mortgage at 8.75% and 3 discount points. The annual property tax is $1,940, and the hazard insurance premium is $1,460. When Adam signed the original sales contract, he put down a deposit of $10,000, which will be credited to his down payment. In addition, at the time of closing, he must pay the following expenses:

Appraisal fee	$165
Credit report	$75
Attorney's fees	$490
Roof inspection	$50
Termite inspection	$88
Title search	$119
Mortgage insurance premium	1.2% of amount financed
Documentary stamps	$\frac{1}{4}$% of amount financed

As Adam's real estate agent, he has asked you the following questions:

a. What is the total monthly PITI of the mortgage loan?

b. What is the total amount of interest that Adam will pay on the loan?

c. How much is due at the time of the closing?

d. If the sellers are responsible for the 6% broker's commission, $900 in closing costs, and the existing first mortgage with a balance of $45,000, what proceeds will be received on the sale of the property?

18. Martin Ellingham is negotiating to buy a vacation cottage in Port Wenn. The seller of the cottage is asking $186,000. Martin offered him a cash deal, owner-seller (no broker) only if the seller would reduce the price by 12%. The seller agreed. Martin must pay a 10% down payment upon signing the agreement of sale. At closing, he must pay the balance of the agreed-upon sale price, a $500 attorney's fee, a $68 utility transfer fee, a title search and transfer fee of $35 plus $\frac{3}{4}$% of the selling price, and the first six months of the annual insurance of $1,460 per year. How much does Martin owe at closing?

19. The Randolphs own a home that recently appraised for $161,400. The balance on their existing first mortgage is $115,200. If their bank is willing to loan up to 70% of the appraised value, what is the amount of credit available to the Randolphs on a home equity line of credit?

20. Jonathan and Kimberly Schwartz live in a home to which they want to make major improvements. They plan to replace the existing heating and cooling system, remodel the kitchen, and add a room above the garage. To pay for this renovation, they plan to get a home equity line of credit. Their home currently appraises for $298,000. They owe $68,340 on the first mortgage. How much credit will their bank provide if the limit is 75% of their home's value?

21. Phil Armstrong earns a gross income of $5,355 per month. He has submitted an application for a fixed-rate mortgage with a monthly PITI of $1,492. Phil has other financial obligations totaling $625 per month.

a. What is his housing expense ratio?

b. What is his total obligations ratio?

c. According to the Lending Ratio Guidelines on page 473, for what type of mortgage would Phil qualify, if any?

22. Magda Leon is applying for a home mortgage with a monthly PITI of $724. She currently has a gross income of $2,856 and other monthly expenses of $411.

a. What is Magda's housing expense ratio?

b. What is her total obligations ratio?

c. According to the lending ratio guidelines, for what type of mortgage would Magda qualify, if any?

"OKAY, WIPE THAT 30-YEAR FIXED SCOWL OFF YOUR FACE, AND GIVE US YOUR SHORT-TERM ADJUSTABLE GRIN!"

© Harley Schwadron. Reproduction rights obtainable from www.CartoonStock.com

BUSINESS DECISION: FOR WHAT SIZE MORTGAGE CAN YOU QUALIFY?

23. You are applying for a conventional mortgage from the Americana Bank. Your monthly gross income is $3,500, and the bank uses the 28% housing expense ratio guideline.

a. What is the highest PITI for which you can qualify? *Hint:* Solve the housing expense ratio formula for PITI. Remember, this is an application of the percentage formula, Portion = Rate × Base, where PITI is the portion, the expense ratio is the rate, and your monthly gross income is the base.

b. Based on your answer from part a, if you are applying for a 30-year, 9% mortgage and the taxes and insurance portion of PITI is $175 per month, use Table 14-1 to calculate the size of the mortgage for which you qualify. *Hint:* Subtract TI from PITI. Divide the PI by the appropriate table factor to determine the number of $1,000s for which you qualify.

c. Based on your answer from part b, if you are planning on a 20% down payment, what is the most expensive house you can afford? *Hint:* Use the percentage formula again. The purchase price of the house is the base, the amount financed is the portion, and the percent financed is the rate.

COLLABORATIVE LEARNING ACTIVITY

The Hypothetical Mortgage

Speak with the loan officers at mortgage lending institutions in your area and ask for their help with a business math class project.

Your assignment is to research the various types of financing deals currently being offered for a hypothetical condominium you plan to buy. The following assumptions apply to this project:

- The purchase price of the condo you plan to buy is $200,000.
- The condo was recently appraised for $220,000.
- You plan to make a 25% down payment ($50,000) and are seeking a $150,000 mortgage.
- You have a job that qualifies you for that size mortgage.

As a team, your assignment is to compare the current interest rates, costs, and features associated with a 15-year fixed-rate mortgage, a 30-year fixed-rate mortgage, and an adjustable-rate mortgage.

a. What are the current interest rates and discount points of the 15- and 30-year fixed-rate mortgages?
b. What are the monthly payments of the fixed-rate mortgages?
c. What is the initial (teaser) rate, discount points, adjustment period, rate caps, margin, and index for the adjustable-rate mortgage?
d. What are the fees or charges for the loan application, property appraisal, survey, credit report, inspections, title search, title insurance, and document preparation?
e. What other charges or fees can be expected at closing?
f. Which type of mortgage does your team think is the best deal at this time? Why?
g. Which bank would you choose for the mortgage? Why?

Answers to *Business Decisions* are not included.

Chapter 1: Whole Numbers

SECTION I

1. 22,938—Twenty-two thousand, nine hundred thirty-eight   **3.** 184—One hundred eighty-four   **5.** 2,433,590—Two million, four hundred thirty-three thousand, five hundred ninety   **7.** 183,622   **9.** $40,000,000,000   **11.** d   **13.** c   **15.** 1,760
17. 235,400   **19.** 8,000,000   **21.** 1,300,000,000   **23a.** Texas: eight thousand seven hundred ninety-seven megawatts, Iowa: three thousand, fifty-three megawatts
23b. Texas: 8,800 megawatts, Iowa: 3,100 megawatts

SECTION II

1. 91   **3.** 19,943   **5.** 37,648   **7.** 70,928   **9.** estimate 43,100—exact 41,844
11a. 7,000 Vehicles   **11b.** 6,935 Vehicles   **13.** $103,005 Grand Total
15. $1,627   **17.** 4,629   **19.** 278,091   **21.** $138   **23.** $139   **25.** 3,490,700
27. 378   **29a.** 43   **29b.** 22   **29c.** 94

SECTION III

1. 11,191   **3.** 294,300   **5.** 56,969,000   **7.** 13,110   **9.** estimate 100,000—exact 98,980   **11.** estimate 200—exact 187   **13.** $6,985,000   **15a.** $87   **15b.** $13
17. 128 R 20   **19.** 240   **21.** estimate 3—exact 3 R 5   **23.** estimate 578—exact 566 R 68   **25a.** 117   **25b.** 15   **27.** The Royale Hotel is more economical.
29a. $40,272   **29b.** $20,031   **29c.** $20,241

ASSESSMENT TEST

1. 200,049—Two hundred thousand, forty-nine   **3.** 316,229   **5.** 18,300
7. 260,000   **9.** 99   **11.** 44 R 28   **13.** 22,258   **15.** 714   **17.** $12,763   **19a.** 19
19b. 25   **21a.** $11,340   **21b.** $36   **23.** $1,003   **25.** $49,260   **27.** $3,186
29. 15   **31.** $20

2　**Chapter 2: Fractions**

SECTION I

1. Mixed, Twenty-three and four-fifths　**3.** Improper, Fifteen-ninths　**5.** Mixed, Two and one-eighth　**7.** $3\frac{1}{3}$　**9.** $4\frac{4}{15}$　**11.** $1\frac{2}{31}$　**13.** $\frac{59}{5}$　**15.** $\frac{149}{8}$　**17.** $\frac{1,001}{4}$　**19.** $\frac{3}{4}$　**21.** $\frac{27}{115}$　**23.** $\frac{1}{8}$　**25.** $\frac{19}{65}$　**27.** $\frac{13}{16}$　**29.** $\frac{5}{18}$　**31.** $\frac{36}{48}$　**33.** $\frac{44}{64}$　**35.** $\frac{42}{98}$　**37.** $\frac{40}{64}$　**39.** $\frac{126}{182}$　**41.** $\frac{5}{11}$　**43a.** $\frac{1}{9}$　**43b.** $\frac{8}{9}$

SECTION II

1. 15　**3.** 12　**5.** 300　**7.** $1\frac{1}{3}$　**9.** $1\frac{7}{16}$　**11.** $1\frac{13}{20}$　**13.** $2\frac{3}{20}$　**15.** $11\frac{13}{24}$　**17.** $10\frac{17}{40}$　**19.** $10\frac{19}{30}$　**21.** $\frac{2}{3}$　**23.** $\frac{11}{18}$　**25.** $8\frac{4}{15}$　**27.** $26\frac{29}{45}$　**29.** $35\frac{13}{15}$　**31.** $21\frac{1}{8}$　**33.** $1\frac{13}{16}$

SECTION III

1. $\frac{8}{15}$　**3.** $\frac{2}{9}$　**5.** $\frac{10}{19}$　**7.** $2\frac{2}{5}$　**9.** $21\frac{13}{15}$　**11.** $\frac{1}{125}$　**13a.** $\frac{5}{8}$　**13b.** 2,750　**15.** $43\frac{15}{16}$　**17.** 15　**19.** $2\frac{2}{9}$　**21.** $1\frac{1}{15}$　**23.** $\frac{2}{5}$　**25.** $5\frac{17}{35}$　**27.** 19　**29.** $\frac{5}{14}$　**31.** 46　**33a.** 240　**33b.** 90　**35.** 185　**37.** 55　**39a.** $2\frac{17}{64}$　**39b.** 11

ASSESSMENT TEST

1. Improper fraction, Eighteen-elevenths　**3.** Proper fraction, Thirteen-sixteenths　5. 25　**7.** $\frac{86}{9}$　**9.** $\frac{2}{5}$　**11.** $\frac{18}{78}$　**13.** $\frac{25}{36}$　**15.** $5\frac{1}{3}$　**17.** $4\frac{3}{10}$　**19.** $13\frac{1}{3}$　**21.** 69　**23.** $23\frac{5}{8}$　**25.** $10\frac{7}{16}$　**27a.** \$588,000　**27b.** \$49,000　**29a.** 275　29b. 495　31a. 99　31b. 22　31c. \$6,605

Chapter 3: Decimals

1. Twenty-one hundredths **3.** Ninety-two thousandths **5.** Ninety-eight thousand, forty-five and forty-five thousandths **7.** Nine hundred thirty-eight hundred-thousandths **9.** Fifty-seven and one-half hundred-thousandths **11.** .8 **13.** 67,309.04 **15.** 41.057 seconds, 41.183 seconds, 41.507 seconds **17.** 0.448557 = 0.45 **19.** 0.9229388 = 0.9229 **21.** $688.75 = $689 **23.** 88.964 = 89.0 **25.** 1.344 = 1.34

1. 58.033 **3.** $45.27 **5.** 152.784494 **7.** 16.349 **9.** $.87 **11.** 116.278—One hundred sixteen and two hundred seventy-eight thousandths **13.** 80.482 **15a.** $30.25 **15b.** $27.75 **17.** $11.14 **19a.** 900,000 **19b.** 11,800,000 **21.** 400.2129 **23.** 1,120,050 **25.** 15.152256 **27.** 33,090 **29.** .07 **31.** $2.72 **33.** 6 **35.** 217.39 **37a.** $2,480.98 **37b.** $15,590.00 **37c.** $230 **39a.** $250,000,000 **39b.** $2,700,000 **41a.** $2,104.32 **41b.** $920.06 **43.** $16 **45a.** 1,152 **45b.** $1,440 **45c.** 12-ounce size

1. $\frac{1}{8}$ **3.** $\frac{1}{125}$ **5.** $14\frac{41}{50}$ **7.** 5.67 **9.** 1.22 **11.** 58.43 **13.** 5 **15a.** 16 **15b.** $190.24 **17a.** $489.26 **17b.** 32.7¢ **19.** $2,520.50

ASSESSMENT TEST

1. Sixty-one hundredths **3.** One hundred nineteen dollars and eighty-five cents **5.** Four hundred ninety-five ten-thousandths **7.** 5.014 **9.** $16.57 **11.** 995.070 **13.** 4.7 **15.** $37.19 **17.** 7.7056 **19.** .736 **21.** .000192 **23.** .4 **25.** $20.06 **27.** $\frac{441}{10,000}$ **29.** 3.11 **31.** The box of 40 Blu-ray discs and box of 40 jewel cases is the better buy by $4.93. **33.** $19.89 **35.** $9.25 Savings **37.** $2,161.19 Remains **39a.** 160 **39b.** $6.60

Chapter 4: Checking Accounts

SECTION I

1. $345.54   **3.** for deposit only, Your Signature, 099-506-8, Restrictive Endorsement
5. Pay to the order of, David Sporn, Your Signature, 099-506-8, Full Endorsement
7. $501.03 net deposit   **9a.** $479.20 bal. forward   **9b.** $1,246.10 bal. forward
9c. $1,200.45 bal. forward   **9d.** $1,075.45 bal. forward   **9e.** $205.45 bal. forward
9f. $1,555.45 bal. forward   **9g.** $691.05 bal. forward

SECTION II

1. $1,935.90 reconciled balances   **3.** $471.84 reconciled balances

ASSESSMENT TEST

1. $24,556.00   **3.** $935.79 net deposit   **5a.** $463.30 bal. forward   **5b.** $395.52 bal. forward   **5c.** $145.52 bal. forward   **5d.** $270.97 bal. forward   **5e.** $590.97 bal. forward   **5f.** $467.87 bal. forward   **7.** $1,538.32 reconciled balances

Chapter 5: Using Equations to Solve Business Problems

1. 13   **3.** 90   **5.** 3   **7.** $7\frac{1}{2}$ **9.** 4   **11.** 3   **13.** 4   **15.** 5   **17.** 1   **19.** $5F + 33$
21. $HP + 550$ **23.** $8Y - 128$ **25.** $\frac{3}{4}B + 40$ **27.** $X = 5B + C$
29. $\$5.75R = \$28.75$ **31.** $5X + 4 + 2X = X + 40$

1. 39 Kathy's sales   **3.** $21,700 Last year's salary   **5.** 8 iPod Nanos, 24 iPod Shuffles
7a. 170 Large size, 280 Small size   **7b.** Large size = $3,400, Small size = $3,920
9. $5,000 = Each grandchild's share, $15,000 = Each child's share, $60,000 = Wife's share
11. 288 Total transactions   **13a.** 220 Pounds of peanut butter cookies, 310 Pounds
of oatmeal cookies   **13b.** $352 Sales of peanut butter cookies, $403 Sales of oatmeal
cookies   **15.** 100 Senators, 435 Representatives   **17.** $485.80 Total cost to ship order
19. 44 Cones to be placed around the area   **21.** 3,080 Pounds of fruit   **23.** 21 Eggs
needed for recipe   **25.** 43 People per job   **27.** 72 Passenger flights   **29a.** 12 Pages of
news, 36 Pages of advertising   **29b.** 4 Pages classified, 12 Pages national, 20 Pages
retail   **29c.** Retail = $450,000, National = $270,000, Classified = $90,000
29d. $14,400 Bonus

ASSESSMENT TEST

1. 65   **3.** 15   **5.** 8   **7.** 8   **9.** 15   **11.** $4R - 108$ **13.** $ZW + 24$ **15.** $X = 4C + L$
17. $3F - 14 = 38$ **19.** 14 Boats sold by Pelican Marine, 19 Boats sold by Boater's
Paradise   **21.** $55 Cost per phone   **23.** 95 Watts for energy-saver bulb
25a. 225 Long-sleeve shirts, 150 Short-sleeve shirts   **25b.** $6,412.50 Long-sleeve
shirts, $3,450.00 Short-sleeve shirts   **27.** 25 Words   **29.** $104,000 Equipment
inventory   **31.** $3\frac{1}{3}$ Quarts of water   **33a.** 45 Pizzas   **33b.** 180 People served

6 Chapter 6: Percents and Their Applications in Business

SECTION I

1. .28 **3.** .134 **5.** .4268 **7.** .0002 **9.** 1.2517 **11.** 350% **13.** 4,600%

15. .935% 17. 16,400% 19. 533% **21.** $\frac{1}{20}$ **23.** $\frac{89}{100}$ **25.** $\frac{19}{50}$ **27.** $\frac{5}{8}$

29. $1\frac{1}{4}$ **31.** 75% **33.** 240% **35.** 125% **37.** 18.75% **39.** 35% **41.** .53, $\frac{53}{100}$

43. .15, $\frac{3}{20}$ **45.** .05, $\frac{1}{20}$

SECTION II

1. 57 **3.** 90 **5.** 85.5 **7.** 64.77 **9.** 56.88 **11.** 32% **13.** 250% **15.** 13.5%
17. 29.9% **19.** 26.0% **21.** 460 **23.** 34.86 **25.** 363.64 **27.** 400 **29.** $53.65
31a. $59,200 **31b.** $594.50 **33.** 2,220 Square feet **35.** $13,650 **37.** 2,820
39a. $150 **39b.** Server $111.00, Host $7.50, Bartender $9.00, Busser $22.50
41. 1,700 **43.** $61,230.75 **45.** $32.3 billion **47.** 60,000 Police vehicles

SECTION III

1. 37.5% **3.** 25.2% **5.** 60 **7.** 15 **9.** 10,000 **11.** 53.7% Decrease **13a.** 1,105
Racquets **13b.** Metal Alloy: 442 Racquets, Graphite: 663 Racquets **15.** 49 Million
uninsured people **17.** $658,762 **19.** 50% **21a.** 32.4% Increase **21b.** 17.35%
Decrease

ASSESSMENT TEST

1. .88 **3.** .5968 **5.** .005625 **7.** 68.1% **9.** 2,480% **11.** $\frac{19}{100}$ **13.** $\frac{93}{1,250}$

15. $\frac{127}{500}$ **17.** 55.56% **19.** 5,630% **21.** 408 **23.** 103.41 **25.** 180% **27.** 69

29. 2,960 31. 1,492 33. $122.48 Savings 35a. $72,000 Total cost
35b. $0.24 Per mile 35c. 25% Savings per mile 35d. 195% Increase
37. 21.0% Increase **39a.** 133,695 Vehicles **39b.** 2.9% Increase
41. 18.1% Increase **43.** $3,016,000 **45.** $40,583.33 Total shipment
47. 158.2% **49.** $229.9 Million

Chapter 7: Invoices, Trade Discounts, and Cash Discounts

SECTION I

1. Box **3.** Drum **5.** Gross **7.** Thousand **9.** Panorama Products **11.** June 16, 20XX **13.** J. M. Hardware Supply **15.** 2051 W. Adams Blvd., Lansing, MI 48901 **17.** Gilbert Trucking **19.** $61.45 **21.** $4,415.12

SECTION II

1. $258.00 **3.** $7.93 **5.** $44.13 **7.** $53.92, $80.87 **9.** $527.45, $431.55 **11.** 76%, $429.65 **13.** 87.25%, $4.01 **15.** $120.50, 34.9% **17.** $239.99 **19.** $1,950 **21a.** $8,653 **21b.** $16,797 **23.** $1,512 **25.** $17

SECTION III

1. .792, $285.12 **3.** .648, $52.97 **5.** .57056, $4.14 **7.** .765, .235 **9.** .59288, .40712 **11.** .51106, .48894 **13.** .6324, .3676, $441.12, $758.88 **15.** .65666, .34334, $303.34, $580.16 **17.** .5292, .4708, $1,353.53, $1,521.42 **19.** .49725 **21a.** .6 **21b.** $54,300 **23a.** Northwest **23b.** $4,500 Savings per year **25a.** $1,494.90 **25b.** $687.65 **25c.** $807.25 **27a.** $851.05 **27b.** $392.72

SECTION IV

1. $474.00, $15,326.00 **3.** $96.84, $2,324.16 **5.** $319.25, $8,802.19 **7.** $474.23, $870.37 **9.** $5,759.16, $1,472.92 **11.** May 8, June 22 **13.** 2% Feb. 8, 1% Feb. 18, Mar. 30 **15.** Jan. 10, Jan. 30 **17.** Oct. 23, Nov. 12 **19.** June 25, July 15 **21a.** April 27, May 27 **21b.** $21.24 **21c.** $1,148.76 **23a.** March 22 **23b.** April 11 **25a.** $32,931.08 **25b.** May 19

ASSESSMENT TEST

1. Leisure Time Industries **3.** 4387 **5.** $46.55 **7.** $2,558 **9.** $11,562.45 **11.** $1,485 **13.** 33.76% **15.** Fancy Footwear **17a.** .6052 **17b.** .3948 **19a.** April 24 **19b.** May 9 **19c.** May 15 **19d.** June 4 **21.** $14,563.80

8 **Chapter 8: Markup and Markdown**

SECTION I   **1.** $138.45, 85.7%   **3.** $6,944.80, 77.8%   **5.** $156.22, $93.73   **7.** $2,149.00, 159.2%   **9.** $.75, $1.33   **11.** $85.90   **13.** $195   **15a.** $4.19   **15b.** 71.7%   **17a.** $60.63   **17b.** 104.1%   **19.** $77.88   **21.** $1,029.41   **23.** $21.88

SECTION II   **1.** $115.00, 43.5%   **3.** $61.36, $136.36   **5.** 37.5%   **7.** $94.74, 133%, 57.1%   **9.** $9,468.74, $24,917.74, 61.3%   **11.** 60%   **13a.** $1.74   **13b.** 34.9%   **13c.** $2.09, 41.9%   **15.** $366.12   **17.** $125   **19.** 75.4%   **21a.** $30.49   **21b.** 141.8%   **21c.** 58.6%

SECTION III   **1.** $161.45, 15%   **3.** $1.68, 23.2%   **5.** $41.10, $16.44   **7.** $80.27, 30.7%   **9.** $559.96, $1,039.92   **11a.** $1,750   **11b.** 18.0%   **13a.** $.70   **13b.** 41.4%   **13c.** $1.39   **15.** $30   **17.** $6,018.75   **19.** $469.68   **21.** $233.99   **23a.** $65.00, 40.6%   **23b.** $85.00, 53.1%   **23c.** $396.41   **23d.** Answers will vary.

ASSESSMENT TEST

1. $152.60   **3.** $18.58   **5.** $6.28, 52.9%   **7.** $15.95   **9a.** $778   **9b.** 21.3%   **11.** $216.06   **13a.** $56.25   **13b.** $64.68   **15a.** $2,499.99   **15b.** $1,000   **15c.** 60%   **15d.** 36%

Chapter 9: Payroll

SECTION I

1. $1,250.00, $625.00, $576.92, $288.46   **3.** $8,333.33, $4,166.67, $3,846.15, $1,923.08   **5.** $34,800, $2,900.00, $1,338.46, $669.23   **7.** $17,420, $1,451.67, $725.83, $670.00   **9.** $1,115.38   **11.** $1,329.23   **13.** 36, 0, $313.20, 0, $313.20
15. 48, 8, $290.00, $87.00, $377.00   **17.** $711.90   **19.** $320.25
21. $1,170.90   **23.** $5,790.40   **25.** $1,565   **27.** $352.66

SECTION II

1. $51.15 Social security, $11.96 Medicare   **3a.** $607.60 Social security, $142.10 Medicare   **3b.** November   **3c.** $545.60 Social security, $142.10 Medicare
5. $212.16, $49.62.   **7.** $99.20, $68.15   **9.** $18.96   **11.** $567.21   **13.** $151.24
15. $3,258.47 Paycheck   **17.** $109.53   **19.** $572.21

SECTION III

1a. $282.72 Total social security, $66.12 Total Medicare   **1b.** $3,675.36 Social security for the first quarter, $859.56 Medicare for the first quarter   **3.** $17,184.96
5. $5,282.40 Social security, $1,235.40 Medicare   **7a.** $378   **7b.** $56
9a. $347.92, $51.54   **11a.** $3,770.40   **11b.** 15%   **11c.** $196,060.80
13a. $23,485.80   **13b.** Form 1040-ES, *Quarterly Estimated Tax Voucher for Self-Employed Persons*

ASSESSMENT TEST

1a. $67,200   **1b.** $2,584.62   **3.** $898.70   **5.** $656.25   **7.** $1,011.71   **9.** $6,963
11. $2,284.10   **13.** $44.95 Social security, $10.51 Medicare   **15a.** $2,034.55
15b. $2,193.00   **15c.** $2,487.29   **17.** $1,062.19   **19a.** $1,693.03 Social security, $395.95 Medicare   **19b.** $44,018.78 Social security, $10,294.70 Medicare
21a. $378   **21b.** $56   **23a.** $58,589.20   **23b.** 20.8%   **23c.** $3,046,638.40

10 Chapter 10: Simple Interest and Promissory Notes

SECTION I

1. $800.00 **3.** $19,050.00 **5.** $206.62 **7.** $1,602.74, $1,625.00 **9.** $1,839.79, $1,865.34 **11.** $15.16, $15.38 **13.** $60.82, $61.67 **15.** $882.88, $895.15 **17.** $12,852.00, $66,852.00 **19.** $2,362.50, $36,112.50 **21.** $22,929.60, $79,129.60 **23.** $1,770.00 **25.** $1,330,000.00 **27.** $155,043.00 **29.** 98 **31.** 289 **33.** 55 **35.** December 3 **37.** June 24 **39.** February 23 **41.** October 2 **43.** $62,005.48 **45.** $403.89 **47.** $14.97

SECTION II

1. $1,250 **3.** $50,000 **5.** $12,000 **7.** $26,000 **9.** 14 **11.** 12.8 **13.** 10.3 **15.** 158 days **17.** 308 days **19.** 180 days **21.** 88 days **23.** $13,063.16, $13,403.16 **25.** $2,390.63, $27,890.63 **27a.** 166 Days **27b.** September 29 **29.** $10,000 **31.** 11.6% **33.** $66,620.99 **35.** $12,370.68 **37a.** 12.5 Years **37b.** 10 Years

SECTION III

1. $292.50, $4,207.50 **3.** $231.25, $1,618.75 **5.** $232.38, $7,567.62 **7.** 84, $171.50, $4,828.50 **9.** 100, $34.31, $1,265.69 **11.** $132.30, $2,567.70, 14.72 **13.** $214.28, $3,585.72, 15.37 **15.** $4,683.85, $52,816.15, 13.88 **17.** Jan. 31, $4,057.78, 12, $4,037.49 **19.** Aug. 8, $8,180, 34, $8,101.20 **21.** $195, $14,805, 5.27 **23.** $964, $79,036, 4.88 **25.** $2,075.00, $97,925.00, 4.24 **27.** 13.61% **29a.** $484.62 **29b.** $149,515.38 **29c.** 4.21%

ASSESSMENT TEST

1. $641.10 **3.** $672.93 **5.** $24,648.00 **7.** 107 **9.** Jan. 24 **11.** $11,666.67 **13.** 9.1 **15.** 72 **17.** 190, $13,960.00 **19.** 15.2, $2,795.00 **21.** Jan. 20, $20,088.54, $854,911.46 **23.** $10,544.72, $279,455.28, 12.35 **25.** Aug. 25, $5,642.31, 34, $5,569.30 **27.** $686.00, $27,314.00, 5.02 **29.** $99.37 **31.** 15.3% **33.** $9,393.88 **35a.** $28,970.83 **35b.** November 12 **35c.** 13.46% **37a.** $752 **37b.** $63,248 **37c.** 4.76%

Chapter 11: Compound Interest and Present Value

11

1. 3, 13 **3.** 24, 4 **5.** 16, 3.5 **7.** 3, 3 **9.** $11,255.09, $1,255.09 **11.** $2,524.95, $524.95 **13.** $24,774.09, $13,774.09 **15.** $95,776.50, $28,776.50 **17.** $450.86, $50.86 **19.** 1.43077, $18,600.01 **21.** 5.61652, $194,893.24 **23.** 8.71525, $8,715.25 **25.** $260.00, 13.00% **27.** $82.43, 8.24% **29a.** 6.14% **29b.** $4,288.50 **31.** $16,174.20 **33.** 97 Sheep **35.** $ 5,904.40, $904.40 **37.** $3,024.73, $224.73 **39.** $71,875

1. $4,633.08, $1,366.92 **3.** $437.43, $212.57 **5.** $3,680.50, $46,319.50 **7.** $6,107.07, $3,692.93 **9.** $209.10, $40.90 **11.** .20829, $2,499.48 **13.** .24200, $338.80 **15.** .26355, $28,990.50 **17a.** $2,549.58 **17b.** $950.42 **19.** $15,742,200 **21.** 47 Million songbirds **23.** $3,466.02, $1,033.98 **25.** $15,643.55, $3,256.45 **27a.** $5,385 **27b.** $615

ASSESSMENT TEST

1. $31,530.66, $17,530.66 **3.** $3,586.86, $586.86 **5.** 5.61652, $112,330.40 **7.** $1,078.06, 12.68% **9.** $6,930.00, $143,070.00 **11.** $658.35, $241.65 **13.** .62027, $806.35 **15.** $81,392.40, $45,392.40 **17.** $17,150.85, $2,150.85 **19.** $92,727.70 **21a.** 12.55% **21b.** $17,888.55 **23.** $48,545.40 **25a.** $37,243.34 **25b.** $14,243.34 **27.** 3.7 Million fleet miles **29.** $25,910.82, $4,110.82 **31.** $11,218.11, $1,588.11 **33.** $77,380.73, $2,819.27 **35.** $2,263.80, $176.20 **37.** $97,129 **39.** $17,795

12 Chapter 12: Annuities

SECTION I

1. $18,639.29 **3.** $151,929.30 **5.** $74,951.37 **7.** $13,680.33 **9.** $100,226.90
11. $2,543.20 **13.** $2,956.72 **15.** $15,934.37 **17.** $36,848.56 **19.** $42,082.72
21. $83,581.92 **23a.** $8,101.04 **23b.** $28,442.52

SECTION II

1. $2,969.59 **3.** $27,096.86 **5.** $79,773.10 **7.** $16,819.32 **9.** $110,997.88
11. $9,025.15 **13.** $380,773 **15.** $7,900.87 **17.** $5,865.77 **19.** $6,696.93
21. $21,856.03 **23.** $100,490.79

SECTION III

1. $2,113.50 **3.** $55.82 **5.** $859.13 **7.** $336.36 **9.** $1,087.48 **11a.** $245,770.96
11b. $2,135,329.28 **13a.** $3,769.04 **13b.** $2,385.76 **15.** $12,802.39 **17.** $53.96
19. $3,756.68 **21.** $78.95 **23.** $169.11 **25a.** $13,787.95 **25b.** $172,723

ASSESSMENT TEST

1. $121,687.44 **3.** $86,445.14 **5.** $42,646.92 **7.** $11,593.58 **9.** $993.02
11. $255.66 **13.** $20,345.57 **15.** $6,081.72 **17.** $368.62 **19.** $40,012.45
21. $7,639.68 **23.** $5,431.63 **25.** $69,840.21 **27.** $32,115.31 **29.** $5,913.62
31. $2,468.92 **33a.** $11,261.18 **33b.** $12,321.12 **35.** $1,454.65

Chapter 13: Consumer and Business Credit

1. 1.5%, $2.52, $335.90 **3.** 21%, $7.96, $544.32 **5.** .75%, $25.64, $2,573.14
7a. $1.20 **7b.** $259.13 **9.** $636.17, $11.13, $628.75 **11.** $817.08, $14.30, $684.76
13. $677.84 **15.** $158.51 **17a.** 12.4% **17b.** 15.5% **17c.** 14.65% **17d.** 11.15%

1. $1,050.00, $582.00, $1,982.00 **3.** $10,800.00, $2,700.00, $14,700.00
5. $7,437.50, $2,082.34, $10,832.34 **7.** $15,000.00, $9,577.20, $29,577.20
9. $1,350.00, $270.00, $67.50 **11.** $15,450.00, $8,652.00, $502.13 **13.** $11,685.00,
$3,154.95, $412.22 **15.** $322.00, $14.00, 13% **17.** $223.50, $12.02, 14.75%
19. $825.20, $12.60, 11.75% **21.** $31.00, 11.25% **23.** $4,940.00, 16.6%
25. $15,130.00, 14.71% **27.** $29.97, $1,498.50, $135.39 **29.** $6.20, $111.60, $159.30
31. $13.82, $1,686.04, $578.59 **33.** 8, 36, 78, $\frac{36}{78}$ **35.** 15, 120, 300, 120/300
37. 40, 820, 1,176, 820/1,176 **39.** 120/300, $360.00, $2,077.50, **41.** 78/1,176,
$219.94, $2,984.06 **43.** 55/465, $260.22, $4,139.78 **45a.** $1,709.10, $2,120.40,
$411.30 **45b.** $2,310.30 **47.** $68.75 **49a.** $729.52 **49b.** $8,329.52
51. $216.45, $63.19 **53a.** 300 **53b.** 465 **55a.** $504 **55b.** $152.25
55c. 14.64%, 14.75% **55d.** $1,157.52

ASSESSMENT TEST

1a. 1.33% **1b.** $4.59 **1c.** $440.38 **3a.** $4.46, $724.12 **3b.** $724.12, $12.09,
$839.64 **3c.** $839.64, $14.02, $859.61 **5a.** $694.76 **5b.** $7.50 **5c.** $864.74
7a. $9,920 **7b.** $39,120 **9a.** $10,384 **9b.** 19.25% **11a.** $66,300
11b. $4,646.67 **13a.** $14,144 **13b.** $1,428 **13c.** 11.75% **13d.** $32,906.45
15a. $30,686.75 **15b.** $24,686.75 **15c.** $8,733.25 **15d.** $39,420 **15e.** 12.75%

14

Chapter 14: Mortgages

SECTION I

1. 80, 9.00, $720.00, $92,800.00   **3.** 130.9, 8.06, $1,055.05, $185,615.00   **5.** 96.8, 7.17, $694.06, $153,061.60   **7.** 184.3, 8.58, $1,581.29, $100,332.20   **9.** $639.47, $821.39
11. $1,189.79, $1,601.21   **13.** $1,067.61, $1,458.78   **15a.** $1,736.46
15b. $275,328   **17a.** Fortune Bank, $115,950; Northern Trust Bank, $120,000
17b. Fortune Bank, $121,950; Northern Trust Bank, $120,000 (Better deal, $1,950 Less)
19a. 7.35%   **19b.** 12.35%   **21a.** 8.55%   **21b.** 14.75%

14

SECTION II

1. $89,025, $21,125   **3.** $112,960, $13,860   **5.** $63,700, 0   **7.** $930,300, $416,120
9. 14.32, 24.05   **11.** 26.04, 35.00   **13.** 27.01, 38.24   **15a.** Parker, Martin, and Jameson   **15b.** Parker and Martin   **17.** 0   **19.** $19,200, No to the addition
21a. 25.75%   **21b.** 39.13%   **21c.** FHA   **21d.** $425.28

ASSESSMENT TEST

1. 134.9, 7.56, $1,019.84, $171,052.00   **3.** Month 1 loan bal: $145,966.57, Month 2 loan bal: $145,832.41, Month 3 loan bal: $145,697.53   **5.** $1,321, $1,596.67   **7.** $41,200, $13,800   **9.** 24.30, 40.15   **11.** FHA, FHA and Conventional   **13a.** $4,269.20   **13b.** Month 1 loan bal: $519,089.13, Month 2 loan bal: $518,172.38   **13c.** $5,221.70   **13d.** $14,578.30   **15a.** $703,639.20, $651,744.00   **15b.** Foremost is better by $34,457.70
17a. $1,230.98   **17b.** $120,236   **17c.** $22,557.40   **17d.** $80,060   **19.** 0
21a. 27.86%   **21b.** 39.53%   **21c.** FHA

BUSINESSS MATH TIMES

Brainteaser solutions

1. page 90   A decimal point 1.2

2. page 190   20 nines   Don't forget 90, 91, 92 , 93, . . . 99!

3. page 306   24 days   Let X = days worked

Let $(30 - X)$ = days not worked
$55X - 66(30 - X) = 924$
$X = 24$ Days

4. page 408   866 miles high   If 4 inches equals \$1 million, then a foot equals \$3 million.

A mile equals \$15.84 billion (5,280 ft × \$3 million)

$1 \text{ trillion} = \left(\dfrac{1{,}000}{15.84}\right) = 63.13 \text{ miles}$

$13.72 \times 63.13 = 866.14 = 866 \text{ miles}$

INDEX